GCSE
Physics

The Complete Course for Edexcel

CGP

How to get your free Online Edition

Go to **cgpbooks.co.uk/extras** and enter this code...

2479 0787 4573 5543

This code will only work once. If someone has used this book before you,
they may have already claimed the Online Edition.

Published by CGP

From original material by Paddy Gannon.

Editors:
Sharon Keeley-Holden, Frances Rooney, Sarah Williams and Dawn Wright.

Contributors:
Gemma Hallam

ISBN: 978 1 78294 816 2

With thanks to Ana Pungartnik for the copyright research.

Printed by Elanders Ltd, Newcastle upon Tyne.
Clipart from Corel®

Contents

How to use this book

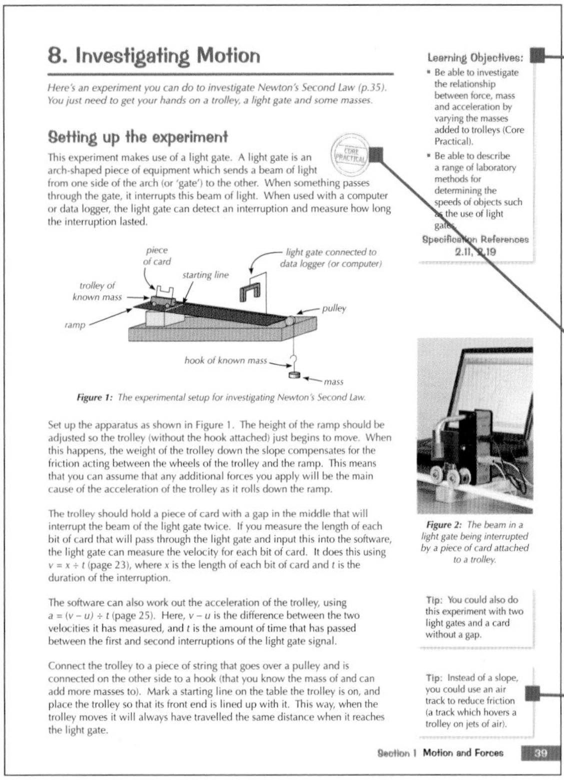

The following is a reproduction of a sample book page:

8. Investigating Motion

Here's an experiment you can do to investigate Newton's Second Law (p.35). You just need to get your hands on a trolley, a light gate and some masses.

Setting up the experiment

This experiment makes use of a light gate. A light gate is an arch-shaped piece of equipment which sends a beam of light from one side of the arch (or 'gate') to the other. When something passes through the gate, it interrupts this beam of light. When used with a computer or data logger, the light gate can detect an interruption and measure how long the interruption lasted.

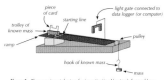

Figure 1: The experimental setup for investigating Newton's Second Law.

Set up the apparatus as shown in Figure 1. The height of the ramp should be adjusted so the trolley (without the hook attached) just begins to move. When this happens, the weight of the trolley down the slope compensates for the friction acting between the wheels of the trolley and the ramp. This means that you can assume that any additional forces you apply will be the main cause of the acceleration of the trolley as it rolls down the ramp.

The trolley should hold a piece of card with a gap in the middle that will interrupt the beam of the light gate twice. If you measure the length of each bit of card that will pass through the light gate and input this into the software, the light gate can measure the velocity for each bit of card. It does this using $v = x \div t$ (page 23), where x is the length of each bit of card and t is the duration of the interruption.

The software can also work out the acceleration of the trolley, using $a = (v - u) \div t$ (page 25). Here, $v - u$ is the difference between the two velocities it has measured, and t is the amount of time that has passed between the first and second interruptions of the light gate signal.

Connect the trolley to a piece of string that goes over a pulley and is connected on the other side to a hook (that you know the mass of and can add more masses to). Mark a starting line on the table the trolley is on, and place the trolley so that its front end is lined up with it. This way, when the trolley moves so that it reaches the light gate, it will always have travelled the same distance when it reaches the light gate.

Learning Objectives:
- Be able to investigate the relationship between force, mass and acceleration by varying the masses added to trolleys (Core Practical).
- Be able to describe a range of laboratory methods for determining the speeds of objects such as the use of light gates.

Specification References 2.11, 2.19

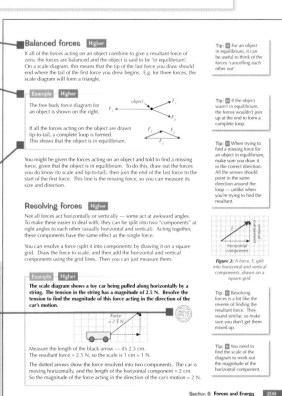

Figure 2: The beam in a light gate being interrupted by a piece of card attached to a trolley.

Tip: You could also do this experiment with two light gates and a card without a gap.

Tip: Instead of a slope, you could use an air track to reduce friction (a track which hovers a trolley on jets of air).

Section 1 Motion and Forces **39**

Learning Objectives
- These tell you exactly what you need to learn, or be able to do, for the exam.
- There are specification references at the bottom that link to the Edexcel specification.

Core Practicals
There are some Core Practicals that you'll be expected to do throughout your course. You need to know all about them for the exams. They're all marked with stamps like this:

Tips and Exam Tips
- There are tips throughout this book to help you understand the theory.
- There are also exam tips to help you with answering exam questions.

Higher Exam Material
- Some of the material in this book will only come up in the exam if you're sitting the higher exam papers.
- This material is clearly marked with boxes that look like this:

Higher **H** **Q1**

Examples
These are here to help you understand the theory.

Maths Skills
- There's a range of maths skills you could be expected to apply in your exams. The section on pages 340-350 is packed with plenty of maths that you'll need to be familiar with.
- Examples that show these maths skills in action are marked up with this symbol.

(MATHS SKILLS)

The following is a reproduction of another sample book page:

Balanced forces *Higher*

If all of the forces acting on an object combine to give a resultant force of zero, the forces are balanced and the object is said to be 'in equilibrium'. On a scale diagram, this means that the tip of the last force you draw should end where the tail of the first force you drew begins. E.g. for three forces, the scale diagram will form a triangle.

Example *Higher*

The free body force diagram for an object is shown on the right.

If all the forces acting on the object are drawn tip-to-tail, a complete loop is formed. This shows that the object is in equilibrium.

You might be given the forces acting on an object and told to find a missing force, given that the object is in equilibrium. To do this, draw out the forces you do know (to scale and tip-to-tail), then join the end of the last force to the start of the first force. This line is the missing force, so you can measure its size and direction.

Resolving forces *Higher*

Not all forces act horizontally or vertically — some act at awkward angles. To make these easier to deal with, they can be split into two "components" at right angles to each other (usually horizontal and vertical). Acting together, these components have the same effect as the single force.

You can resolve a force (split it into components) by drawing it on a square grid. Draw the force to scale, and then add the horizontal and vertical components using the grid lines. Then you can just measure them.

Figure 2: A force, F, split into horizontal and vertical components, drawn on a square grid.

Example *Higher*

The scale diagram shows a toy car being pulled along horizontally by a string. The tension in the string has a magnitude of 2.5 N. Resolve the tension to find the magnitude of this force acting in the direction of the car's motion.

Measure the length of the black arrow — it's 2.5 cm. The resultant force = 2.5 N, so the scale is 1 cm = 1 N.

The dotted arrows show the force resolved into two components. The car is moving horizontally, and the length of the horizontal component = 2 cm. So the magnitude of the force acting in the direction of the car's motion = 2 N.

Tip: For an object in equilibrium, it can be useful to think of the forces 'cancelling each other out'.

Tip: If the object wasn't in equilibrium, the forces wouldn't join up at the end to form a complete loop.

Tip: When trying to find a missing force for an object in equilibrium, make sure you draw it in the correct direction. All the arrows should point in the same direction around the loop — unlike when you're trying to find the resultant.

Tip: Resolving forces is a bit like the reverse of finding the resultant force. They sound similar, so make sure you don't get them mixed up.

Tip: You need to find the scale of the diagram to work out the magnitude of the horizontal component.

Section 8 Forces and Energy **209**

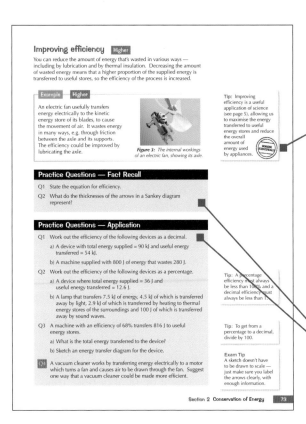

Working Scientifically

- Working Scientifically is a big part of GCSE Physics. There's a whole section on it at the front of the book.

- Working Scientifically is also covered throughout this book wherever you see this symbol.

Practical Skills

There's also a whole section on pages 333-339 with extra details on practical skills you'll be expected to use in the Core Practicals, and apply knowledge of in the exams.

Practice Questions

- Fact recall questions test that you know the facts needed for GCSE Physics.

- Annoyingly, the examiners also expect you to be able to apply your knowledge to new situations — application questions give you plenty of practice at doing this.

- All the answers are in the back of the book.

Exam-style Questions

- Practising exam-style questions is really important — this book has some at the end of every topic to test you.

- They're the same style as the ones you'll get in the real exams.

- All the answers are in the back of the book, along with a mark scheme to show you how you get the marks.

- Higher-only questions are marked like this: **(a)**

Topic Checklist

Each topic has a checklist at the end with boxes that let you tick off what you've learnt.

Glossary

There's a glossary at the back of the book full of definitions you need to know for the exam, plus loads of other useful words.

Exam Help

There's a section at the back of the book stuffed full of things to help you with the exams.

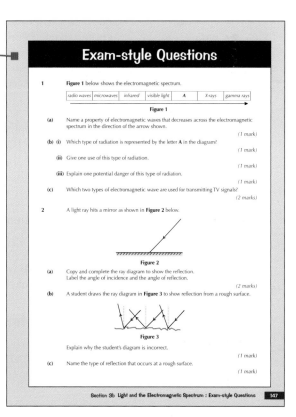

1. The Scientific Method

Science is all about finding things out and learning things about the world we live in. This section is all about the scientific process — how a scientist's initial idea turns into a theory that is accepted by the wider scientific community.

Hypotheses

Scientists try to explain things. Everything. They start by observing something they don't understand — it could be anything, e.g. planets in the sky, a person suffering from an illness, what matter is made of... anything.

Then, they come up with a **hypothesis** — a possible explanation for what they've observed. (Scientists can also sometimes form a model — a description or a representation of what's physically going on — see page 3).

The next step is to test whether the hypothesis might be right or not. This involves making a **prediction** based on the hypothesis and testing it by gathering evidence (i.e. data) from investigations. If evidence from experiments backs up a prediction, you're a step closer to figuring out if the hypothesis is true.

> **Tip:** Investigations include lab experiments and studies.

Testing a hypothesis

Normally, scientists share their findings in peer-reviewed journals, or at conferences. **Peer-review** is where other scientists check results and scientific explanations to make sure they're 'scientific' (e.g. that experiments have been done in a sensible way) before they're published. It helps to detect false claims, but it doesn't mean that findings are correct — just that they're not wrong in any obvious way.

Once other scientists have found out about a hypothesis, they'll start basing their own predictions on it and carry out their own experiments. They'll also try to reproduce the original experiments to check the results — and if all the experiments in the world back up the hypothesis, then scientists start to think the hypothesis is true.

However, if a scientist somewhere in the world does an experiment that doesn't fit with the hypothesis (and other scientists can reproduce these results), then the hypothesis is in trouble. When this happens, scientists have to come up with a new hypothesis (maybe a modification of the old hypothesis, or maybe a completely new one).

> **Tip:** Sometimes it can take a really long time for a hypothesis to be accepted.

Accepting a hypothesis

If pretty much every scientist in the world believes a hypothesis to be true because experiments back it up, then it usually goes in the textbooks for students to learn. Accepted hypotheses are often referred to as **theories**.

Our currently accepted theories are the ones that have survived this 'trial by evidence' — they've been tested many, many times over the years and survived (while the less good ones have been ditched). However... they never, never become hard and fast, totally indisputable fact. You can never know... it'd only take one odd, totally inexplicable result, and the hypothesising and testing would start all over again.

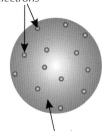

negatively-charged electrons

sphere of positive charge

Figure 1: *The plum pudding model of the atom.*

Example

- The ancient Greek, Democritus, proposed that everything was made up of solid lumps that couldn't be split up, called "atomos".

- About 200 years ago, John Dalton developed Democritus's hypothesis, suggesting that each element was made up of a different type of atom.

- Towards the end of the 19th century, the electron was discovered. This meant the earlier hypothesis of the atom was revised, and atoms were thought of as lumps of positive charge with negative electrons sat inside them (see Figure 1) — this was the plum pudding model (p.149).

- After more evidence was gathered, the hypothesis was changed again and we developed the nuclear model of the atom — a tiny positive nucleus, orbited by negative electrons (see p.151).

Models

Models are used to describe or display how an object or system behaves in reality. They're often based on evidence collected from experiments and can predict what will happen in other, similar experiments. There are different types of models that scientists can use to describe the world around them. Here are just a few:

- A descriptive model describes what's happening in a certain situation, without explaining why. It won't necessarily include details that could be used to predict the outcome of a different scenario. For example, a graph showing the measured resistance of a device at different temperatures would be a descriptive model.

- A representational model is a simplified description or picture of what's going on in real life. It can be used to explain observations and make predictions. E.g. the current nuclear model is a simplified way of showing the arrangement of electrons in an atom (see p.151). It can be used to explain how electrons move between different energy levels.

- Spatial models are used to summarise how data is arranged within space. For example, a map showing where high levels of radiation from rocks is found (see Figure 2) would be a spatial model.

- Computational models are simulations of complex real-life processes, such as climate change, made using computers. They're used when there are a lot of different variables (factors that change) to consider, and because you can easily update them to take into account new data.

- Mathematical models can be used to describe the relationship between variables in numerical form (e.g. as an equation), and therefore predict outcomes of a scenario. For example, an equation can be written to predict the energy transferred to or from a material's thermal energy stores when it changes temperature. This depends on the change in temperature of the material, its mass and its specific heat capacity (see page 304).

Tip: Like hypotheses, models have to be tested before they're accepted by other scientists. You can test models by using them to make a prediction, and then carrying out an investigation to see whether the results match the prediction.

higher

lower

Figure 2: *A spatial model showing radiation from rocks in the United Kingdom. The scale shows how the level of radiation from rocks in different areas varies.*

Tip: Mathematical models are made using patterns found in data and also using information about known relationships between variables.

Tip: Like hypotheses, models are constantly being revised and modified, based on new data.

All models have limitations on what they can explain or predict. The Big Bang model (a model used to describe the beginning of the Universe — see page 193) can be used to explain why everything in the Universe is moving away from us. One of its limitations is that it doesn't explain the moments before the Big Bang.

Communicating results

Some scientific discoveries show that people should change their habits, or they might provide ideas that could be developed into new technology. So scientists need to tell the world about their discoveries.

Tip: New scientific discoveries are usually communicated to the public in the news or via the internet. They might be communicated to governments and large organisations via reports or meetings.

| Example |

Radioactive materials are used widely in medicine for imaging and treatment (see p.169-172). Information about these materials needs to be communicated to doctors so they can make use of them. The patients also need to be told of the risks involved so they can make informed decisions about their treatment.

Reports about scientific discoveries in the media (e.g. newspapers or television) aren't peer-reviewed. This means that, even though news stories are often based on data that has been peer-reviewed, the data might be presented in a way that is over-simplified or inaccurate, leaving it open to misinterpretation.

Tip: If you're reading an article about a new scientific discovery, always think about how the study was carried out. It may be that the sample size was very small, and so the results aren't representative (see page 11 for more on sample sizes).

It's important that evidence isn't presented in a **biased** way. An example of bias is overemphasising a relationship in the data. This sort of thing may be done by someone deliberately to make a point, or accidentally, without them even realising they're doing it. There are lots of reasons why people might present data in a biased way:

| Examples |

- Researchers might want to keep the organisation that's funding the research happy. If the results don't show what the organisation had hoped they'd show, it might not give any more money to fund research.

- Governments might want to persuade voters, other governments or journalists to agree with their policies about a certain issue.

- Companies might want to 'big up' their products, or make impressive safety claims.

- Environmental campaigners might want to persuade people to behave differently.

Tip: An example of bias is a newspaper article describing details of data supporting an idea without giving any of the evidence against it.

There's also a risk that if an investigation is done by a team of highly-regarded scientists it'll be taken more seriously than evidence from less well-known scientists. Even if the scientists involved do have experience, authority or fancy qualifications, it doesn't necessarily mean their evidence is good. The only way to tell is to look at the evidence scientifically (e.g. is it repeatable, valid, etc. — see page 9).

2. Scientific Applications and Issues

New scientific discoveries can lead to lots of exciting new ways of using science in our everyday lives. Unfortunately, these developments may also come with problems that need to be considered.

Using scientific developments

Lots of scientific developments go on to have useful applications.

Examples

- The discovery of electromagnetic induction (which turns movement into potential difference) allowed people to develop machines to easily generate electricity. This is the basis for the widespread electricity supplies we have today.

- As scientists investigated the effects of radiation, they found they had damaging effects on the body, which could be used to kill cancer cells (see pages 171-172).

Tip: **H** See p.280 for more on electromagnetic induction.

Issues created by science

Scientific knowledge is increased by doing experiments. And this knowledge leads to scientific developments, e.g. new technologies or new advice. These developments can create a whole host of issues though.

Examples

- **Economic issues**: Society can't always afford to do things scientists recommend (e.g. investing heavily in renewable energy sources) without cutting back elsewhere.

- **Social issues**: Decisions based on scientific evidence affect people — e.g. should fossil fuels be taxed more highly (to encourage investment in renewable energy sources)? Should alcohol be banned (to prevent health problems)? Would the effect on people's lifestyles be acceptable?

- **Environmental issues**: Human activity often affects the natural environment — e.g. burning fossil fuels may be cheaper than using renewable energy sources, but it has a large negative impact on the environment.

- **Personal issues**: Some decisions will affect individuals. For example, someone might support renewable energy sources, but object if a wind farm is built next to their house.

Figure 1: *The ATLAS detector at CERN, part of the Large Hadron Collider (LHC). The LHC has greatly advanced our knowledge of subatomic particles, but it also cost a lot of money to build and run.*

3. Limitations of Science

Science has taught us an awful lot about the world we live in and how things work — but science doesn't have the answer for everything.

Questions science hasn't answered yet

We don't understand everything. And we never will. We'll find out more, for sure — as more hypotheses are suggested, and more experiments are done. But there'll always be stuff we don't know.

> **Examples**
>
> - Today we don't know as much as we'd like about the impacts of global warming. How much will sea levels rise? And to what extent will weather patterns change?
> - We also don't know anywhere near as much as we'd like about the Universe. Are there other life forms out there? And what is most of the Universe made of?

In order to answer scientific questions, scientists need data to provide evidence for their hypotheses. Some questions can't be answered yet because the data can't currently be collected, or because there's not enough data to support a theory. But eventually, as we get more evidence, we probably will be able to answer these questions. By then there'll be loads of new questions to answer though.

Questions science can't answer

There are some questions that all the experiments in the world won't help us answer — for example, the "should we be doing this at all?" type questions.

> **Example**
>
> Take the idea of space exploration and the search for alien life — some people think it's a good idea. It increases our knowledge of the Universe and the new technologies developed to explore space can be useful on Earth too. For example, a lot of developments within space exploration has led to improvements of MRI machines — these are used in hospitals to image the inside of the body. It also inspires young people to get into science.
>
> Other people say it's a bad idea. They think we should concentrate on understanding our own planet better first, or spend the vast amounts of money on solving more urgent problems here on Earth — things like providing clean drinking water and curing diseases in poor countries.

The question of whether something is morally or ethically right or wrong can't be answered by more experiments — there is no "right" or "wrong" answer. The best we can do is get a consensus from society — a judgement that most people are more or less happy to live by. Science can provide more information to help people make this judgement, and the judgement might change over time. But in the end it's up to people and their conscience.

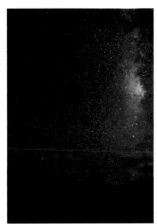

Figure 1: *The night sky. We can use high powered telescopes to observe some of the Universe but we still have little idea what most of it is made of or how it was formed.*

Tip: Some experiments have to be approved by ethics committees before scientists are allowed to carry them out. This stops scientists from getting wrapped up in whether they <u>can</u> do something, before anyone stops to think about whether they <u>should</u> do it.

4. Risks and Hazards

A lot of things we do could cause us harm. But some things are more hazardous than they at first seem, whereas other things are less hazardous than they at first seem. This may sound confusing, but it'll all become clear...

What are risks and hazards?

A **hazard** is something that could potentially cause harm. All hazards have a **risk** attached to them — this is the chance that the hazard will cause harm.

The risks of some things seem pretty obvious, or we've known about them for a while, like the risk of causing acid rain by polluting the atmosphere, or of having a car accident when you're travelling in a car.

New technology arising from scientific advances can bring new risks. These risks need to be thought about alongside the potential benefits of the technology, in order to make a decision about whether it should be made available to the general public.

> **Example**
>
> Imaging technologies, like CT scans, can be used to see inside the body. These technologies can allow doctors to diagnose medical conditions.
>
> These scans use ionising radiation, so there's a chance that they'll cause cancer in the patient. The risk of the scan causing cancer has to be weighed against the risk of leaving the suspected medical condition undiagnosed and untreated. Often the risk from the medical condition far outweighs the risk from the scan, so the scan goes ahead.

Tip: In a CT scan, lots of X-ray images are taken from different angles to build up a detailed picture of inside the body. A CT scan exposes the patient to much more radiation than having a single X-ray image taken does, but it provides doctors with a lot more information.

Figure 1: *A patient being prepared for a CT scan.*

Estimating risk

You can estimate the risk based on how many times something happens in a big sample (e.g. 100 000 people) over a given period (e.g. a year). For example, you could assess the risk of a driver crashing by recording how many people in a group of 100 000 drivers crashed their cars over a year.

However, this estimate wouldn't give you an idea of the severity of the risk — i.e. how bad the harm caused by the hazard was. To make a decision about how dangerous an activity is, we don't just need to take into account the chance of the activity causing harm, but also how serious the consequences would be if it did.

The general rule is that, if an activity involves a hazard that's very likely to cause harm, with serious consequences if it does, that activity is considered high-risk.

> **Example 1**
>
> If you go for a run, there's a reasonably high chance you'll pull a muscle. But most pulled muscles recover within a few days, so even if the chance of harm is quite high, running is generally considered a low-risk activity.

If you go skiing, you may fall and break a bone. There may be a fairly low chance of this happening, but broken bones take many weeks to heal, and may cause further complications later on in life. So skiing is usually considered higher risk than running (even if the actual chance of injury isn't any higher).

Perceptions of risk

Not all risks have the same consequences, e.g. if you chop vegetables with a sharp knife you risk cutting your finger, but if you go scuba-diving you risk death. You're much more likely to cut your finger during half an hour of chopping than to die during half an hour of scuba-diving. But most people are happier to accept a higher probability of an accident if the consequences are short-lived and fairly minor.

Tip: Risks people choose to take are called 'voluntary risks'. Risks that people are forced to take are called 'imposed risks'.

People tend to be more willing to accept a risk if they choose to do something (e.g. go scuba diving), compared to having the risk imposed on them (e.g. having a nuclear power station built next door).

People's perception of risk (how risky they think something is) isn't always accurate. They tend to view familiar activities as low-risk and unfamiliar activities as high-risk — even if that's not the case. For example, cycling on roads is often high-risk, but many people are happy to do it because it's a familiar activity. Air travel is actually pretty safe, but a lot of people perceive it as high-risk. People may incorrectly estimate the risk of things with long-term or invisible effects, e.g. ionising radiation.

Reducing risk in investigations

Tip: You can find out about potential hazards by looking in textbooks, doing some internet research, or asking your teacher.

Part of planning an investigation is making sure that it's safe. To make sure your experiment is safe you must identify all the hazards. Hazards include:

- Lasers: e.g. if a laser is directed into the eye, this can cause blindness.

- Gamma radiation: e.g. gamma-emitting radioactive sources can cause cancer.

- Fire: e.g. an unattended Bunsen burner is a fire risk.

- Electricity: e.g. faulty electrical equipment could give you a shock.

Once you've identified the hazards you might encounter, you should think of ways of reducing the risks from the hazards.

- If you're working with springs, always wear safety goggles. This will reduce the risk of the spring (or a fragment of it) hitting your eye if the spring snaps.

- If you're using a Bunsen burner, stand it on a heat proof mat. This will reduce the risk of starting a fire.

Figure 2: *A scientist wearing safety goggles to protect her eyes during an experiment.*

5. Designing Investigations

To be a good scientist you need to know how to design a good experiment, including how to make sure you get good quality results.

Making predictions from a hypothesis

Scientists observe things and come up with hypotheses to explain them. To decide whether a hypothesis might be correct you need to do an investigation to gather evidence, which will help support or disprove the hypothesis. The first step is to use the hypothesis to come up with a prediction — a statement about what you think will happen that you can test.

> **Example**
>
> If your hypothesis is "aluminium foil is a better thermal insulator than newspaper", then your prediction might be "a cup of hot water wrapped in newspaper will cool down to a lower temperature than a cup of hot water wrapped in aluminium foil will over a period of five minutes".

Once a scientist has come up with a prediction, they'll design an investigation to see if there are patterns or relationships between two variables. For example, to see if there's a pattern or relationship between the variables 'insulating material used' and 'change in temperature'.

Tip: For more on thermal insulation, see page 69.

Tip: A variable is just something in the experiment that can change.

Repeatable and reproducible results

Results need to be **repeatable** and **reproducible**. Repeatable means that if the same person does an experiment again using the same methods and equipment, they'll get similar results. Reproducible means that if someone else does the experiment, or a different method or piece of equipment is used, the results will be similar.

> **Example**
>
> In 1989, two scientists claimed that they'd produced 'cold fusion' (the energy source of the Sun but without the high temperatures). If it was true, it would have meant free energy for the world forever. However, other scientists couldn't reproduce the results, so 'cold fusion' wasn't accepted as a theory.

Tip: Data that's repeatable and reproducible is <u>reliable</u> and scientists are more likely to have confidence in it.

Figure 1: *Stanley Pons and Martin Fleischmann — the scientists who allegedly discovered cold fusion.*

Ensuring the test is valid

Valid results are repeatable, reproducible and answer the original question.

> **Example**
>
> **Do power lines cause cancer?**
>
> Some studies have found that children who live near overhead power lines are more likely to develop cancer. What they'd actually found was a **correlation** (relationship) between the variables "presence of power lines" and "incidence of cancer". They found that as one changed, so did the other.
>
> But this data isn't enough to say that the power lines cause cancer, as there might be other explanations. For example, power lines are often near busy roads, so the areas tested could contain different levels of pollution. As the studies don't show a definite link they don't answer the original question.

Tip: Peer review (see page 2) is used to make sure that results are valid before they're published.

Tip: See page 17 for more on correlation.

Ensuring it's a fair test

Tip: For the results of an investigation to be <u>valid</u> the investigation must be a <u>fair test</u>.

In a lab experiment you usually change one variable and measure how it affects another variable. To make it a fair test, everything else that could affect the results should stay the same (otherwise you can't tell if the thing you're changing is causing the results or not — the data won't be valid).

Example

To investigate how the length of a wire affects its resistance, you must only change the wire length. You need to keep, for example, the temperature the same, otherwise you won't know if any change in the resistance was caused by the change in length, or the change in temperature.

The variable you change is called the **independent variable**. The variable you measure when you change the independent variable is called the **dependent variable**. The variables that you keep the same are called **control variables**.

Example

In the resistance experiment above, the length of the wire is the independent variable, the resistance is the dependent variable, and the control variables are the temperature, supplied potential difference, wire thickness, etc.

Control experiments and control groups

Tip: Control experiments let you see what happens when you don't change anything at all.

In some investigations it's useful to have a **control experiment** — an experiment that's kept under the same conditions as the rest of the investigation, but doesn't have anything done to it. This allows you to see exactly what effect changing the independent variable has in the investigation.

Tip: The control experiment in this example could also account for any systematic errors (see page 13) that may be affecting all of your results.

Example

You can investigate how different materials act as thermal insulators by wrapping each material round a beaker of hot water and recording how much the temperature of the water has dropped by after a given time period. However, you would also carry out the experiment without any insulating material — the control experiment. This gives you a point of comparison, so you can evaluate by how much a thermal insulator has slowed down the cooling process. Without it, you wouldn't know if the insulators were actually slowing down the cooling rate.

It's important that a study (an investigation that doesn't take place in a lab) is a fair test, just like a lab experiment. It's a lot trickier to control the variables in a study than it is in a lab experiment though. Sometimes you can't control them all, but you can use a **control group** to help. This is a group of whatever you're studying (e.g. people) that's kept under the same conditions as the group in the experiment, but doesn't have anything done to it.

Example

If you were studying the link between CT scans and thyroid cancer, you'd take one group of people who have had CT scans, and another group (the control group) who haven't. Both groups should be of roughly the same age, live in the same area, have similar lifestyles, etc.

The control group will help you try to account for other variables like people's diet, which could affect the results.

Sample size

Data based on small samples isn't as good as data based on large samples. A sample should be representative of the whole population (i.e. it should share as many of the various characteristics in the population as possible) — a small sample can't do that as well.

Tip: It's hard to spot anomalies if your sample size is too small.

The bigger the sample size the better, but scientists have to be realistic when choosing how big.

Example

If you were studying how exposure to sunlight affects people's risk of skin cancer it'd be great to study everyone in the UK (a huge sample), but it'd take ages and cost a bomb. Studying a thousand people with a mixture of ages, gender and race would be more realistic.

Trial runs

It's a good idea to do a **trial run** (a quick version of your experiment) before you do the proper experiment. Trial runs are used to figure out the range (the upper and lower limits) of independent variable values to be used in the proper experiment. If there was no change in the dependent variable between your upper and lower values in the trial run, then you might increase the range until there was an observable change. Or if there was a large change, you might want to make your higher and lower values closer together.

Tip: Trial runs are also know as pilot experiments.

Tip: If you don't have time to do a trial run, you could always look at the data other people have got doing a similar experiment and use a range and interval values similar to theirs.

Example

In the experiment on p.327, masses are added to a spring to find how the force acting on the spring is related to its extension. Doing a trial run on the spring (or an identical one) ensures that your lowest independent variable value (the smallest mass) doesn't stretch the spring too far, but is large enough to cause a notable extension.

Enough data points need to be collected before the spring stretches beyond its limit of proportionality. A trial run allows you to check that this is possible with the range of independent variable values you're planning to use.

Trial runs can be used to figure out the appropriate intervals (gaps) between the values too. The intervals can't be too small (otherwise the experiment would take ages), or too big (otherwise you might miss something).

Example

If, in the experiment in the example above, the spring extended a lot when you added a 100 g mass, you may be better using 10 g masses instead.

Trial runs can also help you figure out whether or not your experiment is repeatable. If you repeat it three times and the results are all similar, the experiment is repeatable.

6. Collecting Data

Once you've designed your experiment, you need to get on and do it. Here's a guide to making sure the results you collect are good.

Getting good quality results

When you do an experiment you want your results to be repeatable, reproducible and as **accurate** and **precise** as possible.

To check repeatability you need to repeat the readings and check that the results are similar — you should repeat each reading at least three times. To make sure your results are reproducible you can cross check them by taking a second set of readings with another instrument (or a different observer).

Your data also needs to be accurate. Really accurate results are those that are really close to the true answer. The accuracy of your results usually depends on your method — you need to make sure you're measuring the right thing and that you don't miss anything that should be included in the measurements. For example, estimating the wavelength of water waves produced by a signal generator by counting the number waves in a set distance isn't very accurate because you might miss some of the waves as they're moving. It's more accurate to use a strobe light to show a 'frozen' shadow pattern of the waves and then count the number of shadows (each shadow represents one wave). See page 96 for more on this experiment.

Your data also needs to be precise. Precise results are ones where the data is all really close to the **mean** (average) of your repeated results (i.e. not spread out).

Tip: Sometimes, you can work out what result you should get at the end of an experiment (the theoretical result) by doing a bit of maths. If your experiment is accurate there shouldn't be much difference between the theoretical result and the result you actually get.

Tip: For more on means see page 14.

> **Example**
>
> Look at the data in this table. Data set 1 is more precise than data set 2 because all the data in set 1 is really close to the mean, whereas the data in set 2 is more spread out.
>
> | Repeat | Data set 1 | Data set 2 |
> |--------|-----------|-----------|
> | 1 | 12 | 11 |
> | 2 | 14 | 17 |
> | 3 | 13 | 14 |
> | Mean | 13 | 14 |

Choosing the right equipment

When doing an experiment, you need to make sure you're using the right equipment for the job. The measuring equipment you use has to be sensitive enough to measure the changes you're looking for.

> **Example**
>
> If you need to measure changes of 1 cm^3 you need to use a measuring cylinder that can measure in 1 cm^3 steps — it'd be no good trying with one that only measures 10 cm^3 steps, it wouldn't be sensitive enough.

The smallest change a measuring instrument can detect is called its **resolution**. For example, some mass balances have a resolution of 1 g, some have a resolution of 0.1 g, and some are even more sensitive.

Figure 1: Different types of measuring cylinder and glassware — make sure you choose the right one before you start an experiment.

Also, equipment needs to be **calibrated** by measuring a known value. If there's a difference between the measured and known value, you can use this to correct the inaccuracy of the equipment.

Tip: Calibration is a way of making sure that a measuring device is measuring things accurately — you get it to measure something you know has a certain value and set the device to say that amount.

> **Example**
>
> If a known mass is put on a mass balance, but the reading is a different value, you know that the mass balance has not been calibrated properly.

Errors

Random errors

The results of an experiment will always vary a bit due to **random errors** — unpredictable differences caused by things like human errors in measuring.

> **Example**
>
> Errors made when reading from a measuring cylinder are random. You have to estimate or round the level when it's between two marks — so sometimes your figure will be a bit above the real one, and sometimes a bit below.

You can reduce the effect of random errors by taking repeat readings and finding the mean. This will make your results more precise.

Systematic errors

If a measurement is wrong by the same amount every time, it's called a **systematic error**.

Tip: If there's no systematic error, then doing repeats and calculating a mean can make your results more accurate.

> **Example**
>
> If you measured from the very end of your ruler instead of from the 0 cm mark every time, all your measurements would be a bit small.

Just to make things more complicated, if a systematic error is caused by using equipment that isn't zeroed properly it's called a **zero error**. You can compensate for some of these errors if you know about them though.

Tip: A zero error is a specific type of systematic error.

> **Example**
>
> If a mass balance always reads 1 gram before you put anything on it, all your measurements will be 1 gram too heavy. This is a zero error. You can compensate for this by subtracting 1 gram from all your results.

Tip: Repeating the experiment in the exact same way and calculating a mean won't correct a systematic error.

Anomalous results

Sometimes you get a result that doesn't seem to fit in with the rest at all. These results are called **anomalous results** (or outliers).

> **Example**
>
> Look at the data in this table. The entry that has been circled is an anomalous result because it's much larger than any of the other data values.
>
> | Experiment | A | B | C | D | E | F |
> |---|---|---|---|---|---|---|
> | Acceleration (m/s²) | 1.05 | 1.12 | 1.08 | (8.54) | 1.06 | 1.11 |

Tip: There are lots of reasons why you might get an anomalous result, but usually they're due to human error rather than anything crazy happening in the experiment.

You should investigate anomalous results and try to work out what happened. If you can work out what happened (e.g. you measured something totally wrong) you can ignore them when processing your results.

7. Processing Data

Once you've collected some data, you might need to process it.

Organising data

It's really important that your data is organised. Tables are dead useful for organising data. When you draw a table, use a ruler, make sure each column has a heading (including the units) and keep it neat and tidy.

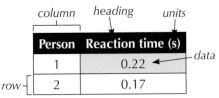

Person	Reaction time (s)
1	0.22
2	0.17

Figure 1: *Table showing the time taken to react to a stimulus for two people.*

Processing your data

When you've collected data from a number of repeats of an experiment, it's useful to summarise it using a few handy-to-use figures.

Mean and range

When you've done repeats of an experiment you should always calculate the **mean** (a type of average). To do this add together all the data values and divide by the total number of values in the sample.

You might also need to calculate the **range** (how spread out the data is). To do this find the largest number and subtract the smallest number from it.

> **Example**
>
> Look at the data in the table below. The mean and range of each set of data has been calculated.
>
> | Trolley | Repeat (m/s) | | | Mean (m/s) | Range (m/s) |
> |---------|---|---|---|------------|-------------|
> | | 1 | 2 | 3 | | |
> | A | 3.1 | 3.6 | 3.2 | (3.1 + 3.6 + 3.2) ÷ 3 = 3.3 | 3.6 − 3.1 = 0.5 |
> | B | 4.7 | 5.1 | 5.8 | (4.7 + 5.1 + 5.8) ÷ 3 = 5.2 | 5.8 − 4.7 = 1.1 |

Median and mode

There are two more types of average, other than the mean, that you might need to calculate. These are the **median** and the **mode**.

- To calculate the median, put all your data in numerical order — the median is the middle value.

- The number that appears most often in a data set is the mode.

> **Example**
>
> **The results of a study investigating the reaction times (in seconds) of students are shown below:**
> **0.10, 0.25, 0.20, 0.15, 0.25, 0.15, 0.25, 0.20, 0.30**
>
> First put the data in numerical order:
> 0.10, 0.15, 0.15, 0.20, 0.20, 0.25, 0.25, 0.25, 0.30
>
> There are nine values, so the median is the 5th number, which is 0.20.
>
> 0.25 comes up three times. No other numbers come up more than twice. So the mode is 0.25.

Uncertainty

When you repeat a measurement, you often get a slightly different figure each time you do it due to random error. This means that each result has some **uncertainty** to it. The measurements you make will also have some uncertainty in them due to limits in the resolution of the equipment you use. This all means that the mean of a set of results will also have some uncertainty to it. Here's how to calculate the uncertainty of a mean result:

Tip: There's more about errors on page 13.

$$\text{uncertainty} = \frac{\text{range}}{2}$$

The larger the range, the less precise your results are and the more uncertainty there will be in your results. Uncertainties are shown using the '±' symbol.

> ### Example
>
> The table below shows the results of an experiment to determine the resistance of a piece of wire in a circuit.
>
> | Repeat | 1 | 2 | 3 | mean |
> |---|---|---|---|---|
> | Resistance (Ω) | 4.20 | 3.80 | 3.70 | 3.90 |
>
> 1. The range is: 4.20 – 3.70 = 0.50 Ω
>
> 2. So the uncertainty of the mean is: range ÷ 2 = 0.50 ÷ 2 = 0.25 Ω
>   You'd write this as 3.90 ± 0.25 Ω

Tip: Since uncertainty affects precision, you'll need to think about it when you come to evaluating your results (see page 21).

Measuring a greater amount of something helps to reduce uncertainty. For example, for radioactive decay, measuring the count rate over a longer period compared to a shorter period reduces the percentage uncertainty in your results.

Rounding to significant figures

The first **significant figure** (s.f.) of a number is the first digit that isn't a zero. The second, third and fourth significant figures follow on immediately after the first (even if they're zeros). When you're processing your data you may well want to round any really long numbers to a certain number of s.f..

> ### Example
>
> 0.6874976 rounds to **0.69 to 2 s.f.** and to **0.687 to 3 s.f.**

Exam Tip
If a question asks you to give your answer to a certain number of significant figures, make sure you do this, or you might not get all the marks.

Tip: This covers GCSE physics specification point 1.4, "use significant figures where appropriate".

When you're doing calculations using measurements given to a certain number of significant figures, you should give your answer to the lowest number of significant figures that was used in the calculation. If your calculation has multiple steps, only round the final answer, or it won't be as accurate.

Tip: Remember to write down how many significant figures you've rounded to after your answer.

> ### Example
>
> For the calculation: 1.2 ÷ 1.85 = 0.648648648...
>
> 1.2 is given to 2 significant figures. 1.85 is given to 3 significant figures. So the answer should be given to 2 significant figures.
>
> Round the final significant figure (0.6<u>4</u>8) up to 5: 1.2 ÷ 1.85 = 0.65 (2 s.f.)

Tip: When rounding a number, if the next digit after the last significant figure you're using is less than 5 you should round it <u>down</u>, and if it's 5 or more you should round it <u>up</u>.

The lowest number of significant figures in the calculation is used because the fewer significant figures a measurement has, the less accurate it is. Your answer can only be as accurate as the least accurate measurement in the calculation.

8. Graphs and Charts

It can often be easier to see trends in data by plotting a graph or chart of your results, rather than by looking at numbers in a table.

Plotting your data on a graph or chart

One of the best ways to present your data after you've processed it is to plot your results on a graph or chart. You need to know these rules about drawing graphs and charts:

- Draw it nice and big (covering at least two-thirds of the graph paper).
- Label both axes and remember to include the units.
- If you've got more than one set of data include a key.
- Give your graph a title explaining what it is showing.

Whatever type of graph or chart you draw, make sure you follow the rules above. There are lots of different types you can use. The type you should use depends on the type of data you've collected.

Bar charts and histograms

Bar charts can be used to show **categoric**, **discrete** or **continuous data**.

- If the data is categoric or discrete, include gaps between the bars (see Figure 1).
- If the data is continuous, the bars should be touching.

Whatever the data type, bars in a bar chart must always be the same width.

Histograms are a useful way of displaying frequency data when the independent variable is continuous and the data is grouped together in classes.

Histograms may look like bar charts, but it's the area of the bars that represents the frequency (rather than the height) so the bars can be different widths, see Figure 1.

The height of each bar is called the **frequency density**. This is found by dividing the frequency by the class width. (The class width is just the width of the bar on the histogram.)

Tip: Categoric data is data that comes in distinct categories, e.g. 'state of matter (solid, liquid, gas)' and 'type of material (e.g. wood metal, paper)'. Discrete data is numerical data that can only take certain values, because there are no in-between values, e.g. 'number of people' (because you can't have half a person). Continuous data is numerical data that can have any value within a range, e.g. length, volume, temperature.

Tip: Frequency is just the number of times that something occurs. It's often shown in a frequency table.

Tip: Don't be fooled by the height of the bars in a histogram — the tallest bar doesn't always belong to the class with the greatest frequency.

Tip: A frequency diagram is a histogram where the width of all the bars are the same and frequency is plotted on the y-axis, rather than frequency density.

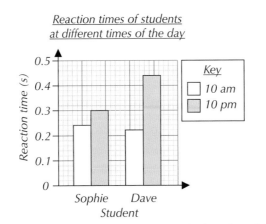

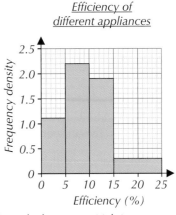

Figure 1: *An example of a bar chart (left) and a histogram (right).*

Plotting points

If the independent and the dependent variables are continuous you should plot points on a graph to display the data. Here are the golden rules specifically for plotting points on graphs:

- Put the independent variable (the thing you change) on the *x*-axis.
- Put the dependent variable (the thing you measure) on the *y*-axis.
- To plot the points, use a sharp pencil and make a neat little cross.

Tip: The *x*-axis is the horizontal axis and the *y*-axis is the vertical axis.

In general, you shouldn't join the crosses up. Only specific graphs, such as distance-time graphs (page 27) and velocity-time graphs (page 30), will need you to connect every point you plot. Otherwise, you'll need to draw a line of best fit (or a curve of best fit if your points make a curve). When drawing a line (or curve), try to draw the line through or as near to as many points as possible, ignoring anomalous results. When you draw a line of best fit, there should be roughly as many points above the line as underneath it.

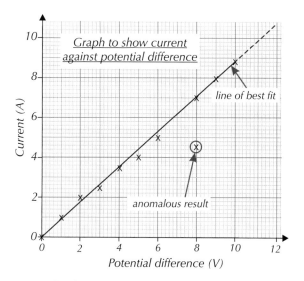

Tip: Use the biggest data values you've got to draw a sensible scale on your axes. Here, the highest current is 8.8 A, so it makes sense to label the *y*-axis up to 10 A.

Tip: If you're not in an exam, you can use a computer to plot your graph and draw your line of best fit for you.

Figure 2: *An example of a graph with points plotted and a line of best fit drawn.*

Correlations

Graphs are used to show the relationship between two variables. Data can show three different types of correlation (relationship).

Tip: Just because two variables are correlated doesn't mean that the change in one is causing the change in the other. There might be other factors involved, or it could be due to chance — see pages 20-21 for more.

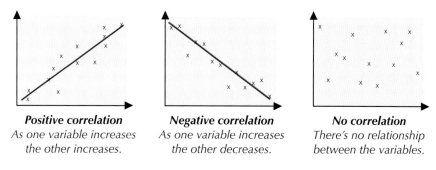

Positive correlation	**Negative correlation**	**No correlation**
As one variable increases the other increases.	*As one variable increases the other decreases.*	*There's no relationship between the variables.*

Figure 3: *Examples of different types of correlations shown on a graph.*

9. Units

Using the correct units is important when you're drawing graphs or calculating values with an equation. Otherwise your numbers don't really mean anything.

S.I. units

Tip: S.I. stands for 'Système International', which is French for 'international system'.

Tip: This covers GCSE physics specification point 1.1, "recall and use the SI units for physical quantities".

Lots of different units can be used to describe the same quantity. For example, volume can be given in terms of cubic feet, cubic metres, litres or pints. It would be quite confusing if different scientists used different units to define quantities, as it would be hard to compare people's data. To stop this happening, scientists have come up with a set of standard units, called **S.I. units**, that all scientists use to measure their data. Here are some S.I. units you'll see in physics:

Quantity	S.I. Unit
mass	kilogram, kg
length	metre, m
time	second, s
electric current	ampere, A

Figure 1: Some common S.I. units used in physics.

Scaling prefixes

Quantities come in a huge range of sizes. For example, the volume of a swimming pool might be around 2 000 000 000 cm³, while the volume of a cup is around 250 cm³. To make the size of numbers more manageable, larger or smaller units are used. Figure 2 shows the prefixes which can be used in front of units (e.g. metres) to make them bigger or smaller:

Tip: This covers GCSE physics specification point 1.2, "recall and use multiples and sub-multiples of units, including giga (G), mega (M), kilo (k), centi (c), milli (m), micro (μ) and nano (n)".

prefix	tera (T)	giga (G)	mega (M)	kilo (k)	deci (d)	centi (c)	milli (m)	micro (μ)	nano (n)
multiple of unit	10^{12}	10^9	1 000 000 (10^6)	1000	0.1	0.01	0.001	0.000001 (10^{-6})	10^{-9}

Figure 2: Scaling prefixes used with units.

These prefixes are called **scaling prefixes** and they tell you how much bigger or smaller a unit is than the original unit. So one kilometre is one thousand metres.

Converting between units

Exam Tip
If you're going from a smaller unit to a larger unit, your number should get smaller.
If you're going from a larger unit to a smaller unit, your number should get larger.
This is a handy way to check you've done the conversion correctly.

To swap from one unit to another, all you need to know is what number you have to divide or multiply by to get from the original unit to the new unit — this is called the **conversion factor** and is equal to the number of times the smaller unit goes into the larger unit.

- To go from a bigger unit to a smaller unit, you multiply by the conversion factor.

- To go from a smaller unit to a bigger unit, you divide by the conversion factor.

There are some conversions that'll be particularly useful for GCSE Physics. Here they are...

Mass can have units of kg and g.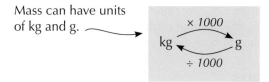

Exam Tip
Before you put values into an equation, you need to make sure they have the right units.

Length can have lots of units, including mm, μm and nm.

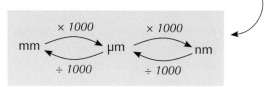

Tip: This covers GCSE physics specification point 1.3, "Be able to convert between different units, including hours to seconds".

Time can have units of hours (hr), minutes (min) and s.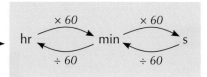

Area can have units of m², cm² and mm².

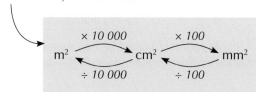

Exam Tip
Being familiar with these common conversions could save you time when it comes to doing calculations in the exam, and will help you get the right answer.

Volume can have units of m³, dm³ and cm³.

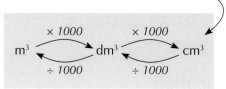

Tip: Volume is also often given in l (litres) or ml (millilitres). To convert, you'll need to remember that 1 ml = 1 cm³ and so 1 l = 1000 cm³.

Examples

- To go from dm³ to cm³, you'd multiply by 1000.

  2 dm³ is equal to 2 × 1000 = **2000 cm³**

- To go from grams to kilograms, you'd divide by 1000.

  3400 g is equal to 3400 ÷ 1000 = **3.4 kg**

10. Conclusions and Evaluations

So... you've planned and carried out an amazing experiment, got your data and have processed and presented it in a sensible way. Now it's time to figure out what your data actually tells you, and how much you can trust what it says.

How to draw conclusions

Drawing conclusions might seem pretty straightforward — you just look at your data and say what pattern or relationship you see between the dependent and independent variables.

But you've got to be really careful that your conclusion matches the data you've got and doesn't go any further. You also need to be able to use your results to justify your conclusion (i.e. back up your conclusion with some specific data).

When writing a conclusion you need to refer back to the original hypothesis and say whether the data supports it or not.

Example

This table shows the count rate detected when one of two different materials (A and B) is placed between a radioactive sample and the detector.

Material	Count rate (counts per second)
A	85
B	13
No material	98

The conclusion of this experiment would be that material B blocks more of the radiation from the sample than material A.

The justification for this conclusion is that the count rate was much lower using material B compared with using material A.

You can't conclude that material B blocks more radiation from any other radioactive sample — the results might be completely different.

Correlation and causation

Tip: Graphs are useful for seeing whether two variables are correlated (see page 17).

If two things are correlated (i.e. there's a relationship between them) it doesn't necessarily mean that a change in one variable is causing the change in the other — this is really important, don't forget it. There are three possible reasons for a correlation:

1. Chance

Tip: Causation just means one thing is causing another.

Even though it might seem a bit weird, it's possible that two things show a correlation in a study purely because of chance.

Example

One study might find a correlation between the number of people suffering from insomnia (trouble sleeping) and the distance they live from a wind farm. But other scientists don't get a correlation when they investigate it — the results of the first study are just a fluke.

---

2. They're linked by a third variable

A lot of the time it may look as if a change in one variable is causing a change in the other, but it isn't — a third variable links the two things.

> **Example**
>
> There's a correlation between water temperature and shark attacks. This isn't because warm water makes sharks crazy. Instead, they're linked by a third variable — the number of people swimming (more people swim when the water's hotter, and with more people in the water shark attacks increase).

3. Causation

Sometimes a change in one variable does cause a change in the other.

> **Example**
>
> There's a correlation between exposure to radiation and cancer. This is because radiation can damage body cells and cause cancer.

You can only conclude that a correlation is due to cause if you've controlled all the variables that could be affecting the result. (For the radiation example, this would include age and exposure to other things that cause cancer.)

Evaluation

An evaluation is a critical analysis of the whole investigation. Here you need to comment on the following points about your experiment and the data you gathered:

- **The method**: Was it valid? Did you control all the other variables to make it a fair test?

- **The quality of your results:** Was there enough evidence to reach a valid conclusion? Were the results repeatable, reproducible, accurate and precise?

- **Anomalous results**: Were any of the results anomalous? If there were none then say so. If there were any, try to explain them — were they caused by errors in measurement? Were there any other variables that could have affected the results? You should comment on the level of uncertainty in your results too.

Once you've thought about these points you can decide how much confidence you have in your conclusion. For example, if your results are repeatable, reproducible and valid and they back up your conclusion then you can have a high degree of confidence in your conclusion.

You can also suggest any changes to the method that would improve the quality of the results, so that you could have more confidence in your conclusion. For example, you might suggest changing the way you controlled a variable, or increasing the number of measurements you took. Taking more measurements at narrower intervals could give you a more accurate result.

You could also make more predictions based on your conclusion, then further experiments could be carried out to test them.

Tip: Lots of things are correlated without being directly related. E.g. the level of carbon dioxide (CO_2) in the atmosphere and the amount of obesity have both increased over the last 100 years, but that doesn't mean increased atmospheric CO_2 is causing people to become obese.

Tip: When suggesting improvements to the investigation, always make sure that you say why you think this would make the results better.

Learning Objectives:

- Be able to explain that a scalar quantity has magnitude (size) but no specific direction.
- Be able to explain that a vector quantity has both magnitude (size) and a specific direction.
- Be able to recall that velocity is speed in a stated direction.
- Be able to explain the difference between vector and scalar quantities.
- Be able to recall vector and scalar quantities, including: displacement, distance, velocity, speed, acceleration, force, weight, mass, momentum, energy.
- **H** Be able to explain that an object moving in a circular orbit at constant speed has a changing velocity (qualitative only).
- Be able to recall some typical speeds encountered in everyday experience for wind and sound, and for walking, running, cycling and other transportation systems.
- Be able to recall and use the equations:
  a (average) speed = distance ÷ time,
  b distance travelled = average speed × time.

Specification References
2.1-2.6, 2.12, 2.20

1. Distance, Displacement, Speed and Velocity

Some of your bread and butter physics here — it's all about things that are moving. Make sure you really understand it, otherwise things could get tricky.

Vectors and scalars

Some physical quantities have magnitude (size) but no direction. These are called **scalar** quantities. For example, speed describes how fast an object is going and distance describes how far something has travelled. Other examples of scalar quantities are distance, mass, energy and time.

Vector quantities have a magnitude and a direction. For example, **velocity** is a vector quantity. It describes the speed of an object in a certain direction.

Lots of other quantities are vectors too — some examples are force, **displacement** (distance in a given direction), acceleration (page 25), weight (page 37) and momentum (page 44).

The direction of a vector can be given in various ways, e.g. towards a fixed point or as a bearing (which is a three-digit angle from north, e.g. 035°).

Example

A person walks 5 m north and then 5 m south.
Calculate the distance they travel and their displacement.

Distance travelled = 5 + 5 = 10 m
Displacement = 0 m as they have ended up back at their starting position.

Example

The cars below are all travelling at the same speed of 0.5 m/s, but they're all moving in different directions, so all have a different velocity.

Moving in a circle [Higher]

You can have objects travelling at a constant speed with a changing velocity. This happens when the object is changing direction whilst staying at the same speed.

An object moving in a circle at a constant speed has a constantly changing velocity, as the direction is always changing, for example a car going around a roundabout.

Figure 1: *People on a Ferris wheel will have a constant speed but a changing velocity as the wheel turns.*

Everyday speeds

Objects rarely travel at a constant speed. E.g. when you walk, run or travel in a car, your speed is almost always changing. Whilst every person, train, bus etc. is different, there is usually a typical speed that each object travels at. Remember these typical speeds for everyday objects:

A person walking — 1.5 m/s	A car in a built up area — 13 m/s
A person running — 3 m/s	A car on the motorway — 30 m/s
A person cycling — 6 m/s	A train — 55 m/s
Wind speed — 5-20 m/s	A plane — 250 m/s
Speed of sound in air — 340 m/s	A ferry 15 m/s

Lots of different things can affect the speed something travels at. For example, the speed at which a person is cycling may depend on their fitness, their age, the terrain (what kind of land they're moving over, e.g. roads, fields), and so on.

Tip: It might help to remember that running is typically about half the speed of cycling, and walking is about half the speed of running.

Tip: Lots of everyday speeds are given in miles per hour (mph) instead of m/s. A rough way to get from mph to m/s is to divide the value by two — e.g. 20 mph is roughly 10 m/s.

Calculating speed

As the speeds of objects aren't usually constant, the average speed across a given distance is usually calculated:

$$\text{(average) speed} = \text{distance} \div \text{time}$$

You can also find the distance travelled by an object if you assume that it travels at an average speed for a given amount of time:

$$\text{distance travelled} = \text{average speed} \times \text{time}$$

You may sometimes see these equations written in symbols. For example:

Tip: You need to know the best ways to measure distances and times when doing experiments — see page 41 for more.

Tip: You can use formula triangles to help you rearrange equations. There's more about them on page 345. For this equation, the triangle would be:

x = distance travelled (m) $x = v \times t$ v = average speed (m/s) t = time (s)

Practice Questions — Fact Recall

Q1   State whether the following quantities are scalars or vectors.

   a) displacement   b) speed   c) velocity   d) distance

Q2   How can an object have a constant speed and a changing velocity?

Q3   Give a typical speed for when someone is:

   a) cycling,   b) running,   c) walking.

Q4   Give the equation that relates speed, distance and time, for an object travelling at a constant speed. Give the units of each term.

Practice Questions — Application

Q1   A car drives 16 m east, then 25 m south, then 16 m west.

   a) Calculate the distance travelled by the car.

   b) Calculate the displacement of the car.

Q2   A person walks for 18 s. Estimate the distance that they will have walked during this time.

Q3   A train travels from station A to station B at an average speed of 45 m/s. It takes the train 120 s to reach station B. The train then travels at an average speed of 60 m/s to station C. Stations B and C are 16.8 km apart.

   a) Calculate how far apart stations A and B are.

   b) Calculate how long it takes for the train to travel from station B to station C.

   c) Find the average speed of the train between stations A and C.

2. Acceleration

How quickly an object changes its speed is all to do with its acceleration.

What is acceleration?

Acceleration is definitely not the same as velocity or speed:

- Acceleration is how quickly the velocity is changing.

- This change in velocity can be a change in speed, or a change in direction, or both.

You can calculate the acceleration of an object using the formula below. If acceleration isn't constant, this will give you the average acceleration over that period.

a = acceleration (m/s²) ⟶ $a = \dfrac{(v - u)}{t}$ ⟵ $(v - u)$ = change in velocity (m/s)

t = time taken (s)

Here, $v - u$ is just 'final velocity (v) – initial velocity (u)'. So if an object is slowing down, the change in velocity will be negative, giving a negative acceleration. A negative acceleration is called deceleration.

The units of acceleration are m/s² — don't get them confused with the units for speed and velocity, m/s.

Example

Find the average acceleration of a dog whose velocity goes from 2 m/s to 6 m/s in 5 s.

$$a = \frac{(v - u)}{t} = \frac{(6 - 2)}{5} = 0.8 \text{ m/s}^2$$

Everyday accelerations

You might have to estimate the acceleration (or deceleration) of an object. To do this, you'll need to use the typical speeds from page 23.

Example

It takes a cyclist 4 seconds to reach his top speed from rest.
Estimate the acceleration of the cyclist.

First, give a sensible speed for the cyclist to be travelling at. The ~ symbol just means it's an approximate value (or answer).

A typical speed for a cyclist is ~6 m/s.

Put these numbers into the acceleration equation.

$$a = \frac{(v - u)}{t} = \frac{(6 - 0)}{4} = 1.5 \text{ m/s}^2$$

Learning Objectives:

- Be able to recall and use the equation:
  $a = \dfrac{(v - u)}{t}$.
- Be able to estimate the magnitudes of everyday accelerations.
- Be able to use the equation:
  $v^2 - u^2 = 2 \times a \times x$
- Be able to recall that the acceleration, g, in free fall is 10 m/s².

Specification References
2.8, 2.9, 2.13

Tip: If you struggle to remember what u and v stand for — u comes before v in the alphabet, so u is initial velocity and v is final velocity.

Tip: You might see change in velocity written as Δv.

Figure 1: *When cheetahs start running, they get to a high velocity very quickly, which means they have a very high acceleration.*

Exam Tip
Examiners accept a range of answers for estimate questions, so don't panic too much if you can't remember the exact speeds from page 23. Just make a sensible guess.

Uniform acceleration

Constant acceleration is sometimes called uniform acceleration. You can use this equation for uniform acceleration:

v = final velocity (m/s)

u = initial velocity (m/s)

a = acceleration (m/s²)

x = distance (m)

$$v^2 - u^2 = 2 \times a \times x$$

Tip: Free fall means that you are assuming that only gravity is acting on the object as it falls. You ignore any other forces (like air resistance).

Acceleration due to gravity (g) is uniform for all objects in free fall. It's roughly equal to 10 m/s² near the Earth's surface and has the same value as gravitational field strength.

Example

A ball has been dropped from the top of a building. The velocity of the ball when it is 2.25 m from the ground is 6.0 m/s. Calculate the velocity of the ball when it reaches the ground. You can assume there is no air resistance.

First, rearrange the equation so v^2 is on one side: $v^2 = 2 \times a \times x + u^2$

Then put the numbers in. Remember, acceleration, $a = g = 10$ m/s².

$v^2 = (2 \times 10 \times 2.25) + 6.0^2 = 81$

Finally, square root the whole thing to get v:

$v = \sqrt{81} = 9$ m/s

Practice Questions — Fact Recall

Q1 What is the equation for calculating acceleration from the change in an object's velocity and the time taken for this change.

Q2 What are the units of acceleration?

Q3 What is the value of acceleration due to gravity?

Practice Questions — Application

Q1 A car is travelling forwards at 25 m/s and the driver applies the brakes. The car's velocity drops steadily for 5 seconds until it becomes 10 m/s. Find its acceleration during this time.

Q2 A cheetah begins from rest and accelerates at an average acceleration of 4 m/s² over a period of 5 s. Calculate the speed of the cheetah after this time.

Tip: If an object starts from rest, its initial velocity is 0 m/s.

Q3 A runner is running at a steady velocity of 5.6 m/s. When she is 38.1 m away from the finish line, she accelerates at a constant rate. If her velocity at the finish line is 7.1 m/s, what was her acceleration as she approached the finish line?

Q4 An apple falls from a tree and hits the ground at a speed of 6.0 m/s. Calculate the height the apple fell from. You can assume there is no air resistance.

Tip: Remember acceleration due to gravity is about 10 m/s².

3. Distance/Time Graphs

Distance/time graphs show how far an object has travelled in a given time. They're useful in physics because they help keep track of an object's motion.

Learning Objective:
- Be able to analyse distance/time graphs including determination of speed from the gradient.

Specification Reference 2.7

What are distance/time graphs?

Distance/time graphs are a good way of describing the motion of something travelling in a straight line. They have time on the horizontal axis and distance on the vertical axis.

Average speed = distance ÷ time (see page 23), so the gradient (slope) of a distance-time graph tells you how fast your object is travelling. This is because the gradient is the change in the distance (vertical axis) divided by the change in time (horizontal axis).

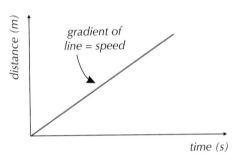

distance (m)

gradient of line = speed

time (s)

Figure 1: *A basic distance/time graph.*

Drawing and interpreting distance/time graphs

You need to be able to draw and interpret distance/time graphs in the exam. Here are some important points to remember about the distance/time graph for an object:

1. Gradient = speed.

2. Straight uphill sections mean it is travelling at a steady speed.

3. The steeper the graph, the faster it's going.

4. Flat sections are where it's stationary — it's stopped.

5. Curves represent acceleration (speeding up) or deceleration (slowing down) (page 25).

6. A steepening curve means it's accelerating/speeding up — the gradient is increasing.

7. A levelling off curve means it's decelerating/slowing down — the gradient is decreasing.

Tip: Take a look at page 346 for how to calculate the gradient of a straight-line graph.

Tip: The speed of the object is faster in the first 20 s compared to the speed of the object in the last 30 s. You can tell because the gradient is steeper in the first 20 s.

Tip: Be careful with the units on the axes of these graphs. Here you have distance in m and time in s, so the gradient is speed in m/s. But you may have to deal with graphs with axes in other units of distance (e.g. kilometres) and time (e.g. hours).

Tip: Take a look at page 348 for more on drawing tangents.

Tip: You can also calculate the average speed of an object when it has non-uniform motion (i.e. it's accelerating) by dividing the total distance travelled by the time it takes to travel that distance.

Tip: When drawing a tangent, always make it as long as possible, so it's easier to work out the gradient.

Example

This distance/time graph shows an object that moves off from its starting point at a steady speed for 20 s, then stops for 20 s. It then accelerates for 25 s and decelerates for 25 s before resuming a steady speed for 30 s.

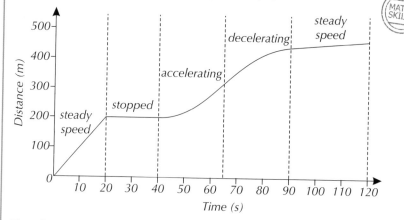

The object's speed during the first 20 s can be found from the gradient:

$$\text{gradient} = \frac{\text{change in the vertical}}{\text{change in the horizontal}} = \frac{200 - 0}{20 - 0} = 10 \text{ m/s}$$

Calculating speed for accelerating objects

If an object is changing speed (accelerating), you can find its speed at a point by finding the gradient of the tangent to the curve at that point.

Example

The graph below is the distance/time graph for a bike accelerating for 30 s and then travelling at a steady speed for 5 s.

The speed of the bike at 25 s can be found by drawing a tangent to the curve (shown by the red line) at 25 s and then finding the gradient of the tangent:

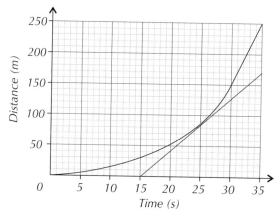

$$\text{gradient} = \frac{\text{change in the vertical}}{\text{change in the horizontal}} = \frac{170 - 0}{35 - 15} = 8.5 \text{ m/s}$$

Practice Questions — Fact Recall

Q1   What does the gradient of a distance/time graph represent?

Q2   What does a flat section on a distance/time graph tell you?

Q3   What does a curved section on a distance/time graph represent?

Q4   How would you calculate the speed of an accelerating object at a given time from its distance-time graph?

Practice Questions — Application

Q1   For this distance/time graph, say what's happening to the speed of the object in each of the sections labelled A, B, C and D.

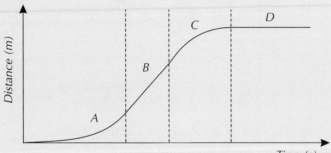

Q2   An object moving in a straight line accelerates for 10 seconds and then moves at a steady speed for 5 seconds. Describe the distance-time graph for the object during this time.

Q3   Look at this table showing the distance travelled (in a straight line) by a toy car over a period of time. The car initially moves with a constant speed, then decelerates to rest over 8 seconds.

Time (s)	0	2	4	6	8	10	12	14	16
Distance (m)	0.0	2.0	4.0	5.8	7.0	7.8	8.0	8.0	8.0

a) Plot these values and join the points on a distance/time graph to represent the car's motion.

b) Calculate the speed of the car between 0 and 4 seconds.

c) Estimate the speed of the car at 8 seconds.

- Be able to analyse velocity/time graphs to:
  a compare acceleration from gradients qualitatively.
  b calculate the acceleration from the gradient (for uniform acceleration only).
  c determine the distance travelled using the area between the graph line and the time axis (for uniform acceleration only).

Specification Reference 2.10

4. Velocity/Time Graphs

You just saw how an object's motion can be shown on a distance/time graph. You can also show motion on a velocity/time graph. Woohoo...

Velocity/time graphs

You can plot a **velocity/time graph** to show an object's motion. Time goes on the horizontal axis and velocity goes on the vertical axis.

Acceleration is the change in an object's velocity over time (see page 25). So the gradient of a velocity/time graph tells you the acceleration of your object. The steeper the line, the greater the acceleration of the object.

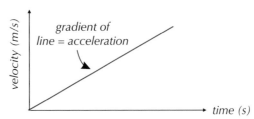

Figure 1: A basic velocity/time graph.

Here are some important things about velocity/time graphs:

1. The gradient of a velocity/time graph gives the object's acceleration.

2. Flat sections represent steady speed.

3. The steeper the graph, the greater the acceleration or deceleration.

4. Uphill sections show acceleration.

5. Downhill sections show deceleration.

6. A curve means changing acceleration.

Tip: Make sure you don't get confused between velocity/time graphs and distance/time graphs (which you met on page 27).

> ### Example
>
> This velocity/time graph shows an object that accelerates from rest to 20 m/s in 20 seconds then travels at a steady velocity for 20 seconds. It then accelerates at an increasing rate for 30 seconds, travels at a steady 40 m/s for a further 30 seconds and finally decelerates back to rest in 20 seconds.
>
>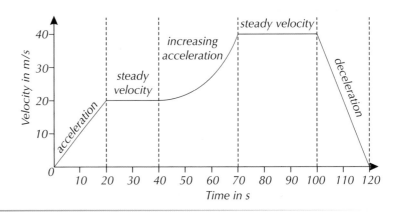

Tip: If an object wasn't moving, its velocity/time graph would just be a straight line along the x-axis, i.e. velocity = 0 m/s.

Acceleration on a velocity/time graph

The acceleration of an object can be found by calculating the gradient of its velocity/time graph.

Tip: This is the same method as finding the speed from a distance/time graph (see page 28).

Example

This is a velocity/time graph for a race car accelerating from 0 to 50 m/s. Calculate the acceleration of the car between 3 and 6 seconds.

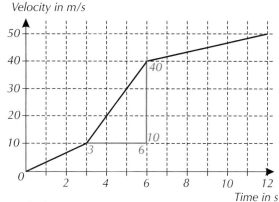

$$\text{acceleration} = \text{gradient}$$
$$= \frac{\text{change in vertical}}{\text{change in horizontal}} = \frac{(40 - 10)}{(6 - 3)} = 10 \, \text{m/s}^2$$

Distance travelled on a velocity/time graph

The area beneath a velocity/time graph gives the distance travelled. The distance travelled in any time interval is equal to the area under the velocity/time graph in that interval.

Example

For the same car as in the previous example, calculate the distance travelled between 3 and 6 seconds.

- The distance travelled is equal to the area under the graph, so look at the graph between 3 and 6 seconds. It might seem difficult to work out the area of this part of the graph, but you can make it easier by splitting the area into a triangle (**A**) and a rectangle (**B**).

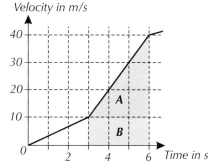

Tip: You could also use the 'counting the squares method' (see page 349) to find the area under the graph.

- You can then calculate the area of each shape individually:

$$\text{Area}_A = \frac{1}{2} \times \text{base} \times \text{height} \qquad \text{Area}_B = \text{base} \times \text{height}$$
$$= \frac{1}{2} \times 3 \times 30 = 45 \qquad\qquad\quad = 3 \times 10 = 30$$

- Then just find the total area by adding Area$_A$ and Area$_B$ together:

   distance travelled = total area under graph = 45 + 30 = 75 m

Tip: Remember to check the units of any information you read from a graph — it can be easy to miss a prefix, which could mess up your calculation.

Q1 What does the gradient of a velocity/time graph represent?

Q2 What does the area under a velocity/time graph represent?

Practice Questions — Application

Q1 For this velocity/time graph, say what's happening to the acceleration of the object in each of the sections labelled A, B, C and D.

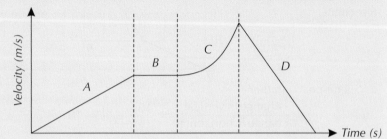

Q2 Below is a velocity/time graph for a cyclist during a race.

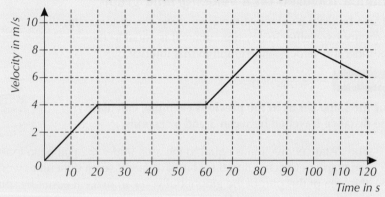

a) What's the cyclist's velocity at 40 seconds?

b) During which part(s) of the race is the cyclist decelerating?

c) What's the cyclist's acceleration between 60 and 80 seconds?

d) How far does the cyclist travel in the first 60 seconds of the race?

Q3 A car travels forwards at 25 m/s for 3 s before the driver applies the brakes. The car decelerates steadily for 5 seconds until its velocity becomes 10 m/s. Plot a velocity/time graph to show this and, using the graph, find its acceleration whilst it's slowing down.

Tip: Remember, acceleration can have a negative value (in which case it can be called deceleration).

5. Newton's First Law

Newton was a pretty smart guy, who came up with three famous laws of motion. Lucky for you, you have to learn all of them. Let's start with the first...

Resultant forces

If you have a number of forces acting at a single point, you can replace them with a single force which has the same effect as all the original forces acting together. This single, overall force is called the **resultant force**. In some cases, the resultant force is zero.

What is Newton's First Law?

Newton's First Law says that a resultant force is needed to change the motion of an object. In other words, a force is needed to make something move, or to change the speed it's moving at or direction it's moving in.

Zero resultant force

Objects don't just start moving on their own — if there's no resultant force acting on a stationary object, there's no acceleration and it will just stay put.

> If the resultant force on a stationary object
> is zero, the object will remain stationary.

If there's no resultant force acting on an object, it won't change velocity. That means if it's already moving, it will just keep moving at the same velocity.

> If the resultant force on a moving object is zero,
> it'll just carry on moving at the same velocity.

If any object (be it a train, a car, a horse, or anything else really) is moving at a constant velocity then the forces on it must all be balanced. Never let yourself stray down the path of thinking that things need a constant resultant force to keep them moving — this is a common misconception.

To keep going at a steady velocity, there must be zero resultant force. This doesn't mean there must be no driving force — it means the driving force is balanced by other forces, like friction and air resistance.

Example

A van travelling at a steady velocity has zero resultant force acting on it. This is because the driving force from the engine is balanced by friction forces.

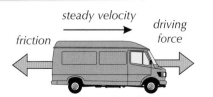

steady velocity

friction   driving force

Learning Objective:

- Be able to recall Newton's first law and use it in the following situations:
  a where the resultant force on a body is zero, i.e. the body is moving at a constant velocity or is at rest.
  b where the resultant force is not zero, i.e. the speed and/ or direction of the body change(s).

Specification Reference 2.14

Tip: Objects experiencing a zero resultant force are said to be in equilibrium. There's more about this on page 209.

Tip: Don't forget, velocity is a vector (see page 22). So in order for an object to have a constant velocity, the object must keep moving at the same speed <u>and</u> in the same direction.

Non-zero resultant force

In most situations, there will be a resultant force acting on an object.

Tip: Remember — when an object accelerates, its velocity changes, and a change in velocity means a change in speed or direction of motion (or both) (see page 25).

> If there is a non-zero resultant force on an object, its velocity will change (it will accelerate in the direction of the force).

This applies to both stationary objects and ones that are already moving. When a resultant force acts on an object, the change in velocity it experiences can take five different forms:

- starting
- stopping
- changing direction
- speeding up
- slowing down

Tip: ▣ On a free body force diagram (see page 207), if there's a resultant force, then the total size of the arrows in one direction will be different to the total size of the arrows in the opposite direction.

Example — continued

The van driver presses the accelerator pedal, which increases the driving force produced by the engine.

There is now a resultant force on the van and its speed increases.

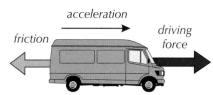

Figure 1: *When a rocket is launched, there needs to be a force acting upwards that is larger than the weight of the rocket, so that it accelerates away from Earth.*

Practice Question — Fact Recall

Q1 Say what will happen to the object in each of the following cases:

a) No resultant force acting on a stationary object.

b) A resultant force acting on a stationary object.

c) No resultant force acting on a moving object.

d) A resultant force acting on a moving object in the same direction as its motion.

e) A resultant force acting on a moving object in the opposite direction to its motion.

Practice Question — Application

Q1 If a rocket is moving through space at a steady velocity, what can you say about the resultant force acting on the rocket?

6. Newton's Second Law and Inertia

So you've seen from Newton's First Law that an object will accelerate if there's a non-zero resultant force acting on it. You can find the size of the acceleration using Newton's Second Law.

What is Newton's Second Law?

Newton's Second Law has two points that you need to know:

- The larger the force acting on an object, the more the object accelerates — the force and the acceleration are **directly proportional**. You can write this as $F \propto a$.

- Acceleration is also inversely proportional to the mass of the object — so an object with a larger mass will accelerate less than one with a smaller mass (for a fixed resultant force).

There's an incredibly useful formula that describes Newton's Second Law:

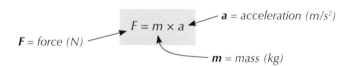

$$F = m \times a$$

F = force (N)

a = acceleration (m/s²)

m = mass (kg)

Tip: If you need to, you can use this formula triangle for $F = m \times a$:

Example 1

A car with a mass of 920 kg accelerates from rest with an initial acceleration of 2.5 m/s².
Calculate the force required to produce this acceleration.

Simply substitute in the values to $F = m \times a$

$F = m \times a = 920 \times 2.5 = 2300$ N

Example 2

A car has a mass of 1250 kg. At 70 mph the resultant force acting on the car is 110 N, in the car's direction of motion. Find its acceleration at 70 mph.

Rearrange the equation for a:

$a = F \div m$

Then substitute in the values:

$a = 110 \div 1250 = 0.088$ m/s²

Circular motion Higher

You saw on page 23 that an object travelling in a circle is constantly changing velocity and therefore accelerating. This means that a resultant force must constantly be being applied to the object. This resultant force acts towards the centre of the circle and is called the **centripetal force**.

Figure 1: *A car going round a roundabout experiences a resultant force that acts towards the centre of the roundabout.*

Inertia Higher

Figure 2: *A full trolley will accelerate less for a given pushing force then an empty one would, as it has a larger mass.*

You saw on pages 33-34 that until acted upon by a resultant force, objects at rest stay at rest and objects moving at a steady speed will stay moving at that speed. This is Newton's First Law. This tendency to continue moving at the same velocity is called **inertia**.

An object's **inertial mass** measures how difficult it is to change the velocity of the object. Imagine that a bowling ball and a golf ball roll towards you with the same velocity. It would require a larger force to stop the bowling ball than the golf ball in the same time. This is because the bowling ball has a larger inertial mass.

Inertial mass can be found using Newton's Second Law, $F = m \times a$. Rearranging this gives:

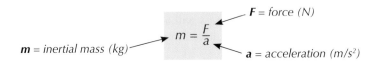

$$F = \text{force (N)}$$
$$m = \frac{F}{a}$$
$$m = \text{inertial mass (kg)}$$
$$a = \text{acceleration (m/s}^2\text{)}$$

So inertial mass is defined as the ratio of force over acceleration.

Practice Questions — Fact Recall

Q1 Write down the formula used for calculating the force acting on an object from its mass and its acceleration. Say what each term represents and the units it's measured in.

Q2 a) What is the name of the resultant force acting on objects moving in a circle?

b) In what direction does this force act?

Q3 What is inertial mass?

Practice Questions — Application

Q1 Two identical remote-control cars take part in a straight race across flat ground. One of the cars is loaded with a large rock. Which of the two will win the race? Explain your answer.

Q2 When a catapult is released, it applies 303 N of force to a rock with a mass of 1.5 kg. Find the acceleration of the rock at this point.

7. Weight, Mass and Gravity

Gravity is pretty important. It not only gives everything a weight, it also keeps us glued to Earth.

Gravitational force

Gravitational forces act between all masses, but you only notice them when one or more of the masses are really big, e.g. a planet. Anything near a planet or star is attracted to it very strongly. This has two important effects:

1. On the surface of a planet, it makes all things accelerate (see page 25) towards the ground.

2. It gives everything a weight (see below).

Weight and mass

Weight and mass are not the same — mass is just the amount of 'stuff' in an object. For any given object this will have the same value anywhere in the universe.

Weight is the force acting on an object due to gravity (the gravitational force on the object). This force is caused by gravitational fields, and the size of the force depends on the object's mass and the strength of the gravitational field that the object is in.

Weight is directly proportional to both mass and gravitational field strength. In other words, if the mass of an object is increased, its weight will increase by the same proportion — e.g. doubling the mass doubles the weight. And if the gravitational field the object is in gets stronger, its weight will increase by the same proportion.

Gravitational field strength can vary with location — this means that the weight of an object can change with its location.

> **Example**
>
> A 1 kg mass will have a mass of 1 kg on both the Earth and the Moon.
>
> But it will have a weight of about 10 N on the Earth, and a weight of about 1.6 N on the Moon. This is because the gravitational field strength on the surface of the Moon is less than on the surface of the Earth.

Calculating weight

You can calculate the weight of an object if you know its mass (*m*) and the strength of the gravitational field at that point (*g*):

$$W = m \times g$$

W = weight in N

m = mass in kg

g = gravitational field strength in N/kg

Learning Objectives:
- Be able to define weight.
- Be able to describe the relationship between the weight of a body and the gravitational field strength.
- Be able to recall and use the equation: $W = m \times g$.
- Be able to describe how weight is measured.

Specification References 2.16-2.18

Tip: Weight is a non-contact force caused by the gravitational fields around the planet and the object interacting (page 205).

Exam Tip
For the Earth, *g* is equal to 10 N/kg. You'll always be given a value of *g* to use in your exam.

Tip: The weight equation is just a special case of $F = m \times a$ (p.35).

Example 1

What is the weight, in newtons, of a 5 kg mass, both on Earth (g = 10 N/kg) and on the Moon (g = 1.6 N/kg)?

Just use the formula $W = m \times g$ in each case:

On Earth:	On the Moon:
$W = m \times g = 5 \times 10$	$W = m \times g = 5 \times 1.6$
$= 50$ N	$= 8$ N

Tip: You can use a formula triangle to help rearrange the equation:

There's more on formula triangles on page 345.

Example 2

The value of g on Mars is 3.71 N/kg. What is the mass of a buggy if its weight on Mars is 4452 N?

Just rearrange the formula to make mass the subject, then plug in the correct numbers:

$$W = m \times g, \text{ so } m = W \div g = 4452 \div 3.71 = 1200 \text{ kg}$$

Figure 1: *Measuring the weight of an apple using a newton meter.*

Measuring weight

You can measure an object's weight directly with a newton meter (sometimes called a spring balance). To do this, secure the newton meter so that it hangs vertically downwards. Attach the item you want to weigh to the hook on the bottom of the newton meter (see Figure 1). Make sure that the object hangs freely (e.g. it isn't resting on a table). Wait until the object has stopped swinging or bouncing, then read off the weight from the scale on the newton meter.

Practice Questions — Fact Recall

Q1 Define weight.

Q2 Describe how the weight of an object is related to the strength of the gravitational field it is in.

Q3 State the formula used to calculate the weight of an object.

Q4 What apparatus is used to measure the weight of an object on Earth?

Practice Question — Application

Q1 A rock on Earth has a mass of 15 kg. g on Earth = 10 N/kg.

a) Calculate the weight of the rock on Earth.

b) What would happen to the mass of the rock if it was moved to the surface of the Moon?

8. Investigating Motion

Here's an experiment you can do to investigate Newton's Second Law (p.35). You just need to get your hands on a trolley, a light gate and some masses.

Setting up the experiment

This experiment makes use of a light gate. A light gate is an arch-shaped piece of equipment which sends a beam of light from one side of the arch (or 'gate') to the other. When something passes through the gate, it interrupts this beam of light. When used with a computer or data logger, the light gate can detect an interruption and measure how long the interruption lasted.

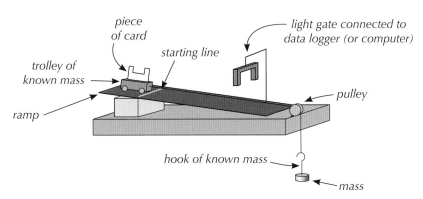

Figure 1: *The experimental setup for investigating Newton's Second Law.*

Set up the apparatus as shown in Figure 1. The height of the ramp should be adjusted so the trolley (without the hook attached) just begins to move. When this happens, the weight of the trolley down the slope compensates for the friction acting between the wheels of the trolley and the ramp. This means that you can assume that any additional forces you apply will be the main cause of the acceleration of the trolley as it rolls down the ramp.

The trolley should hold a piece of card with a gap in the middle that will interrupt the beam of the light gate twice. If you measure the length of each bit of card that will pass through the light gate and input this into the software, the light gate can measure the velocity for each bit of card. It does this using $v = x \div t$ (page 23), where x is the length of each bit of card and t is the duration of the interruption.

The software can also work out the acceleration of the trolley, using $a = (v - u) \div t$ (page 25). Here, $v - u$ is the difference between the two velocities it has measured, and t is the amount of time that has passed between the first and second interruptions of the light gate signal.

Connect the trolley to a piece of string that goes over a pulley and is connected on the other side to a hook (that you know the mass of and can add more masses to). Mark a starting line on the table the trolley is on, and place the trolley so that its front end is lined up with it. This way, when the trolley moves it will always have travelled the same distance when it reaches the light gate.

Figure 2: *The beam in a light gate being interrupted by a piece of card attached to a trolley.*

Tip: You could also do this experiment with two light gates and a card without a gap.

Tip: Instead of a slope, you could use an air track to reduce friction (a track which hovers a trolley on jets of air).

Tip: Remember — always carry out a risk assessment before doing a practical. In this experiment, the string may snap, so it's a good idea to remain standing up so that you can quickly get out of the way before the masses land on your toes.

You should make sure the string and table are the right length so that your trolley passes through the light gate before the masses hit the floor or the trolley hits the pulley, otherwise the accelerating force will be removed before the acceleration has been recorded.

The weight of the hook and any masses attached to it will provide the accelerating force that causes the trolley to move when released. This force is equal to the total mass of the hook and masses (m) × acceleration due to gravity (g) — which is just $W = m \times g$ (see page 37).

Carrying out the experiment

Hold the trolley so the string between the trolley and pulley is straight and taut (not loose and touching the ramp). Next, release the trolley and record the acceleration measured by the light gate as the trolley passes through it. This is the acceleration of the whole system (trolley, hook and masses). Repeat this twice more and calculate the average acceleration (see page 14).

You can use this setup to investigate the effect that varying the force and mass has on the trolley's acceleration.

Varying the mass

To investigate the effect of varying the mass, add masses to the trolley one at a time. This will increase the mass of the system. Don't add masses to the hook, or you'll change the force. Record the average acceleration each time you add a mass.

Varying the force

To investigate the effect of varying the force, you need to keep the total mass of the system the same, but change the weight on the hook. To do this, start with all the masses loaded onto the trolley, and transfer the masses to the hook one at a time, recording the new acceleration each time you transfer one of the masses. This will increase the accelerating force while keeping the mass of the system the same, as you're only transferring the masses from one part of the system (the trolley) to another (the hook).

Tip: Remember, the force acting on the system (the trolley, hook and masses) is equal to the weight of the hook and the masses attached to it. So adding masses to the hook changes the weight, which changes the force.

Tip: A system is just the object or objects that you're looking at — it sounds fancy, but don't let it worry you. There's more about systems over on page 61.

The results

You can use Newton's Second Law, $F = m \times a$, to explain the results. In this case, F = weight of the hanging masses and hook, m = mass of the whole system (trolley, hook and any added masses) and a = acceleration of the system.

By adding masses to the trolley, you increase the mass of the whole system, but keep the force applied to the system the same. This should lead to a decrease in the acceleration of the trolley, as acceleration is inversely proportional to mass ($a = F \div m$).

By transferring masses from the trolley to the hook, you are increasing the accelerating force without changing the mass of the system. Increasing the force should lead to an increase in the acceleration of the trolley, because a is directly proportional to F. If you were to plot a graph of acceleration against force, the graph should be a straight line through the origin.

Tip: $F = m \times a$ was introduced on page 35.

Suitable equipment

The best equipment to use to find an object's speed depends on the situation. For example, a 30 cm ruler is suitable for measuring short distances and light gates are often the best option for measuring short time intervals. This is because measurements from light gates aren't affected by reaction times like ones from stopwatches are.

For finding something like a person's walking speed, the distances and times you'll measure are quite large. You can use a metre ruler and markers to measure and mark out distances. For any times longer than five seconds, you can use a regular stopwatch, as the reaction time of the person using the stopwatch will only be a small percentage of the time measured by the stopwatch.

If you're feeling a bit high-tech, you could use a video camera to determine an object's speed (like in Figure 3). If you know how many frames per second the camera records, you can find the distance travelled by an object in a given number of frames and the time that it takes to do so.

Tip: Choosing the right method and equipment to make sure an investigation is accurate and reliable is an important part of Working Scientifically.

WORKING SCIENTIFICALLY

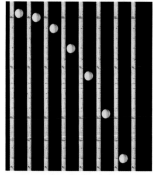

Figure 3: *Multiple frames of a video, showing the distance travelled by a falling ball over time.*

Practice Question — Application

Q1 A student uses the set-up below to calculate the relationship between mass and acceleration.

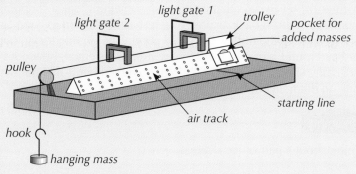

a) Suggest one safety precaution the student should consider in her risk assessment.

b) Explain why the student has used an air track.

The student lines the trolley up with the starting line, then lets go of the hook. The trolley moves along the air track.

c) The length of the trolley is 0.10 m. The trolley interrupts the beam of light gate 1 for 0.2 seconds. Calculate the velocity of the trolley as it passes through light gate 1.

d) The velocity of the trolley as it passes through light gate 2 is 2.0 m/s. It takes the trolley 0.75 seconds to travel between light gate 1 and light gate 2. Calculate the acceleration of the trolley between the two light gates.

The student repeats the experiment, each time adding a mass to the trolley and keeping the mass on the hook the same.

e) How would you expect the acceleration of the trolley between the two light gates to change as the mass of the trolley is increased?

Tip: Remember speed = distance ÷ time from page 23 and $a = (v - u) \div t$ from page 25.

9. Newton's Third Law

Learning Objective:

- Be able to recall and apply Newton's third law to equilibrium situations.

Specification Reference 2.23

Newton's Third Law is just as important as the other two. If it wasn't true, then we'd never be able to sit anywhere without falling to the centre of the Earth.

What is Newton's Third Law?

When two objects interact, they apply forces to each other. These forces are of the same type and always act in the opposite direction to each other. You've probably heard the law in physics that "every action has an equal and opposite reaction" — this is **Newton's Third Law**, which is defined as:

> When two objects interact, they exert equal but opposite forces of the same type on each other.

Tip: H Newton's Third Law relates to conservation of momentum — there's more about this on page 47.

There is always a pair of forces acting on two touching objects, caused by them touching. These forces are **normal contact forces**. They obey Newton's Third Law — they are equal in size but act in opposite directions. Have a look below and at the next page for examples showing them.

Newton's Third Law says that if you push something, say a shopping trolley, the trolley will push back against you, just as hard. And as soon as you stop pushing, so does the trolley. So far so good. The slightly tricky thing to get your head round is this — if the forces are always equal, how does anything ever go anywhere? The important thing to remember is that the two forces are acting on different objects.

Figure 1: *British physicist Sir Isaac Newton, who is famous for his three laws.*

Example

Think about a pair of ice skaters.

Skater A   mass = 55 kg

Skater B   mass = 65 kg

When skater A pushes on skater B with a force, she feels an equal and opposite force from skater B's hand (the normal contact force). Both skaters feel the same sized force, in opposite directions, and so accelerate away from each other.

Skater A will be accelerated more than skater B, though, because she has a smaller mass — $a = F \div m$ (see page 35).

Tip: In this example, the two objects interacting are the two skaters.

Equilibrium

It's easy to get confused with Newton's Third Law and an object in **equilibrium**. You need to be careful about which forces you say are equal and opposite.

Tip: Objects in equilibrium are experiencing a zero resultant force.

Example 1

An example of Newton's Third Law in an equilibrium situation is a man applying a force to a wall.

The man pushes on the wall and the wall pushes back on him. Both of these forces are the same type — normal contact forces. They are also the same size.

Tip: In this example, the two objects interacting are the man and the wall.

Example 2

A book resting on a table is in equilibrium. The weight of the book (W_B) is equal to the normal contact force from the table on the book (N_B). But this is NOT Newton's Third Law because the two forces are different types, and are both acting on the book.

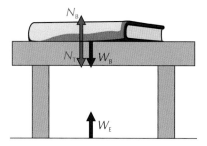

In this situation, Newton's Third Law is:

- The normal contact force acting on the book (from the table), N_B, is equal to the normal contact force acting on the table (from the book), N_T.

- The weight of the book being pulled down by Earth, W_B, is equal to the weight of the Earth being pulled up by the book, W_E.

Tip: Both of these bullet points are examples of Newton's Third Law because each of them is describing forces that are the same type and size and acting on different objects.

Practice Question — Fact Recall

Q1 What is Newton's Third Law?

Practice Question — Application

Q1 A ball hanging on the end of a piece of string is in equilibrium. It only has two forces acting on it — its weight acting downwards and tension in the string acting upwards. State whether these two forces are an example of Newton's Third Law.

10. Momentum Higher

Learning Objectives:
- H Be able to define momentum and recall and use the equation: $p = m \times v$.
- H Be able to describe examples of momentum in collisions.
- H Be able to use Newton's second law as $F = \frac{(mv - mu)}{t}$.
- H Be able to recall and apply Newton's third law to collision interactions and relate it to the conservation of momentum in collisions.

Specification References
2.23-2.26

If something is moving along, it'll have some momentum. How much depends on its mass and velocity. If it collides with something, it'll 'share' its momentum with it...

Momentum

Momentum is a property of moving objects. The greater the mass of an object and the greater its velocity (see p.22), the more momentum the object has. You can work out the momentum of an object using:

$$\boldsymbol{p} = \text{momentum (kg m/s)} \longrightarrow p = m \times v \longleftarrow \boldsymbol{v} = \text{velocity (m/s)}$$
$$\boldsymbol{m} = \text{mass (kg)}$$

Momentum is a vector quantity (see page 22) — so make sure you include the direction when you talk about the momentum of an object.

Example 1 — Higher

A 1800 kg rhino is running north at 9.50 m/s. How much momentum does it have?

$p = m \times v = 1800 \times 9.50 = 17\ 100$ kg m/s to the north

---

Tip: H Use this formula triangle to help you rearrange the formula:

Example 2 — Higher

A 40.0 kg rock that is falling off a cliff has 484 kg m/s momentum. What is the rock's velocity?

Rearranging $p = m \times v$, $v = p \div m = 484 \div 40.0 = 12.1$ m/s downwards

---

Conservation of momentum

In a closed system, the total momentum before an event (e.g. a collision or an explosion) is the same as after the event. This is called **conservation of momentum**.

Tip: H Here, a closed system is just a fancy way of saying that no external forces act.

In some collisions, the objects bump into one another and stay stuck together (for example, if you throw a lump of clay at a wall). In other collisions, the objects bounce off each other (e.g. when snooker balls hit each other). In both types of collision, the momentum is always conserved (if it's a closed system).

If the momentum before an event is zero, then the momentum after will also be zero. For example, if a stationary balloon is popped, the pieces of the balloon will fly off in different directions so that the momentums of the pieces cancel each other out and the total momentum is zero.

In the exam, you might be asked to describe or calculate how the momentums of objects change in simple collisions and explosions.

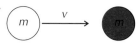 

In snooker, balls of the same size and mass, m, collide with each other. Each collision is an event where the momentum of each ball changes, but the overall momentum stays the same (momentum is conserved).

Before:  **After:**

In the diagram, the red ball is initially stationary, so it has zero momentum. The white ball is moving with a velocity v, so it has a momentum of $p = m \times v$.

The white ball then hits the red ball, causing it to move. The red ball now has momentum. The white ball continues moving, but at a much smaller velocity (and so it has a much smaller momentum).

The combined momentum of the red and white ball is equal to the original momentum of the white ball, $m \times v$.

Tip: **H** You can think of the momentum of the white ball being 'shared out' between the two balls after the collision. That's why the white ball's velocity decreases.

Example 2 — Higher

Two skaters, Ed and Sue, approach each other, collide, and move off together as shown. What is their combined momentum before the collision?

2 m/s   *1.5 m/s*

Ed   *Sue*

80 kg   *60 kg*   *(80 + 60) kg*

Before collision   *After collision*

Figure 1: *Ice skaters rely on momentum to keep themselves moving across the ice.*

- Choose which direction is positive.

    Let's say "positive" means "to the right".

- Next, work out the total momentum before the collision:

    Total momentum = momentum of Ed + momentum of Sue

    $= (m_{Ed} \times v_{Ed}) + (m_{Sue} \times v_{Sue})$

    $= (80 \times 2) + (60 \times (-1.5)) = 70$ kg m/s to the right

Tip: **H** Sue's velocity has a minus sign in front of it because she's moving to the left.

velocity (v)

At what velocity do Ed and Sue move after the collision?

- Work out what the total momentum after the collision is:

    Total momentum = momentum of Ed and Sue together

    $= m_{Ed+Sue} \, v_{Ed+Sue}$

    $= (80 + 60) \times v$

    $= 140v$

(80 + 60) kg

After collision

- Finally, find out what v is using conservation of momentum:

    Momentum before collision = momentum after collision

    $70 = 140v$

    $v = 70 \div 140 = 0.5$ m/s to the right

Tip: **H** The final velocity is positive, so it's to the right.

Force and change in momentum

You know that when a non-zero resultant force acts on a moving object (or an object that can move), it causes its velocity to change (page 34). This means there is a change in momentum.

You also know $F = m \times a$, and $a = \frac{(v - u)}{t}$ (see page 35 and page 25).

So $F = m \times \frac{(v - u)}{t}$. This can be written as:

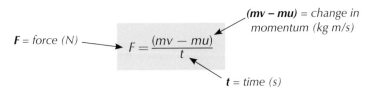

$F = force$ (N) $F = \frac{(mv - mu)}{t}$ $(mv - mu) = change\ in\ momentum\ (kg\ m/s)$

$t = time$ (s)

So the force causing the change of velocity is equal to the rate of change of momentum. A larger force means a faster change in momentum.

Exam Tip $\boxed{H}$
Don't worry about memorising this equation — it'll be given to you in the exam on the Physics Equation Sheet. You just need to remember the units.

Tip: Crashing cars undergo a large change of momentum very quickly, so the forces on the cars and passengers are very large. See p.53 for more about this.

| Example | Higher |

A 400 g football is travelling horizontally towards a player at 10 m/s. The player kicks the ball back along the same line at a speed of 15 m/s, as shown below. The kick lasts 0.010 s.

Calculate the size and direction of the force exerted on the ball by the player.

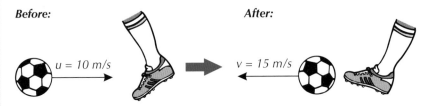

Before: $u = 10$ m/s   *After:* $v = 15$ m/s

Take right as the positive direction.

This makes the 15 m/s velocity negative, as the ball is travelling to the left.

$$m = 0.40\ kg,\ t = 0.010\ s,\ v = -15\ m/s,\ u = 10\ m/s$$

Now just substitute the values into $F = \frac{(mv - mu)}{t}$:

$$F = \frac{(0.40 \times -15) - (0.40 \times 10)}{0.010}$$
$$= \frac{(-6) - 4}{0.010}$$
$$= \frac{-10}{0.010}$$
$$= -1000\ N\ or\ 1000\ N\ to\ the\ left.$$

Tip: It doesn't matter which way you define as positive — so long as you make it clear what you have done.

Newton's Third Law

Newton's Third Law says that whenever two objects interact, they exert equal but opposite forces on each other. Because a force causes a change of momentum, these equal but opposite forces are what lead to momentum being conserved in collisions (when no external forces act).

Tip: You saw Newton's Third Law on page 42.

Usually, one force acts to reduce the momentum of one object, and the second force acts to increase the momentum of the other object. Take the snooker balls from example 1 on page 45:

Example — Higher

A white snooker ball collides with a red snooker ball. Each ball has a mass of 0.15 kg. Initially, the white ball is moving with a velocity of 4.0 m/s and the red ball is stationary. A collision occurs, lasting 0.10 seconds.

After the collision, the white ball is moving with a velocity of 1.0 m/s and the red ball begins moving with a velocity of 3.0 m/s.

a) Calculate the force that caused the change in velocity of each ball and show that Newton's Third Law is true in this situation.

b) Show that momentum is conserved in the collision.

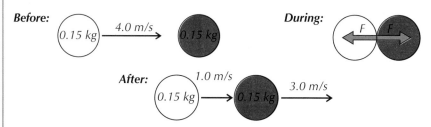

Figure 2: Cannons recoil (move backwards) when they are fired. The cannon feels a force equal to the force it exerts on the cannon ball, but it moves much slower than the cannon ball because it has a much larger mass (and $F = m \times a$, p.35).

a) For the white ball:

$u = 4.0$ m/s, $v = 1.0$ m/s

$$F = \frac{(mv - mu)}{t} = \frac{(0.15 \times 1.0) - (0.15 \times 4.0)}{0.10} = \frac{-0.45}{0.10} = -4.5 \text{ N}$$

For the red ball:

$u = 0.0$ m/s, $v = 3.0$ m/s

$$F = \frac{(mv - mu)}{t} = \frac{(0.15 \times 3.0) - (0.15 \times 0.0)}{0.10} = \frac{0.45}{0.10} = 4.5 \text{ N}$$

The forces that act on the two balls during the collision are equal in size but act in opposite directions — Newton's Third Law.

b) Find the total momentum before and after the collision. If they are equal then momentum has been conserved.

Before the collision:

$$p_{white} + p_{red} = (0.15 \times 4.0) + (0.15 \times 0.0) = 0.6 \text{ kg m/s}$$

After the collision:

$$p_{white} + p_{red} = (0.15 \times 1.0) + (0.15 \times 3.0) = 0.15 + 0.45 = 0.6 \text{ kg m/s}$$

So momentum has been conserved.

Tip: Newton's Third Law and the conservation of momentum are <u>always</u> true for a closed system.

Practice Questions — Fact Recall

Q1 What does the momentum of an object depend on?

Q2 What is the formula for calculating the momentum of an object? Say what units each term is measured in.

Practice Questions — Application

Tip: H Remember, momentum is a vector quantity, so your answers should include a direction.

Q1 Work out the momentum of the following:

a) A 100 g magnet moving north at 0.6 m/s.

b) A 0.80 g bug travelling to the left at 12 m/s.

c) A 5.2 kg rock falling vertically downwards 8.0 m/s.

Q2 A stationary gas canister explodes. What is the momentum of the system before and after the explosion? Explain how you know.

Q3 A ball undergoes a change in momentum of 27 kg m/s. This change in momentum takes 3 seconds to occur. Calculate the size of the force on the ball which causes this change in momentum.

Q4 What is the velocity of the following?

a) A 0.95 kg turtle swimming south with 3.04 kg m/s momentum.

b) A 2000 kg car travelling east with 45 000 kg m/s of momentum.

Q5 What is the mass of the following?

a) A child skiing at 0.75 m/s with 31.5 kg m/s momentum.

b) A dog running at 7.5 m/s with 210 kg m/s of momentum.

Q6 A force of 20 N is applied to an object, which experiences a change in momentum of 32 kg m/s. Calculate the time for which the force was applied.

Q7 A bullet is fired from a stationary gun. This causes the 1 kg gun to move backwards at 2 m/s. The bullet moves forwards at 200 m/s. What is the mass of the bullet?

Tip: The motion of skiers C and D is all along the same line.

Q8 Two skiers (C and D) crash into each other and move off together to the left at 1.50 m/s after the collision. Skier C has a mass of 56.0 kg and was moving right at 1.30 m/s before the collision. Skier D has a mass of 70.0 kg. What was the velocity of skier D before the collision?

Tip: Remember to check the units of any data carefully before you do any calculations.

Q9 A paint ball fired from a gun experiences a force of 100 N, applied over 0.05 seconds. The mass of the paint ball is 50 g.

a) Calculate the speed at which the paint ball leaves the gun.

b) The gun recoils at a speed of 2.0 m/s. Calculate the mass of the paint ball gun.

11. Stopping Distances

Stopping distances are important — awareness of them can make the difference between crashing and not. It's easy to get stopping, braking and thinking distances confused, so make sure you learn what each one means.

Stopping distance

In an emergency (e.g. a hazard ahead in the road), a driver may perform an emergency stop. This is where maximum force is applied by the brakes in order to stop the car in the shortest possible distance. The longer it takes to perform an emergency stop, the higher the risk of crashing into whatever's in front.

The total **stopping distance** of a vehicle is the distance covered in the time between the driver first spotting a hazard and the vehicle coming to a complete stop. The total stopping distance is the sum of the thinking distance and the braking distance.

> **stopping distance = thinking distance + braking distance**

The **thinking distance** is the distance the vehicle travels during the driver's **reaction time** (the time between seeing a hazard and applying the brakes).

The **braking distance** is the distance the vehicle travels after the brakes are applied until it comes to a complete stop, as a result of the braking force.

Example

A driver sees a hazard on the road and brakes. His thinking distance is 11 m and his braking distance is 32 m. Find his stopping distance.

Stopping distance = thinking distance + braking distance
$$= 11 + 32 = 43 \text{ m}$$

Many factors affect your total stopping distance — and you can break it down into thinking distance and braking distance to look at the factors that affect each of these.

Thinking distance

Thinking distance is affected by two main factors:

1. The speed of the vehicle — whatever your reaction time, the faster you're going, the further you'll go in that time.

2. How quick to respond you are, i.e. your reaction time — this can be affected by tiredness, drugs, alcohol and distractions.

Learning Objectives:

- Be able to recall that the stopping distance of a vehicle is made up of the sum of the thinking distance and the braking distance.

- Be able to explain that the stopping distance of a vehicle is affected by a range of factors including: the mass of the vehicle; the speed of the vehicle; the driver's reaction time; the state of the vehicle's brakes; the state of the road; the amount of friction between the tyre and the road surface.

- Be able to describe the factors affecting a driver's reaction time including drugs and distractions.

Specification References 2.28-2.30

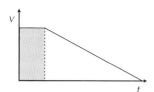

Figure 1: *You can show thinking and braking distance on a velocity/time graph (page 31). The blue area is the thinking distance, the yellow is braking distance.*

Tip: Bad visibility can delay when you spot a hazard. It doesn't directly affect thinking distance, but it means you won't start to think about stopping until later, making you more likely to crash.

Tip: There's more about how speed affects braking distance on the next page.

Figure 2: *A deep tyre tread helps to clear water between the tyre and the road.*

Figure 3: *Petrol spills on roads can reduce grip and cause tyres to skid, increasing the braking distance.*

Braking distance

Braking distance is affected by four main factors:

1. How fast you're going — the faster you're going, the further it takes to stop.

2. The mass of the vehicle — vehicles with a larger mass (e.g. lorries, cars full of passengers) will take longer to stop.

3. How good your brakes are — all brakes must be checked and maintained regularly. Worn or faulty brakes won't be able to apply as much force as well-maintained brakes and could let you down catastrophically just when you need them the most, i.e. in an emergency.

4. The amount of friction between the vehicle's tyres and the road surface. The less friction there is between the tyres and the road, the more likely the vehicle is to skid, which increases stopping distance. The amount of friction is affected by:

   - How good the tyres are — tyres should have a minimum tread depth of 1.6 mm. In wet conditions, the tread pattern helps to stop water getting trapped between the tyres and the road — they provide a channel through which the water can 'escape'. With too little tread, the tyres may lose contact with the ground, causing the vehicle to slide.

   - The state of the road — water, ice, leaves, diesel spills, muck on the road etc. can result in reduced friction between the tyres and the road and so can greatly increase the braking distance.

Practice Questions — Fact Recall

Q1 Define stopping distance, thinking distance and braking distance.

Q2 Other than speed, name three factors that affect braking distance.

Q3 Say whether each of the following would affect the thinking distance or the braking distance of a vehicle:
   a) Ice on the road   b) Alcohol intake of the driver
   c) Tiredness of the driver   d) Petrol spills

Practice Question — Application

Q1 A driver in a car has a thinking distance of 15 m and a braking distance of 38 m. What's the stopping distance of the car?

12. Stopping Safely

Braking works by transferring energy away from the kinetic energy store of the car due to work done against friction. During emergency stops, the braking force is large and causes a large deceleration which can be dangerous.

Speed and stopping distance

Speed affects braking distance more than thinking distance. As a car speeds up, the thinking distance increases at the same rate as the speed — so they're directly proportional. For example, if speed doubles (increases by a scale factor of 2), thinking distance also doubles (increases by a factor of 2).

This is because the reaction time (how long it takes the driver to apply the brakes) stays pretty constant — but the higher the speed, the more distance you cover in that same time, using $x = v \times t$ from page 23.

Braking distance, however, increases faster the more you speed up. This is because it depends on the amount of energy in a vehicle's kinetic energy store ($KE = \frac{1}{2} \times m \times v^2$ — see next page). So if speed doubles, braking distance increases 4-fold (2^2). And if speed trebles, braking distance increases 9-fold (3^2). So the braking distance increases with the square of the scale factor of the speed increase.

You need to be able to estimate how the stopping distance of a vehicle changes for a range of speeds.

Example

When travelling at 20 mph, a driver's thinking distance is 6.0 m and their braking distance is 6.0 m. Estimate their total stopping distance at 80 mph.

First work out the scale factor of the speed increase: $80 \div 20 = 4$

Look at the thinking and braking distances separately.
Start with the thinking distance — it's directly proportional to speed, so simply multiply the thinking distance at 20 mph by the scale factor:

$$6.0 \times 4 = 24 \text{ m}$$

Now look at the braking distance — it increases by the square of the scale factor of the speed increase, so multiply the original braking distance by the scale factor squared:

$$6.0 \times 4^2 = 96 \text{ m}$$

Finally, stopping distance is the sum of thinking and braking distance, so:

$$\text{Stopping distance at 80 mph} = 24 + 96 = 120 \text{ m}$$

Figure 2 on the next page shows some typical thinking and braking distances for a car at different speeds. These are taken from the Highway Code.

Learning Objectives:

- Be able to estimate how the distance required for a road vehicle to stop in an emergency varies over a range of typical speeds.
- Be able to carry out calculations on work done to show the dependence of braking distance for a vehicle on initial velocity squared (work done to bring a vehicle to rest equals its initial kinetic energy).
- Be able to explain the dangers caused by large decelerations.
- **H** Be able to estimate the forces involved in typical situations on a public road.

Specification References 2.31-2.33

Figure 1: *Speed limits are very important, because of how speed affects stopping distance. Areas where there are lots of hazards, like outside of schools, often have a low speed limit to reduce the risk of collisions.*

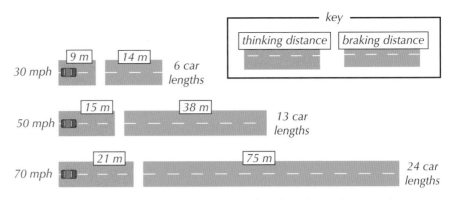

Figure 2: Typical stopping distances taken from the Highway Code.

Braking and friction

Tip: Work done is on page 199 and is equal to force × distance.

Braking relies on friction between the brakes and the wheels. When the brake pedal is pushed, it causes brake pads to be pressed onto parts of the wheels. This contact causes friction, which causes work to be done.

The **work done** transfers energy from the kinetic energy store of the vehicle to the thermal energy stores of the brakes and wheels. To stop a vehicle, all of the energy in its kinetic energy store must be transferred to other stores.

In other words, the work done by the brakes to stop the car must equal the energy in the kinetic energy store of the car before the brakes were applied. You can write this as:

$$\tfrac{1}{2} \times m \times v^2 = F \times d$$

d = braking distance (m)

m = mass (kg)

v = speed (m/s)

F = force (N)

Figure 3: When you apply the brakes on a bicycle, the brake pad is squeezed onto the rim of the tyre. The friction caused does work and slows down the wheel (and so the bike).

Example

A 1000 kg car is travelling at 25 m/s. The driver of the car sees a hazard ahead and applies his brakes. The brakes exert a force of 6250 N to bring the car to a stop. Calculate the distance travelled by the car between the brakes being applied and the car coming to a stop.

Rearrange $\tfrac{1}{2} \times m \times v^2 = F \times d$ for distance, d:

$d = (m \times v^2) \div (2 \times F)$

Then substitute in the values:

$d = (1000 \times 25^2) \div (2 \times 6250) = 625\,000 \div 12\,500 = 50$ m

This explains why the braking distance of any given vehicle depends on the initial speed of the vehicle squared — the faster a vehicle is travelling before it brakes, the longer it will travel before it comes to a stop.

Dangers of large decelerations

You know from page 25 that acceleration is the rate of change of speed. So a large deceleration is caused by a vehicle slowing down by a large amount in a very short time. For example, in an emergency stop or more dramatically, in a car crash.

A large deceleration causes a large force (as $F = m \times a$). This large force can result in serious injuries to the passengers of the vehicles. Large decelerations can also be dangerous as large forces can cause brakes to overheat (so they won't work as well) or vehicles to skid — both of which increases the stopping distance and chance of a collision.

Tip: The work done by the brakes transfers energy to the thermal energy stores of the brakes, which causes them to heat up. Transferring too much energy to thermal energy stores too quickly can cause the brakes to overheat.

Estimating forces for large decelerations Higher

You need to be able to make estimates of the forces involved in everyday road situations. This includes calculating the forces for large decelerations.

Example — **Higher**

Estimate the force on a car as it decelerates from a typical motorway speed to rest in 3.5 s.

Force is given by the equation $F = \frac{(mv - mu)}{t}$ (p.46)

First you need to estimate the mass and initial speed of the car. You can use the typical speeds from page 23.

A typical speed of a car is ~30 m/s. Mass of a car is ~1000 kg.

Then use the equation given above to calculate the force. You know that the final speed of the car, v, is 0 m/s.

$F = \frac{(mv - mu)}{t} = \frac{(1000 \times 0) - (1000 \times 30)}{0.35} = -85\ 714.2... \text{ N}$

So $F \sim -90\ 000$ N

Figure 4: *Safety features in cars, like airbags, are designed to slow passengers down more slowly, reducing the force that acts on them.*

Exam Tip
Knowing some typical vehicle masses could come in very handy in the exam:
A car ~ 1000 kg.
A single-decker bus ~ 10 000 kg.
A loaded lorry ~ 30 000 kg.

Practice Questions — Application

Q1 Explain why large decelerations are dangerous.

Q2 A car driver, travelling at 30 mph, makes an emergency stop. Their thinking distance is 9.0 m and their braking distance is 14.0 m. The driver then accelerates to a new speed of 60 mph. Estimate:

a) the thinking distance at 60 mph.

b) the braking distance at 60 mph.

Q3 A 12 000 kg bus performs an emergency stop. A braking force of 10 000 N is applied constantly whilst the bus slows down. The braking distance of the bus is 15 m. Calculate the speed of the bus just before the brakes were applied.

Q4 A car is travelling at 12 m/s. The driver is distracted and hits a stationary bus at this speed. Estimate the force that acts on the car as it comes to a stop.

Tip: For Q4, just make a sensible guess for any values you use. Basic collisions are over fairly quickly, usually taking less than a second.

13. Reaction Times

Learning Objective:
- Be able to explain methods of measuring human reaction times and recall typical results.

Specification References 2.27

Reaction time is an important factor in determining thinking distance. You can measure reaction times in the classroom really easily.

Testing reaction times

Everyone's reaction times are different, and are affected by many different factors (see page 49). Typical reaction times are between 0.2 seconds and 0.9 seconds, so you haven't got a chance of measuring one with a stopwatch.

However, you can do simple experiments to investigate reaction time. One way of measuring reaction times is to use a computer-based test (e.g. clicking a mouse when the screen changes colour). Another is the ruler-drop test.

Tip: The longer your reaction time, the longer your thinking distance when driving a car. This is the distance travelled between spotting a hazard and applying the brakes (page 49).

The ruler-drop test

Sit with your arm resting on the edge of a table (this should stop you moving your arm up or down during the test). Get someone else to hold a ruler so it hangs between your thumb and forefinger, lined up with zero. You may need a third person to be at eye level with the ruler to check it's lined up.

Figure 1: The minimum reaction time for a human is thought to be 0.1 seconds. In high-level races, any athlete starting within 0.1 s of the starting gun is considered to have false-started. This is measured by computerised sensors built into the starting blocks.

Without giving any warning, the person holding the ruler should drop it. At this point, close your thumb and finger to try and catch the ruler as quickly as possible.

The measurement on the ruler at the point where it's caught is how far the ruler dropped in the time it took you to react. The longer the distance, the longer the reaction time.

Tip: A 30 cm ruler should work for measuring most people's reaction times. However, you could use a metre ruler if necessary.

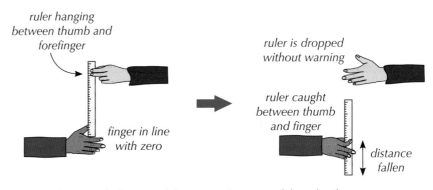

Figure 2: A diagram of the two main stages of the ruler-drop test.

You can calculate how long the ruler falls for (the reaction time) because acceleration due to gravity is constant (roughly 10 m/s²). See the next page for an example calculation.

Tip: For a refresher on calculations with acceleration due to gravity, see page 26.

Example

Say you catch the ruler at 20 cm.

From page 26, you know: $v^2 - u^2 = 2 \times a \times x$.

$$u = 0, \ a = 10 \text{ m/s}^2 \text{ and } x = 0.2 \text{ m}.$$

Rearrange for v:

$$v = \sqrt{(2 \times a \times x) + u^2} = \sqrt{2 \times 10 \times 0.2 + 0} = 2 \text{ m/s}$$

v is equal to the change in velocity of the ruler.
From page 25 you know that $a = (v - u) \div t$. Rearrange for t.

$$t = (v - u) \div a = 2 \div 10 = 0.2$$

This gives you your reaction time of 0.2 s.

Tip: Remember — the distance must be in metres to use this equation. To convert from cm to m, you divide by 100.

It's pretty hard to do this experiment accurately, so you should do a lot of repeats. The results will be better if the ruler falls straight down — you might want to add a blob of modelling clay to the bottom to stop it from waving about. Make sure it's a fair test — use the same ruler for each repeat and have the same person dropping it.

You could try to investigate some factors affecting reaction time, e.g. you could introduce distractions by having some music playing or by having someone talk to the person being tested while the test takes place. Remember to still do lots of repeats and calculate the mean reaction time with distractions, which you can compare to the mean reaction time without distractions.

Tip: See page 49 for other factors that can affect reaction times and increase the thinking distance of someone driving a vehicle.

Tip: Collecting lots of results and calculating a mean will reduce the amount of random error in your results as well.

WORKING SCIENTIFICALLY

Practice Question — Fact Recall

Q1 Describe the main steps involved in measuring a person's reaction time using the ruler-drop test.

Practice Question — Application

Q1 A student's reaction time is tested using the ruler drop test. She repeats the test three times, grabbing the ruler at 3.0 cm, 5.0 cm and 7.0 cm.

  a) Calculate the average distance, in centimetres, at which the student grabbed the ruler.

  b) Using your answer to part a), calculate their reaction time. Use $g = 10 \text{ m/s}^2$.

  c) The student later repeated the test at the end of the school day. The average reaction time was longer than that from earlier in the day. Suggest a reason for this.

Section 1 Checklist — Make sure you know...

Distance, Displacement, Speed and Velocity

- ☐ That scalar properties only have a size, not a direction.
- ☐ That speed, distance, mass and energy are all scalar quantities.
- ☐ That a vector has a size and a direction.
- ☐ That velocity, displacement, force, acceleration, weight and momentum are all vectors.
- ☐ **H** That objects moving in a circle can move at a constant speed, but will always have a constantly changing velocity because the direction they are travelling in is always changing.
- ☐ That the typical walking speed is about 1.5 m/s, running speed is 3 m/s and cycling speed is 6 m/s.
- ☐ The typical speed of sound in air, which is about 340 m/s.
- ☐ The typical speed of wind.
- ☐ The typical speeds of different types of transportation.
- ☐ The equation (average) speed = distance ÷ time, and how to use it.
- ☐ The equation distance travelled = average speed × time, and how to use it.

Acceleration

- ☐ The equation $a = \frac{(v - u)}{t}$ and how to use it.
- ☐ How to estimate the acceleration of everyday objects like vehicles.
- ☐ How to use the equation $v^2 - u^2 = 2 \times a \times x$.
- ☐ That the acceleration due to gravity of an object in free fall is 10 m/s^2.

Distance/Time Graphs

- ☐ How to use a distance/time graph to describe a journey.
- ☐ How to interpret distance/time graphs.
- ☐ That the gradient of a distance/time graph is the speed at which the object is travelling.
- ☐ How to calculate the gradient of a distance/time graph.

Velocity/Time Graphs

- ☐ How to use a velocity/time graph to describe a journey.
- ☐ How to interpret velocity/time graphs.
- ☐ That the gradient of a velocity/time graph is the acceleration of the object, and how to compare accelerations by comparing gradients of velocity/time graphs.
- ☐ That the area under a velocity/time graph for a given time interval is the distance travelled by the object during that time period ,and how to calculate this for uniformly accelerating objects.

cont...

Newton's First Law

☐ Newton's First Law — that a resultant force is needed to change the motion (the speed or direction) of an object.

☐ That a resultant force of zero acting on a stationary object means that the object stays still.

☐ That a resultant force of zero acting on a moving object means that the object's speed or direction of travel will stay the same.

☐ That if a non-zero resultant force acts on an object, it will start to move, speed up, slow down, stop moving or change direction.

Newton's Second Law and Inertia

☐ That the acceleration of an object is directly proportional to the resultant force acting on it and inversely proportional to the object's mass — this is Newton's Second Law.

☐ The equation $F = m \times a$ and how to use it.

☐ H That objects travelling in a circle are always accelerating, so a resultant force must always be acting on them. This resultant force always acts towards the centre of the circle.

☐ H That the resultant force acting on an object travelling in a circle is called the centripetal force.

☐ H That an object's inertial mass describes how difficult it is to change the object's velocity.

☐ H That inertial mass is the ratio of force over acceleration, i.e. $m = F \div a$.

Weight, Mass and Gravity

☐ That weight is a force acting on an object due to gravity.

☐ That weight is directly proportional to the mass of an object and to the gravitational field strength of the gravitational field that the object is in.

☐ The equation $W = m \times g$ and how to use it.

☐ That weight can be measured using a newton meter, which is also called a spring balance.

Investigating Motion

☐ How to investigate Newton's Second Law by changing the mass of and force acting on a trolley.

☐ How to use a range of equipment, e.g. light gates, to find the speed of an object.

Newton's Third Law

☐ Newton's Third Law — that when two objects interact, they exert equal but opposite forces on each other. These forces are the same type.

☐ How to apply Newton's Third Law to objects in equilibrium, e.g. a book on a table.

cont...

Momentum

- [ ] **H** The definition of momentum.
- [ ] **H** The equation $p = m \times v$ and how to use it.
- [ ] **H** How to describe how the momentum of each object has changed in a collision and how to show that the total momentum is unchanged.
- [ ] **H** That momentum is always conserved in collisions when no external forces act.
- [ ] **H** That a force is needed to change the momentum of an object, and the size of this force can be found using $F = \frac{(mv - mu)}{t}$.
- [ ] **H** How the equal but opposite forces described in Newton's Third Law link to the conservation of momentum in a collision.

Stopping Distances

- [ ] That the stopping distance of a vehicle is the distance covered between the driver spotting a hazard and the vehicle coming to a stop. It is the sum of the thinking distance and braking distance.
- [ ] That thinking distance is the distance the vehicle travels during the driver's reaction time.
- [ ] That braking distance is the distance travelled whilst the vehicle's brakes are applied.
- [ ] That the thinking distance is affected by the speed of the vehicle and the driver's reaction time.
- [ ] That a driver's reaction time is affected by factors including tiredness, drugs and distractions.
- [ ] That the braking distance is affected by the speed and mass of the vehicle, how good the vehicle's brakes are, how good the grip is between the vehicle and the road (because of the condition of the tyres and the state of the road).

Stopping Safely

- [ ] How to estimate stopping distances for vehicles for a range of speeds.
- [ ] That when a vehicle brakes, friction does work and transfers energy away from the kinetic energy store of the vehicle.
- [ ] That when a car is brought to a complete stop, the work done during braking is equal to the energy in the kinetic energy store of the car just before the brakes were applied ($\frac{1}{2} \times m \times v^2 = F \times d$).
- [ ] That large decelerations are dangerous because they exert large forces on passengers which can cause injuries, and because they can cause brakes to overheat, or vehicles to skid.
- [ ] **H** How to estimate the forces acting on vehicles and passengers during an emergency stop or a collision.

Reaction Times

- [ ] That the typical human reaction time is between 0.2-0.9 seconds.
- [ ] How to measure reaction times, including using computer-based tests and the ruler-drop test.

Exam-style Questions

1   **Figure 1** is a velocity/time graph for a car during a journey to the local shops.

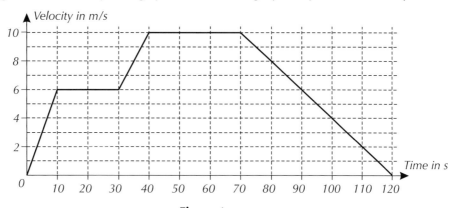

Figure 1

(a)   During which time period(s) does the graph show a negative acceleration?

(1 mark)

(b)   Calculate the acceleration of the car between 30 and 40 seconds.
Show clearly how you work out your answer. Give your answer in m/s^2.

(3 marks)

(c)   If the car has a mass of 980 kg, calculate the resultant force acting on the car between 30 and 40 seconds. Write down any equations you use. Give your answer in N.

(3 marks)

(d)   Use the graph to calculate how far the car travels between 30 and 40 seconds.
Show clearly how you work out your answer. Give your answer in m.

(3 marks)

2   An astronaut in his space suit has a weight of 2300 N on Earth.
The gravitational field strength near to the surface of Earth is 10 N/kg.

(a) (i)   State the equation that links weight, mass and gravitational field strength.

   (ii)   On the Moon, the astronaut has a weight of 368 N.
Calculate the gravitational field strength of the Moon. Give your answer in N/kg.

(4 marks)

The astronaut goes on a spacewalk from a space station, where gravitational forces and air resistance acting on him are assumed to be 0 N. He pushes against the side of the space station with a force, *F*. The push lasts for 1.4 seconds and causes the astronaut to move away from the space station at a velocity of 0.42 m/s.

(b)   Calculate the acceleration of the astronaut.
Write down any equations you use. Give your answer in m/s^2.

(3 marks)

(c)   Calculate the size of force *F*. Write down any equations you use.
Give your answer in N.

(3 marks)

3   A white snooker ball collides with a stationary blue snooker ball. Both balls have a mass of 0.16 kg. Before the collision, the white ball is moving to the right at 0.5 m/s, as shown in **Figure 2**.

Before collision

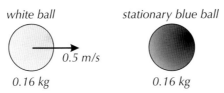

white ball   stationary blue ball

0.5 m/s

0.16 kg   0.16 kg

Figure 2

(a)   What is meant by the conservation of momentum?

(1 mark)

(b) (i)   State the equation that links momentum, mass and velocity.

(1 mark)

(ii)   Calculate the total momentum of the system before the collision.
Give your answer in kg m/s.

(2 marks)

(iii)   After the collision, the white ball moves right at 0.1 m/s.
Calculate the velocity of the blue ball after the collision. Give your answer in m/s.

(3 marks)

4   A 25 000 kg truck is travelling along a straight, flat road at 20 m/s.
The truck then uniformly accelerates over a distance of 125 m to a speed of 25 m/s.

(a)   Calculate the acceleration of the truck as it accelerates from 20 m/s to 25 m/s. Give
your answer in m/s^2. Use the correct equation from the equations listed on page 404.

(1 mark)

The truck then continues travelling at 25 m/s.

(b) (i)   State the equation that links speed, distance and time.

(1 mark)

(ii)   Calculate how long it takes the truck to travel 450 m at this speed.
Give your answer in s.

(3 marks)

The maximum force that can be applied by the trucks brakes is 125 000 N.

(c)   Calculate the braking distance of the truck when it is travelling at 30 m/s.

(4 marks)

The truck driver performs an emergency stop whilst travelling at 30 m/s. It takes 10
seconds for the truck to come to a complete stop once the brakes have been applied.

(d)   Calculate the force acting on the truck driver during the emergency stop. Give your
answer in N. Use the correct equation from the equations listed on page 404.

(2 marks)

1. Energy Stores and Transfers

Energy is what makes everything happen. It can be transferred between stores, and different things happen depending on which stores it is moving between.

Energy stores

When energy is transferred to an object, the energy is stored in one of the object's **energy stores**. You can think of energy stores as being like buckets that energy can be poured into or taken out of. Here are the stores you need to know, and some examples of objects with energy in each of these stores:

Energy store	Objects with energy in this store
Kinetic	Anything moving has energy in its kinetic energy store.
Thermal	Any object. The hotter it is, the more energy it has in this store.
Chemical	Anything that can release energy by a chemical reaction, e.g. food, fuels.
Gravitational Potential	Anything that has mass and is inside a gravitational field.
Elastic Potential	Anything that is stretched (or compressed) e.g. springs.
Electrostatic	Anything with electric charge that is interacting with another electric charge — e.g. two charges that attract or repel each other.
Magnetic	Anything magnetic that is interacting with another magnet — e.g. two magnets that attract or repel each other.
Nuclear	Atomic nuclei have energy in this store that can be released in nuclear reactions.

Energy transfers

A **system** is just a fancy word for a single object (e.g. the air in a piston) or a group of objects (e.g. two colliding vehicles) that you're interested in.

A **closed system** is one that doesn't let energy in or out of it. Energy can be transferred between different energy stores within the system, but no energy is transferred to the system and no energy is transferred away from the system. This means that there is no net change in energy in a closed system — in other words, the total change in energy of a closed system is always zero.

For example, a pan of soup heating on a hob isn't a closed system. Energy is being transferred to the soup from the hob and away from the soup to the surroundings. However, soup inside a sealed thermos flask can be treated as a closed system. Energy cannot be transferred to or away from the soup, so it remains hot and the net change in the energy of the system is zero.

Learning Objectives:

- Be able to explain that where there are energy transfers in a closed system there is no net change to the total energy in that system.
- Be able to analyse the changes involved in the way energy is stored when a system changes, including: an object projected upwards or up a slope; a moving object hitting an obstacle; an object being accelerated by a constant force; a vehicle slowing down; bringing water to a boil in an electric kettle.
- Be able to explain what is meant by conservation of energy.
- Be able to explain, using examples, how in all system changes energy is dissipated so that it is stored in less useful ways.
- Be able to explain that mechanical processes become wasteful when they cause a rise in temperature, so dissipating energy in heating the surroundings.
- Be able to draw and interpret diagrams to represent energy transfers.

Specification References 3.3-3.8

When a system changes, energy is transferred. It can be transferred into or away from a system, between different objects in the system, or between different types of energy stores.

Energy can be transferred between stores in four main ways:

- Mechanically — an object moving due to a force acting on it, e.g. pushing, pulling, stretching or squashing.

- Electrically — a charge (current) moving through a potential difference, e.g. charges moving round a circuit.

- By heating — energy transferred from a hotter object to a colder object, e.g. heating a pan of water on a hob.

- By radiation — energy transferred by waves, e.g. energy from the Sun reaching Earth by light.

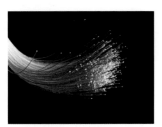

Figure 1: *Energy is transferred through fibre optic cables by radiation.*

Tip: See Section 3b for more on energy transfers by radiation.

Tip: Energy is transferred electrically by the moving charges doing work against the electrical resistance of the heating element — see page 243.

| Example |

If you're boiling water in a kettle — you can think of the water as the system. Energy is transferred to the water's thermal energy store by heating, causing the temperature of the water to rise.

You could also think of the kettle's heating element and the water together as a two-object system. Energy is transferred electrically to the thermal energy store of the kettle's heating element, which transfers energy by heating to the water's thermal energy store.

Work done

Work done is just another way of saying energy transferred — they're the same thing. Work can be done electrically by a moving charge (see page 242) or mechanically by a force moving an object through a distance (see page 199).

Here are some examples of energy transfers involving work:

| Examples |

- The initial force exerted by a person to throw a ball upwards does work. It causes an energy transfer from the chemical energy store of the person's arm to the kinetic energy store of the arm and the ball. Energy is then transferred to the gravitational potential energy store of the ball.

- A ball dropped from a height is accelerated by gravity. The gravitational force does work. It causes energy to be transferred mechanically from the ball's gravitational potential energy store to its kinetic energy store (see page 68).

Figure 2: *Throwing a ball upwards transfers energy mechanically.*

- When a car slows down without braking, the friction between a car's tyres and the road does work. Energy in the kinetic energy store of the car is transferred mechanically, and then by heating, to the thermal energy stores of the car and road.

- In a collision between a car and a stationary object, the normal contact force between the car and the object does work. It causes energy to be transferred mechanically from the car's kinetic energy store to other energy stores, e.g. the elastic potential and thermal energy stores of the object and the car body. Some energy will also be transferred away by sound waves (p.103).

Exam Tip
In the exam, they can ask you to describe the energy transfer in any system. If you understand a few different examples, it'll be much easier to think through whatever they ask you about in the exam.

The conservation of energy principle

Energy always obeys the **conservation of energy principle**:

> Energy can be transferred usefully, stored, or dissipated, but can never be created or destroyed.

Tip: Dissipated is a fancy way of saying spread out and lost.

You can use the conservation of energy principle to calculate how much energy is transferred to certain stores when a system is changed. You'll see lots of examples of this, and you can only do these calculations because of conservation of energy.

Tip: You can calculate energy transferred by heating (page 304) or when work is done by a force (page 199) or by moving charges (page 242) using the formulas given on those pages.

Example

A ball rolling up a slope eventually comes to a stop.

- The energy in the kinetic energy store of the ball is transferred to its gravitational potential energy store.

- All the energy in the kinetic energy store is transferred, so by conservation of energy, it must be moved to other stores.

- You can calculate the energy transferred, it's just the energy that the ball had in its kinetic energy store to start with (using $\frac{1}{2} \times m \times v^2$, see p.66).

- If you assume all of the energy is transferred to the ball's gravitational potential energy store, then you can calculate the energy in this store when the ball stops.

- You'll see on page 67 that the energy in an object's gravitational potential energy store can be found using $m \times g \times \Delta h$, so you can let $\frac{1}{2} \times m \times v^2 = m \times g \times \Delta h$ in this transfer and work out things like Δh, the change in vertical height.

Tip: Another example of using conservation of energy in this way is when an object is falling (without air resistance) — see page 68.

Useful energy stores

When energy is transferred between stores, not all of the energy is transferred usefully to the store that you want it to go to. Some energy is always dissipated when an energy transfer takes place. Dissipated energy is sometimes called 'wasted energy' because the energy is stored in a way which is not useful (usually energy has been transferred into thermal energy stores of the surroundings).

The conservation of energy principle means that:

total energy input = useful energy output + wasted energy

Figure 3: A mobile phone transfers some energy from the chemical energy store of the battery to the thermal energy store of the phone, causing it to feel warm.

Example

A mobile phone is a system.

- When you use the phone, some energy is usefully transferred from the chemical energy store of the battery in the phone.

- Some energy is dissipated to the thermal energy store of the phone (you may have noticed your phone feels warm if you've been using it for a while).

- The total energy transferred from the chemical energy store of the phone's battery is equal to the useful energy transferred to operate the phone, plus the energy dissipated to thermal energy stores.

Whenever work is done mechanically, some work has to be done against frictional forces. As work done is the same as energy transferred, this means that some energy must be transferred to overcome the frictional forces. This causes energy to be transferred to thermal energy stores (of the object doing the work and the surroundings).

This means that all mechanical processes are being wasteful when they raise the temperature of the surroundings, because energy is being dissipated rather than transferred usefully.

Tip: The less energy that's wasted, the more efficient the device is said to be. The amount of energy that's wasted can often be reduced — see page 69.

Example

Figure 4 shows a motor lifting a load.

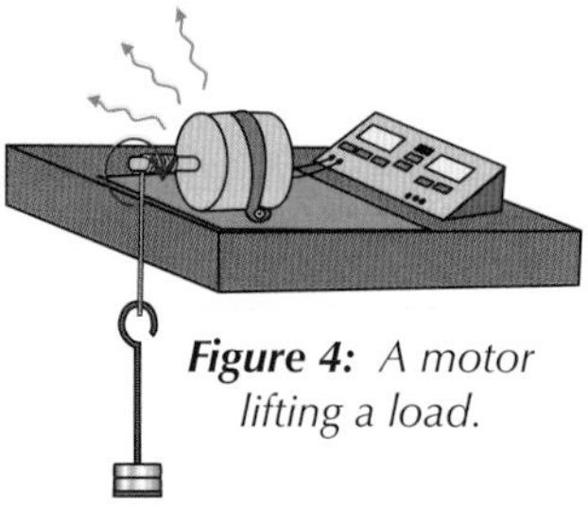

The motor transfers energy usefully from its kinetic energy store to the kinetic and gravitational potential energy stores of the load.

Figure 4: A motor lifting a load.

It also transfers energy mechanically to the thermal energy stores of its moving parts, and electrically to the thermal energy stores of its circuits. This energy is then transferred by heating to the surroundings.

Energy transfer diagrams

Diagrams can make it easier to see what's going on when energy is transferred. Boxes are used to represent energy stores, and arrows are used to show energy transfers.

Example

The diagram below shows the energy transferred when a ball is thrown upwards, taking air resistance into account.

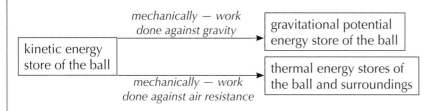

Exam Tip
You may have to use or draw a diagram like this in the exam, so make sure you understand what it's showing.

Practice Questions — Fact Recall

Q1 State eight different forms of energy store.

Q2 What is the net change in energy for a closed system?

Q3 State the conservation of energy principle.

Practice Questions — Application

Q1 Describe the main energy transfer between stores that occurs, including the way in which energy is transferred, when each of the following things happen:

a) An arrow is released from a bow (as in Figure 5).

b) A gas camping stove is used to heat soup.

c) A battery-powered fan is used.

Q2 A ball is allowed to roll freely down a hill. At the top, the ball has 50 J of energy in its gravitational potential energy store. At the bottom, 40 J of this has been transferred usefully to its kinetic energy store.

Explain why the energy in the kinetic energy store is less than the amount of energy in the gravitational potential energy store. Draw a diagram to show the energy transfers involved.

Figure 5: An archer pulls an arrow back on the string of a bow before releasing it.

Learning Objectives:

- Be able to recall and use the equation to calculate the amounts of energy associated with a moving object: $KE = \frac{1}{2} \times m \times v^2$.
- Be able to recall and use the equation to calculate the change in gravitational PE when an object is raised above the ground: $\Delta GPE = m \times g \times \Delta h$.

Specification References
3.1, 3.2

Exam Tip
You're not given this equation on the data sheet so make sure you learn it.

Figure 2: A heavy van will have more kinetic energy than a lighter moped travelling at the same speed.

Exam Tip
Use this formula triangle (see page 345) to rearrange the equation:

2. Kinetic and Potential Energy Stores

Some of the most common and straightforward energy transfers are between kinetic energy stores and gravitational potential energy stores. They have handy formulas so you can easily calculate how much energy is gained or lost.

Kinetic energy stores

Anything that is moving has energy in its **kinetic energy store**. Energy is transferred to this store when an object speeds up and is transferred away from this store when an object slows down.

The energy in the kinetic energy store depends on the object's mass and speed. The greater its mass and the faster it's going, the more energy there will be in its kinetic energy store. It's got a slightly tricky formula, so you'll need to concentrate a bit harder on this one:

 KE = kinetic energy (J) $\longrightarrow KE = \frac{1}{2} \times m \times v^2 \longleftarrow v^2 = (speed)^2\ ((m/s)^2)$

m = mass (kg)

*small mass, low speed —
small amount of energy
in kinetic energy store*

*large mass, high speed —
large amount of energy
in kinetic energy store*

Figure 1: A diagram to show how the energy in the kinetic energy store of a moving object depends on its mass (m) and speed (v).

Example 1

**A van of mass 2450 kg is travelling at 40.0 m/s.
Calculate the energy in its kinetic energy store.**

You just plug the numbers into the formula — but watch the 'v^2'.

$$KE = \frac{1}{2} \times m \times v^2 = \frac{1}{2} \times 2450 \times 40.0^2 = 1\ 960\ 000\ J$$

Example 2

A moped with 1.17×10^4 J of energy in its kinetic energy store travels at 12.0 m/s. What is the mass of the moped?

$KE = 1.17 \times 10^4$ J, $v = 12.0$ m/s

Rearranging $KE = \frac{1}{2} \times m \times v^2$,

$$m = (2 \times KE) \div v^2 = (2 \times 1.17 \times 10^4) \div 12.0^2$$
$$= 162.5 = 163\ kg\ (to\ 3\ s.f.)$$

Gravitational potential energy stores

Lifting an object in a gravitational field requires work. This causes a transfer of energy to the **gravitational potential energy (GPE) store** of the raised object. The higher an object is lifted, the more energy is transferred to this store.

The amount of energy in an object's GPE store depends on its mass, its height and the strength of the gravitational field the object is in. The amount of energy that is transferred to an object's gravitational potential energy store when it's raised through a certain height can be found by:

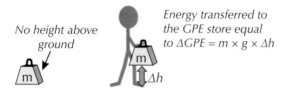

g = gravitational field strength (N/kg)

$\mathbf{\Delta GPE}$ = change in gravitational potential energy (J)

$$\Delta GPE = m \times g \times \Delta h$$

$\mathbf{\Delta h}$ = change in vertical height (m)

$\mathbf{m}$ = mass (kg)

On Earth, the gravitational field strength (g) is approximately 10 N/kg.

No height above ground

Energy transferred to the GPE store equal to $\Delta GPE = m \times g \times \Delta h$

Δh

m

Figure 3: *A diagram showing how the energy in the gravitational potential energy store of a mass (m) increases when it is lifted to a height (Δh) in a gravitational field.*

Example 1

A 50 kg mass is slowly raised through a height of 6.0 m. Find the energy transferred to its gravitational potential energy store. The gravitational field strength is 10 N/kg.

Just plug the numbers into the formula:
$$\Delta GPE = m \times g \times \Delta h = 50 \times 10 \times 6.0 = 3000 \text{ J}$$

Example 2

A flea of mass 1.0×10^{-3} g jumps vertically from the ground. The gravitational field strength is 10 N/kg. At the top of the jump the flea has gained 1.96×10^{-6} J of energy in its GPE store. How high has the flea jumped?

$\Delta GPE = 1.96 \times 10^{-6}$ J
$m = 1.0 \times 10^{-3}$ g = 1.0×10^{-6} kg

Rearranging $\Delta GPE = m \times g \times \Delta h$,

$$\Delta h = \Delta GPE \div (m \times g) = 1.96 \times 10^{-6} \div (1.0 \times 10^{-6} \times 10)$$
$$= 0.196 = 0.20 \text{ m (to 2 s.f.)}$$

Figure 4: A zipline. As the person descends, energy is transferred from their GPE store to their kinetic energy store, increasing their speed.

Energy transfer for falling objects

When something falls, energy from its gravitational potential energy store is transferred to its kinetic energy store. The further it falls, the faster it goes.

For a falling object when there's no air resistance, you can use the principle of conservation of energy to get:

Energy lost from the GPE store = Energy gained in the kinetic energy store

You can use this to make calculations of energy transfers when an object falls, using the equations on the previous pages.

Example

The flea from the example on the previous page falls from the top of its jump. Assuming there is no air resistance, calculate the speed of the flea when it hits the ground. Give your answer to 2 significant figures.

All the energy the flea gained in its GPE store by jumping will be transferred back to its kinetic energy store as it falls towards the ground, so *GPE* at the top of the jump will equal *KE* when it hits the ground.

$\Delta GPE = 1.96 \times 10^{-6}$ J $= KE$
$m = 1.0 \times 10^{-6}$ kg

$KE = \frac{1}{2} \times m \times v^2$, so rearrange for v:

$$v = \sqrt{\frac{2 \times KE}{m}} = \sqrt{\frac{2 \times 1.96 \times 10^{-6}}{1.0 \times 10^{-6}}} = 1.979... = 2.0 \text{ m/s (to 2 s.f.)}$$

Practice Questions — Fact Recall

Q1   What is the formula for calculating the energy in an object's kinetic energy store? What does each term represent and what units should it be in?

Q2   What is the formula for working out the energy transferred to an object's gravitational potential energy store? What does each term represent and what units should it be in?

Practice Questions — Application

Q1   A 25 000 kg plane takes off and climbs to a height of 12 000 m above its take off point. How much energy has been transferred to its gravitational potential energy store? $g = 10$ N/kg.

Q2   A 12.5 g ball with 40 J of energy in its kinetic energy store is travelling horizontally through the air. How fast is it moving?

Q3   A 1 kg potato falls to the ground and loses 450 J of energy from its gravitational potential energy store. Assuming no air resistance, what is the speed of the potato as it hits the ground?

3. Reducing Unwanted Energy Transfers

Some energy is always transferred to energy stores which are not useful. This is a pain, but there are a number of ways that we can reduce these unwanted transfers and maximise the energy in the useful energy stores.

Thermal conductivity and insulation

When one side of an object is heated, the particles in the hotter part vibrate more and collide with each other. This transfers energy from their kinetic energy stores to the kinetic energy stores of other particles, which then vibrate faster. This process is called **conduction**. It transfers energy through the object.

All materials have a **thermal conductivity** — it describes how well a material transfers energy by conduction. For example, metals have a high thermal conductivity and gases (like air) have a low thermal conductivity.

In a building, the lower the thermal conductivity of its walls, the slower the rate of energy transfer through them. Thicker walls help too — the thicker the wall, the slower the rate of energy transfer. So thick walls with a low thermal conductivity cause a building to cool slowly.

You can also help reduce the amount of energy lost from a building using **thermal insulators**, which are objects made from materials that have a low thermal conductivity. Figure 1 shows some examples.

Learning Objectives:
- Be able to describe the effects of thickness and thermal conductivity of the walls of a building on its rate of cooling qualitatively.
- Be able to explain ways of reducing unwanted energy transfer including through lubrication and thermal insulation.

Specification References
3.9, 3.10

Tip: Make sure you understand the ideas behind these common examples of insulation so that you can explain how they work.

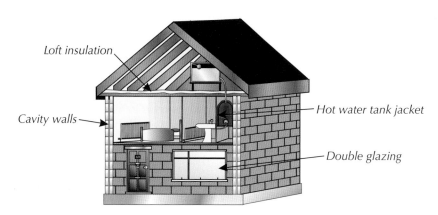

Loft insulation

Cavity walls

Hot water tank jacket

Double glazing

Figure 1: *Different methods of insulating a home.*

Cavity walls and double glazing

Some houses have cavity walls, made up of an inner and an outer wall with an air gap in the middle. The air gap reduces the amount of energy transferred by conduction through the walls, because air has a low thermal conductivity. Double-glazed windows work in the same way — they have an air gap between two sheets of glass to prevent energy transfer by conduction through the windows.

Figure 2: *Sleeves on coffee cups are another example of thermal insulation. They stop your hand getting too hot. They're often made of cardboard with air pockets, as air is a good insulator.*

Figure 3: Loft insulation.

Loft insulation

Fibreglass is an insulating material made of thin strands of glass that trap pockets of air. A thick layer of fibreglass wool laid out across the whole loft floor reduces conduction to the attic space, as the material (and the trapped air) are insulators.

Hot water tank jacket

Putting fibreglass wool around a hot water tank reduces the energy transferred by conduction from the tank's thermal energy store to the surroundings.

Lubrication

Whenever something moves, there's usually at least one frictional force acting against it. This transfers energy mechanically (work is done against friction) to the thermal energy stores of the objects involved, which is then dissipated by heating to the surroundings. For example, pushing a box along the ground causes energy to be transferred mechanically to the thermal energy stores of the box and the ground. This energy is then radiated away to the thermal energy store of the surroundings.

For objects that are touching each other, **lubricants** can be used to reduce the friction between the objects' surfaces when they move. Lubricants are usually liquids (like oil), so they can flow easily between objects and coat them.

Figure 4: A well-oiled bicycle chain allows a bicycle to reach higher speeds with less effort, because a higher proportion of the energy supplied is transferred to the bike's kinetic energy store.

Examples

- Cars need a good supply of engine oil to lubricate the moving parts in the engine and reduce the work done against friction. Without it, the engine will overheat as more work has to be done against friction, which causes more energy to be transferred to useless thermal energy stores (p.64).

- Sewing machines have fast-moving parts which need to be lubricated with oil or grease to keep them working efficiently. When they are well lubricated, more of the energy supplied is transferred to the kinetic energy stores of the parts instead of being wasted to thermal energy stores.

Practice Questions — Fact Recall

Q1 Explain how the thermal conductivity and thickness of the walls of a building affect how quickly the building cools.

Q2 Explain how each of the following helps reduce unwanted energy transfers.

   a) Cavity walls

   b) Double glazing

   c) A hot water tank jacket

Q3 Give one example of when lubrication is used to decrease unwanted energy transfers.

4. Efficiency

Efficiency is a good way to compare devices, as it tells you how much energy is usefully transferred as a proportion of the total energy supplied.

What is efficiency?

Efficiency compares the energy supplied to a device to the energy that is usefully transferred. The less energy that is 'wasted', the more efficient the device is said to be.

The efficiency of an energy transfer can be worked out using this equation:

$$\text{efficiency} = \frac{\text{useful energy transferred by the device}}{\text{total energy supplied to the device}}$$

This equation gives you the efficiency as a decimal, but you may be asked to express it as a percentage. To do that, simply multiply your result by 100, and stick the % symbol on the end.

You also need to remember that:

> No device is 100% efficient and the wasted energy is usually transferred to useless thermal energy stores.

Learning Objectives:
- Be able to recall and use the equation: efficiency = (useful energy transferred by the device) ÷ (total energy supplied to the device).
- Be able to draw and interpret diagrams to represent energy transfers.
- **H** Be able to explain how efficiency can be increased.

Specification References
3.3, 3.11, 3.12

Exam Tip
You shouldn't calculate an efficiency equal to or larger than 1 (or 100%). If you do, redo your calculation.

Example 1

A motor is supplied with 3000 kJ of energy.
600 kJ of that is transferred to useless thermal energy stores.
What is the efficiency of the motor as a percentage?

(MATHS SKILLS)

Total energy supplied to the device = 3000 kJ

Useful energy transferred by the device
= total energy in − wasted energy transfer
= 3000 − 600 = 2400 kJ

Start by working out the efficiency as a decimal:

$$\text{efficiency} = \frac{\text{useful energy transferred by the device}}{\text{total energy supplied to the device}}$$
$$= \frac{2400}{3000}$$
$$= 0.8$$

Then, multiply this by 100 to get the efficiency of the motor as a percentage:
$$\text{efficiency} = 0.8 \times 100 = 80\%$$

Tip: Efficiency is just a number, so it doesn't matter what units your energy values are in. As long as the values for energy supplied and energy transferred are in the same units, you'll get the right answer.

Tip: See page 342 for more on percentages.

Example 2

Exam Tip
Make sure you think
carefully about which
value is total energy
supplied, and which
is useful energy
transferred. It's easy to
get them mixed up.

A lamp with an efficiency of 0.740 is supplied with 350 J of energy. How much energy is usefully transferred by the lamp?

Rearrange $\text{efficiency} = \dfrac{\text{useful energy transferred by the device}}{\text{total energy supplied to the device}}$ to give:

useful energy transferred by the device
$$= \text{efficiency} \times \text{total energy supplied to the device}$$
$$= 0.740 \times 350$$
$$= 259 \text{ J}$$

Showing efficiency on energy transfer diagrams

You can use diagrams like the one in Figure 1 below to show the different energy transfers made by a device. These diagrams can be used to calculate efficiency.

Tip: You might see diagrams like this referred to as Sankey diagrams. You can also use sketches instead of scale diagrams like this one.

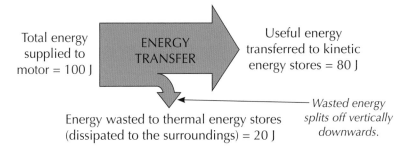

Total energy supplied to motor = 100 J

ENERGY TRANSFER

Useful energy transferred to kinetic energy stores = 80 J

Wasted energy splits off vertically downwards.

Energy wasted to thermal energy stores (dissipated to the surroundings) = 20 J

Figure 1: Diagram for an electric motor with 80% efficiency.

The thickness of the arrows represents how much energy is being transferred, the length has nothing to do with it. The total energy supplied is always shown by the base of the arrow, with any wasteful energy transfers splitting off downwards from the main arrow.

Example

12 000 J is supplied to an electric shaver. Figure 2 shows the energy transfer diagram for the shaver as it's used. Calculate the efficiency of the shaver.

First, find out how much 1 square represents:

The base of the arrow is 10 squares, which is equal to 12 000 J. So:

1 square = 12 000 ÷ 10 = 1200 J

Now calculate the useful energy transferred by the motor:

Thickness of useful arrow = 6 squares

6 × 1200 = 7200 J

Now calculate the efficiency :

$$\text{efficiency} = \frac{\text{useful energy transferred by the device}}{\text{total energy supplied to the device}} = \frac{7200}{12\,000} = 0.6$$

Figure 2: Energy transfer diagram for an electric shaver.

Tip: You could also calculate the efficiency by comparing the thicknesses of the base and the useful energy transfer arrow. For Figure 2, this would be 6 squares ÷ 10 squares = 0.6. If you're not confident doing this, go through each step one at a time like in the example.

Improving efficiency Higher

You can reduce the amount of energy that's wasted in various ways — including by lubrication and by thermal insulation. Decreasing the amount of wasted energy means that a higher proportion of the supplied energy is transferred to useful stores, so the efficiency of the process is increased.

Example — **Higher**

An electric fan usefully transfers energy electrically to the kinetic energy store of its blades, to cause the movement of air. It wastes energy in many ways, e.g. through friction between the axle and its supports. The efficiency could be improved by lubricating the axle.

Figure 3: The internal workings of an electric fan, showing its axle.

Tip: Improving efficiency is a useful application of science (see page 5), allowing us to maximise the energy transferred to useful energy stores and reduce the overall amount of energy used by appliances.

Practice Questions — Fact Recall

Q1   State the equation for efficiency.

Q2   What do the thicknesses of the arrows in a Sankey diagram represent?

Practice Questions — Application

Q1   Work out the efficiency of the following devices as a decimal.

   a) A device with total energy supplied = 90 kJ and useful energy transferred = 54 kJ.

   b) A machine supplied with 800 J of energy that wastes 280 J.

Q2   Work out the efficiency of the following devices as a percentage.

   a) A device where total energy supplied = 36 J and useful energy transferred = 12.6 J.

   b) A lamp that transfers 7.5 kJ of energy, 4.5 kJ of which is transferred away by light, 2.9 kJ of which is transferred by heating to thermal energy stores of the surroundings and 100 J of which is transferred away by sound waves.

Q3   A machine with an efficiency of 68% transfers 816 J to useful energy stores.

   a) What is the total energy transferred to the device?

   b) Sketch an energy transfer diagram for the device.

Q4   A vacuum cleaner works by transferring energy electrically to a motor which turns a fan and causes air to be drawn through the fan. Suggest one way that a vacuum cleaner could be made more efficient.

Tip: A percentage efficiency must always be less than 100% and a decimal efficiency must always be less than 1.

Tip: To get from a percentage to a decimal, divide by 100.

Exam Tip
A sketch doesn't have to be drawn to scale — just make sure you label the arrows clearly, with enough information.

5. Energy Sources and Their Uses

Tip: See pages 81-82 for more on non-renewable fuels.

There are lots of different energy sources that we use today for all sorts of things. But first you need to know your non-renewables from your renewables.

Non-renewable energy sources

Non-renewable energy sources are the three **fossil fuels** and **nuclear fuels**:

- Coal
- Oil
- (Natural) gas
- Nuclear fuels (e.g. uranium and plutonium)

Fossil fuels are natural sources that form underground over millions of years. They are typically burnt to provide energy.

Non-renewable fuels are not being made at the same rate as they are being used and will all run out one day. They all do damage to the environment through emissions or because of issues with their mining, storage and disposal, but they do provide most of our energy.

Renewable energy sources

Renewable energy sources are:

- Wind
- Tides
- Hydro-electricity
- The Sun (solar)
- Bio-fuel

Tip: Lots of people are now trying to use more renewable energy sources — see page 83.

Renewable energy sources can be made at the same rate as they're being used and therefore will never run out. Using most of them does damage to the environment, but in less nasty ways than most non-renewables. The trouble is they often don't provide as much energy as non-renewable sources and some of them are unreliable because they depend on the weather.

Use of energy sources

Energy sources, both renewable and non-renewable, are mostly used to generate electricity. There's more about this on pages 76-82, but two other major uses are transport and heating.

Transport

Transport is one of the most obvious places where fuels are used. Traditionally, non-renewable energy sources have been the main fuel used in transportation:

- Petrol and diesel — fuel created from oil used to power many vehicles (including most cars).

- Coal — used in some old-fashioned steam trains to boil water to produce steam.

Figure 1: *A bio-fuels filling station in Spain.*

Recently, more methods of transportation have started using renewable energy sources, such as bio-fuels. Some vehicles run on pure bio-fuels (see p.79) or a mix of a bio-fuel and petrol or diesel.

Heating

Energy sources are also used for heating things like your home.
Non-renewable sources used for heating include:

- Natural gas — this is the most widely used fuel for heating homes in the UK. The gas is burned to heat water, which is then pumped into radiators throughout the home.

- Oil — some homes are heated by burning oil from a tank instead of gas, especially in remote places where it is difficult to connect to the gas supply.

- Coal — this is commonly burnt in fireplaces.

Solar power is an example of a renewable energy source used for heating. Solar water heaters use electromagnetic radiation (see page 127) from the Sun to heat water which is then pumped into radiators in the building.

> **Tip:** You might come across other energy sources used for heating. For example, wood-burning stoves are fashionable in the UK, and most homes in Iceland are heated using 'geothermal' energy from hot springs underground.

Electric transport and heating

Both renewable and non-renewable energy sources can also be used to generate electricity used in transport and heating. Cars, trains and trams can all be powered by electricity, and storage heaters are a common electrical heater.

Figure 2: The tram network in Manchester is powered by electricity.

Practice Questions — Fact Recall

Q1 What are the three fossil fuels?

Q2 a) Name four renewable energy sources.

   b) Give one reason why renewable energy sources aren't always used instead of non-renewable energy sources.

Q3 Give one renewable and one non-renewable source used directly for transport (without the need for generating electricity).

Q4 How can solar power be used to heat buildings without the need for generating electricity?

Here's the first of many pages looking at using different renewable energy sources to generate electricity. First up: wind and solar power...

Wind power

Generating electricity from wind involves putting up lots of wind turbines (see Figure 1) where they're exposed to the weather, like on moors or around coasts.

Each wind turbine has its own generator inside it. The electricity is generated directly from the wind turning the blades, which turns the generator.

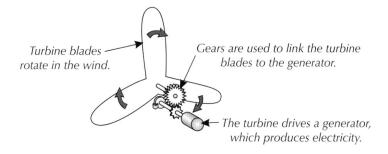

Turbine blades rotate in the wind.

Gears are used to link the turbine blades to the generator.

The turbine drives a generator, which produces electricity.

Figure 1: *The structure of a wind turbine. The blades of the wind turbine rotate in the wind and directly drive a generator, which generates electricity.*

Wind turbines produce no pollution (except for a little bit when they're manufactured), but according to some they do spoil the view (see Figure 2). You need about 1500 wind turbines to replace one coal-fired power station and 1500 of them cover a lot of ground — which would have a big effect on the scenery.

Wind turbines can be very noisy, which can be annoying for people living nearby. There's no permanent damage to the landscape though — if you remove the turbines, you remove the noise and the view returns to normal.

Figure 2: *A wind farm in the countryside.*

There are also problems with reliability. There's no power when the wind stops and it's impossible to increase supply when there's extra demand. Wind turbines also have to be stopped if the wind is very strong, as they could be damaged. Wind turbines typically produce electricity 70-85% of the time.

The initial costs (to build and set up the wind turbines) are quite high, but there are no fuel costs and minimal running costs.

Solar cells

Solar cells generate electric currents directly from the Sun's radiation (see Figure 3). Solar cells cause no pollution, although they do need quite a lot of energy to manufacture in the first place. Initial costs are high but after that the energy is free and running costs almost nil.

The solar cell generates electric current directly from the Sun's radiation and so can be used to charge batteries that can power electrical devices.

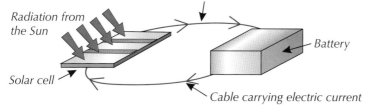

Radiation from the Sun

Battery

Solar cell

Cable carrying electric current

Figure 3: *A solar cell generating electric current from the Sun's radiation, being used to charge a battery which can later power a device.*

Solar cells are often the best source of energy for devices that don't use a lot of energy, or in remote places where it would be difficult to get power from other sources.

Figure 4: *A solar panel generates electricity during the day to power the lights on the speed warning sign through the day and night.*

Examples

- Calculators, road signs and watches don't use much electricity, so solar cells are ideal for powering them — see Figure 4.

- Space is probably the ultimate remote location — you can't just nip up to a space satellite and top it up with fuel. Instead, satellites use large solar panels to generate the electricity they need.

In sunny countries, solar power is a very reliable source of energy, although it can only generate electricity during the daytime, and you can't increase the output when there's more demand. Solar power can still be cost-effective in cloudy countries like Britain. Solar cells are usually used to generate electricity on a relatively small scale, e.g. powering individual homes (see Figure 5).

Figure 5: *Solar cells and a wind turbine being used to power a house in Hamburg, Germany.*

Practice Questions — Fact Recall

Q1 How is electricity generated by a wind turbine?

Q2 Give one issue associated with the reliability of using wind power.

Q3 Why are solar cells often used to power devices in remote locations?

Practice Question — Application

Q1 For each situation below, suggest an appropriate method of generating electricity and explain your answer.

a) Street lights in a remote part of Australia.

b) An illuminated road sign on an exposed hillside in the UK.

Learning Objective:
- Be able to describe the main energy sources available for use on Earth, including bio-fuel, hydro-electricity and the tides.

Specification Reference 3.13

7. Renewable Sources: Hydro-electricity, Tides and Bio-fuels

Although hydro-electricity and tidal power both use water in a similar way, you need to know the details of each, and how they're different. You also need to know about bio-fuels — renewable sources which are burnt like fossil fuels.

Hydro-electric power stations

Generating electricity using **hydro-electric power** usually requires the flooding of a valley by building a big dam. Water is allowed out at a controlled rate through turbines — see Figure 2.

Figure 1: *The Hoover Dam on the Colorado River in the USA — possibly the most well-known hydro-electric power station in the world.*

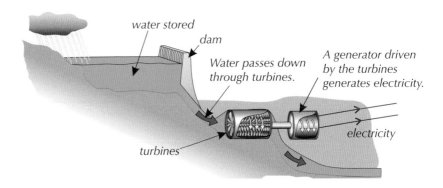

water stored

dam

Water passes down through turbines.

A generator driven by the turbines generates electricity.

electricity

turbines

Figure 2: *A hydro-electric power station. Water is held back behind a dam. When it's released it passes through turbines, which turn a generator and generates electricity.*

Tip: Methane and carbon dioxide contribute to global warming — see page 81.

There is no pollution, but there is a big impact on the environment. The flooding of the valley leads to rotting vegetation (which releases methane and carbon dioxide) and possible loss of habitat for some species (both animals and humans). Sometimes whole villages are evacuated and flooded to build a dam.

The reservoirs can also look very unsightly when they dry up. Putting hydro-electric power stations in remote valleys tends to reduce their impact on humans.

Tip: For more on the national grid, see page 290.

A big advantage is they can provide an immediate response to an increased demand for electricity. There's no problem with reliability except in times of drought. Initial costs are high, but there's no fuel costs and minimal running costs. It can be a useful way to generate electricity on a small scale in remote areas. However, in these cases it's often not practical or economical to connect it to the national grid.

> ### Example
>
> Almost all of the electricity generated in Norway is hydro-electric. Norway is very mountainous with lots of rivers and valleys, making it ideal for hydro-electric power.

Tidal barrages

Tides are produced by the gravitational pull of the Sun and Moon. They are used in lots of ways to generate electricity. The most common method is building a **tidal barrage**.

Tidal barrages are big dams built across river estuaries, with turbines in them. The turbines, as ever, are connected to electrical generators which turn and generate electricity. As the tide comes in it fills up the estuary to a height of several metres and is held back by the barrage. This water can then be allowed out through the turbines at a controlled speed when there's a height difference of water between the two sides of the barrage.

Tip: H See page 282 for more on how generators produce electricity.

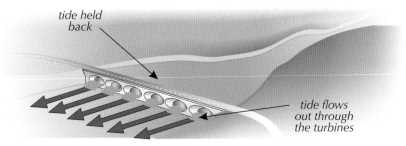

tide held back

tide flows out through the turbines

Figure 3: *The structure of a tidal barrage. Tide water is held back behind the barrage, then allowed to flow through turbines connected to generators, generating electricity.*

This form of electricity generation causes no pollution — the main problems are preventing free access by boats, spoiling the view and altering the habitat of the wildlife, e.g. wading birds, sea creatures and beasties who live in the sand.

Figure 4: *A tidal barrage on the Rance River in France.*

Tides are pretty reliable in the sense that they happen twice a day without fail, and always near to the predicted height. The only drawback is that the height of the tide is variable, so lower (neap) tides will provide significantly less energy than the bigger (spring) tides. They also don't work when the water level is the same either side of the barrage — this happens four times a day because of the tides.

Initial costs are moderately high, but there are no fuel costs and minimal running costs. Even though only some estuaries are suitable for tidal barrages, tidal power has the potential for generating a significant amount of energy.

Bio-fuels

Bio-fuels are renewable energy sources — they're created from either plant products or animal dung. They can be solid, liquid or gas and can be burnt to produce electricity or run cars in the same way as fossil fuels — see Figure 6 on the next page.

Figure 5: *Cow pats are dried out to make solid 'cakes' which can be burnt.*

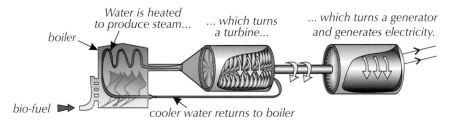

Water is heated to produce steam...

boiler

bio-fuel

cooler water returns to boiler

... which turns a turbine...

... which turns a generator and generates electricity.

Figure 6: *A diagram of how bio-fuels are used to generate electricity. Bio-fuels are burned to heat water, which produces steam. The steam drives a turbine, which drives a generator and generates electricity.*

Bio-fuels are fairly reliable, as crops take a relatively short time to grow and different crops can be grown all year round. However, they cannot respond to immediate energy demands. To combat this, bio-fuels are continuously produced and stored for when they are needed.

The cost to refine bio-fuels is very high and some worry that growing crops specifically for bio-fuels will mean there isn't enough space or water to meet the demands for crops that are grown for food.

Bio-fuels made from plants are theoretically **carbon neutral**:

- The plants that grow to produce the bio-fuel absorb CO_2 from the atmosphere as they are growing.

- When the bio-fuel is burned, this CO_2 is re-released into the atmosphere. So it has a neutral effect on atmospheric CO_2 levels (although this only really works if you keep growing plants at the same rate you're burning things).

However, there is still debate regarding the impact of bio-fuels on the environment, once all aspects of production are considered. For example, fossil fuels are used in the transport of seeds and crops, and in some regions large areas of forest have been cleared to make room to grow bio-fuels (see Figure 7). This results in lots of species losing their natural habitats and the decay and burning of this vegetation also increases CO_2 and methane emissions.

There is also some debate as using bio-fuels to generate electricity doesn't just produce carbon dioxide. Bio-fuel production also creates methane emissions. This is more of a problem when using animal dung as a bio-fuel, as animals such as cows produce large amounts of methane over their lifetime.

Bio-fuels have potential, but their use is limited by the amount of available farmland that can be dedicated to their production.

Figure 7: *An oil palm plantation in Indonesia. These crops can be used to make biodiesel.*

Practice Questions — Fact Recall

Q1   Explain why hydro-electric dams are often built in remote areas.

Q2   State one advantage and one disadvantage of using a tidal barrage to produce electricity.

Q3   What limits the use of bio-fuels as a main source of energy?

8. Non-renewable Sources

Fossil fuels and nuclear fuels will eventually run out. However, we use them to generate most of our electricity, so it's important that you know how they're used, as well as some of the benefits and downsides to using them.

Fossil fuels

Most of the electricity we use is generated from fossil fuels (coal, oil, and gas) in big power stations. Figure 1 shows how electricity is generated in a typical fossil fuel power station.

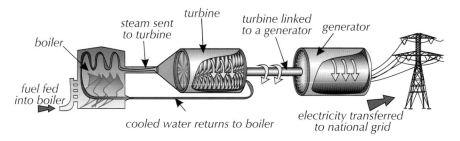

boiler
fuel fed into boiler
steam sent to turbine
turbine
turbine linked to a generator
generator
cooled water returns to boiler
electricity transferred to national grid

Figure 1: *Electricity generation in a fossil fuel power station.*

Fossil fuels provide a cost-effective energy source, that produces large amounts of energy and is readily available. While setup costs of power plants can be higher than other sources, the running costs and fuel extraction costs are fairly low.

They're also reliable — there's enough fuel to meet current demand, and they are extracted from the Earth at a fast enough rate that power plants always have fuel in stock. This means that the power plants can respond quickly to changes in demand. However, these fuels are slowly running out. If no new sources are found, some fossil fuel stocks may run out within a hundred years.

All three fossil fuels (coal, oil and gas) release CO_2 into the atmosphere when they're burned. For the same amount of energy produced, coal releases the most CO_2, followed by oil then gas. All this CO_2 adds to the **greenhouse effect** and contributes to global warming. The greenhouse effect is where gases in the Earth's atmosphere (known as greenhouse gases) block radiation from the Sun from leaving the atmosphere. This causes the overall temperature of the atmosphere to rise (i.e. global warming).

Oil spillages cause serious environmental problems, affecting animals that live in and around the sea. We try to avoid them, but there's always a chance they'll happen.

Example

In 2010, an explosion at the oil drilling station Deepwater Horizon in the Gulf of Mexico resulted in the largest accidental oil spill in history. This resulted in thousands of miles of coastline being covered in crude oil, making the area uninhabitable for many local species of animals and plants.

Figure 2: *A pelican covered in oil from the Deepwater Horizon oil spill.*

Burning coal and oil releases sulfur dioxide, which causes acid rain. Acid rain can be harmful to trees and soils and can have far-reaching effects in ecosystems. Acid rain can be reduced by taking the sulfur out of the fuel before it is burned, or by cleaning up the emissions before they're released into the atmosphere.

Coal mining makes a mess of the landscape, especially "open-cast mining" where huge pits are dug on the surface of the Earth.

Nuclear fuels

Tip: Fission is the process where atoms split and release energy, see page 173.

Tip: The radiation produced by radioactive materials can be very dangerous to humans. See page 165 for more details.

A nuclear power station is mostly the same as the one used for burning fossil fuels (see previous page), but the fuel isn't burnt. Nuclear fission of nuclear fuels such as uranium or plutonium releases the energy to heat water into steam which drives turbines. Nuclear power stations take the longest time of all the power stations to start up.

Nuclear power is 'clean', in that it doesn't cause the release of any harmful gases or other chemicals into the atmosphere. It's also reliable — there's enough fuel to meet current demand.

The biggest problem with generating electricity using nuclear fuel is that the nuclear waste produced is very dangerous and difficult to dispose of. This is because it stays highly radioactive (see page 161) for a long time and so needs to be stored safely far away from people's homes.

Nuclear fuel (e.g. uranium and plutonium) is relatively cheap but the overall cost of nuclear power is high due to the cost of the power station and final decommissioning — shutting down the power station so it's completely safe and poses no risk to people or the environment.

Nuclear power always carries the risk of a major catastrophe, like the Chernobyl disaster in 1986 or the Fukushima disaster in 2011.

Figure 3: *A nuclear power station at night with steam condensing into water vapour as it leaves the cooling tower.*

Practice Questions — Fact Recall

Q1 Name two harmful gases that are released into the atmosphere by burning coal.

Q2 a) Which non-renewable source doesn't directly release harmful gases into the atmosphere when used to generate electricity?

   b) Give two problems with using this fuel to generate electricity.

9. Trends in Energy Source Use

Learning Objective:
- Be able to explain patterns and trends in the use of energy resources.

Specification Reference 3.14

Environmental issues related to energy sources have led us to change the sources we use over time. But it's not always easy to do so...

Reliance on fossil fuels

Over the 20th century, the electricity use of the UK hugely increased as the population got bigger and people began to use electricity for more things.

Since the beginning of the 21st century, electricity use in the UK has been decreasing (slowly), as we get better at making appliances more efficient (p.71) and try to be more careful with energy use in our homes.

Most of our electricity is produced using fossil fuels (mostly coal and gas) and from nuclear power. Generating electricity isn't the only reason we burn fossil fuels — oil (diesel and petrol) is used to fuel cars, and gas is used to heat homes and cook food. However, renewable energy sources can be used for these purposes as well. Bio-fuels can be used to exclusively power vehicles, and solar water heaters can be used to heat buildings.

We are trying to increase our use of renewable energy sources (the UK aims to use renewable sources to provide 15% of its total yearly energy by 2020).

Movement towards renewable energy sources

We now know that burning fossil fuels has a lot of negative effects on the environment (p.81-82). This makes many people want to use more renewable energy sources that affect the environment less.

People and governments are also becoming increasingly aware that non-renewables will run out one day. Many people think it's better to learn to get by without non-renewables before this happens.

Pressure from other countries and the public has meant that governments have begun to introduce targets for using renewable sources. This in turn puts pressure on energy providers to build new power plants that use renewable sources to make sure they don't lose business and money.

Figure 1: *Protest movements have applied pressure to governments to change their energy policies.*

Car companies have also been affected by this change in attitude towards the environment. Electric cars and hybrids (cars powered by two fuels, e.g. petrol and electricity) are already on the market and their popularity is increasing.

Factors limiting change

Although scientists know about the negative environmental effects of energy sources, they can only give advice and don't have the power to make people, companies or governments change their behaviour. The environmental issues aren't the only ones that matter, either. There are other political, social, ethical and economic issues to consider too (see page 5).

For example, the use of renewables is usually limited by reliability and money. Building new renewable power plants costs money, so some smaller energy providers are reluctant to do this — especially when fossil fuels are such a cost effective way of meeting demand.

Even if new power plants are built, there are a lot of arguments over where they should be. For example, many people don't want to live next to a wind farm, which can lead to them protesting.

Some energy sources like wind power are not as reliable as traditional fossil fuels and cannot increase their power output on demand. This would mean either having to use a combination of different power plants (which would be expensive) or researching ways to improve reliability.

Research into improving the reliability and reducing the cost of renewable sources takes time and money. This means that, even with funding, it might be years before improvements are made. In the meantime, dependable power stations using non-renewable sources have to be used.

Making personal changes can also be quite expensive. Hybrid cars are generally more expensive than equivalent petrol cars and things like solar panels for your home are still quite pricey. The cost of these things is slowly going down, but they are still not an option for many people.

Figure 2: *Offshore (at sea) wind turbines are relatively expensive to build and maintain but usually have fewer complaints from locals.*

Practice Questions — Fact Recall

Q1 Why has electricity usage in the UK been decreasing slowly since the start of the of the 21st century?

Q2 Give two limitations on using more renewable energy sources.

Section 2 Checklist — Make sure you know...

Energy Stores and Transfers

☐ That energy can be transferred to and from the following energy stores of an object: kinetic, thermal, chemical, gravitational potential, elastic potential, electrostatic, magnetic and nuclear.

☐ The definition of a system.

☐ That when energy is transferred in a closed system, there is no net change to its total energy.

☐ The different ways that energy can be transferred.

☐ The energy transfers in situations such as: boiling water in an electric kettle; a ball being thrown upwards or falling down; and a car slowing down or hitting an obstacle.

☐ The conservation of energy principle — that energy can be transferred usefully, stored, or dissipated, but can never be created or destroyed.

☐ How and why mechanical processes are wasteful — some energy is always dissipated to thermal energy stores; as well as some examples that show this.

☐ How to interpret and draw energy transfer diagrams.

cont...

Kinetic and Potential Energy Stores

- ☐ That the energy stored in a moving object's kinetic energy store is equal to $\frac{1}{2} \times$ mass $\times$ speed^2.
- ☐ That the change in energy in an object's GPE store when it's raised above the ground is equal to mass $\times$ gravitational field strength $\times$ change in height.
- ☐ How to use both of these equations to make calculations of energy transfer between the two stores.

Reducing Unwanted Energy Transfers

- ☐ That the thicker a building's walls, and the lower their thermal conductivity, the slower the building will cool.
- ☐ How thermal insulation is used to reduce unwanted energy transfers.
- ☐ How lubrication reduces unwanted energy transfers in mechanical processes.

Efficiency

- ☐ That the efficiency of a device can be calculated by the equation:
  efficiency = useful energy transferred by the device ÷ total energy supplied to the device.
- ☐ How to give efficiency as both a decimal and a percentage.
- ☐ That no devices are 100% efficient.
- ☐ How to interpret energy transfer diagrams that show the efficiency of a process.
- ☐ **H** Ways to improve the efficiency of devices by reducing the amount of energy they waste.

Energy Sources and Their Uses

- ☐ The difference between renewable and non-renewable energy sources, and examples of each.
- ☐ The different ways in which energy sources are used.

Renewable and Non-renewable Sources

- ☐ About renewable sources of energy: the wind, the Sun, hydro-electricity, tides and bio-fuels.
- ☐ The advantages and disadvantages of using these renewable sources of energy.
- ☐ How fossil and nuclear fuel are used for energy, and their advantages and disadvantages.

Trends in Energy Source Use

- ☐ Why, currently, the UK mainly uses non-renewables, but is trying to use more renewables.
- ☐ The different environmental, political, social, ethical and economic factors that affect the energy sources that are used.

1   A bowling ball has a mass of 5.0 kg.
It is raised through a vertical height of 0.8 m by a conveyor belt on a slope.

(a)   How much energy has been transferred to the gravitational potential energy store of the ball when it reaches the top of the slope?

The gravitational field strength on Earth is 10 N/kg.
Write down any equations you use. Give your answer in joules.

(3 marks)

(b)   The conveyor belt moves the ball up the slope at a constant speed.
The total energy in the ball's kinetic energy store as it moves is 10 J.

    (i)   Which equation relates kinetic energy to mass and speed?

        A $KE = m \times v^2$ **B** $KE = \frac{1}{2} \times m \times v$

        C $KE = m^2 \times v$ **D** $KE = \frac{1}{2} \times m \times v^2$

(1 mark)

    (ii)   Calculate the ball's speed as it moves up the slope. Give your answer in m/s.

(3 marks)

(c)*   The ball reaches the top of the slope and loses contact with the conveyor belt.
The ball rolls down the other side of the slope, then rolls along a flat surface back to the start of the bowling lane.

Describe the energy transfers that take place between the ball losing contact with the conveyor belt and it arriving at the start of the bowling lane. Refer to energy stores and transfers between energy stores in your answer.

(6 marks)

2   **Figure 1** shows the energy transferred when water is boiled in an electric kettle.
The efficiency of the kettle is 62.5%.

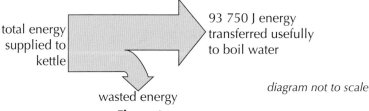

93 750 J energy transferred usefully to boil water

total energy supplied to kettle

wasted energy

diagram not to scale

Figure 1

(a)   Calculate the total energy supplied to the kettle.

Use the equation: $\text{efficiency} = \dfrac{\text{useful energy transferred by the device}}{\text{total energy supplied to the device}}$.

Give your answer in kJ.

(3 marks)

(b)   Suggest **one** way to improve the efficiency of the kettle.

(1 mark)

3   Jack's house cools very quickly when the heating is switched off.

(a)   Which **two** properties of the walls of the house affect how fast it cools?

(2 marks)

(b)   Loft insulation is a thick, thermally insulating material that is laid along the floor in the lofts of houses. Explain how installing loft insulation will improve the efficiency of Jack's house.

(2 marks)

4   **Figure 2** shows the percentage of the total electricity produced from each of six energy sources in two different countries.

	Coal	Oil	Gas	Nuclear	Solar	Wind
Country 1	49.9%	2.4%	20.3%	19.6%	6.0%	1.8%
Country 2	3.9%	4.0%	4.5%	3.1%	84.2%	0.3%

Figure 2

(a) (i)   Define a non-renewable energy source.

(1 mark)

(ii)   What percentage of electricity in Country 1 is generated from non-renewable energy sources?

(2 marks)

(b)   Both countries generate the same amount of electricity each year.
Suggest which country will emit more pollution by generating electricity.
Explain your answer.

(2 marks)

(c)   Country 1 is considering reducing the amount of coal it burns and using more renewable sources instead.

(i)   Give **one** environmental impact of using coal to generate electricity.

(1 mark)

(ii)   Suggest another use of coal as an energy source, other than for generating electricity.

(1 mark)

(iii)   Suggest **one** renewable energy source which would be a suitable alternative to coal to produce electricity on the island, which is not listed in **Figure 2**.

(1 mark)

(iv)   Give **one** reason why the renewable alternative given in **(iii)** may not be able to entirely replace coal as an option for generating the country's electricity.

(1 mark)

Learning Objectives:
- Be able to recall that waves transfer energy and information without transferring matter.
- Be able to describe the difference between longitudinal and transverse waves by referring to sound, electromagnetic, seismic and water waves.
- Be able to describe evidence that with water and sound waves it is the wave and not the water or air itself that travels.

**Specification References
4.1, 4.2, 4.5**

Tip: Information transferred by waves includes computer data, and TV and radio programmes.

Tip: [H] Seismic waves are covered in more detail on pages 109-110.

Tip: Compressions are regions of <u>high pressure</u> (they have lots of particles). Rarefactions are regions of <u>low pressure</u> (they have fewer particles).

1. Wave Basics

Waves move through substances carrying energy and information from one place to another — and once they've gone, it's as if they were never there.

What is a wave?

A **wave** is an oscillation (vibration) that transfers energy and information without transferring any matter, by making the particles of the substance (or fields) that it is travelling through oscillate.

Waves can be either transverse or longitudinal. These words sound complicated but they describe something simple — the direction of the wave oscillations.

Transverse waves

Transverse waves oscillate at right angles to the direction that they travel in. The direction they travel in is also the direction they transfer energy and information in.

> In transverse waves the oscillations are perpendicular (at 90°) to the direction of travel of the wave.

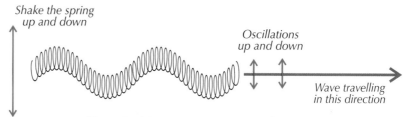

Shake the spring up and down

Oscillations up and down

Wave travelling in this direction

Figure 1: *A transverse wave on a spring.*

Examples of transverse waves include: light and all other electromagnetic waves (p.127), ripples on water, and waves on strings or springs when wiggled up and down (see Figure 1). S-waves (a type of seismic wave produced by earthquakes) are also transverse.

Longitudinal waves

Longitudinal waves have oscillations along the same line as they travel in, and they transfer energy and information in the same direction too. This type of wave has areas of compression, in which the particles are bunched together, and areas of rarefaction, in which the particles are spread out — see Figure 2.

> In longitudinal waves the oscillations are parallel to the direction of travel of the wave.

Examples of longitudinal waves include sound waves (page 103), a spring when you push the end (see Figure 2) and P-waves (another type of seismic wave produced by earthquakes).

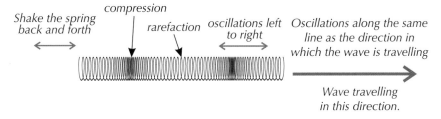

Shake the spring back and forth   *compression*   *rarefaction*   *oscillations left to right*   *Oscillations along the same line as the direction in which the wave is travelling*

Wave travelling in this direction.

Figure 2: *A longitudinal wave on a spring.*

Waves and matter

Waves transfer energy and information in the direction in which they are travelling, but they don't transfer matter. When waves travel through a medium (a material), such as air or water, the particles of the medium oscillate and transfer energy and information between each other, but overall the particles stay in the same place — only energy and information is transferred. You need to be able to describe some observations that provide evidence for this idea, so make sure you know these examples.

Figure 3: *The energy transferred by earthquake waves can be seen in the damage they cause.*

Examples

- Ripples on a water surface cause floating objects, e.g. twigs or birds, to just bob up and down. They don't move the object across the water to the edge. This is evidence that the wave travels but not the water.

- If you strum a guitar string and create sound waves, the sound waves don't carry the air away from the guitar to create a vacuum (completely empty space).

Tip: Waves that need a medium to travel in are classed as mechanical waves. They include water waves, waves in springs and strings, seismic waves and sound waves. Electromagnetic waves are an example of non-mechanical waves (see page 127).

Practice Questions — Fact Recall

Q1   Which of the following is not transferred by waves?

    A matter   **B** information   **C** energy

Q2   Waves can be transverse or longitudinal.

    a) Describe the difference between transverse and longitudinal waves.

    b) Give an example of a transverse wave.

Q3   Which two of the following waves are longitudinal?

    A light   **B** sound   **C** water ripples   **D** seismic P-waves

Q4   Do water waves cause water molecules to travel across the water's surface? Describe an observation which supports your answer.

2. Features of Waves

Learning Objectives:

- Be able to use the terms amplitude, period and wavefront as applied to waves.
- Be able to define and use the terms frequency and wavelength as applied to waves.

Specification References 4.3, 4.4

Describing a wave as 'really big and fast' might work for surfers, but physicists need a more accurate way — and that's what this page is about.

Representing waves

A wave can be represented on a set of axes — a line is drawn to show the displacement of the particles of the medium the wave is travelling through from their undisturbed positions at a moment in time. Crests and troughs are just points of maximum positive and maximum negative displacement from the particle's rest position.

Tip: Remember, the medium is just the substance the wave is travelling through.

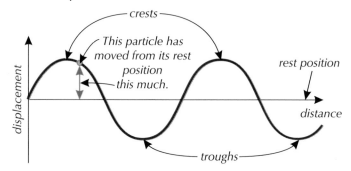

Figure 1: *A diagram showing the displacements of particles along a wave.*

Tip: You might see a wave represented with the horizontal axis showing time instead of distance.

This shows the displacement of a single particle as time passes. Oscilloscope traces are often like this (p.282).

Wavefronts

Wavefronts are imaginary lines drawn through identical points on waves, e.g. through each crest, (see Figure 2). They're perpendicular (at right angles) to the direction in which the wave is moving.

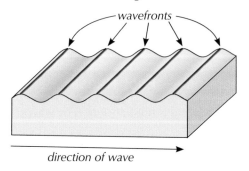

Figure 2: *Five wavefronts marked on a water wave.*

A **wavefront diagram** can be used to represent a wave (see Figure 3). The distance between each wavefront is equal to the wavelength of the wave. See the next page for more on wavelengths.

Tip: Wavefront diagrams are a useful way of showing refraction — see p.101.

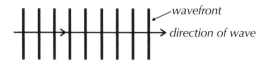

Figure 3: *A wavefront diagram.*

Wave measurements

There are a few measurements that you can use to describe waves...

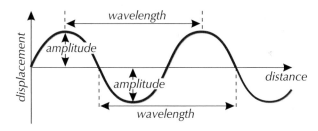

Figure 4: *A diagram showing the amplitude and wavelength of a wave.*

- The **amplitude** of a wave is the maximum displacement of a point on the wave from its undisturbed (or rest) position. In other words it's the displacement from the undisturbed position to a crest or a trough.

- The **wavelength** is the distance between the same point on two adjacent waves. So on a transverse wave it may be the distance between the crest of one wave and the crest of the next wave.

- The **frequency** is the number of waves produced by a source each second. It can also be defined as the number of complete waves passing a certain point per second. It is measured in hertz (Hz). 1 Hz is 1 wave per second.

Tip: Amplitude is <u>not</u> the distance from a trough to a crest — it's an easy mistake to make, so watch out...

Figure 5: *On a longitudinal wave, the distance between the centres of two adjacent compressions is the wavelength.*

The period of a wave

The **period** of a wave is the amount of time it takes for a full cycle of the wave to be completed. In other words, it's the length of time between one crest passing a point and the next crest passing the same point.

You can find the period of a wave from the frequency using this equation:

$$\text{Period} = \frac{1}{\text{frequency}} \qquad \text{or:} \qquad T = \frac{1}{f}$$

T = period (s) f = frequency (Hz)

Exam Tip
You aren't required to know this equation for the exam, but it's worth learning as it makes finding the period a breeze.

Example

A buoy measures the frequency of an ocean wave as 0.2 Hz. Calculate the period of this wave.

The frequency is in the correct unit (Hz), so 0.2 Hz can be substituted directly into the formula $T = \frac{1}{f}$:

$T = \frac{1}{f} = \frac{1}{0.2} = 5$ seconds

Tip: You can use a formula triangle to rearrange the equation.

Practice Questions — Fact Recall

Q1 What is:

  a) the amplitude of a wave?

  b) the wavelength of a wave?

  c) the frequency of a wave?

  d) the period of a wave?

Q2 What are wavefronts?

Practice Questions — Application

Q1 The diagram below shows a man shaking a spring up and down to produce a wave. What is the wavelength of the wave?

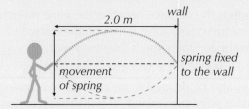

Q2 An oscilloscope is used to display the wave below.

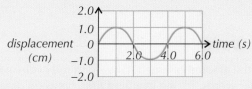

  a) What is the amplitude and the period of the wave shown?

  b) Calculate the frequency of the wave.

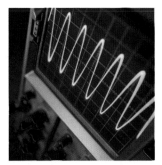

Figure 6: An oscilloscope screen showing a waveform. The amplitude, wavelength and frequency can be found from it.

3. Wave Speed

A wave's speed is how fast it moves, and there are two formulas you can use to calculate it. The first you'll have seen before — you can use it to find the speed of anything. The second is just for finding wave speed.

Using the speed equation for waves

Wave speed is how fast a wave moves, or how fast it transfers energy or information. You can use the usual speed equation from page 23 to work out wave speed if you know the distance it has travelled in a certain time:

$$\boldsymbol{v} = \text{wave speed (m/s)} \longrightarrow v = \frac{x}{t} \begin{matrix} \nearrow & \boldsymbol{x} = \textit{distance (m)} \\ \searrow & \boldsymbol{t} = \textit{time (s)} \end{matrix}$$

You can also use this formula to calculate **wave velocity**, which is just the speed of a wave in a certain direction.

Example

A firework is fired straight upwards. It explodes 272 m above the ground. It takes the sound wave from the firework 0.8 s to reach the ground. Calculate the speed of sound in air.

Simply substitute in the values given into the equation:

$v = x \div t = 272 \div 0.8 = 340$ m/s

Finding distance using reflected waves   Higher

You might be given a question in which a wave bounces back from a surface, e.g. a sound wave echoing off a cliff face, or an ultrasound wave reflecting from the sea bed (see page 108).

The important thing to remember with these questions is that the distance travelled by the wave is not the distance between the wave source and the reflective surface. If you are asked to find the distance between the wave's source and the reflective surface, first find the total distance travelled by the wave using the equation above. Then divide this distance by 2.

Example — Higher

A water wave is generated by a wave machine in a pool. The wave travels to the end of the pool, is reflected, and travels back to the wave machine. It takes 8.0 seconds for the wave to return to the machine once it has been generated. The wave travels at a speed of 4.5 m/s. How far from the end of the pool is the wave machine?

First, rearrange the equation above and substitute the values into it to find the total distance travelled by the water wave:

$v = \frac{x}{t} \Rightarrow x = v \times t = 4.5 \times 8.0 = 36$ m

Now divide this distance by 2 to find the distance between the machine and the end of the pool:

$36 \div 2 = 18$ m

Learning Objectives:

- Be able to use the term wave velocity as applied to waves.
- Be able to recall and use the equation $v = x \div t$ for all waves.
- **H** Calculate distance from time and wave velocity.
- Be able to recall and use the equation $v = f \times \lambda$ for all waves.

Specification References
4.4, 4.6, 4.8

Tip: Make sure you can rearrange the formula to calculate either distance or time. Here's the formula triangle.

$$\frac{x}{v \times t}$$

Figure 1: *The difference in speed between sound and light waves is the reason why you see a firework explode before you hear it.*

Tip: Question 6 on the next page involves reflected waves.

Tip: The symbol for wavelength is the Greek letter λ, which is called 'lambda'.

The wave equation

If you know the wave's frequency and wavelength, you can calculate its speed using the wave equation:

v = wave speed (m/s) ⟶ $v = f \times \lambda$ ⟵ λ = wavelength (m)

f = frequency (Hz)

Example 1

A paddle vibrating up and down in a pool is used to produce waves on the water. The wavelength of each wave is 1.2 m and exactly 2 complete waves are produced per second. Calculate the speed of the wave.

The number of waves produced per second is the frequency.

So $f = 2$ Hz and $\lambda = 1.2$ m.

Substitute these into the wave equation:

$v = f \times \lambda = 2 \times 1.2 = 2.4$ m/s

MATHS SKILLS

Tip: You need to be able to rearrange this formula too. Here's the formula triangle for it.

Example 2

A wave has a frequency of 4.0×10^7 Hz and a speed of 3.0×10^8 m/s. Find its wavelength.

MATHS SKILLS

You're trying to find λ using f and v, so you've got to rearrange the equation.

So $\lambda = v \div f = (3.0 \times 10^8) \div (4.0 \times 10^7) = 7.5$ m

---

Practice Questions — Fact Recall

Q1 Write down the equation for wave speed that you would use if you know the distance a wave has travelled and how long it has taken to travel that distance. Give the units each quantity is measured in.

Q2 Write down the wave equation. Give the units of each quantity.

Practice Questions — Application

Q1 Calculate the speed of a wave which travels 100 m in 0.5 s.

Q2 Calculate the speed of a wave with a wavelength of 0.45 m and a frequency of 15 Hz. Give your answer to 2 significant figures.

Q3 A meteor burns up 90 km above the Earth's surface. After how long does the light from the burning meteor reach the Earth's surface? Assume that light travels through air at 3×10^8 m/s.

Q4 The speed of sound in a seawater sample is known to be 1500 m/s. A sound wave with a frequency of 3 kHz is produced under water. Calculate the wavelength of this sound wave.

Q5 A light wave has a wavelength of 7.5×10^{-7} m and travels at 3.0×10^8 m/s. What is its frequency?

Q6 A boy blows a whistle. The sound wave produced is reflected back from a mountain and is heard by the boy 1.5 s later. How far is the mountain from the boy? Assume that sound travels at 340 m/s in air.

Tip: 🅗 Watch out in Q6 — the sound wave has travelled to the mountain and back again. It's often useful to draw a quick diagram so you don't get muddled about how far a wave has travelled.

4. Measuring Waves

Finding the speed of a wave is a bit trickier than finding the speed of, say, a car. Luckily, there are some cunning methods you can use, which is what the next few pages are about.

Measuring the speed of sound in air

To measure the speed of sound, you need to find the frequency and the wavelength of a sound wave — you can then use the wave equation $v = f \times \lambda$ (see page 94).

You can generate a sound wave with a specific frequency by attaching a signal generator to a speaker. This sound wave can then be detected by microphones, which convert it to a trace on an oscilloscope.

Method

Set up your equipment as shown below, with both microphones next to the speaker. The detected wave at each microphone can be seen as separate traces on the oscilloscope.

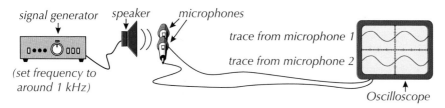

Figure 1: *The initial set-up of apparatus when measuring the speed of sound in air.*

Slowly move one microphone away from the speaker. Its trace will shift sideways on the oscilloscope. Keep moving it until the two traces on the oscilloscope are aligned once more. At this point the microphones will be exactly one wavelength apart, so measure the distance between them to measure the wavelength (λ).

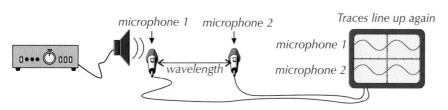

Figure 2: *Arrangement of apparatus when the microphones are one wavelength apart.*

You can then use the formula $v = f \times \lambda$ to find the speed (v) of the sound wave passing through the air — the frequency (f) of the wave will be equal to the frequency set by the signal generator.

The speed of sound in air is around 340 m/s, so check that your results roughly agree with this.

Learning Objectives:
- Be able to describe how to measure the velocity of sound in air and ripples on water surfaces.
- Be able to investigate the suitability of equipment to measure the speed, frequency and wavelength of a wave in a solid and a fluid (Core Practical).

Specification References 4.7, 4.17

Tip: Remember — you should carry out a risk assessment before you do a practical.

Tip: The traces on the oscilloscope line up with each other as both microphones are the same distance from the speaker.

Tip: The traces are both of the same wave, just one has travelled further.

Tip: Don't forget you need the wavelength in metres and the frequency in Hz to use the wave equation.

Tip: When you state the speed of sound, you should say what it's travelling through. Sound moves at different speeds through different materials — see p.103.

Measuring the speed of water ripples

You can see water ripples, but they tend to move a bit too quickly for their measurements to be taken. This method is basically a way to get a still image of them. Again, you use a signal generator to produce waves of a known frequency, but this time you attach it to the dipper of a ripple tank.

A ripple tank is a shallow glass tank used to show the properties of waves. The glass bottom of a ripple tank means a light can be shone on the tank from above to project the wave pattern onto a screen below. This makes it much easier to measure the waves without disturbing them (see Figure 3).

Method

Set up your equipment as shown in Figure 3. Fill your ripple tank with water to a depth of around 5 mm. Connect your dipper to the signal generator and set it off at a known frequency. Dim the lights and turn on the strobe light — you'll see a wave pattern made by the shadows of the wave crests on the screen below the tank.

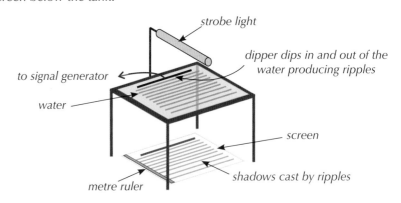

Figure 3: Apparatus for measuring the speed of ripples using a strobe light.

Increase the frequency of the strobe light until the wave pattern on the screen appears to 'freeze' and stop moving. This happens when the frequency of the waves and the strobe light are equal — the waves appear not to move because they are being lit at the same point in their cycle each time.

The distance between each shadow line is equal to one wavelength. Measure the distance between shadow lines that are 10 wavelengths apart using a metre ruler, then divide this distance by 10 to find the average wavelength. This is a suitable method for measuring small wavelengths (see page 333).

Depending on the exact set up of your apparatus, the waves seen on the screen may be magnified. In this case you'll need to work out the scale factor before you can find the wavelength. An easy way to do this it to stick a piece of tape of a known length, e.g. 10 cm, to the bottom of the ripple tank. Then measure the length of its shadow. If the shadow is longer than the tape, then what you're seeing on the screen is magnified. The length of the tape's shadow divided by the actual length of the tape will give you the scale factor.

You can then use the formula $v = f \times \lambda$ to find the speed (v) of the ripples, where f is the frequency of the signal generator and strobe light.

Tip: More practicals mean more risk assessments. Make sure you do one for this experiment and the one on the next page. For this practical, take care when using electronics like the strobe light and signal generator near the water in the ripple tank.

Tip: The strobe light is a good piece of equipment to use because it allows you to measure a still pattern instead of a constantly moving one. However, it should be used with care as some people are sensitive to flashing lights.

Tip: Measure the wavelength by looking at the screen from underneath the ripple tank — don't look at it through the water. Your view will be distorted by refraction (see page 99).

Tip: You can also find the frequency using a regular light. The wave shadows will be moving, so count how many waves pass a mark on the screen in a given time, then divide this by the time in seconds to find the frequency.

Tip: The shadow lines may be very close together, so you'll get a more accurate measurement for wavelength if you measure ten spaces and divide, rather than try to measure one space.

Finding the speed of a wave in a solid

When you hit a metal rod with a hammer, waves are produced along the rod. These waves make the rod vibrate and produce sound waves in the air around the rod. These sound waves have the same frequencies as the waves in the rod.

The waves produced along the rod have lots of different frequencies and wavelengths, but they all travel at the same speed. To find this speed, you need to know the frequency and wavelength of a single wave. This is where the peak frequency of the rod comes in handy. It's equal to the frequency of the loudest sound wave, which can be identified using computer software.

Figure 5 shows the peak frequency wave of the rod.
The length of the rod is equal to half the wavelength of this wave.

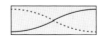

Figure 5: *The peak frequency wave of a rod.*

You can investigate wave speed in a solid using the apparatus shown in Figure 6. Make sure you measure the length of the rod before you start, and to secure the rod at its centre with the elastic bands.

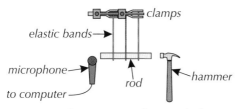

Figure 6: *Apparatus for measuring the speed of a wave in a rod.*

Tap the end of the rod with the hammer and use the microphone and computer to measure the peak frequency sound wave produced (and so the peak frequency wave in the rod). Repeat this three times to get an average peak frequency. Calculate the speed of the wave using $v = f \times \lambda$, where λ is equal to twice the length of the rod.

Figure 4: *A percussion triangle produces its sound in the same was as the rod in this experiment*

Tip: A wavelength is the length of a full cycle of a wave, e.g. from crest to crest (see page 91). The wave along the rod in Figure 5 runs from trough to crest, so its length is half a wavelength.

Tip: The peak frequency wave <u>always</u> has λ = rod length × 2, whatever the rod is made from. So this set up is suitable for finding the wave speed in any type of solid material.

Practice Questions — Fact Recall

Q1 Describe a way of measuring: a) the speed of sound in air.

Q2 Explain how to find the speed of waves along a solid metal rod.

Practice Question — Application

Q1 A signal generator connected to the paddle in a ripple tank is set to 100 Hz. The frequency of a strobe light above the tank is adjusted until the shadows of the ripples on the screen below are stationary. A 1.0 cm line is drawn on the bottom of the ripple tank. The diagram shows the line's shadow and part of the shadow pattern of the ripples.

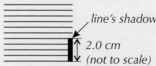

a) Use the diagram to calculate the wavelength of the ripples.

b) Calculate the speed of the ripples.

Tip: For Q1a, compare the actual length of the line on the bottom of the ripple tank to the length of its shadow to find the magnification of the shadows on the screen.

- Be able to describe
  the effects of
  reflection,
  transmission and
  absorption of waves at
  material interfaces.
- **H** Be able to
  recall that different
  substances may
  absorb, transmit,
  refract or reflect waves
  in ways that vary with
  wavelength.

**Specification References
4.9 and 4.11**

Figure 1: *Light waves reflect
from a mirror, allowing you
to see an image in it.*

Tip: There's lots
about electromagnetic
radiation on
pages 127-129.

5. Wave Behaviour at Boundaries

*When a wave hits the boundary between the substance it's moving through
and a new substance, it doesn't just continue on in exactly the same way.
There are a few different things that can happen to it.*

Waves at a boundary

Waves travel through different materials, e.g. air, water, glass. When they
arrive at a boundary between two different materials (a **material interface**),
three things can happen:

Absorption — The waves may be absorbed by the second material. This
transfers energy to the material's energy stores (see p.61). Often, the energy
is transferred to a thermal energy store, which leads to heating (this is how a
microwave oven works, see page 133).

Reflection — The waves may bounce back from the second material
(see p.115). This is how echoes are created.

Transmission — The waves may carry on travelling through the new material,
e.g. light shining through a window. However, they often undergo **refraction**
— there's more on this on the next page.

In reality, a combination of all three of these will usually occur at a boundary.

What factors decide what happens to a wave?

What exactly happens to a wave when it meets at boundary depends on its
wavelength and the properties of the materials involved.

> **Example** ── **Higher**
>
> The Earth's atmosphere absorbs some wavelengths of electromagnetic
> radiation from the Sun and transmits others. For example, gamma rays
> have a very short wavelength and are absorbed by the atmosphere,
> which helps to protect us from their harmful effects. However, visible
> light has a longer wavelength and is transmitted by the atmosphere,
> which is why we can see things.

Practice Questions — Fact Recall

Q1   When a wave hits a material interface, it can be absorbed, reflected
      or transmitted by the second material. Describe what happens in
      each of these cases.

Q2   Why might a material transmit some waves, while absorbing or
      reflecting other waves?

6. Refraction

Refraction is all about bending waves. It's how glasses work and how prisms create pretty rainbows, and it's used in tonnes of other applications too. Who said you won't use what you learn in physics in the real world...

Refraction basics

A wave can refract (change direction) when it meets a boundary between two different materials — see Figure 1.

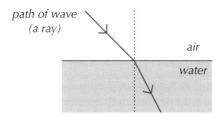

path of wave (a ray)

air

water

Figure 1: *The path of a wave as it travels across the boundary between air and water.*

In Figure 1, the dotted line is called the **normal**. This is just an imaginary line that is at 90° to the boundary between the two materials. Refraction only occurs if the wave isn't travelling along the normal — see Figure 2.

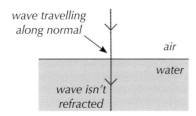

wave travelling along normal

air

water

wave isn't refracted

Figure 2: *The path of a wave as it travels across the boundary between air and water along the normal. The wave is not refracted.*

You can use the normal to describe how a wave has been refracted. You can say the refracted wave has bent towards or away from the normal.

Showing refraction with a ray diagram

A **ray** is a straight line showing the path that a wave, such as light, travels along. You can show the path taken by a wave by drawing a ray diagram (see Figure 4 for a labelled example of one). Here's how you do it:

1. Draw the boundary between the two materials and then add in the normal. The normal is usually shown as a dotted line.

2. Draw an incoming (incident) ray that meets the normal at the boundary. The angle between the ray and the normal is the **angle of incidence**. (If you're given this angle, make sure to draw it carefully with a protractor.)

3. Now draw the refracted ray on the other side of the boundary. It should start exactly where the incident ray meets the boundary. The angle that the refracted ray makes with the normal is called the **angle of refraction**.

Learning Objectives:
- Be able to describe the effects of refraction of waves at material interfaces.
- Be able to explain how waves will be refracted at a boundary in terms of the change of direction.
- Be able to explain refraction with the aid of ray diagrams.
- Be able to investigate refraction in rectangular glass blocks in terms of the interaction of electromagnetic waves with matter (Core Practical).
- **H** Be able to explain how waves will be refracted at a boundary in terms of the change of speed.

Specification References 4.9, 4.10, 5.1, 5.9

Figure 3: *The light waves being reflected by the striped surface are refracted by the glass and the water before they reach your eyes — which is why the image looks distorted.*

Tip: Ray diagrams are mainly used to show the refraction of light, but any type of wave can refract. How much a wave refracts at a boundary depends on its wavelength. Remember, not all waves will refract — they may be absorbed or reflected instead.

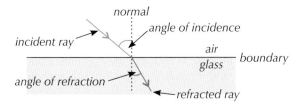

Figure 4: *Refraction of a light ray moving from air into glass. When the light refracts, it bends towards the normal.*

If the refracted ray bends towards the normal, the angle of refraction will be smaller than the angle of incidence. If it bends away from the normal, the angle of refraction will be larger than the angle of incidence.

Investigating refraction

Tip: You'll need to do a risk assessment before you start.

You can investigate the refraction of light at the boundary between air and glass using a transparent rectangular glass block and a ray box or laser.

The first thing to do is place the glass block on a piece of paper and trace around it. Then use the ray box (or laser) to shine a ray of light at the middle of one side of the block.

Figure 5: *A ray box is basically a lamp with a metal box around it. In one of the sides you can insert a metal plate with one or more narrow slits to produce narrow beams of light.*

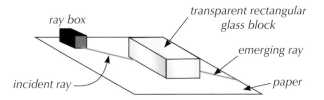

Figure 6: *Set-up of the equipment needed to investigate the refraction of light as it travels between air and glass.*

Trace the incident ray on the paper, and do the same for the light ray that emerges on the other side of the block. Remove the block and, with a straight line, join up the lines for the incident ray and the emerging ray. This shows the path of the refracted ray through the block.

Tip: Make sure you trace the light rays (and join them up) using a ruler and sharp pencil.

Draw the normal at the point where the light ray entered the block. Use a protractor to measure the angle between the incident ray and the normal (the angle of incidence, *I*) and the angle between the refracted ray and the normal (the angle of refraction, *R*).

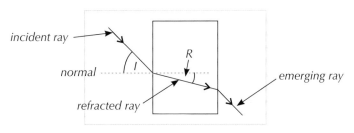

Figure 7: *Rays and angles marked on the piece of paper.*

Repeat this three times, keeping the angle of incidence as the ray enters the block the same. Calculate an average for each of the angles.

It's important to remember that all waves can be refracted — this experiment uses visible light so that you can actually see the ray being refracted as it travels through the block.

Tip: Light is an electromagnetic (EM) wave — see p.127 for more about other types of EM wave. All EM waves can be refracted.

More on refraction `Higher`

Refraction occurs because waves travel faster in some materials than others, so the speed of a wave can change as it crosses a boundary between two materials.

Which way the wave bends depends on whether it moves faster or slower in the medium it travels into.

- If a wave slows down at a boundary, it bends towards the normal.

- If a wave speeds up at a boundary, it bends away from the normal.

When a wave enters a new material, its speed changes, but its frequency remains the same. Since the speed, wavelength and frequency of a wave are all related by the wave equation ($v = f \times \lambda$ — see page 94), if the speed changes but the frequency is constant, the wavelength must change. If the speed of the wave increases, its wavelength increases. If the speed decreases, so does the wavelength.

Tip: 'Medium' is just a word for what the wave is travelling through. 'Media' is a plural of it.

Tip: H 'Optical density' is a term you may see when talking about the refraction of light. The more optically dense a material is, the slower light (and other EM waves) travel through it.

Using wavefronts to show refraction `Higher`

Figure 8 is a wavefront diagram showing light waves travelling along the normal to a boundary. The waves travel more slowly in material 2 than in material 1, meaning the wavelength decreases. This decrease is shown by the wavefronts becoming closer together.

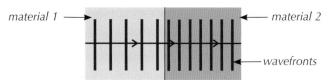

Figure 8: A wavefront diagram showing light travelling along a normal to a boundary.

Tip: Wavefronts are imaginary lines drawn through identical points along a wave, e.g. through each crest. This means each wavefront is exactly one wavelength apart — see page 90.

Tip: H The wave travelling along the normal isn't refracted, but its speed and wavelength still change.

Wavefront diagrams are useful for explaining why refraction happens. When a wave crosses a boundary at an angle to the normal, one end of the wavefront will cross the boundary before the rest of the wavefront. This means that one end of the wavefront changes speed before the rest of the wavefront.

Think about the case of a wave slowing down as it crosses a boundary (as shown in Figure 9 on the next page). When one part of the wavefront crosses the boundary, that part travels slower than the rest of the wavefront.

So by the time the whole wavefront crosses the boundary, the faster part of the wavefront will have travelled further than the slower part of the wavefront.

Tip: ⊞ Imagine driving a go-kart in the direction of the wave, and that the material 2 is a pool of mud. One side of the go-kart will reach the mud first and slow down. The other side of the go-kart isn't yet in the mud so it carries on moving quickly, causing the go-kart to swing round, changing direction.

This difference in distance travelled (caused by the difference in speed) between the ends of wavefronts causes the wave to change direction and bend towards the normal.

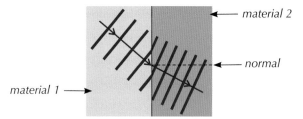

Figure 9: *A wave slowing down as it crosses a boundary at an angle to the normal.*

Figure 10 shows a wave speeding up as it crosses a boundary. When the first part of the wavefront crosses the boundary it speeds up, so it will travel further than the rest of the wavefront in a given time. This again causes the wave to change direction. However, this time the wave bends away from the normal.

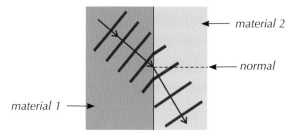

Figure 10: *A wave speeding up as it crosses a boundary at an angle to the normal.*

Practice Questions — Fact Recall

Q1 What is refraction and under what circumstances does it occur?

Q2 Draw a ray diagram to show a wave bending towards the normal. Mark on the angles of incidence and refraction.

Q3 Describe an experiment you could do to investigate the refraction of light as it travels between air and glass.

Q4 Describe the refraction of a wave that crosses a boundary at an angle to the normal and speeds up.

Q5 What happens to the wavelength and frequency of a wave as it crosses into a different medium and speeds up?

Practice Questions — Application

Q1 Draw a ray diagram to show a light wave hitting a boundary between two substances with an angle of incidence of 40° and an angle of refraction of 60°.

Q2 A light ray hits a boundary between two materials with an angle of incidence of 30°. It travels into the new material and is refracted. The angle of refraction is 40°. Explain how the speed of the light ray has changed between the two materials.

7. Sound

Sound waves are basically vibrations that pass through matter. If they get to your ear, they make bits inside it vibrate, causing the sensation of hearing.

What are sound waves?

Sound waves are longitudinal waves (see page 88) of vibrating particles caused by vibrating objects. These vibrations are passed through the surrounding matter as a series of compressions and rarefactions. The surrounding matter can be solid, liquid or gas. Sound generally travels faster in solids than in liquids, and faster in liquids than in gases.

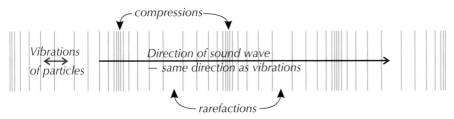

Figure 1: *A sound wave made up of compressions and rarefactions of the particles in a medium.*

Sound waves in different materials

Sound waves will refract (change direction — see page 99) as they enter different materials. However, since sound waves spread out a lot, the change in direction is hard to spot under normal circumstances.

When a sound wave enters a denser medium it speeds up. Its frequency stays the same, so for the wave equation speed = frequency × wavelength (see page 94) to stay true the wavelength of the sound wave must change too. If its speed increases, its wavelength also increases. If its speed decreases, then its wavelength decreases too.

Example

A guitar string produces a sound wave with a wavelength of 0.68 m and a speed of 340 m/s in air. The sound wave then enters water where its speed changes to 1500 m/s. Calculate its new wavelength.

In air, $v = 340$ m/s and $\lambda = 0.68$ m.
Rearrange the wave equation, $v = f \times \lambda$ to find frequency: $f = v \div \lambda$

   So $f = 340 \div 0.68 = 500$ Hz

The frequency stays the same in the water, so $f = 500$ Hz and $v = 1500$ m/s.
Rearrange the wave equation to find wavelength: $\lambda = v \div f$

   So $\lambda = 1500 \div 500 = 3$ m

Learning Objectives:

- Be able to describe how changes, if any, in velocity, frequency and wavelength, in the transmission of sound waves from one medium to another are inter-related.

- **H** Be able to describe the processes which convert wave disturbances between sound waves and vibrations in solids, and
  a) explain why such processes only work over a limited frequency range.
  b) use this to explain the way the human ear works.

**Specification References
4.12, 4.16**

Tip: Remember — the word 'medium' just refers to the material that a wave is travelling through.

Tip: Sound waves will be reflected by hard, flat surfaces. Echoes are just reflected sound waves.

Tip: Sound can't travel in space because it's mostly a vacuum (there are no particles to move or vibrate).

Hearing Higher

To understand how sound waves are heard by the ears, you need to understand how sound travels through solids. Figure 3 shows how sound travels through air and then through a solid. The paper diaphragm in a speaker vibrates backwards and forwards, which causes the surrounding air to vibrate. This creates compressions and rarefactions — a sound wave.

When the sound wave meets a solid object, the air particles hitting the object (and producing changes in pressure — page 310) cause the closest particles in the solid to move back and forth (vibrate). These particles hit the next particles along and so on. This series of vibrations passes the sound wave through the object.

Tip: Compressions are areas of high pressure and rarefactions are areas of low pressure.

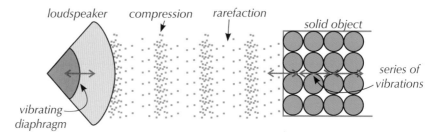

Figure 3: The conversion of sound waves to vibrations in a solid.

Figure 2: In a string telephone, the sound wave is passed through the string as a series of vibrations.

Sometimes, sound waves can cause the entire solid object to vibrate. Not all sound waves will be converted to vibrations of a solid in this way. It depends on the object's size, shape and structure and the frequency of the sound wave. Most materials and objects will only convert sound waves within a certain frequency range into vibrations.

Tip: H Microphones work in a similar way to the ear. In a microphone, sound waves cause a diaphragm to vibrate and this movement is transferred into an electrical signal.

Sound waves of certain frequencies that reach your **ear drum** cause it to vibrate. These vibrations are passed on to tiny bones in your ear called ossicles, through the semicircular canals and to the cochlea. The cochlea turns these vibrations into electrical signals which get sent to your brain and allow you to hear the sound.

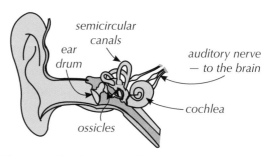

Figure 4: The structure of the ear.

Tip: H The exact range of frequencies that can be heard varies a lot between individuals. Also, as we age, the upper limit decreases.

Humans can only hear sounds with frequencies between 20 Hz and 20 kHz. The limits are caused by the size and shape of our ear drum, as well as the structure of all the parts within the ear that vibrate to transfer the energy from the sound wave.

Practice Questions — Fact Recall

Q1 How does the frequency and wavelength of a sound wave change when the sound wave enters a new medium and speeds up?

Q2 Give one factor that limits the vibrations of an object's particles that occur when a sound wave strikes the object.

Q3 Explain the process by which a stereo speaker produces a sound wave, and how the sound wave travels to and is heard by a person.

Practice Questions — Application

Q1 The density of lead is 11 g/cm^3 and the density of aluminium is 2.7 g/cm^3 at room temperature. Predict what will happen to a sound wave's frequency, wavelength and speed when it moves from the lead to the aluminium.

Q2 Dog whistles produce high-frequency sound waves that dogs can hear, but humans cannot. Why can humans not hear high-frequency sound waves, such as those produced by these whistles?

Figure 5: *Dog whistles are used to train dogs without disturbing humans.*

- **H** Be able to recall that sound with frequencies greater than 20 000 hertz, Hz, is known as ultrasound.
- **H** Be able to explain uses of ultrasound, including sonar and foetal scanning.
- **H** Be able to calculate depth from time and wave velocity.

Specification References 4.8, 4.13, 4.15

8. Ultrasound

Ultrasound waves are high frequency sound waves. How they reflect at boundaries makes them a useful tool for imaging things we can't see directly.

What is ultrasound?

Ultrasound waves are sound waves with frequencies greater than 20 000 Hz (20 kHz). Ultrasound cannot be heard by people, as it is outside the normal range of human hearing.

Ultrasound waves are fairly easy to produce. Electrical devices can be made which produce electrical oscillations of a large range of frequencies. These can easily be converted into mechanical vibrations to produce sound waves with frequencies above 20 kHz.

Properties of ultrasound

When waves pass from one medium into another, some of the waves are reflected by the boundary between the two media, and some are transmitted (and possibly refracted). This is partial reflection.

Tip: See page 98 for more about what can happen to a wave when it reaches the boundary between two media.

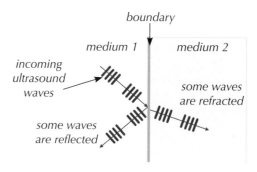

Figure 1: *A diagram of ultrasound waves undergoing partial reflection at a boundary.*

What this means is that you can point a pulse (short burst) of ultrasound at an object, and wherever there are boundaries between one substance and another, some of the ultrasound gets reflected back.

When sound waves are reflected by surfaces, there is a delay between you hearing the original sound and the reflected sound. This is because the reflected sound waves have to travel further, taking longer to reach your ears. The reflected wave is known as an echo.

The same goes for ultrasound, the pulse takes time to return. The time it takes for the reflections to reach a detector can be used to measure how far away the boundary is.

Figure 2: *Some animals, including dolphins and bats, emit ultrasound and use the reflected waves to navigate and find food.*

Exploring structures with waves

As you've seen on page 98, waves have different properties (e.g. speed) depending on the material they're travelling through.

When a wave arrives at a boundary between materials, a number of things can happen. It can be completely reflected or partially reflected (as above), continue travelling in the same direction but at a different speed, or be refracted or absorbed (p.98).

Studying the properties and paths of waves through structures can give you clues to some of the properties of the structure that you can't see by eye. You can do this with lots of different waves — ultrasound and seismic waves (page 109) are two good, well-known examples.

Tip: H Waves which have been transmitted could go on to be partially reflected and transmitted at another boundary. So if you have a set of boundaries one after the other, the wave will undergo partial reflection at each boundary. This allows you to work out the distances between boundaries, based on when you detect the reflected waves.

Exploring structures with ultrasound

Partial reflection means that ultrasound has a number of useful applications. These chiefly involve imaging or locating objects that we can't directly see. Ultrasound can be used for medical purposes, as well as in sonar, which can be used in the military or in commercial fishing.

Tip: H Ultrasound is also used in industry to see inside materials. For example, it can be used to find flaws in objects such as pipes.

Foetal scanning

Ultrasound is used in foetal scanning to produce an image of an unborn baby. This allows any problems with the baby's development to be identified at an early stage.

Ultrasound waves can pass through the body, but whenever they reach a boundary between two different media (like fluid in the womb and the skin of the foetus) some of the waves are reflected back and detected (see Figure 3). The exact timing and distribution of these echoes are processed by a computer to produce a video image of the foetus.

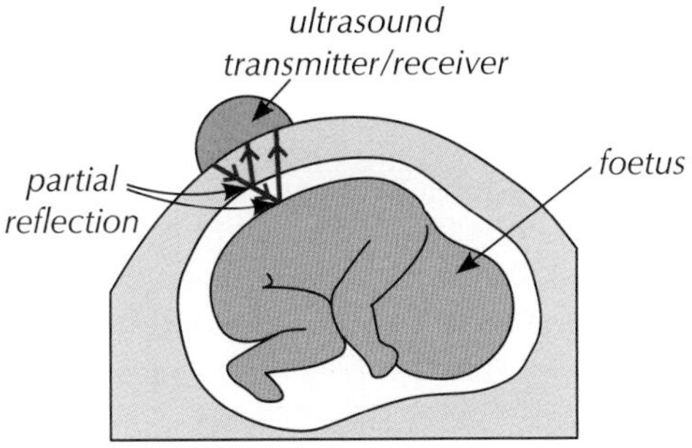

Figure 3: *Ultrasound waves being used to produce an image of a foetus.*

Ultrasound has many other applications in medical imaging. Being able to "see" inside the body allows doctors to check how the body is functioning and diagnose medical conditions (see Figure 4).

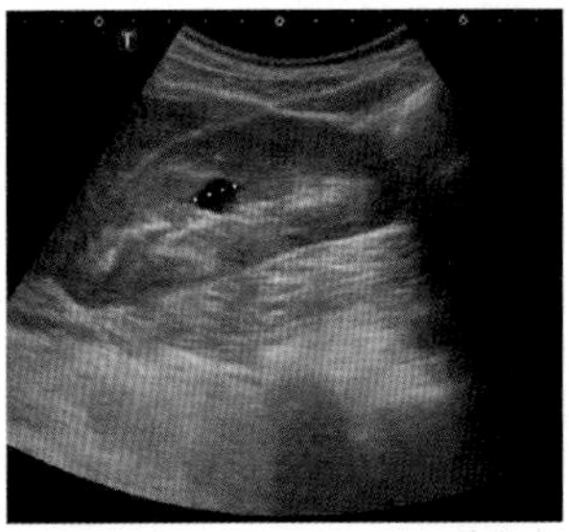

Figure 4: *An ultrasound image of a kidney. The black area marked with yellow dots is a cyst.*

Active sonar

Active sonar (also known as echo sounding) is a type of sonar used by boats and submarines, where high-frequency sound waves (including ultrasound) are used to find out the depth of the water they are in, or to locate objects in deep water.

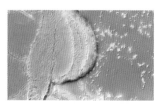

Figure 5: *An image of the Mariana Trench, produced by sonar. The darker the blue, the lower the sea bed.*

A pulse of sound waves is emitted by the boat or submarine, and the time taken for the echo to return is measured. Then if you know the speed of sound in the water, you can calculate the depth of the object using the equation from page 93: $v = \frac{x}{t}$.

Example — Higher

A pulse of ultrasound takes 4.50 seconds to travel from a submarine to the sea bed and back again. If the speed of sound in seawater is 1520 m/s, how far away is the submarine from the sea bed?

MATHS SKILLS

First rearrange the equation: $v = \frac{x}{t} \Rightarrow x = v \times t$

Then substitute in the values:
$x = 1520 \times 4.50 = 6840$ m

But, this is a reflection question — the pulse travelled to the sea bed AND back in 4.50 s. So you need to divide your distance by 2.

Distance to seabed = 6840 ÷ 2 = 3420 m

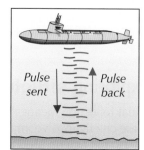

Pulse sent   Pulse back

Practice Questions — Fact Recall

Q1 What is ultrasound?

Q2 Explain how ultrasound allows an image of a foetus to be produced.

Q3 Explain how ultrasound is used by a submarine to determine how far it is above the ocean floor.

Practice Questions — Application

Q1 A food manufacturer discovers that some of their tins of syrup have been contaminated with shards of plastic. Suggest how ultrasound might be used to detect which tins contain shards of plastic.

Q2 An ultrasound pulse is directed into a solid block of material, as shown in the diagram. A reflected pulse is detected 15.0 µs later.

Tip: µs means microseconds. One microsecond is equal to 1×10^{-6} s. (See page 18 for more on prefixes like this.)

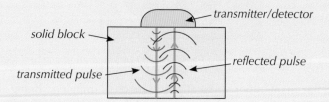

solid block   *transmitter/detector*

transmitted pulse   *reflected pulse*

The ultrasound pulse travels at 1720 m/s through the material. What is the distance (in mm) between the transmitter and the boundary from which the pulse is reflected?

9. Infrasound Higher

You've just seen how ultrasound waves can help us create an image of things we can't see on a fairly small scale. But what about structures as big as the Earth itself? That's where seismic waves come in.

What is infrasound?

Infrasound waves are sound waves with a frequency below 20 Hz. This frequency is too low for humans to hear. Studying infrasound can allow scientists to detect distant volcanic eruptions or to find out information about meteors which enter our atmosphere. One common use of infrasound is in exploring the structure and properties of the Earth's core.

Seismic waves

Earthquakes produce **seismic waves** which travel out through (or across the surface of) the Earth. We can use seismic waves, some of which are infrasound, to explore the structure of the Earth.

There are two different types of seismic waves you need to know about — P-waves and S-waves. P-waves are longitudinal waves. They can travel through both solids and liquids. Like sound waves, P-waves travel much faster in solids than in liquids. S-waves are transverse waves. They aren't able to pass through liquid materials. P-waves always travel faster than S-waves, and both will travel faster through denser materials than they will through less dense ones.

Exploring the Earth's structure

Seismic waves from an earthquake can be detected at different points on the surface of the planet using detectors called seismometers. Seismologists (scientists who study earthquakes) work out the time it takes for the waves to reach each seismometer. They also note which parts of the Earth don't receive the waves at all. They can use the data they gather to form an understanding of the inner structure of the Earth.

Like all waves, when seismic waves reach a boundary between two different materials, they can be absorbed, reflected, transmitted and refracted. Most of the time, as seismic waves travel through the Earth, they change speed gradually (as the density of the material they are moving through is also gradually changing). This causes the waves to follow a slightly curved path. But when the medium the waves are travelling through changes suddenly (like at the boundary between two different materials), the direction changes abruptly, and the path has a kink (see Figure 2).

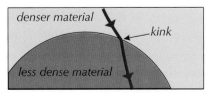

Figure 2: A diagram showing the 'kink' in the path when a seismic wave refracts at a boundary between two materials.

Learning Objectives:
- **H** Be able to recall that sound with frequencies less than 20 hertz, Hz, is known as infrasound.
- **H** Be able to explain uses of infrasound, including exploration of the Earth's core.

Specification References 4.14, 4.15

Figure 1: Some animals, such as elephants and whales, communicate using infrasound. By detecting this, scientists are able to track these animals for conservation purposes.

Tip: **H** P-waves and S-waves are 'body waves' — they travel through the Earth, not across its surface.

Figure 3: A seismograph, attached to a seismometer. Seismic waves cause the needle to move, and draw out a graph of the waves.

By measuring the seismic waves detected at various points on Earth, seismologists can build up a picture of the paths the waves have travelled along from the point of origin (the earthquake) to the points of detection. This allows them to work out where any boundaries between different materials occur within the Earth.

Tip: ⬛ The P-waves travelling directly downwards from the source to the opposite side of the Earth don't change direction. This is because they hit the core at 90° — and waves that hit a boundary at 90° (i.e. along the normal) don't refract (see page 99).

Tip: ⬛ P-waves are 'primary waves' — they arrive at the detectors first. S-waves are 'secondary waves' — they travel slower, and so are detected second. It's a good way to remember the difference between the two.

Tip: ⬛ The mantle (see Figure 6) isn't quite solid — but it's close enough to solid that S-waves can still travel through it.

Example — Higher

An earthquake produces seismic waves which travel through the inside of the Earth. Figure 4 shows the path of the P-waves.

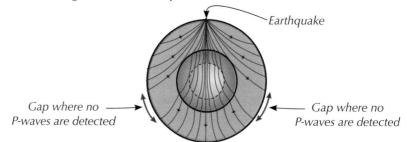

Earthquake

Gap where no P-waves are detected *Gap where no P-waves are detected*

Figure 4: *A diagram showing how P-waves travel through the Earth.*

Some P-waves are detected on the other side of the Earth to the earthquake, which means they have been able to pass through the Earth's interior. But there are some gaps where no waves are detected. At these points, the waves must have abruptly changed direction (i.e. refracted) at a boundary somewhere along the way. This suggests that the Earth has a 'core' inside it, made of a different material to the rest of the Earth.

Figure 5 shows the path of the S-waves generated by the earthquake.

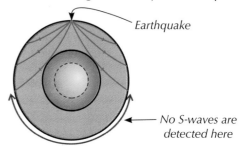

Earthquake

No S-waves are detected here

Figure 5: *A diagram showing how S-waves travel through the Earth.*

There's a large area on the opposite side of the Earth to the earthquake where no S-waves are detected. This indicates that, whatever the 'core' is made of, the S-waves cannot pass through it. So the core must be (at least partially) made from a liquid material, as S-waves cannot pass through liquids. This would also help explain the motion of P-waves — they travel slower in liquids, which is why their paths change abruptly at the boundary.

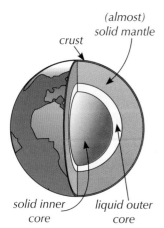

(almost) solid mantle

crust

solid inner core   liquid outer core

Figure 6: *The internal structure of the Earth.*

Different observations such as the one described above have led seismologists to develop a model (page 3) of the internal structure of the Earth — see Figure 6.

Practice Questions — Fact Recall

Q1 Explain what is meant by infrasound.

Q2 Describe one way that infrasound waves have helped scientists to learn about the Earth's core.

Q3 State two types of seismic waves.

Practice Question — Application

Q1 A seismometer is placed at the bottom of a lake to detect S-waves and P-waves created by earthquakes. Suggest why the seismometer cannot be placed at the surface of the lake.

Section 3a Checklist — Make sure you know...

Wave Basics

☐ That waves transfer energy and information (but not matter) by causing oscillations in the substance (or fields) they are travelling through.

☐ That the vibrations in transverse waves are perpendicular to the direction of travel of the wave.

☐ That electromagnetic waves, water waves and seismic S-waves are all examples of transverse waves.

☐ That the vibrations in longitudinal waves are parallel to the direction of travel of the wave.

☐ That sound waves and seismic P-waves are examples of longitudinal waves.

☐ Examples that show that waves don't transfer matter. E.g. water ripples don't cause floating objects to move across the water's surface, and sound waves don't create a vacuum around a speaker.

Features of Waves

☐ The meaning of the word 'wavefront' and how to use wavefront diagrams to represent waves.

☐ The meanings of the words 'amplitude', 'wavelength', 'frequency' and 'period'.

Wave Speed

☐ That wave speed is the speed at which energy or information is transferred by the wave (or the speed the wave is moving at) and that wave velocity is just the wave speed in a certain direction.

☐ The equation $v = x \div t$, and how to use it.

☐ The wave equation $v = f \times \lambda$, and how to use it.

cont...

Measuring Waves

☐ How to measure the speed of sound in air by determining the frequency and wavelength of the wave.

☐ How suitable equipment is used to find the speed, frequency and wavelength of water ripples and a wave in a solid.

Wave Behaviour at Boundaries

☐ That waves can be reflected, transmitted or absorbed when they meet a material interface, and what each of these terms mean.

☐ H That what happens when a wave meets a particular material interface depends on the wavelength of the wave.

Refraction

☐ What the term 'refraction' means.

☐ How to draw ray diagrams to show the refraction of waves as they move between different materials.

☐ How to investigate refraction using a glass block.

☐ H That waves travel at different speeds in different substances, and this can cause refraction.

Sound Waves

☐ That when a sound wave moves from one medium to another, its frequency stays the same but its wavelength and speed change.

☐ H How the conversion between sound waves and vibrations in a solid happens.

☐ H That vibrations in a solid will only be produced by sound waves within a certain frequency range. This frequency range depends on a solid object's size, shape and what it's made of.

☐ H How sound waves causing your ear drum to vibrate leads to hearing.

Ultrasound

☐ H That ultrasound waves have frequencies greater than 20 000 Hz.

☐ H How ultrasound is used, including in foetal scanning and in sonar.

☐ H How to calculate the distance to a boundary from the time taken for a wave of known speed to be reflected back from the boundary, e.g. to find the distance to the sea bed using active sonar.

Infrasound

☐ H That infrasound waves have frequencies of less than 20 Hz.

☐ H Some uses of infrasound, including how observations of seismic S-waves and P-waves can be used to explore the structure of the Earth's core.

1   **Figure 1** below shows a transverse wave on a rope.

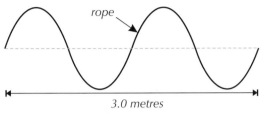

Figure 1

(a)   What is the wavelength of the wave on the rope?

     A   6.0 m   **B**   3.0 m   **C**   1.5 m   **D**   0.75 m

(1 mark)

(b)   The number of complete waves passing a point on the rope each second is the

     A   period   **B**   frequency   **C**   amplitude   **D**   wavelength

(1 mark)

The frequency of the wave is 2 Hz.

(c)   Calculate the period of the wave. Give your answer in seconds.

(2 marks)

(d)   State the equation linking wave speed, wavelength and frequency.

(1 mark)

(e)   Calculate the speed of the waves. Give your answer in m/s.

(2 marks)

(f)   A wave on a rope is a transverse wave. Waves can be transverse or longitudinal. Give **one** similarity between transverse and longitudinal waves.

(1 mark)

(g)   List A in **Figure 2** shown below, gives the names of three different waves. List B gives two possible wave types.

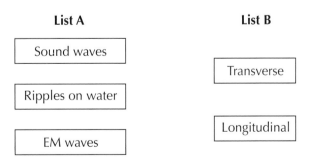

Figure 2

Draw lines to match each wave in List A to the correct wave type(s) in List B.

(2 marks)

2   A student is investigating the speed of waves produced in a brass rod
when the brass rod is struck with a hammer. The rod is 80 mm long.

(a)   Equipment is used to measure the frequency of the loudest sound wave produced. This
sound wave is produced by the peak frequency wave in the rod.
What is the wavelength of the peak frequency wave?
Give your answer in metres.

(2 marks)

(b)   The experiment is repeated three times and the peak sound wave frequency
measurements recorded are: 1.3 kHz, 1.8 kHz, 2.0 kHz.
Use these results to calculate the average speed of the waves produced in the rod.
Give your answer to 2 significant figures.

(4 marks)

3   An ultrasonic scanner is a device that emits and detects ultrasound waves. It can be
used to monitor pregnancies.

(a)   Which of the following describes ultrasound?

A   Sound with frequencies greater than 20 000 Hz.

B   Sound with frequencies greater than 20 000 kHz.

C   Sound with frequencies less than 20 000 Hz.

D   Sound with frequencies less than 20 000 kHz.

(1 mark)

A pregnant patient has an ultrasound scan to produce an image of the foetus. A pulse
of ultrasound is transmitted into her abdomen. A reflected pulse is detected by the
scanner 20 μs later.

(b)   Calculate the distance between the scanner and the boundary from which the pulse is
reflected. You can assume that ultrasound travels at 1500 m/s in the abdomen.
Give your answer in metres.

(3 marks)

4   **Figure 3** shows the Earth. An earthquake occurs at point A.
It produces P-waves and S-waves, which travel through the Earth.

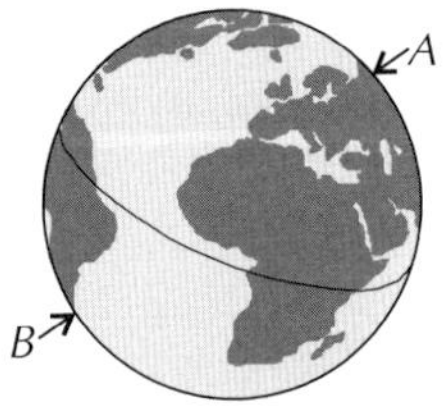

(a)   Some P-waves are classed as infrasound waves.
Explain what infrasound waves are.

(1 mark)

(b)   At point B, P-waves are detected but no S-waves are detected.
Explain what this suggests about the structure of the Earth.

(3 marks)

Figure 3

5   A sound wave with a wavelength of 3.3 m travels through a concrete block at 3300 m/s.
The vibrations then pass into a steel beam, and the wave speed changes to 6000 m/s.
Calculate the wavelength of the sound wave in the steel beam.

(4 marks)

1. Reflection and TIR

Learning Objectives:
- Be able to explain, with the aid of ray diagrams, reflection, including the law of reflection.
- Be able to explain the difference between specular and diffuse reflection.
- Be able to explain, with the aid of ray diagrams, total internal reflection (TIR), including the critical angle.

Specification References 5.1 and 5.2

You met ray diagrams on page 99 when talking about refraction. Turns out, they're pretty handy and you can use them to show reflection too...

Ray diagrams of reflections

A wave can be reflected when it meets a boundary between two different materials. To draw a ray diagram showing reflection, you need to draw the incident ray, the normal and the reflected ray like in Figure 1.

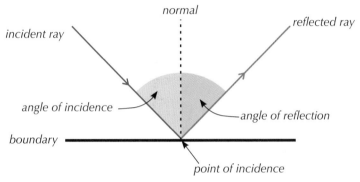

Figure 1: A ray diagram to show the reflection of a wave at a surface.

Tip: The steps for drawing ray diagrams are covered on page 99.

Remember, the angle between the ray and the normal is the angle of incidence. The **angle of reflection** is the angle between the reflected ray and the normal. The **law of reflection**, which applies to every reflected wave, is:

angle of incidence = angle of reflection

Tip: This rule is true for <u>all</u> reflected waves, not just light waves.

So, a reflected wave always bounces off a boundary at the same angle to the normal as it hit the boundary (but on the other side of the normal).

Types of reflection

Waves are reflected at different boundaries in different ways.

Specular reflection happens when parallel waves are reflected in a single direction by a smooth surface. E.g. when light is reflected by a mirror you get a nice clear reflection.

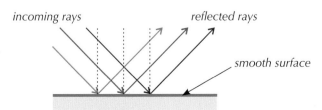

Figure 3: A ray diagram showing specular reflection.

Figure 2: A beam of light being specularly reflected by a mirror.

Diffuse reflection is when parallel waves are reflected by a rough surface (e.g. a piece of paper) and the reflected rays are scattered in lots of different directions.

Figure 4: A beam of light being diffusely reflected by a piece of paper.

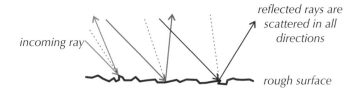

Figure 5: A ray diagram showing diffuse reflection.

The angle of incidence is still equal to the angle of reflection for each ray. However, the tiny bumps on the surface mean that the normal for each ray is different. Therefore, the angle of incidence is different for each ray.

When light is reflected by a rough surface, the surface appears matt (not shiny) and you don't get a clear reflection of objects.

Total internal reflection (TIR)

Tip: Ⓗ Remember, optical density is how much light is slowed down by a material (page 101).

Tip: Optical fibres (page 132) use total internal reflection to bounce waves back and forth along the fibre. This allows them to transfer information across long distances.

You saw on page 99 that when a wave travels into a new material, it can be refracted. When a wave is travelling into a less dense material, the ray can be refracted so much that **total internal reflection** occurs. This is where the ray is reflected back into the first material instead of being transmitted into the new material.

This happens when the angle of incidence is larger than the **critical angle** of the material (see Figure 9). Every material has its own, different critical angle.

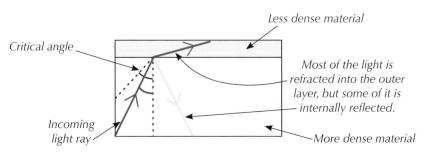

Figure 6: A diagram showing a ray travelling into a less dense material at an angle less than the critical angle, and being mostly refracted.

Figure 7: An endoscope is a medical device that uses total internal reflection to see inside a patient's body without the patient having to undergo major surgery.

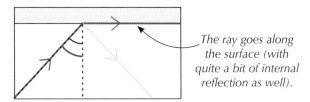

Figure 8: A diagram showing a ray travelling into a less dense material at the critical angle of the material.

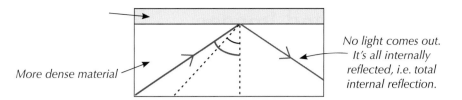

More dense material

No light comes out. It's all internally reflected, i.e. total internal reflection.

Tip: The internally reflected ray follows the law of reflection (p.115).

Figure 9: *A diagram showing a ray travelling into a less dense material at an angle larger than the critical angle of the material. Total internal reflection occurs.*

Practice Questions — Fact Recall

Q1 Sketch a diagram showing a reflected ray. Label the normal, the angle of incidence and the angle of reflection.

Q2 Explain the difference between specular and diffuse reflection.

Q3 What is total internal reflection?

Practice Questions — Application

Q1 Construct a ray diagram to show the reflection of a ray with an angle of incidence of 40°.

Q2 A beam of light is shone onto a piece of polystyrene. A second identical beam of light is shone onto a sheet of aluminium foil. In both cases, the angle of incidence is 30°. Describe the difference in the way that light rays are reflected from each surface.

Q3 Glass has a critical angle of 42°. Sketch the path of a light ray travelling from glass to air when:

a) The angle of incidence is 30°.

b) The angle of incidence is 45°.

Learning Objectives:

- Be able to explain the effects of different types of lens in producing real and virtual images.
- Be able to relate the power of a lens to its focal length and shape.

Specification References 5.4 and 5.6

Tip: When a ray enters any lens, it bends towards the normal. When it leaves, it bends away from the normal (page 100).

Tip: You might see converging lenses called convex lenses.

2. Lenses and Images

Lenses use refraction to bend light rays to form an image. They're used in things like glasses, magnifying glasses and cameras. This topic is all about the different types of lenses and the images they produce.

Lenses

Lenses form images by refracting light and changing its direction. There are two main types of lens — converging and diverging. They have different shapes and have opposite effects on light rays.

The **axis** of a lens is a line passing through the middle of the lens, perpendicular to the lens. There is a principal focus on each side of a lens (Figures 3 and 6). The distance from the centre of a lens to its principal focus is called the **focal length** of the lens.

Converging lenses

A **converging lens** is a lens which bulges outwards. It causes rays of light which are parallel to the axis of the lens (see Figure 1) to converge (come together) at a point on the other side of the lens. The **principal focus of a converging lens** is the point where rays hitting the lens parallel to the axis all meet.

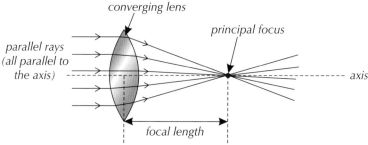

Figure 1: *A converging lens focusing parallel rays at the principal focus.*

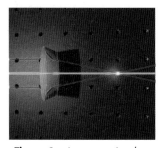

Figure 2: *A converging lens focusing laser beams at the principal focus (yellow). The light is coming from the left.*

Tip: In reality, the line passing through the centre of the lens will refract slightly as it enters and leaves the lens, but the deflection is so small that it can be ignored and just drawn as a straight line.

Three important rules for converging lenses

1. An incident ray travelling parallel to the axis refracts through the lens and passes through the principal focus on the other side.

2. An incident ray passing through the centre of the lens carries on in the same direction.

3. An incident ray passing through the principal focus before meeting the lens refracts through the lens and travels parallel to the axis.

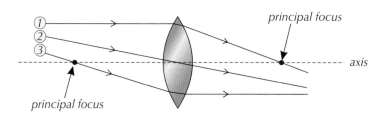

Figure 3: *Three rays passing through a converging lens.*

Diverging lenses

A **diverging lens** is a lens which caves inwards. It causes parallel rays of light to diverge (spread out). The **principal focus of a diverging lens** is the point where rays hitting the lens parallel to the axis appear to all come from — you can trace them back until they all appear to meet up at a point behind the lens (see Figure 4).

Tip: You might see diverging lenses called concave lenses.

Tip: Virtual rays are rays that aren't actually there. They show the path that it <u>looks like</u> the light has taken.

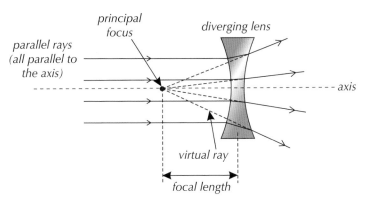

Figure 4: A diverging lens diverging parallel rays so that they appear to have come from the principal focus.

Tip: Diagrams that show the paths of rays are called ray diagrams. You'll learn how to draw them for lenses on pages 122-125.

Three important rules for diverging lenses

1. An incident ray travelling parallel to the axis refracts through the lens and travels in line with the near-side principal focus (so it appears to have come from the principal focus).

2. An incident ray passing through the centre of the lens carries on in the same direction.

3. An incident ray passing through the lens towards the far-side principal focus refracts through the lens and travels parallel to the axis.

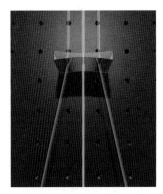

Figure 5: A diverging lens refracting beams of laser light. The light is coming from above.

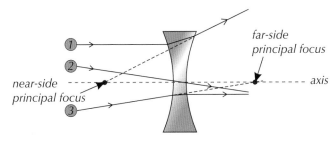

Figure 6: Three rays passing through a diverging lens.

Images

Different lenses can produce different kinds of image. There are two types of image — **real images** and **virtual images**. It's all to do with whether two light rays coming from the same point on an object will eventually meet.

Tip: Diverging lenses <u>always</u> produce virtual images. Converging lenses can produce both types of image — see pages 124-126.

Real images

A real image is formed when the light rays from a point on an object come together to form an image. The light rays actually pass through the same point. A real image can be captured on a 'screen' — like the image formed on an eye's retina (the 'screen' at the back of an eye) or the image formed on a projector screen.

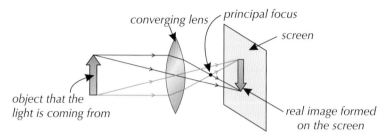

Figure 7: *A real image, formed by a converging lens, being projected onto a screen.*

Virtual images

A virtual image is formed when the light rays don't actually come together to form an image. The image is created where the light rays from a point on an object appear to come together, but the light rays don't actually pass through that point. This means that you can't project a virtual image on a screen. Virtual images occur when the light rays from a point diverge after they have left the lens. This is why diverging lenses always produce virtual images.

You can get a virtual image when looking at an object through a magnifying lens. The virtual image looks bigger than the object actually is (see Figure 8).

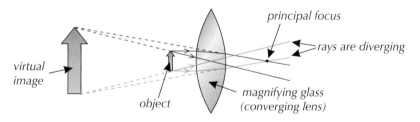

Figure 8: *A virtual image formed by looking through a magnifying glass (a converging lens).*

Describing an image

To describe an image properly, you need to say three things:

- How big it is compared to the object.
- Whether it's upright or inverted (upside down) relative to the object.
- Whether it's real or virtual.

> **Example**
>
> In Figure 8, the image is larger than the object, the right way up and virtual.

Lens power

The more powerful a lens is, the better it is at refracting light. So the more powerful a lens is, the shorter its focal length. The curvature of a lens affects its power — the more curved a lens is, the more powerful it is (see Figure 10).

Figure 9: *The prescriptions for glasses state the power each lens should be.*

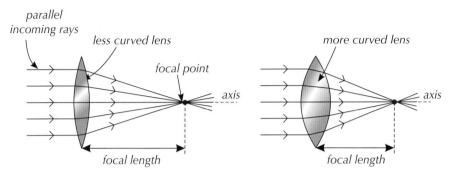

Figure 10: *The refraction of light rays by two lenses of different curvatures.*

So to increase the power of a lens made from a certain material, you have to make it with more strongly curved surfaces.

Tip: Some materials are better at refracting light than others, which means that the power of a lens can also depend on what material it's made from.

Practice Questions — Fact Recall

Q1 What is meant by the focal length of a lens?

Q2 What sort of lens spreads out rays of light?

Q3 Sketch a converging lens and a diverging lens.

Q4 Define the principal focus of a converging lens and of a diverging lens.

Q5 Name the two types of images produced by lenses.

Q6 What three things do you need to say to describe an image formed by a lens?

Q7 How is the power of a lens related to its focal length?

Q8 Give one way to increase the power of a lens made from a given material.

Practice Question — Application

Q1 The eye contains a lens like the one shown in the diagram.

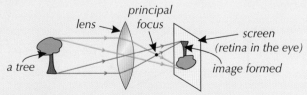

a) What kind of lens does the eye contain?

b) Describe the image formed in the diagram.

- Be able to use ray diagrams to show the similarities and differences in the refraction of light by converging and diverging lenses.
- Be able to explain the effects of different types of lens in producing real and virtual images.

Specification References 5.5 and 5.6

3. Ray Diagrams for Lenses

You're not done with lenses yet. You need to be able to know how to draw ray diagrams for lenses. These are pretty useful — you can use them to work out what sort of image is formed, its size, its position and its orientation.

Lenses in ray diagrams

Converging lenses are drawn like this in a ray diagram:

And diverging lenses are drawn like this:

Ray diagrams for converging lenses

Drawing ray diagrams is pretty straightforward — just follow these four steps:

1. Draw a ray through the lens centre

Draw a ray from the top of the object that passes straight through the centre of the lens without changing direction at all (see Figure 1).

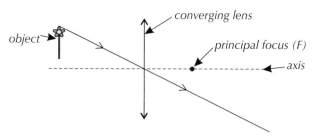

Figure 1: *A diagram showing step 1 of the method for drawing a ray diagram for a converging lens.*

2. Draw a ray parallel to the axis

Draw a second ray from the top of the object that travels parallel to the axis. The ray should refract at the lens so that it passes through the principal focus of the lens. There are two things that can happen when you do this.

One possibility is that the two rays will meet on the far side of the lens — see Figure 2. If this happens, you're done with this step.

Tip: With this type of diagram you draw each ray only changing direction once as it passes through the lens. But the rays actually change direction twice, once on entering and once on leaving the lens.

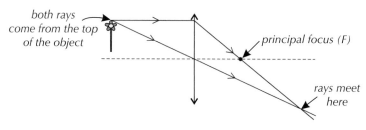

Figure 2: *A diagram of step 2 of the method for drawing a ray diagram for a converging lens, showing the refracted rays meeting.*

The other possibility is that the rays don't meet (see Figure 3). In this case, you'll need to extend the refracted rays back on the near-side of the lens as virtual rays (dotted lines). They will eventually meet.

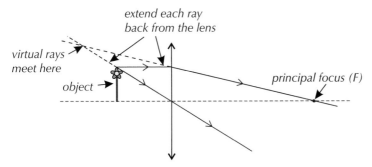

Figure 3: A diagram of step 2 of the method for drawing a ray diagram for a converging lens showing what to do if the refracted rays don't meet.

Tip: You should always draw arrows on real rays but not on virtual rays.

3. Repeat the process

Repeat steps 1 and 2 for the bottom of the object. If the rays met in step 2 the first time round, they'll meet this time too. If they didn't meet before, they won't this time either and you'll need to extend them back again.

Exam Tip
It's sometimes possible to draw a third incident ray passing through the principal focus on the way to the lens (it will refract so that it goes parallel to the axis — see rule 3 on p.118). In the exam, you can get away with two rays though, unless they ask for three.

4. Draw the image

Draw in the image. The point where the two rays from the top of the object meet is where the top (in this case, the petals) of the image is formed. The point where the two rays from the bottom of the object meet is where the bottom (in this case, the stalk) of the image is formed.

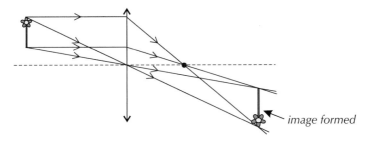

Figure 4: A diagram of steps 3 and 4 of the method for drawing a ray diagram for a converging lens.

Tip: Figure 4 only shows what to do when the rays meet. If the rays don't meet, you draw the image where the virtual rays meet.

When the bottom of the object is on the axis, the bottom of the image is also on the axis. In this case you only need to draw the top set of rays — see Figure 5.

Tip: The rules that describe how rays travel through converging lenses are on page 118.

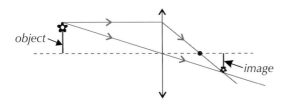

Figure 5: A ray diagram showing the image formed by a converging lens of an object that is 'sitting' on the axis of the lens.

Images formed by converging lenses

The type of image formed by a converging lens depends on where the object is placed in relation to the principal focus (F). Make sure you learn these four situations:

Tip: 2F just means twice the focal length away from the lens.

Beyond 2F

An object beyond 2F will produce a real, inverted (upside down) image that is smaller than the object. It will sit between F and 2F on the far side of the lens (see Figure 6).

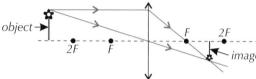

Figure 6: A real, inverted and smaller image is formed by a converging lens when an object is placed beyond 2F.

At 2F

An object placed at 2F will produce a real, inverted (upside down) image that is the same size as the object. It will sit at 2F on the far side of the lens (see Figure 8).

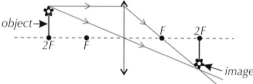

Figure 8: A real, inverted image of the same size as the object is formed by a converging lens when an object is placed at 2F.

Figure 7: A converging lens forming a real and inverted, but smaller, image of the woman.

Between F and 2F

An object placed between F and 2F will form a real, inverted image that's bigger than the object. It will sit beyond 2F on the far side of the lens (see Figure 9).

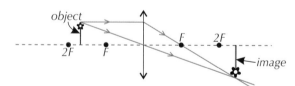

Figure 9: A real, inverted and larger image is formed by a converging lens when an object is placed between F and 2F.

Between the lens and F

An object placed closer to the lens than F will make a virtual image that is the right way up, but bigger than the object and on the same side of the lens as the object (see Figure 11).

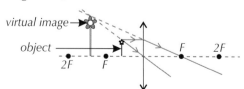

Figure 11: A virtual, upright and larger image is formed by a converging lens when an object is placed closer to the lens than F.

Figure 10: A converging lens forming a virtual, upright and larger image of the eye.

Ray diagrams for diverging lenses

Drawing ray diagrams for diverging lenses is similar to drawing them for converging ones — it's just step 2 that works slightly differently.

1. Draw a ray through the lens centre

Draw a ray from the top of the object that passes straight through the centre of the lens without changing direction at all (see Figure 12).

Tip: The rules that describe how rays travel through diverging lenses are on page 119.

2. Draw a ray parallel to the axis

Draw a second ray from the top of the object that travels parallel to the axis. The ray should refract at the lens so that it appears to have come from the near-side principal focus. Draw a virtual ray (dotted line) from that principal focus to where that ray meets the lens (see Figure 12).

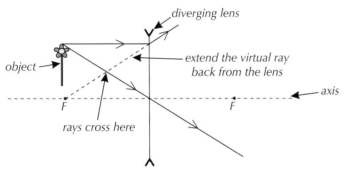

Figure 12: A diagram of steps 1 and 2 of the method for drawing a ray diagram for a diverging lens.

Tip: You can draw a third incident ray in the direction of the principal focus on the far side of the lens if you want to. Just remember that it refracts to travel parallel to the axis.

3. Repeat the process

Repeat steps 1 and 2 for the bottom of the object. If the bottom of the object is on the axis, the bottom of the image will be too (see page 123).

4. Draw the image

Draw in the image. Where the real and the virtual rays from the top of the object meet is where the top of the image is formed. Where the real and virtual rays from the bottom of the object meet is where the bottom of the image is formed.

Exam Tip
In the exam, you can get away with two rays from each point on the object. Just choose whichever two are easiest to draw — don't try to draw a ray that won't actually pass through the lens.

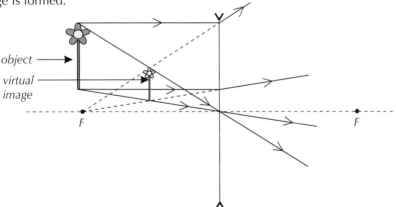

Figure 13: A diagram of steps 3 and 4 of the method for drawing a ray diagram for a diverging lens.

Tip: It is sometimes difficult to work out where the image should be drawn. The top and bottom of the image should be where two rays from <u>the same point</u> on the object cross.

Images formed by a diverging lens

Remember, a diverging lens always produces a virtual image. The image is the right way up, smaller than the object, and on the same side of the lens as the object — no matter where the object is.

Comparing lenses using ray diagrams

You can use ray diagrams to show the similarities and differences between how different lenses refract light and form images. Remember:

- Converging lenses converge light whereas diverging lenses diverge light.
- Rays parallel to the axis converge onto the far-side principle focus of a converging lens.
- Rays parallel to the axis diverge so that they appear to have come from the near-side principal focus of a diverging lens.
- Converging lenses can product real or virtual images, whilst diverging lenses only produce virtual images.

Tip: Remember, a ray that goes straight through the centre of a lens doesn't change direction — this is true for both converging and diverging lenses.

Practice Questions — Fact Recall

Q1 The principal focus of a converging lens is F. Describe the image produced by a converging lens if the object is placed:

a) beyond 2F, b) at 2F, c) between F and 2F, d) closer than F.

Q2 The principal focus of a diverging lens is F. Describe the image produced by the lens if the object is placed at 2F.

Practice Questions — Application

Q1 The principal focus of the lens in this diagram is F. A pencil is placed in front of the lens between F and 2F, as shown.

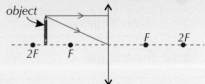

a) Complete the ray diagram to show the image being formed.

b) Describe the image produced by the lens.

c) What sort of lens is shown in the diagram?

Q2 A straight arrow is placed pointing upwards, perpendicular to the axis of a converging lens with a focal length of 3 cm, so that the bottom end of the arrow is touching the axis. The object is 1 cm from the lens.

a) Sketch a ray diagram to show the image being formed.

The converging lens is then replaced with a diverging lens, with a focal length of 3 cm. The straight arrow is kept at a distance of 1 cm from the lens.

b) Describe the difference between how converging and diverging lenses refract light.

c) Draw a ray diagram showing the image formed by the diverging lens.

d) Describe the image formed by the diverging lens.

Tip: Remember focal length is the distance between the centre of the lens and the principal focus.

4. The Electromagnetic Spectrum

Electromagnetic (EM) waves are a group of waves that are made from vibrating fields. All the different wavelengths of EM waves form a spectrum.

What is the electromagnetic spectrum?

Electromagnetic waves are a group of transverse waves (see page 88). They are sometimes called electromagnetic radiation. They consist of vibrating electric and magnetic fields, which is why they can travel through a vacuum — they don't rely on vibrating matter. When travelling through a vacuum, all EM waves travel at the same speed — about 3×10^8 m/s.

EM waves form a spectrum of waves with different wavelengths, from around 10^{-15} m to more than 10^4 m. The spectrum is continuous — meaning there's no gaps in it.

> The **electromagnetic (EM) spectrum** is a continuous spectrum of all the possible wavelengths of electromagnetic waves.

As electromagnetic waves with longer wavelengths have lower frequencies, you can also say that it's a spectrum of all the possible frequencies of electromagnetic waves.

EM waves are grouped into seven basic types according to their wavelength (or frequency), but remember the spectrum is continuous — so the different regions actually merge into each other, see Figure 1.

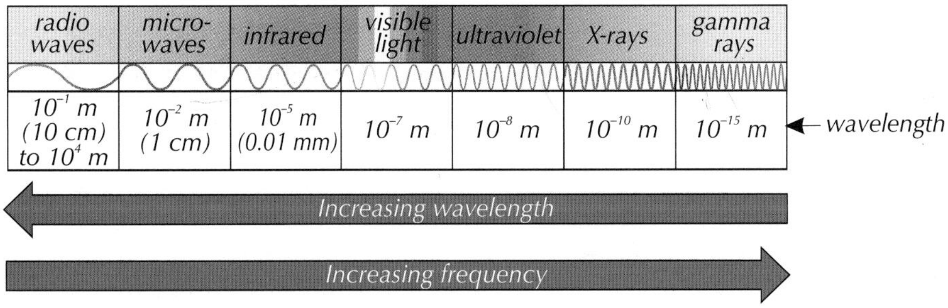

radio waves	micro- waves	infrared	visible light	ultraviolet	X-rays	gamma rays
10^{-1} m (10 cm) to 10^4 m	10^{-2} m (1 cm)	10^{-5} m (0.01 mm)	10^{-7} m	10^{-8} m	10^{-10} m	10^{-15} m

← wavelength

Increasing wavelength →

Increasing frequency →

Figure 1: *The electromagnetic spectrum, with decreasing wavelength and increasing frequency from left to right.*

Our eyes can only detect electromagnetic waves in the visible light part of the spectrum. Different colours of visible light have different wavelengths — from longest to shortest, they are: red, orange, yellow, green, blue, indigo, violet.

Practice Questions — Fact Recall

Q1   Are electromagnetic waves transverse or longitudinal?

Q2   What is the electromagnetic spectrum?

Q3   Write down the seven main types of electromagnetic radiation in order of increasing wavelength.

Q4   Which type of electromagnetic wave has the highest frequency?

Learning Objectives:
- Be able to recall that all electromagnetic waves are transverse.
- Be able to recall that all electromagnetic waves travel at the same speed in a vacuum.
- Be able to describe the electromagnetic spectrum as continuous from radio waves to gamma rays and that the radiations within it can be grouped in order of decreasing wavelength and increasing frequency.
- Be able to recall the main groupings of the continuous electromagnetic spectrum including (in order) radio waves, microwaves, infrared, visible (including the colours of the visible spectrum), ultraviolet, X-rays and gamma rays.
- Be able to recall that our eyes can only detect a limited range of frequencies of electromagnetic radiation.

Specification References 5.7, 5.10-5.12

Exam Tip
You need to know the order of the EM spectrum in terms of wavelength and frequency, but you don't need to know the actual wavelengths.

- Be able to recall that changes in atoms and nuclei can generate radiations over a wide frequency range and be caused by absorption of a range of radiations.

- Be able to explain, with examples, that all electromagnetic waves transfer energy from source to observer.

- **H** Be able to recall that different substances may absorb, transmit, refract or reflect electromagnetic waves in ways that vary with wavelength.

- **H** Be able to explain the effects of differences in the velocities of electromagnetic waves in different substances.

Specification References
5.8, 5.13, 5.14, 5.24

5. Properties of EM Waves

EM waves have different properties and are generated in different ways.

Generation of electromagnetic waves

Electromagnetic waves can be produced by changes inside atoms. These could be changes to the arrangement of electrons or changes within the nucleus.

Electron changes

If an atom absorbs energy, some of its electrons move to higher **energy levels** within the atom (see page 153 for more on this). When each electron falls back down to a lower level, an electromagnetic wave is produced.

The electron absorbs energy and is excited to a higher energy level.   *The electron falls back down and the excess energy is released as an electromagnetic wave.*

Figure 1: *Electromagnetic waves are produced when excited electrons fall back down.*

Different atoms have different energy levels, so there are lots of possible changes that can happen within atoms and molecules. This is why electromagnetic waves produced in this way have such a large range of frequencies. The higher the frequency of an electromagnetic wave, the more energy it transfers. So an atomic change that releases a lot of energy will produce a high-frequency electromagnetic wave.

The huge number of possible changes within atoms also allows a wide range of frequencies of electromagnetic radiation to be absorbed by electrons.

Nuclear changes

Gamma rays are high-energy electromagnetic waves which come from changes in the nuclei of atoms. Gamma rays are emitted when the nucleus needs to get rid of some extra energy (usually after it has emitted a particle, p.156-157). It does this by releasing a gamma ray.

Electromagnetic waves and energy

All electromagnetic waves transfer energy from a source to an absorber.

Example 1

A hot object (the source) transfers energy by emitting infrared radiation, which is absorbed by the surroundings.

Example 2   Higher

Oscillating electrons (the source) in a radio transmitter produce radio waves. These transfer energy to a receiver where it causes the electrons in the receiver to oscillate — see page 130.

Figure 2: *Neon signs work by passing electricity through neon gas. This excites electrons in the neon atoms. When the electrons fall back down, waves from the visible light part of the EM spectrum are produced.*

Electromagnetic waves and matter Higher

When any wave meets a boundary between two different materials, it can be reflected, absorbed or transmitted (see page 98). Electromagnetic waves of different wavelengths may be reflected, absorbed or transmitted differently when they meet a boundary. This is one of the reasons why different types of electromagnetic waves have different uses (see pages 130-135).

Also, EM waves with different wavelengths are refracted (see page 99) by different amounts. This is because different wavelengths of EM radiation travel at different velocities in different materials. This leads to dispersion (the separating out of different wavelengths) — see below for an example of this.

> **Tip:** See pages 137-139 for how differences in behaviour when light waves meet a boundary determine the colour or transparency of an object.

Example — **Higher**

White light is made up of all the wavelengths of electromagnetic radiation in the visible part of the spectrum. Each narrow band of wavelengths corresponds to a different colour, from red to violet. The different wavelengths all bend (refract) by different amounts when they enter and leave a prism, so the colours are separated out.

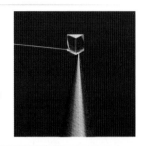

Practice Questions — Fact Recall

Q1 Describe two types of atomic change that produce electromagnetic waves.

Q2 Give an example of a situation in which electromagnetic waves transfer energy from a source to an absorber.

Q3 What can happen to an electromagnetic wave when it meets the boundary between two substances? Will the exact same thing always happen to any type of electromagnetic wave when it meets the same boundary?

Q4 Name one effect caused by electromagnetic radiation travelling at different speeds in different materials.

- **H** Be able to recall that radio waves can be produced by, or can themselves induce, oscillations in electrical circuits.

- Be able to describe some uses of electromagnetic radiation, including:
  a radio waves in broadcasting, communications and satellite transmissions;
  b microwaves in communications and satellite transmissions;
  c infrared in short range communications, optical fibres and television remote controls.

Specification References
5.22, 5.23

Tip: Oscillating means moving back and forth, i.e. vibrating.

Tip: See p.246 for more on alternating current.

6. EM Radiation for Communication

Different wavelengths of EM radiation have different properties, which means they have many different uses. Radio waves, microwaves and infrared waves can all be used for communication.

How are radio waves produced?

You can produce radio waves using an alternating current (a.c.) in an electrical circuit. Alternating currents are made up of oscillating charges (electrons). As the charges oscillate, they produce oscillating electric and magnetic fields, i.e. electromagnetic waves, which is what radio waves are (see page 127). The frequency of the radio waves produced will be equal to the frequency of the alternating current. The object in which charges oscillate to create the radio waves is called a transmitter.

How are radio waves received? Higher

When transmitted radio waves reach a receiver, the radio waves are absorbed. The energy carried by the waves is transferred to the kinetic energy stores of the electrons in the material of the receiver. This causes the electrons to oscillate and, if the receiver is part of a complete electrical circuit, it generates an alternating current. This current has the same frequency as the radio wave that generated it.

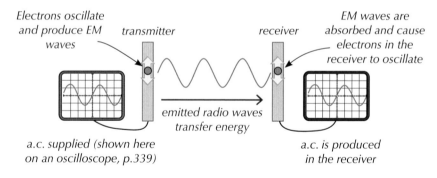

Figure 1: A diagram showing how radio waves are produced, transmitted and received.

Using radio waves for communication

Radio waves are used mainly for radio and TV signals (broadcasting). They are sent out by transmitters and received by TV or radio aerials (receivers). Different wavelengths of radio wave are used in different ways.

Tip: There are more uses of EM radiation on pages 133-135.

Long-wave radio

Long-wave radio can be transmitted and received halfway round the world because long wavelengths diffract (bend) around the curved surface of the Earth (see Figure 3 on the next page). Long-wave radio wavelengths can also diffract around hills, into tunnels and all sorts. This diffraction effect makes it possible for radio signals to be received even if the receiver isn't in the line of sight of the transmitter.

Short-wave radio

Short-wave radio signals don't diffract around the Earth's curve, but they can still be received at large distances from the transmitter. They are reflected between the Earth and the atmosphere (see Figure 3).

Bluetooth® uses short-wave radio waves to send data over short distances between devices without wires (e.g. wireless headsets so you can use your phone while driving a car).

TV signals and FM radio

The radio waves used for TV and FM radio transmissions have very short wavelengths. To get reception, you must be in direct sight of the transmitter — the signal doesn't bend around hills or travel far through buildings.

Figure 2: A television aerial raised high above a house to increase the signal quality. The aerial needs to be in direct sight of the transmitter as the radio waves used for TV signals do not diffract around large obstacles.

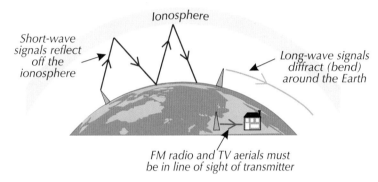

Ionosphere

Short-wave signals reflect off the ionosphere

Long-wave signals diffract (bend) around the Earth

FM radio and TV aerials must be in line of sight of transmitter

Figure 3: A diagram showing how different wavelength radio waves travel.

Tip: The type of TV that's transmitted by radio waves is known as terrestrial TV. It's different from satellite TV, which uses microwaves relayed by satellites in space and cable TV, where the signal travels through wires.

Satellite communication

Communication to and from satellites usually uses microwaves but can sometimes be relatively high frequency radio waves. This is because these waves can pass easily through the Earth's atmosphere without really being reflected, refracted, diffracted or absorbed, which means they can reach satellites. Satellite communications have a range of applications, e.g. satellite TV, satellite phones and internet, and military communications.

For all types of satellite communications, the signal from a transmitter is transmitted into space, where it's picked up by the satellite's receiver orbiting high above the Earth. The satellite transmits the signal back to Earth in a different direction, where it's received by a satellite receiver on the ground. There is a slight time delay between the signal being sent and received because of the long distance the signal has to travel.

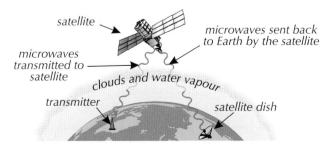

satellite

microwaves sent back to Earth by the satellite

microwaves transmitted to satellite

clouds and water vapour

transmitter

satellite dish

Figure 5: A diagram showing how microwaves are used for satellite communication.

Figure 4: The TV satellite dishes on this roof point in a specific direction in order to receive the signal from a space satellite.

Using infrared radiation for communications

Infrared radiation can also be used for communications. For example, it can be used to send files between mobile phones or laptops. The distances must be fairly small and the receiver must be in the line of sight of the emitter. This is also how TV remote controls work. In fact, some mobile phones now have built in software which means that you can use your phone as a TV remote.

Optical fibres are thin glass or plastic fibres that can carry data (e.g. from telephones or computers) over long distances. Pulses of infrared radiation can be used, because when the radiation hits the walls of the fibres, it's reflected back into the fibre. They usually use a single wavelength of infrared radiation to prevent dispersion (page 129), which can otherwise cause some information to be lost.

Figure 6: *A fibre optic cable which contains a bundle of optical fibres.*

Tip: Optical fibres work by total internal reflection (p.116). The infrared signal is refracted so much that it is bent back into the fibre, instead of being transmitted out of the fibre.

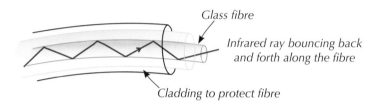

Glass fibre

Infrared ray bouncing back and forth along the fibre

Cladding to protect fibre

Figure 7: *An optical fibre transmitting a pulse of infrared radiation.*

Practice Questions — Fact Recall

Q1 Describe how radio waves can be produced and detected using electrical circuits.

Q2 What types of electromagnetic radiation can be used in satellite communications?

Q3 Give two uses of infrared radiation.

7. More Uses of EM Radiation

And you're not done yet I'm afraid. Electromagnetic radiation is also used for cooking, security, imaging and sterilisation... And you get to learn all about it...

Cooking using microwaves

The wavelengths of microwaves used in satellite communications pass through the Earth's watery atmosphere (page 131). However, the microwaves used in microwave ovens have wavelengths which allow them to be absorbed by water molecules in food.

These microwaves penetrate up to a few centimetres into the food before being absorbed and transferring the energy they are carrying to the thermal energy stores of the water molecules in the food, causing the water to heat up. The water molecules then transfer this energy to the rest of the molecules in the food, which quickly cooks it.

Infrared radiation

Going along the EM spectrum in order of decreasing wavelength, infrared (IR) radiation comes next. Its uses are related to temperature.

Thermal imaging

Infrared (IR) radiation is given out by all objects — and the hotter the object, the more IR radiation it gives out in a given time. Infrared cameras can be used to detect infrared radiation and monitor temperature. The camera detects the IR radiation and turns it into an electrical signal, which is displayed on a screen as a picture. This process is sometimes called thermal imaging.

> **Example**
>
> The heat loss through different parts of a house can be detected using an infrared camera.
>
> Colour coding is used to show different amounts of infrared.

hot

cold

Security systems

Infrared cameras can also be used in security systems. If infrared radiation is detected (e.g. from an intruder), an alarm sounds or a security light turns on.

Cooking

Absorbing IR radiation causes objects to get hotter. This means that food can be cooked using IR radiation — the temperature of the food increases when it absorbs IR radiation, e.g. from a toaster's heating element, see Figure 1.

Learning Objective:

- Be able to describe some uses of electromagnetic radiation, including:
  b microwaves in cooking;
  c infrared in cooking, thermal imaging and security systems;
  d visible light in vision, photography and illumination;
  e ultraviolet in security marking, fluorescent lamps, detecting forged bank notes and disinfecting water;
  f X-rays in observing the internal structure of objects, airport security scanners and medical X-rays;
  g gamma rays in sterilising food and medical equipment, and the detection of cancer and its treatment.

Specification Reference 5.22

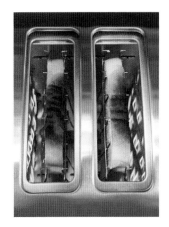

Figure 1: *The element of a toaster heats up and emits lots of infrared radiation. This is absorbed by the bread, causing it to 'toast'.*

Visible light

Visible light is the light that we can see. So it's only natural that we use it for illuminating things so that we can see them.

Tip: Photographic film has to be handled in complete darkness, to stop the photos being ruined by any light.

Photography is another common use of visible light. Photographic film reacts to light to form an image. This is how traditional cameras create photographs. Digital cameras contain image sensors, which detect visible light and generate an electrical signal. This signal is then converted into an image that can be stored digitally or printed.

Ultraviolet radiation

Security

Tip: Ultraviolet radiation is a type of ionising radiation (p.156) meaning it has enough energy to remove electrons from atoms.

Fluorescence is a property of certain chemicals. When ultraviolet (UV) radiation hits them, it's absorbed and visible light is emitted. That's why fluorescent colours look so bright — they actually emit light.

Security pens can be used to mark valuable items, such as laptops, with fluorescent ink. Under UV light the ink will glow (fluoresce), but it's invisible otherwise. This can help the police identify your property if it's stolen.

Fluorescent ink is also used as a security feature in banknotes. The notes feature patterns that only show up under UV light, so forged (fake) bank notes are easier to detect — see Figure 2.

Figure 2: *Banknotes contain a fluorescent ink pattern, making them harder to forge. It only shows up under UV light of the correct frequency.*

Fluorescent lamps

Fluorescent lamps and bulbs use fluorescence too. They have glass tubes which are coated on the inside with a fluorescent material and then filled with a mixture of mercury and noble gases such as neon and argon.

When the electrical current is switched on, electrons in the mercury atoms are excited to higher energy levels. When they fall back down, the energy is released as UV radiation (see page 153). The UV radiation hits the fluorescent coating and is converted into visible light. A lamp of this type is far more energy efficient than an older-style incandescent lamp containing a wire filament.

Disinfecting water

Tip: Gamma radiation is also used for sterilisation — see the next page.

Ultraviolet radiation transfers enough energy that it can damage and kill cells (see page 165). So UV radiation is sometimes used to sterilise water. It kills bacteria in the water, making it safe to drink.

X-rays

X-rays can be used to view the internal structure of objects and materials, including our bodies. They affect photographic film in the same way as light, meaning you can take X-ray photographs. But X-ray images are usually formed electronically these days.

Medical imaging

Radiographers in hospitals take X-ray 'photographs' of people to see if they have any broken bones. X-rays pass easily through flesh but not so easily through denser material like bone or metal.

X-rays are directed through a patient towards film. The film starts off clear, and the bits that are exposed to the fewest X-rays (i.e. the areas where X-rays have been absorbed by bone on the way through the patient) remain clear and uncoloured. The bits where the X-rays have passed through soft tissue without being absorbed turn black. So an X-ray image is really a negative image — the amount of radiation that's not absorbed gives you the image.

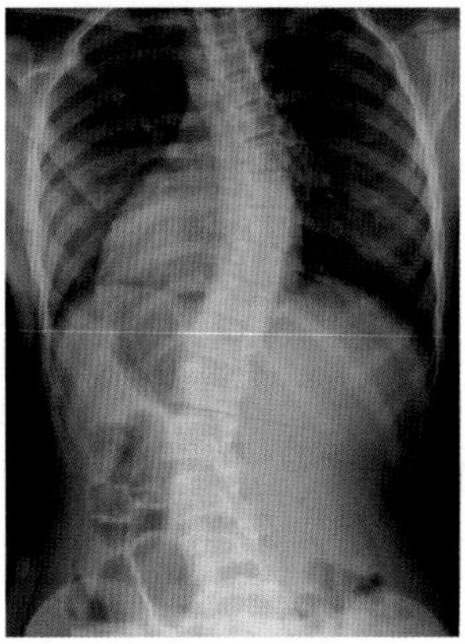

Airport security

X-rays are used in airports to detect hidden objects that can't be found with metal detectors. X-rays are used to check all bags going on to a plane, and any suspicious bags are then inspected. This is much quicker than opening every bag and looking through it.

Gamma rays

Sterilisation

Food can be sterilised before being sold to kill microbes that make the food go bad, so it doesn't rot as quickly. Medical equipment is also sterilised to prevent the spread of infection. Boiling is one method of sterilisation, but the high temperatures can damage food (e.g. fresh fruit) or plastic instruments — so gamma radiation is used instead. Gamma rays transfer lots of energy when they are absorbed, which can damage or kill cells (like bacteria).

Detecting and treating cancer

Gamma rays can be used to treat cancer in the same way as they are used to sterilise equipment. Gamma rays are directed towards a tumour and are absorbed by the cancer cells, killing them.

Cancer can also be detected using gamma rays. A substance that emits gamma rays can be injected into or drunk by a patient. The gamma rays emitted by the substance can be detected outside the patient's body. Doctors can track where the substance goes and how much of the substance different parts of the body use. They can use this information to detect a tumour.

Figure 3: *An X-ray showing a curved spine. Few X-rays have passed through the bones, so those parts of the plate remain clear and uncoloured. They appear white when a white light is shone behind them.*

Tip: As gamma rays carry enough energy to kill cells, this means that they are dangerous for humans to be exposed to. There's more about the dangers of gamma rays on the next page and on p.165-167.

Tip: There's loads about using radiation to detect illnesses and treat cancer in Section 4 — have a look at pages 169-172.

Practice Questions — Fact Recall

Q1   What two types of EM radiation are commonly used in cooking?

Q2   Describe how infrared cameras work.

Q3   What type of EM radiation does traditional photography use?

Q4   Name the type of EM radiation used to detect forged bank notes.

Q5   Give two uses of X-rays.

Q6   Name one use of gamma radiation.

Learning Objectives:
- Be able to recall that the potential danger associated with an electromagnetic wave increases with increasing frequency.
- Be able to describe the harmful effects on people of excessive exposure to electromagnetic radiation, including:
  a microwaves: internal heating of body cells.
  b infrared: skin burns.
  c ultraviolet: damage to surface cells and eyes, leading to skin cancer and eye conditions.
  d X-rays and gamma rays: mutation or damage to cells in the body.

Specification References 5.20 and 5.21

Tip: Ionising radiation is radiation that knocks electrons off of atoms. There's more about the dangers of it on p.165.

Figure 1: *Suncream prevents UV radiation from being absorbed by the skin, reducing the risk of skin cancer.*

8. Dangers of EM Radiation

As you've seen on pages 130-135, electromagnetic radiation is really useful. However, it can be pretty harmful too.

Which types of EM radiation are most damaging?

When EM radiation enters living tissue (like you) it's often harmless, but sometimes it creates havoc. The effects of each type of radiation are based on how much energy the wave transfers. The higher the frequency of the radiation, the more energy it transfers and so the more dangerous it is.

For example, low frequency waves, like radio waves, don't carry much energy. There is a low chance they will cause cell damage if they are absorbed. Whereas high frequency waves like gamma rays transfer lots of energy, meaning they are much more dangerous.

Heating and burns

Some wavelengths of microwaves are absorbed by water molecules, which causes them to heat up. Cells in the body contain lots of water, so being exposed to microwaves (e.g. from mobiles and wireless internet) can cause cells to heat up. There is some debate about if this is harmful.

Infrared radiation is mostly reflected by your skin, but some is absorbed, causing heating. This can lead to burns if your skin gets too hot.

Skin cancer and eye conditions

Ultraviolet (UV) radiation is also absorbed by the skin. It's a type of ionising radiation (p.156) and when absorbed it can cause damage to cells on the surface of your skin, which could lead to skin cancer. It can also damage cells in your eyes and cause a variety of eye conditions or even blindness.

Cancer and radiation sickness

X-rays and gamma rays are also ionising, so they can cause mutations (changes) and damage cells too (which can lead to cancer). But they have even higher frequencies, so transfer even more energy, causing even more damage.

This means that sometimes they kill cells entirely, which can lead to radiation sickness (which causes vomiting and hair loss, p.165).

Practice Questions — Fact Recall

Q1   Describe how the frequency of electromagnetic radiation is linked to the risk of harm from that radiation.

Q2   State a harmful effect infrared radiation may have on the human body.

Q3   What type of EM radiation is a potential cause of skin cancer?

9. Visible Light and Colour

Visible light is the only type of EM radiation that our eyes can detect. Like the other types of EM radiation, visible light is actually a band of wavelengths. It's these differing wavelengths that makes the world a colourful place.

The visible light spectrum

As you saw on page 127, EM waves cover a very large spectrum. We can only see a tiny part of this — the visible light spectrum. Within this, narrow bands of wavelengths (and frequencies) correspond to certain colours. For example, violet is at one end, with wavelengths in the range of around 380-450 nm. Red is at the other end, with wavelengths in the range of around 620-750 nm.

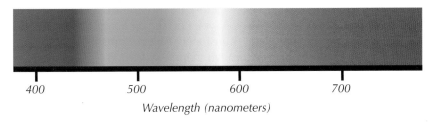

Wavelength (nanometers)

Figure 1: *Diagram showing the colours corresponding to the different wavelengths across the visible light spectrum.*

Colours can also be created by mixing different wavelengths of light. This is because the eyes contain three types of 'cone' cells that are used for detecting colour. Each type of cone is better than the other two at detecting certain colours of light. Generally speaking, one type of cone detects mainly red light, one detects mainly green light and one detects mainly blue light.

When light that isn't red, green or blue enters the eye, it is detected by more than one cone. For example, yellow light is detected by both the red and green cones. This means that you also see 'yellow' when a mixture of red and green light from an object enters your eye, as it causes the same reaction in your eye cells. Figure 2 shows some colour combinations and the colour of light produced by each mixture. Red, green and blue light are often called the primary colours of light.

Colour of opaque objects

When any wave (including visible light) meets an object, it can either be transmitted, absorbed or reflected by it (page 98). **Opaque objects** are objects that do not transmit light. When visible light waves hit them, some wavelengths of light are absorbed and some are reflected. The colour of an object depends on which wavelengths of light are most strongly reflected.

> ### Example
>
> A red apple appears to be red because the wavelengths corresponding to the red part of the visible spectrum are most strongly reflected. The other wavelengths of light are absorbed.
>
>

Learning Objective:

- Be able to explain how colour of light is related to the differential absorption at surfaces and the transmission of light through filters.

Specification Reference 5.3

Tip: 1 nanometre (nm) is equal to 1×10^{-9} m. So 400 nm = 4×10^{-7} m.

Tip: Waves with longer wavelengths have lower frequencies. So the violet end of the visible light spectrum is the high frequency end.

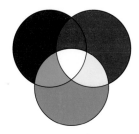

Figure 2: *A diagram showing how different colours of light add together. Red and blue light makes magenta light, blue and green light makes cyan light and red and green light makes yellow light.*

Tip: The reflection of light from a surface might be specular (in one direction) or diffuse (scattered), depending on how smooth the surface is — see pages 115-116.

For opaque objects that aren't red, green or blue, they may be reflecting either the wavelengths of light corresponding to that colour or the wavelengths of the colours that can mix together to make that colour. So a banana may look yellow because it's reflecting yellow light or because it's reflecting both red and green light.

White objects reflect all of the wavelengths of visible light equally, which is why they appear white in white light. Objects that appear black are those that absorb all the wavelengths of visible light. Your eyes see black as the lack of any visible light (i.e. the lack of any colour).

Tip: It doesn't matter if the white light shone on a white object is made up of just red, green and blue light, or all of the wavelengths of visible light. It will reflect all the wavelengths that hit it equally and appear white.

Transparent and translucent objects

Objects which transmit light are either transparent or translucent. Transparent objects transmit light in straight lines so you can see an image clearly through them, e.g. still water or clear glass. Translucent objects transmit light, but also scatter it, so you can't see clearly through them, e.g. frosted glass.

Transparent and translucent objects do not necessarily transmit all wavelengths of light — they may still absorb or reflect some. A transparent or translucent object's colour is related to the wavelengths of light transmitted and reflected by it.

Colour filters

A colour filter is a transparent object that only transmits certain wavelengths (colours) and absorbs all other wavelengths. This has the effect of only letting some colours through — it lets through colours that match the filter's colour.

If you look at a blue object through a blue colour filter, it will still look blue. This is because the blue light reflected from the object's surface is transmitted by the filter. However, if the object was e.g. red (or any colour not made from blue light), the object would appear black when viewed through a blue filter. All of the light reflected by the object will be absorbed by the filter.

Filters that aren't red, green or blue let through both the wavelengths of light for that colour and the wavelengths of the colours that can be added together to make that colour. For example, cyan can be made from blue and green light mixed together. So a cyan colour filter will let through the wavelengths of light that correspond to cyan, blue and green.

Figure 3: Frosted glass is translucent to provide privacy while still letting light through.

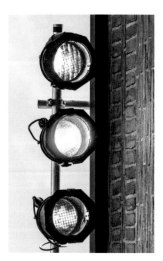

Figure 4: Coloured filters are used on spotlights at discos and in theatres.

Example

A red hat appears black when viewed through a blue filter.

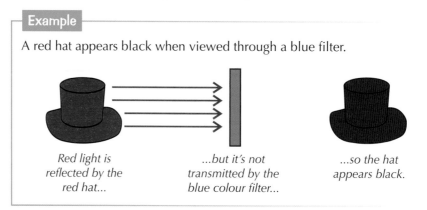

Red light is reflected by the red hat...   *...but it's not transmitted by the blue colour filter...*   *...so the hat appears black.*

Q1   What determines the colour of a wave of visible light?

Q2   What happens to visible light when it hits an opaque object?

Q3   Which wavelengths are reflected by an object that appears:

    a) black?

    b) white?

Q4   What is the difference between an opaque material and a translucent material, in terms of what happens to visible light incident on it?

Q5   What effect does a coloured filter have on visible light?

> **Tip:** If a question talks about radiation incident on something, it just means radiation that hits it.

Practice Questions — Application

Q1   Explain why an opaque green cup appears green.

Q2   A boy is wearing glasses with red filters for lenses. He looks at a set of lights at a pedestrian crossing, as shown below. What colour will each of the lights (red and green) appear to him?

Q3   A student looks at a red bag with a blue buckle through a blue colour filter. Describe and explain the appearance of the bag and the buckle when the student looks through the filter.

- Be able to explain
  that all bodies
  emit radiation,
  that the intensity
  and wavelength
  distribution of any
  emission depends on
  their temperature.

- **H** Be able to explain
  what happens to a
  body if the average
  power it radiates is
  less or more than the
  average power that it
  absorbs.

- **H** Be able to explain
  that for a body to
  be at a constant
  temperature it needs
  to radiate the same
  average power that it
  absorbs.

- **H** Be able to explain
  how the temperature
  of the Earth is affected
  by factors controlling
  the balance between
  incoming radiation
  and radiation emitted.

- Be able to investigate
  how the nature of a
  surface affects the
  amount of thermal
  energy radiated
  or absorbed (Core
  Practical).

Specification References
5.15-5.19

10. Radiation and Temperature

When you feel the warmth of the sun, it's actually the radiation emitted by it that you're feeling. The warmth you feel from other hot objects is radiation too — it just hasn't had such a long journey to reach you.

Radiation emitted by objects

All objects emit radiation with a range of wavelengths and frequencies. For a given object, you can plot a graph of **intensity** against wavelength of the radiation it emits. Intensity is power per unit area, i.e. how much energy is transferred to a given area in a certain amount of time. So the graph shows how much energy is being transferred by each wavelength of radiation emitted by the object each second.

Intensity-wavelength distributions have a general shape, shown in Figure 1. The graph has a peak at a **peak wavelength** (the wavelength that's emitted with the highest intensity), with a spread of lower intensities either side. The further you go from the peak wavelength, the lower the intensity of that wavelength (see Figure 1).

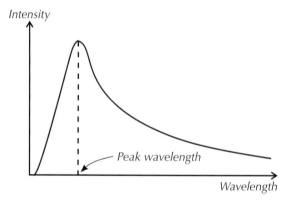

Figure 1: *Graph showing the intensity and distribution of the wavelengths emitted by an object.*

The shape of the graph depends on the temperature of the object.

Intensity of wavelengths emitted

The intensity of radiation emitted by an object depends on its temperature:

> As the temperature of an object increases, the intensity of every emitted wavelength increases.

In other words, a hotter object gives out more of every wavelength of radiation than a cooler object does in a given time. This is shown in Figure 2 on the next page — the curve for the hotter object is higher up than the curve for the cooler object. If the intensity of visible wavelengths emitted increases, the object will appear brighter.

Distribution of wavelengths emitted

The distribution (the spread of intensities) of the wavelengths emitted by an object also depends on the object's temperature:

As the temperature of an object increases, the peak wavelength decreases.

As objects get hotter, the intensity of the radiation they emit increases more rapidly for shorter wavelengths than for longer wavelengths. So a larger proportion of the radiation emitted by a hotter object has a short wavelength, compared to that emitted by a cooler object.

This means that the peak wavelength is at a lower wavelength for a hotter object when compared to a cooler object. You can see this in Figure 2 — the peak of the curve for the hotter object is further to the left than the peak for the cooler object.

Tip: You see this effect when using a Bunsen burner. The large, orange flame isn't as hot as the smaller, blue flame. The peak wavelength of radiation emitted by the flame has moved from the orange part of the visible spectrum to the blue end.

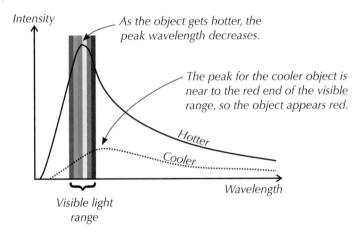

Figure 2: Graph showing how the intensity and distribution of the wavelengths emitted by an object depends on its temperature.

Radiation and temperature   Higher

All objects are constantly emitting and absorbing radiation. The temperature of an object depends on the balance between the amount of radiation it absorbs and the amount of radiation it emits.

The average power is the mean energy transferred each second. If the average power radiated (emitted) by an object is larger than the average power absorbed by the object, the object will cool down. This is because the object is losing energy over time.

Example — Higher

Hot chocolate (and the mug it is in) is warmer than the air around it. Each second it gives out more energy than it absorbs, which is why it cools down over time (see Figure 3).

Figure 3: A mug full of hot chocolate radiating more energy per second (red arrows) than it absorbs (orange arrows).

If the average power radiated is smaller than the average power absorbed, the object heats up. When an object is at a constant temperature, the average power radiated and absorbed are equal.

Radiation and the Earth's temperature $\quad$ Higher

Tip: H The atmosphere protects us from lots of the harmful wavelengths in solar radiation, such as gamma rays, by absorbing them.

Radiation from the Sun (solar radiation) consists of wavelengths from across the EM spectrum. Some of the solar radiation transmitted to Earth is reflected back to space by the atmosphere, clouds or bright surfaces such as snow. The rest is absorbed by the atmosphere or by Earth's surface. The atmosphere and surface then emit the radiation as infrared.

The overall temperature of the Earth depends on the rates at which radiation is reflected, absorbed and emitted. During the day, more radiation is absorbed than is emitted. This causes an increase in local temperature (i.e. an increase in temperature at the points on Earth where it is currently daytime).

Tip: H Cloudy nights are generally warmer than clear nights. This is because the water droplets that clouds consist of are really good absorbers of IR radiation. So the IR radiation emitted upwards by Earth's surface gets absorbed by the clouds. The clouds then emit radiation in all directions, including back down towards Earth.

At night, less radiation is absorbed than is emitted, which causes a decrease in the local temperature. Even though local temperatures vary, the overall temperatures of the Earth's surface and atmosphere stay fairly constant. That's because the overall amount of radiation absorbed from space is equal to the amount reflected or emitted into space.

You can show the flow of radiation for the Earth on a diagram:

Some radiation is reflected by the atmosphere, clouds and the Earth's surface.

Some radiation is emitted by the atmosphere

Some of the radiation emitted by the surface is reflected or absorbed (and later emitted) by the clouds.

Some radiation is absorbed by the atmosphere, clouds and the Earth's surface.

Figure 4: *Diagram showing the flow of radiation to and from Earth.*

Tip: H Changes to the atmosphere can cause a change to the Earth's overall temperature. If the atmosphere starts to absorb more radiation without emitting the same amount, the overall temperature will rise until absorption and emission are equal again.

Radiation and type of surface

It's the surface of an object that absorbs and emits radiation.
Some colours and surfaces absorb and emit radiation better than others.
For example, a black surface is better at absorbing and emitting radiation than a white one, and a matt (non-shiny) surface is better at absorbing and emitting radiation than a shiny one.

Tip: So a matt black surface would be the best absorber and emitter.

> ### Example
>
> Houses in hot countries are painted white because white surfaces are poor absorbers of radiation. This means that the houses heat up less than if the natural, dark brick was exposed to the sun.
>
>

Investigating emission

CORE PRACTICAL

You can investigate how well different surfaces emit radiation with a simple experiment. Wrap four identical test tubes with material, e.g. paper. The material covering each test tube should be the same, but each one should have a different surface or be a different colour. For example, you could use matt black paper, matt white paper, gloss (shiny) black paper and gloss white paper.

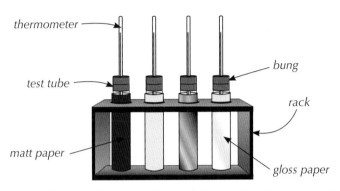

thermometer — *bung*

test tube — *rack*

matt paper — *gloss paper*

Figure 6: *The setup of an investigation into the amount of radiation emitted by different surfaces.*

Figure 5: *Runners often wrap themselves in space blankets after a race. They're light coloured and shiny to reduce heat loss by radiation.*

Boil water in a kettle and fill each test tube with the same volume of water. Seal them with identical bungs each containing a thermometer. Use the thermometers to measure the temperature of the water in each test tube every minute.

It's important to be careful when you're doing this experiment. Don't try to move the test tubes when they're full of boiling water — you might burn your hands. Also, take care when carrying the kettle of boiling water and when pouring the water into the test tubes.

Tip: As with all practical investigations, make sure you do a risk assessment before you start either of these experiments.

Results

The temperature of the water will decrease quicker for the test tubes surrounded by surfaces that are good emitters of radiation. You should find that matt surfaces are better emitters than shiny ones and that black surfaces emit radiation better than white ones. As always, you should do the experiment more than once.

Tip: Doing the experiment more than once lets you see if your results are <u>repeatable</u> or not. Valid experiments must be both repeatable and reproducible.

WORKING SCIENTIFICALLY

Investigating absorption

CORE PRACTICAL

You can do an experiment to investigate how different surfaces affect absorption, using a Bunsen burner and some candle wax.

- Set up the equipment as shown in Figure 7. Two ball bearings are each stuck to one side of a metal plate with solid pieces of candle wax. The other sides of these plates are then faced towards the flame.

- The sides of the plates that are facing towards the flame each have a different surface colour — one is matt black and the other is silver.

- The ball bearing on the black plate will fall first as the black surface absorbs more radiation — transferring more energy to the thermal energy store of the wax. This means the wax on the black plate melts before the wax on the silver plate.

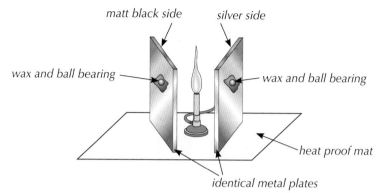

Figure 7: *The setup of an investigation into the amount of infrared radiation absorbed by different surfaces.*

Practice Questions — Fact Recall

Q1 What types of objects emit radiation?

Q2 Describe how the intensity and distribution of wavelengths emitted by an object changes as the object's temperature increases.

Q3 Explain whether the following statement is true or false: 'Objects only absorb radiation if they're cooler than their surroundings.'

Q4 What is the relationship between the power being emitted and the power being absorbed over a certain time for an object at constant temperature?

Q5 Why does the temperature at a point on Earth decrease at night?

Q6 Describe an investigation to investigate how the surface of a material affects how it absorbs radiation.

Practice Questions — Application

Q1 The peak wavelength of light from the Sun is about 500 nm. The peak wavelength of light from a second star is about 850 nm. Which star is hotter? Explain your answer.

Q2 Explain, in terms of radiation emission and absorption, what happens to the temperature of a bowl of ice cream that is left on a counter in a warm room.

Section 3b Checklist — Make sure you know...

Reflection and TIR

☐ How to draw a ray diagram to show reflection.

☐ That the law of reflection is 'angle of incidence = angle of reflection' and that it is true for all waves.

☐ That specular reflection occurs when waves are reflected by a smooth surface. Parallel waves are reflected in a single direction.

☐ That diffuse reflection occurs when waves are reflected by a rough surface. Parallel waves are scattered in lots of different directions.

☐ That total internal reflection occurs when a wave is travelling into a less dense material, with an angle of incidence that is larger than the critical angle of the material.

Lenses, Images and Ray Diagrams

☐ That there are two types of lenses — converging (convex) and diverging (concave).

☐ That real images are formed where rays of light come together to form the image. Real images can be projected on to a screen.

☐ That virtual images are formed where rays of light appear to come together. Virtual images cannot be projected on to a screen.

☐ That the more powerful a lens, the shorter its focal length.

☐ That the more curved a lens is, the more powerful it is.

☐ The symbols representing converging and diverging lenses in a ray diagram.

☐ How to draw ray diagrams for lenses, to show how they bend light.

The Electromagnetic Spectrum and Properties of EM Waves

☐ That all electromagnetic waves are transverse and in a vacuum they all travel at the same speed.

☐ That electromagnetic waves form a continuous spectrum, which can be split into seven main groups: radio waves, microwaves, infrared, visible light, ultraviolet, X-rays, gamma rays.

☐ The order of the main groups of EM waves, based on wavelength and frequency.

☐ That we can only see waves in the 'visible light' part of the spectrum.

☐ That the colours we see in the visible light spectrum can be ordered in terms of their frequency and wavelength. From long wavelength to short, they are: red, orange, yellow, green, blue, indigo, violet.

☐ That EM waves can be generated by electrons moving between energy levels in atoms, or by rearrangements in the nuclei of atoms.

☐ That atoms can generate and absorb a wide range of EM waves, which can cause changes in them.

☐ That all EM waves transfer energy, and examples that show this.

☐ ⓗ That the wavelength of an electromagnetic wave affects whether it is absorbed, transmitted, refracted or reflected by a material.

☐ ⓗ That waves travel at different speeds in different materials, which can lead to refraction or dispersion.

cont...

EM Radiation for Communication

- [ ] **H** That an alternating current is made of oscillating charges, which can produce radio waves. When radio waves are absorbed, they cause charges to oscillate, which can create an alternating current.
- [ ] That radio waves are used for communications, including radio and TV signals.
- [ ] That radio waves and microwaves are used for communications with satellites.
- [ ] That infrared radiation is used in short range communication, optical fibres and by TV remotes.

More Uses of EM Radiation

- [ ] That microwaves can be used to cook food by transferring energy to water molecules in the food.
- [ ] That infrared radiation can be used by infrared cameras, security systems and in cooking.
- [ ] That visible light is used to see things, to light things up and in photography.
- [ ] That UV radiation is used in security marking, testing bank notes, fluorescent lamps and to disinfect water.
- [ ] That X-rays are used to see inside things, and are used by airport scanners and in medicine.
- [ ] That gamma rays are used to sterilise food and equipment, as well as to detect and treat cancer.

Dangers of EM Radiation

- [ ] That the higher the frequency of EM radiation, the more danger it potentially poses to a person.
- [ ] That microwaves heat up internal body cells and infrared radiation can cause skin burns.
- [ ] That UV radiation damages eyes and surface cells, leading to eye problems and skin cancer.
- [ ] That X-rays and gamma rays kill or damage cells. Damaging cells may cause them to mutate, leading to cancer.

Visible Light and Colour

- [ ] That an object reflects light that matches the colour of the object, and absorbs all other wavelengths.
- [ ] That a colour filter transmits light that matches the colour of the filter, and absorbs all others.

Radiation and Temperature

- [ ] That all objects emit radiation, and that the distribution of the intensity of radiation against wavelength depends on the temperature of the object.
- [ ] **H** That if an object radiates more power than it absorbs, it cools down; if it absorbs more than it radiates, it warms up; and if the powers are equal, it remains at a constant temperature.
- [ ] **H** That the temperature of the Earth is determined by the balance between incoming and outgoing radiation, which is affected by factors like the atmosphere, clouds and the Earth's surface.
- [ ] How to investigate how the surface of an object affects how well it radiates and absorbs radiation.

Exam-style Questions

1   **Figure 1** below shows the electromagnetic spectrum.

radio waves	microwaves	infrared	visible light	A	X-rays	gamma rays

Figure 1

(a)   Name a property of electromagnetic waves that decreases across the electromagnetic spectrum in the direction of the arrow shown.

(1 mark)

(b) (i)   Which type of radiation is represented by the letter **A** in the diagram?

(1 mark)

(ii)   Give one use of this type of radiation.

(1 mark)

(iii)   Explain one potential danger of this type of radiation.

(1 mark)

(c)   Which two types of electromagnetic wave are used for transmitting TV signals?

(2 marks)

2   A light ray hits a mirror as shown in **Figure 2** below.

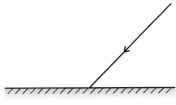

Figure 2

(a)   Copy and complete the ray diagram to show the reflection.
Label the angle of incidence and the angle of reflection.

(2 marks)

(b)   A student draws the ray diagram in **Figure 3** to show reflection from a rough surface.

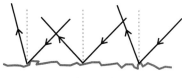

Figure 3

Explain why the student's diagram is incorrect.

(1 mark)

(c)   Name the type of reflection that occurs at a rough surface.

(1 mark)

3 **Figure 4** shows the apparatus for an investigation into the amount of radiation emitted by different surfaces. Half of a shiny aluminium can is painted matt black and the can is filled with boiling water. A radiation sensor is used to record the radiation emitted by each side of the can. The results of the investigation are shown in the table below.

Figure 4

	Matt black	Shiny silver
Temperature reading (°C)	92	92
Average radiation reading (W/m²)	41	5

(a) Explain why the results from the radiation sensor are different for each surface, while the temperature readings are the same for each surface.

(2 marks)

The water was left in the can.
Radiation and temperature readings were taken again 15 minutes later.

(b) Describe how you would expect these readings to compare to the earlier ones, giving reasons for your answer.

(3 marks)

4* Some colour filters are set up and a white ball with a thick red stripe is viewed from different points, as shown in **Figure 5**.

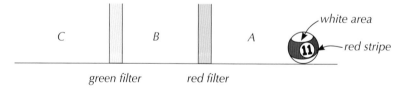

Figure 5

Describe how the red and white parts of the ball will appear when viewed from points A, B and C. Explain why this is, in terms of how the light is reflected and transmitted.

(6 marks)

5 A 5 cm tall object is placed upright and perpendicular to the axis of a diverging lens, with its base on the axis 10 cm from the lens. The lens has a focal length of 5 cm.

(a) Describe the image of the object that is produced by the diverging lens.

(3 marks)

(b) Draw a ray diagram to show the formation of the image. Draw your diagram to scale.

(5 marks)

(c) State the height of the image formed.

(1 mark)

1. Atomic Models

You'll be learning about the current 'nuclear model' of the atom shortly. But first it's time for a trip back in time to see how scientists came up with it. And it's got a bit to do with plum puddings.

The plum pudding model

The Greeks were the first to think about **atoms**. A man called Democritus in the 5th century BC thought that all matter was made up of identical lumps called "atomos". But that's about as far as the theory got until the 1800s...

In 1804 John Dalton agreed with Democritus that matter was made up of tiny spheres ("atoms") that couldn't be broken up, but he reckoned that each element was made up of a different type of "atom".

Nearly 100 years later, J. J. Thomson discovered particles called **electrons** that could be removed from atoms. So Dalton's theory wasn't quite right (atoms could be broken up). Thomson suggested that atoms were spheres of positive charge with tiny negative electrons stuck in them like fruit in a plum pudding — this is called the "plum pudding model".

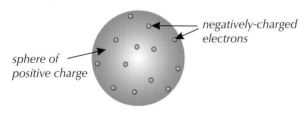

sphere of positive charge
negatively-charged electrons

Figure 1: *The plum pudding model of the atom.*

That "plum pudding" theory didn't last very long though...

The alpha particle scattering experiment

In 1910, scientists in Rutherford's lab tried firing a beam of **alpha particles** (see page 156) at thin gold foil — they used a set-up similar to Figure 3. A circular detector screen surrounds the gold foil and the alpha source, and is used to detect alpha particles deflected by any angle. This was the alpha particle scattering experiment.

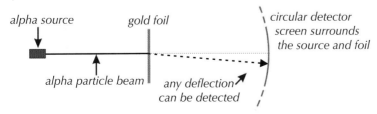

alpha source
gold foil
circular detector screen surrounds the source and foil
alpha particle beam
any deflection can be detected

Figure 3: *The experimental set-up for detecting whether alpha particles have been scattered by gold foil.*

Learning Objectives:

- Be able to describe how and why the atomic model has changed over time, including reference to the plum pudding model and Rutherford alpha particle scattering leading to the Bohr model.

- Be able to describe an atom as a positively charged nucleus, consisting of protons and neutrons, surrounded by negatively charged electrons, with the nuclear radius much smaller than that of the atom and with almost all of the mass in the nucleus.

- Be able to recall the typical size (order of magnitude) of atoms and small molecules.

Specification References 6.1, 6.2, 6.17

Figure 2: *The New Zealand physicist Ernest Rutherford.*

They expected that the positively-charged alpha particles would go straight through or be slightly deflected by the electrons if the plum pudding model was true.

In fact, most of the alpha particles did go straight through the foil, but some were deflected more than they had expected and the odd one came straight back at them. This was frankly a bit of a shocker. The results of the alpha particle scattering experiment showed that atoms must have small, positively-charged **nuclei** at the centre (see Figure 4).

Tip: 'Nuclei' is the plural of 'nucleus'.

Here's why:

- Most of the atom must be empty space because most of the alpha particles passed straight through the foil.

Tip: Remember, like charges repel each other (page 255).

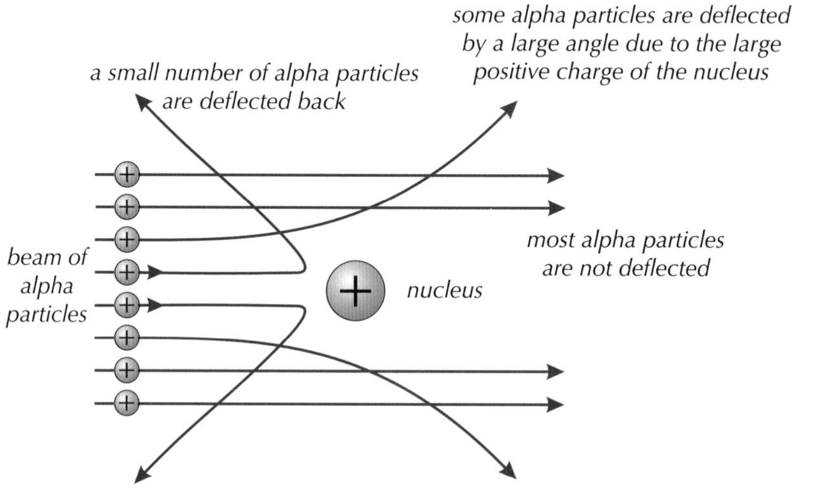

- The nucleus must have a large positive charge as some positively-charged alpha particles were repelled and deflected by a big angle.

- The nucleus must be small as very few alpha particles were deflected back.

Tip: These results provided new evidence, causing the accepted model of the atom to be changed — see pages 2-3 for more on how new theories are accepted with new evidence. **WORKING SCIENTIFICALLY**

some alpha particles are deflected by a large angle due to the large positive charge of the nucleus

a small number of alpha particles are deflected back

beam of alpha particles

nucleus

most alpha particles are not deflected

Figure 4: *A diagram showing some positively-charged alpha particles passing straight through a gold atom and some being deflected by the atom's nucleus.*

This led Rutherford to come up with the first **nuclear model** of the atom (see Figure 6).

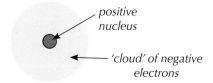

positive nucleus

'cloud' of negative electrons

Figure 6: *Rutherford's nuclear model of the atom.*

Figure 5: *The Danish physicist Niels Bohr.*

Bohr's development of the nuclear model

Rutherford's nuclear model still needed fine-tuning. Electrons are negatively charged, and protons are positively charged (p.152), so scientists realised that electrons in a 'cloud' around the nucleus of an atom would be attracted to the nucleus. This would cause the atom to collapse (fall inwards).

Niels Bohr adapted Rutherford's model to fix this. He concluded that electrons orbiting the nucleus can only do so at certain distances, and nowhere in between. These fixed orbits are called energy levels, or 'shells' (see page 153). Bohr's theoretical calculations were found to agree with experimental data, so the model was accepted.

The current nuclear model

Further experiments tweaked Bohr and Rutherford's model even more, leading to the current nuclear model that we use today (see Figure 7).

Just like in the previous models, there is a tiny, central, positively-charged nucleus that contains most of the atom's mass, with negatively-charged electrons orbiting it in fixed energy levels. However, in the current model, the nucleus is made up of **protons**, which are positively-charged particles, and **neutrons,** which are neutral (they have no charge).

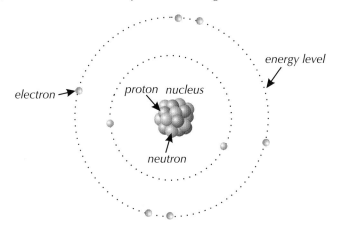

Figure 7: The atom (not to scale).

Tip: We're currently pretty happy with this model, but there's no saying it won't change. Just like for the plum pudding model, new experimental evidence sometimes means we have to change or scrap current models.

WORKING SCIENTIFICALLY

Atomic sizes

Current measurements give the radius of an atom as about 1×10^{-10} m. The radius of the nucleus is about 10 000 times smaller than the radius of the atom. Atoms can also join together to form **molecules** — e.g. molecules of oxygen gas are made up of two oxygen atoms bonded together. Small molecules like this aren't that much bigger than an atom. They are said to be of the same order of magnitude — which is often given as just 10^{-10} m.

Tip: 1×10^{-10} is written in standard form. For more on standard form, see page 340.

Practice Questions — Fact Recall

Q1 Describe the plum pudding model of the atom.

Q2 Describe Rutherford's nuclear model. State the problem with the location of the electrons in this model.

Q3 How did Bohr adapt Rutherford's nuclear model?

Q4 a) Name the three particles that make up an atom.

b) Describe their position according to the current nuclear model.

Q5 What is the typical size of an atom or small molecule?

Learning Objectives:
- Be able to recall the relative masses and relative electric charges of protons, neutrons and electrons.
- Be able to recall that in an atom the number of protons equals the number of electrons and the atom is therefore neutral.
- Be able to recall the relative masses and relative electric charges of positrons.

Specification References 6.5 and 6.6

Tip: Compared to a proton or a neutron, the mass of an electron is tiny — 2000 times smaller in fact.
As protons and neutrons are found in the nucleus of an atom, this shows why almost all of the atom's mass is at its centre.

Tip: The mass of an electron or a positron is so small that you can often treat its relative mass as 0.

2. Subatomic Particles

Now you've seen atoms, it's time to learn about some even smaller particles known as 'sub-atomic' particles.

Relative mass and charge

As you saw on page 151, atoms are made up of protons, neutrons and electrons. Each particle has a relative mass and a relative charge. Relative just means in relation to the other particles — it's so you can compare their masses and charges easily. Figure 1 shows the relative masses and charges of protons, neutrons and electrons.

particle	mass	charge
proton	1	+1
neutron	1	0
electron	$\frac{1}{2000}$	−1

Figure 1: *The relative masses and charges of the particles in the atom.*

Atoms have the same number of protons and electrons. As you can see in Figure 1, the charge on an electron is the same size as the charge on a proton — but opposite. This means that atoms have no charge overall, so we say they are neutral.

Positrons

Another particle you need to know about is the **positron.** Positrons are not found in atoms. They're basically the opposite of an electron — they have the same mass as an electron, but a relative charge of +1. They can be emitted when an atom undergoes radioactive decay (see page 156).

Practice Questions — Fact Recall

Q1   What particle has a relative mass of 1 and a relative charge of 0?

Q2   What is the relative charge of an electron?

Q3   What is the relative mass and charge of a positron?

Practice Question — Application

Q1   An atom contains 10 protons.
How many electrons does the atom contain?

3. Electron Energy Levels

So, you know that electrons are found in energy levels around the nucleus. The next thing you need to know is how they can move between these levels.

Moving between energy levels

Electrons in an atom sit in different energy levels or shells. Each energy level is a different distance from the nucleus. The furthest energy level from the nucleus is called the outer energy level (or shell), and all of the levels closer to the nucleus are called inner energy levels.

The energy level that an electron is in depends on how much energy the electron has. The further from the nucleus an electron is, the more energy it has. Electrons can move between energy levels by gaining or releasing energy.

If electrons located in inner shells gain energy, they move to higher energy levels, further from the nucleus (see Figure 1). When this happens, the electrons are said to be 'excited'.

Electrons gain energy by absorbing electromagnetic (EM) radiation. However, they can only absorb electromagnetic radiation that carries the exact amount of energy that will make them move between energy levels. In other words, the energy carried by the EM radiation must equal the difference in energy between two energy levels, or it won't be absorbed.

Example

The difference in energy between the first and second energy levels of an atom is 1.6×10^{-18} J.

An electron could only move from the first to the second energy level if it absorbed EM radiation that carried exactly 1.6×10^{-18} J of energy.

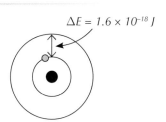

$\Delta E = 1.6 \times 10^{-18}$ J

If electrons release EM radiation, they lose energy and fall to lower energy levels that are closer to the nucleus (see Figure 1). The part of the EM spectrum the radiation emitted is from depends on its energy, which depends on the energy levels the electron has moved between. A higher energy means a higher frequency of EM radiation — p.128.

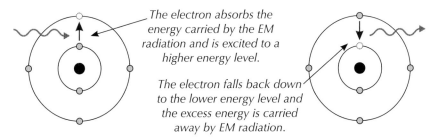

The electron absorbs the energy carried by the EM radiation and is excited to a higher energy level.

The electron falls back down to the lower energy level and the excess energy is carried away by EM radiation.

Figure 1: *A model of how electrons move between energy levels.*

Learning Objectives:

- Be able to recall that in each atom the electrons orbit the nucleus at different set distances from the nucleus.
- Be able to explain that electrons change orbit when there is absorption or emission of electromagnetic radiation.
- Be able to explain how atoms may form positive ions by losing outer electrons.

Specification References 6.7-6.9

Tip: You met electromagnetic radiation on page 127.

Tip: Remember, Δ just means 'change in'.

As you move further out from the nucleus, the energy levels get closer together, so the difference in energy between two levels next to each other gets smaller. This means that an excited electron falling from the third energy level to the second would release less energy than an excited electron falling from the second energy level to the first.

So the frequency of the generated radiation decreases as you get further from the nucleus. This means that a range of electromagnetic radiation can be generated by changes within atoms (page 128).

Tip: Changes within the nucleus itself lead to the production of high energy, high frequency gamma rays (p.128).

Ions

If an electron in the outer energy level of an atom absorbs radiation with enough energy, it can move so far that it leaves the atom. It is now a free electron and the atom is said to have been ionised.

Tip: Atoms and ions of the same element have the same number of protons in their nuclei. An element is defined by the number of protons in the nuclei of its ions or atoms, e.g. an ion or atom with eight protons in its nucleus is the element oxygen.

The atom has become a positive **ion**. It's positively charged because there are now more protons than electrons. An atom can lose more than one electron. The more electrons it loses, the greater its positive charge.

Tip: Ionising radiation is any radiation that can knock electrons from atoms. How likely it is that each type of radiation will ionise an atom varies. You can see more about the different types of ionising radiation on pages 156-157.

> **Example**
>
>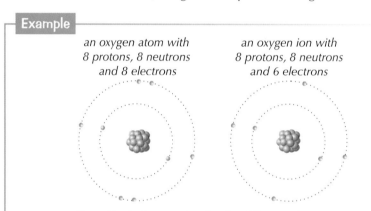
>
> an oxygen atom with 8 protons, 8 neutrons and 8 electrons
>
> an oxygen ion with 8 protons, 8 neutrons and 6 electrons
>
> **Figure 2:** A diagram showing the difference between an uncharged oxygen atom (left) and a positive oxygen ion (right).

Practice Questions — Fact Recall

Q1 How does an electron move to a higher energy level within an atom?

Q2 What happens to an electron when it absorbs EM radiation if it is in the outer energy level of the atom?

Practice Question — Application

Q1 Particle A has 17 protons, 18 neutrons and 16 electrons. Explain how you know that particle A is an ion.

4. Isotopes and Radioactive Decay

Many elements have different forms called isotopes. Some of these isotopes are unstable and decay, giving out various types of radiation.

Atomic number and mass number

The number of protons in the nucleus of an atom is called the **atomic (proton) number**. The number of protons plus the number of neutrons in the nucleus of an atom is called the **mass (nucleon) number**.

An element can be described using the mass number and atomic number of its atoms. The notation looks like this:

mass number $\longrightarrow A$
$\mathbf{X}$ $\longleftarrow$ *symbol of the element,*
atomic number $\longrightarrow Z$ *e.g. O is the symbol for oxygen*

Examples

- An atom of carbon with 6 protons and 6 neutrons would be $^{12}_{6}C$.

- An atom of oxygen with 8 protons and 9 neutrons would be $^{17}_{8}O$.

Elements and isotopes

Isotopes are different forms of the same element, which have the same number of protons but a different number of neutrons. This means they have the same atomic number, but different mass numbers.

Because isotopes of an element always have the same number of protons, they always have the same nuclear charge. However, because they have different numbers of neutrons, their atoms always have different masses. To make it clear which isotope is being referred to, the mass number is added on to the element's name, e.g. oxygen-17.

Example

Carbon-12 and carbon-14 are good examples of isotopes:

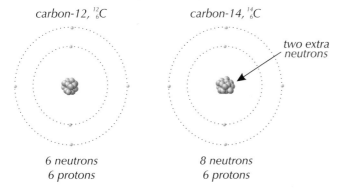

carbon-12, $^{12}_{6}C$ *carbon-14, $^{14}_{6}C$*

two extra neutrons

6 neutrons   8 neutrons
6 protons   6 protons

Figure 1: *Two isotopes of carbon — carbon-12 (left) and carbon-14 (right).*

Learning Objectives:

- Be able to describe the structure of nuclei of isotopes using the terms atomic (proton) number and mass (nucleon) number and using symbols in the format $^{13}_{6}C$.

- Be able to recall that the nucleus of each element has a characteristic positive charge, but that isotopes of an element differ in mass by having different numbers of neutrons.

- Be able to recall that alpha, β– (beta minus), β+ (positron), gamma rays and neutron radiation are emitted from unstable nuclei in a random process.

- Be able to recall that alpha, β– (beta minus), β+ (positron) and gamma rays are ionising radiations.

- Be able to recall that an alpha particle is equivalent to a helium nucleus, a beta particle is an electron emitted from the nucleus and a gamma ray is electromagnetic radiation.

- Be able to compare alpha, beta and gamma radiations in terms of their abilities to penetrate and ionise.

- Be able to recall that nuclei that have undergone radioactive decay often undergo nuclear rearrangement with a loss of energy as gamma radiation.

Specification References
6.3, 6.4, 6.10, 6.11, 6.15, 6.16, 6.21

Unstable isotopes and radioactive decay

All elements have different isotopes, but there are usually only one or two stable ones. Isotopes can be unstable when they have a large imbalance between the numbers of protons and neutrons in the nucleus. Unstable isotopes tend to decay into other elements and give out radiation as they try to become more stable. This process is called **radioactive decay**. Radioactive decay is entirely random, so you can't predict exactly when it will happen (page 161).

Radioactive substances emit **ionising radiation** when they decay. Ionising radiation is radiation that knocks electrons off atoms, creating positive ions (see page 154). The ionising power of a radiation source tells you how easily it can do this. The types of ionising radiation you need to know about are alpha, beta-minus, beta-plus and gamma rays.

Tip: Unstable isotopes are sometimes called 'undecayed isotopes' because they haven't yet undergone radioactive decay to become stable.

Figure 2: The age of an archeological sample can be estimated by measuring the amount of carbon-14 it contains. Carbon-14 is a radioactive isotope that gives out beta-minus particles.

Alpha decay

Alpha decay is when an **alpha particle**, α, is emitted from the nucleus. An alpha particle is two neutrons and two protons — the same as a helium nucleus. So alpha particles have a relative charge of +2 and a relative mass of 4 (see page 152 for more about relative mass and charge).

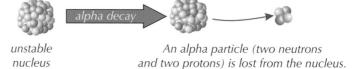

unstable nucleus

An alpha particle (two neutrons and two protons) is lost from the nucleus.

Figure 3: An unstable nucleus decaying by emitting an alpha particle.

Alpha particles are relatively big, heavy and slow-moving. They are strongly ionising — they bash into a lot of atoms and knock electrons off them before they slow down, which creates lots of ions.

Being strongly ionising means they don't penetrate very far into materials and are stopped quickly. They only travel a few centimetres in air and are absorbed by a sheet of paper.

Figure 4: Alpha radiation is used in household smoke detectors — see page 168.

Beta decay

A **beta-minus particle**, β-, (sometimes just called a 'beta particle') is simply a fast-moving electron released by the nucleus (when an neutron turns into a proton). It has virtually no mass and a relative charge of –1.

Tip: Make sure you know that the electron comes from the nucleus. It's not just one of the electrons that are whizzing around outside the nucleus jumping off.

unstable nucleus

A neutron turns into a proton and a beta-minus particle (electron) is released.

Figure 5: An unstable nucleus decaying by emitting a beta-minus particle.

A **beta-plus particle** (β+) is a fast-moving positron released from the nucleus. The positron is the antiparticle of the electron. This just means it has exactly the same mass as the electron, but a positive (+1) charge.

Both types of beta particle move quite fast and are quite small. They are both moderately ionising. Beta-minus particles have a range in air of a few metres and are absorbed by a sheet of aluminium (around 5 mm thick). Positrons have a smaller range, because when they hit an electron the two destroy each other and produce gamma rays — this is called annihilation.

Gamma decay

Gamma rays, γ, (short wavelength electromagnetic radiation, see page 127) have no mass and no charge. They are emitted by a nucleus to get rid of some energy so the nucleus goes into a more stable state. This process is called gamma decay.

Gamma decay often happens after a nucleus has undergone a different type of radioactive decay (e.g. after an alpha decay). The nucleus undergoes some nuclear rearrangement and loses energy by emitting gamma rays.

Gamma rays penetrate far into materials without being stopped and travel a long distance through air. This means they are weakly ionising because they tend to pass through rather than collide with atoms. Eventually they hit something and cause ionisation. They can be absorbed by thick sheets of lead or several metres of concrete.

Neutron radiation

Unstable isotopes can also release neutrons (n). This type of decay allows atoms to create a more stable balance between their atomic and mass numbers.

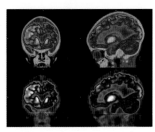

Figure 6: *An image of a brain generated by positron emission tomography (a PET scan), which uses electron-positron annihilation — see page 170.*

Tip: There's more on neutron radiation on page 160.

Practice Questions — Fact Recall

Q1 What is meant by atomic number and mass number?

Q2 What can you say about the charge on nuclei of the same element?

Q3 a) Name five types of radiation that can be emitted by a nucleus.

   b) Which of these is equivalent to a helium nucleus?

   c) Which type has the strongest ionising power?

Practice Questions — Application

Q1 An iodine atom (chemical symbol I) has 53 protons and 82 neutrons.

   a) Use symbol notation ($^{A}_{Z}X$) to represent this atom.

   b) Which of the following is an isotope of iodine: $^{135}_{82}I$, $^{123}_{53}I$, $^{53}_{82}I$, or $^{134}_{52}I$?

Q2 This diagram shows the paths of three types of ionising radiation, A, B and C, being directed towards a human hand and a thick metal sheet.

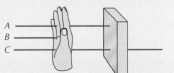

   a) Which radiation (A or B) is more penetrating? How can you tell?

   b) Which radiation (A or B) is likely to be alpha radiation? Why?

   c) Explain what radiation C is likely to be and how you know.

- Be able to use given data to balance nuclear equations in terms of mass and charge.

- Be able to explain the effects on the atomic (proton) number and mass (nucleon) number of radioactive decays (α, β, γ and neutron emission).

- Be able to describe the process of $\beta-$ decay (a neutron becomes a proton plus an electron).

- Be able to describe the process of $\beta+$ decay (a proton becomes a neutron plus a positron).

Specification References
6.18-6.20, 6.22

Tip: Remember, in the notation $^A_Z X$, A is the mass number (the total number of protons and neutrons) and Z is the atomic number (the number of protons).

5. Nuclear Equations

When an atom gives out alpha or beta radiation, its atomic number changes and it becomes a new element. You can show these processes using balanced nuclear equations.

What are nuclear equations?

You can write radioactive decays as **nuclear equations** using symbol notation. They are written in the following form:

> atom before decay → atom after decay + radiation emitted

The mass and atomic numbers have to balance on both sides of the equation (before and after decay). In other words, the total mass and charge must stay the same. You'll need to be familiar with the notation on page 155, and how each type of radiation can be written in this notation:

- Alpha particles are 2 protons and 2 neutrons. They are written as $^4_2\alpha$.

- Beta-minus particles are electrons with (almost) no mass and a charge of −1. They are written as $^0_{-1}\beta$ or $^0_{-1}e^-$.

- Beta-plus particles are positrons with (almost) no mass and a charge of +1. They are written as $^0_1\beta$ or $^0_1e^+$.

- Neutrons are written as ^1_0n, because they have no charge and a mass of 1.

- Gamma radiation is written as $^0_0\gamma$, because it has no mass and no charge.

Alpha decay

Tip: In alpha decay, a new element will be formed, as the number of protons in the nucleus (the atomic number) changes.

As protons have a relative charge of +1, alpha emission decreases the charge on the nucleus (and the atomic number) by 2. The mass number decreases by 4, as protons and neutrons each have a relative mass of 1.

Example 1

Uranium-238 can decay into thorium-234 by emitting an alpha particle. Uranium has 92 protons and thorium has 90 protons.

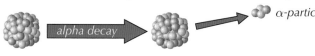

uranium-238   *thorium-234*   *α-particle*

alpha decay

The nuclear equation for this decay looks like this:

$$^{238}_{92}U \rightarrow {}^{234}_{90}Th + {}^4_2\alpha$$

On the left-hand side:

- The mass number is 238.

- The atomic number is 92.

On the right-hand side:

- The total of the mass numbers is: 234 + 4 = 238.

- The total of the atomic numbers is: 90 + 2 = 92.

So both sides of the equation balance.

Example 2

Balance the following equation: $^{238}_{94}\text{Pu} \longrightarrow \,^{234}\text{U} \; + \,^{...}_{2}\alpha$

Make these equations balance: $238 \longrightarrow 234 \; + \; .....$

$\qquad\qquad\qquad\qquad\qquad\quad 94 \longrightarrow \; ..... \; + \; 2$

Balancing mass numbers, $238 = 234 + \mathbf{4}$, so the mass number of α is 4.

Balancing atomic numbers, $94 = \mathbf{92} + 2$, so the atomic number of U is 92.

The full equation is: $^{238}_{94}\text{Pu} \longrightarrow \,^{234}_{92}\text{U} \; + \,^{4}_{2}\alpha$

Exam Tip
You won't have to work out what the elements are (e.g. Pu, U) in nuclear equations. You only need to be able to balance the atomic and mass numbers and identify the type of decay.

Beta-minus decay

When a nucleus decays by beta-minus decay, a neutron turns into a proton and an electron. The electron is emitted from the atom. This increases the charge on the nucleus (and the atomic number) by 1 but leaves the mass number unchanged.

Example

Carbon-14 can decay into nitrogen-14 by emitting a beta-minus particle (when a neutron turns into a proton and an electron).

$\bigcirc$ β-minus particle

carbon-14   nitrogen-14

The equation is: $^{14}_{6}\text{C} \longrightarrow \,^{14}_{7}\text{N} + \,^{0}_{-1}\beta$

and the mass and atomic numbers balance on each side. Brill.

Tip: As with alpha decay, beta-minus decay forms a new element because the atomic number changes.

Beta-plus decay

In beta-plus decay, a proton changes into a neutron and a positron. The positron is emitted from the atom. The mass number doesn't change, as it has lost a proton but gained a neutron. The atomic number (and so the nuclear charge) decreases by 1, because it has one less proton.

Tip: Remember, for beta-minus decays you can use $^{0}_{-1}\text{e}^{-}$ instead of $^{0}_{-1}\beta$, and for beta-plus decays, you can use $^{0}_{1}\text{e}^{+}$ instead of $^{0}_{1}\beta$.

Example

Show that the decay of fluorine-18 to oxygen-18 in the equation below emits beta-plus radiation:

$$^{18}_{9}\text{F} \longrightarrow \,^{18}_{8}\text{O} + \; ?$$

Make these equations balance: $18 \longrightarrow 18 + ...$
$\qquad\qquad\qquad\qquad\qquad\quad 9 \longrightarrow \; 8 + ...$

$18 = 18 + \mathbf{0}$, so the emitted particle must have a mass number of 0.
$9 = 8 + \mathbf{1}$, so the particle must have an atomic number of 1.

The emitted particle has a mass number of 0 and an atomic number of 1, which means that it's a beta-plus particle $^{0}_{1}\beta$.

Gamma decay

When a nucleus emits a gamma ray, it is getting rid of excess energy. The charge and mass of the nucleus remain unchanged, so the atomic and mass numbers don't change.

Tip: You might sometimes see this as $^{99}_{43}Tc* \rightarrow ^{99}_{43}Tc + ^{0}_{0}\gamma$. The asterisk means the atom is excited (so it has excess energy).

Example

Technetium-99 releases energy as a gamma ray:

$$^{99}_{43}Tc \rightarrow ^{99}_{43}Tc + ^{0}_{0}\gamma$$

Neutron emission

When a nucleus emits a neutron the mass number decreases by 1, as it has lost a neutron. The atomic number stays the same though, so the charge on the nucleus remains unchanged. The nucleus just becomes a different isotope of the element.

Tip: See page 155 for more on isotopes.

Example

Beryllium-13 emits a neutron when it decays to beryllium-12, as shown in the equation below:

$$^{13}_{4}Be \rightarrow ^{12}_{4}Be + ^{1}_{0}n$$

Practice Questions — Fact Recall

Q1 What can you say about the total mass and total charge on each side of a nuclear equation?

Q2 What happens to the mass and charge of a nucleus when it emits a neutron?

Q3 Describe what happens in the nucleus during:

a) beta-minus decay,

b) beta-plus decay.

Practice Questions — Application

Q1 Americium-241 decays into neptunium-237. The nuclear equation for this decay is: $^{241}_{95}Am \rightarrow ^{237}_{93}Np + ^{4}_{2}?$. What type of decay is this?

Q2 Radium-228 decays into actinium-228 by emitting an electron from its nucleus.

a) What is the name of this type of decay?

b) Complete the following nuclear equation for this decay:

$$^{....}_{88}Ra \rightarrow ^{228}_{....}Ac + ^{0}_{-1}\beta$$

Q3 Carbon-11 ($^{11}_{6}C$) undergoes beta-plus decay. What is the mass number and atomic number of the new element formed?

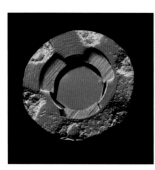

Figure 1: *Americium is the radioactive source used in a smoke detector.*

6. Activity and Half-life

Radioactive samples give out less and less radiation over time, but they never stop giving out radiation altogether.

Activity

Radioactive substances will give out radiation from the nuclei of their atoms — no matter what. This radiation can be measured with a **Geiger-Muller tube** and counter (see Figure 1), which records the count-rate — the number of radiation counts reaching it per second. You can also detect radiation using photographic film. The more radiation the film's exposed to, the darker it becomes (just like when you expose it to light).

Radioactive decay is entirely random. So you can't predict exactly which nucleus in a sample will decay next, or when any one of them will decay. But you can find out the time it takes for the amount of radiation emitted by a source to halve, this is known as the **half-life**. It can be used to make predictions about radioactive sources, even though their decays are random.

Half-life can be used to find the rate at which a source decays — its **activity**. Activity is measured in becquerels, Bq (where 1 Bq is 1 decay per second).

Half-life

The activity of a sample always decreases over time. Each time a radioactive nucleus decays to become a stable nucleus, the activity as a whole will decrease — so older sources emit less radiation.

How quickly the activity drops off varies a lot. For some isotopes, it takes just a few hours before nearly all of the unstable nuclei have decayed, whilst others last for millions of years.

The problem with trying to measure this is that the activity never reaches zero. However, the half-life of a radioactive isotope is constant, which is why you can use the idea of half-life to measure how quickly the activity drops off.

Learn these definitions of half-life:

The half-life of a radioactive isotope is the time taken for the activity of a source to decay by half.	The half-life of a radioactive isotope is the time taken for half the undecayed nuclei to decay.

Learning Objectives:

- Be able to describe methods for measuring and detecting radioactivity limited to photographic film and a Geiger–Müller tube.
- Be able to explain that it cannot be predicted when a particular nucleus will decay but half-life enables the activity of a very large number of nuclei to be predicted during the decay process.
- Be able to recall that the unit of activity of a radioactive isotope is the Becquerel, Bq.
- Be able to describe how the activity of a radioactive source decreases over a period of time.
- Be able to explain that the half-life of a radioactive isotope is the time taken for half the undecayed nuclei to decay or the activity of a source to decay by half.
- Be able to use the concept of half-life to carry out simple calculations on the decay of a radioactive isotope, including graphical representations.

Specification References
6.14, 6.23-6.27

Figure 1: *A Geiger-Müller tube and counter being used to measure the radioactivity of tomatoes.*

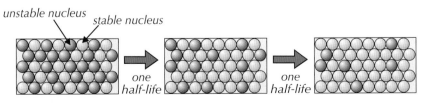

unstable nucleus stable nucleus one half-life one half-life

Figure 2: *A diagram showing how the number of unstable (undecayed) nuclei of a radioactive isotope in a sample decreases over two half-lives.*

A short half-life means the activity of a source falls quickly, because the nuclei are very unstable and rapidly decay. A long half-life means the activity falls more slowly because most of the nuclei don't decay for a long time — the source just releases small amounts of radiation over a longer period.

Calculating half-life

You can work out the half-life of a radioactive isotope if you're given a little information. Or if you know the half-life, you can work out how long it will take for the activity to drop a certain amount.

Half-life is maybe a little confusing, but exam calculations on it are straightforward as long as you do them slowly, step by step. Like this:

Example 1

The activity of a radioactive isotope is 640 cpm (counts per minute). Two hours later it has fallen to 80 cpm. Find the half-life of the sample.

You must go through it in short simple steps like this:

	after one half-life	after two half-lives	after three half-lives
initial count			

640   (÷2)   320   (÷2)   160   (÷2)   80

It takes three half-lives for the activity to fall from 640 to 80. Hence two hours represents three half-lives, so the half-life is 120 mins ÷ 3 = 40 minutes.

Example 2   Higher

The initial activity of a sample is 640 Bq. Calculate the percentage reduction in activity after two half-lives.

Find the activity after each half-life.

> 1 half-life: 640 ÷ 2 = 320 Bq
> 2 half-lives: 320 ÷ 2 = 160 Bq

So the reduction in activity is: 640 − 160 = 480 Bq

Then write this as a percentage: $\frac{480}{640} \times 100 = \textbf{75\%}$

Using graphs

You can plot or use a graph of activity against time to work out the half-life of a radioactive isotope.

The data for the graph will usually be several readings of activity. The graph will always be shaped like the one shown in Figure 4.

The half-life is found from the graph by finding the time interval on the bottom axis corresponding to a halving of the activity on the vertical axis.

Example

Figure 4 shows how the activity of a radioactive sample decreases with time. The half-life can be found from the graph as follows:

- The initial activity is 80 Bq, so after one half-life it will be 40 Bq (and after two it will be 20 Bq and after three it will be 10 Bq).

- To find the half-life of the sample, draw a line from 40 Bq on the activity axis across to the curve and down to the time axis (green dotted line). This tells you that the half-life is 4 hours.

- You can check you were right by doing the same for an activity of 20 Bq and checking that you get a time of 8 hours, and so on...

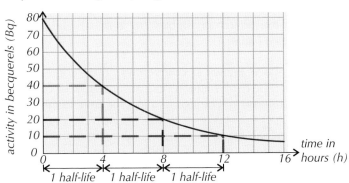

Figure 4: A graph of activity against time for a radioactive isotope, taking into account background radiation (see page 164).

Figure 3: You can do an experiment to simulate half-life using cubes with one black face. The cubes represent unstable nuclei and if they land black-side up, they have 'decayed'. Take note of how many cubes you start with and throw them all, removing any that 'decay'. Count the number remaining, then throw those remaining cubes again. Plotting your results on a graph will allow you to calculate the 'half-life' in 'number of throws'. The more cubes you start with, and the more rolls you do, the closer the results will model radioactive decay. However, unlike the activity of a radioactive sample, the number of cubes will eventually fall to zero.

Practice Questions — Fact Recall

Q1 State the units of activity, and describe how the activity of a radioactive source changes over time.

Q2 Why can't we measure the time it takes for a source to fully decay?

Q3 Write down two definitions of half-life.

Practice Questions — Application

Q1 The activity of a source is 32 Bq. After how many half-lives will the activity have dropped to 4 Bq?

Q2 Find the half-life of the radioactive isotope from this graph of the activity of the radioactive isotope against time.

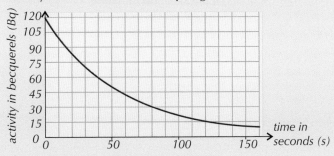

Tip: Make sure you read the axes carefully — you don't want to be saying the half-life is 'so many' hours when it's actually 'so many' seconds.

Learning Objectives:

- Be able to explain what is meant by background radiation.

- Be able to describe the origins of background radiation from Earth and space.

Specification References 6.12, 6.13

7. Background Radiation

No matter where you are, you're always being exposed to a small amount of radiation called background radiation.

What is background radiation?

Background radiation is low-level radiation that is present at all times, all around us, wherever you go. The background radiation we receive comes from many sources, including:

- Radioactivity of naturally occurring unstable isotopes which are all around us — in the air, in food, in building materials and in the rocks under our feet (see Figure 1).

- Radiation from space, known as **cosmic rays**. These come mostly from the Sun. Luckily, the Earth's atmosphere absorbs a lot of cosmic rays, but at very high altitudes you'll be exposed to a lot more of them.

- Radiation due to man-made sources, e.g. fallout from nuclear weapons tests, nuclear accidents (such as Chernobyl — see Figure 2) or dumped nuclear waste.

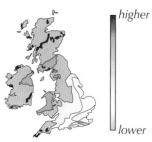

higher

lower

Figure 1: *A map of the United Kingdom showing radiation from rocks. The scale shows how the level of radiation from rocks in different areas varies.*

| Example |

More than half of the background radiation that a typical person in the UK is exposed to comes from radioactive radon gas produced by rocks. Some homes in areas with a greater chance of high levels of radon (see Figure 1) have radon detectors fitted, to warn occupants if the levels of radon in their house go above a certain amount.

As background radiation is always present, it means that when you measure the count-rate of a source, background radiation will contribute towards your measurement. To avoid systematic errors (p.13), you should always measure the count-rate due to background radiation and then subtract this figure from your measurement of the count-rate of a source.

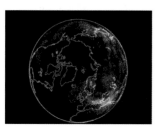

Figure 2: *A simulation of the radiation (pink) in the Northern hemisphere 10 days after the Chernobyl disaster in which a nuclear power plant in Ukraine exploded in 1986 and released lots of radiation.*

Practice Questions — Fact Recall

Q1 What is background radiation?

Q2 Give three main sources of background radiation.

8. Dangers of Ionising Radiation

Ionising radiation can be incredibly useful (pages 168-172) — it can even save lives. Sadly it can also be very dangerous and can cause harm to your body. How dangerous a radiation source is depends on which type of radiation it emits and how you're using it.

Dangers of radiation

If your body is exposed to radiation, radiation is hitting or entering your body. The amount of radiation your body absorbs (and so the amount of energy it absorbs) is the **absorbed radiation dose**. Exposure to radiation can be very harmful. Alpha, beta and gamma radiation can enter living cells and collide with molecules. These collisions cause ionisation (p.156), which damages or destroys the molecules and can lead to tissue damage.

Lower doses of radiation tend to cause minor damage without killing the cell. This can give rise to mutant cells which divide uncontrollably — see Figure 1. The cells keep dividing, making more cells — this uncontrolled cell division is cancer.

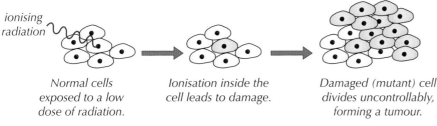

ionising radiation

| *Normal cells exposed to a low dose of radiation.* | *Ionisation inside the cell leads to damage.* | *Damaged (mutant) cell divides uncontrollably, forming a tumour.* |

Figure 1: *A cell being damaged by a low dose of radiation, leading to it multiplying uncontrollably.*

Higher amounts tend to kill cells completely, which causes **radiation sickness** if a lot of (otherwise healthy) body cells are killed at once. Radiation sickness causes vomiting, tiredness and hair loss.

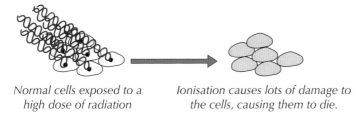

Normal cells exposed to a high dose of radiation   *Ionisation causes lots of damage to the cells, causing them to die.*

Figure 2: *Cells being killed by a high dose of radiation.*

Irradiation

If radiation from a radioactive source reaches an object (such as your body), the object is being irradiated. For example, all objects (including your body) are always being irradiated by background radiation sources.

High levels of irradiation from all sources are dangerous for humans, but especially from ones that emit beta and gamma radiation. This is because beta and gamma can penetrate the body and get to the delicate organs. Alpha irradiation is less dangerous because it can't penetrate the skin and is easily blocked by air.

Learning Objectives:

- Be able to describe the dangers of ionising radiation in terms of tissue damage and possible mutations and relate this to the precautions needed.
- Be able to describe the differences between contamination and irradiation and compare the hazards associated with these two.
- Be able to explain the precautions taken to ensure the safety of people exposed to radiation, including limiting the dose for patients and the risks to medical personnel.
- Be able to explain how the dangers of ionising radiation depend on half-life and relate this to the precautions needed.

Specification References 6.29-6.32

Precautions to reduce the risk of harm from irradiation

- Radioactive sources should be kept in lead-lined boxes. Lead blocks a lot of radiation, preventing exposure by irradiation to anyone near the box.

- People using a radioactive source can reduce the amount they are irradiated by standing behind barriers or wearing shielding, which will absorb some or all of the radiation before it reaches their bodies. They could also use remote-controlled arms to handle sources or operate machines from another room.

- When working with a radioactive source, you should try to stay as far away from the source as possible. The greater the distance away from the source, the lower a person's absorbed radiation dose.

- Medical staff who work with radiation wear photographic film badges to monitor their exposure by irradiation and make sure it doesn't get too high.

- Patients being treated with radiation should have their dose limited by wearing shielding over healthy areas of their body, in order to prevent damage to healthy cells.

Figure 3: *A hospital employee preparing a radioactive treatment from behind shielding, whilst wearing a protective suit and gloves.*

Tip: There's more about how radiation is used in medical tests and treatments on pages 169-172.

Contamination

If unwanted radioactive atoms get onto or into a material (or your body), it is said to be **contaminated**. E.g. if you touch a radioactive source without wearing gloves, your hands would be contaminated. These contaminating atoms might then decay, releasing radiation which could cause you harm. Even when the original source has been removed, you're still exposed to the radiation.

Contamination is especially dangerous inside your body. Alpha sources are the most dangerous inside the body because they are the most ionising. They do all their damage in a very localised area. Beta and gamma sources are less dangerous inside the body because they mostly pass straight out without doing much damage (they have a lower ionising power). So contamination, rather than irradiation, is the major concern when working with alpha sources.

Precautions to reduce the risk of harm from contamination

- Gloves and tongs should be used when handling radioactive sources, to avoid contamination from particles getting stuck to your skin or under your nails.

- Some industrial workers wear protective suits to prevent contamination through breathing in particles or getting any on their normal clothes or their skin. They can also wash away any particles stuck to the protective suits using a decontamination shower, as shown in Figure 4.

- In medicine, radioactive sources are sometimes put inside a patient's body (p.169-172). The sources chosen need to have appropriate half-lives to reduce the risk of damaging the patient's healthy cells. The half-life needs to be long enough to be effective for the medical procedure, but short enough so the activity falls to a safe level within a reasonable time.

Figure 4: *A decontamination shower, used to wash away radioactive particles to prevent them being carried away from the site and contaminating other people and places.*

Effect of half-life on potential danger of a source

The lower the activity (see p.161) of a radioactive source, the safer it is to be around. If two sources that produce the same type of radiation start off with the same activity, the one with the longer half-life will always be more dangerous. This is because, after any given time, the activity of the source with a short half-life will have fallen more than the activity of the source with a long half-life.

If the two sources have different initial activities, the danger associated with them changes over time. Even if its initial activity is lower (so it is initially safer), the source with the longer half-life will be more dangerous after a certain period of time because its activity falls more slowly.

Tip: Remember, activity is the rate at which a source decays. So a higher activity means more decays in a given time, and so more radiation being released by the source in that time.

> ### Example
>
> **Source A has an activity of 20 kBq and a half-life of 5 days.** **Source B has an activity of 200 kBq and a half-life of 1 day. Which source is more dangerous initially, and after 5 days?**
>
> Initially, source B is the most dangerous because its activity is highest.
>
> After 5 days:
>
> Source A has had one half-life, so its activity is 20 kBq ÷ 2 = 10 kBq.
>
> Source B has had five half-lives, so its activity has halved 5 times:
> 200 kBq ÷ 2 = 100 kBq, 100 kBq ÷ 2 = 50 kBq, 50 kBq ÷ 2 = 25 kBq, 25 kBq ÷ 2 = 12.5 kBq, 12.5 kBq ÷ 2 = 6.25 kBq
>
> So after 5 days, source A is the most dangerous, because its activity is now higher than that of source B.

When choosing a radioactive source for an application, it's important to find a source that has the right level of activity for the right amount of time, but that isn't too dangerous for too long. This means choosing a source that has an appropriate half-life.

The half-life and the type of radiation emitted, as well as whether the source is to be used inside or outside of a person's body, affects the precautions that should be taken when using a source.

Tip: Careful planning for how radioactive sources will be disposed of is needed, especially for sources with long half-lives as they remain radioactive for a long time.

Practice Questions — Fact Recall

Q1 Give one danger of exposure to ionising radiation.

Q2 State what is meant by the terms irradiation and contamination.

Practice Questions — Application

Q1 A nurse has to inject a patient with a radioactive source for a medical procedure. Explain two ways in which the nurse can protect himself from harmful exposure to radiation during the procedure.

Q2 Two radioactive sources have the same activity and emit the same type of radiation, but have different half-lives. Source A has a half-life of 8 minutes, and source B has a half-life of 5 hours. Which source is potentially more dangerous? Explain your answer.

- Be able to describe uses of radioactivity, including: household fire (smoke) alarms; irradiating food; sterilisation of equipment; tracing and gauging thicknesses; and diagnosis and treatment of cancer.
- Be able to explain some of the uses of radioactive substances in diagnosis of medical conditions, including PET scanners and tracers.
- Be able to explain why isotopes used in PET scanners have to be produced nearby.
- Be able to compare and contrast the treatment of tumours using radiation applied internally or externally.

Specification References
6.28, 6.30, 6.33-6.35

Tip: There's more on half-life on page 161.

9. Uses of Ionising Radiation

Ionising radiation gets loads of bad press, but it is pretty essential in all sorts of everyday situations, especially medicine. In fact, you're probably not too far away from a radioactive source right now...

Fire (smoke) alarms

The properties of alpha radiation make it ideal for use in household fire alarms. A weak source of alpha radiation is placed inside a smoke detector, close to two electrodes. The alpha particles are highly ionising, so they cause ionisation of the air between the electrodes. This allows a current to flow through the air between the electrodes. If there is a fire then the smoke will block the flow of ions, stopping the current. An alarm sounds whenever the current stops, signalling a fire.

As alpha particles are highly ionising, they can only travel a few centimetres in air and are stopped by the plastic casing of the fire alarm. This means that the alpha radiation produced by the source can't reach anyone, and the fire alarm is safe to use. The half-life of the source needs to be long, so the fire alarm doesn't need to be replaced often.

Thickness gauges

Beta radiation is used in industry where thickness control is needed — for example, in the manufacture of paper or aluminium foil.

Example

Figure 1 shows part of the paper manufacturing process.

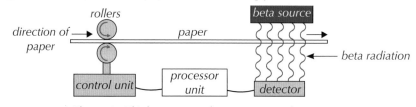

Figure 1: *Thickness control in paper manufacture.*

Radiation is directed through the paper to a detector, connected to a control unit. When the amount of detected radiation changes, it means the paper is coming out too thick or too thin, so the control unit adjusts the rollers to give the correct thickness.

The source in a thickness gauge needs to emit beta radiation, so that it is partly blocked by the paper or foil (see p.157). If all the radiation goes through (or none of it does), then the reading on the detector won't change as the thickness changes.

Thickness gauges are often part of an automated process, meaning that workers in the factory do not need to be close to the beta source, which reduces their chance of irradiation. The beta sources used should have long half-lives so they don't need to be replaced often.

Sterilisation

Food and medical equipment are irradiated with a high dose of gamma rays, which sterilises them (page 135). The radioactive source used for this needs to be an emitter of gamma rays with a high activity, and a reasonably long half-life (at least several months) so that it doesn't need replacing too often. The sterilising equipment is used in a shielded room, to prevent irradiation of nearby people (p.165).

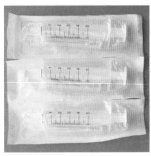

Figure 2: *Single-use syringes are sterilised by radiation whilst in sealed packages, so they remain sterile until they are opened.*

Industrial tracers

Gamma emitting sources are used in industry as **tracers** to detect leaks in underground pipes. The source is added to the fluid in the pipe, and the radiation is then detected above the ground. A higher level of radiation will be detected at the point above a leak, as the radiation will be able to pass through the hole in the pipe and also because a pool of leaked fluid will form. The half-life of the source needs to be just long enough to carry out the trace, without leaving the area radioactive for a long time as this could cause harm to nearby animals or people.

Medical tracers

Certain radioactive isotopes can be injected into people (or they can just swallow them) and their progress around the body can be followed using an external detector. Isotopes used in this way are known as medical tracers.

A computer converts the readings from the external detector to a display showing where the strongest readings are coming from. This can help doctors to investigate whether a patient's internal organs are functioning as they should be. If not, it may lead the doctor to diagnose the patient with a medical condition or illness, including cancer.

Example

A well-known example is the use of iodine-123 or iodine-131. These are absorbed by the thyroid gland in the neck just like normal iodine-127, but give out gamma radiation. The radiation can be detected to indicate whether the thyroid gland is taking in iodine as it should.

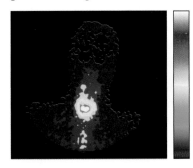

high

intensity of gamma
radiation detected

low

Figure 3: *An image of the gamma radiation detected from a person who has been injected with gamma-emitter iodine-131. The image shows that most gamma radiation is coming from the thyroid, indicating that the iodine-131 has collected there.*

Tip: The intensity of gamma radiation means the amount detected per unit time.

Figure 4: *A patient being injected with a radioactive tracer. The nurse is wearing a protective apron to reduce her exposure to radiation (see page).*

Tip: A positron is a beta-plus particle — look back at pages and for more on beta-plus decay.

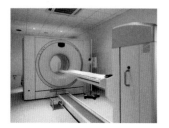

Figure 5: *PET scanning equipment.*

All isotopes which are taken into the body must be gamma or beta emitters, so that the radiation passes out of the body. Alpha sources should never be used as they are highly ionising and do their damage in a localised area — see page 156. The source should have a short half-life too, so that the activity falls quickly, and patients (and people around them) aren't exposed to radiation for any longer than necessary to limit the damage done to their cells.

Positron emission tomography

Positron emission tomography, or PET scanning, is a technique used to show tissue or organ function, and can be used to diagnose medical conditions.

The patient is injected with a glucose-like substance that can be used by the body but also contains a positron-emitting radioactive isotope to act as a tracer. The isotope used must have a short half-life, e.g. ^{11}C, ^{13}N, ^{15}O or ^{18}F. Over an hour or so, the tracer moves through the body and is taken up by the organs, to varying degrees.

Positrons emitted by the isotope meet electrons in an organ and annihilate (see page 157), emitting high-energy gamma rays in opposite directions that are detected. Detectors around the body (or the head, as shown in Figure 6) detect each pair of gamma rays, forming an image of the places where the tracer has been taken up by the organs. By detecting at least three pairs, the location of the places where the take up is high can be accurately found by triangulation.

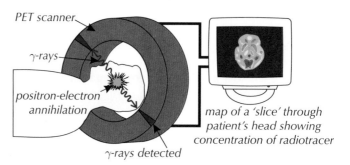

PET scanner

γ-rays

positron-electron annihilation

map of a 'slice' through patient's head showing concentration of radiotracer

γ-rays detected

Figure 6: *Diagram of a PET scan on a patient's head.*

Example

PET scans can identify cancer because cancer cells have a much higher metabolism than healthy cells as they're growing much more rapidly. Glucose provides cells with energy, so cancer cells will absorb more of the glucose-like substance that emits positrons than healthy cells.

The distribution of radioactivity detected by the PET scanner matches up with the metabolism of the cells. So if the PET scan image shows an area of intense radiation in one part of the body, this could indicate the location of a tumour.

The isotopes used in PET scanning have short half-lives, so it's important that they're made close to where they'll be used. Some hospitals have their own cyclotron to make the isotopes on-site. Otherwise, if the isotopes had to be transported over a large distance, their activity could be too low by the time they arrived at the hospital, making them no longer useful.

Radiotherapy

Radiotherapy is the treatment of cancer using ionising radiation, e.g. gamma rays. It can be used to control or destroy cancer cells. High doses of radiation will kill all living cells, including cancer cells. The radiation has to be given at just the right dosage so as to kill the cancer cells without damaging too many healthy cells.

A radioactive source can be used externally, by directing radiation at a person's body from the outside, or internally by implant or injection.

Exam Tip
You need to be able to describe the similarities and differences between treating tumours externally and internally.

External radiotherapy

Tumours can be treated externally using radiation aimed at the tumour from a source outside of the body. Gamma radiation is used because it can penetrate through the patient's body.

The radiation is carefully focused on the tumour (see Figure 8) to ionise the cancer cells, killing them off. Some damage is still done to surrounding healthy cells, although shielding can be placed on other areas of the patient's body to reduce this.

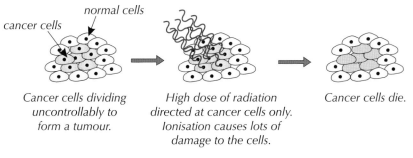

Cancer cells dividing uncontrollably to form a tumour.　　*High dose of radiation directed at cancer cells only. Ionisation causes lots of damage to the cells.*　　*Cancer cells die.*

Figure 8: *Radiation being used to kill cancer cells.*

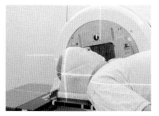

Figure 7: *A person undergoing radiotherapy for brain cancer. The laser crosshair marks the point where the radiation should be focused, and a head brace is worn to keep the head perfectly still.*

The sources used in external radiotherapy treatments should have long half-lives. This is so they don't have to be replaced often in the machines in the hospital. The source itself never enters the patient's body, so it can't continue to damage cells after the treatment has stopped. However, these sources emit lots of radiation, putting the people close to the machines at risk of irradiation. The machines are usually surrounded by shielding and kept in a designated room to reduce the risk to staff and patients in the hospital.

Tip: Some medical staff wear photographic film badges to monitor their exposure to radiation in hospitals. See page 166 for more about the precautions taken by people who work with radiation.

Internal radiotherapy

With internal radiotherapy, a radioactive material is placed inside the body into or near a tumour. This can be done in many ways, e.g. by injecting a small amount of a radioactive substance into the tumour or by placing a radioactive implant near the tumour.

Example — Injection

Alpha emitters are usually injected into the tumour. As alpha particles are strongly ionising, they do lots of damage to the nearby area (the cancerous cells), but the damage to normal tissue surrounding the tumour is limited because they have such a short range.

Beta emitters are often used in implants placed inside or next to a tumour. Beta radiation is able to penetrate the casing of the implant (unlike alpha particles, which would be stopped) in order to damage nearby cancerous cells. A disadvantage of using beta radiation is that beta particles have a longer range than alpha particles, so they can damage healthy cells further away from the cancerous cells.

Tip: Some implants can be left inside the patient permanently because they have a short enough half-life. Others have to be removed.

Unlike external radiotherapy, the half-lives of the sources used for internal treatments are usually short, to limit the absorbed radiation dose of healthy cells.

Weighing up the risks

WORKING SCIENTIFICALLY

For every situation, it's worth considering both the benefits and risks of using radioactive materials. For example, tracers can be used to diagnose life-threatening conditions, while the risk of cancer from one use of a tracer is very small.

Whilst prolonged exposure to radiation poses risks and causes many side effects, many people with cancer choose to have radiotherapy as it may get rid of their cancer entirely. For them, the potential benefits outweigh the risks.

Practice Questions — Fact Recall

Q1 Describe a non-medical use of each type of ionising radiation.

Q2 a) Explain how medical tracers work.

b) Which types of ionising radiation sources can be used in medical tracers and why?

Q3 Why might hospitals need to make the isotopes used in PET scanners on-site?

Q4 Explain the differences in the radioactive sources used for external and internal radiotherapy in terms of:

a) the type of radiation they emit,

b) the half-life of the source.

Exam Tip
In the exam you could be asked to explain why certain radioactive sources are chosen for certain tasks. Just think about the properties of each one (p.156-157), and how that would make them useful. Think about the half-life too.

Practice Question — Application

Q1 Carbon-11 is a beta-plus emitter with a half-life of around 20 minutes. Cobalt-60 is a gamma emitter with a half-life of around 5 years. Suggest a medical use for each of these isotopes. Explain your answer.

10. Nuclear Fission and Fusion

Nuclear fusion and nuclear fission are two different nuclear reactions which release large amounts of energy. Harnessing this energy isn't so easy though...

Nuclear fission

Nuclear fission is a type of nuclear reaction that is used to release energy from large and unstable atoms (e.g. uranium-235 or plutonium-239) by splitting them into smaller atoms.

Uranium-235 fission

Spontaneous (unforced) fission rarely happens. Usually, the nucleus has to absorb a neutron before it will split. A neutron can be easily absorbed by the nucleus because it has no charge, so it won't be repelled by the positive charge of the nucleus.

In the fission of uranium-235 (U-235), a slow-moving neutron is fired at a large, unstable U-235 nucleus. The neutron is absorbed by the nucleus, which makes the atom more unstable and causes it to split.

When the U-235 atom splits it forms two new lighter elements that are roughly the same size. These are called daughter nuclei. There are lots of different pairs of daughter nuclei that uranium can split into — Figure 1 shows krypton-91 and barium-143 being produced. All the new nuclei produced in a fission reaction are radioactive.

Two or three neutrons are also released when the U-235 atom splits (see Figure 1). If any of these neutrons are moving slowly enough to be absorbed by another uranium nucleus, they can cause more fission to occur. This is a **chain reaction**. Chain reactions can only occur when the type of particle released (in this case a neutron) is the same type of particle as that which caused the fission in the first place.

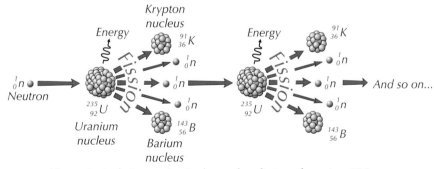

Figure 1: *A chain reaction in the nuclear fission of uranium-235.*

Each fission is accompanied by a release of energy. This is why nuclear chain reactions are used to generate power in nuclear power plants (see the next page). In a nuclear power plant, chain reactions take place inside nuclear reactors. The nuclear fission chain reaction needs to be carefully controlled, so each fission reaction generates one new fission reaction. This ensures energy is released at a steady rate.

Learning Objectives:
- Be able to explain how the fission of U-235 produces two daughter nuclei and the emission of two or more neutrons, accompanied by a release of energy.
- Be able to recall that the products of nuclear fission are radioactive.
- Be able to explain the principle of a controlled nuclear chain reaction.
- Be able to explain how the chain reaction is controlled in a nuclear reactor, including the action of moderators and control rods.
- Be able to explain the difference between nuclear fusion and nuclear fission.
- Be able to describe nuclear fusion as the creation of larger nuclei resulting in a loss of mass from smaller nuclei, accompanied by a release of energy, and recognise fusion as the energy source for stars.
- Be able to explain why nuclear fusion does not happen at low temperatures and pressures, due to electrostatic repulsion of protons.
- Be able to relate the conditions for fusion to the difficulty of making a practical and economic form of power station.

Specification References 6.38-6.40, 6.42-6.46

Controlling chain reactions in nuclear reactors

Tip: The energy released in the fission reaction is transferred to the coolant, and then used to heat water, making steam to turn turbines to generate electricity — see page 283.

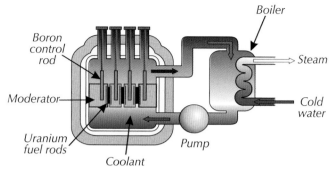

Figure 2: A diagram to show the control methods used in a nuclear reactor.

Tip: The potential for catastrophic explosions, such as the Chernobyl disaster in Ukraine in 1986, is one argument against nuclear power. See page 82 for more about the advantages and disadvantages of using nuclear power to produce electricity.

Figure 3: A 'mushroom cloud' from a nuclear explosion. This was produced during nuclear weapons testing by the US in the Pacific Ocean in 1952.

The neutrons released by fission reactions in a nuclear reactor (see Figure 2) have a lot of energy. They will only cause other nuclear fissions (and cause a chain reaction) if they are moving slowly enough to be captured by the uranium nuclei in the fuel rods. These slow-moving neutrons are called thermal neutrons. The uranium fuel rods are placed inside a **moderator**, such as graphite, which slows down the fast-moving neutrons. Without a moderator to control the speed of the neutrons, fewer fissions would occur and the chain reaction would slow or stop.

Control rods, often made of boron, are placed in between the fuel rods and are raised and lowered into the reactor to control the chain reaction. The control rods absorb excess neutrons, preventing them from being absorbed by and splitting other uranium nuclei. This creates a steady rate of nuclear fission, where one new neutron produces another fission.

If the chain reaction in a nuclear reactor is left to continue unchecked, large amounts of energy are released in a very short time. Many new fissions will follow each fission, causing a runaway reaction which could lead to an explosion. This is how atomic bombs work.

Nuclear fusion

Nuclear fusion is the opposite of nuclear fission. In nuclear fusion, two light nuclei collide at high speed and join (fuse) to create a larger, heavier nucleus. For example, hydrogen nuclei can fuse to produce a helium nucleus.

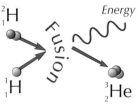

Figure 4: A diagram to show the formation of a helium nucleus from the nuclear fusion of two hydrogen nuclei. Energy is released in this process.

This heavier nucleus does not have as much mass as the two separate, light nuclei did. Some of the mass of the lighter nuclei is converted into energy (don't panic, you don't need to know how). This energy is then released as radiation. Nuclear fusion is the reaction which generates energy in stars (see page 187).

So far, scientists haven't found a way of using fusion to generate energy for us to use. Fusion only happens at really high pressures and temperatures (about 10 000 000 °C). This is because the positively charged nuclei have to get very close to fuse, so the strong force due to electrostatic repulsion (p.255) has to be overcome. Overcoming this force takes a lot of energy.

It's really hard to create the right conditions for fusion to happen in a lab or power station, so trying to build a fusion reactor is very difficult and expensive. There are a few experimental reactors around at the moment, but none of them are generating electricity yet — they take more power to create and control the fusion reaction than the reactor produces, so it is not an economical (cost effective) source of energy.

Figure 5: *The inside of the JET Tokamak fusion research reactor at the Culham Centre for Fusion Energy in Oxfordshire.*

Practice Questions — Fact Recall

Q1 Describe the process of nuclear fission of a uranium-235 atom.

Q2 What is the term used to describe the nuclei produced by a fission reaction?

Q3 Describe nuclear fusion. How does it differ from nuclear fission?

Q4 What type of nuclear reaction occurs in stars?

Q5 Why do we not currently use nuclear fusion to generate electricity?

Practice Question — Application

Q1 Chain reactions have to be carefully controlled inside a nuclear reactor. Describe the control method used to:

a) prevent runaway fission chain reactions that could lead to explosions,

b) keep the fission chain reaction going.

- Be able to recall that nuclear reactions, including fission, fusion and radioactive decay, can be a source of energy.

- Be able to describe how thermal (heat) energy from a chain reaction is used in the generation of electricity in a nuclear power station.

- Be able to evaluate the advantages and disadvantages of nuclear power for generating electricity, including the lack of carbon dioxide emissions, risks, public perception, waste disposal and safety issues.

Specification References 6.36, 6.37, 6.41

Tip: Look back at pages 61-65 for a recap on energy stores and energy transfer.

11. Nuclear Power

You've already seen the different energy resources we can use to generate electricity in Section 2. Here's a closer look at how nuclear power is used, and some of the issues associated with using it.

Energy transfer in nuclear power stations

All reactions that involve changes to the nuclei of atoms can be a source of energy. This includes radioactive decay (p.156), fission (p.173) and fusion (p.174). Nuclear power stations use the energy released during controlled fission reactions to generate electricity (see Figure 1).

The energy released by the chain reaction inside the reactor (see p.174) is transferred to the thermal energy store of the moderator. Some of this energy is then transferred to the thermal energy store of the coolant. The coolant flows around to the boiler and transfers energy to the thermal energy store of cold water passing through the boiler. This causes the water to boil, generating steam. This steam turns a turbine connected to a generator and the turning generator produces electricity.

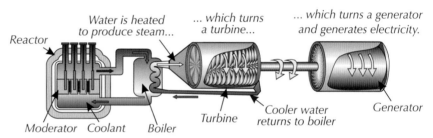

Figure 1: Electricity generation in a nuclear power station.

Using nuclear power

Using nuclear fission to produce electricity can be controversial. There are several arguments both for and against using nuclear power.

Advantages

Nuclear power is a reliable alternative to fossil fuels (i.e. coal, oil and gas). Fossil fuels all release carbon dioxide (CO_2) when they're burnt. This adds to the greenhouse effect and global warming. Burning coal and oil also releases sulfur dioxide that can cause acid rain. Nuclear fission doesn't release these gases, so in this way it is a very clean source of energy.

Huge amounts of energy can be generated from a relatively small amount of nuclear fuel — as shown in Figure 2. Uranium is also relatively cheap and readily available.

Disadvantages

Public perception of nuclear power can be very negative, and it's seen by many to be very dangerous. This is because of the risk of radiation or radioactive materials leaking out from power stations or nuclear waste storage facilities. There is also a very small risk of a major catastrophe like those at Chernobyl and Fukushima, but generally nuclear power is very safe.

Figure 2: This shows the size of nuclear fuel pellets and their injection rod. One pellet can produce the same amount of energy as around 3 tonnes of coal.

Some people worry that nuclear waste can never be disposed of safely. The waste products from nuclear fission have very long half-lives, meaning they'll be radioactive for hundreds or thousands (even millions) of years. There is always a danger that they could leak out and pollute land, rivers and oceans.

Although nuclear fuel is relatively cheap compared to fossil fuels (for the same amount of energy), the overall cost of nuclear power is high. This is because of the high costs of setting up the power plant, as well as decommissioning the plant when it's no longer useful. Dismantling a nuclear plant safely takes decades.

Figure 3: *An anti-nuclear demonstration in Japan. 'Don't forget Fukushima' refers to the 2011 disaster at a nuclear power plant, initiated by a tsunami.*

Practice Questions — Fact Recall

Q1   Name three types of nuclear reaction that are a source of energy.

Q2   Describe how electricity is generated from the energy produced in a nuclear chain reaction.

Q3   Evaluate the use of nuclear power to generate electricity.

Section 4 Checklist — Make sure you know...

Atomic Models

☐ What the plum pudding model of the atom looked like and how the model was developed.

☐ How the results of Rutherford's alpha particle scattering experiment led to the nuclear atomic model.

☐ How and why Bohr adapted the nuclear model following Rutherford's experiment.

☐ That in the current nuclear model of the atom, protons and neutrons form a positively charged nucleus at the centre of the atom, orbited in fixed energy levels by negatively charged electrons.

☐ That in the current nuclear model, the nucleus has a radius about 10 000 times smaller than the radius of the atom, but contains most of the mass.

☐ That the radius of an atom or small molecule is typically around 1×10^{-10} m.

Subatomic Particles

☐ That protons and neutrons have a relative mass of 1, whilst electrons have a relative mass of $\frac{1}{2000}$ (which is usually ignored as it's so small).

☐ The relative electric charge on: a proton (+1), a neutron (0), an electron (–1).

☐ That atoms have no overall charge because they have the same number of protons and electrons.

☐ That positrons have an identical relative mass to an electron, but an opposite (+1) relative charge.

Electron Energy Levels

☐ That electrons orbit the nucleus of an atom at different set distances called energy levels.

☐ That electrons absorb electromagnetic (EM) radiation to move to a higher energy level, and emit EM radiation to move back to a lower energy level.

cont...

☐ That an outer electron might absorb enough EM radiation to leave the orbit of the nucleus completely, which turns the atom into a positively charged ion. This is called ionisation.

Isotopes and Radioactive Decay

☐ That the atomic number is the number of protons, and the mass number is the total number of protons and neutrons in the nucleus of an atom.

☐ That an element can be described using $^A_Z X$ notation, where X is the chemical symbol of the element, A is its mass (nucleon) number, and Z is its atomic (proton) number.

☐ That the nucleus of each element has a unique positive charge.

☐ That isotopes of an element have the same number of protons and so the same positive nuclear charge, but different numbers of neutrons and so different masses.

☐ That unstable nuclei will emit ionising radiation (alpha, beta-minus, positron and gamma rays) or neutrons at random.

☐ That an alpha particle is made of 2 protons and 2 neutrons, which is the same as a helium nucleus.

☐ That alpha particles are strongly ionising, but are easily stopped by a few cm of air, or by paper.

☐ That a beta-minus particle is a fast moving electron emitted from the nucleus.

☐ That a beta-plus particle is a fast moving positron emitted from the nucleus.

☐ That beta radiation is moderately ionising, and can penetrate a few metres of air, but is stopped by a sheet of aluminium.

☐ That a gamma ray is a type of EM radiation, and can be emitted when a nucleus decays and undergoes rearrangement.

☐ That gamma rays are weakly ionising, can travel long distances in air, and are only stopped by several metres of concrete or a very thick lead sheet.

Nuclear Equations

☐ How the atomic and mass numbers of a nucleus are affected by different types of radioactive decay.

☐ How to balance nuclear equations for the different types of decay in terms of mass and charge.

☐ That during beta-minus decay, a neutron turns into a proton and an electron, and the electron is emitted from the nucleus.

☐ That during beta-plus decay, a proton turns into a neutron and a positron, and the positron is emitted.

Activity and Half-life

☐ That radioactivity can be measured using photographic film and a Geiger-Müller tube and counter.

☐ Why you can't predict when a single nucleus will decay, but half-life allows you to make predictions about the activity of a large sample of nuclei.

☐ That the activity of a radioactive isotope is measured in Becquerels, Bq.

☐ How the activity of a radioactive source decreases over time.

cont...

☐ The definition of half-life as the time taken for half the undecayed nuclei to decay or the activity of a source to decay by half.

☐ How to carry out simple calculations using half-life, including reading off a graph.

☐ **H** How to find the reduction in activity after a number of half-lives as a percentage.

Background Radiation

☐ That background radiation is a constant source of low-level radiation, from naturally-occuring radioactive isotopes, cosmic rays, and the fallout from nuclear weapons tests or accidents.

Dangers of Ionising Radiation

☐ How ionising radiation causes cells to mutate (leading to cancer) or die.

☐ The difference between exposure to radiation through irradiation and contamination.

☐ The reasons for the different safety precautions taken to limit a person's exposure to radiation.

☐ How the half-life of a radioactive source affects how safe it is.

Uses of Ionising Radiation

☐ How radioactivity is used in household fire alarms, for sterilising food and medical equipment, in thickness gauges, in industrial and medical tracers, in PET scanners, and in radiotherapy.

☐ Why the radioactive isotopes used in PET scanners are usually produced on-site in hospitals.

☐ The differences between the isotopes used for externally and internally applied treatment for cancer.

Nuclear Fission and Fusion

☐ What fission is, and the nuclear fission chain reaction for uranium-235.

☐ That the products of a fission reaction are radioactive.

☐ How chain reactions are controlled in a nuclear reactor using control rods and moderators.

☐ That nuclear fusion is the joining of two nuclei, whereas fission is the splitting of a nucleus.

☐ That there is a loss in mass and a subsequent release of energy duing nuclear fusion, and that this is the energy source for stars.

☐ That nuclear fusion requires high temperatures and pressures to overcome the electrostatic repulsion of protons in the nuclei, and that this currently makes fusion power stations inefficient.

Nuclear Power

☐ That nuclear reactions (fission, fusion and radioactive decay) can be a source of energy.

☐ How electricity is generated in a nuclear power station, and the pros and cons of nuclear power.

Exam-style Questions

1   **Figure 1** shows two atoms.

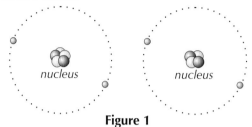

Figure 1

(a)   Put these three words into the following sentences.
You may only use each word once.

| protons | neutrons | electrons |

The nucleus contains _____ and _____.

The numbers of protons and _____ in a neutral atom are equal.

(2 marks)

(b)   The two atoms shown in **Figure 1** are isotopes of the same element.
Describe the similarities and differences in the nuclei of the two atoms.

(1 mark)

2   **Figure 2** gives some information about three types of ionising radiation.

Radiation type:	Made up of:	Stopped by:
Alpha particles		Thin paper
	Electrons emitted from the nucleus	Thin aluminium
Gamma rays	Short-wavelength EM waves	Thick lead

Figure 2

(a)   Complete the table shown in **Figure 2**.

(2 marks)

(b)   Alpha sources are the most dangerous radioactive sources when inside the body.
Explain why.

(1 mark)

(c)   Describe how the atomic and mass numbers of a nucleus change when it emits an alpha particle.

(2 marks)

(d)   State what happens in a nucleus when it emits a beta-minus particle.

(1 mark)

3   In March 2011, the Fukushima nuclear power plant in Japan was damaged by a tsunami and leaked some nuclear radiation into the air. One of the radioactive isotopes that was leaked in this incident was caesium-137, which has a half-life of 30 years.

(a)   Explain what it means for caesium-137 to have a half-life of 30 years.

(1 mark)

(b)   A sample containing caesium-137 is found to have an activity of 24 Bq.
Calculate what the activity of the sample will be in 90 years' time.

(3 marks)

Shortly after the disaster, the Japanese government decided to evacuate all people from their homes within a 12 mile radius of the power plant, because the background radiation was significantly higher than average due to the disaster.

(c)   Name **two** sources of background radiation, other than man-made nuclear sources.

(2 marks)

(d)   Describe **one** method that could be used to detect and measure radioactivity.

(1 mark)

Caesium-137 decays into barium-137.
The following incomplete equation shows this decay:

$$^{137}_{55}\text{Cs} \longrightarrow \, ^{137}_{\ldots}\text{Ba} + \, ^{0}_{-1}\ldots$$

(e)   What type of radiation is being given out in this decay?

(1 mark)

(f)   Complete the nuclear equation for this decay.

(1 mark)

4*   An underground pipe is thought to be cracked, so that the substance carried by the pipe is leaking out. An engineer intends to use a radioactive isotope to locate the cracks. The isotope is put into the substance carried by the pipe. A radiation detector on the ground is moved along above the pipe, as shown in **Figure 3**.

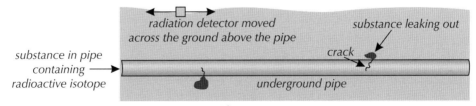

Figure 3

Describe how the engineer would be able to tell where there was a crack in the pipe. Explain what type of radiation the isotope in the pipe should emit and what the half-life of the source should be.

(6 marks)

5   A patient is undergoing radiotherapy to treat a cancerous tumour.
         Plastic pellets containing a beta source are placed inside the tumour.

(a)   Describe how ionising radiation kills cancer cells.

(2 marks)

(b) (i)   Explain why a beta source is suitable for this procedure.

(2 marks)

      (ii)   The plastic pellets are left in the patient's body permanently.
           State and explain what this indicates about the half-life of the beta source.

(2 marks)

           External radioactive sources can also be used to treat cancer.

(c)   The patient may feel very ill during this treatment. Explain why this is the case.

(1 mark)

(d)   Explain **two** ways in which the radioactive source used for external radiotherapy
          will differ from the source used for implants.

(4 marks)

(e)   Explain why machines used for external radiotherapy are kept in shielded rooms.

(1 mark)

6   A nuclear fission power station uses the energy released when uranium-235 nuclei
         split in two to generate electricity.

(a)   The reaction that occurs in a nuclear reactor is a chain reaction.

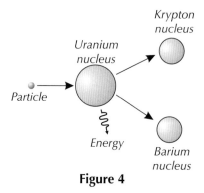

Figure 4

      (i)   Give the name of the particle shown in **Figure 4** that initiates the fission reaction.

(1 mark)

      (ii)   Complete the diagram in **Figure 4** to illustrate how the chain reaction occurs, assuming
           the fission products are moving slowly enough to cause further fission.

(2 marks)

(b)   Compare nuclear fission and fossil fuel power stations in terms of their
          environmental effects.

(2 marks)

(c)   Describe the methods used in a nuclear fission power plant to control the chain
          reaction of uranium-235.

(4 marks)

1. The Solar System and Orbits

The Solar System is made up of the Sun at the centre, everything that orbits around it — and everything else which orbits around them. These pages are all about our Solar System, and how objects are kept in orbits.

Models of the Solar System

Over time, there have been lots of different models of the **Solar System**. One of the first models was the **geocentric model**. It suggested that the Earth was the centre of the Solar System and the Sun, Moon, planets and stars all orbited the Earth in perfect circles. An **orbit** is the path on which one object moves around another (see Figure 1). The geocentric model arose because people on Earth didn't have telescopes and saw the Sun and Moon travelling across the sky in the same way every day and night. It was the accepted model of the Universe from the time of the ancient Greeks until the 1500s.

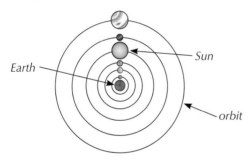

Figure 1: *A diagram showing the geocentric model of the Solar System.*

Next up was the **heliocentric model**, which had the Sun at the centre of the Solar System. It said that the Earth and all of the planets orbited the Sun in perfect circles. Galileo found one of the best pieces of evidence for this theory — the moons around Jupiter. Whilst looking at Jupiter with a telescope, he noticed some stars in a line near the planet. When he looked again, he saw these 'stars' never moved away from Jupiter and seemed to be carried along with the planet. This showed not everything was in orbit around the Earth, and provided evidence that the geocentric model was incorrect.

Gradually, evidence for the heliocentric model increased thanks to more technological advances. The current model still says that the planets in our Solar System orbit the Sun — but that these orbits are actually elliptical (a very stretched out circle) rather than circular.

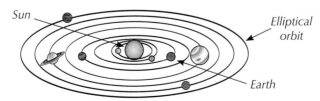

Figure 2: *A diagram showing our current model of the Solar System.*

Learning Objectives:

- Be able to describe how ideas about the structure of the Solar System have changed over time.
- Be able to recall that our Solar System consists of the Sun (our star), eight planets and their natural satellites (such as our Moon); dwarf planets; asteroids and comets.
- Be able to recall the names and order, in terms of distance from the Sun, of the eight planets.
- Be able to describe the orbits of moons, planets, comets and artificial satellites.
- Be able to explain for circular orbits how the force of gravity can lead to changing velocity of a planet but unchanged speed.
- Be able to explain how and why both the weight of any body and the value of *g* differ between the surface of the Earth and the surface of other bodies in space, including the Moon.
- Be able to explain how, for a stable orbit, the radius must change if orbital speed changes (qualitative only).

Specification References 7.1-7.7

The Solar System

Our Solar System contains one star — the Sun. The rest is made up of everything that orbits the Sun. The Sun is orbited by:

Tip: One way of remembering the order of the planets is to use the sentence 'my very excellent mother just served us nachos'.

- **Planets** — these are large objects which orbit a star. There are eight of them orbiting the Sun. In order, from the Sun outwards, they are Mercury, Venus, Earth, Mars, Jupiter, Saturn, Uranus and Neptune. They have to be large enough to have "cleared their neighbourhood". This means that their gravity is strong enough to have pulled in any nearby objects apart from their natural satellites.

- **Dwarf planets** — e.g. Pluto. These are planet-like objects that orbit stars, but are too small to meet all of the rules for being a planet.

- **Satellites** — these are objects that orbit a second more massive object. For example:

  1. **Natural satellites** — these are natural (i.e. not man-made) objects. The Moon is an example of a natural satellite.

  2. **Artificial satellites** are satellites that humans have built. There are lots orbiting the Earth and some orbiting the Sun and other planets.

- **Asteroids** — these are lumps of rock and metals that orbit the Sun. They're usually found in the asteroid belt between Mars and Jupiter.

- **Comets** — e.g. Halley's comet. These are lumps of ice and dust that orbit the Sun.

Figure 3: *Jupiter is the largest planet in our Solar System.*

Tip: Our solar system is just one of many in our galaxy. We are in the Milky Way galaxy, which is a collection of billions of stars and objects held together by gravity. By looking at light from objects in other galaxies, scientists can observe how the Universe itself is behaving (see p.191).

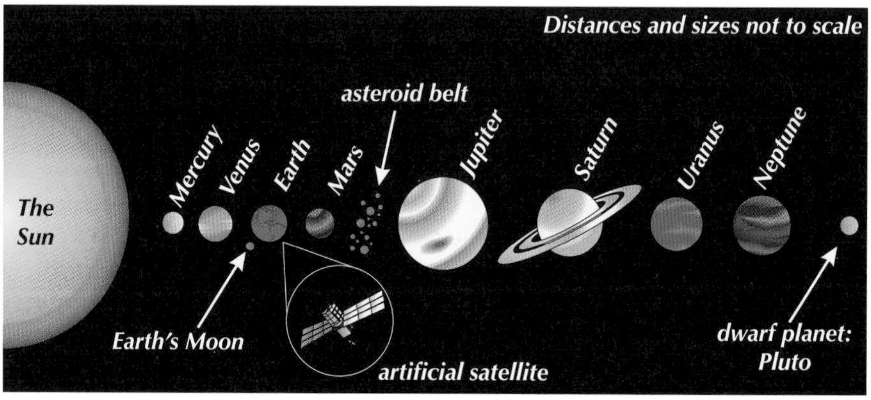

Figure 4: *A diagram of our Solar System, showing the eight planets in order and examples of a dwarf planet, a natural satellite and an artificial satellite.*

Orbits — the basics

The planets move around the Sun in almost circular orbits. The same is true for moons and artificial satellites orbiting planets. The orbits of comets around the Sun are usually highly elliptical — some travel from near to the Sun to the outskirts of our Solar System.

For all of these objects, gravity is the force that keeps it in orbit.

Circular motion in orbits

If an object is travelling in a circle, it is constantly changing direction, which means it is constantly accelerating (just like a car going round a roundabout, page 23). This also means that it is constantly changing velocity but not changing speed.

Tip: Velocity is a vector quantity (page 22) — it has a magnitude and a direction.

For an object to accelerate, there must be a force acting on it (page 33). For circular motion, this force is called the centripetal force and it is directed towards the centre of the circle. In the Solar System, the centripetal force is the gravitational force (gravity) between a planet and the Sun (or a planet and its satellites).

An orbit is a balance between the force providing the acceleration and the forward motion (**instantaneous velocity**) of the object. The object keeps accelerating towards what it's orbiting, but the instantaneous velocity (which is at right angles to the acceleration and to the force of gravity) keeps it travelling in a circle — see Figure 5. So for a planet in a circular orbit, gravity leads to the velocity of the planet constantly changing whilst its speed remains constant.

Tip: As the orbits of planets around the Sun are almost circular, we treat them as perfectly circular to make calculations easier.

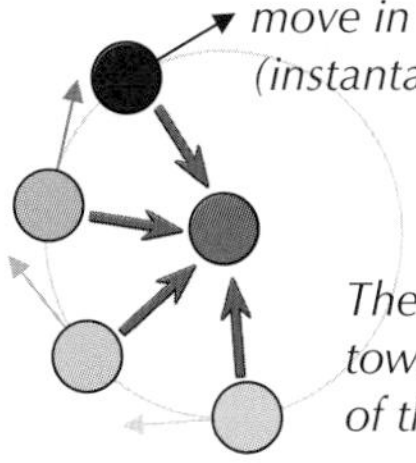

The planet is 'trying' to move in this direction (instantaneous velocity).

The force is always towards the centre of the circle.

Figure 5: A diagram of a planet orbiting around the Sun, showing its instantaneous velocity (black arrows) and the gravitational force (blue arrows).

Orbital speed and radius

Back on page 37 you saw that the weight (i.e. the force on an object due to gravity) of any object varies depending on the strength (g) of the gravitational field that it is in.

Gravitational field strength depends on the mass of the body creating the field. The larger the mass of the body, the stronger its gravitational field.

Figure 6: Johannes Kepler came up with three laws to describe orbits, including the idea that the smaller the orbital radius, the faster the orbiting object must travel.

Example

The Moon has a mass of about 7.3×10^{22} kg. Its gravitational field strength is about 1.6 N/kg. The Earth, on the other hand, has a much bigger mass of around 6.0×10^{24} kg. So it creates a much stronger gravitational field — g on Earth is around 9.8 N/kg.

This means the weight of any given object on the surface of Earth would be less if the object was on the surface of the Moon.

Tip: The fact that
different planets orbit
the Sun at different
speeds means that the
distances between
planets vary over time.

Gravitational field strength also varies with distance. The closer you get to a
star or planet, the stronger the gravitational force. The stronger the force, the
larger the instantaneous velocity needed to balance it. So the closer to a star
or planet an object gets, the faster it needs to go to remain in orbit.

This means that for an object in a stable orbit, if the speed of the object
changes, the size (radius) of its orbit must do so too. If the object moves faster,
the radius of its orbit must be smaller. If it moves slower, the radius must be
larger — see Figure 7.

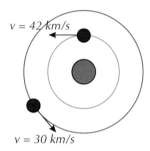

Figure 7: *A diagram of two different orbits around a body,
showing how distance (radius) affects speed.*

Practice Questions — Fact Recall

Tip: If you struggle to
remember the difference
between the geocentric
and heliocentric models,
think of the word
geography (studying the
Earth) to help.

Q1 Describe the geocentric model of the Solar System.
Explain how this is different to the current model of the Solar System.

Q2 Name the planets in our Solar System, in order of their distance from
the Sun.

Q3 State what is meant by a 'natural satellite', and give one example.

Q4 What type of object orbits the Sun with a highly elliptical orbit?

Q5 What causes the centripetal force that keeps the Earth in orbit around
the Sun?

Practice Question — Application

Q1 If the Earth moved towards the Sun, what would happen to the speed
of its orbit, provided it were to remain in a stable orbit? Why?

2. The Life Cycle of Stars

Stars give out a huge amount of energy — this is fuelled by nuclear fusion inside the star. These pages are all about how stars are formed and what happens to stars once all of their fuel runs out.

The formation of stars

Stars initially form from a cloud of dust and gas (mainly hydrogen) called a **nebula**. The force of gravity makes the gas and dust spiral in together to form a **protostar** — see Figure 4. Gravitational attraction causes the density of the protostar to increase and particles within the protostar to collide with each other more frequently, so the temperature rises.

When the temperature gets high enough, hydrogen nuclei begin to undergo nuclear fusion (see pages 174-175) to form helium nuclei in the core of the star. This gives out massive amounts of energy which keeps the core of the star hot. At this point, a star is born. Smaller masses of gas and dust around the star may also be pulled together to make planets that orbit the star.

Main sequence stars

Once a star has been formed, it immediately enters a long stable period. During this time it is described as being on the main sequence. The energy released by the nuclear fusion provides an outward pressure that tries to expand the star (thermal expansion), which balances the force of gravity pulling everything inwards. It is in equilibrium and so does not expand or contract. In this stable period it's called a **main sequence star**.

This stage typically lasts several billion years, but the more mass a star has, the shorter its time on the main sequence. This is because more massive stars use up fuel in their cores much quicker than smaller stars, even though they contain more fuel than smaller stars. The Sun is a stable main sequence star in the middle of this stable period.

The death of stars

Eventually the hydrogen in the core of a star begins to run out. The force due to gravity becomes larger than the pressure of thermal expansion. The star is compressed, until it is dense and hot enough that the energy released makes the outer layers of the star expand.

Stars about the same mass as the Sun

A small to medium-sized star, with a mass similar to the Sun will expand into a **red giant** when it starts to run out of hydrogen. It becomes red because the surface cools.

It then becomes unstable and ejects its outer layer of dust and gas as a planetary nebula. This leaves behind a hot, dense solid core — a **white dwarf**. As a white dwarf cools down, it emits less and less energy and eventually it will disappear from sight.

Learning Objectives:

- Be able to describe the evolution of stars of similar mass to the Sun through the following stages:
  a nebula
  b star (main sequence)
  c red giant
  d white dwarf.
- Be able to explain how the balance between thermal expansion and gravity affects the life cycle of stars.
- Be able to describe the evolution of stars with a mass larger than the Sun.

Specification References 7.16-7.18

Figure 1: *Our Sun is a main sequence star. It will spend a total of about 10 billion years on the main sequence.*

Figure 2: *A star cluster — the orange star in the centre is a red giant.*

Stars with a much larger mass than the Sun

Stars that are larger and have more mass than the Sun expand into **red supergiants** when they start to run out of hydrogen. Red supergiants are much bigger and brighter than regular red giants. They expand and contract several times, forming elements as heavy as iron in various nuclear reactions.

Eventually they run out of elements to fuse and become unstable. They explode in a **supernova**, forming elements heavier than iron and ejecting them into the Universe to form new planets and stars.

The exploding supernova throws the outer layers of dust and gas into space, leaving a very dense core called a **neutron star**. If the star is big enough, it will become a **black hole** instead — a super dense point in space that nothing can escape from (see Figure 4).

Figure 3: *The remnants of a supernova.*

Tip: Black holes don't emit any light, so you can't actually see them.

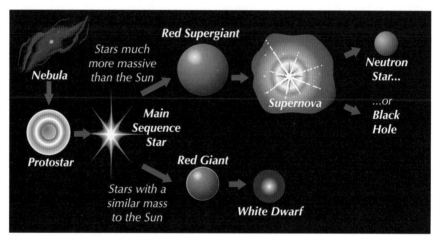

Figure 4: *A flow diagram to show the life cycles of stars that are about the same mass as the Sun and stars with a much greater mass than the Sun.*

Practice Questions — Fact Recall

Q1   How are stars formed?

Q2   Explain why main sequence stars are stable.

Q3   Describe the stages that a star with the same mass as the Sun will go through when it stops being a main sequence star.

Practice Question — Application

Q1   Melnick-34 is a star that has a much larger mass than the Sun. State whether it will form a white dwarf, or a black hole.

3. Observing the Universe

Learning Objective:

- Be able to describe
how methods
of observing the
Universe have
changed over time
including why some
telescopes are located
outside the Earth's
atmosphere.

**Specification Reference
7.19**

*The invention of telescopes completely changed how the Solar System was
viewed, but it didn't stop there. Advancements in technology have allowed us
to see further and to form theories on how the Universe itself was created.*

Optical telescopes

Telescopes help you to see distant objects clearly and are used to observe the
Universe. There are loads of different kinds and they all work in different ways
(see below). The one you're most likely to have seen is an optical telescope —
ones that detect visible light.

There are three main types of optical telescopes: refracting telescopes which
use lenses, reflecting telescopes which use mirrors and telescopes that use a
combination of lenses and mirrors.

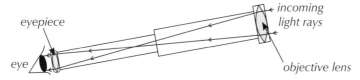

eyepiece *incoming
light rays*

eye *objective lens*

Figure 2: *A basic diagram of light being refracted in a refracting telescope.*

Figure 1: *An optical
telescope.*

Evolution of telescopes over time

The earliest type of telescope was the optical telescope. But from the
1940s onwards, telescopes were developed to detect other parts of the
electromagnetic (EM) spectrum (page 127). These modern telescopes mean
we can now 'see' parts of the Universe that we couldn't see before and learn
more about the Universe, e.g. its structure.

> **Examples**
>
> X-ray telescopes are a good way to 'see' violent, high-temperature events
> in space, like exploding stars. And radio telescopes were responsible for
> the discovery of the cosmic microwave background radiation (page 192)
> — this helped scientists to learn more about the origins of the Universe.

Telescopes are improving all the time — bigger telescopes give us better
resolution (i.e. a lot of detail) and can gather more light, so we can see things
we couldn't before as they were too faint. Improved magnification means we
can now look further into space — leading to more and more galaxies being
discovered.

Figure 3: *A radio telescope,
similar to the one used to
detect cosmic microwave
background radiation.*

Modern telescopes often work alongside computers. Computers help create
clearer and sharper images and make it easy to capture these pictures so
they can be analysed later. Computers also make it possible to collect
and store huge amounts of data, 24 hours a day, without having to rely on
humans. They also make it easier and quicker to analyse all this data.

Image quality

The quality of the image produced by a telescope can be affected by the telescope itself. The diameter of the objective lens (the **aperture** of the telescope) and its quality both affect image quality — using a larger aperture or a higher quality lens (e.g. one that is made from glass that has few imperfections) will improve the image produced.

The location of the telescope can also have a large effect on image quality. The Earth's atmosphere absorbs a lot of the electromagnetic radiation coming from space before it can reach telescopes on the Earth's surface. To observe the frequencies absorbed, you have to go above the atmosphere.

The atmosphere also distorts the EM radiation that does reach telescopes on the Earth's surface, by refracting it (p.99) multiple times. Refraction of visible light is what makes stars appear to 'twinkle'. The less atmosphere there is above a telescope, the less distortion there is in the image seen through the telescope.

On Earth, light pollution (light thrown up into the sky from street lamps, etc.) makes it hard to pick out dim objects in the sky. And air pollution (smoke, dust, etc.) can reflect and absorb light (and other radiation) coming from space.

So to get the best view possible from Earth, a telescope should be on top of a mountain (where there's less atmosphere above it), and in a dark place away from cities (e.g. on Hawaii).

To avoid these issues entirely, some telescopes are put into space, most often in orbits around the Earth. One of the most famous space telescopes is the Hubble Space Telescope, shown in Figure 4. Its images have led to numerous scientific advances, including helping to determine the age of the Universe (page 193).

Tip: If you're taking a photo through a telescope, increasing the exposure time increases the quality of the image.

Figure 4: *The Hubble Space Telescope was launched in 1990.*

Practice Questions — Fact Recall

Q1 How does the aperture of a telescope affect its image quality?

Q2 Describe how methods of observing electromagnetic radiation from space have changed over time.

Q3 Explain why many telescopes on Earth are situated high up on mountains, away from towns and cities.

4. Red-shift and CMB Radiation

Learning Objectives:
- Be able to describe that if a wave source is moving relative to an observer there will be a change in the observed frequency and wavelength.
- Be able to describe the red-shift in light received from galaxies at different distances away from the Earth.
- Be able to explain why the red-shift of galaxies provides evidence for the Universe expanding.
- Be able to compare the Steady State and Big Bang theories.
- Be able to explain how both the Big Bang and Steady State theories of the origin of the Universe both account for red-shift of galaxies.
- Be able to describe evidence supporting the Big Bang theory, limited to red-shift and the cosmic microwave background (CMB) radiation.
- Be able to explain how the discovery of the CMB radiation led to the Big Bang theory becoming the currently accepted model.
- Be able to recall that as there is more evidence supporting the Big Bang theory than the Steady State theory, it is the currently accepted model for the origin of the Universe.

Specification References 7.8-7.15

Red-shift and cosmic microwave background radiation have allowed scientists to gain a better understanding of how the Universe is behaving, as well as supporting theories describing the creation of the Universe...

Red-shift and the Doppler effect

You'll have experienced the **Doppler effect** loads of times with sound waves. Imagine a police car driving past you. As it moves towards you its siren sounds higher-pitched than it would if it were stationary. As it moves away from you, its pitch is lower. This change in frequency and wavelength is called the Doppler effect.

The frequency and the wavelength change because the waves bunch together in front of the source and stretch out behind it (see Figure 1). The amount of stretching or bunching together depends on the speed of the source.

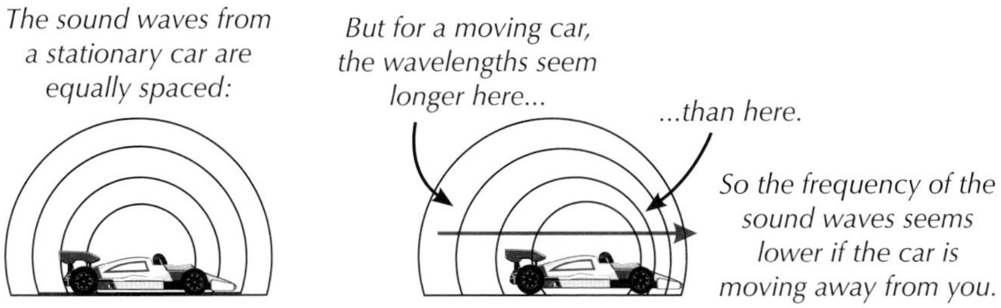

The sound waves from a stationary car are equally spaced:

But for a moving car, the wavelengths seem longer here...

...than here.

So the frequency of the sound waves seems lower if the car is moving away from you.

Figure 1: *A diagram showing the Doppler effect for sound.*

The Doppler effect happens with all waves, including electromagnetic waves like light. When we look at light from many distant galaxies (a collection of lots of stars held together by gravity) we find that its wavelength is longer than it should be. The light we detect is shifted towards the red end of the visible spectrum (see page 137). In other words, the light that we receive from the galaxy is redder than the actual light emitted by the galaxy.

This effect is called **red-shift**. It shows us that the galaxy the light has come from is moving away from the Earth. The faster the galaxy is moving away from us, the larger the red-shift.

Measuring red-shift

You can measure red-shift by looking at **absorption spectra**. These are patterns of dark lines in the visible light spectrum that are caused by certain wavelengths of light being absorbed. Each element absorbs particular wavelengths of visible light, so the pattern of lines it creates is always the same.

Scientists compare absorption spectra from distant galaxies to absorption spectra in their lab to see how much red-shift has occurred. They take a particular pattern — e.g. the pattern made by helium — and look at how far each matching absorption line has moved in the galaxy's absorption spectra (see Figure 2 on the next page). The scientists can measure the change in wavelength that lets them calculate red-shift.

Light on Earth

Light from distant galaxy

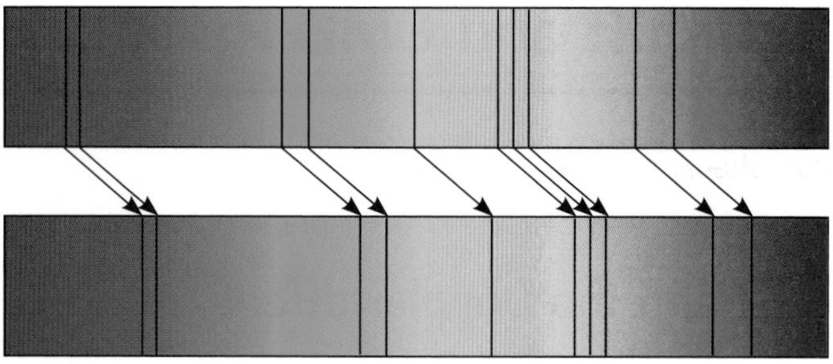

Figure 2: *An absorption spectrum for light from a distant galaxy compared to an absorption spectrum for light on Earth.*

Tip: The more the absorption lines have moved, the more the light from the galaxy is red-shifted and the faster it's moving away from us.

The expansion of the Universe

As the light from the majority of distant galaxies has been red-shifted, this suggests that the galaxies are moving away from us. Measurements of the red-shift indicate that most distant galaxies are moving away from us (receding) very quickly — and it's the same result whatever direction you look in.

Tip: You can think of space 'stretching' as it expands — which 'stretches out' light waves as they travel between two objects, causing red-shift.

More distant galaxies have a greater red-shift than nearer ones. This means that more distant galaxies are moving away faster than the nearer ones. This suggests that all galaxies are moving away from each other. The conclusion of these results is that the whole Universe (space itself) is expanding.

Example

To understand the expansion of the Universe, imagine a balloon covered with pompoms. As you blow into the balloon, it stretches. The pompoms move further away from each other, but each pompom stays the same size.

The balloon represents the Universe, and each pompom is a galaxy. As time goes on, space stretches and expands, moving galaxies away from each other. The galaxies are held together by gravity and so don't stretch themselves.

This is a simple model (balloons only stretch so far, and there would be galaxies 'inside' the balloon too) but it shows how the expansion of space makes it look like galaxies are moving away from us.

Cosmic microwave background radiation

Astronomers using radio telescopes in the 1960s unexpectedly discovered low-frequency EM radiation that was present in all of their measurements, no matter the time of day. This radiation comes from all parts of the Universe and is mainly in the microwave part of the electromagnetic spectrum. It's known as **cosmic microwave background radiation** (CMB radiation).

Figure 3: *Arno Penzias and Robert Wilson, the two astronomers who discovered CMB radiation.*

Theories of the origin of the Universe

Over time there have been many different theories to explain how the Universe and everything in it began. The ones you need to know are the **Steady State theory** and the **Big Bang theory**.

The Steady State theory

The Steady State theory says that the Universe has no beginning and no end. It has always existed as it is now, and it always will do.

It's based on the idea that the Universe looks pretty much the same in all directions from any point (i.e. it's uniform on a large scale). The theory says that as the Universe expands, new matter is constantly being created, so the density of the Universe is always roughly the same.

The Big Bang theory

All galaxies are moving away from each other at great speed — suggesting something must have got them going. That something was probably a big explosion — the Big Bang. The **Big Bang theory** says:

- Initially, all matter in the Universe occupied a very small space. This tiny space was very dense (page 296) and so was very hot.

- Then it 'exploded' — space started expanding, and so got less dense, and the expansion is still going on.

This theory gives a finite age to the Universe — around 13.8 billion years.

Evidence supporting the theories

Red-shift can be used as evidence for both the Steady State and Big Bang theories. Both theories account for the Universe expanding, so red-shift would be present in any measurements taken in either model.

CMB radiation is theorised to be leftover energy from an initial explosion that has cooled over time. This suggests that the Universe had a beginning, which provides evidence in support of the Big Bang theory and disproves the Steady State theory. As there is currently more evidence to support the Big Bang theory than the Steady State theory, the Big Bang theory is the currently accepted model of how the Universe began.

Exam Tip
WORKING SCIENTIFICALLY
You may be asked to explain how a piece of evidence supports a theory, or how it could lead to other theories being abandoned.

Practice Questions — Fact Recall

Q1 a) How is the light observed from a distant galaxy different from the light that the galaxy actually emits?

b) What is the name given to this effect?

c) How does this effect generally depend on the distance from the galaxy to the Earth?

Q2 a) Compare the Steady State and Big Bang theories.

b) State one observation which contradicts the Steady State theory, and explain why it contradicts the theory.

The Solar System and Orbits

☐ How ideas about the structure of the Solar System have changed over time, to include information about both geocentric and heliocentric models.

☐ That our Solar System has one star, the Sun, which is orbited by eight planets, dwarf planets, asteroids and comets.

☐ The order of the planets from the Sun: Mercury, Venus, Earth, Mars, Jupiter, Saturn, Uranus and Neptune.

☐ That planets orbit the Sun in roughly circular orbits, but comets have highly elliptical orbits.

☐ That natural satellites (e.g. moons) and artificial satellites orbit planets in roughly circular orbits.

☐ That the force of gravity is the centripetal force that acts on planets as they orbit the Sun.

☐ That the velocity of a planet changes whilst its speed remains unchanged.

☐ How and why the weight of an object changes depending on where it is in the Solar System.

☐ How and why gravitational field strength differs between the surface of the Earth and the surface of other bodies in space.

☐ That if an object is in a stable orbit, a change in its speed will cause the radius of its orbit to change.

The Life Cycle of Stars

☐ That a star begins as a cloud of dust and gas called a nebula.

☐ That nebulae are pulled together by gravity to create protostars, which become main sequence stars when their temperature is high enough for fusion to occur.

☐ That fusion of hydrogen occurs in the centre of stars, which creates an outwards pressure in the star, called thermal expansion.

☐ That thermal expansion outwards balances the force of gravity trying to collapse the star inwards whilst the star is on the main sequence.

☐ That when a main sequence star begins to run out of fuel in its core, thermal expansion and gravity are no longer balanced and the star begins to collapse.

☐ That this collapse increases the temperature of the star, causing fusion of heavier elements, which results in thermal expansion becoming larger than the force of gravity. This causes the star's outer layers to expand and cool.

☐ That a star will become a red giant if it has a similar mass to the Sun.

☐ That red giants eject their outer layers and become white dwarfs.

☐ That stars much larger than our Sun become red supergiants.

☐ That red supergiants eventually explode in a supernova.

☐ That supernovae leave behind a neutron star or a black hole.

cont...

Observing the Universe

- [ ] That telescopes allow us to see distant objects.
- [ ] That the Earth's atmosphere absorbs some frequencies of electromagnetic radiation.
- [ ] That light and air pollution reduce the quality of an image seen through a telescope on Earth.
- [ ] That to avoid issues caused by the atmosphere and pollution, some telescopes are placed in space.
- [ ] That telescopes have developed over time to be able to detect electromagnetic radiation outside of the visible spectrum.
- [ ] That the use of computers has made it easier and quicker to collect and analyse data from telescopes.

Red-shift and CMB Radiation

- [ ] That whenever a source of waves is moving relative to an observer, the observed frequency (and wavelength) will be different to the frequency (and wavelength) of the waves emitted.
- [ ] That light from distant galaxies has longer wavelengths than expected, an effect known as red-shift.
- [ ] That the faster a light source moves, the greater the observed red-shift.
- [ ] That red-shift measurements suggest that most galaxies are moving away from us.
- [ ] That galaxies further away appear to be moving away faster than nearer galaxies.
- [ ] That more distant galaxies receding quicker suggests that the Universe is expanding.
- [ ] That cosmic microwave background (CMB) radiation is present across the Universe.
- [ ] That the Steady State theory says the Universe has no beginning and no end, and that the Universe has always been as it appears and always will be.
- [ ] That the Steady State theory says matter is continuously created so the density of the Universe remains constant.
- [ ] That the Big Bang theory says the Universe started in a very small space that was hot and dense and that this small space then exploded, space expanded and it is still expanding now.
- [ ] That the Big Bang theory gives a finite age to the Universe and states that the Universe had a beginning — unlike the Steady State theory.
- [ ] That red-shift measurements of galaxies support both the Steady State theory and the Big Bang theory, because both theories include an explanation of the Universe expanding.
- [ ] That CMB radiation supports the Big Bang theory but not the Steady State theory because it provides evidence that the Universe had a beginning.
- [ ] That the Big Bang theory is the currently accepted model for the origin of the Universe because there is more evidence to support it than there is to support the Steady State theory.

Exam-style Questions

1   The Sun is a main sequence star in the middle of its stable period.
The hydrogen fuel in the Sun's core is expected to run out in about 5 billion years.

   (a)   Explain why a main sequence star does not collapse due to gravitational attraction.

(2 marks)

   (b)   A main sequence star evolves and eventually becomes a black hole. Describe this evolution from a main sequence star to the point of becoming a black hole.

(4 marks)

   (c)   Will the Sun ever become a black hole? Explain your answer.

(1 mark)

   (d)   Suggest whether a star created at around the same time as the Sun, with a mass of half that of the Sun, will have run out of fuel in 5 billion years time.
Explain your answer.

(2 marks)

2*   A planet is orbiting around a star in a stable, circular orbit.
Explain why the planet orbits the star in this way and how the speed of the planet's orbit relates to the radius of its orbit.

(6 marks)

3   Light from most distant galaxies is observed to have been red-shifted.
The more distant a galaxy is, the larger its red-shift.

   (a)   Explain what is meant by the term red-shift, and state when it occurs.

(2 marks)

   (b)   Explain what this observation suggests about our Universe.

(2 marks)

       Measurements of red-shift from a distant galaxy are taken at an observatory on the Earth's surface.

   (c)   The angular resolution of a telescope describes the smallest distance between objects that the telescope can distinguish. The telescope used at the observatory has an aperture of 10.0 m.

       Calculate its angular resolution for light with a wavelength of $\lambda = 650$ nm.
Give your answer in radians. Use the equation:

$$\text{Angular resolution (in radians)} = \frac{\text{wavelength (in metres)}}{\text{aperture (in metres)}}$$

(2 marks)

   (d)   The observatory also uses a space telescope to detect radiation from the same galaxy.
Explain the benefits of using a telescope located in space rather than on Earth.

(3 marks)

1. Energy Transfers and Systems

*How energy is stored and transferred should be familiar to you
from pages 61-65. It's really important for this section too.*

(see page 65)

Systems and energy transfers

Whenever a system (p.61) changes, energy is transferred. A system can be
changed by forces doing work, electrical equipment doing work or by heating.
Remember that a closed system is one that's defined so that the net change in
energy is zero.

You can use diagrams such as Figure 1 to show energy transfers between
different energy stores (see page 65).

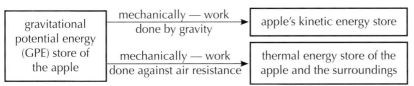

Figure 1: *An energy transfer diagram for an apple falling from a tree.
The boxes represent energy stores, and the arrows show energy transfers.*

Whenever a system changes, some energy is dissipated (stored in less useful
ways). The efficiency of a transfer is the proportion of the total energy
supplied that ends up in useful energy stores (p.64). Figure 2 is a type of
energy transfer diagram that shows energy transfers to scale, and which can be
used to calculate efficiency.

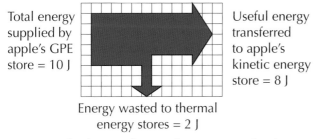

Total energy supplied by apple's GPE store = 10 J

Useful energy transferred to apple's kinetic energy store = 8 J

Energy wasted to thermal energy stores = 2 J

Figure 2: *Energy transfer diagram showing the energy transfers for an apple falling
from a tree. The width of each arrow represents the amount of energy transferred.*

Work done by forces

Energy is transferred mechanically when work is done by or against a force
(see page 199 for more on work done).

> **Example**
>
> A box is lifted up off of the floor. The box is the system. As the box is
> lifted, work is done against gravity. This causes energy to be transferred
> to the box's kinetic and gravitational potential energy stores.

Learning Objectives:

- Be able to describe the changes involved in the way energy is stored when systems change.
- Be able to explain that where there are energy transfers in a closed system there is no net change to the total energy in that system.
- Be able to draw and interpret diagrams to represent energy transfers.
- Be able to identify the different ways that the energy of a system can be changed through work done by forces, in electrical equipment and in heating.

**Specification References
8.1-8.4**

Tip: The type of diagram shown in Figure 2 can be used to calculate the efficiency of a process. See p.72 for more about this.

Tip: If the box was dropped, the gravitational force would do work to transfer energy from the box's GPE store to its kinetic energy store.

Electrical equipment

Electrical devices work by transferring energy between different energy stores.

> **Example 1**
>
> An electric toothbrush is a system. It transfers some energy electrically from the chemical energy store of its battery to the kinetic energy store of its bristles. Some energy is transferred out of the system to the surroundings by sound and by heating.

> **Example 2**
>
> A hair dryer is a system. It transfers energy into the system electrically from the mains supply to the kinetic energy store of the fan inside of it.
>
> It also transfers energy electrically to the thermal energy store of the heating element and some energy is transferred away by sound.

Figure 3: *An electric toothbrush. The toothbrush is powered by a battery during use, but is shown here being charged by electricity from the mains supply.*

Heating

Heating is the transfer of energy from the thermal energy store of a hotter object to the thermal energy store of a colder object.

> **Example**
>
> Figure 4 shows a pan of water being heated on a gas camping stove.
>
> When the system is the pan of water, energy is transferred into the system by heating to the thermal energy stores of the pan and the water, which increases their temperature.
>
> When the system is the camping stove and the pan, energy is transferred from the chemical energy store of the gas to the thermal energy stores of the pan and the water, increasing their temperature.

Figure 4: *A pan of water being heated on a gas camping stove. You could define the system as just the pan of water, or the stove, or both.*

Practice Questions — Fact Recall

Q1   What is a closed system?

Q2   Give three ways that the energy of a system can be changed.

Practice Questions — Application

Q1   Draw an energy transfer diagram for an electric kettle. Treat the kettle, and the water and air inside it as a system.

Q2   Describe the energy transfers in the following systems:

a) a skier skiing down a slope,

b) a Bunsen burner being used to heat a beaker of water.

2. Work Done

If a force moves an object from one position to another, energy must be transferred from one energy store to another.

What is work done?

In physics 'work done' has a specific meaning, and you need to know what that is.

> Work done is the energy transferred when a force moves an object through a distance.

Whenever something moves, something else might be providing some sort of 'effort' to move it, as shown in Figure 1. The thing putting the effort in needs a source of energy (like fuel or food etc.). It then does 'work' by moving the object — energy is transferred mechanically from one store to another.

Energy is transferred from the chemical energy store of the person to their kinetic energy store.

Energy is transferred to the kinetic energy store of the broom, causing it to move through a distance, so work is done.

Figure 1: *A diagram showing how work is done when a person supplies energy to a broom and sweeps.*

Whether this energy is transferred 'usefully' (e.g. by pushing a broom) or is 'wasted' (e.g. transferred to the thermal energy stores of the surroundings), you can still say that 'work is done'.

So work done is simply the energy transferred when a force acts on an object. You can work out how much work is done using the following formula:

$$E = \text{work done (J)} \longrightarrow E = F \times d \longleftarrow \begin{array}{l} F = \text{force (N)} \\ d = \text{distance moved in the direction of the force (m)} \end{array}$$

One joule of work is done when a force of one newton causes an object to move a distance of one metre. So one joule is equal to one newton-metre.

Example

Some kids drag a tractor tyre 5.0 m over the ground. They pull with a resultant force of 340 N in the direction of motion. Find the work done to move the tyre.

Force = 340 N   Distance = 5.0 m

Then put the numbers into the formula for work done:

$$E = F \times d = 340 \times 5.0 = 1700 \text{ J}$$

Learning Objectives:
- Be able to describe how to measure the work done by a force and understand that energy transferred (joule, J) is equal to work done (joule, J).
- Be able to recall and use the equation: $E = F \times d$.
- Be able to recall and use the equation to calculate the change in gravitational PE when an object is raised above the ground: $\Delta GPE = m \times g \times \Delta h$.
- Be able to recall and use the equations to calculate the amounts of energy associated with a moving object: $KE = \frac{1}{2} \times m \times v^2$.
- Be able to describe and calculate the changes in energy involved when a system is changed by work done by forces.

Specification References
8.5-8.9

Tip: The amount of work done is not affected by how fast the object is moving, just the size of the force and the distance moved.

Tip: The formula triangle for this equation is:

Calculating energy transfers

When work is done, energy is transferred. Usually, you'll be dealing with examples where this energy is transferred to useful stores (stores you want energy to be in), like kinetic or gravitational potential energy stores.

You'll need to know the following equations from p.66 and p.67 in order to calculate how doing work changes the energy of a system:

from p.66 and p.67

ΔGPE = change in gravitational potential energy (J) → $\Delta GPE = m \times g \times \Delta h$ ← Δh = change in vertical height (m)

m = mass (kg) g = gravitational field strength (N/kg)

KE = kinetic energy (J) → $KE = \frac{1}{2} \times m \times v^2$ ← m = mass (kg) v^2 = (speed)^2 ((m/s)^2)

Figure 2: A wheelchair user pushing the wheels of her chair. She does work against friction by transferring energy from her chemical energy store, to her kinetic energy store and then to the kinetic energy store of the chair.

Example

A brick is lifted using a resultant upwards force of 45 N. The brick moves a vertical distance of 1.4 m. Find the mass of the brick, assuming all of the energy is transferred to the brick's GPE store. (g = 10 N/kg.)

Calculate work done: $E = F \times d = 45 \times 1.4 = 63$ J

So the energy transferred to the GPE store, $\Delta GPE = 63$ J, and $\Delta h = 1.4$ m.

Rearranging $\Delta GPE = m \times g \times \Delta h$,

$$m = \Delta GPE \div (g \times \Delta h) = 63 \div (10 \times 1.4) = 4.5 \text{ kg}$$

Practice Questions — Application

Q1   A child pulls a sledge across snow for 14 m. The resultant horizontal force applied over this distance is 24 N. Calculate the work done to move the sledge.

Q2   a) A bike is pushed 20 m using a steady force of 250 N in the direction of motion. How much energy is transferred?

b) If the bike continues to be pushed with the same force, calculate how far the bike will move if 750 J of work is done.

c) The bike has a mass of 10 kg. Find its speed after the first 2 m of being pushed, assuming that all the energy supplied is transferred to the bike's kinetic energy store.

Q3   A ball of mass 0.1 kg is pushed up a slope by a force. It moves a distance of 0.5 m in the direction of the force, and is raised through a vertical height of 0.3 m. Find the size of the force, assuming all of the work done by the force transfers energy to the ball's GPE store. (g = 10 N/kg.)

3. Dissipation of Energy

Whenever energy is transferred by a device, it's likely that some will be dissipated (wasted) instead of being put to good use. Efficiency is a great way to see how well (or how uselessly) a device transfers energy.

How is energy 'dissipated'?

A force doing work often causes a rise in temperature as some energy is dissipated to the thermal energy stores of the moving object and its surroundings.

When you push something along a rough surface (like a carpet) you are doing work against frictional forces. Energy is transferred to the kinetic energy store of the object because it starts moving, but some is also transferred to the thermal energy stores of the object, the surface and the surroundings due to friction. This causes the overall temperature of the object and surface to increase.

> **Example**
>
> When you rub your hands together, the work done against friction causes energy to be transferred to your hand's thermal energy stores. In this case, the energy transfer is useful, as you want to warm up your hands.

When mechanical processes cause this rise in temperature, we usually say they are 'wasteful', because less of the total energy supplied can be transferred to useful energy stores, such as gravitational potential and kinetic energy stores.

> **Example**
>
> A motor will feel warm to the touch after it has been running for a while. This is because of the work done against friction between touching parts of the motor as it spins. This energy is dissipated to the thermal energy stores of the motor and the air around it, leaving less energy to be transferred to useful stores (like the kinetic energy stores of blades of a fan).

Lubrication

For objects that are being rubbed together, lubricants can be used to reduce the friction between the objects' surfaces when they move, which reduces the energy dissipated. There's more about lubricants and reducing unwanted energy transfers over on page 70.

Efficiency of a device

The less wasteful an energy transfer process, the higher its efficiency:

$$\text{efficiency} = \frac{\text{useful energy transferred by the device}}{\text{total energy supplied to the device}}$$

Learning Objectives:

- Be able to explain that mechanical processes become wasteful when they cause a rise in temperature so dissipating energy in heating the surroundings.

- Be able to explain, using examples, how in all system changes energy is dissipated so that it is stored in less useful ways.

- Be able to explain ways of reducing unwanted energy transfer through lubrication.

- Be able to recall and use the equation: efficiency = (useful energy transferred by the device) ÷ (total energy supplied to the device).

Specification References 8.10, 8.11, 8.15, 9.10

Tip: Air resistance causes a frictional force on an object moving through the air.

Tip: Look back at pages 71-73 if you need a recap on efficiency — it's covered in much more detail in Section 2.

Example 1

A motor does 10 J of work to accelerate a toy car from rest to a speed of 4 m/s. The car has a mass of 1 kg. Calculate the efficiency of the motor.

Energy supplied to the car = work done by motor = 10 J

Energy usefully transferred to the car's kinetic energy store:

$$KE = \frac{1}{2} \times m \times v^2 = \frac{1}{2} \times 1 \times 4^2 = 8 \text{ J}$$

Substitute these values into the equation:

$$\text{efficiency} = \frac{\text{useful energy transferred by the device}}{\text{total energy supplied to the device}} = \frac{8}{10} = 0.8$$

Tip: You need to know how to find efficiency as a percentage as well as a decimal — see p.342.

Example 2

An electric fan is supplied with 2000 kJ of energy. 600 kJ of that is dissipated. What is the efficiency of the fan as a percentage?

Total energy transferred = 2000 kJ

Useful energy transferred = 2000 − 600 = 1400 kJ

Start by working out the efficiency as a decimal:

$$\text{efficiency} = \frac{\text{useful energy transferred by the device}}{\text{total energy supplied to the device}} = \frac{1400}{2000} = 0.7$$

Then, multiply this by 100 to get the efficiency of the fan as a percentage:

$$\text{efficiency} = 0.7 \times 100 = 70\%$$

Figure 1: *An electric fan. Friction between the moving parts will cause them to heat up, wasting some of the energy supplied.*

Practice Questions — Fact Recall

Q1 Explain why mechanical processes are wasteful.

Q2 State the equation for calculating the efficiency of a device.

Practice Question — Application

Q1 A motorised lift does 500 kJ of work to raise a total mass of 2000 kg through a height of 15 m.

a) What is the efficiency of the lift, as a percentage? (g = 10 N/kg.)

b) Suggest a way to reduce unwanted energy transfers in the lift.

Tip: Remember, the energy transferred to an object's gravitational potential energy store can be found using:
$\Delta GPE = m \times g \times \Delta h$.

4. Power

Power is a really important concept that pops up all over the place because power is all about how quickly energy is transferred.

What is power?

Power is the rate of energy transfer, or the rate of doing work — in other words, how much energy is transferred or how much work is done every second. Power is measured in watts, W. One watt is equivalent to one joule transferred per second (J/s).

You can calculate power using this equation:

$$P = \frac{E}{t}$$

P = power (W)
E = work done (J)
t = time taken (s)

Learning Objectives:

- Be able to define power as the rate at which energy is transferred and use examples to explain this definition.
- Be able to recall that one watt is equal to one joule per second, J/s.
- Be able to recall and use the equation: $P = E \div t$.

Specification References 8.12-8.14

Example 1

A rock climber does 4.8 kJ of work scaling a rock face in 2 minutes. Find her power.

Work done = 4.8 kJ = 4.8 × 1000 = 4800 J
Time taken = 2 minutes = 2 × 60 s = 120 s

$$P = \frac{E}{t} = \frac{4800}{120} = 40 \text{ W (or 40 J/s)}$$

Tip: Watch out for common prefixes in units. Here 1 kJ = 1000 J, because the prefix 'kilo' means '1000'. See page 18 for more on this.

Example 2

Lifting a box onto a shelf requires 11 J of work. How long would it take a person to lift one box with a power of 55 W?

Rearranging $P = E \div t$,
$t = E \div P$
$= 11 \div 55$
$= 0.2$ s

Tip: This formula triangle might help with rearranging the power equation:

A powerful machine is not necessarily one which can exert a strong force (although it usually ends up that way). A powerful machine is one which transfers a lot of energy (or does a lot of work) in a short space of time.

Example

Consider two cars that are identical in every way apart from the power of their engines. Both cars race the same distance along a straight race track to a finish line. The car with the more powerful engine will reach the finish line faster than the other car — i.e. it will transfer the same amount of energy, but over less time.

Figure 1: *'Supercars' have engine powers of 400-500 kW — around 5 times higher than a typical car.*

Figure 2: *Lifting machines, such as this cherry picker, exert a force against a person's weight to move them through a vertical height. A more powerful machine could lift a larger weight in the same time, or the same weight in a shorter time.*

Example

It takes 8000 J of work to lift a stunt performer to the top of a building. Motor A can lift the stunt performer to the correct height in 50 s. Motor B would take 300 s to lift the performer to the same height. Which motor is most powerful? Calculate the power of this motor.

Both motors do the same amount of work, but motor A would do it quicker than motor B. So, motor A is the more powerful motor.

Plug the time taken and work done for motor A into the equation $P = E \div t$ and find the power.

$$P = E \div t = 8000 \div 50 = 160 \text{ W}$$

Practice Questions — Fact Recall

Q1 What is meant by the term 'power'?

Q2 State the equation for power. What does each term represent and what units are they measured in?

Practice Questions — Application

Q1 Find the power of the following:

a) A hill walker who does 1500 J of work in 37.5 s.

b) A weightlifter who does 7.98 kJ of work in 42 s.

c) A motor that does 6840 kJ of work in 9.5 minutes.

Q2 Two lifts, A and B, operate between the ground floor and the second floor of a building. Lift A's motor has a power of 4800 W, and lift B's motor has a power of 5200 W. They are otherwise identical and have the same efficiency. State which of the two lifts will carry a given load up the two floors in the least time, and explain why.

Q3 How long does it take for a 525 W motor to do 1344 J of work?

Q4 How much work is done by a machine with a power of 1240 W running for 35 s?

Tip: Remember —
1 kJ = 1000 J (see p.18).

5. Force Basics

You've met forces before in Section 1, so you should recall that they are vectors because they have a magnitude and a direction. Here we'll be looking at some examples of contact and non-contact forces.

Vectors and scalars

Force is a vector quantity — vector quantities have a magnitude (size) and a direction. Lots of physical quantities are vector quantities — some examples are force, velocity, displacement, acceleration and momentum.

Some physical quantities have magnitude but no direction. These are called scalar quantities, and some examples are speed, distance, mass, temperature and time.

Contact and non-contact forces

A force is a push or a pull on an object that is caused by it interacting with something. All forces are either **contact** or **non-contact forces**.

When two objects have to be touching for a force to act, that force is called a contact force. For example, friction, air resistance, tension in ropes and the normal contact force (page 42) are all contact forces.

Examples

- For a moving car, friction acts between the tyres and the road, and air resistance acts between the body of the car and the air. Both forces act in the opposite direction to the car's movement.

- When a person sits on a stool, there is a normal contact force between the person and the stool, opposing the person's weight.

- Tension acts when something is pulled or stretched. A dog pulling on a lead held by a dog-walker will produce a tension force in the lead.

If the objects do not need to be touching for the force to act, the force is a non-contact force. This type of force is usually caused by interacting fields. Magnetic forces, gravitational forces and electrostatic forces are all non-contact forces.

Examples

- The gravitational attraction between the Earth and the Moon is caused by their gravitational fields interacting.

- Magnetic fields (p.269) cause attraction or repulsion between two bar magnets, depending on which poles are facing each other.

- The electrostatic force causing attraction and repulsion between electrical charges (p.264) is due to interactions between their electric fields. Brushing your hair can lead to a build-up of electrical charges on individual hairs so that they repel each other and stand on end.

Learning Objectives:

- Be able to explain the difference between vector and scalar quantities using examples.

- Be able to describe, with examples, how objects can interact by contact, including normal contact force and friction.

- Be able to describe, with examples, how objects can interact at a distance without contact, linking these interactions to the gravitational, electrostatic and magnetic fields involved.

- Be able to describe, with examples, how objects can interact producing pairs of forces which can be represented as vectors.

Specification References 9.1, 9.2

Tip: All touching objects experience normal contact forces. The normal contact force is sometimes called the reaction force.

Figure 1: *A sledge being pulled. The friction and normal contact force between the sledge and the snow, and the tension in the rope, are all contact forces.*

When two objects interact, there is a force produced on both objects. An interaction pair is a pair of forces that are equal and opposite and act on two interacting objects. (This is basically Newton's Third Law — see p.42.) The two forces are the same type of force (e.g. both gravitational).

You can represent interaction pairs, just like all forces, using arrows — the length of the arrow shows the magnitude, and the direction of the arrow shows the direction of the force.

Tip: All vector quantities can be represented by an arrow.

Tip: The attraction between the Sun and the Earth is what causes the Earth to move around (orbit) the Sun. See pages 185-186 for more.

Tip: ⬛ These are not free body force diagrams as the forces are acting on different objects. Free body force diagrams are coming up on the next page.

Examples

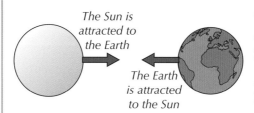

The Sun is attracted to the Earth

The Earth is attracted to the Sun

The Sun and the Earth are attracted to each other by a gravitational force. This is a non-contact force. An equal but opposite force of attraction is felt by both the Sun and the Earth.

A chair exerts a force (its weight) on the ground, whilst the ground pushes back at the chair with the same force (the normal contact force). Equal but opposite forces are felt by both the chair and the ground.

Ground pushes on chair

Chair pushes on ground

Practice Questions — Fact Recall

Q1 What is the difference between a vector quantity and a scalar quantity?

Q2 State whether the following are vector quantities or scalar quantities:

a) force   b) acceleration   c) speed   d) velocity

Q3 Give an example of a contact force.

Q4 Give an example of a non-contact force.

Practice Question — Application

Q1 A swimmer pushes off against the wall of a pool (see Figure 2). Describe the interacting forces between the swimmer's feet and the wall as they make contact. You may use a sketch in your answer.

Figure 2: *A swimmer pushing off in a backstroke race.*

6. Finding the Resultant Force

You should remember from page 33 that numerous forces acting on an object can be replaced with a single resultant force. You can calculate the size of this resultant force using free body force diagrams.

Free body force diagrams

A **free body force diagram** shows all the forces acting on an isolated object or a system — i.e. every force acting on the object or system but none of the forces the object or system exerts on the rest of the world.

Each force on the diagram is represented by an arrow — the lengths of the arrows show the relative magnitudes of the forces and the directions of the arrows show the directions of the forces. Free body force diagrams can help you see if there is a resultant (net) force on an object (a single force which has the same effect as all the original forces acting all together, p.33).

Learning Objectives:
- **H** Be able to draw and use free body force diagrams.
- **H** Be able to explain examples of the forces acting on an isolated solid object or a system where several forces lead to a resultant force on an object and the special case of balanced forces when the resultant force is zero.
- **H** Be able to use vector diagrams to illustrate resolution of forces, a net force, and equilibrium situations (scale drawings only).

Specification References 9.3-9.5

Example — **Higher**

This free body force diagram shows the forces acting on a person who's running.

Air resistance acts in the opposite direction to the forwards thrust.

The person's weight acts downwards and the normal contact force acts upwards.

normal contact force from ground

air resistance *thrust*

weight

The weight and normal contact arrows are the same length, so these two forces balance and the resultant vertical force is zero.

The thrust arrow is longer than the air resistance arrow, so there is a resultant force in the direction of motion (forwards).

If the air resistance arrow was the same length as the thrust arrow, then they would balance too. There would be no resultant force and the person would be in equilibrium (see page 209 for more on this).

You can use free body force diagrams to calculate the size of a resultant force, if you know the scale used to draw the diagram (e.g. 1 cm = 100 N). See below for more on how to do this.

Tip: If the runner was in equilibrium, he would move at a constant speed. This is Newton's First Law — see p.33.

Calculating the resultant force

Forces along the same line

If the forces on an object all act along the same line (in the same or opposite directions), the resultant force is found by calculating the sum of all the forces.

To do this, set a direction as being positive. Then add together the magnitudes of all the forces acting in that direction. Subtract the magnitudes of all the forces acting in the opposite direction. The number you are left with is the size of the resultant force, and whether it is positive or negative will tell you what direction it acts in.

Figure 1: *A tug of war is an example of two forces acting in opposite directions. If the two forces have the same magnitude, the rope will not move (see page 33).*

A vintage sports car is driving along with a driving force of 1000 N. Air resistance of 600 N is acting in the opposite direction. What is the resultant horizontal force on the car?

First, draw a free body force diagram for the situation.
We're only interested in the horizontal forces, so we can leave off weight and the normal contact force. You should have a diagram like this:

air resistance
600 N

driving force
1000 N

Set to the right as the positive, then add any forces in this direction and subtract any forces in the opposite direction.

So the resultant force = 1000 − 600 = 400 N (forwards).

Tip: The car is accelerating because a resultant force is acting on it (see page 34).

Scale drawings

For objects where the forces are not all acting in the same line, you can use scale drawings to find the resultant force. First draw all the forces acting on an object 'tip-to-tail', making sure they're to scale and in the correct directions.

Then draw a straight line from the start of the first force to the end of the last force — this is the resultant force. Measure the length of the resultant force on the diagram to find the magnitude and measure the bearing of the force to find its direction (see below).

Tip: H Drawing forces 'to scale' means each unit of length represents the same quantity. E.g. each centimetre drawn represents 1 N of force.

A man is travelling on an electric bicycle. To the right is the free body force diagram for the man.

Find the magnitude and direction of the resultant force.

Start by doing a scale drawing of the forces acting, tip-to-tail. Make sure you choose a sensible scale (e.g. 1 cm = 1 N).

Draw the resultant from the tail of the first arrow to the tip of the last arrow. Measure the length of the resultant with a ruler and use the scale to find the force in N.

Then use a protractor to measure the direction as a bearing.

The resultant force is 5 N on a bearing of 037°.

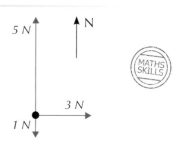

5 N

N

3 N

1 N

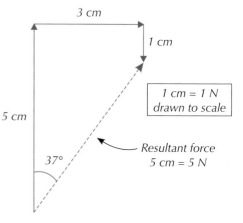

3 cm

1 cm

1 cm = 1 N
drawn to scale

5 cm

Resultant force
5 cm = 5 N

37°

Tip: H You can use any scale you like to work out the resultant force, so long as you scale every force up or down in the same way (e.g. divide all of them by 10). Choose a scale that gives you a clear diagram that's easy to work from.

Tip: H A bearing is an angle measured clockwise from north, given as a 3 digit number, e.g. 10° = 010°.

Balanced forces

If all of the forces acting on an object combine to give a resultant force of zero, the forces are balanced and the object is said to be 'in equilibrium'. On a scale diagram, this means that the tip of the last force you draw should end where the tail of the first force you drew begins. E.g. for three forces, the scale diagram will form a triangle.

Tip: 🅷 For an object in equilibrium, it can be useful to think of the forces 'cancelling each other out'.

Example — Higher

The free body force diagram for an object is shown on the right.

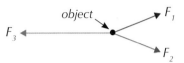

If all the forces acting on the object are drawn tip-to-tail, a complete loop is formed. This shows that the object is in equilibrium.

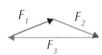

Tip: 🅷 If the object wasn't in equilibrium, the forces wouldn't join up at the end to form a complete loop.

You might be given the forces acting on an object and told to find a missing force, given that the object is in equilibrium. To do this, draw out the forces you do know (to scale and tip-to-tail), then join the end of the last force to the start of the first force. This line is the missing force, so you can measure its size and direction.

Tip: 🅷 When trying to find a missing force for an object in equilibrium, make sure you draw it in the correct direction. All the arrows should point in the same direction around the loop — unlike when you're trying to find the resultant.

Resolving forces

Not all forces act horizontally or vertically — some act at awkward angles. To make these easier to deal with, they can be split into two "components" at right angles to each other (usually horizontal and vertical). Acting together, these components have the same effect as the single force.

You can resolve a force (split it into components) by drawing it on a square grid. Draw the force to scale, and then add the horizontal and vertical components using the grid lines. Then you can just measure them.

Figure 2: A force, F, split into horizontal and vertical components, drawn on a square grid.

Example — Higher

The scale diagram shows a toy car being pulled along horizontally by a string. The tension in the string has a magnitude of 2.5 N. Resolve the tension to find the magnitude of this force acting in the direction of the car's motion.

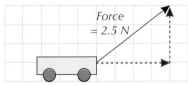

Measure the length of the black arrow — it's 2.5 cm.
The resultant force = 2.5 N, so the scale is 1 cm = 1 N.

The dotted arrows show the force resolved into two components. The car is moving horizontally, and the length of the horizontal component = 2 cm.
So the magnitude of the force acting in the direction of the car's motion = 2 N.

Tip: 🅷 Resolving forces is a bit like the reverse of finding the resultant force. They sound similar, so make sure you don't get them mixed up.

Tip: 🅷 You need to find the scale of the diagram to work out the magnitude of the horizontal component.

Practice Questions — Fact Recall

Q1 What is a free body force diagram?

Q2 Describe how a scale diagram of all the forces acting on an object can be used to determine whether the object is in equilibrium.

Q3 What is meant by 'resolving a force'?

Practice Questions — Application

Q1 A bike is being pushed. The magnitude of the force pushing the bike forwards is equal to 87 N. A resistive force with a magnitude of 24 N is acting in the opposite direction. Find the magnitude and direction of the resultant of these forces.

Q2 A boat is being pulled by three tugboats. The boat also experiences a frictional force from the current. These forces are shown to scale on the diagram below. Using a scale diagram, work out whether the boat is in equilibrium.

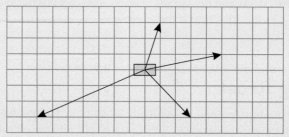

Tip: **H** Don't forget to include the weight and normal contact force in your free body force diagram.

Q3 A box is being dragged along a table. The direction of the force that is pulling the box is parallel to the surface of the table. Draw a free body force diagram to show all the forces acting on the box. (You can assume there is no friction between the box and the table.)

Q4 A train is being pulled along a track (shown in blue) with a force of 20 N. A frictional force and a reaction force from the side of the track act on the train. A scale diagram of the train, as viewed from above, is shown below. By resolving forces, find the resultant force acting on the train in its direction of motion.

Tip: **H** When finding the resultant force in the direction of motion, you don't need to take into account any components that are at right angles to the direction of motion.

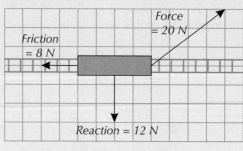

7. Moments

If you apply a force to an object that have a pivot point, like the hands on a clock, it will start turning around the pivot point. This turning effect is important for understanding how levers and gears work.

What is a moment?

A force, or several forces, can cause an object to rotate. The turning effect of a force is called its **moment**. You can calculate the moment of a force using:

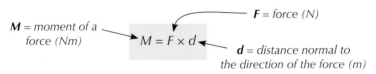

M = moment of a force (Nm)

F = force (N)

$M = F \times d$

d = distance normal to the direction of the force (m)

The distance 'normal' to the direction of the force means the distance between where the force is applied and the pivot, along a line that makes a right angle with the direction of the force — see Figure 1.

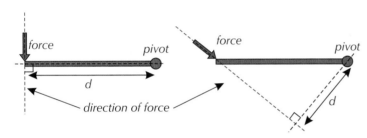

Figure 1: *The same force applied to the same pivoted object at two different angles. Changing the angle at which the force is applied changes the normal distance between the applied force and the pivot (d).*

Examples

The force on this spanner causes a turning effect or moment on the nut (which acts as pivot). A larger force would mean a larger moment.

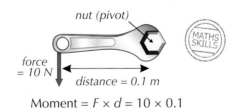

nut (pivot)

force = 10 N

distance = 0.1 m

Moment = $F \times d$ = 10 × 0.1
= 1 Nm

To get the maximum moment (or turning effect) you need to push at right angles (perpendicular) to the spanner.

Pushing at any other angle means a smaller moment because the normal distance between the applied force and the pivot is smaller.

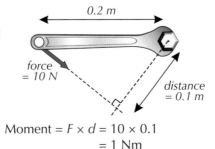

0.2 m

force = 10 N

distance = 0.1 m

Moment = $F \times d$ = 10 × 0.1
= 1 Nm

Learning Objectives:

- Be able to recall and use the equation: moment of a force = force × distance normal to the direction of the force.
- Be able to describe situations where forces can cause rotation.
- Be able to recall and use the principle of moments in situations where rotational forces are in equilibrium: the sum of clockwise moments = the sum of anti-clockwise moments.
- Be able to explain how levers and gears transmit the rotational effects of forces.

Specification References 9.6-9.9

Tip: **H** Changing the angle of the applied force changes the moment because a force can be split into horizontal and vertical components (p.209). Only one of these components will act to turn the object, so as these components change, so does the size of the moment.

Tip: The distance *d* in these examples is measured to the centre of the nut/pivot.

Tip: Using a longer spanner means the same force can exert a larger moment because the distance from the pivot is greater.

Calculating an overall moment

In cases where more than one moment is acting on an object, you can calculate the overall moment on an object. To do this, add together all of the moments that will turn the object clockwise. Then add together all of the moments that will turn it anticlockwise. The difference between these two values is the overall moment on the object.

Objects that have no overall moment won't turn. They're said to be in equilibrium. The **principle of moments** states that for any object in equilibrium:

> the sum of clockwise moments = the sum of anti-clockwise moments

You can combine the principle of moments with the equation from the previous page to find a missing force or distance for an object in equilibrium.

Centre of mass

In some cases, the weight of the object might contribute to the overall moment acting on it. The weight of the object acts downwards from the centre of mass — a single point that you assume the whole mass is concentrated at. For uniform shapes, this point is at their centre.

Most of the time, the pivot is assumed to be at the centre of mass of an object, so you don't have to worry about the object's weight causing a moment.

Figure 2: A spanner being used to tighten a nut on a construction site. The spanner transmits the turning effect of the force, ensuring the nut can be screwed in as tightly as possible.

Tip: To work out which moments are clockwise and which are anticlockwise, think about which direction the force would cause the object to turn if it was the only force acting.

Tip: The centre of mass is usually in the middle of the object unless you're told otherwise — so here it is halfway along the girder's length.

Example

A uniform 6 m long steel girder weighing 1000 N rests horizontally in equilibrium on a pole 1 m from one end. What is the tension in a supporting cable attached vertically to the other end?

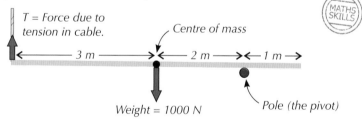

Take moments about the pole:
Anticlockwise: force = weight = 1000 N, distance = 2 m.
So anticlockwise moment = $F \times d$ = 1000 × 2 = 2000 Nm.

Clockwise: force = tension = T, distance = 3 + 2 = 5 m.
So clockwise moment = $F \times d$ = T × 5.

For the girder to balance, the total anticlockwise moment should equal the total clockwise moment. So: 2000 = T × 5

Rearrange for tension: T = 2000 ÷ 5 = 400 N

Levers

Levers transmit the turning effect of a force, and make it easier for us to do work (e.g. lift a heavy object). Levers increase the distance from the pivot at which the force is applied — so a small 'input' force creates a large moment. This moment is equal to the moment created on the other side of the pivot. Usually the distance between the heavy object and the pivot is small, so a large 'input' moment creates a large 'output' force on the object, which lifts the object.

Figure 3: Using a screwdriver to prise open a tin of paint is an example of a lever. The pivot is the lip of the tin.

Example

A lever is used to lift a heavy rock.

The input force of 20 N creates a moment of:
$20 \times 2.0 = 40$ Nm

This creates a force of:
$F = M \div d = 40 \div 0.5 = 80$ N
on the rock, which will cause it to lift.
So an input force of 20 N can lift a load of 80 N.

0.5 m   2.0 m
input force = 20 N
pivot
load = 80 N

Figure 4: Scissors use a combination of two levers to let you cut through objects.

Gears

Gears are circular discs with 'teeth' around their edges. Their teeth interlock so that turning one causes another to turn in the opposite direction. They are used to transmit the rotational effect of a force from one place to another (see Figure 6).

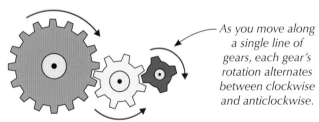

As you move along a single line of gears, each gear's rotation alternates between clockwise and anticlockwise.

Figure 6: Three linked gears all turn together when one gear is turned.

Figure 5: Gears on a bicycle. They're connected by a chain, rather than being in contact with each other.

Two adjacent, interlocking gears will spin in opposite directions, as shown in Figure 6. If the sizes of the gears are different, the rotational speed of the gears will be different. A larger gear will turn slower than a smaller gear. You can use the number of teeth to work out the relative speeds of interconnected gears.

Tip: Gears can be used to change the moment of a force.
A force transmitted to a larger gear will cause a bigger moment, as the distance from the edge of the gear to the pivot is greater.

Example

In Figure 6, the largest gear has 16 teeth, and the medium gear has 8 teeth. The ratio of teeth between the largest gear and the medium gear is 16 : 8 = 2 : 1.

This means that the medium gear is turning twice as fast as the large gear. For every turn the largest gear does, the medium gear will do 2 turns.

Tip: Lubricating gears helps to reduce the energy wasted due to friction between them — see page 70.

Practice Questions — Fact Recall

Q1 What is the moment of a force?

Q2 Give the equation for calculating the moment of a force, including the units of any variables.

Q3 What condition must be satisfied in order for an object with a pivot to be in equilibrium?

Q4 How does a lever reduce the force needed to lift or turn something?

Q5 Describe what a gear is and what function it serves in machinery.

Practice Questions — Application

Q1 In the setup of gears below, which gears will turn clockwise if gear A is turned anticlockwise?

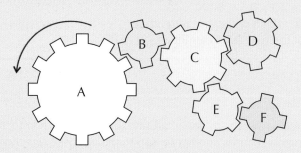

Q2 A plank of wood of length 2.70 m has a pivot at one end. If a force of 60.0 N is applied to its other end (perpendicular to the plank of wood), calculate the moment of the force about the pivot.

Q3 Two children with weights of 350 N and 420 N are sat on a seesaw as shown in the diagram. The pivot is at the seesaw's centre of mass.

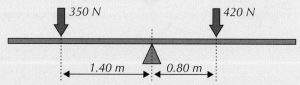

Where should a third child, with a weight of 308 N, sit in order to balance the seesaw?

Tip: For Q3, think about whether a clockwise or anticlockwise moment is needed to make the seesaw balance.

Q4 The diagram shows a lever being used to lift a large load. Give two changes that could be made in order to reduce the force needed to lift the load.

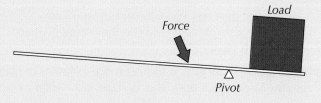

Section 6 Checklist — Make sure you know...

Energy Transfers and Systems

- [ ] How to describe the energy transfers that occur when a system changes.
- [ ] That a closed system is one where there is no net change to the total energy in that system.
- [ ] How to draw and interpret energy transfer diagrams.
- [ ] How the energy of a system can be changed through work done by forces, by electrical equipment and by heating.

Work Done

- [ ] That 'work done' is the same as energy transferred.
- [ ] The equation $E = F \times d$, and how to use it to calculate the work done by a force.
- [ ] The equation to calculate the change in energy stored in the GPE store when an object is raised above the ground ($\Delta GPE = m \times g \times \Delta h$) and how to use it.
- [ ] The equation to calculate the amount of energy stored in the kinetic energy store of a moving object ($KE = \frac{1}{2} \times m \times v^2$) and how to use it.
- [ ] How to describe and calculate energy changes in a system due to work done by forces.

Dissipation of Energy

- [ ] That whenever a system changes, some energy is always dissipated so that it is stored in less useful ways.
- [ ] Some examples of systems where energy is dissipated.
- [ ] How lubrication can reduce unwanted energy transfers.
- [ ] That mechanical processes become wasteful when they heat the surroundings.
- [ ] The equation: efficiency $= \dfrac{\text{useful energy transferred by the device}}{\text{total energy supplied to the device}}$ and how to use it.
- [ ] How to express efficiency as a decimal and percentage.

Power

- [ ] That power is the rate of energy transfer, and is measured in watts.
- [ ] That 1 watt is equivalent to 1 joule per second.
- [ ] The equation $P = E \div t$, and how to use it.
- [ ] Examples to explain that for two otherwise identical devices, the device with the higher power will transfer the same amount of energy in less time.

cont...

Force Basics

- [ ] The difference between vector and scalar quantities.
- [ ] Examples of both vector and scalar quantities.
- [ ] The meaning of the term 'contact force', including examples showing how objects can interact when they touch.
- [ ] Examples of contact forces such as friction, the normal contact force, air resistance and tension.
- [ ] The meaning of the term 'non-contact force', including examples showing how objects can interact without touching.
- [ ] Examples of non-contact forces caused by interacting gravitational, electrostatic and magnetic fields.
- [ ] How to describe and represent the pairs of forces produced when objects interact.

Finding the Resultant Force

- [ ] H How to draw and interpret free body force diagrams showing the forces acting on an isolated object.
- [ ] H How to explain, using free body force diagrams, how several forces acting on an object can result in a resultant force on the object.
- [ ] H That when an object is in equilibrium, there is no resultant force acting on it.
- [ ] H How to use scale vector diagrams to find a resultant force.
- [ ] H How to use scale vector diagrams to show that an object is in equilibrium, or to find unknown forces acting on an object in equilibrium.
- [ ] H How to resolve a force into horizontal and vertical components using a scale vector diagram.

Moments

- [ ] That a moment (with units of Nm) is the rotational effect of a force.
- [ ] The equation $M = F \times d$ and how to use it. Here F (in N) is the applied force and d (in m) is the distance between the applied force and the pivot, normal to the direction of the force.
- [ ] Examples of situations where forces can cause rotation.
- [ ] That when the total clockwise moments acting on an object equal the total anticlockwise moments acting on the object, then the object is in equilibrium. (This is the principle of moments.)
- [ ] How to use moments to calculate unknown forces and distances for objects in equilibrium.
- [ ] How levers and gears work by causing rotations.

Exam-style Questions

1   A girl pushes her little brother to the top of a playground slide.
The energy transfers for this process are shown in **Figure 1**.

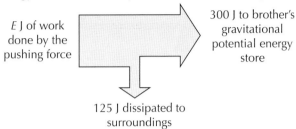

E J of work done by the pushing force

300 J to brother's gravitational potential energy store

Diagram not to scale

125 J dissipated to surroundings

Figure 1

(a)   Explain why the girl's brother is not a closed system.

(2 marks)

(b)   Describe how energy could be dissipated to the surroundings in this situation.

(2 marks)

(c)   The girl exerted a constant pushing force on her brother, which caused him to travel 2.50 m up the slide in the direction of the force.

(i)   Use Figure 1 to calculate the work done by the pushing force.
Give your answer in J.

(1 mark)

(ii)   Calculate the size of the pushing force.
Write down any equations you use. Give your answer in N.

(4 marks)

2   Light bulb A has a power of 60 W, and an efficiency of 3%.
Light bulb B has a power of 10 W, and an efficiency of 9%.

(a)   Describe the differences in the total energy transferred due to A being more powerful than B.

(1 mark)

(b)   Describe the differences in the proportion of energy transferred usefully due to B being more efficient than A.

(1 mark)

(c)   Light bulb B is switched on for one minute.

(i)   Find the total energy transferred in this time.
Write down any equations you use. Give your answer in J.

(4 marks)

(ii)   Calculate the amount of energy transferred usefully by the bulb in this time.
Use the equation: $\text{efficiency} = \dfrac{\text{useful energy transferred by the device}}{\text{total energy supplied to the device}}$.
Give your answer in J.

(3 marks)

3   A plank of wood is resting on a pivot located at its centre of mass.
Three forces are applied to it, as shown in **Figure 2**.

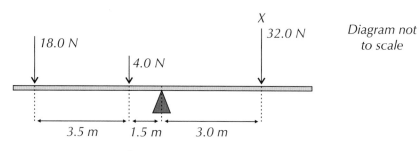

Figure 2

(a) (i)   State the equation that relates the moment of a force to the force and the distance
normal to the direction of the force.

(1 mark)

   (ii)   Calculate the moment of force X about the pivot. Give your answer in Nm.

(2 marks)

(b)   Is the plank of wood balanced?

(5 marks)

(c)   Explain what would happen if force X was applied at a different angle.

(2 marks)

4   A canal boat is towed along by two horses, one on each bank. Each horse is pulling
the canal boat with a different force. **Figure 3** shown is to scale.

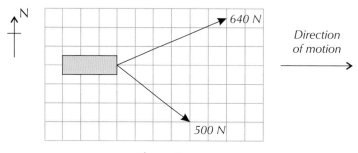

Figure 3

(a)   Are the horses pulling the canal boat with a contact force or a non-contact force?

(1 mark)

(b)   Calculate the total force provided by the horses in the direction of the
canal boat's motion.

(4 marks)

(c)   There is a resistive force on the boat acting in the opposite direction to its motion.
If the resultant force acting on the boat in the direction of its motion is 800 N,
calculate the magnitude of this resistive force.

(1 mark)

1. Circuit Basics

You need to get the basics right before you can move on to the more complicated bits of electricity. So let's have a bit of circuit training...

Circuit symbols

You need to know (and be able to draw) each of the following circuit symbols. You'll learn a bit more about some of them later in this section.

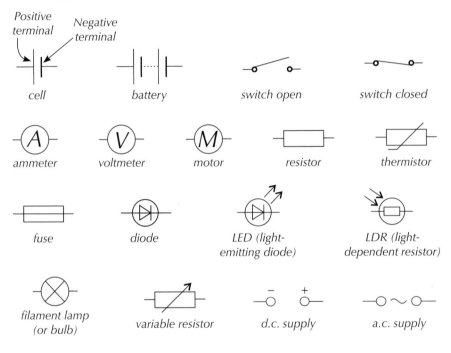

Positive terminal *Negative terminal*

cell   battery   switch open   switch closed

ammeter   voltmeter   motor   resistor   thermistor

fuse   diode   LED (light-emitting diode)   LDR (light-dependent resistor)

filament lamp (or bulb)   variable resistor   d.c. supply   a.c. supply

Figure 1: *Circuit symbols for a variety of circuit components.*

Circuit diagrams

You might be asked to draw a circuit, or to find a problem with one. One thing to make sure of is that your circuit is complete. If a component isn't connected in a circuit properly, it won't work. A circuit is complete if you can follow a wire from one end of the battery (or other power supply), through any components to the other end of the battery (ignoring any switches) — see Figure 2.

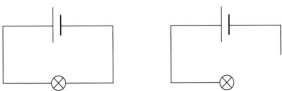

Figure 2: *(Left) A complete circuit. All the wires are joined to something at both ends and the lamp will light. (Right) An incomplete circuit. The lamp won't light.*

Learning Objectives:

- Be able to draw and use electric circuit diagrams representing them with the conventions of positive and negative terminals, and the symbols that represent cells, including batteries, switches, voltmeters, ammeters, resistors, variable resistors, lamps, motors, diodes, thermistors, LDRs and LEDs.

- Be able to recall that a voltmeter is connected in parallel with a component to measure the potential difference (voltage), in volt, across it.

- Be able to recall that an ammeter is connected in series with a component to measure the current, in amp, in the component.

Specification References 10.2, 10.4, 10.7

Tip: Wires are just represented by straight lines.

Tip: Switches allow you to turn circuits (and so components) on and off. You can ignore them when working out if a circuit is complete, because they can always be closed to complete the circuit.

Another thing to watch out for is that the terminals of your power supplies are aligned correctly. Current flows from positive terminals to negative terminals. If you put two cells opposite ways in a circuit, a current can't flow and the circuit won't work (see Figure 3).

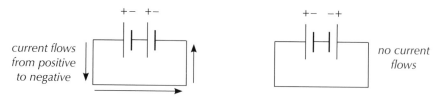

Figure 3: A diagram showing the correct alignment of cells.

Voltmeters and ammeters

Tip: Voltmeters have very large resistances, and ammeters have very small resistances, which is why it's important that they're connected the right way around — otherwise your circuit won't work properly.

Voltmeters and ammeters always have to be connected in a circuit in a certain way, as shown in Figure 4, otherwise they won't do what they are meant to.

▪ A **voltmeter** measures potential difference (voltage). It is always connected 'across' a component — this is known as 'in parallel' (p.235).

▪ An **ammeter** measures current. It is always connected 'in line' with a component — this is known as 'in series' (page 231).

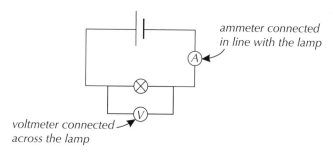

Figure 4: A circuit with a voltmeter and an ammeter connected correctly.

Figure 5: Multimeters can be set up to act as a voltmeter or an ammeter (as well as other electrical components).

Practice Questions — Application

Q1 Draw a complete circuit containing a cell, a lamp, and an open switch which can be used to turn the lamp on and off.

Q2 Draw a complete circuit containing a battery, a resistor and a voltmeter measuring the voltage across the resistor.

Q3 Draw a circuit containing a cell, a thermistor and an ammeter.

Q4 In which of these circuits will the lamp be lit up?

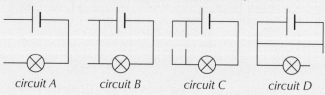

circuit A   circuit B   circuit C   circuit D

2. Current and Potential Difference

Learning Objectives:
- Be able to explain that an electric current is the rate of flow of charge and the current in metals is a flow of electrons.
- Be able to recall and use the equation: $Q = I \times t$.
- Be able to describe that when a closed circuit includes a source of potential difference there will be a current in the circuit.
- Be able to explain that potential difference (voltage) is the energy transferred per unit charge passed and hence that the volt is a joule per coulomb.
- Be able to recall and use the equation: $E = Q \times V$.

Specification References
10.5, 10.6, 10.8-10.10

Current flows around a circuit when charges get a 'push' from a source of potential difference. The size of the current depends on how many charges get pushed through a circuit in a given amount of time.

What is current?

Electric **current** is the rate of flow of charge. In other words, how many charged particles pass a point every second. In metals, the current is the rate of flow of electrons (see page 223). It's measured in amperes, A.

When current flows past a point in a circuit for a length of time then the charge that has passed is given by this formula:

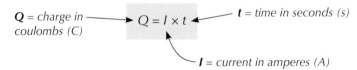

$$Q = I \times t$$

Q = charge in coulombs (C)   *t = time in seconds (s)*   *I = current in amperes (A)*

Example

A battery charger passes a current of 2.5 A through a cell over a period of exactly 4 hours. How much charge does the charger transfer to the cell altogether?

You've got I = 2.5 A and t = 4 × 60 × 60 s = 14 400 s.

$Q = I \times t = 2.5 \times 14\ 400 = 36\ 000$ C

Potential difference

Potential difference (or voltage) can be thought of as the driving force that pushes the charge around. Electrical charge will only flow around a complete (closed) circuit if there is a potential difference. In a simple circuit, this is usually provided by a cell or battery.

Potential difference (p.d.) is the energy transferred per unit charge passed — i.e. how much energy each coulomb of charge transfers as it passes between two points in a circuit. So the p.d. across a component is the amount of energy transferred by that component for every coulomb passed. Potential difference is measured in volts, where one volt is one joule per coulomb (1 V = 1 J/C).

Tip: Energy is transferred by a charge as it does work (p.242).

You can calculate the energy transferred by a given amount of charge using:

Tip: You can turn this equation into a formula triangle (page 345):

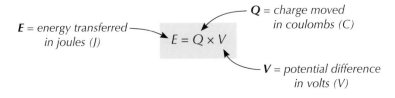

$$E = Q \times V$$

E = energy transferred in joules (J)   *Q = charge moved in coulombs (C)*   *V = potential difference in volts (V)*

The motor in an electric toothbrush is attached to a 3.0 V battery. The total charge that passes a point in the motor circuit during use is 140 C. Calculate the energy transferred by the motor.

To calculate the energy transferred you need to use the formula $E = Q \times V$:

charge = 140 C, potential difference = 3.0 V

$E = Q \times V = 140 \times 3.0 = 420$ J

Practice Questions — Fact Recall

Q1   What charges move in metals to form a current?

Q2   What is the equation linking charge, current and time?
Write down the units each quantity is measured in.

Q3   What is needed for a current to flow in a closed circuit?

Q4   What is potential difference? What is it measured in?

Q5   Write down the equation linking energy transferred, charge moved and potential difference.

Practice Questions — Application

Q1   A motor is connected to a 12 V power supply. Over time, 3600 J of energy is transferred to the motor. Calculate the charge that passes through the motor in this time.

Q2   The current through a lamp is 0.20 A. Calculate the time taken for 50.0 C of charge to pass through the lamp.

3. Resistance

Resistance is how much a component in a circuit slows down the flow of current. It's different for each component, and it's related to p.d. and current.

What is resistance?

Resistance is anything in the circuit which reduces the flow of current. It is measured in ohms, Ω. The current flowing through a component depends on the potential difference across it, and the resistance of the component. The greater the resistance of a component, the smaller the current that flows (for a given potential difference across the component).

The resistance of a component is linked to potential difference across it and current through it by the following formula:

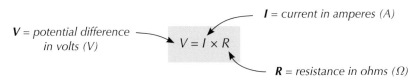

I = current in amperes (A)

V = potential difference in volts (V) —— $V = I \times R$

R = resistance in ohms (Ω)

Example

Voltmeter *V* reads 6.0 V and resistor *R* has a resistance of 4.0 Ω. What is the current through ammeter *A*?

Rearrange the formula for $V = I \times R$.

You need to find *I*, so rearrange the equation to get $I = V \div R$.

$I = V \div R = 6.0 \div 4.0 = 1.5$ A

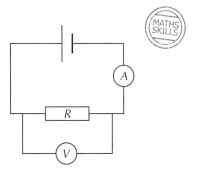

MATHS SKILLS

Resistance and temperature

In most cases, if the temperature of an electrical component increases, its resistance increases. To understand this, you have to understand what's actually happening to the atoms within the component.

Atomic structure in metals

All atoms contain positively charged protons and neutral neutrons in the nucleus at their centre, with negatively charged electrons orbiting the nucleus. You've met atomic structure before on page 151, so go back if you need a reminder.

The atoms in metals are bonded in such a way that metals are made up of a lattice (a grid) of positive ions (p.154) surrounded by free electrons. These electrons are free to move through the whole metal (see Figure 1). The current in metals is the flow of these free electrons.

Learning Objectives:

- Be able to recall and use the equation: $V = I \times R$.

- Be able to describe the structure of the atom, limited to the position, mass and charge of protons, neutrons and electrons.

- Be able to recall that, when there is an electric current in a resistor, there is an energy transfer which heats the resistor.

- Be able to explain that electrical energy is dissipated as thermal energy in the surroundings when an electrical current does work against electrical resistance.

- Be able to explain the energy transfer described above as the result of collisions between electrons and the ions in the lattice.

Specification References
10.1, 10.13, 10.22-10.24

Tip: Thermistors (p.225) are an exception to this rule — as the temperature of a thermistor increases, its resistance decreases.

Tip: Make sure you learn the relative masses and charges for protons, neutrons and electrons on page 152.

Tip: Current is described as flowing from positive to negative (see page 220) — this is known as conventional current. This can be a bit confusing, as the electrons actually move from the negative to positive terminals. However, current was described before people knew about electrons, so the idea of it flowing from positive to negative has stuck.

Tip: Most electrical components are made from metal because metals are really good at conducting electricity.

Tip: Rearranging $V = I \times R$ gives $I = V \div R$. Using this you can see that if the p.d. is kept constant, the current will decrease as the temperature (and so resistance) increases.

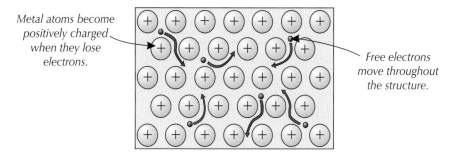

Metal atoms become positively charged when they lose electrons.

Free electrons move throughout the structure.

Figure 1: *Electrons and ion lattice within a metal.*

Temperature and resistance in metal

When an electrical charge flows through a component, there will usually be an electrical transfer of energy. Some of this energy is transferred usefully, but work done against resistance will cause energy to be transferred and dissipated to the thermal energy stores of the component and the surroundings. So when a current flows through a component, like a resistor, the component heats up.

This happens because the free electrons collide with the ions that make up the lattice. These collisions transfer energy from the electrons to the ions, making the ions vibrate and causing the resistor to heat up.

This increase in the resistor's temperature increases its resistance. The more the ions vibrate, the harder it is for electrons to pass through the resistor (because they end up colliding with ions more often). Eventually, the resistor will get so hot that electrons can't get through, so no current will flow.

Practice Questions — Fact recall

Q1   What is resistance? What unit is resistance measured in?

Q2   Explain why a resistor heats up when a current flows through it, in terms of the movement and collisions of electrons in the resistor.

Tip: $V = I \times R$ comes up a lot in electricity. It might be handy for you to remember it as a formula triangle.

Practice Question — Application

Q1   A current of 0.015 A is flowing through a 2.0 Ω resistor. What is the potential difference across the resistor?

4. LDRs and Thermistors

LDRs and thermistors are just fancy resistors. Their resistances depend on the conditions that they're in, which makes them handy in certain applications.

Thermistors

Thermistors are a type of resistor whose resistance depends on their temperature. A thermistor's resistance decreases as the temperature increases.

- In hot conditions, the resistance drops (see Figure 1).

- In cool conditions, the resistance goes up.

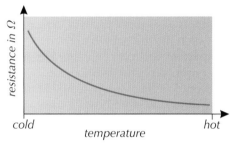

Figure 1: *A graph of resistance against temperature for a thermistor.*

Thermistors are useful in temperature detectors called thermostats. They are connected in a circuit where their resistance can be measured. As resistance varies with temperature, knowing the resistance means you can detect the temperature of the thermistor (and its surroundings). Thermostats can be used in car engine temperature sensors to make sure the engine isn't overheating.

Light-dependent resistors (LDRs)

An **LDR** is a resistor that is dependent on the intensity of light. Simple really.

- In bright light, the resistance falls (see Figure 3).

- In darkness, the resistance is highest.

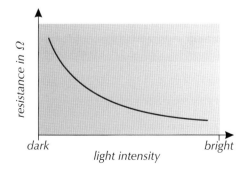

Figure 3: *A graph of resistance against light intensity for a light-dependent resistor (LDR).*

LDRs can be used where a function depends on light levels, e.g. when you want a component to only work in the dark.

Learning Objectives:

- Be able to describe how the resistance of a thermistor varies with change of temperature (negative temperature coefficient thermistors only).

- Be able to describe how the resistance of a light-dependent resistor (LDR) varies with light intensity.

- Be able to explain how the design and use of circuits can be used to explore the variation of resistance in thermistors and LDRs.

Specification References 10.19-10.21

Figure 2: *An example of one type of thermistor (top), and its circuit symbol (bottom).*

Tip: Intensity is the power per unit area (in other words the energy transferred to a given area each second). You came across it on page 140.

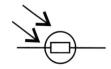

Figure 4: *The circuit symbol of an LDR.*

Investigating the resistance of LDRs and thermistors

Thermistors

You can use the circuit shown in Figure 5 to investigate how a thermistor's resistance varies with temperature.

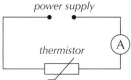

Figure 5: Circuit used to investigate the resistance of a thermistor.

Tip: Remember to do a risk assessment (p.336) before these experiments. Be very careful when using electronics near water, as it can break components or lead to an electric shock.

Tip: Water baths allow objects to be heated more evenly.

A good way of controlling the temperature of the thermistor is to use a water bath (only if the thermistor is waterproof though). Place the thermistor in the bath and pour enough water into the bath to fully cover the thermistor. Turn on the water bath, so the water begins to heat up. Measure and record the temperature of the water using a digital thermometer, and measure the current through the circuit for every 5 °C increase in temperature. The potential difference across the thermistor needs to be kept constant throughout the experiment.

Use the p.d. of the power supply and the values of current you recorded to calculate the resistance of the thermistor at each temperature, using $R = V \div I$ (p.223). You should find that as the temperature increases, the resistance decreases (and so the current will increase).

LDRs

You can use the circuit in Figure 5 to investigate the resistance of an LDR — just replace the thermistor with an LDR.

In a darkened room, use a torch to shine light on the LDR. Record the distance between the torch and the LDR. Gradually move the torch away from the LDR, so the intensity of the light hitting the LDR will decrease. Record the current through the LDR for, e.g. every 10 cm you move the torch. Then use $R = V \div I$, where V is the p.d. of the power source and I is your measurement of current, to calculate the resistance of the LDR for different light intensities. You should find as the torch moves further away, less light hits the torch and the LDR's resistance increases (and the current through it decreases).

Figure 6: LDRs are used in automatic street lights.

Practice Questions — Fact Recall

Q1 Sketch a graph of resistance against temperature for a thermistor.

Q2 How can you lower the resistance of an LDR?

Q3 Describe an experiment you could do to investigate the resistance of a thermistor with temperature.

Practice Question — Application

Q1 Draw the circuit you could use to investigate the resistance of an LDR with light intensity.

5. I-V Graphs

Get your crocodile clips out, it's time for a practical investigating how current and potential difference are related, and how you can see this on I-V graphs.

What do I-V graphs show?

I-V graphs show how the current (*I*) varies as you change the potential difference (*V*) across a component. As $R = V \div I$ (p.223), you can calculate the resistance at a point by reading off and substituting values of potential difference (p.d.) and current into the equation. You can also use I-V graphs to compare the resistances of components — the shallower the gradient of an I-V graph, the greater the resistance of the component.

Example

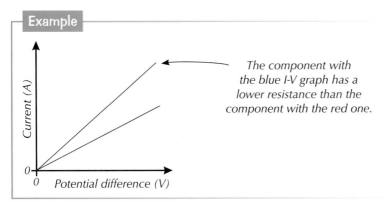

The component with the blue I-V graph has a lower resistance than the component with the red one.

Linear components have I-V graphs that are straight lines. Their resistances remain constant as the current through them is changed.

Non-linear components, on the other hand, have curved I-V graphs — the resistance changes depending on the current.

Investigating I-V graphs

CORE PRACTICAL

You can investigate the I-V graph for a component yourself using the test circuit displayed in Figure 1. You need to be able to do this experiment for a fixed resistor and a filament lamp, but you can use the circuit in Figure 1 to investigate other components too, like LDRs, thermistors and diodes.

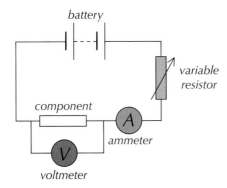

Figure 1: *A circuit diagram of a test circuit used to investigate the I-V graph of a component.*

- Be able to construct electrical circuits to investigate the relationship between potential difference, current and resistance for a resistor and a filament lamp (Core Practical).
- Be able to explain how the design and use of circuits can be used to explore the variation of resistance in the following devices: filament lamps, diodes, thermistors and LDRs.
- Be able to explain how changing the resistance in a circuit changes the current and how this can be achieved using a variable resistor.
- Be able to explain how current varies with potential difference for the following devices and how this relates to resistance: filament lamps, diodes and fixed resistors.

Specification References
10.12, 10.17, 10.18, 10.21

Tip: Again, make sure you do a risk assessment for this practical.

Figure 2: *A type of variable resistor. They can be used to control the amount of current flowing in a circuit.*

To find a component's *I-V* graph, begin to increase the resistance of the variable resistor. As $I = V \div R$, this reduces the current flowing through the circuit, and changes the potential difference across the component.

Each time you use the variable resistor to alter the current, record the potential difference across the component and the current through it. Repeat each reading twice more and calculate an average p.d. for each current.

Swap over the wires connected to the battery to reverse the direction of the current. Measure negative values of current and potential difference using the same method as described above.

Now you can use your measurements to plot a graph of current against potential difference for the component. This is your *I-V* graph. Read on to see some examples of *I-V* graphs for different components.

Tip: To make this a fair test (p.10), do this experiment in constant conditions. This means keeping things like room temperature and light levels the same.

Tip: Once you've swapped over the wires at the battery, the readings will be negative because the current is flowing through the components in the opposite direction to before.

Figure 3: *Different sizes of resistors could be used in this investigation. They typically look like this.*

Fixed resistors

The current through a fixed resistor (at constant temperature) is directly proportional to potential difference, so you get a straight line (linear) *I-V* graph. The resistance of the resistor is constant and doesn't depend on the current.

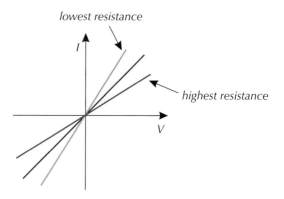

Figure 4: *I-V graphs for fixed resistors with different resistances.*

Filament lamps

When an electrical charge flows through a filament lamp, it transfers some energy to the thermal energy store of the filament (page 61), which is designed to heat up and glow. Resistance increases with temperature, so as more current flows through the lamp, the lamp heats up more and the resistance increases. This means less current can flow per unit potential difference, so the graph gets shallower, hence the curve of the *I-V* graph shown in Figure 6.

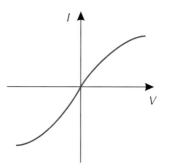

Figure 6: *An I-V graph for a filament lamp.*

Figure 5: *A filament lamp.*

Diodes

A **diode** is a component that only lets current pass through it in one direction. The resistance of a diode depends on the direction of the current — it will happily let current flow through it one way, but will have a very high resistance if the current is reversed.

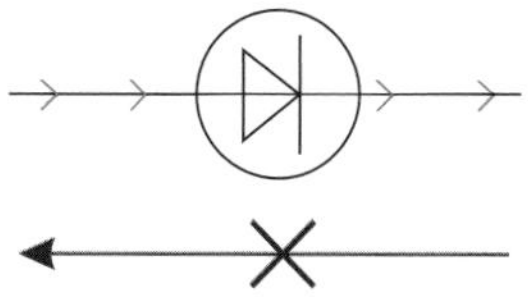

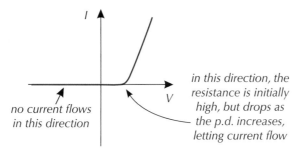

current flows in
the forward direction

no current
flows this way

Figure 7: A diagram illustrating which way current is able to flow in a diode.

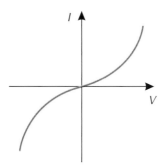

in this direction, the resistance is initially high, but drops as the p.d. increases, letting current flow

no current flows in this direction

Figure 8: An I-V graph for a diode. Current only flows in one direction.

Thermistors

The *I-V* graph for a thermistor (p.225) gets steeper as the current through it increases. The explanation for this is similar to that for the filament lamp. As a current flows through the thermistor, the thermistor heats up. This causes the resistance of the thermistor to decrease, so the *I-V* graph becomes steeper.

Figure 9: Electric kettles contain thermistors to switch them off once the water inside has started to boil.

Figure 10: An I-V graph for a thermistor at a constant external temperature.

Tip: External conditions change the resistance of LDRs and thermistors (p.225). These *I-V* graphs are for LDRs and thermistors in <u>constant conditions</u>.

LDRs

The resistance of an LDR only depends on light intensity, not the current through it. So if the light level is kept constant during the experiment, an LDR will behave like a fixed resistor and produce a linear *I-V* graph.

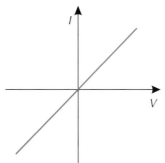

Figure 12: An LDR.

Figure 11: An I-V graph for an LDR at a constant light level.

Practice Questions — Fact Recall

Q1   How do you calculate the resistance of a component at a given potential difference from its *I-V* graph?

Q2   Draw a circuit diagram of a circuit you could use to find the *I-V* graph of a component.

Q3   Sketch an *I-V* graph for:

a) a fixed resistor at a constant temperature   b) a diode

Q4   Describe the resistance of a diode as the current through it flows in:

a) the forwards direction.   b) the backwards direction.

Practice Questions — Application

Q1   A student tests component A using a suitable test circuit and plots a graph of his data, shown below. What would you expect component A to be?

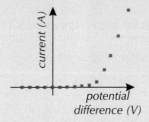

Q2   The graph below shows the *I-V* graph of a resistor at a constant temperature. Calculate its resistance.

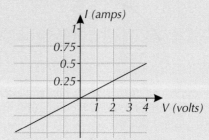

6. Series Circuits

So you've got the basics of circuit components covered... but how are you going to connect them? Components can either be connected in series or parallel. First up, series circuits — they're basically just big loops.

Components in series

In **series circuits**, the different components are connected in a line, end to end, between the positive and negative ends of the power supply (except for voltmeters, which are always connected across a component — see page 220).

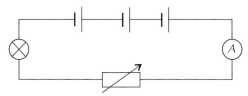

Figure 1: *A circuit in which each component is connected in series — you can draw a single line that travels along the wires and passes through every component once before returning to your starting point.*

If you remove or disconnect one component, the circuit is broken and they all stop. This is generally not very handy, and in practice very few things are connected in series. However, series circuits are often designed and built to test and measure components (e.g. the test circuit on page 227) because the potential difference, current and resistance are quite easy to change, measure and calculate.

Potential difference in series circuits

There is a bigger potential difference (p.d.) when more cells are connected in series, provided the cells are all connected the same way. For example, when two cells with a potential difference of 1.5 V are connected in series, they supply 3 V between them (see Figure 3 on the next page). You just add up all the individual cell p.d.s to find the total power source p.d..

In series circuits the total potential difference of the supply is shared between the various components. So the potential differences round a series circuit always add up to equal the source potential difference. If two or more components are the same, the p.d. across them will also be the same.

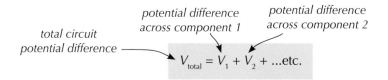

total circuit potential difference

potential difference across component 1

potential difference across component 2

$$V_{total} = V_1 + V_2 + ...etc.$$

Learning Objectives:

- Be able to explain the design and construction of series circuits for testing and measuring.

- Be able to calculate the currents, potential differences and resistances in series circuits.

- Be able to explain why, if two resistors are in series, the net resistance is increased.

**Specification References
10.14-10.16**

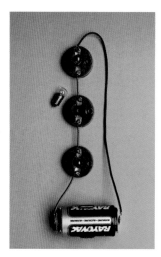

Figure 2: *Three lamps connected in series. When one lamp is removed, the other two go out.*

Tip: Ammeters are always connected in series with the components that they are measuring the current through — even if the circuit is not a series circuit (p.220).

Example

In the diagram, two cells and two lamps are connected in series. The total potential difference across the circuit is the sum of the p.d.s of the two batteries, so:

$$V = 1.5\,V + 1.5\,V = 3.0\,V$$

The potential differences, V_1 and V_2, of the two lamps add up to 3.0 V:

$$V = V_1 + V_2 = 3.0\,V$$

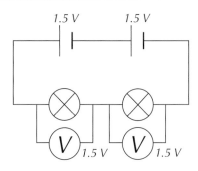

Figure 3: A circuit diagram containing two cells and two identical lamps connected in series. The potential difference from the cells is split evenly across the lamps.

Figure 4: Christmas tree lights are often connected in series. The bulbs can be very small because the mains voltage is shared out between them.

Current in series circuits

In series circuits the same current flows through all parts of the circuit:

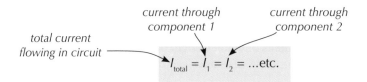

The size of the current is determined by the total potential difference of the cells and the total resistance of the circuit, using the equation $V = I \times R$ (from page 223).

Example

In the diagram, two lamps are connected in series. The current through each lamp (and in fact the whole circuit) is exactly the same.

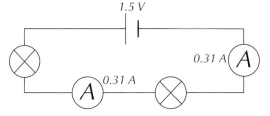

Figure 5: A series circuit containing two lamps and two ammeters, showing that the current is the same throughout the circuit.

Resistance in series circuits

In series circuits the total (net) resistance is just the sum of all the resistances:

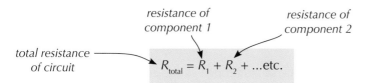

resistance of
component 1

resistance of
component 2

total resistance
of circuit

$$R_{total} = R_1 + R_2 + ...etc.$$

This is because by adding a resistor in series, the two resistors have to share the total p.d.. The potential difference across each resistor is lower, so the current through each resistor is also lower. In a series circuit, the current is the same everywhere so the total current in the circuit is reduced when a resistor is added. This means that the total resistance of the circuit increases.

The bigger the resistance of a component, the bigger its share of the total potential difference.

Example

Find the total resistance of this circuit.

MATHS
SKILLS

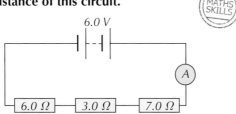

6.0 V

A

6.0 Ω   3.0 Ω   7.0 Ω

The total resistance of a series circuit is the sum of the resistances of each component:

$$R = 6.0\ \Omega + 3.0\ \Omega + 7.0\ \Omega = 16\ \Omega$$

Tip: The resistance of the ammeter and wires is so small that you don't need to worry about it.

Find the current through the circuit.

- The total potential difference in the circuit is equal to the battery potential difference: $V = 6.0$ V.

- Rearrange the equation $V = I \times R$ and plug in the values of V and R to find the total current:

$$I = V \div R = 6.0 \div 16 = 0.375\ A = 0.38\ A \text{ (to 2 s.f.)}$$

Find the potential difference across the 6.0 Ω resistor.

- The current is the same everywhere in the circuit, so the current through the 6.0 Ω resistor is $I = 0.375$ A.

- The resistance of the resistor is clearly (I hope...) $R = 6.0\ \Omega$.

- Use the equation $V = I \times R$:

$$V = I \times R = 0.375 \times 6.0 = 2.25\ V = 2.3\ V \text{ (to 2 s.f.)}$$

Summary of series circuits

There are four simple rules to remember for series circuits:

- The p.d. of the cells adds up to the source p.d..

- The source p.d. is split across the components.

- The current is the same through all the components.

- The total resistance of the circuit is the sum of all the resistances of the separate components.

You'll need to be able to use these rules in all sorts of circuit examples in the exam, so make sure you know them.

Practice Questions — Fact Recall

Q1 What does 'connected in series' mean?

Q2 How should you connect extra cells in a circuit in order to increase the total potential difference across the circuit?

Q3 True or false? Every component connected in series has the same potential difference across it.

Q4 What can you say about the current through each component connected in series?

Q5 What type of circuit component must always be connected in series?

Q6 Explain why adding a resistor in series increases the total resistance.

Practice Question — Application

Q1 The circuit shown has a 7.0 Ω resistor and a filament lamp in series. Ammeter A reads a constant value of 1.5 A.

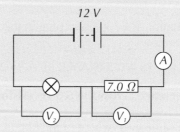

Tip: Remember the total V across the circuit will be equal to $V_1 + V_2$.

a) What is the current through the filament lamp?

b) What potential difference will voltmeter V_1 measure?

c) What potential difference will voltmeter V_2 measure?

d) What is the resistance of the filament lamp?

7. Parallel Circuits

In parallel circuits, components or groups of components are on their own separate loop or branch. They're much more useful than series circuits because you can turn off each loop separately, without turning off the rest.

Components in parallel

Unlike components in series, components connected in **parallel** each have their own branch in a circuit connected to the positive and negative terminals of the supply (except ammeters which are always connected in series). If you remove or disconnect one of them, it will hardly affect the others at all. This is because current can still flow in a complete loop (page 219) from one end of the power supply to the other through the branches that are still connected.

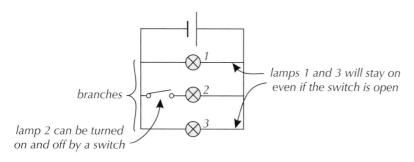

branches

lamps 1 and 3 will stay on even if the switch is open

lamp 2 can be turned on and off by a switch

Figure 1: *A circuit diagram with three lamps connected in parallel, one of which can be switched on and off by a switch.*

This is obviously how most things must be connected, for example in cars and in household electrics. You have to be able to switch everything on and off separately. Everyday circuits often include a mixture of series and parallel parts (see page 238).

Potential difference in parallel circuits

In parallel circuits, all components get the full source p.d.. Each branch in a parallel circuit has the same potential difference as the power supply, so the potential difference is the same across all components connected in parallel:

potential difference across component 1

potential difference across component 2

source potential difference

$$V_{total} = V_1 = V_2 = ...etc.$$

This means that identical lamps connected in parallel will all be as bright as if a single lamp was in the circuit.

Learning Objectives:

- Be able to recall that current is conserved at a junction in a circuit.

- Be able to explain why, if two resistors are in series, the net resistance is increased, whereas with two in parallel the net resistance is decreased.

- Be able to describe the differences between series and parallel circuits.

Specification References
10.3, 10.11, 10.14

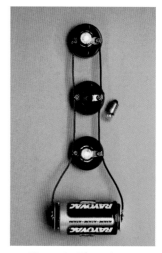

Figure 2: *Three lamps connected in parallel. When one lamp is removed, the other two remain lit.*

Tip: Voltmeters must be connected in parallel with the component that they're measuring because that's the only way they'll have the same p.d. across them as the component.

Figure 3: A car dashboard. Everything that you can turn on and off from your dashboard will be on its own parallel circuit branch connected to the car battery.

Tip: (M) is the symbol for a motor.

Example

Everything electrical in a car is connected in parallel. Parallel connection is essential in a car, so everything can be turned on and off separately. It also means that everything always has the full p.d. of the battery across it. This is useful because it means that you can listen to the radio on full blast without it having much effect on the brightness of your lights.

The only slight effect is that when you turn lots of things on the lights may briefly go a bit dim because the battery can't provide full potential difference under heavy load. This is normally a very slight effect. You can spot the same thing at home when you turn a kettle on, if you watch very carefully.

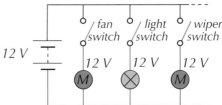

Figure 4: A circuit diagram to give an idea of how the electronic components in a car are connected in a parallel circuit.

Current in parallel circuits

In parallel circuits the total current flowing around the circuit is equal to the total of all the currents through the separate branches.

total current flowing in the circuit → $I_{total} = I_1 + I_2 + ...etc.$ ← *current through branch 1* / *current through branch 2*

Tip: This makes sense, because as charges move around a circuit they don't get used up or lost, so the number of charges flowing into a junction must equal the number of charges flowing out of it. As current is the rate of flow of charge, the current in must equal the current out too.

This means that unlike voltage, the current going through each branch is less than the total current in the circuit. Whenever the circuit splits into one or more branches, a certain amount of the current flows through each branch.

The current through each component inside a branch is the same — it's like a mini series circuit. The same amount of current that entered the branch must then leave the branch when it rejoins the rest of the circuit.

Example

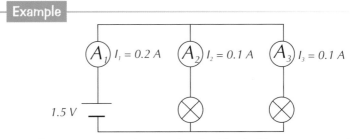

Figure 5: A circuit diagram showing identical lamps connected in parallel.

Lamps connected in parallel will share the total current in the circuit.
In Figure 5: $I_1 = I_2 + I_3$ 0.2 A = 0.1 A + 0.1 A

Resistance in parallel circuits

If you have two resistors in parallel, their total resistance is less than the resistance of the smallest of the two resistors. So adding a resistor in parallel reduces the total resistance. This can be tough to get your head around, but think about it like this:

In parallel, both resistors have the same potential difference across them as the source. This means the 'pushing force' making the current flow is the same as the source p.d. for each resistor you add.

But by adding another additional loop, the current has more than one direction to go in. This increases the total current that can flow around the circuit. Using $V = I \times R$, an increase in current means a decrease in the total resistance of the circuit.

Tip: This last bit is important — adding another loop to the circuit increases the current in the circuit (because there are more paths where charge is flowing).

Example

In the circuit shown in Figure 6, there are three resistors connected in parallel.

In a parallel circuit, the total resistance is smaller than the smallest resistance on an individual branch. Therefore, the total resistance of the circuit in Figure 6 is less than 4 Ω.

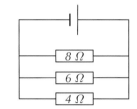

Figure 6: A circuit diagram showing three resistors connected in parallel.

Tip: You might see the answer in this example written as $R_{total} < 4\ \Omega$. This just means that the total resistance is less than 4 Ω.

Summary of parallel circuits

There are three rules for parallel circuits. Know them well:

- The p.d. across each branch is the same as the source p.d..

- The current is split across the branches, and the total current is the sum of the current of each branch.

- The total resistance of a parallel circuit is less than the smallest resistance of an individual circuit branch.

Tip: Remember for parallel circuits:
$I_{total} = I_1 + I_2 + $ ...etc. and
$V_{total} = V_1 = V_2 = $ ...etc.

Comparing series and parallel circuits

Make sure you know and can describe the differences between series and parallel circuits:

- **Current** — The current through all components in series is the same. The current through components in parallel depends on the resistance of each component.

- **Potential difference** — The total p.d. is shared across components in series, and the p.d. across each component depends on its resistance. The p.d. across components in parallel is equal to the source potential difference.

- **Resistance** — The total resistance of components in series is the sum of all the component's resistances. The total resistance of components in parallel decreases as more components are added (you don't need to know how).

Mixed series and parallel circuits

Tip: Look back at pages 231-234 for series circuit rules.

You will often use a circuit that contains components connected in series and in parallel. When this happens, focus on one branch at a time, and work out whether you need to use series or parallel rules for it.

Example

Determine the current measured by ammeter A$_2$.

First, find the combined resistance
of the two resistors in series,
using series rules from page 233:
$R = 8.0\ \Omega + 4.0\ \Omega = 12\ \Omega$

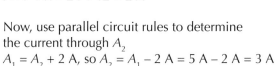

Now, determine the current through
the branch containing the resistors
using $V = I \times R$ (p.223)
$I = V \div R = 24 \div 12 = 2$ A

Now, use parallel circuit rules to determine
the current through A_2
$A_1 = A_2 + 2$ A, so $A_2 = A_1 - 2$ A $= 5$ A $- 2$ A $= 3$ A

Practice Questions — Fact Recall

Q1 What does 'connected in parallel' mean?

Q2 What can you say about the potential difference across all the components connected in parallel with a power supply? Assume each component is on a branch with no other components.

Q3 If you know the current in every branch of a parallel circuit, how can you work out the total current in the circuit?

Q4 Describe how the total resistance of a circuit changes when two components that are connected in series are moved so they are connected in parallel.

Practice Question — Application

Q1 Look at the circuit shown below.

a) If switch S is open, ammeter A reads 0.70 A.
Find the potential difference across the battery.

b) If switch S is closed, ammeter A reads 0.50 A.

   i) Find the potential difference across lamp B.

   ii) Find the potential difference across resistor R$_2$.

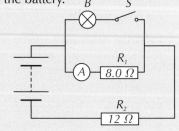

8. Investigating Circuits

Learning Objective:
- Be able to construct electrical circuits to test series and parallel circuits using resistors and filament lamps (Core Practical).

Specification Reference
10.17

You can investigate the properties of a circuit by adding identical resistors and lamps in series and parallel and seeing the effects.

Investigating resistors in series and parallel

Before you get started, you'll need to make sure you have at least four identical resistors.

Series

1. Start by constructing the circuit shown in Figure 1 using one of the resistors. Make a note of the potential difference of the battery (*V*).

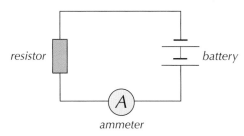

resistor   *battery*

ammeter

Figure 1: *A circuit diagram of the initial circuit for investigating resistance of resistors in series, with a single resistor connected in series.*

2. Measure the current through the circuit using the ammeter. Use this and the p.d. of the battery to calculate the resistance of the circuit using $R = V \div I$ (from $V = I \times R$, see page 223).

3. Add another resistor, in series with the first (as shown in Figure 2).

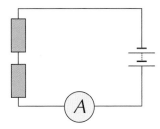

Figure 2: *A circuit diagram of the circuit in Figure 1, with a second resistor added in series with the first.*

4. Again, measure the current through the circuit and use this and the p.d. of the battery to calculate the overall resistance of the circuit.

5. Repeat steps 2 and 3 until you've added all of your resistors.

With your results, plot a graph of the number of identical resistors against the total resistance of the circuit. Your graph should look similar to the one shown in Figure 3.

Tip: Remember to do a risk assessment before doing these experiments. The risks of working with electronics include electric shocks (page 247), burns from hot equipment and causing electrical fires if equipment is left unattended or used improperly.

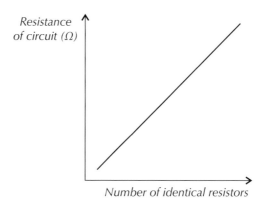

Figure 3: A graph of total resistance of a circuit against number of identical resistors connected in series.

Tip: To refresh your memory on how current, potential difference and resistance behave in series circuits, check out pages 231-234.

You should find that adding resistors in series increases the total resistance of the circuit — i.e. adding a resistor decreases the total current through the circuit. The more resistors you add, the larger the resistance of the whole circuit.

Parallel

Use the same equipment as you did to investigate resistors in series (so the experiment is a fair test). Build the same initial circuit shown in Figure 1, and carry out the following steps:

1. Measure the total current through the circuit and calculate the resistance of the circuit using $R = V \div I$ (again, V is the potential difference of the battery).

2. Next, add another resistor, in parallel with the first, as shown in Figure 4.

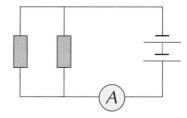

Figure 4: A circuit diagram of the circuit in Figure 1, with a second resistor added in parallel with the first.

Tip: Remember, fixed resistors only have a constant resistance at a constant temperature. Disconnecting the battery between readings will stop your circuit getting too hot, which could affect your results.

3. Measure the total current through the circuit and use this and the potential difference of the battery to calculate the overall resistance of the circuit.

4. Repeat steps 2 and 3 until you've added all of your resistors.

Just like before, use your results to plot a graph of the number of identical resistors in the circuit against the total resistance. You should get a graph which looks like the one shown in Figure 5 on the next page.

When you add resistors in parallel, the total current through the circuit increases — so the total resistance of the circuit has decreased. The more resistors you add, the smaller the overall resistance becomes.

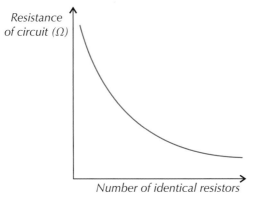

Figure 5: A graph of total resistance of a circuit against number of identical resistors connected in parallel.

Tip: You need to be able to explain why the resistance decreases when a component is added in parallel (see page 237).

Investigating lamps in series and parallel

CORE PRACTICAL

You can also investigate series and parallel circuits using identical lamps. Gradually add the lamps in series and note down how bright they appear each time a new bulb is added. Do the same with the lamps in parallel.

When adding lamps in series, you should see that the brightness decreases each time a lamp is added. This is because the same potential difference is being shared out between the lamps, so each lamp has a lower p.d. across it. These results agree with the rules for series circuits on page 231.

When you add lamps in parallel, their brightnesses don't change. This is because each branch (and so each lamp) has the same potential difference as the battery. These results agree with the rules for parallel circuits on page 235.

Tip: The brightness of a lamp depends on its potential difference. The larger the p.d. the more energy is being transferred to the lamp (see page 242).

Practice Question — Application

Q1 A student wants to investigate how the resistance of a circuit changes as they connect more resistors in parallel. They have six identical 1 Ω resistors, a battery and an ammeter.

a) Draw a circuit diagram of the circuit they should construct to find the total resistance of the circuit when three resistors are connected in parallel.

b) The student's results are displayed in the table below.

Number of 1 Ω resistors	Total resistance (Ω)
1	1.00
2	0.50
3	0.33
4	0.25
5	0.20
6	0.17

Plot a graph of their results, and draw a line of best fit.

c) Explain the trend shown by the results.

- Be able to describe how, in different domestic devices, energy is transferred from batteries and the a.c. mains to the energy of motors and heating devices.

- Be able to use the equation: $E = I \times V \times t$.

- Be able to explain that electrical energy is dissipated as thermal energy in the surroundings when an electrical current does work against electrical resistance.

- Be able to explain ways of reducing unwanted energy transfer through low resistance wires.

- Be able to describe the advantages and disadvantages of the heating effect of an electric current.

Specification References
10.23, 10.25-10.27,
10.32

9. Energy in Circuits

All the useful things electricity can do are due to the transfer of energy. Energy is transferred between stores electrically (like you saw on page 62) by electrical appliances.

Energy transfers in electrical appliances

You know from page 221 that electric current is the flow of electric charge. When a charge moves, it transfers energy. This is because the charge does work against the resistance of the circuit, and work done is the same as energy transferred. Electrical appliances are designed to transfer energy to components in a circuit when a current flows.

> **Example**
>
> - Kettles transfer energy electrically from the mains a.c. supply to the thermal energy store of the heating element inside the kettle.
>
> - Energy is transferred electrically from the battery of a handheld fan to the kinetic energy store of the fan's motor.

You can find the energy transferred to an electrical appliance using:

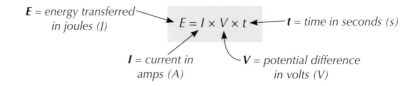

E = energy transferred in joules (J) $E = I \times V \times t$ t = time in seconds (s)

I = current in amps (A) V = potential difference in volts (V)

Tip: This equation comes from the definitions of current and p.d. from page 221. $E = Q \times V$ and $Q = I \times t$, so $E = (I \times t) \times V$.

> **Example**
>
> **A student uses an immersion heater to heat a beaker of water. The heater is connected to a power supply at 24 V, and a current of 10 A flows through it.**
>
> a) **Calculate the energy transferred to the heater in 2.5 minutes.**
>
>   Convert the time to seconds: 2.5 minutes = 150 seconds
>
>   Then just substitute in the values:
>
> $E = I \times V \times t = 10 \times 24 \times 150 = 36\ 000$ J
>
> b) **The student calculates it will take 168 480 J of energy to begin boiling the water. What is the minimum time that the heater must be used for in order to heat the water to its boiling point?**
>
>   Rearrange the equation to get $t = E \div (I \times V)$
>
>   Then substitute in the values:
>
> $t = 168\ 480 \div (12 \times 24) = 585$ s (= 9 minutes 45 seconds)

Heating

Whenever a current flows through anything with electrical resistance (which is pretty much everything) the charges do work and energy is transferred to the thermal energy stores of the components and then the surroundings. The higher the current or resistance, the more energy is transferred to these thermal energy stores.

Often, this is heating effect is unwanted. It can reduce the efficiency of a process (p.71) as less energy is being transferred to useful energy stores. It can also cause components in a circuit to melt, meaning the circuit stops working or doesn't work properly. Using low-resistance wires is one way of reducing unwanted energy transfers and these negative effects.

However, there are advantages to this heating effect. **Fuses** are components that help to protect circuits and people. They melt and break the circuit if the current gets too high — preventing fires and electrical shocks (p.247). And of course, if you want to heat something, energy transferred to thermal energy stores is useful.

Tip: Charges do work against resistance and causing heating — see p.224 for more on this.

Tip: The national grid uses low-resistance wires and transmits electricity at a low current to reduce energy losses (page 290).

Figure 1: The glowing wires within a toaster.

Example

Toasters contain wires with a really high resistance.
When a current passes through a wire, its temperature increases so much that it glows (see Figure 1). The wire gives off lots of infrared radiation, which transfers energy to the bread and toasts it.

Practice Questions — Fact Recall

Q1 a) How is energy wasted when electric charge flows through a circuit component with electrical resistance?

b) Suggest one way to reduce the amount of wasted energy.

Q2 Give one useful application of electrical heating.

Practice Questions — Application

Q1 A watch contains a small battery. Describe the energy transfers that occur within the watch.

Q2 A washing machine is connected to the mains supply at 230 V. An average current of 3.0 A flows through the machine during an hour-long cycle. Calculate the energy transferred to the washing machine during this cycle.

Q3 An electric heater transfers 52 800 J of energy to heat a block of metal by 30 °C. The heater is connected to a 24 V power supply and a current of 8.0 A flows through it. Calculate the time taken to heat the block by 30 °C.

Tip: How much a material's temperature increases for a given amount of energy depends on its specific heat capacity, over on page 304.

Learning Objectives:
- Be able to describe power as the energy transferred per second and recall that it is measured in watt.
- Be able to recall and use the equation: $P = \frac{E}{t}$.
- Be able to describe, with examples, the relationship between the power ratings for domestic electrical appliances and the changes in stored energy when they are in use.
- Be able to explain how the power transfer in any circuit device is related to the potential difference across it and the current in it.
- Be able to recall and use the equations: $P = I \times V$ and $P = I^2 \times R$.

Specification References
10.28-10.31, 10.42

10. Power of Electrical Appliances

The power of an appliance tells us how quickly it transfers energy.

Power and energy transfer

The total energy transferred by an appliance depends on how long the appliance is on for and the power at which it's operating. The power of an appliance is the energy that it transfers per second.

The power of an electrical appliance is given by:

$$P = \frac{E}{t}$$

P = power in watts (W)
E = energy transferred in joules (J)
t = time taken in seconds (s)

Example

If a 2.5 kW kettle is on for 5 minutes, how much energy is transferred by the kettle?

First make sure the numbers are in the right units:

power = 2.5 kW = 2500 W   time = 5 minutes = 300 s

Then rearrange the power equation and substitute in the values:

$E = P \times t = 2500 \times 300 = 750\,000$ J

Appliances are often given a **power rating** — they're labelled with the maximum safe power that they can operate at. You can usually take this to be their maximum operating power. The power rating tells you the maximum amount of energy transferred between stores per second when the appliance is in use. This helps customers choose between models — the lower the power rating, the less electricity an appliance uses in a given time, so the cheaper it is to run.

But a higher power doesn't necessarily mean that it transfers more energy usefully. An appliance may be more powerful than another, but less efficient, meaning that it might still only transfer the same amount of energy (or even less) to useful stores (see page 71).

Figure 1: *A label showing the voltage and power rating of an electrical appliance.*

Power, potential difference and current

The power of an appliance also depends on the p.d. across it and the current through it. The higher the p.d. or current, the more powerful the appliance. You can calculate power using this formula:

$$P = I \times V$$

P = electrical power (W)
V = potential difference (V)
I = current (A)

Example

What's the power input of a light bulb that draws 0.20 A of current from a 230 V supply?

Just put the numbers into the equation:

$P = I \times V = 0.20 \times 230 = 46$ W

You can also find the power if you don't know the potential difference. To do this, stick $V = I \times R$ from page 223 into $P = I \times V$, giving:

$\boldsymbol{P}$ = electrical power (W) $\longrightarrow P = I^2 \times R \longleftarrow$ $\boldsymbol{R}$ = resistance (Ω)

I^2 = current squared (A^2)

> **Tip:** These equations are useful when looking at the efficiency of devices. The efficiency of the national grid is discussed on page 290.

Example

The motor in a toy car has a resistance of 25 Ω and an operating power of 64 W. Find the current it draws from the battery.

You don't know the potential difference, so you'll have to use $P = I^2 \times R$. Rearrange the equation for power to make current the subject:

$P = I^2 \times R$, so $I = \sqrt{\dfrac{P}{R}}$

Then put the numbers in:

$I = \sqrt{\dfrac{P}{R}} = \sqrt{\dfrac{64}{25}} = 1.6$ A

Practice Questions — Application

Q1 A homeowner is choosing a cooker. Cooker A is rated at 9800 W and cooker B is rated at 10 200 W. Which cooker will use the most energy in 20 minutes?

Q2 An appliance draws 3.0 A of current from the mains supply (230 V). What's the power of the appliance?

Q3 A 2.0 kW heater is on for 30 minutes. How much energy does it transfer?

Q4 A 0.2 A current flows through a 40 W filament lamp. Calculate the resistance of the filament lamp.

Q5 Microwave A is rated at 900 W and takes 4 minutes to cook a ready meal. Microwave B is rated at 650 W and takes 6 minutes to cook a ready meal. Assuming both microwaves are working at maximum power, which transfers the most energy in cooking the meal?

- Be able to describe
  that in alternating
  current (a.c.) the
  movement of charge
  changes direction.

- Be able to recall
  that in the UK the
  domestic supply is
  a.c., at a frequency of
  50 Hz and a voltage
  of about 230 V.

- Be able to describe
  direct current (d.c.) as
  movement of charge
  in one direction only
  and recall that cells
  and batteries supply
  direct current (d.c.).

- Be able to explain the
  difference between
  direct and alternating
  voltage.

- Be able to explain the
  difference in function
  between the live and
  the neutral mains
  input wires.

- Be able to recall the
  potential differences
  between the live,
  neutral and earth
  mains wires.

- Be able to explain the
  dangers of providing
  any connection
  between the live wire
  and earth.

- Be able to explain
  why switches and
  fuses should be
  connected in the live
  wire of a domestic
  circuit.

- Be able to explain the
  function of an earth
  wire and of fuses or
  circuit breakers in
  ensuring safety.

Specification References
10.33-10.41

11. Electricity in the Home

We use electricity all the time without thinking about it but there's actually a lot to think about. There are two types of electricity, a.c. and d.c., and there's a lot of clever wiring in all our appliances that keep us safe.

A.c. and d.c. supplies

There are two types of electricity supplies — **alternating current (a.c.)** and **direct current (d.c.)**. In a.c. supplies the charges are constantly changing direction. Alternating currents are produced by alternating voltages (page 282) in which the positive and negative ends of the p.d. keep switching.

The UK domestic mains supply (the electricity in your home) is an a.c. supply at around 230 V. The frequency of the a.c. mains supply (how often the current changes direction) is 50 cycles per second or 50 Hz (hertz).

By contrast, cells and batteries supply direct current (d.c.). Direct current is a current in which the charges only move in one direction. It's created by a direct voltage — where, unlike for an alternating voltage, the positive and negative ends of the source are fixed.

Three-core cables

Most electrical appliances are connected to the mains supply by **three-core cables**. This means that they have three wires inside them, each with a core of copper and a coloured plastic coating. The colour of the insulation on each cable shows its purpose — the colours are always the same for every appliance. This is so that it is easy to tell the different wires apart.

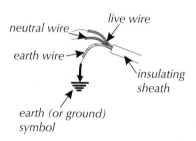

Figure 1: *A three-core electrical cable showing the live, neutral and earth wires.*

- The brown **live wire** is what provides the electricity from the mains supply. Current flows in through the live wire. It is at 230 V.

- The blue **neutral wire** completes the circuit and carries away current. It is around 0 V.

- The green and yellow **earth wire** is also at 0 V. It is for protecting the wiring and for safety — it stops the appliance casing from becoming live. It doesn't usually carry a current — only when there's a fault.

The potential difference between the live and the neutral wire is 230 V. The p.d. between the live and the earth is also 230 V, and there is no p.d. between the neutral and the earth wires, as they are both at 0 V.

The live wire

Your body (just like the earth) is at 0 V. This means that if you touch the live wire, a large potential difference is produced across your body and a current flows through you. This causes a large electric shock which could injure or even kill you.

Any connection between the live wire and the earth can be dangerous. If the link creates a low resistance path to the earth, a huge current will flow, which could result in a fire.

Components that are used to break circuits (like switches and fuses) should always be connected to the live wire. This is so if there is a problem, the supply of electricity to the appliance can be cut off. If a switch was in e.g. the earth wire, electricity would still flow through to the appliance via the live wire and away via the neutral wire, so the appliance wouldn't be turned off by a break in the earth wire. And if a fuse was connected in the neutral wire, in the event of a fault (see next page), electricity would flow in through the live wire and away via the earth wire. Both of these cases could lead to a shock or a fire.

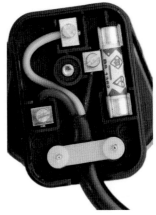

Figure 2: *The three wires in a plug. A fuse is connected to the live wire.*

Fuses

To reduce the risk of fires and electric shocks, fuses are used in circuits. Small fuses are placed inside most electrical appliances in the UK, and larger ones are used in fuseboxes to protect household circuits.

Fuses contain a thin piece of wire. When a current flows through the wire, the wire heats up (page 224). If the current increases beyond a certain point (called the fuse rating), the wire gets too hot and melts. The fuse 'blows', the circuit is broken and electricity cannot flow.

Fuses should be rated slightly above, but as near as possible to their operating current. The larger the current, the thicker the cable you need to carry it (to stop the cable getting too hot and melting). So the fuse rating for cables usually increases with cable thickness.

Figure 3: *You can see the thin wire in some fuses.*

Example

An electrician has a 3 A, a 5 A and a 10 A fuse. He is replacing a broken fuse in an appliance.

The appliance has a power rating of 1000 W and it is plugged into the mains supply, at 230 V. Determine the fuse that should be used in the appliance.

First, calculate the normal operating current of the appliance, using the power equation from page 244:

$P = I \times V$ so $I = P \div V$

$I = 1000 \div 230 = 4.34...$ A

So the electrician should fit the 5 A fuse.

Tip: If you put in fuses that had a rating below the normal operating current of the device, the fuses would keep blowing and the device wouldn't work.

Sudden increases in current, called current surges, can be due to a number of reasons, including changes in the national grid and faulty appliances.

Faulty appliances

All electrical appliances that have a metal casing contain an earth wire. The earth wire is connected to the metal casing, which provides a low-resistance path for a current to travel down in the event of a fault. As the resistance is low, a large current flows, causing a current surge which melts the fuse.

Tip: An appliance with a plastic casing doesn't need an earth wire. This is because plastic is a poor conductor of electricity, so you cannot get an electric shock from touching the casing. However, many of these devices still use fuses to protect them against current surges caused by other events.

Example

Figure 4 shows how current normally flows through the wires in a toaster.

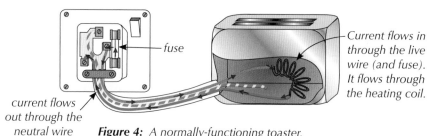

current flows out through the neutral wire

fuse

Current flows in through the live wire (and fuse). It flows through the heating coil.

Figure 4: *A normally-functioning toaster.*

Tip: Remember, the live wire is brown, the neutral wire is blue and the earth wire is green and yellow (page 246).

Figure 5 shows a faulty toaster, where the live wire is able to touch the metal casing. This causes a large current surge as current flows in through the live wire, through the casing and out down the earth wire.

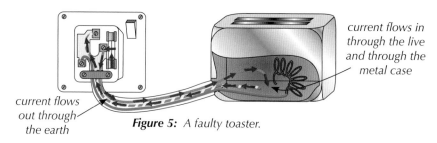

current flows out through the earth

current flows in through the live and through the metal case

Figure 5: *A faulty toaster.*

This surge in current melts the fuse connected to the live wire. The circuit is broken and the appliance is isolated, see Figure 6. So it's now impossible to get an electric shock from the casing and the risk of fire is reduced.

Tip: Isolating the appliance also reduces the risk of a fire, because the appliance won't continue to heat up.

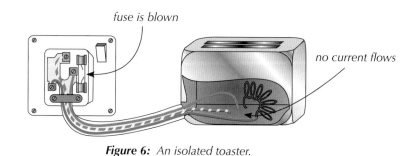

fuse is blown

no current flows

Figure 6: *An isolated toaster.*

Circuit breakers

Figure 7: *Household circuit breakers can be switched on and off.*

Instead of melting a household fuse, a large current may instead 'trip' (turn off) a **circuit breaker**. Circuit breakers are great because they turn off quicker than the time taken for a fuse to melt if there's a current surge. They can also be reset, which is much easier than having to replace a fuse. However, circuit breakers are more expensive than fuses.

Practice Questions — Fact Recall

Q1 What does a.c. stand for? How is it different from d.c.?

Q2 What is the potential difference and frequency of the UK domestic electricity supply?

Q3 State the purpose of each wire in a three-core cable.

Q4 What is the potential difference between the live and neutral wires?

Q5 Explain why it is dangerous to make a connection between the live wire and the earth.

Q6 Name one device, aside from fuses, that is used to make electronic circuits safer.

Practice Questions — Application

Q1 The graph below shows a trace of potential difference against time. State the type of current that could be produced by this potential difference.

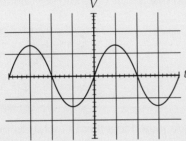

Tip: You'll come across different voltages (and how to produce them) in Section 8b, p.282.

Q2 a) Explain why fuses and switches should be connected to the live wire of an appliance.

b) Explain how using a fuse in an electrical appliance ensures the safety of people using the appliance.

Section 7 Checklist — Make sure you know...

Circuit Basics

☐ How to draw circuit diagrams, including knowing the symbols for a: cell, battery, switch, voltmeter, ammeter, resistor, variable resistor, filament lamp, motor, diode, thermistor, LDR and LED.

☐ That a voltmeter measures potential difference and is always connected in parallel.

☐ That an ammeter measures current and is always connected in series.

Current and Potential Difference

☐ That current is how much charge passes a point in a given time (i.e. the rate of flow of charge).

☐ That the current in metals is the flow of electrons.

☐ The equation $Q = I \times t$ and how to use it.

☐ That a complete circuit needs a source of potential difference in order for a current to flow.

☐ That potential difference between two points is the energy transferred by each coulomb of charge as the charges pass between those points.

☐ That potential difference is measured in volts, and that 1 volt = 1 joule per coulomb.

☐ The equation $E = Q \times V$ and how to use it.

Resistance

☐ The equation $V = I \times R$ and how to use it.

☐ The basic structure of an atom, and how atoms are joined together in metals to form a lattice of ions surrounded by free electrons.

☐ That when a current flows, some energy is dissipated to thermal energy stores, which causes a rise in temperature.

☐ That electron collisions can be used to explain heating caused by a current — electrons collide with the positive ions that make up a component, which gives them energy and heats the component.

LDRs and Thermistors

☐ That the resistance of a thermistor decreases as its temperature increases, and how to test this.

☐ That the resistance of an LDR decreases as light intensity increases, and how to test this.

I-V Graphs

☐ How to create I-V graphs for a range of components, including resistors and filament lamps.

☐ How a variable resistor changes the current through a circuit.

☐ The I-V graphs for resistors, filament lamps, diodes, thermistors and LDRs.

☐ How to use I-V graphs to show how the resistance of a component changes with current.

cont...

Series and Parallel Circuits and Investigating Them

☐ How series circuits are used for testing and measuring circuits.

☐ That in series circuits, the p.d. is shared between components according to their resistances, the current is the same everywhere and the net resistance is the sum of all the resistances.

☐ Why adding two resistors in series increases the net resistance of a circuit.

☐ That in parallel circuits, the p.d. across each branch is the same as the supply p.d. and the total current into a junction equals the total current out of the junction.

☐ That adding two resistors in parallel decreases the net resistance and the reason for this.

☐ How to test series and parallel circuits with resistors and lamps.

Energy in Circuits

☐ How to use the equation $E = I \times V \times t$.

☐ How to describe the energy transfers that occur when electrical devices are used, including the idea that some energy is always dissipated to thermal energy stores of the surroundings.

☐ That an electrical heating effect occurs because charges do work against resistance.

☐ That using low-resistance wires reduces energy losses by heating.

☐ That electrical heating is often unwanted but it can be useful (e.g. in fuses, toasters).

Power of Electrical Appliances

☐ That power is the rate of energy transfer and how to calculate it using $P = \frac{E}{t}$.

☐ That power ratings describe the maximum safe operating power of a device.

☐ That the higher the potential difference across and current through a device, the higher its power.

☐ The equations for electrical power, $P = I \times V$ and $P = I^2 \times R$, and how to use them.

Electricity in the Home

☐ That in a.c. the charges constantly change direction, but in d.c. the charges don't.

☐ That a.c. is created by an alternating voltage (where the positive and negative ends swap), and d.c. is created by a direct voltage (where the positive and negative ends stay the same).

☐ That the UK domestic mains supply is an alternating supply at 230 V and with a frequency of 50 Hz.

☐ That most electrical cables contain three wires: the live, which transmits electricity to a device; the neutral, which transmits electricity away from a device; and the earth, which is used for safety.

☐ That the p.d. between the live wire and the neutral or earth wire is 230 V, and the p.d. between the neutral and the earth wire is 0 V.

☐ How connecting the live wire to earth can cause electric shocks or fires and why switches and fuses are connected to the live wire.

☐ How fuses and circuit breakers work.

Exam-style Questions

1   A physics student is carrying out a series of experiments to investigate the *I-V* graph of component X in constant conditions. He uses the circuit shown in **Figure 1**.

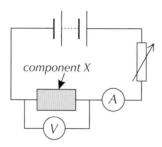

Figure 1

(a)   Explain how the variable resistor is used to change the current in a circuit.

(1 mark)

The student tests an unknown component, X.
The data collected for component X is shown as an *I-V* graph in **Figure 2**.

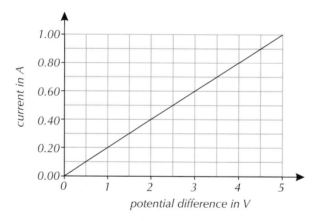

Figure 2

(b)   What is component X?

(1 mark)

(c)   Calculate the resistance of component X. Give your answer in Ω.

(3 marks)

(d) (i)   The student then tests a filament lamp. Sketch the *I-V* graph of a filament lamp.

(1 mark)

(ii)   Explain the shape of the *I-V* graph sketched in part (i).

(3 marks)

2   **Figure 3** shows an electric motor and filament lamp connected in parallel to a battery.

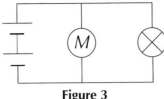

Figure 3

The total size of the electric current in the circuit is 1.2 A. It takes 30 seconds to move 15 C of charge through the motor. The potential difference across the motor is 14 V.

(a)   What is the potential difference across the battery?

(1 mark)

(b) (i)   Write down the equation that links charge, current and time.

(1 mark)

  (ii)   Calculate the current passing through the motor. Give your answer in A.

(3 marks)

(c)   Calculate the energy transferred by the lamp in 240 seconds. Give your answer in J, to 2 significant figures. Use the correct equation from the equations listed on page 404.

(4 marks)

3   A kitchen contains a 2.55 kW oven connected to the UK mains a.c. supply.

(a)   State the potential difference and frequency of the UK mains a.c. supply.

(2 marks)

The oven transfers 7 038 000 J of energy in the time it takes to cook a particular meal.

(b) (i)   Write down the equation that links power, energy transferred and time.

(1 mark)

  (ii)   Calculate how long it takes to cook the meal. Give your answer in s.

(3 marks)

(c)   Calculate the total amount of charge that passes through the oven in the time it takes to cook the meal. Give your answer in C.
Write down any equations you use.

(4 marks)

4   A kettle with a metal casing is linked to the mains electricity using a three-core cable. The three-core cable has a live wire, an earth wire and a neutral wire inside it.

(a)   The kettle operates at 230 V and has a power of 575 W.
Calculate the resistance of the kettle's heating element. Give your answer in Ω.
Write down any equations you use.

(5 marks)

(b)*   The kettle's cable is frayed, and the live wire is exposed so that it touches the metal casing. Explain how this could cause a fire and how a fuse can be used to reduce this risk.

(6 marks)

Learning Objectives:
- Be able to explain how an insulator can be charged by friction, through the transfer of electrons.
- Be able to explain how the material gaining electrons becomes negatively charged and the material losing electrons is left with an equal positive charge.
- Be able to recall that like charges repel and unlike charges attract.
- Be able to explain common electrostatic phenomena in terms of movement of electrons, including attraction by induction such as a charged balloon attracted to a wall and a charged comb picking up small pieces of paper.

Specification References
11.1-11.4

1. Static Electricity

Static electricity is the cause of all sorts of fun and games and you get the pleasure of learning all about it — joy.

Insulators and conductors

Electrical charges can move easily through some materials, and less easily through others.

- If electrical charges can easily move through a material, it is called an electrical **conductor**. Metals are known to be good conductors.

- If electrical charges cannot easily move through a material, it is called an electrical **insulator**. Plastics and rubbers are usually good insulators.

> **Example**
>
> Electrical wires and cables are usually made up of both electrical insulators and conductors. They have a core made out of an electrical conductor so that electric charge can flow through it easily, and a casing made of an electrical insulator to stop you getting an electric shock (p.247) by touching the wire or cable.

Static charge

A **static charge** is an electric charge which cannot move. Static charges are often (but not always) found on electrical insulators where charge cannot flow freely. They can be positive (+ve) or negative (–ve). A static charge can build up on a conductor if it's isolated — in other words, if there's nowhere for the charge to flow to.

When certain insulating materials are rubbed together, friction causes negatively charged electrons to be scraped off one and dumped on the other.

This will leave a positive static charge on the one that loses electrons and a negative static charge on the one that gains electrons. Which way the electrons are transferred depends on the two materials involved — see the examples on the next page.

Both positive and negative electrostatic charges are only ever produced by the movement of electrons. Protons definitely do not move.

A positive static charge is always caused by electrons moving away elsewhere. The material that loses the electrons loses some negative charge, and is left with an equal positive charge.

Tip: There's more about electrons and protons on page 152.

Tip: This is really important, so make sure you remember it — <u>only</u> electrons move, not protons. A positive charge is gained by losing electrons, <u>not</u> gaining protons.

The classic examples of static build up are polythene and acetate rods being rubbed with a cloth duster.

- With the polythene rod, electrons move from the duster to the rod. The rod becomes negatively charged and the cloth has an equal positive charge.

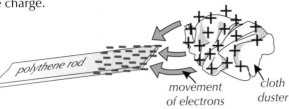

Figure 1: *A polythene rod being rubbed with a cloth duster to create static charge.*

- With the acetate rod, electrons move from the rod to the duster. The rod becomes positively charged and the cloth has an equal negative charge.

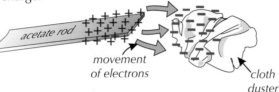

Figure 2: *An acetate rod being rubbed with a cloth duster to create static charge.*

Electrostatic attraction and repulsion

When two electrically charged objects are brought close together they exert a force on one another, as shown in Figure 3.

- Two things with opposite electric charges are attracted to each other.

- Two things with the same electric charge will repel each other.

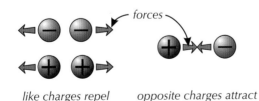

like charges repel   *opposite charges attract*

Figure 3: *A diagram showing the forces that different electric charges exert on one another.*

These **electrostatic forces** will cause the objects to move if they are able to do so. This is known as electrostatic attraction/repulsion. Electrostatic forces are non-contact forces (the objects don't need to touch, see page 205) and they get weaker the further apart the two things are.

If a rod with a known charge is suspended from a piece of string (so it is free to move) and another rod with the same charge is placed nearby, they will repel each other. The suspended rod will swing away. If an oppositely charged rod is placed nearby instead, they will attract and the suspended rod will swing towards it.

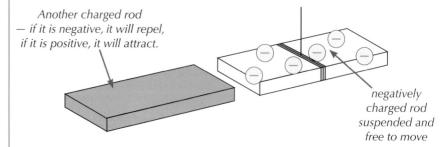

Another charged rod — if it is negative, it will repel, if it is positive, it will attract.

negatively charged rod suspended and free to move

Figure 5: *A diagram of a method to demonstrate electrostatic attraction and repulsion.*

Figure 4: *A demonstration of electrostatic attraction between a balloon and hair. When you rub your hair with a balloon, electrons are transferred from your hair to the balloon. The balloon and your hair then become oppositely charged, so they will attract each other.*

Tip: Induction in physics means a field is created by a second, nearby field. Here, an electric field is being created (page 263) but a similar thing can happen with magnets too (page 267). Make sure you always use correct terminology when talking about scientific observations.

WORKING SCIENTIFICALLY

Uncharged objects

Electrostatic attraction can occur between a charged and an uncharged object. This is called **attraction by induction**. It occurs because charges on the surface of an object are able to move slightly.

If a static negative charge is brought close to a neutral object, the negative charges in the neutral object are repelled by the static charge. This creates a small positive charge on the surface of the uncharged object. This positive charge attracts the negative static charge and the two objects stick together.

If a static positive charge is brought close to a neutral object, negative charges in the object are attracted to the positive charge and move towards it. This creates a negative charge on the surface of the uncharged object, which attracts the positive static charge.

Example 1

Rubbing a balloon against your hair or clothes transfers electrons to the balloon, leaving it with a negative charge. If you then hold the balloon to a wall, the negative charges on the balloon repel the negative charges on the surface of the wall. This leaves a positive charge on the surface, which attracts the negatively charged balloon — the balloon 'sticks' to the wall.

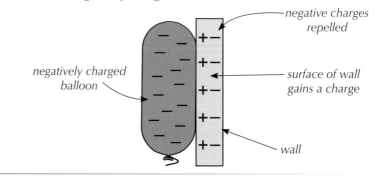

negative charges repelled

negatively charged balloon

surface of wall gains a charge

wall

Example 2

If you run a comb through your hair, electrons will be transferred from your hair to the comb, making it negatively charged. It can then be used to pick up little pieces of uncharged paper. Holding it near the little pieces of paper causes induction in the paper, causing the paper pieces to 'jump up' and stick to the comb.

Figure 6: *You can see attraction by induction by placing a charged comb next to a tap — the water is attracted towards the comb. This causes the stream of water from the tap to bend.*

Practice Questions — Fact Recall

Q1   How may some insulators become positively charged when they are rubbed against another insulator?

Q2   Say whether the following objects will attract, repel, or feel no force when brought close together:

a) Two positively charged objects.

b) A negatively charged object and a positively charged object.

Practice Questions — Application

Q1   A woman uses a plastic hair brush to brush her hair. Both the hair brush and her hair become electrically charged.

a) When the woman looks in the mirror, her hair is standing on end. Explain why.

b) The hair brush has a charge of −0.5 nC. What is the total charge on the woman's hair?

Q2   A cleaner wipes a TV screen with an anti-static cloth, which prevents a static charge building up on the screen. Explain how this keeps the screen free from dust for longer.

Tip: Plastic and hair are both electrical insulators.

Tip: 1 nC = 1×10^{-9} C (it's short for nano-coulomb). There's more about prefixes on page 18.

Learning Objective:
- Be able to explain some of the uses of electrostatic charges in everyday situations, including insecticide sprayers.

Specification Reference
11.6

2. Uses of Static Electricity

Static electricity is used more than you'd think — in photocopiers, printers and even when painting cars. You need to be able to explain how static electricity is used in different processes.

Common uses of static electricity

Tip: Photocopiers work in a similar way to laser printers.

Example 1

Laser printers use static electricity to print documents. Inside the printer, an object called the image drum is given a positive charge. A laser is then shone onto the drum, creating a negative charge on parts of the drum (see Figure 1). This negative charge is in the shape of whatever is to be printed.

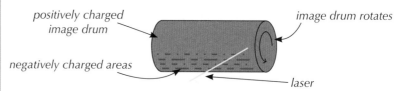

positively charged image drum

image drum rotates

negatively charged areas

laser

***Figure 1:** A laser being shone onto a positively charged image drum.*

Powdered ink (toner) inside the printer is given a positive charge, so it is attracted towards the negatively charged areas of the image drum. Negatively charged paper is then rolled across the image drum.

The charge on the paper is stronger than the charge on the image drum, so the powdered ink on the drum sticks to the paper (Figure 3). The paper is then heated, fusing the ink powder to the paper.

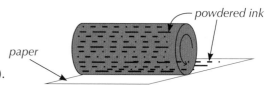

powdered ink

paper

***Figure 3:** Paper being rolled across the image drum and attracting the ink.*

***Figure 2:** Printer ink cartridges are filled with coloured powder (toner). Printers use a mixture of toners to create documents.*

Example 2

Filters in chimneys work by passing smoke through an electrically charged grid. The particles in the smoke gain electrons from the grid and become negatively charged (see Figure 4).

The sides of the chimney have positively charged plates, which attract the negatively charged smoke particles. The particles stick to the plates instead of travelling out of the chimney and into the atmosphere.

Particles are attracted to the positively charged plates

Negatively charged smoke particle

Negatively charged grid

Uncharged smoke particle

***Figure 4:** An air filter in a chimney.*

Electrostatic sprayers

Electrostatic sprayers are used in various industries to give an even coat of whatever's being sprayed. The spray gun is charged, so that the droplets it sprays all gain a static charge. As all of the droplets have the same charge, they repel each other, creating a fine, even spray.

Figure 5: An aeroplane being used to spray crops with insecticides.

Example 1

Insecticides are chemicals that are sprayed onto crops to kill insects. Insecticide sprayers use static electricity to get a wider, more even distribution of insecticide onto crops.

Often, crops are sprayed with insecticides from a low-flying aeroplane. This creates some problems, as the insecticide may fall unevenly onto the crops, so different areas of a field receive different concentrations of the chemicals.

By using an electrostatic sprayer, the insecticide spray spreads out evenly above the crops, giving them an even coverage. The insecticide is also attracted to the plants, due to attraction by induction (page 256), meaning less will be blown away by the wind.

Example 2

Bicycle frames are painted using electrostatic paint sprayers.

The spray gun is charged, which charges the small drops of paint as they are sprayed out of the gun. The frame is given the opposite charge to the gun. This is easy to do as the frame is usually made from metal (which is a conductor), and means that the paint is attracted towards the bicycle frame.

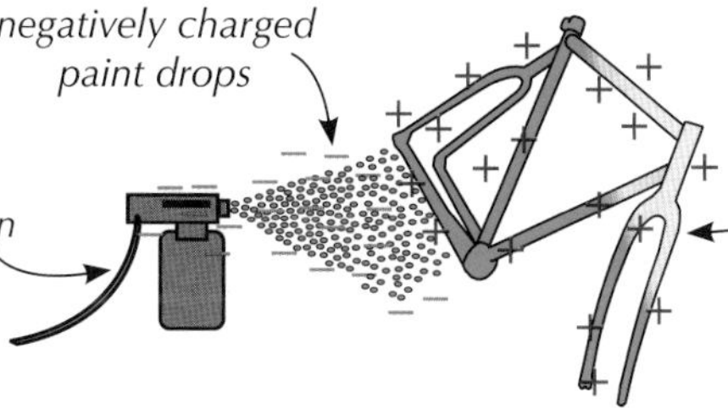

negatively charged paint drops

positively charged bike frame

spray gun

Figure 6: An electrostatic sprayer used for painting a bicycle frame.

This prevents paint being wasted and means that parts of the bicycle frame pointing away from the spray gun still receive paint, i.e. there are no paint shadows.

Tip: There's more on how electrostatic paint sprayers work on page 264.

Tip: The examples on these pages will work with the charges either way around — e.g. if the paint drops were positively charged and the bike frame was negatively charged, the paint would still be attracted to the frame.

Practice Question — Application

Q1 Explain how electrostatic sprayers use electrostatic charge to form an even spray of liquid droplets.

Learning Objectives:
- Be able to explain common electrostatic phenomena in terms of movement of electrons, including shocks from everyday objects and lightning.
- Be able to describe some of the dangers of sparking in everyday situations, including fuelling cars, and explain the use of earthing to prevent dangerous build-up of charge.
- Be able to explain how earthing removes excess charge by movement of electrons.

Specification References
11.4, 11.5, 11.7

Tip: When describing sparks (or any other event caused by static electricity) make sure you talk about the movement of the electrons. You may also need to include information about the electric fields (page 263) in your answer.

3. Sparking and the Dangers of Static Electricity

Static electricity can be painful and even dangerous when sparks are created. Thankfully, you can earth objects to reduce these risks.

What is sparking?

As electric charge builds up on an object, the potential difference (p.221) between the object and the earth (which is at 0 V) increases. If the potential difference gets large enough, electrons can jump across the gap between the charged object and the earth — this is a **spark**.

Electrons can also jump between a charged object and any nearby conductor connected to the ground, which is why you can get static shocks from clothes or from getting out of cars. Usually sparks happen when the gap is fairly small, but sparks can occur across large distances (e.g. lightning, see below).

> **Example**
>
> You may have felt a static shock when opening a door.
>
> A negative charge builds up on your body, due to the friction between your shoes and the floor as you walk around.
>
> When you go to open a door that has a metal handle, electrons jump from you to the metal, and you get a shock.

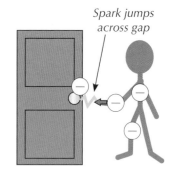

Spark jumps across gap

Figure 1: *A spark jumping between a person's handle and a door handle.*

Lightning

Lightning is just a really big spark. When raindrops and bits of ice bump together inside storm clouds, friction between them causes the top of the cloud to become positively charged and the bottom of the cloud to become negatively charged. This creates a huge potential difference. Electrons usually travel within the cloud or between clouds, creating lightning across the sky. However, some sparks are large enough that the electrons can travel between the cloud and the ground.

Lightning strikes can be very dangerous, as they can damage homes or start fires when they hit the ground. They can also be fatal if they hit a person — but this is very uncommon.

Figure 2: *Lightning striking the ground.*

Dangers of static electricity

Static charges build up on objects whether they're wanted or not. This can be inconvenient and sometimes even dangerous if it leads to sparking.

As a plane flies through the air, friction between the air and the plane causes electrons to be transferred and the plane becomes charged. This build up of static charge can interfere with communication equipment.
Modern planes are fitted with static dischargers, which control the amount of static charge that builds up on a plane as it flies.

Example 2

Static charges can build up when refuelling vehicles, especially large tankers and planes, which can be very dangerous. Sparks can cause the fuel to ignite, causing a fire or even an explosion.

As fuel flows out of a filler pipe into a fuel tank, a static charge can build up on the fuel. This causes a potential difference, which eventually could lead to a spark. For large vehicles like aircraft where lots of fuel flows into the tank in a short time, chemicals are added to the fuel to make it more conductive so it is less likely to build up a static charge.

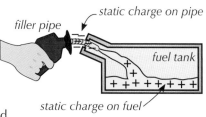

Figure 3: Static charge created when refuelling.

Figure 4: A car being refuelled by a filler pipe.

There is also a danger from any static charges on the surface of the vehicle. You saw in example 1 that a static charge builds up on a plane as it flies. So before an aircraft is refuelled this static charge must be removed, e.g. by earthing (see below).

Earthing

Dangerous sparks can be prevented by connecting a charged object to the ground using a conductor (e.g. a copper wire) — this is called **earthing**. Earthing provides an easy route for electrons to travel between the object and the ground. This removes any excess charge that could give you a shock or make a spark.

The electrons flow down the conductor to the ground if the static charge on the object is negative and flow up the conductor from the ground if the static charge is positive (see Figures 6 and 7).

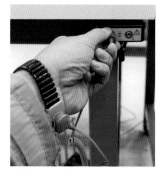

Figure 5: Anti-static wrist straps ground the wearer. These are used when people are working with sensitive equipment that may be damaged by sparks.

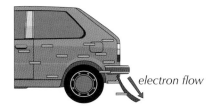

electron flow

Figure 6: Electrons flowing from a charged car to the ground.

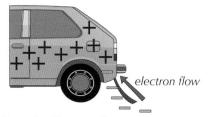

electron flow

Figure 7: Electrons flowing from the ground to a charged car.

Practice Questions — Fact Recall

Q1 What is a spark?

Q2 Describe the cause of lightning striking the ground.

Q3 Give one example of how static electricity can be dangerous.

Q4 What is 'earthing'?

Practice Questions — Application

Q1 A positively charged object is connected to the ground by a conductor. Describe the movement of electrons between the object and the ground.

Q2 A student is walking up a carpeted staircase. As they reach out to touch the metal hand-rail, they receive a small shock. Explain how this happens.

Q3 Tall buildings usually have a lightning rod on their roof. This is a metal rod placed on the top of the building that is connected to a wire which runs down the building and into the ground. Explain how this helps to protect the building.

4. Electric Fields

Everything with an electric charge has an electric field. Field interactions explain the non-contact forces between charged objects, as well as sparks.

What is an electric field?

An **electric field** is created around any electrically charged object. It's the region around a charged object where, if a second charged object was placed inside it, a force would be exerted on both of the charges (see next page). The closer to the object you get, the stronger the field is (and the further you are from it, the weaker it is).

You can show an electric field around an object using field lines. Electric field lines point away from positive charge and towards negative charge, and they're always at right angles to a charged object's surface. You can think of field lines as showing you the path that a positively charged particle would move along in an electric field. The closer together the lines are, the stronger the field is.

The electric field around a point charge

You have to know the shape and direction of the field lines around an isolated point charge (Q), as shown in Figure 1.

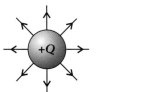

Figure 1: *The electric field pattern of a positive point charge (left) and a negative point charge (right).*

As you can see from Figure 1, the field lines radiate out from the centre of the point charge. The closer to the charge you are, the closer together the lines are and so the stronger the field is. (And the further from the charge you go, the further apart the lines get, so the weaker the field is).

The electric field between parallel plates

You also need to be able to draw the electric field between two oppositely charged parallel plates. The field between parallel plates is a **uniform field**, which means that it has the same strength everywhere (this only stops being true at the very edges of the plates). You can see this in Figure 2 — the field lines are straight, at right angles to the plates and evenly spaced, so the strength of the field is the same everywhere.

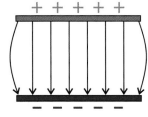

Figure 2: *The electric field pattern between two oppositely charged parallel plates.*

Learning Objectives:
- Be able to define an electric field as the region where an electric charge experiences a force.
- Be able to describe the shape and direction of the electric field around a point charge and between parallel plates and relate the strength of the field to the concentration of lines.
- Be able to explain how the concept of an electric field helps to explain the phenomena of static electricity.

Specification References
11.8-11.10

Tip: 'Isolated' means that the point charge isn't interacting with anything.

Tip: When drawing the field for an isolated point charge, make sure you draw at least eight equally spaced field lines.

Tip: When drawing uniform fields, draw at least three straight, equally spaced parallel lines.

Tip: There are lots of similarities between electric fields and electrostatic forces, and magnetic fields and magnetic forces.
See page 267 for more on magnetic fields.

Electrostatic forces

When a charged object is placed in the electric field of another charged object, it feels a non-contact force (like on page 205). This force is caused by the electric fields of each charged object interacting with each other.

If the field lines between the charged objects point in the same direction, the field lines 'join up' and the objects are attracted to each other (Figure 4). When the field lines between the charged objects point in opposite directions, the field lines 'push against' each other and the objects repel each other (see Figures 3 and 5).

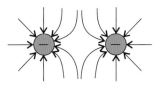

Figure 3: *Interacting fields between two negative charges that are repelling each other.*

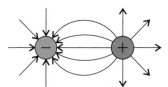

Figure 4: *Interacting fields between two opposite charges that are attracting each other.*

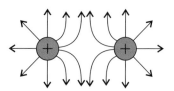

Figure 5: *Interacting fields between two positive charges that are repelling each other.*

Tip: You can think of electric field lines as 'lines of force' — they show the direction of the force that would act on a positive charge placed at that point.

The size of the force between the objects is linked to the strength of the electric field at that point. You can see in Figure 1 that the further from a point charge you go, the further apart the lines are and so the weaker the field is. So, as you increase the distance between the charged objects, the strength of the field decreases and the force between them gets smaller.

Explaining electrostatic events

Electric fields help to describe electrostatic events like attraction by induction. When an object becomes statically charged, it generates an electric field. This field interacts with the electric fields of nearby electrons in other objects. This interaction causes an attractive electrostatic force — the two objects move towards or stick to each other, (like the balloon and the wall on p.256).

Exam Tip
Make sure you understand how interacting electric fields cause a force. In the exam you might have to apply your knowledge of electric fields to explain examples of static electricity that you've not seen before.

This also explains how electrostatic sprayers work — in the paint example from page 259, the electric field created around the bicycle frame interacts with the fields around the negatively charged droplets of paint. The field lines 'join up' and the droplets and the frame are attracted to each other. The droplets of paint are free to move, so they follow the field lines of the electric field produced by the bicycle frame, until they touch the frame. This is why no paint shadows are created — the field lines touch all parts of the frame, so all parts of the frame receive paint.

Electric fields can also be used to explain sparks. As you've seen on page 260, sparks are caused when there is a high enough potential difference between a charged object and the earth (or an earthed object). A high potential difference causes a very strong electric field between the charged object and the earthed object.

The strong electric field interacts with the electric fields of electrons in air particles. This creates a force so strong that it removes electrons from the air particles (a process known as ionisation). Air is normally an insulator, but when it is ionised it is much more conductive, so charge can flow through it. This is the spark — the flow of charge through the ionised air.

Practice Questions — Fact Recall

Q1　What direction do electric field lines point in?

Q2　Draw the field lines between two oppositely charged parallel plates.

Q3　Explain, with respect to electric fields, how a build up of static charge can lead to a spark.

Section 8a Checklist — Make sure you know...

Static Electricity and Uses of Static Electricity

☐ That a static charge is a charge which cannot move.

☐ That rubbing two insulating materials together causes friction, which can cause negatively charged electrons to move from one to the other, giving both materials an equal but opposite charge.

☐ That a material which loses electrons is left with a positive charge and a material that gains electrons becomes negatively charged.

☐ That electrically charged objects exert a force on one another — objects with the same charge repel each other and objects with opposite charges attract each other.

☐ That a charged object can repel or attract electrons on the surface of a second, neutral object to create a small charge on the surface of the second object. This causes attraction by induction. Examples of this are a balloon sticking to a wall and scraps of paper being attracted to a charged comb.

☐ How static electricity is used in a number of situations, including electrostatic sprayers.

Sparking and the Dangers of Static Electricity

☐ That if a build up of static creates a high enough p.d. between a charged object and earth (or an earthed conductor), a spark can be created. This is where electrons jump between the object and the earth. Lightning is just an example of a very large spark.

☐ That sparks can be dangerous, especially when refuelling vehicles.
One way of reducing this danger is to earth objects.

☐ That electrons travel to or from the ground and stop a charge building on an earthed object.

Electric Fields

☐ That all charged objects have an electric field around them, which is the area around a charge where a second charge will feel a force.

☐ That field lines can be used to represent electric fields, and the closer together the field lines are the stronger the electric field is.

☐ How to draw the electric field around a point charge and the field between two oppositely charged parallel plates.

☐ How to explain attraction by induction and sparks using the idea of electric fields.

Exam-style Questions

1   Electrostatic spray-painting is a method used to paint car bodies that uses electrostatic charges. The car body is given a negative charge, and a paint gun gives each paint droplet a positive charge.

  (a)   Suggest why giving the paint droplets and the car opposite charges reduces the amount of paint wasted when a car is spray-painted.

(2 marks)

  (b)   An engineer holds his hand close to the car and gets a small electric shock.
Explain how this happens with reference to electric fields.

(5 marks)

2   Large, metal storage tanks are used to store petrol at depots. Petrol from these tanks is pumped into lorries which transport the fuel to petrol stations.

  (a)   Explain the risks caused by static electricity at depots.

(2 marks)

  (b)   The storage tanks are connected to a metal bar driven deep into the ground.
Explain how this reduces the risks described in part (a).

(3 marks)

  (c)   A worker at the depot gains a small, positive static charge from the friction between his shoes and the floor. He then touches the storage tank.
Describe what happens, in terms of the movement of charge.

(2 marks)

3   A student rubs a balloon against a scarf.
The student determines that the scarf is negatively charged.

  (a)   Explain how the scarf has become negatively charged.

(1 mark)

        The student predicts that the balloon must be positively charged.
To test this, the student suspends the balloon from a string and brings a positively charged rod near to the balloon.

  (b)   Explain what the student would expect to see when the rod is brought close, based on their prediction.

(2 marks)

  (c)   The student's prediction is correct. The student then places the balloon onto a wall. The balloon sticks to the wall.
Explain what has happened in terms of the electric fields involved.

(3 marks)

  (d)   Sketch the electric field around the balloon. You may assume the balloon's field is the same as the field around an isolated point charge.

(1 mark)

1. Magnets and Magnetic Fields

Chances are, you've come across magnets before. Whilst some of this may seem familiar, make sure you learn it as you'll need the ideas from these pages in order to understand the rest of the section...

Permanent and induced magnets

All magnets produce a **magnetic field**. A magnetic field is a region around the magnet where other magnets experience a non-contact force acting on them — see page 268.

There are two types of magnet — **permanent magnets** and **induced** (or **temporary**) **magnets**. Permanent magnets (e.g. bar magnets) produce their own magnetic field all the time. Induced magnets only produce a magnetic field when they're in another, external magnetic field. When the external field is removed, induced magnets quickly lose their magnetism (or most of it).

Magnets are made from magnetic materials. There are three common magnetic elements — iron, nickel and cobalt. Some alloys and compounds of these metals are also magnetic. For example, steel is magnetic because it contains iron.

The 'softness' of a material affects how quickly it loses its magnetism. Permanent magnets are made from **permanent magnetic materials** like steel. They are magnetically 'hard' because they take a long time to lose their magnetism. **Temporary magnetic materials** are magnetically 'soft', they lose their magnetism fairly quickly. Pure iron and nickel-iron alloys are examples of temporary magnetic materials.

> **Example**
>
> Transformers work by rapidly magnetising and demagnetising a metal core. This core is usually made from iron, as it is soft and so can easily lose its magnetism. There's more about transformers on pages 285-286.

Drawing magnetic fields

A magnetic field can be represented by a field diagram. A field diagram is just a series of lines that show where a magnetic field exists and its direction.

All magnets have two poles — a north pole and a south pole. Magnetic field lines have arrows on them that always point from north to south. The direction of the field lines show the direction of the force a north pole would feel if it was placed in that location. The stronger the magnetic field at any point, the closer together the field lines are.

You need to know the field diagrams for bar magnets and uniform fields.

Learning Objectives:

- Be able to explain the difference between permanent and induced magnets.

- Be able to describe permanent and temporary magnetic materials including cobalt, steel, iron and nickel.

- Be able to describe the shape and direction of the magnetic field around bar magnets and for a uniform field, and relate the strength of the field to the concentration of lines.

- Be able to recall that unlike magnetic poles attract and like magnetic poles repel.

- **H** Be able to explain that magnetic forces are due to interactions between magnetic fields.

- Be able to describe the use of plotting compasses to show the shape and direction of the field of a magnet and the Earth's magnetic field.

- Be able to explain how the behaviour of a magnetic compass is related to evidence that the core of the Earth must be magnetic.

Specification References 12.1-12.6, 12.11

Bar magnets

Tip: ■H Magnetic forces are strongest at the poles too.

The magnetic field is strongest at the poles of a magnet. So field lines for magnets are closest together at the poles, as shown in Figure 1. The further away from a magnet you get, the weaker the field is.

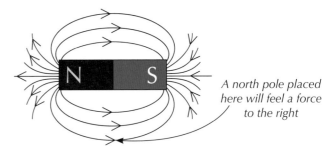

A north pole placed here will feel a force to the right

Tip: When drawing field lines, draw at least three and make sure they give an overall idea of the whole shape of the field. And of course, don't forget to label the direction of the field lines.

Figure 1: *A field diagram showing the magnetic field around a bar magnet.*

Uniform magnetic fields

Tip: You met uniform fields on page 263.

Uniform magnetic fields are created between two opposite magnetic poles. Uniform fields have the same strength everywhere — so the field lines are evenly spaced, parallel, straight lines (see Figure 2).

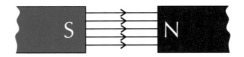

Tip: To see the shape of a magnetic field, place a piece of card over a magnet and sprinkle iron filings onto it. The filings line up with the field lines — but they won't show you the direction of the field.

Figure 2: *A field diagram showing a uniform magnetic field.*

Forces between magnets

The force between two permanent magnets can be attractive or repulsive. Two poles that are the same (these are called 'like poles') will repel each other. Two different poles ('unlike poles') will attract each other.

The force between a permanent and an induced magnet is always attractive.

> ### Example
>
> The iron block on the right becomes magnetised when it is brought near the permanent bar magnet on the left. The south pole of the permanent magnet induces a north pole in the iron bar, so there is an attractive force between the two magnets.

Tip: You don't need to know how magnetic materials (page 267) become induced magnets, just that they do. Remember that the force between a permanent and an induced magnet is always attractive to help you work out the induced poles.

permanent magnet   *induced magnet*

Figure 3: *A diagram of magnetic poles induced in a magnetic material when it is brought near to a bar magnet.*

Interacting magnetic fields Higher

Forces between magnets are caused by interacting magnetic fields. When you bring two like poles near to each other, their magnetic field lines overlap and some cancel each other out. The remaining field causes the repulsive force that pushes the two poles apart (see Figure 4).

When two unlike poles are brought close to each other, their field lines add together. A uniform field is created between the two poles, causing the attractive force that pulls the two poles together (see Figure 5).

Tip: Interacting electric fields cause electrostatic forces, which you saw on page 264. There are a lot of similarities between electric and magnetic fields, so understanding one will help you with the other.

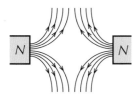

Figure 4: *The magnetic field between two like poles repelling each other.*

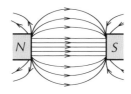

Figure 5: *The magnetic field between two unlike poles attracting each other.*

Compasses

Inside a compass is a tiny bar magnet called a needle. The north pole of this magnet is attracted to the south pole of any other magnet it is near. So the compass points in the direction of the magnetic field it is in.

You can find the shape and direction of a magnetic field by using a compass. First, put the magnet on a piece of paper and draw round it. Then, place the compass on the paper near the magnet. Mark the direction of the compass needle by drawing two dots — one at each end of the needle. Move the compass so that the tail (south) end of the needle is where the tip (north) of the needle was. Put another dot by the tip of the needle. Repeat this around the magnet and then join up the marks you've made — you'll end up with a drawing of one field line around the magnet. Repeat this method at different points around the magnet to get several field lines.

When they're not near a magnet, compasses always point north. This is because the Earth generates its own magnetic field (where the North Pole is actually a magnetic south pole). This shows that the inside (core) of the Earth must be magnetic.

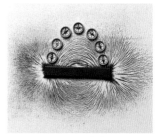

Figure 6: *A series of compasses pointing along the magnetic field lines of a bar magnet, which are also shown by iron filings.*

Tip: Remember to draw the direction on to any field lines you draw.

Practice Questions — Fact Recall

Q1 What is a magnetic field?

Q2 Describe what is meant by an 'induced magnet'.

Q3 Name three magnetic materials.

Q4 Draw the magnetic field lines around a bar magnet and state where the field is strongest.

Q5 a) Do like poles attract or repel each other?

b) What causes this force?

Q6 How do we know that the Earth's core is magnetic?

- Be able to describe
  how to show that a
  current can create
  a magnetic effect
  around a long
  straight conductor,
  describing the shape
  of the magnetic field
  produced and relating
  the direction of the
  magnetic field to
  the direction of the
  current.
- Be able to recall that
  the strength of the
  field depends on the
  size of the current
  and the distance
  from the long straight
  conductor.
- Be able to explain
  how inside a solenoid
  (an example of an
  electromagnet) the
  fields from individual
  coils add together to
  form a very strong
  almost uniform field
  along the centre of the
  solenoid and cancel
  to give a weaker field
  outside the solenoid.
- Be able to describe
  the uses of permanent
  and temporary
  magnetic materials.

Specification References
12.2, 12.7-12.9

2. Electromagnetism

Magnets aren't the only things with magnetic fields — anything that's carrying an electric current also has one. This can have some clever applications.

The magnetic field around a current-carrying wire

When a current (see p.221) flows through a long, straight conductor like a wire, a magnetic field is created around it. The field is made up of concentric circles (circles which share the same centre) perpendicular to the conductor, with the conductor in the centre (see Figure 1).

You can see this by placing a compass near a conductor which is carrying a current. As you move the compass, it will trace the direction of the magnetic field.

Changing the direction of the current changes the direction of the magnetic field — use the **right-hand thumb rule** to work out which way it goes:

The right-hand thumb rule

Using your right hand, point your thumb in the direction of the current, and curl your fingers. The direction of your fingers is the direction of the field.

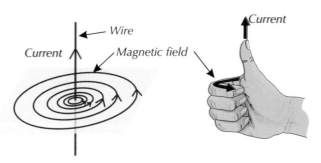

Figure 1: *A diagram showing how a magnetic field is created around a current-carrying wire, alongside a demonstration of the right-hand thumb rule.*

The strength of the magnetic field produced changes with the current and the distance from the wire. The larger the current through the wire, or the closer to the wire you are, the stronger the field is.

Solenoids

You can increase the strength of the magnetic field that a wire produces by wrapping the wire into a coil called a **solenoid** (see Figure 2). This happens because the field lines around each loop of wire line up with each other, as shown on the next page in Figure 4.

A solenoid is an example of an **electromagnet** — a magnet whose magnetic field can be turned on and off by an electric current.

Figure 2: *Copper wire wrapped into a solenoid.*

The magnetic field around a single loop of wire is shown in Figure 3.

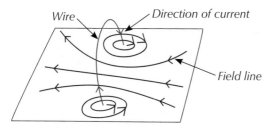

Figure 3: *The magnetic field lines around a single loop of wire.*

When the wire is wrapped into multiple loops, the field lines overlap and interact — see Figure 4. This leads to them either 'adding together' or 'cancelling out'.

Inside the solenoid, lots of field lines all point in the same direction, so the resulting magnetic field is strong and almost uniform. Outside of the solenoid, a lot of the overlapping field lines cancel each other out — so the field is weak apart from at the ends of the solenoid. You end up with a field that looks like the one around a bar magnet, shown in Figure 5.

Tip: H You can think of magnetic field lines as 'lines of force' as they show the direction of the force a north pole would feel if it was placed in that location. So you can treat interacting magnetic field lines in the same way as you'd treat forces (p.207). Field lines pointing in the same direction 'add together' and field lines pointing in opposite directions 'cancel out'.

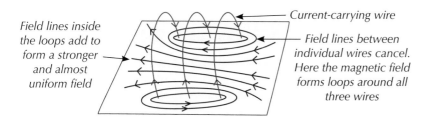

Figure 4: *The magnetic field lines around multiple loops of wire (a solenoid).*

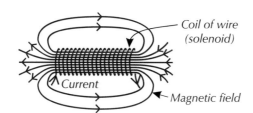

Figure 5: *A field diagram showing the magnetic field created around a current-carrying solenoid.*

Figure 6: *Iron filings showing the magnetic field lines around a current-carrying solenoid.*

You can increase the strength of the magnetic field of a solenoid even more by putting a block of iron in the centre of the coil. The iron core becomes an induced magnet whenever current is flowing. The magnetic field of the core and the coil combine, making a stronger magnet overall.

Uses of magnets

Magnets have lots uses. For example, the force of attraction between two permanent magnets is used to keep fridge doors closed. Magnets are also used in magnetic separators, which are used in recycling plants to sort metal items (like cans).

Figure 7: A scrap yard crane that uses an electromagnet.

Many modern objects use electromagnets because the magnetic field they produce can be turned on and off.

Example

Electromagnets are used in some cranes, e.g. in scrap yards and steel works. They can be turned on to attract and pick up magnetic materials such as iron and steel. When you want to release them, you simply turn the electromagnet off.

Practice Questions — Fact Recall

Q1 The current through a wire is increased. How does this change the magnetic field around the wire?

Q2 How does the strength of the magnetic field produced by a current in a wire vary with distance from the wire?

Q3 Describe what an electromagnet is.

Q4 Give one use of magnetic materials.

Practice Questions — Application

Tip: You'll need to use the right-hand thumb rule to find the direction of the current.

Q1 A current-carrying wire (shown by the red dot) produces the following magnetic field pattern when viewed from above.

a) What direction is the current flowing in?

b) In what direction would the field lines point if the current began flowing in the opposite direction?

Q2 An electromagnet is used in an electric door lock, as shown. Normally, the circuit has a current flowing through it and the iron bolt is pulled across the doorway, stopping the door from being opened. When the correct code is typed into the keypad, the circuit is broken.

a) Explain why the bolt is pulled across the door when current flows through the circuit.

b) Explain why breaking the circuit allows the door to be opened.

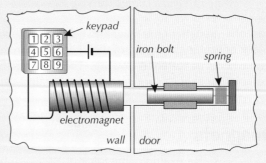

3. The Motor Effect Higher

If the magnetic field produced by a current-carrying conductor is put within a second magnetic field, the interacting fields can make things start to move...

What is the motor effect?

As you know from page 270, passing an electric current through a conductor produces a magnetic field around the conductor. If you put that conductor into another magnetic field, you end up with two magnetic fields interacting. The result is that the conductor and the magnet exert equal but opposite forces on each other (an example of Newton's 3rd law, page 42).

These forces often result in movement, which is why this known as the **motor effect**.

→— Normal magnetic field of wire
→— Normal magnetic field of magnets
→— Deviated magnetic field of magnets

Figure 1: *A diagram of the magnetic field interactions which lead to the motor effect. The red dot represents a wire carrying current out of the page (towards you).*

Increasing the strength of the magnetic field, or the size of the current flowing through the wire, will increase the size of the force.

To experience the full force, the wire has to be at 90° to the magnetic field (see Figure 3). If the wire runs along parallel to the magnetic field it won't experience any force at all. At angles in between it'll feel some force.

Example Higher

A straight current-carrying wire will experience a force if it is placed at right angles to a magnetic field. The force will be at 90° to both the wire and the magnetic field.

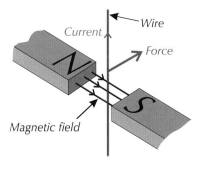

Figure 3: *A diagram showing the force on a current-carrying wire placed at 90° to a magnetic field.*

Learning Objectives:

- **H** Be able to explain that magnetic forces are due to interactions between magnetic fields.
- **H** Be able to recall that a current carrying conductor placed near a magnet experiences a force and that an equal and opposite force acts on the magnet.
- **H** Be able to use the equation: $F = B \times I \times l$.
- **H** Be able to recall and use Fleming's left-hand rule to represent the relative directions of the force, the current and the magnetic field for cases where they are mutually perpendicular.

Specification References 12.10-12.13

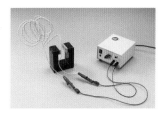

Figure 2: *An experiment showing the motor effect in action. The coil of yellow current-carrying wire leaps into the air due to interaction between its magnetic field, and that of the magnet.*

Calculating the size of the force

The force acting on a conductor in a magnetic field depends on three things:

Tip: Magnetic flux density is largest at the poles of a bar magnet.

Tip: N/Am is newtons per ampere-metre. Tesla is much more common though.

Tip: H Don't worry about memorising this equation — it'll be given to you on the equations sheet in the exam (see page 404). However, you won't be given the units, so you need to remember them.

- The **magnetic flux density** — how many field (flux) lines there are in a region (area). This shows the strength of the magnetic field. It is represented by the symbol B and is measured in tesla (T) or N/Am.

- The size of the current through the conductor, I.

- The length of the conductor that's in the magnetic field, l.

When the current is at 90° to the magnetic field it is in, then you can calculate the size of the force using the equation:

I = current (A)

F = force on a conductor at right angles to a magnetic field carrying a current (N)

$$F = B \times I \times l$$

l = length (m)

B = magnetic flux density (T or N/Am)

> **Example** — **Higher**
>
> **A 10 cm length of wire carrying a current of 3 A sits inside a magnetic field. The current flows at 90° to the direction of the magnetic field. It experiences a force of 0.12 N from the motor effect.**
>
> **Calculate the magnetic flux density of the magnet field.**
>
> (MATHS SKILLS)
>
> First, convert the length into metres.
>
> $$l = 10 \text{ cm} = 0.1 \text{ m}$$
>
> You're looking for the magnetic flux density, so rearrange $F = B \times I \times l$ to find B, then substitute in the values you're given.
>
> $$F = B \times I \times l, \text{ so } B = F \div (I \times l)$$
> $$= 0.12 \div (3 \times 0.1) = 0.4 \text{ T}$$

Fleming's left-hand rule

If a current is flowing at 90° to a magnetic field, you can tell which way the force on the conductor due to the motor effect will act using **Fleming's left-hand rule** (see Figure 4).

Here's what you do:

- Using your left hand, point your **F**irst finger (your index finger) in the direction of the **F**ield.

- Point your se**C**ond finger (your middle finger) in the direction of the **C**urrent.

- Stick your thu**M**b out so it's at 90° to the other two fingers. It will then point in the direction of the force (**M**otion).

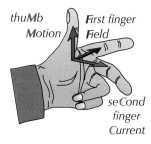

*thu**M**b*   ***F**irst finger*
Motion   ***F**ield*

*se**C**ond finger*
***C**urrent*

Figure 4: *A diagram showing Fleming's left-hand rule.*

If the direction of the current or magnetic field is reversed, then the direction of the force is reversed too (try it).

Tip: H You can use Fleming's left-hand rule to find the missing direction of force, current or the magnetic field — as long as you know the other two.

Example **Higher**

Draw in the direction of the force acting on this wire.

- Start by drawing in the current arrows and the magnetic field lines. Current goes from positive to negative and magnetic fields go from north to south. Then use Fleming's left-hand rule to work out the direction of the force (motion).

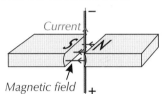

seCond finger
Current

First finger
Field

thuMb

Motion

- Finally, draw in the direction of the force.

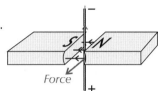

Force

Exam Tip H
You need to practise this before you get into the exam — you might need to use it to answer an exam question. It's no good pointing all over the place and ending up with the wrong answer because you can't remember which hand you're supposed to be using or what each finger represents.

Practice Questions — Fact Recall

Q1 What is the size of the force due to the motor effect on a current-carrying wire if it's parallel to a magnetic field?

Q2 For the motor effect, give two ways the force on a current-carrying wire at 90° to a magnetic field can be increased.

Q3 In Fleming's left-hand rule, what do the middle finger, index finger and thumb each represent?

Practice Questions — Application

Q1 In each of the situations below, the current-carrying wire is at 90° to the magnetic field. Give the direction of the force on the wire.

a) *Current*

b) *Current*

c) *Current*
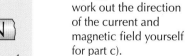

Tip: H You'll have to work out the direction of the current and magnetic field yourself for part c).

Q2 Give the direction of the force on the wire in Q1 c) if the direction of the current is swapped and the poles of the magnets are swapped.

Q3 A wire carrying a current of 5.0 A through a 0.20 T magnetic field (at 90° to the field) experiences a force of 0.25 N.
Calculate the length of the wire, in cm, inside the magnetic field.

4. Using the Motor Effect   Higher

The motor effect has many useful applications. It becomes really handy once you start using it to turn an axle.

Learning Objectives:

- **H** Be able to explain how the force on a conductor in a magnetic field is used to cause rotation in electric motors.
- **H** Be able to explain the action of converting variations in current in electrical circuits into pressure variations in sound waves, as used in loudspeakers and headphones.

Specification References 12.14 and 13.4

The simple d.c. electric motor

You know from page 273 that the motor effect is when a current-carrying conductor experiences a force in a magnetic field. Electric motors use the motor effect to produce rotation — and that rotation is the basis of an awful lot of appliances.

How it works

A loop of wire that's free to rotate about an axis is placed in a magnetic field (see Figure 1).

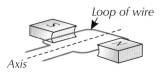

Figure 1: *A loop of wire in a magnetic field free to rotate about its axis.*

Tip: Remember, direct current (d.c.) is current that only flows in one direction, see page 246.

When a direct current flows through the loop, the two side arms, which are at 90° to the field, each experience a force due to the motor effect. They experience forces in opposite directions because the direction of the current in each arm is opposite (see Figure 2). The loop will start to rotate around its axis because the forces act one up and one down.

Tip: **H** Fleming's left-hand rule can be used to find the direction of each force — see page 274 if you need a reminder.

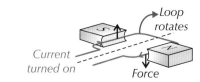

Figure 2: *A loop of wire in a magnetic field rotating when current flows through it.*

When the wire loop reaches a vertical position the forces will still be acting one up and one down on the same arms of the loop, so the loop gets stuck (see Figure 3).

Tip: **H** The loop will actually vibrate back and forth slightly as it'll have some momentum, but you don't need to worry about that.

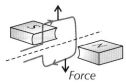

Figure 3: *A loop of wire getting stuck in the same position due to the forces acting on it.*

For the motor to keep rotating in the same direction, the forces acting on the arms of the loop need to swap direction.

Reversing the direction of the current reverses the direction of the force (see page 275). A split-ring commutator is a clever way of doing this — it swaps the contacts of the loop every half turn, reversing the current — see Figures 4 and 5.

A split-ring commutator is just a conducting ring with a gap between the two halves. As it rotates, the part of the commutator that is touching each contact changes every half turn.

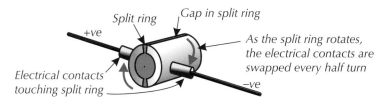

Figure 4: A split-ring commutator.

By linking each end of the loop to one half of a split-ring commutator, you change the electrical contacts of the loop (and so the direction of the current) every half turn. This means that the force acting on each arm of the loop will swap every half turn, allowing rotation to continue in the same direction.

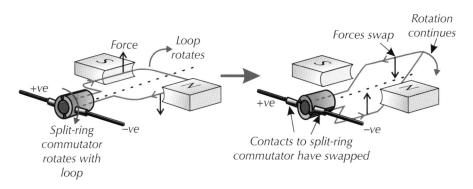

Figure 5: A d.c. electric motor using a split-ring commutator to swap the direction of the current, and so the forces, every half turn.

Tip: ⊞ You can have an a.c. (alternating current) electric motor too, in which case you don't need a split-ring commutator — it just has to rotate at or close to the frequency of the current.

And that's it — a simple d.c. electric motor. Make sure you understand how it uses the motor effect to work.

Speed of a simple electric motor

The speed of an electric motor can be increased in two main ways:

- by increasing the current.
- by increasing the strength of the magnetic field.

Both of these factors increase the force experienced by the wire due to the motor effect, so it rotates faster.

Using a coil of wire instead of a single loop will also increase the force caused by the motor effect. It's simple really — the sides of each individual loop experience a force, so the more loops you have, the larger the total force on the sides of the coil. So, if you're calculating the force on a coil of wire in a magnetic field, you need to first calculate the force on a single loop (using the equation on p.274) and then multiply it by the number of loops in the coil.

Figure 6: The spinning coil of wire inside an electric drill motor.

Direction of a simple electric motor

The direction that a motor turns in can be found using Fleming's left-hand rule, and can be reversed either by:

- swapping the polarity of the direct current (d.c.) supply, or

- swapping the magnetic poles over.

Example — **Higher**

Is the electric motor turning clockwise or anticlockwise?

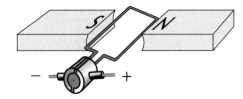

- Start by drawing in the magnetic field lines from north to south, and the direction of the current from positive to negative.

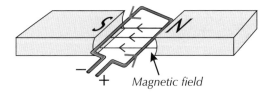

Magnetic field

Tip: H The first step of this method should look familiar — it's the same one that was used on page 275 to find the direction of the force on a straight wire in a magnetic field.

- Then use Fleming's left-hand rule on one side of the loop to work out the direction of the force (motion). Let's use the right side of the loop.

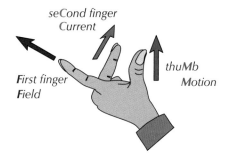

seCond finger
Current

First finger
Field

thuMb
Motion

- Finally, draw in the direction of the force.

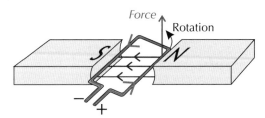

Force
Rotation

- So — the motor is turning anticlockwise.

Loudspeakers

Loudspeakers work due to the motor effect. Loudspeakers and headphones (which are just tiny loudspeakers) both use electromagnets.

Tip: **H** This type of loudspeaker is known as a moving-coil loudspeaker.

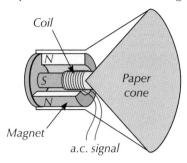

Figure 7: A diagram of the internal workings of a loudspeaker.

An alternating current (a.c.) is sent through a coil of wire attached to the base of a paper cone (see Figure 7). The coil surrounds one pole of a permanent magnet, and is surrounded by the other pole, so the current causes a force on the coil (which causes the cone to move).

When the current reverses, the force acts in the opposite direction, which causes the cone to move in the opposite direction too. So variations in the current make the cone vibrate, which makes the air around the cone vibrate and creates the variations in air pressure that form a sound wave (see page 103).

The frequency of the sound wave produced is the same as the frequency of the a.c., so by controlling the frequency of the a.c. you can alter the sound wave.

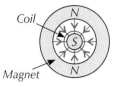

Figure 8: A diagram of a cylindrical magnet, as used in a loudspeaker, showing the magnetic field.

Figure 9: A cross-section of a loudspeaker, showing the outer ring of the magnet, and the copper coil, attached to a paper cone, surrounding the inner pole of the magnet.

Practice Questions — Fact Recall

Q1 Why is a split-ring commutator needed in an electric motor that uses direct current?

Q2 Give two ways the direction of rotation of a simple electric motor can be reversed.

Q3 How do loudspeakers use the motor effect to produce sound waves?

Practice Question — Application

Q1 Look at this diagram of a simple electric motor.

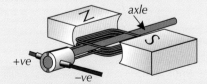

a) Which direction is the axle turning — clockwise or anticlockwise?

b) What will happen to the speed of the axle if the current is increased?

c) What will happen if the magnetic poles are reversed?

- **H** Be able to explain how to produce an electric current by the relative movement of a magnet and a conductor on a small scale in the laboratory.

- **H** Be able to recall the factors that affect the size and direction of an induced potential difference, and describe how the magnetic field produced opposes the original change.

- **H** Be able to explain how electromagnetic induction is used in alternators to generate current which alternates in direction (a.c.) and in dynamos to generate direct current (d.c.).

- **H** Be able to explain how to produce an electric current by the relative movement of a magnet and a conductor in the large-scale generation of electrical energy.

- **H** Be able to explain the action of the microphone in converting the pressure variations in sound waves into variations in current in electrical circuits.

Specification References 13.1-13.4

Tip: H The movement causes the magnetic field through the conductor to change, which induces a p.d. and a current.

5. Electromagnetic Induction Higher

Electromagnetic induction is quite a tricky idea to get your head around. It's really important though — it's how we generate most of our electricity.

What is electromagnetic induction?

You've already seen on page 273 that a magnetic field can create a force that causes a current-carrying conductor to move.

Well, it works the other way round too. An electrical conductor that is moving relative to a magnetic field can induce (create) a potential difference (p.d.) across the conductor. Similarly, a p.d. can also be induced if there is a change in an external magnetic field (i.e. one other than the conductor's) around a conductor. If the conductor is part of a complete circuit, current will flow.

When a potential difference is created like this it's called **electromagnetic induction** (or sometimes 'the generator effect').

> Electromagnetic induction is the induction of a potential difference (and current if there's a complete circuit) across a conductor which is experiencing a change in an external magnetic field.

Electromagnetic induction happens when a conductor 'cuts' through the magnetic field lines. So a potential difference across the ends of a conductor can be induced in two ways:

- By moving the electrical conductor in a magnetic field.

- By moving or changing a magnetic field (e.g. moving a magnet) relative to the electrical conductor.

Examples Higher

- Moving a wire in a magnetic field will cause a potential difference to be induced across the ends of the wire.

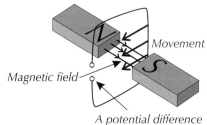

Movement

Magnetic field

A potential difference is induced across the ends of the wire.

- Moving a bar magnet through a coil of wire will induce a potential difference across the ends of the wire.

  If you connect each end of the coil to a bulb, you'll see the bulb light up as the magnet moves.

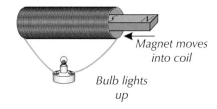

Magnet moves into coil

Bulb lights up

If you move the magnet (or conductor) in the opposite direction, then the potential difference/current will be reversed. Likewise, if the polarity of the magnet is reversed, then the potential difference/current will be reversed too.

Tip: The 'polarity' of a magnet is which way round its north and south poles are.

So, if you keep the magnetic field (or the coil) moving backwards and forwards, you produce a potential difference/current that keeps swapping direction. This is an alternating current (page 246).

Example — **Higher**

You can create the same effect by turning a magnet end to end in a coil, or turning a coil inside a magnetic field.

- As you turn the magnet, the magnetic field through the coil changes. This change in the magnetic field induces a potential difference, which can make a current flow in the wire.

- When you've turned the magnet through half a turn, the direction of the magnetic field through the coil reverses. When this happens, the potential difference reverses, so the current flows in the opposite direction around the coil of wire.

- If you keep turning the magnet in the same direction — e.g. always clockwise — then the potential difference will keep on reversing every half turn and you'll get an alternating current.

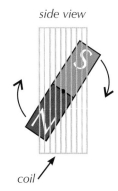

side view

coil

Figure 1: A portable electricity generator. It uses a combustion engine to turn a coil in a magnetic field, and so generate electricity.

If you want to change the size of the induced p.d., you have to change the rate that field lines are being cut. Induced potential difference (and so induced current) can be increased by:

- Increasing the speed of the movement — the field through the coil is changing quicker, so more field lines are being cut in a given time.

- Increasing the strength of the magnetic field (so there are more field lines that can be cut).

- Having more turns per unit length on the coil of wire (so there are more wires to cut the field lines).

Tip: ▣ Increasing the speed also increases the frequency (p.91) of the induced potential difference produced.

Induced current

So, a change in magnetic field can induce a current in a wire. But, as you saw on page 270, when a current flows through a wire, a magnetic field is created around the wire. So you get a second magnetic field — different to the one whose field lines were being cut in the first place.

The magnetic field created by an induced current always acts against the change that made it (whether that's the movement of a wire or a change in the field it's in). Basically, it's trying to return things to the way they were.

This means that the induced current always opposes the change that made it.

Generating electricity

Generators make use of electromagnetic induction to induce a current. They rotate a coil in a magnetic field (or a magnet in a coil). As the coil (or magnet) spins, a current is induced in the coil. Whether they generate an alternating or direct current depends on the device.

Alternators

Alternators generate alternating current (page 246). Their construction is similar to a motor (see pages 276-277). As the coil spins, a p.d. and a current is induced in the coil. Every half-turn, these change direction. Alternators use slip rings and brushes (see Figure 3) so that the contacts don't swap every half-turn — the positive and negative ends keep swapping. This maintains the alternating potential difference.

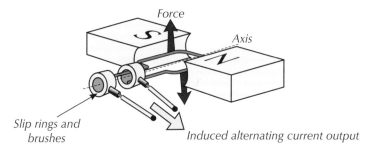

Figure 3: A diagram of a simple alternator.

If you plugged an alternator into an oscilloscope, you could measure the p.d. produced against time. You should see a trace that cycles between positive and negative peaks, and that crosses the horizontal axis (see Figure 4).

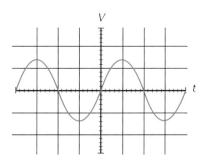

Figure 4: A trace of the potential difference (V) over time (t) generated by an alternator.

Dynamos

Dynamos generate direct p.d. and current. They're similar to alternators, with one important difference — they use a split-ring commutator as their electrical contact (see Figure 5). This swaps the connection every half turn, to keep the current flowing in the same direction and generate a direct p.d. and current.

Tip: [H] Remember — electromagnetic induction works whether the coil or the field is moving. It's how most of our electricity is generated, whether it's in a coal-fired power station or a wind turbine.

Figure 2: Cars use alternators to charge their batteries as they are longer lasting than dynamos. The alternator generates a.c. and a diode system is used to turn the a.c. into d.c..

Tip: Oscilloscopes are electrical devices that show how the potential difference across an object changes over time. They display this as a 'trace' — a real-time representation of the potential difference at that time.

Tip: [H] Split-ring commutators are also used in electric motors — see page 277.

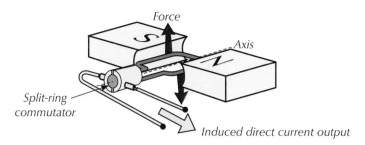

Figure 5: A diagram of a simple dynamo.

Figure 6: Dynamos are used in wind-up torches. The crank turns a coil, which induces a p.d. and powers the bulb.

The induced potential difference doesn't alternate and the charges always flow in the same direction. On an oscilloscope, the trace of p.d. against time never crosses the horizontal axis — see Figure 7. You might expect the direct p.d. trace to be a straight line because it doesn't change direction. But because the dynamo reverses direction every half turn, you still get peaks like in the alternating p.d. trace — they're just all above the horizontal axis.

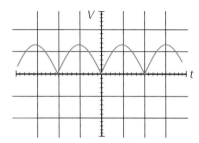

Figure 7: A trace of the potential difference (V) over time (t) generated by a dynamo.

Tip: H The peak value is the maximum p.d. generated by the dynamo. Increasing the speed of the dynamo will increase this value and will increase the frequency of the trace (page 91).

Large-scale generation

Electromagnetic induction is how most of our electricity is generated. Most of the time, fuels are burnt in the boilers of large power stations. The boilers heat water to convert it to steam, which turns a turbine. The turbine is connected to a powerful magnet inside a generator (a huge cylinder wound with coils of copper wire.). As the turbine spins, the magnet spins with it, inducing a large p.d. and alternating current in the coils of the generator — see Figure 8.

Tip: Solar power is the only method of generating electricity that doesn't use electromagnetic induction (pages 76-77).

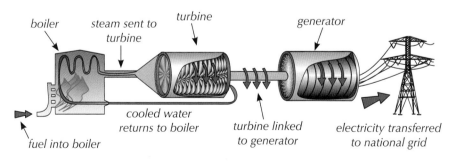

Figure 8: A diagram of a typical power station.

This electricity is then transferred to homes and businesses by the **national grid** (page 290).

Tip: **H** Microphones are basically loudspeakers (see p.279) in reverse.

Microphones

Microphones generate current from sound waves.

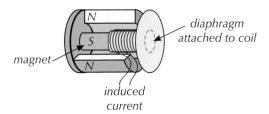

Figure 9: A diagram of the internal workings of a microphone.

Sound waves hit a flexible diaphragm that is attached to a coil of wire, wrapped around a magnet (see Figure 9). This causes the coil of wire to move back and forth in the magnetic field, which generates a current.

The movement of the coil (and so the generated current) depends on the properties of the sound wave (louder sounds make the diaphragm move further). This is how microphones can convert the pressure variations of a sound wave into variations in current in an electric circuit.

Figure 10: A microphone connected to an oscilloscope, displaying the generated p.d. trace.

Practice Questions — Fact Recall

Q1 What is electromagnetic induction?

Q2 Give two ways electromagnetic induction can be used to generate a potential difference across a coil of wire.

Q3 Describe how to reverse the direction of an induced p.d..

Q4 Describe how a microphone converts sound waves into electrical signals.

Practice Question — Application

Q1 The diagram shows how a windmill can be used to power a light bulb. As the axle turns, the slip rings make sure that each end of the coil of wire stays connected to the same end of the bulb circuit.

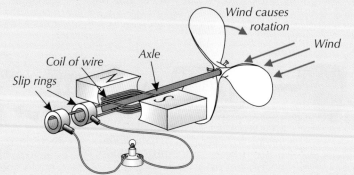

a) Explain how the windmill rotating causes a current to flow in the bulb circuit.

b) What sort of current will flow in the bulb circuit?

6. Transformers

Another nifty use of electromagnetic induction is in transformers. They're handy for changing the potential difference (voltage) of an a.c. supply.

What do transformers do?

Transformers are devices that can change the potential difference (and so the current) of an electrical supply using electromagnetic induction (page 280).

The structure of a transformer

Figure 1 shows the structure of a transformer — it consists of two coils, the primary and the secondary, wrapped around an iron core.

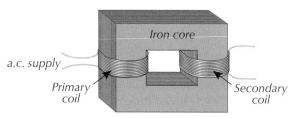

Figure 1: *The structure of a transformer.*

How a transformer works [Higher]

Transformers can only be used to change the size of an alternating voltage (p.d.). Here's how it works:

- As you know from page 270, passing an electric current through a wire produces a magnetic field around it. So, when an alternating current (created by an alternating p.d.) flows through the primary coil in a transformer it produces a magnetic field which magnetises the iron core — see Figure 3 on the next page.

- Because there is alternating current (a.c.) in the primary coil, the magnetic field in the iron core is alternating too — i.e. it is a constantly changing magnetic field.

- This constantly changing magnetic field cuts through the secondary coil.

- The changing field induces an alternating potential difference across the ends of the secondary coil (electromagnetic induction, p.280).

- If the secondary coil is part of a complete circuit, this potential difference causes an alternating current to flow — and it has the same frequency as the alternating current in the primary coil.

- The size of the potential difference induced across the secondary coil depends on the size of the potential difference across the primary coil and the number of turns on each coil (see page 287).

Learning Objectives:

- [H] Be able to recall that a transformer can change the size of an alternating voltage.
- [H] Be able to explain how an alternating current in one circuit can induce a current in another circuit in a transformer.
- [H] Be able to use the turns ratio equation for transformers to calculate either the missing voltage or the missing number of turns:
$$\frac{V_p}{V_s} = \frac{N_p}{N_s}.$$
- Be able to use the power equation (for transformers with 100% efficiency):
$$V_p \times I_p = V_s \times I_s.$$

Specification References 13.5-13.7, 13.10

Tip: Remember, voltage is the same as potential difference.

Tip: [H] Iron is used for the core because it can magnetise and demagnetise quickly.

Figure 2: *The copper coils on a transformer.*

The iron core is purely for transferring the changing magnetic field from the primary coil to the secondary. No electricity flows round the iron core.

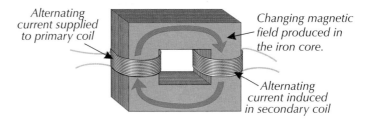

Alternating current supplied to primary coil

Changing magnetic field produced in the iron core.

Alternating current induced in secondary coil

Figure 3: *A transformer using electromagnetic induction to induce an alternating current in the secondary coil.*

If you supplied d.c. to the primary coil, you'd get nothing out of the secondary coil at all. Sure, there'd still be a magnetic field in the iron core, but it wouldn't be constantly changing, so there'd be no induction in the secondary coil because you need a changing field to induce a potential difference.

Step-up and step-down transformers

There are a few different types of transformer. Two that you need to know about are step-up transformers and step-down transformers. In a step-up transformer, the output potential difference is larger than the input potential difference. In a step-down transformer, the output potential difference is smaller than the input potential difference.

Coils on step-up and step-down transformers　Higher

The ratio between the primary and secondary potential differences is the same as the ratio between the number of turns on the primary coil and the number of turns on the secondary coil — see the equation on the next page. This means:

- In a step-up transformer, the number of turns on the secondary coil and the size of the p.d. across it are greater than across the primary coil.

- In a step-down transformer, the number of turns on the secondary coil and the size of the p.d. across it are smaller than across the primary coil.

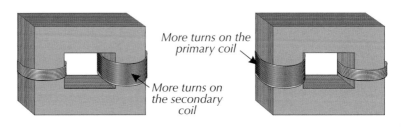

More turns on the primary coil

More turns on the secondary coil

Figure 4: *A step-up transformer (left) and a step-down transformer (right).*

The transformer equation Higher

You can calculate the output potential difference from a transformer if you know the input potential difference and the number of turns on each coil.

This is the equation to use:

$\dfrac{\text{Potential difference across primary coil}}{\text{Potential difference across secondary coil}}$	$=$	$\dfrac{\text{Number of turns on primary coil}}{\text{Number of turns on secondary coil}}$

Tip: H The potential differences can be in any units, as long as they are both in the same units.

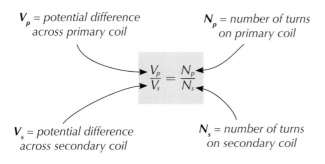

V_p = potential difference across primary coil

N_p = number of turns on primary coil

$$\frac{V_p}{V_s} = \frac{N_p}{N_s}$$

V_s = potential difference across secondary coil

N_s = number of turns on secondary coil

Exam Tip H
This equation is on the equation sheet that you'll be given in the exam, so you don't have to learn it.

Handily, you can write it either way up. So:

$$\frac{V_s}{V_p} = \frac{N_s}{N_p}$$

Tip: H There's less rearranging to do if you put whichever variable you're trying to find on the top of the fraction.

So, for a step-up transformer, $V_s > V_p$ and for a step-down transformer, $V_s < V_p$.

Example 1 — **Higher**

A transformer has 40 turns on the primary coil and 800 on the secondary coil. If the input potential difference is 1000 V, find the output potential difference. What type of transformer is this?

(MATHS SKILLS)

V_p = 1000 V, N_s = 800, N_p = 40

You're looking to find the potential difference across the secondary coil, so use the version of the formula with V_s at the top.

$\dfrac{V_s}{V_p} = \dfrac{N_s}{N_p}$ so $V_s = \dfrac{N_s}{N_p} \times V_p$

$\qquad = \dfrac{800}{40} \times 1000$

$\qquad = 20\,000$ V

This is what you'd expect — there are 20 times as many turns on the secondary coil as on the primary coil, so the output voltage is 20 times the input voltage.

This is a step-up transformer.

Example 2 | Higher

The ratio of the potential difference across the primary coil to the potential difference across the secondary coil of a transformer is 2:1.

The primary coil has 20 turns. How many does the secondary coil have?

The p.d. across the primary coil is twice as big as across the secondary coil. So, the primary coil must have twice as many turns as the secondary coil.

Therefore, the secondary coil has $20 \div 2 = 10$ turns.

The power equation for transformers

Transformers are almost 100% efficient. If we assume that they are, this means their electrical power output is equal to their electrical power input.

You know from page 244 that the formula for electrical power is:

electrical power = current × potential difference (or $P = I \times V$)

This means you can write "electrical power output = electrical power input" as an equation in terms of potential difference and current.

So, for a transformer:

V_p = potential difference across primary coil (V)

I_s = current in secondary coil (A)

$$V_p \times I_p = V_s \times I_s$$

I_p = current in primary coil (A)

V_s = potential difference across secondary coil (V)

$V_p \times I_p$ is the power input at the primary coil, and $V_s \times I_s$ is the power output at the secondary coil. This equation shows why, for a given power, a high p.d. is needed for a low current, which is useful in the national grid (see page 290).

Example 1

A transformer in a travel adaptor steps up a 115 V a.c. mains electricity supply to the 230 V needed for a hair dryer. The current through the hair dryer is 5 A.

Assume the transformer is 100% efficient and calculate how much current is drawn by the transformer from the mains supply.

$V_p = 115$ V, $V_s = 230$ V, $I_s = 5$ A

Rearranging $V_p \times I_p = V_s \times I_s$:

$I_p = (V_s \times I_s) \div V_p = (230 \times 5) \div 115 = 10$ A

Tips (margin)

Tip: There's more about efficiency on pages 71-73.

Tip: Remember, power is measured in watts, W.

Exam Tip
You'll be given this equation in the exam, so don't worry about learning it.

Exam Tip
You might be given the power output at the secondary coil and asked to find the current through the primary coil. You'll just need to do the same calculation as here, but replace $V_s \times I_s$ with the power value you're given.

The current through the primary coil of a step-down transformer is 0.5 A. The potential difference across the primary coil is 200 V. The transformer can be assumed to be 100% efficient.

a) **Find the power output of the transformer.**

The transformer can be considered 100% efficient, which means:

$$\text{power output} = \text{power input}$$

And the power input can be found using the formula $P = I \times V$:

$$\text{power output} = \text{power input}$$
$$= V_p \times I_p = 200 \times 0.5 = 100 \text{ W}$$

b) **The potential difference across the primary coil is doubled, but the current is kept the same.**
What effect will this have on the output power?

If the potential difference across the primary coil is doubled, the input power will also be doubled. Because the transformer can be considered 100% efficient, the output power will be double its original value (i.e. 200 W).

Practice Questions — Fact Recall

Q1 What kind of potential difference must be used with a transformer?

Q2 Explain how a transformer works.

Q3 What can you say about the electrical power input and electrical power output of a transformer if it's assumed to be 100% efficient?

Practice Questions — Application

Q1 A transformer has 15 turns on the primary coil and 30 turns on the secondary coil.

a) Is it a step-up transformer or a step-down transformer? How do you know?

b) Will the output potential difference be greater or smaller than the input potential difference?

Q2 A transformer, assumed to be 100% efficient, has an output potential difference of 12 V and an output current of 10 A. What is the electrical power input?

Q3 A step-up transformer has a potential difference across the primary coil of 4 V. It has 8 turns on the primary coil and 12 turns on the secondary coil. Calculate the potential difference across the secondary coil.

Q4 An ideal transformer has a p.d. of 400 V across the primary coil and a p.d. of 20 V across the secondary coil. The current in the secondary coil is 100 A. What is the current in the primary coil?

Tip: 'Ideal' means you can assume the transformer is 100% efficient.

- Be able to explain
why, in the national
grid, electrical energy
is transferred at high
voltages from power
stations, and then
transferred at lower
voltages in each
locality for domestic
uses as it improves
the efficiency by
reducing heat loss in
transmission lines.

- Be able to explain
where and why step-
up and step-down
transformers are used
in the transmission
of electricity in the
national grid.

- **H** Be able to explain
the advantages of
power transmission in
high voltage cables,
using the equations:
$P = E \div t$, $P = I \times V$,
$P = I^2 \times R$, $\dfrac{V_p}{V_s} = \dfrac{N_p}{N_s}$,
$V_p \times I_p = V_s \times I_s$.

Specification References
13.8, 13.9, 13.11

Tip: Look back to pages
76-82 to see the energy
sources used to generate
electricity.

7. The National Grid

Transformers are used in the national grid to make transmitting electricity more efficient. You need to be able to explain how this works, so get reading...

Distributing electricity

The national grid is a network of wires and transformers across the UK. It transfers electrical energy from power stations anywhere on the grid to anywhere else on the grid where it's needed. To transmit the huge amount of electrical power needed, you need to transmit the electricity at either a high voltage (potential difference) or a high current.

The problem with transmitting electricity at a high current is that you lose loads of energy as the cables heat up. The cables heat up because the electrical charges have to do work against the resistance of the cables (there's more about resistive heating on page 243). Doing work causes energy to be transferred to the thermal energy stores of the cables and the surroundings. The lower the current through the cables, and the lower the resistance of the cables, the less energy is wasted.

So to make the national grid more efficient, high-voltage, low-resistance cables, and transformers are used. Step-up transformers at power stations boost the p.d. up really high (400 000 V) and keep the current low which decreases the energy lost by heating. This makes the national grid an efficient way of transferring energy. Step-down transformers then bring it back down to safe, usable levels at the consumers' end — see Figure 1.

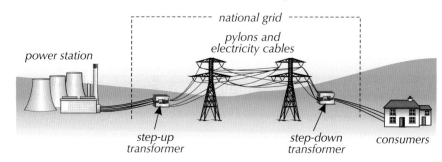

Figure 1: A diagram of the national grid distributing electricity from a power station to consumers.

Tip: Remember,
efficiency shows the
proportion of energy
transferred usefully. The
more of the supplied
energy that's wasted, the
less efficient a process
is, page 71.

Explaining efficiency Higher

As well as explaining how transmitting electricity at a high voltages improves the efficiency of the national grid, you may have to back up your reasoning with calculations using equations you've already met.

- The national grid transfers lots of energy per second, which means it has a high power, as power = energy transferred ÷ time taken ($P = E \div t$, page 244).

- Electrical power = current × p.d. ($P = I \times V$, page 244). So to transmit electricity at a high power, it must either need to be at a high potential difference or a high current.

- The power lost due to resistive heating is found using electrical power = current squared × resistance ($P = I^2 \times R$, page 245) so the energy lost by the national grid is related to the current through the cables and the resistance of the cables.

- The equation p.d. across primary coil × current through primary coil = p.d. across primary coil × current through primary coil ($V_p \times I_p = V_s \times I_s$) shows that increasing the potential difference across the secondary coil decreases the current through the secondary coil. So the potential difference must be increased before transmission in order to lower the current.

- In order to do this, a step-up transformer is used. This is because for a step-up transformer, the number of turns on the secondary coil is larger than the number of turns on the primary coil ($N_s > N_p$) so the p.d. across the secondary coil (V_s) is larger than the p.d. across the primary coil (V_p). You can see this by using the transformer equation:

$$\frac{\text{p.d. across primary coil}}{\text{p.d. across secondary coil}} = \frac{\text{no. turns on primary coil}}{\text{no. turns on secondary coil}} \text{ or } \left(\frac{V_p}{V_s} = \frac{N_p}{N_s}\right).$$

Figure 2: *Transformers are used in electrical substations, which are located across the national grid.*

Practice Questions — Fact Recall

Q1 Why are transformers used in the national grid?

Q2 What does each label A-E represent in this diagram?

Practice Question — Application

Q1 a) Calculate the power lost in a 3.0 Ω cable if it electricity is transmitted through it at a current of 4.0 kA.

The current is passed through a step-up transformer.

b) Explain how using step-up transformers increases the efficiency of the national grid. Support your explanation with equations.

Section 8b Checklist — Make sure you know...

Magnets and Magnetic Fields

☐ That permanent magnets always produce a magnetic field, but induced magnets only do so when they're put into another magnetic field.

☐ That iron, steel, cobalt and nickel are magnetic materials.

☐ That the closer together magnetic field lines are, the stronger the magnetic field is at that point.

☐ That all magnets have two poles, north and south, where the magnetic field is strongest.

☐ How to draw the magnetic field around a bar magnet and how to draw a uniform magnetic field.

☐ That like magnetic poles repel each other and unlike poles attract each other.

☐ H That magnetic fields interact and cause forces on the two objects producing the magnetic fields.

☐ That compasses can be used to plot the shape of magnetic fields, and when they're not near a magnet they always point north, because the Earth's core is made from a magnetic material.

Electromagnetism

☐ That a current creates a magnetic field, which can be seen using a compass. If the current flows through a straight conductor, the shape of the field is concentric circles around the conductor.

☐ How to use the right-hand thumb rule to find the direction of the field around a current-carrying conductor.

☐ That the strength of the field around a current-carrying conductor depends on the size of the current and the distance from the conductor.

☐ That the field lines around a current-carrying conductor interact when the conductor is wrapped into a solenoid. This results in a strong, almost uniform field inside the solenoid and a weak field outside.

☐ Uses of magnets, for example in cranes, sorting machines and magnetic clasps.

The Motor Effect

☐ H That a conductor carrying a current will experience a force if it is placed into an external magnetic field, as long as the directions of the current and field aren't parallel. This is the motor effect.

☐ H That the motor effect causes an equal but opposite force on both objects involved.

☐ H How to use $F = B \times I \times l$ and Fleming's left-hand rule when dealing with examples of the motor effect, where the magnetic field and the current are at right angles to each other.

Using the Motor Effect

☐ H How an electric motor works, using ideas about the motor effect and Fleming's left-hand rule.

☐ H How loudspeakers and headphones convert electrical signals to the motion of a speaker, creating pressure variations in the nearby air — i.e. sound waves.

cont...

Electromagnetic Induction

☐ **H** That moving a magnet and a conductor relative to each other can generate a potential difference, and a current if the conductor is part of a complete circuit.

☐ **H** That the direction of an induced potential difference/current is reversed if the direction of the magnet or conductor's movement is reversed.

☐ **H** That the size of an induced p.d. is increased by increasing the speed of movement, increasing the strength of the magnetic field or using a coiled conductor with more turns per unit length.

☐ **H** That the magnetic field produced by an induced current acts to oppose the change in magnetic field that induced the current.

☐ **H** How alternators generate an alternating potential difference and alternating current.

☐ **H** How dynamos generate a direct potential difference and direct current.

☐ **H** That electromagnetic induction is how a majority of our electricity is created in power stations.

☐ **H** How microphones convert sound waves to electrical signals.

Transformers

☐ **H** That transformers can change the size of an alternating potential difference.

☐ That a transformer consists of a primary coil and a secondary coil wrapped around an iron core.

☐ **H** That the alternating current in a transformer's primary coil creates a changing magnetic field in the core of the transformer. This changing magnetic field creates an alternating p.d. and current in the secondary coil of the transformer.

☐ That a step-up transformer increases potential difference.

☐ **H** That a step-up transformer has more turns on the secondary than the primary coil.

☐ That a step-down transformer decreases potential difference.

☐ **H** That a step-down transformer has more turns on the primary than the secondary coil.

☐ **H** That the ratio of potential differences across the coils is proportional to the ratio of the number of turns of wire on the coils, and how to use $\frac{V_p}{V_s} = \frac{N_p}{N_s}$.

☐ That transformers are assumed to be 100% efficient and so the power input equals the power output.

☐ How to use $V_p \times I_p = V_s \times I_s$.

The National Grid

☐ That the national grid is a network of wires and transformers that transmits electricity across the UK.

☐ That the energy lost due to resistive heating in a wire is proportional to the current through the wire.

☐ That the national grid transmits electricity at a high voltage to keep the current, and thus energy losses, as low as possible. This makes the national grid an efficient way of transferring energy.

☐ Why step-up transformers are used to increase the p.d. of electricity before it is transmitted by the national grid and step-down transformers to reduce the p.d. before it is used by consumers.

☐ **H** How to use the following equations to support the explanation of why the national grid is an efficient way of transferring energy: $P = E \div t$, $P = I \times V$, $P = I^2 \times R$, $V_p \times I_p = V_s \times I_s$ and $\frac{V_p}{V_s} = \frac{N_p}{N_s}$.

1 An alternator is attached to the wheel of an exercise bike.
When the wheel turns, it causes a coil in the alternator to rotate in a magnetic field, and a current is induced in the coil.

(a) A uniform magnetic field is generated between the magnets in the alternator.
Explain what is meant by, and describe the shape of, a uniform magnetic field.

(2 marks)

(b) (i) State the type of current induced in the coil.

(1 mark)

(ii) State which of the oscilloscope traces shown in **Figure 1**, **Figure 2** and **Figure 3**, would be generated by the alternator. Explain your answer.

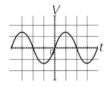

Figure 1

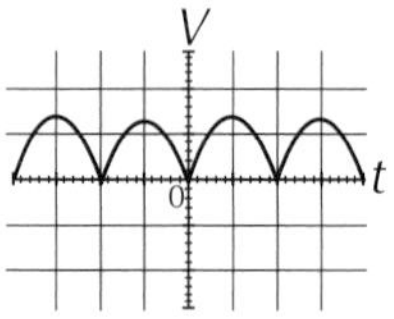

Figure 2

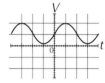

Figure 3

(2 marks)

(c) Explain **one** way to increase the size of the current generated by the alternator.

(2 marks)

2 Transformers are used to change the potential difference of a supply.

(a) A step-down transformer is assumed to be 100% efficient.
It is used to decrease the potential difference of an electricity supply.

The potential difference is decreased from 400 kV to 125 kV.
The initial current is 50 A. Calculate the current after the potential difference has been decreased. Give your answer in amperes.
Use the correct equation from the equations listed on page 404.

(3 marks)

(b)* Explain why transformers are used within the national grid.
Comment on the efficiency of the national grid in your answer.

(6 marks)

(c) Explain why the current in the primary coil of a transformer must be an alternating current.

(2 marks)

(d) A small transformer has 60 turns on the primary coil and 30 turns on the secondary coil. The input potential difference is 100 V.

Calculate the output potential difference. Give your answer in volts.
Use the correct equation from the equations listed on page 404.

(3 marks)

3   A student designs a simple battery-powered screwdriver,
     as shown in **Figure 4**. The coil of wire is placed in a uniform
     magnetic field between two permanent bar magnets.

     The coil is supplied with direct current (d.c.), and a split-ring commutator is used to
     reverse the direction of the current flowing through the coil of wire every half turn.

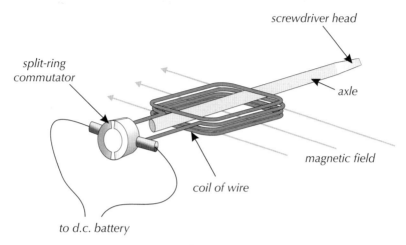

Figure 4

(a) The screwdriver uses the motor effect to produce rotation of the axle.
     Usually, the screwdriver head rotates clockwise. A reverse switch rotates
     the position of the magnets so that the direction of the magnetic field is reversed.

     Explain why this causes the screwdriver head to rotate anticlockwise.

     (2 marks)

(b) The current flowing through the wire is 3.0 A.
     The coil forms a square with sides 0.50 cm long and four wires tall.
     The magnetic flux density of the magnet is 0.20 T.

     Calculate the total force on one of the two sides perpendicular to the magnetic field.
     Give your answer in newtons.
     Use the correct equation from the equations listed on page 404.

     (2 marks)

     The bar magnets used by the drill lose their magnetism over time, so the drill becomes
     gradually less powerful. One way of avoiding this is using electromagnets in place of
     the bar magnets. The electromagnets are made of a coil of wire wrapped around an
     iron core and connected to a d.c. supply.

(c) Explain how turning on the d.c. supply to the electromagnets produces a magnetic
     field around them.

     (2 marks)

(d) Explain why an a.c. supply would not be suitable to power an electromagnet in the
     screwdriver.

     (3 marks)

1. Density

Density is a property that all materials have, and different materials have different densities. It's all to do with how much mass there is in a given space.

Density

Density is a measure of the 'compactness' of a substance. It relates the mass of a substance to how much space it takes up (i.e. it's a substance's mass per unit volume).

There's a formula for finding the density of a substance:

$\rho = density \ (kg/m^3) \longrightarrow \rho = \dfrac{m}{V} \longleftarrow m = mass \ (kg)$
$\longleftarrow V = volume \ (m^3)$

Tip: The symbol for density is a Greek letter, rho. It looks like a 'p' but it isn't.

Density can also be measured in g/cm^3 ($1 \ g/cm^3 = 1000 \ kg/m^3$).

Tip: The formula triangle for the density equation looks like this:

$$\frac{m}{\rho \times V}$$

Example 1

A copper cube has sides of length 5.00 cm. The density of copper is 8.96 g/cm³. Find the mass of the cube in g.

First find the cube's volume: $V = 5.00 \times 5.00 \times 5.00 = 125 \ cm^3$

Now substitute into the rearranged formula:

$m = \rho \times V = 8.96 \times 125 = 1120 \ g$

Example 2

Iron has a density of 7900 kg/m³. A truck is used to transport iron rods. Each rod is 1.0 m long and has a cross-sectional area of 1.2 × 10⁻² m². The truck has a maximum load limit of 2000 kg. How many iron rods, can the truck transport?

First find the volume of one rod:

$V = cross\text{-}sectional \ area \times length = 1.2 \times 10^{-2} \times 1.0 = 1.2 \times 10^{-2} \ m^3$

Now calculate the mass of one rod:

$m = \rho \times V = 7900 \times 1.2 \times 10^{-2} = 94.8 \ kg$

Divide the maximum load mass by the mass of one rod:

$2000 \div 94.8 = 21.09...$ So the truck can transport 21 rods.

Figure 1: *Racing bicycles have many parts built out of carbon fibre. Carbon fibre has a much lower density than materials like steel, so a carbon fibre bicycle will be much lighter than the same sized bike made from steel.*

The density of an object depends on what it's made of. Density doesn't vary with size or shape, it's all to do with how close together the particles in a material are (page 300). The closer together the particles are, the denser the substance.

Measuring density

You need to be able to measure the densities of different substances.

Tip: As with all practicals, make sure you do a risk assessment (p.336) before you start.

Measuring the density of a liquid

Place a measuring cylinder on a balance and zero the balance (see p.333). Pour 10 ml of the liquid into the measuring cylinder and record its mass.

Pour another 10 ml into the measuring cylinder and record the total volume and mass. Repeat this process until the cylinder is full.

Tip: The measuring cylinder will give you the volume in ml. To convert to cm³, use 1 ml = 1 cm³.

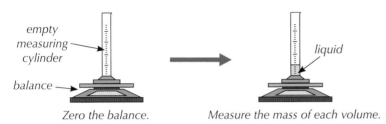

empty measuring cylinder

balance

liquid

Zero the balance.   Measure the mass of each volume.

Figure 2: *Using a balance to find the mass of liquid in a measuring cylinder.*

For each set of measurements, use the formula from the previous page to find the density. Finally, take an average of your calculated densities. This will give you a more precise (p.12) value for the density of the liquid.

Tip: To find the average, add up all the densities, then divide by the number of values. See page 14 for more.

Measuring the density of a solid

First, use a balance to measure the object's mass. You then need to find its volume. If it's a regular solid, like a cuboid, you might be able to measure its dimensions with a ruler and calculate its volume. For an irregular solid, you can find its volume by submerging it in a **eureka can** of water.

Tip: The area and volume formulas for common shapes are on page 350.

A eureka can (or displacement can) is essentially a beaker with a spout — you can see this in Figure 4. To use one, fill it with water so the water level is above the spout. Let the water drain from the spout, leaving the water level just below the start of the spout. (This way, when you put your solid object in, all the water displaced will pass through the spout, giving you the correct volume.)

Place an empty measuring cylinder below the end of the spout. When you put your solid object in the eureka can, it causes the water level to rise and water to flow out of the spout.

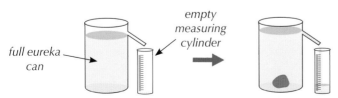

empty measuring cylinder

full eureka can

Figure 3: *A eureka can and measuring cylinder being used to measure a solid's volume.*

Figure 4: *An experiment to measure the density of a solid block. A string is used so the block can easily be removed.*

Once the spout has stopped dripping, you can measure the volume of the water in the measuring cylinder (see page 335 for more on this). This is the volume of your solid object. Now you can substitute the object's mass and volume into the density formula from page 296 to find its density.

Practice Questions — Fact Recall

Q1   What is the formula for density?

Q2   What pieces of apparatus would you need to measure the density of an irregular solid object?

Practice Questions — Application

Q1   A block of material is in the shape of a cuboid. It has sides of length 3.0 cm, 4.5 cm and 6.0 cm, and a total mass of 0.324 kg. Find the density of the block.

Q2   Figure 5 shows a measuring cylinder containing cooking oil. The cylinder was placed on the mass balance, the balance was zeroed and then oil was poured into the measuring cylinder. Calculate the density of the cooking oil in g/cm^3.

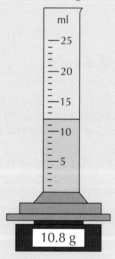

Figure 5: *The apparatus used to determine the density of cooking oil.*

2. States of Matter

The kinetic theory of matter says everything is made up of particles. It's used to help explain the densities of substances and the different states of matter.

Kinetic theory of matter

The **kinetic theory of matter** is a model that explains how the particles (the atoms and the molecules, page 151) that make up matter behave. Kinetic theory models these particles as tiny balls. It explains how matter behaves in terms of how these balls are arranged and how they move around.

The arrangement and movement of the particles depends on attractive forces between the particles. These forces change depending on the substance and the state that the substance is in.

States of matter

Three **states of matter** are solid (e.g. ice), liquid (e.g. water) and gas (e.g. water vapour). The particles of a substance in each state are the same — only the arrangement and energy of the particles are different.

Solids

In solids, strong forces of attraction hold the particles close together in a fixed, regular arrangement. The particles don't have much energy in their kinetic energy stores so they can only vibrate about their fixed positions.

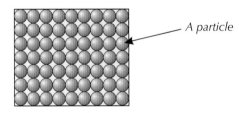
A particle

***Figure 1:** The particles in a solid.*

Liquids

There are weaker forces of attraction between the particles in liquids. The particles are close together, but can move past each other, and form irregular arrangements. They have more energy in their kinetic energy stores than the particles in a solid — they move in random directions at low speeds.

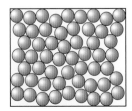

***Figure 3:** The particles in a liquid.*

Learning Objectives:
- Be able to use a simple kinetic theory model to explain the different states of matter (solids, liquids and gases) in terms of the movement and arrangement of particles.
- Be able to explain the differences in density between the different states of matter in terms of the arrangements of the atoms or molecules.

Specification References 14.1 and 14.4

Tip: Head to page 302 for information about changing between states.

Tip: Being able to use a theoretical model, such as kinetic theory, to explain an experimental observation is an important part of Working Scientifically.

WORKING SCIENTIFICALLY

***Figure 2:** The three states of water — ice, water and water vapour.*

Gases

There are almost no forces of attraction between the particles in a gas. The particles have more energy in their kinetic energy stores than those in liquids and solids — they are free to move, and travel in random directions at high speeds.

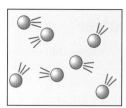

Figure 4: The particle arrangement in a gas.

Density of solids, liquids and gases

Kinetic theory helps to explain the densities of different states of matter. Usually, the density of a substance is highest when it is in solid form. This is because the particles are packed close together — there is a lot of mass in a given volume. As density = mass ÷ volume, this means the density is high.

Liquids are generally less dense than solids because they have fewer particles (and so less mass) in a given volume. As gases have particles spaced far apart, a substance in gas form is usually less dense than when it is a liquid or a solid.

Practice Questions — Fact Recall

Q1   Name the three states of matter.

Q2   Describe the arrangement, movement and energy of particles in the three states of matter.

Practice Question — Application

Q1   The diagram below shows a box filled with small light polystyrene balls. A small fan is fitted at the bottom of the box.

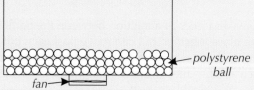

polystyrene ball

fan

a) What state of matter is modelled by the balls at the bottom of the box when the fan is turned off? Explain your answer.

b) The fan is turned on, causing the balls to fly around the inside of the box at high speeds. What state of matter do the balls now model?

c) Use this model to explain the different densities of the two states of matter in parts a) and b).

3. Internal Energy and Changes of State

The state that a substance is in has a lot to do with its temperature and the energy that the particles in the substance have. Read on to find out more.

What is internal energy?

The particles in a system (the objects you're looking at, page 61) vibrate or move around — they have energy in their kinetic energy stores. The more energy they have in their kinetic energy stores, the faster the particles move. They also have energy in their potential energy stores due to their positions. The further apart from each other they are, the more energy the particles have in this store.

The energy stored in a system is stored by its particles. The **internal energy** of a system is the total energy that its particles have in their kinetic and potential energy stores. The energy in the thermal energy store of an object is the energy in just the kinetic energy stores of its particles.

Heating a system transfers energy to its particles, so heating a system always increases its internal energy of the system. This leads to a change in temperature (see below) or a change in state (see next page).

Increasing temperature

Heating a system and increasing its temperature means transferring energy to the thermal energy store of the system. The more energy in an system's thermal energy store, the hotter it is. Temperature measures how hot something is — i.e. how much energy is in thermal energy stores.

Transferring energy to an object's thermal energy store means transferring energy to the kinetic energy stores of the object's particles. So temperature is also related to the average energy in the kinetic energy stores of the particles that make up a system. The hotter a system is, the higher the average energy in the particles' kinetic energy stores.

When a system is heated and its temperature increases, energy is transferred to the kinetic energy stores of the particles in the system, but not the potential energy stores. So when the temperature of a system increases, the particles vibrate or move around faster (as $KE = \frac{1}{2} \times m \times v^2$) but the positions of the particles relative to each other don't really change.

Absolute Zero

If you heat a system, you transfer energy to its particles. In the same way, if you cool a system, you're reducing the energy of its particles. In theory, the coldest that anything can ever get is -273 °C — **absolute zero**. At absolute zero, the particles have as little energy in their kinetic energy stores as it's possible to get — they're pretty much still.

- Be able to explain how heating a system will change the energy stored within the system and raise its temperature or produce changes of state.
- Be able to describe the term absolute zero, −273 °C, in terms of the lack of movement of particles.
- Be able to convert between the Kelvin and Celsius scales.
- Be able to describe that when substances melt, freeze, evaporate, boil, condense or sublimate mass is conserved and that these physical changes differ from some chemical changes because the material recovers its original properties if the change is reversed.

Specification References
14.5, 14.6, 14.14, 14.15

Tip: Here, the internal energy of the system has increased because the energy in kinetic energy stores has increased.

Tip: These scales are basically the same, the only difference is where zero occurs.

Scientists used absolute zero to form the Kelvin scale of temperature — absolute zero is equal to 0 K. A temperature change of 1 °C is also a change of 1 kelvin, so you can convert between the two scales fairly easily.

> Temperature in K = Temperature in °C + 273

> Temperature in °C = Temperature in K − 273

Tip: There's no degree symbol when you write a temperature in kelvins. Just write K, not °K.

Example

A piece of tin is at a temperature of 3.7 °C. State the value of this temperature in K.

3.7 + 273 = 276.7 K

Tip: The same principle is applied to a substance's boiling, freezing and condensing points. Sublimation is a bit trickier — you don't need to know when it occurs, only that it describes a change of state from a solid to a gas.

Changing State

When you heat (or cool) a substance, it can change state. This occurs at certain temperatures, called 'points'. For example, a substance melts once it has reached its melting point. Figure 1 shows the changes of state you need to know:

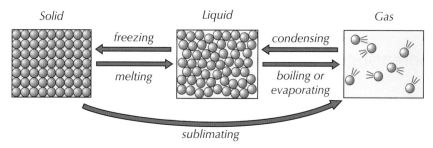

Figure 1: The different changes of state.

When a system is heated and its state changes (e.g. melting, boiling), energy is transferred to the potential energy stores of the particles instead of to their kinetic energy stores. The particles in the system move apart from each other and the forces between the particles get weaker (pages 299-300). However, because the amount of energy in the particles' kinetic energy stores stays the same, the average speed of the particles and the temperature of the system remain constant whilst the substance changes state.

During a change of state due to cooling, the particles lose energy from their potential energy stores. They move closer together and the forces between them get stronger. Their average speed still doesn't change though (so the temperature still remains constant).

Figure 2: As the water boils, the energy transferred to it is used to move particles apart, not to increase temperature.

Reversing changes of state

A change of state is a **physical change** (rather than a chemical change). This means you don't end up with a new substance — it's the same substance as you started with, just in a different form.

If you reverse a change of state (e.g. freeze a substance that has been melted), the particles return to how they were before the change of state. So the substance returns to its original form and gets back its original properties. This is different to most chemical changes.

Mass conservation

During a change of state, the number of particles doesn't change — they're just arranged differently. This means that mass is conserved — none of it is lost when the substance changes state. If you set up your experiment so none of the particles can escape (e.g. by collecting all of the water vapour produced when a liquid boils), you can measure the mass during a change of state and see that it remains constant.

Example

As the ice in Figure 3 melts, the reading on the balance will stay the same. The mass of the beaker's contents will be conserved during the change of state.

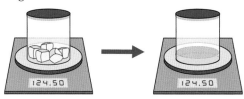

Figure 3: *A beaker of ice melting on a balance.*

Tip: If you were to boil the water from this experiment, you would have to put a lid on the beaker to prevent any water vapour produced from escaping the system.

Practice Questions — Fact Recall

Q1   What is the internal energy of a system?

Q2   Describe what happens to the energy of the particles in a system as it is heated and its temperature increases.

Q3   Explain absolute zero in terms of particle movement.

Q4   Name five different changes of state.

Q5   A change of state is a physical change.
Explain what is meant by the term 'physical change'.

Q6   Does a change of state conserve mass? Explain your answer.

Practice Questions — Application

Q1   Convert 89 kelvin to °C.

Q2   Particles in a system lose energy over time. The particles move closer together, but continue moving at the same speed. What is happening to the system during this time period?

Learning Objectives:

- Be able to define the term specific heat capacity.
- Be able to use the equation: $\Delta Q = m \times c \times \Delta\theta$.
- Be able to investigate the properties of water by determining the specific heat capacity of water (Core Practical).
- Be able to explain ways of reducing unwanted energy transfer through thermal insulation.

Specification References 14.7, 14.8, 14.10, 14.11

Figure 1: *Most metals have low specific heat capacities. This makes them great for cookware as they heat up quickly.*

Tip: Remember, Δ just means 'change in' (see page 344).

4. Specific Heat Capacity

Some materials are easier to heat up than others. Specific heat capacity is a measure of how much energy it takes to change the temperature of a material. Let the fun begin...

What is specific heat capacity?

More energy needs to be transferred to the thermal energy store of some materials to increase their temperature than others. For example, you need 4200 J to warm 1 kg of water by 1 °C, but only 139 J to warm 1 kg of mercury by 1 °C.

Materials that need to have a lot of energy transferred to in their thermal energy stores to warm up also transfer a lot of energy when they cool down.

How much energy needs to be transferred to the thermal energy store of a substance before its temperature increases is determined by its **specific heat capacity (SHC)**.

> Specific heat capacity is the amount of energy needed to raise the temperature of 1 kg of a substance by 1 °C.

The amount of energy transferred to (i.e. stored by) or transferred from (i.e. released by) the thermal energy store of a substance for a given temperature change, $\Delta\theta$, is linked to its specific heat capacity by this equation:

$\boldsymbol{\Delta Q}$ = change in thermal energy (J) ⟶ $$\Delta Q = m \times c \times \Delta\theta$$ ⟵ $\boldsymbol{\Delta\theta}$ = change in temperature (°C)

$\boldsymbol{m}$ = mass (kg) ⟋ $\boldsymbol{c}$ = specific heat capacity (J/kg°C)

Example

Water has a specific heat capacity of 4200 J/kg°C. How much energy is needed to heat 2.00 kg of water from 10.0 °C to 100.0 °C?

First work out the temperature difference, $\Delta\theta$, between the starting and finishing temperatures.

$\Delta\theta = 100.0$ °C $- 10.0$ °C $= 90.0$ °C

Then plug the numbers for m, c and $\Delta\theta$ into the formula to find ΔQ.

$\Delta Q = m \times c \times \Delta\theta = 2.00 \times 4200 \times 90.0 = 756\ 000$ J

You can use the formula above with the conservation of energy, just like on page 68, to make calculations for energy transfers in all sorts of situations. See the example on the next page.

A 3500 kg van travelling at 30.0 m/s applies its brakes and comes to a stop. Estimate the change in temperature of the brakes in this transfer, if their combined mass is 25 kg and their specific heat capacity is 420 J/kg °C.

Assume that all of the energy in the kinetic energy stores of the van is transferred to the thermal energy stores of the brakes. The energy transferred is equal to the energy in the kinetic energy stores (p.66).

$KE = \frac{1}{2} \times m \times v^2 = \frac{1}{2} \times 3500 \times 30.0^2 = 1\ 575\ 000$ J

All this is transferred to the brakes' thermal energy stores, so $\Delta Q = 1\ 575\ 000$ J.

Rearrange $\Delta Q = m \times c \times \Delta\theta$ to give:
$\Delta\theta = \Delta Q \div (m \times c) = 1\ 575\ 000 \div (25 \times 420) = 150$ °C

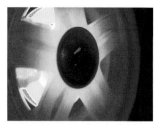

Figure 2: A thermogram showing the temperature differences around a car wheel during braking. White is hottest (where the brakes are) and blue is coolest.

Investigating specific heat capacity

CORE PRACTICAL

You can do an experiment to investigate the specific heat capacity of water. In the experiment, an electric immersion heater is used to heat a container full of water. It is assumed that all of the energy transferred to the heater from the power supply is transferred usefully to the water — i.e. all of the energy transferred heats the water.

First, place your container on a mass balance. Zero the balance and fill the container with water. Record the mass of the water. Then, set up the equipment as shown in Figure 3.

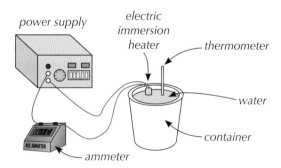

Figure 3: A diagram of the apparatus used to investigate the specific heat capacity of water.

Measure the initial temperature of the water and set the potential difference, V, of the power supply. Turn on the power supply and start a stop watch. As the water heats up, keep an eye on the ammeter — the current through the circuit shouldn't change. After the temperature of the water has increased by, e.g. 10 degrees, stop the stopwatch and turn off the power supply.

Using your measurements of the current, I, the potential difference of the power supply, V, and the time taken to heat the water, t, you can calculate the energy supplied by the heater, E, using $E = I \times V \times t$ from page 242.

As you have assumed that all of the energy supplied by the heater, E, is used to heat the water, you can equate E with ΔQ from $\Delta Q = m \times c \times \Delta\theta$.

Tip: In real life, not all of the energy is used to heat the water. See the next page for ways to reduce energy losses.

Tip: Remember to carry out a risk assessment (page 336) before you do any practical. Be careful not to burn yourself when handling the heater.

Tip: There's another experiment investigating the properties of water on page 308.

Tip: You might use a joulemeter instead of an ammeter. Joulemeters directly measure the energy transferred by the power supply, so you don't have to work out E from I, V and t.

Rearrange $\Delta Q = m \times c \times \Delta\theta$ to give you $c = \Delta Q \div (m \times \Delta\theta)$ and substitute in your measurements to find c.

Example

A student is investigating the specific heat capacity of water. They heat a beaker containing 0.80 kg of water with an electric immersion heater. The current through the heater is 16.8 A, and the potential difference of the power supply is 24.0 V.

It takes 2 minutes and 5 seconds for the water to increase by 15 °C. Calculate the specific heat capacity of water. Give your answer in J/kg °C.

$t = 2 \times 60 + 5 = 125$ seconds

$E = I \times V \times t = 16.8 \times 24.0 \times 125 = 50\ 400$ J

$c = \Delta Q \div (m \times \Delta\theta) = 50\ 400 \div (0.80 \times 15) = 4200$ J/kg °C

Tip: Evaluating experiments and suggesting ways to improve them is an important part of Working Scientifically.

(WORKING SCIENTIFICALLY)

Tip: Another way of improving the experiment is to put a lid on the beaker. This reduces the rate of evaporation.

Improving the experiment

During any process, some energy is always wasted. This means that not all of the energy transferred from the power supply is used to heat the water (although we assume it's true to make calculations easier). Some is lost heating up the wires of the immersion heater and some is transferred by heating to the container and the air around it.

To reduce these unwanted energy transfers and make your result more accurate (p.12), you should wrap the container in a thermally insulating material (e.g. cotton wool) and place it on an insulating surface, like a cork mat. Thermal insulators reduce the rate at which energy is transferred by heating, which means that less energy is transferred to the thermal energy stores of the surroundings. There's more about thermal insulation on page 69.

Practice Questions — Fact Recall

Q1   What is the specific heat capacity of a substance?

Q2   What are the units of specific heat capacity measured in?

Q3   When doing an experiment to find the specific heat capacity of water, why is it important to put the water in a thermally insulated container?

Practice Questions — Application

Q1   A kettle heats 0.200 kg of water from a temperature of 20.0 °C to 100.0 °C. Water has a specific heat capacity of 4200 J/kg°C. How much energy is transferred to the thermal energy store of the water?

Q2   A chef heats 400 g of oil to a temperature of 113 °C. The oil is left to cool until it reaches a temperature of 25 °C. The oil transfers 70.4 kJ of energy to its surroundings during this time. Calculate the specific heat capacity of the oil.

5. Specific Latent Heat

Latent heat is the energy required to move particles apart and change the state of a substance. But there's a bit more to it than that...

What is specific latent heat?

The energy needed to change the state of a substance is called latent heat. **Specific latent heat** (SLH) is the amount of energy needed to change 1 kg of a substance from one state to another without changing its temperature. For cooling, specific latent heat is the energy released by a change in state. Specific latent heat is different for different materials, and for changing between different states.

The specific latent heat for changing between a solid and a liquid (melting or freezing) is called the specific latent heat of fusion. The specific latent heat for changing between a liquid and a gas (evaporating, boiling or condensing) is called the specific latent heat of vaporisation.

You can work out the energy needed (or released) in joules when a substance of mass m changes state using this formula:

$$Q = \text{thermal energy for a change of state (J)} \longrightarrow Q = m \times L \longleftarrow L = \text{specific latent heat (J/kg)}$$
$$m = \text{mass (kg)}$$

Examples

The specific latent heat of vaporisation for water is 2 260 000 J/kg. How much energy is needed to completely boil 1.50 kg of water at 100 °C?

Just plug the numbers into the formula:

$Q = m \times L = 1.50 \times 2\ 260\ 000 = 3\ 390\ 000$ J

A 300 W heater is used to heat a 0.50 kg sample of a solid. Once the solid has reached its melting point, it is heated for 5 minutes and 30 seconds until it is completely melted. Calculate the specific latent heat of fusion for this substance.

First, convert the time into seconds.

5 minutes = $5 \times 60 = 300$ seconds

$300 + 30 = 330$ seconds

Now calculate the energy supplied by the heater during this time (p.244):

energy transferred = power × time taken = $300 \times 330 = 99\ 000$ J

This is equal to the thermal energy for a change of state, Q, so

$L = Q \div m = 99\ 000 \div 0.50 = 198\ 000 = 200\ 000$ J/kg (to 1 s.f.)

Don't get confused with specific heat capacity (page 304), which is the energy associated with a temperature rise of 1 °C. Specific latent heat is about changes of state where there's no temperature change.

Learning Objectives:
- Be able to define the term specific latent heat and explain the differences between it and specific heat capacity.
- Be able to use the equation: $Q = m \times L$.
- Be able to investigate the properties of water by obtaining a temperature-time graph for melting ice (Core Practical).

Specification References
14.7, 14.9, 14.11

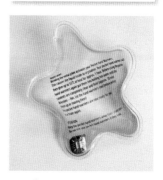

Figure 1: Some hand warmers contain liquid that solidifies when the button is clicked. This releases energy, which heats the surroundings.

Exam Tip
This formula will be given to you on the equations sheet. You can turn it into a formula triangle to help you rearrange it:

Tip: In calculations, your final answer should always be to the same number of significant figures as the data with the lowest number of significant figures.

Figure 2: *Remember to take readings with the scale at eye level if you use an analogue thermometer.*

Investigating changes of state

There's a simple experiment you can do to see how the temperature of ice changes as it is heated. First, fill a beaker with crushed ice and place a thermometer into the beaker. Set up the equipment shown in Figure 3.

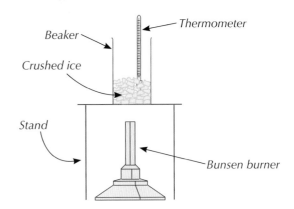

Figure 3: *A diagram of the apparatus used to obtain a temperature-time graph for melting ice.*

Measure the initial temperature of the ice. Then, start a stop watch and turn on the Bunsen burner. Every twenty seconds, record the temperature and the current state of the ice (e.g. partially melted, completely melted).

Continue this process until all of the ice has turned into water and the water then begins to boil. At this point, stop the stopwatch and turn off the Bunsen burner. Using your results, plot a graph of temperature against time for your experiment. You should get a graph similar to the blue sections in Figure 4.

If you continued heating the water and any water vapour that was produced, your graph would also include the purple section of Figure 4. Most substances will have a graph this shape as they are heated.

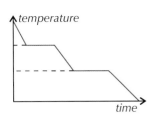

Figure 5: *You'd get a graph this shape if you cooled water vapour to ice.*

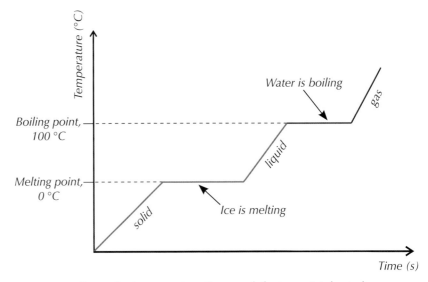

Figure 4: *A temperature-time graph for ice as it is heated.*

There are flat spots on the heating graph in Figure 4. If you compare the times of these to your measurements, you will see this is where a change of state was occurring. This is because during a change of state internal energy changes but the temperature remains constant (page 302).

Practice Questions — Fact Recall

Q1 What is meant by 'specific latent heat'?

Q2 What are the units of specific latent heat?

Q3 Describe the difference between specific latent heat and specific heat capacity.

Q4 Describe an experiment you could do to investigate how the temperature of ice changes as it changes state.

Q5 Sketch a temperature-time graph for ice being heated until it has become liquid water (that has not started to boil).

Practice Questions — Application

Q1 The specific latent heat of fusion for water is 334 000 J/kg. An ice cube of mass 25.0 g is at 0 °C. How much energy is needed to melt the ice cube?

Q2 The specific latent heat of vaporisation for a liquid is 1 550 000 J/kg. What mass of the liquid (already at its boiling point) would be completely boiled by 4 960 000 J of energy?

- Be able to explain the pressure of a gas in terms of the motion of its particles.
- Be able to explain that the pressure of a gas produces a net force at right angles to any surface.
- Be able to explain the effect of changing the temperature of a gas on the velocity of its particles and hence on the pressure produced by a fixed mass of gas at constant volume (qualitative only).
- Be able to explain the effect of changing the volume of a gas on the rate at which its particles collide with the walls of its container and hence on the pressure produced by a fixed mass of gas at constant temperature.
- Be able to use the equation: $P_1 \times V_1 = P_2 \times V_2$ to calculate pressure or volume for gases of fixed mass at constant temperature.
- Be able to explain that gases can be compressed or expanded by pressure changes.
- H Be able to explain why doing work on a gas can increase its temperature, including a bicycle pump.

Specification References
14.12, 14.13, 14.16-14.20

6. Particle Motion in Gases

The temperature of a gas determines the energy in the kinetic stores of its particles. It can also affect the pressure and the volume of the gas.

Gas pressure

As gas particles move about at high speeds, they bang into each other and whatever else happens to get in the way. When they collide with a surface, they exert a force on it. This leads to a resultant (net) force at right angles to the surface. Since pressure is the net force per unit area (p.317), this means they exert a pressure too.

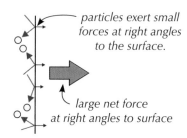

particles exert small forces at right angles to the surface.

large net force at right angles to surface

Figure 1: *Gas pressure on a surface.*

In a sealed container, the outward gas pressure is the total force exerted by all of the particles in the gas on a unit area of the container walls. It is measured in Pascals, Pa.

Pressure and temperature

You saw on page 301 that temperature is related to the average energy in the kinetic energy stores of the particles of a substance. So for a gas, the hotter it is, the faster its particles move. Faster particles and more collisions with the walls of the container in a given time both lead to an increase in net force, and so an increase in gas pressure. Increasing temperature will increase the speed and the number of collisions, and so the pressure (if volume is kept constant). Similarly, decreasing the temperature lowers the gas pressure.

Pressure and volume

If the temperature is kept constant, increasing the volume of a gas means the particles get more spread out. The particles hit the walls of the container less often, so the gas pressure decreases.

Pressure and volume are inversely proportional — when volume goes up, pressure goes down (and when volume goes down, pressure goes up). For a gas of fixed mass at a constant temperature, the relationship is:

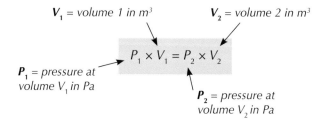

V_1 = volume 1 in m^3 V_2 = volume 2 in m^3

$$P_1 \times V_1 = P_2 \times V_2$$

P_1 = pressure at volume V_1 in Pa

P_2 = pressure at volume V_2 in Pa

A gas is held in a sealed container of volume 11 m³. The pressure of the gas is 84 Pa. The volume of the container is increased and the pressure of the gas changes to 60 Pa. The temperature of the gas is unchanged. What is the new volume of the container?

$P_1 \times V_1 = P_2 \times V_2$

so $V_2 = (P_1 \times V_1) \div P_2$

$= (84 \times 11) \div 60 = 15.4 = 15$ m³ (to 2 s.f.)

Tip: Pressure and volume are inversely proportional. The pressure has decreased, so the volume must have increased. This is a good way to check your answer is along the right lines.

The pressure of a gas results in a net outwards force at right angles to the surface of its container. This can be called the internal or outward pressure. There is also a force on the outside of the container due to the pressure of the air around the container. This is the external or inward pressure.

If a container can easily change its size (e.g. a balloon), then any change in these pressures will cause the container (and so the gas) to compress or expand. The volume of the container and gas is constant when the inwards pressure is equal to the outwards pressure.

You can change the volume of a gas in a container that doesn't have a fixed volume by changing either the internal or external pressure on the container.

Example 1

If a balloon is heated, the temperature of the gas inside the balloon increases. The gas particles gain energy and move around quicker. This increases the pressure of the gas inside the balloon.

The outward pressure of the gas inside the balloon is now larger than the inward pressure caused by the surroundings. The balloon (and so the volume of the gas) expands until the pressures are equal once more.

Tip: Cooling a balloon would have the opposite effect — the outward pressure would become smaller than the inside pressure, so the balloon would shrink.

Example 2

If a helium balloon is released, it rises. Atmospheric pressure decreases with height (page 319), so the pressure outside the balloon decreases. This causes the balloon to expand until the pressure inside drops to the same as the atmospheric pressure.

Figure 2: A balloon in a vacuum chamber. Air is removed from the chamber, so the pressure outside the balloon drops. This makes the air inside the balloon expand, in order to equalise the pressure.

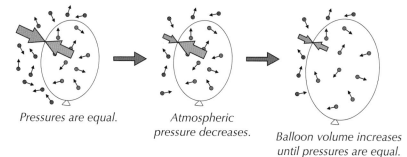

Pressures are equal.   *Atmospheric pressure decreases.*   *Balloon volume increases until pressures are equal.*

Figure 3: A change in external pressure causing the expansion of a balloon.

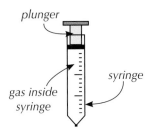

plunger

gas inside syringe

syringe

Figure 4: *An air-tight syringe.*

Tip: There's more about doing work on p.199.

Tip: Remember, temperature of a gas is linked to the average energy in the particles' kinetic stores (p.301).

| Example 3 |

For a gas in an air-tight syringe (see Figure 4), pushing hard on the plunger increases the inward pressure on the gas, so that it is larger than the outward pressure. This causes the gas inside of the syringe to be compressed, increasing the pressure of the gas inside the syringe.

If you remove the force on the plunger, the outwards pressure of the gas is now larger than the inwards pressure (atmospheric pressure, page 319). The plunger rises and the volume of the gas increases until the inward and outward pressures are equal.

Doing work on a gas   Higher

If you transfer energy by applying a force, then you do work. Doing work on a gas increases its internal energy, which can increase its temperature.

| Example — Higher |

You can do work on a gas mechanically, e.g. with a bike pump. The gas applies pressure to the plunger of the pump, and so exerts a force on it. Work has to be done against this force to push down the plunger.

This transfers energy to the kinetic energy stores of the gas particles, increasing the temperature. If the pump is connected to a tyre, you should feel it getting warmer.

Practice Questions — Fact Recall

Q1   A gas is stored inside a sealed container. How does the gas exert an outwards pressure on the walls of the container?

Q2   Explain why increasing the temperature of a fixed volume of gas will increase the pressure of the gas.

Q3   For a fixed mass of gas at a constant temperature, are pressure and volume directly proportional or inversely proportional?

Q4   The volume of a fixed mass of gas is increased. Its temperature remains constant. State what will happen to the pressure of the gas. Explain your answer by referring to the particles involved.

Q5   Work is done on a gas. What effect does this have on the temperature of the gas?

Practice Questions — Application

Tip: Remember, so long as the units of each volume are the same, you don't have to convert them to m².

Q1   A gas is compressed from a volume of 75 cm³ to a volume of 30 cm³. Its temperature remains the same. The pressure of the gas after it has been compressed is 110 Pa. What was the pressure of the gas before it was compressed?

Q2   A helium balloon is inflated, then placed inside a refrigerator. Explain what will happen to the volume of the balloon when it is in the refrigerator.

Density

☐ That density is mass per unit volume.

☐ How to calculate the density of a material, using $\rho = \frac{m}{V}$.

☐ That the closer together the particles in a substance are, the denser the substance is.

☐ How to measure the density of a solid or liquid.

States of Matter

☐ What the kinetic theory model is.

☐ That there are three states of matter — solid, liquid and gas.

☐ That particles in a solid are held close together in a fixed, regular pattern by strong forces.

☐ That the particles in a solid can only vibrate around their fixed positions as they don't have much energy in their kinetic energy stores.

☐ That particles in a liquid are close together but can move past each other to form irregular arrangements, as the forces between the particles are weaker than those for a solid.

☐ That the particles in a liquid move in random directions at low speeds as they have more energy in their kinetic energy stores than the particles in a solid.

☐ That particles in a gas are spread out with almost no forces between particles.

☐ That the particles in a gas can move at high speeds in random directions as they have more energy in their kinetic energy stores than the particles in a liquid.

☐ That particles in a solid are closer together than particles in a liquid, and particles in a liquid are closer together than particles in a gas. This means that solids are usually denser than liquids, and liquids are denser than gases.

Internal Energy and Changes of State

☐ That the energy stored in a system is stored by its particles.

☐ That the internal energy of a system is the total energy that its particles have in their kinetic and potential energy stores.

☐ That heating a system increases the internal energy stored in a system.

☐ That heating a system leads to an increase in temperature or a change in state.

☐ That absolute zero is the temperature at which particles in a system have the lowest possible energy in their kinetic energy stores, so they barely move. Absolute zero is equal to −273 °C.

☐ How to convert between the Kelvin and Celsius scales.

☐ The changes of state — melting, freezing, evaporating, boiling, condensing and sublimating.

☐ That changes of state are physical changes. Physical changes are different from some chemical changes because if you reverse a physical change, the material gets back its original properties.

☐ That when substances change state, mass is conserved.

cont...

Specific Heat Capacity

☐ The meaning of the term specific heat capacity.

☐ How to use the equation $\Delta Q = m \times c \times \Delta\theta$.

☐ How to investigate the properties of water by determining its specific heat capacity

☐ How thermal insulation can be used to reduce unwanted energy transfers.

Specific Latent Heat

☐ The meaning of the term specific latent heat.

☐ The difference between specific latent heat and specific heat capacity.

☐ How to use the equation $Q = m \times L$.

☐ How to investigate the changes of state of water by melting ice and plotting a graph of temperature against time.

Particle Motion in Gases

☐ That the pressure of a gas is caused by the collisions of gas particles.

☐ That the outward pressure of a gas in a container is caused by the gas particles colliding with the surface of the container.

☐ That the net force caused by gas pressure acts at right angles to a surface.

☐ That increasing the temperature of a gas increases the velocity of the gas particles, which increases the rate of collisions. This means that increasing the temperature of a fixed mass and volume of gas increases its pressure.

☐ That gas pressure and volume are inversely proportional, if the temperature remains constant.

☐ How to use the equation $P_1 \times V_1 = P_2 \times V_2$ to calculate pressure or volume changes for a fixed mass of gas at a constant temperature.

☐ That increasing the outwards pressure or decreasing the inwards pressure on a container of gas will cause it to expand, if the container is able to change its size.

☐ That decreasing the outwards pressure or increasing the inwards pressure on a container of gas will cause it to contract, if the container is able to change its size.

☐ H That doing work on a gas (for example, by using a bicycle pump) transfers energy to the kinetic energy stores of its particles, which increases the temperature of the gas.

1 A physicist is carrying out an experiment with a substance which is in solid form. She needs 450 g of the substance for the experiment. The density of the substance when it is a solid is 9 g/cm³.

(a) Which equation relates density to mass and volume?

A $\rho = \dfrac{m}{V}$

B $\rho = \dfrac{V}{m}$

C $\rho = mV$

D $\rho = mV^2$

(1 mark)

(b) Calculate the volume of the solid substance that the physicist needs for the experiment. Give your answer in cm³.

(3 marks)

The physicist heats the substance for 300 seconds. The graph in **Figure 1** shows how the substance's temperature changes over this time period.

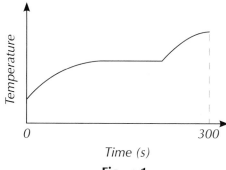

Time (s)

Figure 1

(c) At the end of the time period shown, the temperature of the substance was 72 °C. What is this temperature in kelvins?

A   72 K

B   –72 K

C   345 K

D   –201 K

(1 mark)

(d) In what state of matter is the substance at the end of the time period shown? Explain your answer.

(2 marks)

(e) What is the mass of the substance at the end of the time period shown? Explain your answer.

(2 marks)

2   A 0.132 g sample of gas is stored in a sealed container.
The gas pressure inside the container is 150 Pa.

The gas is then compressed to a volume of 30 cm³.
Following this compression, the sample remains a gas, with a pressure of 220 Pa.

(a)   Calculate the initial volume of the gas before it was compressed.
Use the correct equation from the equations listed on page 404.
Give your answer in cm³.

(3 marks)

(b)   Explain why compressing the gas increases the gas pressure.

(2 marks)

(c)   Calculate how much the density of the gas changed due to the compression.
Give your answer in g/cm³.

(4 marks)

(d)   The container is then cooled. All of the gas in the container condenses into a liquid.

5.0 J of energy is released during the change of state.
Calculate the specific latent heat of vaporisation of the gas.
Use the correct equation from the equations listed on page 404.
Give your answer in kJ/kg to two significant figures.

(3 marks)

3   A student is investigating the specific heat capacity of water.
The student uses an electric immersion heater to heat a beaker of water.
They use a joulemeter to measure the energy transferred by the heater for
a given temperature rise.

(a)   Suggest one safety issue the student should consider when performing a risk
assessment for this experiment.

(1 mark)

(b)   Suggest one way to make the student's experiment more accurate.

(1 mark)

(c)   The student heats 0.50 kg of water from 10.0 °C to 100.0 °C.
189 kJ of energy was transferred to the water.
Calculate the specific heat capacity of water.
Use the correct equation from the equations listed on page 404.
Give your answer in J/kg °C.

(3 marks)

4   An inflatable mattress is pumped up using a foot pump.

(a)   Explain, in terms of pressure, why pumping air into the mattress causes it to inflate.

(3 marks)

(b)   The mattress begins to feel warm as it is pumped up.
Explain why this is the case.

(3 marks)

1. Fluid Pressure

You probably know that liquids are fluids, but so are gases. This means liquid and gas particles can move around, bang into things and create a pressure.

Calculating pressure

If a force is applied to a surface, then there is a pressure on the surface. Pressure is defined as the force exerted normal (at right angles) to a surface per unit area of that surface. It's measured in pascals, Pa.

You can calculate the pressure at a surface using:

P = pressure (Pa) ⟶ $P = \dfrac{F}{A}$ ⟵ F = force normal to a surface (N)

⟵ A = area of that surface (m²)

This equation gives the pressure caused by any force which is applied at right angles to an area, so you can use it for solids, liquids or gases.

Example 1

If a person is wearing high-heels, their weight (force) acts on the ground over a very small area. This causes a large pressure on the ground, which can damage some types of flooring.

Snow shoes have a very large sole, so the person's weight is spread over a large area. This reduces the pressure on the ground and stops the wearer sinking into the snow.

Figure 1: High-heeled shoes have a small area in contact with the ground.

Example 2

A mug is placed on a desk. It has a weight of 7.5 N. The base of the mug has an area of 0.005 m². Calculate the pressure exerted on the desk by the mug.

In this instance, the force causing the pressure is the weight of the mug, so:

Pressure = force ÷ area = 7.5 ÷ 0.005 = 1500 Pa

The mug is then filled with water. The pressure exerted on the desk by the mug is 1600 Pa. Determine the new weight of the mug, in newtons.

Rearrange the pressure equation for force:

Force = pressure × area

Then substitute in the values you've been given:

Force = 1600 × 0.005 = 8 N

Learning Objectives:

- Be able to recall and use the equation: $P = \dfrac{F}{A}$.
- Be able to explain how pressure is related to force and area, using appropriate examples.
- Be able to recall that the pressure in fluids causes a force normal to any surface.
- Be able to describe how pressure in fluids increases with depth and density.
- Be able to describe the pressure in a fluid as being due to the fluid and atmospheric pressure.
- **H** Be able to explain why the pressure in liquids varies with density and depth.
- **H** Be able to use the equation to calculate the magnitude of the pressure in liquids and calculate the differences in pressure at different depths in a liquid: $P = h \times \rho \times g$.
- Be able to explain why atmospheric pressure varies with height above the Earth's surface with reference to a simple model of the Earth's atmosphere.

Specification References
15.7-15.14

What is fluid pressure?

Tip: The attractive forces between particles in solids are stronger than the ones in liquids and gases, which is why solids can't 'flow' (page 299).

Fluids are substances that can 'flow' because their particles are able to move around. A fluid is either a liquid or a gas. As these particles move around, they collide with surfaces and other particles.

Particles have mass, and so when particles in a fluid collide with a surface, they exert a force on it (and so cause a pressure) at right angles to the surface.

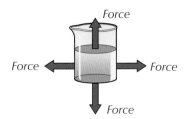

Figure 2: Water in a beaker will exert a force normal to all its surfaces, including the surface in contact with the air.

Tip: For example, water has a density of 1000 kg/m³ and mercury has a density of 13 500 kg/m³. So the pressure exerted by mercury is higher as it has a higher density.

The denser the fluid, or the deeper the point you're looking at, the higher the fluid pressure will be. The total pressure at a point in a fluid is the sum of the pressure due to the fluid itself (i.e. the pressure caused by the particles in the fluid colliding) and the surrounding atmospheric pressure.

Pressure in a liquid   Higher

You need to be able to explain why the pressure in a liquid increases with density and depth.

Density is a measure of how close together the particles in a substance are (page 296). For a given liquid, the density is uniform (the same everywhere) and it doesn't vary with shape or size.

A denser liquid will have more particles in a given volume. This means there are more particles that are able to collide — which means more collisions, a higher total force exerted and so a higher pressure.

As depth increases, the number of particles above that point increases. The weight of these particles adds to the pressure experienced at that point, so liquid pressure increases with depth.

You can show that the pressure of a liquid increases with depth using a tube with equally-sized holes cut into the side of it. When the tube is filled with water, the pressure is greatest at the bottom (i.e. at the deepest point), and so the water spurting out of the hole at the bottom travels faster than the water spurting out of the hole at the top.

Tip: H The higher pressure at the bottom of the tube means the force acting on the sides of the tube is higher at the bottom (per unit area).

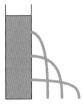

Figure 3: Water spurting out of holes in a tube at different speeds due to differences in pressure at different depths.

You can calculate the pressure at a certain depth due to the column of liquid above that point using:

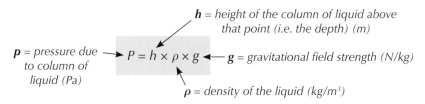

h = height of the column of liquid above that point (i.e. the depth) (m)

p = pressure due to column of liquid (Pa)

$$P = h \times \rho \times g$$

g = gravitational field strength (N/kg)

ρ = density of the liquid (kg/m³)

Tip: $\boxed{\text{H}}$ Be careful — this equation only gives you the pressure due to the column of liquid above a given depth. It doesn't include atmospheric pressure — see below.

Example — Higher

Calculate the change in pressure between a point 20 m below the surface of water and a point 40 m below the surface. The density of water is 1000 kg/m³. Take g to be 10 N/kg.

Calculate the pressure caused by the water at a depth of 20 m:
$P = h \times \rho \times g = 20 \times 1000 \times 10 = 200\ 000$ Pa

Do the same for a depth of 40 m:
$P = h \times \rho \times g = 40 \times 1000 \times 10 = 400\ 000$ Pa

Take away the pressure at 20 m from the pressure at 40 m:
$400\ 000 - 200\ 000 = 200\ 000$ Pa $= 2 \times 10^5$ Pa (or 200 kPa)

Figure 4: Divers can only dive to a certain depth before the pressure gets too high and is dangerous.

Atmospheric pressure

The atmosphere is a layer of air that surrounds Earth. It is thin compared to the size of the Earth. **Atmospheric pressure** is created on a surface by air molecules colliding with the surface. Figure 5 shows that as altitude (height above Earth) increases, atmospheric pressure decreases. This is due to:

1. Density (i.e. how close together the molecules of the atmosphere are). As altitude increases, the atmosphere gets less dense. This means there are fewer air molecules that are able to collide with a surface, which in turn means a lower atmospheric pressure.

2. How much air there is above a certain point. An increasing altitude means fewer air molecules above a surface. This means that the weight of the air above, which contributes to atmospheric pressure, decreases.

Tip: People need to take oxygen tanks with them when climbing high mountains — the density of air decreases with height, so there is less air at the top of the mountain which makes it harder to breathe.

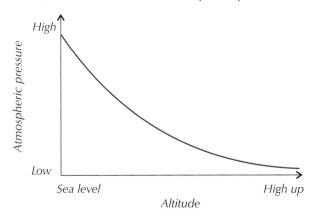

Figure 5: A graph to show how the atmospheric pressure varies with the height above Earth.

Figure 6: Barometers are used to measure atmospheric pressure. Measurements are used to help create weather forecasts.

Practice Questions — Fact Recall

Q1 What is pressure?

Q2 Give the equation that relates pressure, force and area.
Give the units of each variable.

Q3 The pressure of a fluid exerts a force at the surfaces of the fluid.
In what direction does this force act?

Q4 a) Describe how the pressure exerted by a liquid changes with
increasing depth.

    b) Explain your answer to part a).

Q5 Explain how atmospheric pressure changes as the altitude increases.

Tip: Remember, altitude is the height above the Earth's surface.

Practice Questions — Application

Q1 A balloon that is full of water has a surface area of 320.0 cm^2.
The water inside the balloon has a pressure of 101 000 Pa.
Calculate the total force that the water exerts on the balloon.

Q2 A diver swims from the surface of the sea to a depth of 5.0 m.
Calculate the change in pressure that the diver experiences.
The density of the seawater is 1030 kg/m^3 and the gravitational field
strength can be assumed to be 10 N/kg.
Give your answer to 2 significant figures.

Tip: Take a look at pages 18-19 for how to convert between different units.

Exam Tip H
The equation needed for Q2 will be given on your equation sheet in the exam (see page 404).

2. Upthrust Higher

The reason that you feel a lot lighter in a swimming pool than on solid ground is all to do with upthrust. It's the force that pushes up on you and keeps you afloat as you're bobbing along.

What is upthrust?

When an object is submerged in a fluid (either partially or completely), the pressure of the fluid exerts a force on it from every direction.

As pressure increases with depth (see page 318), the force exerted on the bottom of the object is larger than the force acting on the top of the object (because the bottom of the object is deeper in the fluid than the top of it). This causes a resultant force upwards, known as **upthrust**. The upthrust is equal to the weight of fluid that has been displaced (pushed out of the way) by the object.

Example Higher

The upthrust on a pineapple in water is equal to the weight of a pineapple-shaped volume of water.

Pressure

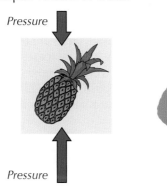

Pressure

Pineapple displaces this much water.

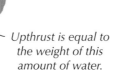

Upthrust is equal to the weight of this amount of water.

Floating and sinking

If the upthrust on an object is equal to the object's weight, then the forces balance and the object floats. If an object's weight is more than the upthrust, the object sinks. Whether or not an object floats depends on its density:

- An object that is less dense than the fluid it is placed in weighs less than the equivalent volume of fluid. This means it displaces a volume of fluid that is equal to its weight before it can become completely submerged. At this point, the upthrust is equal to the object's weight, so the object floats.

- An object that is denser than the fluid it is placed in weighs more than the equivalent volume of fluid. This means it is unable to displace enough fluid to equal its weight (because it will always weigh more than the fluid it displaces). This means its weight is larger than the upthrust, so it sinks.

Learning Objectives:

- **H** Be able to explain why an object in a fluid is subject to an upwards force (upthrust) and relate this to examples including objects that are fully immersed in a fluid (liquid or gas) or partially immersed in a liquid.

- **H** Be able to recall that the upthrust is equal to the weight of fluid displaced.

- **H** Be able to explain how the factors (upthrust, weight, density of fluid) influence whether an object will float or sink.

Specification References 15.15-15.17

Tip: Take a look back at page 317 for a reminder on how pressure relates to force.

Tip: Take a look at page 296 for more on density.

Figure 1: *Rubber ducks float really well on water as they're mostly made of air, and air has a much lower density than water.*

Tip: **H** Saltwater has a higher density than water, so a potato will float in the water if enough salt is added.

Figure 2: *A submarine changes its weight in order to move up and down in the water.*

Examples **Higher**

- An apple will float in water.

This much water weighs the same as the whole apple (because the apple is less dense than water).

The apple has displaced a volume of water equal to its weight, so it floats.

- A potato will sink in water.

This much water weighs less than a potato (because the potato is denser than water).

The potato can never displace a volume of water equal to its weight so it sinks.

Submarines make use of upthrust. To sink, large tanks are filled with water. This increases the weight of the submarine (which increases its average density, as its volume is constant) so that its weight is more than the upthrust. To rise to the surface, the water is expelled (pushed out again) and the tanks are filled with air to reduce the weight so that it's less than the upthrust.

Practice Questions — Fact Recall

Q1 Explain why an object will experience an upthrust in a liquid.

Q2 Will an object float or sink if its weight is equal to the upthrust acting on it?

Q3 Will an object float or sink if its weight is greater than the upthrust acting on it?

Q4 Explain why an object with a higher density than water will sink when it is put in water.

Practice Question — Application

Q1 a) An object with a volume of 0.50 m³ and a uniform density of 1500 kg/m³ is put in water. The density of the water is 1000 kg/m³. Will the object float or sink?

b) The object is then cut in half so that is has a volume of 0.25 m³. Will the object then float or sink?

3. Forces and Elasticity

Applying forces to some objects can cause them to stretch. Stretching an object can either be a permanent change or a temporary change.

Elastic and inelastic distortion

When you apply a force to an object you may cause it to stretch, compress or bend. To change the shape of an object in this way, you need more than one force acting on the object, in different directions (otherwise the object would simply move in the direction of the applied force, instead of changing shape).

> ### Examples
>
> If a spring is supported at the top and a weight is attached to the bottom, it stretches.
>
> Force, F
>
> Original length, l
>
> Extension, x
>
> Force, F
>
> A spring can also be compressed or bent by applying forces at different points.
>
> F
>
> F
>
> F →
>
> ← F
>
> ← F

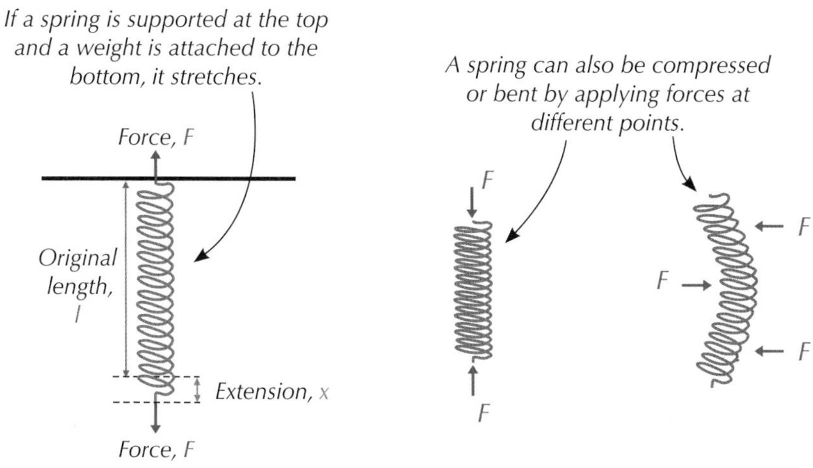

Figure 1: *A spring can be stretched, compressed or bent when more than one force is acting on it. The extension, x, of a stretched spring is the difference between its stretched length and its original length (i.e. with no force applied).*

An object has been **elastically distorted** if it can go back to its original shape and length after the force has been removed. Objects which can be elastically distorted are called **elastic objects** (e.g. a spring).

An object has been **inelastically distorted** if it doesn't return to its original shape and length after the force has been removed (i.e. it's been permanently distorted).

Force and extension

Up to a certain force, the extension of a stretched spring (or other elastic object) is directly proportional to the load or force applied — so $F \propto x$ (p.344).

Whilst $F \propto x$ you can say that the relationship between force and extension is linear. In other words, if you drew a graph of force against extension for the object, the graph would be a straight line (see next page).

Learning Objectives:

- Be able to explain, using springs and other elastic objects, that stretching, bending or compressing an object requires more than one force.

- Be able to describe the difference between elastic and inelastic distortion.

- Be able to recall and use the equation for linear elastic distortion including calculating the spring constant: $F = k \times x$.

- Be able to describe the difference between linear and non-linear relationships between force and extension.

- Be able to use the equation to calculate the work done in stretching a spring: $E = \frac{1}{2} \times k \times x^2$.

Specification References 15.1-15.5

Figure 2: *A bungee jumper. The bungee cord is an elastic object which stretches due to the person's weight. Look back at page 37 for a reminder on weight.*

For linear, elastic distortions, you can use the following equation that relates force and extension:

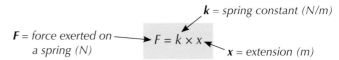

k = spring constant (N/m)

F = force exerted on a spring (N) $\longrightarrow F = k \times x \longleftarrow$ x = extension (m)

The spring constant depends on the material that you are stretching — a stiffer spring has a greater spring constant.

Example

When a lead ball is suspended from a spring, the spring extends by 2.0 cm. If the spring constant k = 60.0 N/m, calculate the weight of the lead ball.

Be careful with units here — the formula uses extension in metres, so make sure you convert any numbers first:

$$2.0 \text{ cm} = 0.020 \text{ m}$$

Then put the numbers into the equation for force:

$$F = k \times x = 60.0 \times 0.020 = 1.2 \text{ N}$$

The limit of proportionality and the elastic limit

There's a limit to the amount of force you can apply to an object for the extension to keep on increasing proportionally. This limit is known as the **limit of proportionality**.

Past this point, the relationship between force and extension is non-linear, (the force-extension graph is no longer a straight line), and you can no longer use the equation $F = k \times x$.

The **elastic limit** of an object is the maximum force that can be applied to an object before it is permanently distorted. The elastic limit is always beyond the limit of proportionality, so all linear distortions are elastic.

Figure 3 shows a graph of force against extension for an object. The limit of proportionality is marked as point P. The elastic limit is marked as point E.

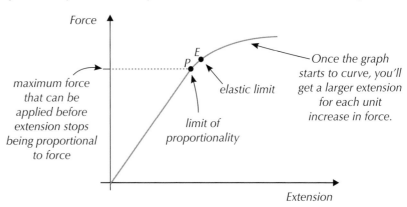

Force

maximum force that can be applied before extension stops being proportional to force

E *P* *elastic limit*

Once the graph starts to curve, you'll get a larger extension for each unit increase in force.

limit of proportionality

Extension

Figure 3: A graph showing the force applied to an object against its extension. The force is proportional to extension up to the limit of proportionality.

Work done in distorting

Work is done when a force stretches or compresses an object. This causes energy to be transferred. If the object is elastically distorted, ALL this energy is transferred to the object's elastic potential energy store.

As long as a spring is not stretched past its limit of proportionality, the energy transferred in stretching or compressing the spring (and so the work done on the spring) can be found using:

k = spring constant (N/m)

E = energy transferred in stretching (J) ⟶ $E = \frac{1}{2} \times k \times x^2$

x = extension (m)

This formula can also be used to calculate the energy stored in a spring's elastic potential energy store.

Tip: If an object is distorted inelastically, some of the work done will transfer energy into other energy stores (e.g. the thermal energy store of the object), not just the elastic potential energy store.

Tip: This formula also works for x being a compression.

Example

A spring has a spring constant of 120 N/m. Its natural length is 15.2 cm. A force is applied to compress the spring. The new length of the spring is 13.8 cm.

Assuming the spring distorts elastically and linearly, calculate the total energy transferred to its elastic potential energy store when it is compressed. Give your answer in mJ.

First, calculate the compression of the spring: 15.2 – 13.8 = 1.4 cm

Now convert this compression to metres: 1.4 ÷ 100 = 0.014 m

Substitute the values into the equation:

$E = \frac{1}{2} \times k \times x^2 = \frac{1}{2} \times 120 \times 0.014^2 = 0.01176$ J

And then convert this answer to mJ:

0.01176 × 1000 = 11.76 mJ = 12 mJ (to 2 s.f.)

Tip: If a stretched spring is released, the energy stored in its elastic potential energy store will be transferred to its kinetic energy store as it springs back to its original size and shape.

Tip: Don't forget to square the compression when calculating the energy transferred to the elastic potential energy store.

Tip: k = 120 N/m is to 2 significant figures, which is the lowest out of all the data, so your final answer should also be to 2 significant figures (page 15).

The work done for a particular force (or extension) can also be found by calculating the area under the force-extension graph up to that force (or extension). Up to the elastic limit, this area is also equal to the energy stored in the elastic potential energy store of the object.

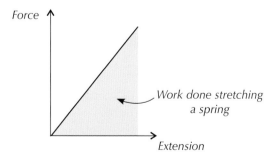

Figure 4: *The area under a force-extension graph for a spring is equal to the work done stretching the spring.*

Tip: See pages 348-349 for more on the area under a graph.

Practice Questions — Fact Recall

Q1 Explain why more than one force needs to be applied to a spring in order to stretch it.

Q2 What is an elastic object?

Q3 Explain the difference between an elastic and an inelastic distortion.

Q4 What is meant by the phrase 'a linear relationship between force and extension'?

Tip: Remember, all linear distortions are elastic.

Q5 Give the equation that relates the force applied to a spring, the spring constant of the spring and the extension of the spring for a linear distortion. Give the units of each term.

Q6 What is the limit of proportionality?

Q7 A spring is elastically distorted.
How much of the energy transferred to the spring is released when the spring is released? Explain your answer.

Practice Questions — Application

Q1 A spring has a spring constant of 34 N/m. Calculate the force required to stretch the spring linearly from 0.50 m to 0.75 m.

Q2 A force-extension graph for a spring is shown below.
Which point marks the spring's limit of proportionality?

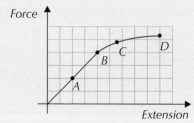

Exam Tip
Remember to make sure all your values are in the right units before you substitute them into an equation. For example, extension, x, should be in metres for Q3.

Q3 a) Spring A is linearly compressed from 16 cm to 12 cm when a force of 0.80 N is applied to it. Calculate the spring constant of spring A.

b) Calculate the work done on spring A as it is compressed.

c) The same force is then applied to spring B. It linearly compresses spring B by a smaller amount than it compressed spring A. Is the spring constant of spring B higher than, lower than or equal to the spring constant of spring A?

4. Investigating Springs

You can investigate the behaviour of a spring and the work done to distort the spring using a simple experiment. Time to get practical...

Apparatus and setup

Set up the apparatus as shown in Figure 1.

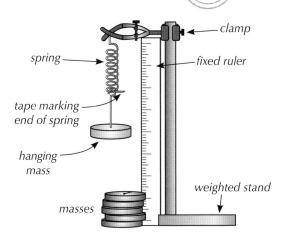

Figure 1: *Experimental setup used to investigate a spring.*

You could do a quick pilot experiment first to check your masses are a suitable size. Using the spring you'll be testing (or an identical one), load it with masses one at a time, up to a total of five masses. Using the ruler, check that the spring extends by the same amount each time. If adding one of these masses causes the spring to stretch by more than the previous ones, you have gone beyond the spring's limit of proportionality. If this happens, you'll need to use smaller masses. Otherwise, you won't end up with enough values to plot your graph later on.

If the spring does go past its limit of proportionality during the pilot experiment, it could start to distort inelastically and so you'll have to replace it with another (identical) spring in the real thing.

Carrying out the experiment

Make sure you have plenty of masses and calculate their weights (the force that will be applied to the spring) using $W = m \times g$ (p.37).

Using the ruler, measure the natural length of the spring (the length when no hanging mass is attached). Make sure you take the reading at eye level and use a marker (e.g. a thin strip of tape, as shown in Figures 1 and 2) to make the reading more accurate.

Add a mass to the spring and allow the spring to come to rest. Measure the spring's new length. Record the weight added and work out the extension (the change in length). Repeat this process, recording the total weight attached and calculating the total extension (total length minus natural length) each time, until you have enough measurements (no fewer than 6).

Learning Objective:
- Be able to investigate the extension and work done when applying forces to a spring (Core Practical).

Specification Reference 15.6

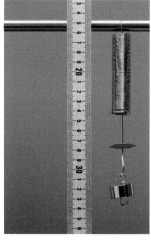

Figure 2: *Using a marker helps you read measurements from the ruler.*

Tip: It's okay to go past the limit of proportionality when you're doing the real thing, but you need to make sure you've recorded enough measurements to plot the linear part of the graph beforehand.

Tip: You should wear safety goggles when carrying out this experiment to protect your eyes in case the spring snaps. Make sure you do a risk assessment to identify any other hazards before you start.

Analysing the results

Plot a force-extension graph of your results and draw a line of best fit. For each measurement, the force you should plot is the total weight of the masses attached to the spring. The extension is the difference between the spring's length with that total weight attached and its natural length. Take a look at pages 16-17 for more information on how to plot graphs.

The graph will only start to curve if you exceed the limit of proportionality when you're adding the masses. Don't worry if yours doesn't start to curve — as long as you've got the straight line bit.

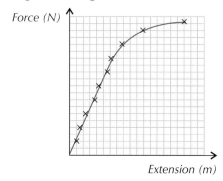

Figure 3: Graph of force against extension for a spring.

Tip: You first saw force-extension graphs on page 324.

You should find that a larger force causes a bigger extension. You can also think of this as more work needing to be done to cause a larger extension. The force doing work is the gravitational force and for elastic distortions, this force is equal to $F = k \times x$.

Work done

You can find the work done by a particular force by calculating the area under the force-extension graph up to that value of force.

Tip: See p.350 for more about the areas of different shapes.

Example

Determine the work done to stretch a spring by 2.0 cm from the force-extension graph.

First, draw a vertical line upwards from an extension of 2.0 cm.

Area under graph = area of triangle

Area = ½ × base × height
Base = 2.0 cm = 0.02 m

Area = ½ × 0.02 × 4 = 0.04 J

Or you can calculate it using the counting squares method (p.349):

Area under graph = 400 small squares

1 small square = 0.001 m × 0.1 N
= 0.0001 J

Work done = 400 × 0.0001 = 0.04 J

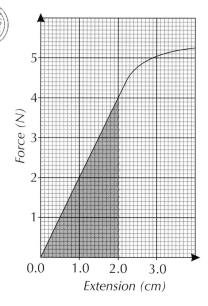

Tip: As the graph is linear up to an extension of 2.0 cm, the work done equals the energy transferred to the object's elastic potential energy store.

Practice Questions — Fact Recall

Q1 When carrying out an experiment to find the work done when stretching a spring, explain why it is a good idea to carry out a pilot experiment first on an identical spring.

Q2 Give a safety procedure that should be carried out when doing an experiment to investigate the relation between force and extension for a spring.

Q3 How is the work done in stretching a spring found from a force-extension graph?

Practice Question — Application

Q1 A student investigates how much work is required to extend a spring. Figure 4 shows their results.

Force (N)	Extension (cm)
0	0
5	0.6
10	1.3
15	1.9
20	2.5
25	3.1
30	3.8
35	4.4
40	5.0

Figure 4: *A table of the student's experimental results.*

a) Plot a force-extension graph for the spring.

b) Calculate the work done to extend the spring by 2.5 cm.

Section 9b Checklist — Make sure you know...

Fluid Pressure

- [ ] How to calculate pressure using the equation $P = \frac{F}{A}$.
- [ ] Examples showing how pressure is related to force and area.
- [ ] That the pressure in fluids causes a force normal to any surface.
- [ ] That pressure in fluids increases with depth.
- [ ] That pressure in fluids increases with the density of the fluid.
- [ ] That the pressure in a fluid is due to the fluid and the surrounding atmospheric pressure.

cont...

- ☐ ⊞ Why the pressure in liquids varies with density and depth.
- ☐ ⊞ How to use the equation $P = h \times \rho \times g$ to calculate pressures (and differences in pressure) in liquids.
- ☐ That atmospheric pressure decreases with altitude (the height above the Earth's surface).
- ☐ Why atmospheric pressure varies with altitude.

Upthrust

- ☐ ⊞ That an object in a fluid experiences upthrust.
- ☐ ⊞ That upthrust is caused by the difference in fluid pressure at the top and bottom of the object for both partially and completely submerged objects.
- ☐ ⊞ That the upthrust on an object is equal to the weight of the fluid displaced by the object.
- ☐ ⊞ That an object floats if its weight is equal to its upthrust.
- ☐ ⊞ That an object sinks if its weight is more than its upthrust.
- ☐ ⊞ That if the density of an object is less than the density of the fluid it is in, the object will float.
- ☐ ⊞ That if the density of an object is more than the density of the fluid it is in, the object will sink.

Forces and Elasticity

- ☐ That to stretch, bend or compress an object, more than one force needs to act on the object.
- ☐ That an elastic distortion is one where an object returns to its original shape after the forces are removed.
- ☐ That an inelastic distortion is one where an object doesn't return to its original shape after the forces are removed (the object is permanently distorted).
- ☐ That the relationship between force and extension is linear when force is directly proportional to extension.
- ☐ The equation $F = k \times x$, and that it can only be used for linear elastic distortions.
- ☐ That the relationship between force and extension is non-linear if the object is distorted past its limit of proportionality.
- ☐ That the work done in stretching a spring can be found using $E = \frac{1}{2} \times k \times x^2$, provided the spring hasn't been stretched past its limit of proportionality.
- ☐ That the area under a force-extension graph shows the work done to stretch a spring.

Investigating Springs

- ☐ How to investigate extension when applying forces to a spring.
- ☐ How to use values of force and extension to calculate the work done in stretching a spring.

Exam-style Questions

1   An object is put on a spring as shown in **Figure 1**. The object compresses the spring, which remains vertical during the compression. The spring has a spring constant of 160 N/m, and the length of the spring changes from 165 mm to 140 mm when the object is put on top of it. The compression of the spring is linear and elastic.

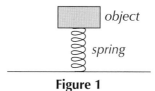

Figure 1

(a) (i) State the equation that links the force exerted on a spring, the spring constant and compression.

(1 mark)

    (ii) Calculate the weight of the object. Give your answer in N.

(3 marks)

(b)   Calculate the energy stored in the elastic potential energy store of the spring. Use the correct equation from the equations listed on page 404. Give your answer in J.

(2 marks)

(c)   The object is removed from the spring and placed on the floor. The area of the surface of the object in contact with the floor is 0.025 m².

    (i) Write down the equation that links pressure, force and area.

(1 mark)

    (ii) Calculate the pressure exerted on the floor by the object. Give your answer in Pa.

(2 marks)

2   A student carries out an experiment to investigate how the extension of a spring changes as an increasing force is applied to it. She plots her results on a force-extension graph and draws a line of best fit. Her results are shown in **Figure 2**.

When drawing the line of best fit, the student assumes the data point recorded when a force of 0.70 N is applied to the spring is anomalous.

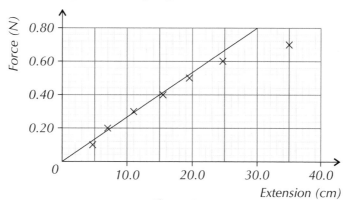

Figure 2

(a) Explain why the student is wrong to assume the data point is anomalous.
Suggest how the student could find out whether it is anomalous or not.

(2 marks)

(b) The student decides to repeat the experiment. Suggest why a second identical spring
should be used rather than the same spring.

(1 mark)

(c) Using the graph in **Figure 2**, calculate the work done to stretch the spring by 15.0 cm.

(3 marks)

3   Barometers are devices that measure atmospheric pressure. Some barometers use a
tube of liquid mercury to indicate the surrounding atmospheric pressure.

(a) The height of the mercury in a barometer is 70.0 cm.
Mercury has a density of 13 500 kg/m³. g = 10.0 N/kg.
Calculate the pressure at the base of the tube due to the mercury above it.
Use a correct equation from the equations listed on page 404. Give your answer in Pa.

(2 marks)

(b)* Atmospheric pressure at sea level is around 101 000 Pa. At the peak of Mount Everest,
this pressure drops to around 34 000 Pa. Explain why the atmospheric pressure is
lower at the top of Mount Everest than at sea level.

(6 marks)

4   A cube with a uniform density of 1200 kg/m³ and weight 6.144 N is placed into a beaker
of liquid. The cube floats when its base is at a depth of 5.00 cm from the liquid's surface,
as shown in **Figure 3** and **Figure 4**.

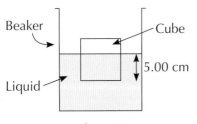

Figure 3

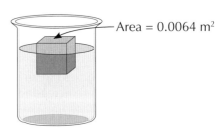

Figure 4

(a) (i) Explain what the behaviour of the cube indicates about the density of the liquid.

(1 mark)

(ii) State the upthrust acting on the cube when it floats in the liquid.
Explain your answer.

(2 marks)

(b) (i) Each surface of the cube has an area of 0.0064 m², as shown in **Figure 4**.
Calculate the pressure on the base of the cube. Give your answer in Pa.

(3 marks)

(ii) Calculate the density of the fluid. Use g = 10.0 N/kg. Use a correct equation
from the equations listed on page 404. Give your answer in kg/m³.

(3 marks)

1. Apparatus and Techniques

As part of GCSE Physics, you'll have to do at least eight practicals, called Core Practicals. You'll need to know how to use various pieces of apparatus and carry out different scientific techniques. And not only do you need to carry out the practicals, you could also be asked about them in the exams. Luckily, all the Core Practicals are covered in this book, and the next few pages cover some of the techniques that you'll need to know about.

Measuring mass

Mass should be measured using a balance. For a solid, set the balance to zero, place your object onto the scale and read off the mass.

If you're measuring the mass of a liquid (or a granular solid, like sand) start by putting an empty container onto the balance. Next, reset the balance to zero, so you don't include the mass of the container in your measurement. Then just pour the substance you want to measure the mass of into the container and record the mass displayed. Easy peasy.

Measuring weight

Remember not to get weight and mass confused. Mass is the amount of 'stuff' in an object. Weight is the force acting on the object due to gravity.

You could calculate the weight of an object by measuring its mass (see above) and then multiplying by the gravitational field strength. But to measure the weight of an object directly, you should use a newton meter (spring balance). Make sure that whatever you're measuring is securely attached to the hook of the newton meter and can hang freely. Remember to wait until it's stopped swinging or bouncing before you read the value from the scale.

Measuring length

In most cases a standard centimetre ruler can be used to measure length. It depends on what you're measuring though — metre rulers are handy for large distances, while micrometers (which have smaller divisions than a standard ruler) are used for measuring tiny things like the diameter of a wire. If you're dealing with something where it's tricky to measure the length of just one accurately (e.g. water ripples, p.96), you can measure the length of ten of them and then divide by ten to find the length of one.

If you're taking multiple measurements of the same object (e.g. to measure changes in length) then make sure you always measure from the same point on the object. It can help to draw or stick small markers onto the object to line up your ruler against — see Figure 1.

The ruler should always be parallel to what you want to measure. You should also make sure the ruler and the object are always at eye level when you take a reading. This stops parallax affecting your results (see next page).

Tip: The Core Practicals in this book are marked with a big stamp like this...

The practicals that you do in class might be slightly different to the ones in this book (as it's up to your teacher exactly what method you use), but they'll cover the same principles and techniques.

Tip: You met weight, including how to calculate and measure it, on pages 37-38.

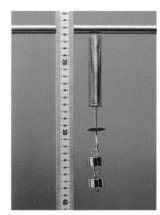

***Figure 1:** A red marker being used to help read a length measurement from a ruler.*

Example

When measuring the length of a spring, you need to make sure you avoid the parallax effect.

Parallax is where a measurement appears to change based on where you're looking from.

In this example, looking from above gives you a longer measurement, while looking from below gives you a shorter one.

The blue line is the measurement taken when the spring is at eye level. It shows the correct length of the spring.

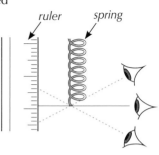

Figure 2: *The parallax effect.*

Measuring angles

You should use a protractor to measure angles. First align the vertex (point) of the angle with the mark in the centre of the protractor. Line up the base line of the protractor with one line that forms the angle and then measure the angle of the other line using the scale on the protractor (see Figure 3).

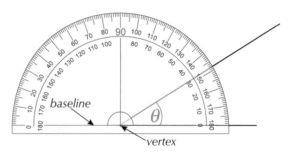

Figure 3: *A protractor, correctly aligned to measure angle θ. The angle is 32°.*

If the lines creating the angle are very thick, align the protractor and measure the angle using the centre of the lines. Using a sharp pencil to trace light rays or draw ray diagrams (page 99) helps to reduce errors when measuring angles.

If the lines are too short to measure easily, you may have to extend them. Again, make sure you use a sharp pencil and a ruler to do this.

Measuring temperature

You measure temperature with a thermometer. To ensure you measure the temperature accurately, make sure the bulb of your thermometer is completely submerged in any substance you're measuring if it's a fluid (a liquid or gas), or held directly against what you're measuring if it's a solid.

If you're taking a single measurement, wait for the temperature to stabilise before you take your reading. If you're measuring how the temperature of a substance is changing, take readings at regular time intervals (e.g. every 10 s).

Again, read your measurement off the scale on a thermometer at eye level.

Figure 4: *The silver bulb of the thermometer should be fully submerged when measuring the temperature of a fluid.*

Measuring time

You should use a stopwatch to measure time in most experiments — they're more accurate than regular watches. You can start and stop the timer whenever you need, or you can set an alarm so you know exactly when to stop an experiment or take a reading.

For some time measurements, you might be able to use a light gate. This will reduce the errors in your experiment. Have a look at page 39 for an example of a light gate being used.

A light gate sends a beam of light from one side of the gate to a detector on the other side. When something passes through the gate, the beam of light is interrupted. The light gate measures how long the beam was interrupted for. Light gates can use their measurements of time to calculate speed and acceleration, given the right information.

Tip: You can also use video software to measure time by looking at an event frame-by-frame. You can then use the measurement to calculate speed — see page 41.

Tip: You can input data into light gate software, for example, the length of the thing that interrupts the beam. This allows it to calculate other quantities such as speed.

Measuring volume

Measuring the volume of a liquid

Measuring cylinders are the most common way to measure the volume of a liquid. They come in all different sizes. Make sure you choose one that's the right size for the measurement you want to make. It's no good using a huge 1 dm^3 (1000 cm^3) cylinder to measure out 2 cm^3 of a liquid — the graduations (markings for scale) will be too big and you'll end up with massive errors (page 13). It'd be much better to use one that measures up to 10 cm^3.

You can also use a pipette to measure volume. Pipettes are used to suck up and transfer volumes of liquid between containers. Graduated pipettes are used to transfer accurate volumes. A pipette filler is attached to the end of a graduated pipette, to control the amount of liquid being drawn up.

Whichever method you use, always read the volume from the bottom of the meniscus (the curved upper surface of the liquid) when it's at eye level — see Figure 5.

Measuring the volume of a solid

Eureka cans (or displacement cans) are used in combination with measuring cylinders to find the volumes of solids. A eureka can is essentially a beaker with a downward spout. A solid object will displace an amount of water equal to its volume, which can then be measured using a measuring cylinder.

Figure 5: *The meniscus of a fluid in a measuring cylinder.*

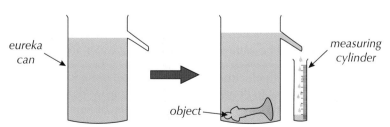

Figure 6: *A eureka can being used to measure volume.*

This method is particularly useful for irregularly shaped objects, where you can't simply measure its dimensions and calculate the volume mathematically. However, this method will only work for objects that sink. If the object floats, it will only displace a volume of water equal to the volume of the object that is submerged. You can see more on how to use a eureka can on page 297.

Tip: **H** There's more on what causes objects to float and sink on pages 321-322.

Good laboratory practice

When it comes to actually doing an experiment, it's important that you use good laboratory practice. This means working safely and accurately. To ensure you get good results, make sure you do the following:

- Measure all your quantities carefully — the more accurately you measure things the more accurate your results will be.

- Try to be consistent — for example, if you're using a piece of apparatus, make sure you use the same one throughout the experiment.

- Don't let yourself get distracted by other people — if you're distracted by what other people are doing you're more likely to make a mistake or miss a reading.

- As you're going along, make sure you remember to fill in your table of results — it's no good doing a perfect experiment if you forget to record the data.

Tip: For lots more info on doing experiments, see the Working Scientifically section at the start of this book.

Working safely

There are always hazards in any experiment, so before you start a practical you should do a risk assessment first. A risk assessment identifies all possible hazards in an experiment and lists the precautions you'll take to deal with them. You should also read and follow any safety precautions provided with the apparatus or by your teacher to do with your method or the apparatus you're using.

The hazards will depend on the experiment and the apparatus you're using, but the examples given here should give you some ideas of things to think about.

Tip: Make sure you wear the correct clothing when doing experiments. For example, you may need to wear safety goggles if there's a risk that equipment you're using might snap or shatter.

Examples

- Stop masses and equipment falling by using clamp stands. Make sure masses are of a sensible weight so they don't break the equipment they're used with. When working with pulleys, use string of a sensible length. That way, any hanging masses won't hit the floor during the experiment.

- When heating materials, make sure to let them cool before moving them, or wear insulated gloves and use tongs to handle them.

- When working with water, clean up any spillages immediately to avoid a slip hazard, and be extra careful when using water around electricity.

- When working with electronics, make sure you use a low enough voltage and current to prevent wires overheating (and potentially melting) and avoid damage to components, like blowing a filament bulb.

Figure 7: *A clamp stand being used in a hanging mass experiment.*

You also need to be aware of general safety in the lab — handle glassware carefully so it doesn't break, don't stick your fingers in sockets and avoid touching frayed wires. That kind of thing.

2. Heating Substances

There are a bunch of ways you can heat a substance, but electric immersion heaters and Bunsen burners are common ones you'll use in your practicals.

Bunsen burners

Bunsen burners are good for heating things quickly. You can easily adjust how strongly they're heating. But you need to be careful not to use them if you're heating flammable materials as the flame means the substance would be at risk of catching fire.

To use a Bunsen burner, you should first connect it to a gas tap, and check that the hole is closed. Place it on a heatproof mat. Next, light a splint (a long strip of wood) and hold it over the Bunsen burner. Now, turn on the gas. The Bunsen burner should light with a yellow flame (see Figure 2).

The more open the hole is, the more strongly the Bunsen burner will heat your substance. Open the hole to the amount you want. As you open the hole more, the flame should turn more blue (see Figure 2). Heat things just above the blue cone, as this is the hottest part of the flame.

Figure 1: *A Bunsen burner being lit.*

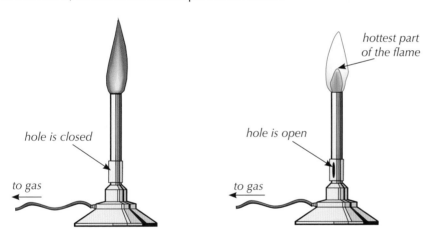

Figure 2: *A Bunsen burner with the hole closed (left) and the hole open (right).*

If your Bunsen burner is alight but not heating anything, make sure you close the hole so that the flame becomes yellow and clearly visible. When you're heating something over the flame (e.g. a beaker), you should put a tripod and gauze over the Bunsen burner before you light it, and place the vessel on this.

Immersion heaters

Immersion heaters good for heating things that are flammable, or when you want to be able to calculate the energy transferred during heating. They use electricity to heat up a metal element, which in turn heats the substance. They're often used in specific heat capacity experiments, like the one on page 305.

3. Working with Electronics

You'll have to do a lot of experiments using electrical circuits. Here's a run down of some of the measurements you'll need to make most often and the equipment you'll need to use to do so.

Circuit diagrams

You need to be able to interpret circuit diagrams. Before you get cracking on an experiment involving any kind of electrical devices, you have to plan and build your circuit using a circuit diagram. You've met circuit symbols and diagrams on pages 219-220, so make sure you learn them well, they're dead important.

Tip: Make sure you draw wires as straight lines, and don't let them cross each other unless there's a connection. This makes your circuit diagrams a lot clearer.

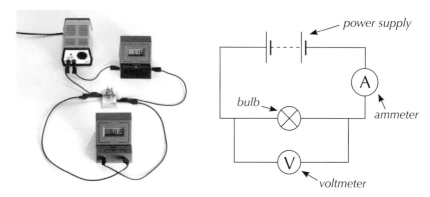

Figure 1: *A photo of a simple electrical circuit, alongside a circuit diagram of the same electrical circuit.*

Making measurements in circuits

Using voltmeters

A voltmeter measures potential difference (see page 221). If you're using an analogue voltmeter, choose the voltmeter with the most appropriate unit for what you're measuring (e.g. V or mV). If you're using a digital voltmeter, you'll most likely be able to switch between them and select the most appropriate unit.

Figure 2: *An example of an analogue voltmeter.*

Connect the voltmeter in parallel (p.235) across the component you want to test. The voltmeter will usually have red (positive) and black (negative) ports, to help you connect them to a circuit correctly. If you get them backwards, your voltage reading will be negative. Once everything's set up, simply read the potential difference from the scale (or from the screen if it's digital).

Using ammeters

Ammeters measure electrical current (see page 221). Just like with voltmeters, choose the ammeter with the most appropriate unit (usually A or mA), unless it's a digital one.

Tip: You should turn your circuit off between readings to prevent wires getting hot and affecting your results.

Connect the ammeter in series (p.231) with the component you want to test, making sure they're both on the same branch. Again, they usually have red and black ports to show you where to connect your wires. Then simply read off the current shown on the scale or by the screen.

Using multimeters

Instead of having a separate ammeter and voltmeter, many circuits use multimeters (see Figure 3). These are devices that measure a range of properties — usually potential difference, current and resistance.

One wire should always be plugged into the black (negative) port. If you want to find potential difference, make sure the other wire is plugged into the red (positive) port that says 'V' (for volts), and connect it like a voltmeter. To find the current, use the red (positive) port labelled 'A' or 'mA' (for amps), and connect it like an ammeter.

The dial on the multimeter should then be turned to the relevant section, e.g. to 'A' to measure current in amps (on Figure 3, the 'DCA' section measures direct current, d.c.). The screen will display the value you're measuring in the units you've chosen with the dial.

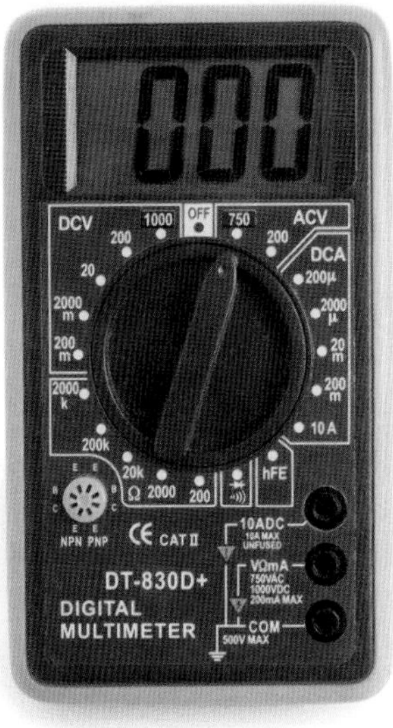

Figure 3: An example of a digital multimeter.

Oscilloscopes

An oscilloscope is basically a snazzy voltmeter. You can use one to 'see' how the potential difference of an electricity supply changes over time (like on page 282). Figure 4 shows an oscilloscope.

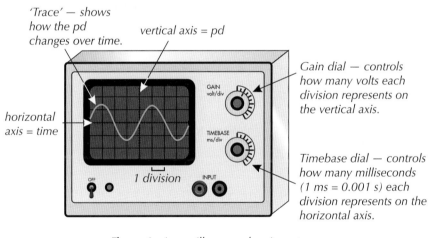

'Trace' — shows how the pd changes over time.

vertical axis = pd

horizontal axis = time

1 division

Gain dial — controls how many volts each division represents on the vertical axis.

Timebase dial — controls how many milliseconds (1 ms = 0.001 s) each division represents on the horizontal axis.

Figure 4: An oscilloscope showing a trace.

Tip: You can see an oscilloscope being used on page 95.

To use an oscilloscope, simply connect it up as you would any voltmeter. You can then read values of the potential difference from the trace displayed.

Each main division (or square) on the screen is usually divided into five smaller divisions so it can be read to a higher resolution. So each minor division is 0.2 of a major division. You'll probably want to adjust the 'gain' and 'timebase' dials to make sure each division represents a sensible value for what you want to measure.

Maths skills for GCSE Physics

Maths crops up quite a lot in GCSE Physics so it's really important that you've mastered all the maths skills needed before sitting your exams. Maths skills are covered throughout this book but here's an extra little section, just on maths, to help you out.

1. Calculations

Sometimes the numbers you use in Physics are just plain awkward — they're either too big, too small or go on forever. The next few pages show how calculations can be made a lot easier.

Standard form

You need to be able to work with numbers that are written in **standard form**. Standard form is used for writing very big or very small numbers in a more convenient way. Standard form must always look like this:

Tip: If a number isn't written in standard form, it's said to be in decimal form — e.g. 0.00012 or 34 500.

This number must always be between 1 and 10. → $A \times 10^n$ ← *This number is the number of places the decimal point moves.*

You can write a standard form number out in full by moving the decimal point. Which direction to move the decimal point, and how many places to move it depends on 'n'. If 'n' is positive, the decimal point needs to move to the right. If 'n' is negative the decimal point needs to move to the left.

Tip: This covers GCSE physics specification point 1.4, "use standard form where appropriate".

Example

Here's how to write out 9.3×10^4 in full.

- Work out which way the decimal point needs to move, by looking at the 'n' number. Here it's a positive number (4) so the decimal point needs to move four places to the right:

$$9.3 \times 10^4 = 9\ 3\ 0\ 0\ 0.$$

- So 9.3×10^4 is the same as 93 000.

Here's how to write out 5.6×10^{-5} in full.

- 'n' is a negative number (−5) so the decimal point needs to move five places to the left.

$$5.6 \times 10^{-5} = .0\ 0\ 0\ 0\ 5\ 6$$

- So 5.6×10^{-5} is the same as 0.000056.

Tip: You need to add a zero into any space left by the decimal point moving.

The key things to remember with numbers in standard form are...

- When 'n' is positive the number is big. The bigger 'n' is, the bigger the number is.

- When 'n' is negative the number is small. The smaller 'n' is (the more negative), the smaller the number is.

- When 'n' is the same for two or more numbers, you need to look at the start of each number to work out which is bigger. For example, 4.5 is bigger than 3.0, so 4.5×10^5 is bigger than 3.0×10^5.

There's a special button on your calculator for using standard form in a calculation — it's the 'Exp' button. So if, for example, you wanted to type in 2×10^7, you'd only need to type in: '2' 'Exp' '7'. Some calculators may have a different button that does the same job, for example it could say 'EE' or '×10^x' instead of 'Exp' — see Figure 1.

Figure 1: *The 'Exp' or '×10^x' button is used to input standard form on calculators.*

Ratios, fractions and percentages

You need to be able to use ratios, fractions and percentages, and know what they mean.

Fractions and ratios

Fractions and ratios are two different things in maths, but they are used to express relationships between quantities in physics in very similar ways.

A fraction is just one number divided by another number, written as $\frac{x}{y}$. They're used all over the place in physics:

Example 1

- $KE = \frac{1}{2} \times m \times v^2$ uses the fraction $\frac{1}{2}$, or 1 divided by 2.

- $\text{Power} = \dfrac{\text{energy transferred}}{\text{time taken}}$ uses a fraction to express power as energy transferred over time.

A ratio is a proportional relationship between two quantities. It tells you how the two quantities are related to each other.

Example 2

Efficiency is a ratio. It is the relationship between the energy usefully transferred by a device to the total energy supplied to a device:

$$\text{Efficiency} = \frac{\text{useful energy transferred by the device}}{\text{total energy supplied to the device}}$$

But it is also a fraction. This is an example of 'ratio' and 'fraction' being used to describe similar things.

Tip: When working with fractions, you might come across the word 'reciprocal'. The reciprocal of a number is just $\dfrac{1}{\text{the number}}$.

Tip: When using the equation $KE = \frac{1}{2} \times m \times v^2$, you could type 0.5 into your calculator instead of $\frac{1}{2}$. Either will work, as $\frac{1}{2} = 0.5$.

Tip: Calculating power is covered on page 203.

Tip: If you'd been asked for the ratio of decayed atoms to undecayed atoms, you'd write the ratio the other way around — $\frac{640}{960}$.

Tip: This ratio means that for every 3 undecayed atoms, there are 2 decayed atoms.

Tip: So in the example above, the ratio of the number of undecayed atoms to the number of decayed atoms would be 960 : 640. This ratio simplifies to 3 : 2.

Example 3

A sample of a radioactive substance has 960 undecayed atoms and 640 decayed atoms. Calculate the ratio of the number of undecayed atoms to the number of decayed atoms. Write your answer in the form $\frac{a}{b}$.

You're told to write the ratio in the form of a fraction — the first quantity in the ratio goes on the top and the second quantity on the bottom.

$$\frac{\text{undecayed atoms}}{\text{decayed atoms}} = \frac{960}{640} = \frac{3}{2}$$

Usually in maths, ratios are expressed in a special form when comparing two quantities.

A colon separates one quantity from the other. $a : b$ *a and b stand for the two quantities.*

To write a ratio in this form, first write down the numbers you have of each thing, separated by a colon. Then divide the numbers by the same amount until they're the smallest they can be whilst still being whole numbers — this is called simplifying the ratio. You can also find what a ratio simplifies to using your calculator.

Example 4

To find the ratio 120 : 150 in its simplest form using your calculator, just type in $\frac{120}{150}$ as a fraction and press equals. Your calculator will give you the most simplified version, which in this case is $\frac{4}{5}$.

So the ratio in its simplest form is 4 : 5.

If your calculator gives a decimal, use the button on your calculator that swaps between fractions and decimals — it'll probably look like one of these: $S\Leftrightarrow D$ $a\,b\!/\!c$ $F\leftrightarrow D$ CHANGE

Percentages

Tip: You may be asked to give efficiency as a percentage — see page 71.

Percent means 'out of 100', so 62% means 62 out of 100.
To find one number as a percentage of another, divide the first number by the second and multiply by 100.

Example 5

A spring has a length of 4.0 cm. It is stretched to a length of 4.4 cm. Calculate the extension of the spring as a percentage of its original length.

First, calculate the extension of the spring: 4.4 − 4.0 = 0.4 cm

Now divide the extension by the original length:
0.4 ÷ 4.0 = 0.1

Multiply this by 100 to get the answer as a percentage: 0.1 × 100 = 10
So the spring has extended by 10% of its original length.

Estimating

Estimating can be a really useful tool in physics. You've already seen that you can use typical values (e.g. speed and mass, see pages 23 and 53) in calculations to give estimates.

You can also use estimating to check if your final answer is sensible or not. When doing this, it is usually helpful to round the data you are given to 1 significant figure.

Example 1

A spring with spring constant 12.05 N/m is extended by 0.98 m. Calculate the energy transferred to its elastic potential energy store. Use the equation: $E = \frac{1}{2} \times k \times x^2$.

Round each value to 1 significant figure.
12.05 N/m = 10 N/m (to 1 s.f.) and 0.98 m = 1 m (to 1 s.f.)

Estimate what the answer should be: $E \approx 0.5 \times 10 \times 1^2 \approx 5$ J

The actual answer is 5.8 J (to 2 s.f.). From the estimated calculation, 5.8 J is a sensible answer. If your answer was 5800 J, you would know that your calculation had gone wrong somewhere.

Estimating can also be useful for choosing apparatus to use in an experiment.

Example 2

The apparatus for measuring the volume of an awards statue is shown on the right.

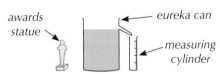

When the statue is put in the eureka can, the water level rises, which causes water to flow into the measuring cylinder. The volume of the statue is equal to the volume of water displaced. To decide what measuring cylinder to use, you should estimate the volume of the object.

An estimate for the volume of the statue can be found if the statue is considered to be a cuboid with a height of 20 cm and a base of 7 cm by 7 cm.

Volume of a cuboid $= w \times h \times d$
$= 7 \times 20 \times 7$
$= 980$ cm³

The measuring cylinder should be able to hold about 1000 cm³.

When estimating values, you can sometimes use order of magnitude estimates. The order of magnitude of a number describes the number to the nearest power of ten. For example, $100 = 10 \times 10 = 10^2$, so 100 has an order of magnitude of 2.

This is useful when doing estimates involving really big or really small numbers. For example, you can estimate the size of 2 528 726 ÷ 0.00845 by doing $10^6 \div 10^{-2} = 10^8$.

Tip: You need to be able to find the volume of an irregularly shaped object in order to find its density. See page 297.

Tip: 2 528 726's nearest power of ten is 1 000 000 or 1×10^6. 0.00845's nearest power of ten is 0.01 or 1×10^{-2}.

2. Algebra

Physics involves a lot of rearranging and substituting values into equations. It can be easy to make simple mistakes, so here's a few things to remember...

Algebra symbols

Here's a reminder of some of the symbols that you may come across:

Symbol	Meaning
=	is equal to
<	is less than
<<	is much less than
>	is greater than
>>	is much greater than
∝	is directly proportional to
~	is approximately
Δ	change in (a quantity)
≈	is approximately equal to

Tip: An example of using ∝ can be found on page 323.

Tip: Δ is the Greek capital letter 'delta'. An example of using Δ can be found on page 304.

Rearranging equations

Being able to rearrange equations is a must in physics — you'll often need to change the subject of an equation. The subject of an equation is just the value that the rest of the equation is equal to (usually a single letter on the left-hand side of the equals sign). For rearranging equations, remember the golden rule — whatever you do to one side of the equation, you must do to the other side.

Figure 1: It can be easy to make a mistake rearranging equations when you're stressed in an exam. It's a good idea to double check rearrangements, especially if it's a tricky one where you've had to combine and rearrange equations.

Example 1

Rearrange the equation for momentum, $p = m \times v$, to make v the subject.

$p = m \times v$

$\dfrac{p}{m} = v$

Divide both sides by m to get v by itself.

So $v = \dfrac{p}{m}$.

Example 2

For an object travelling with a uniform acceleration, the equation that links the initial velocity, final velocity, acceleration and distance travelled is: $v^2 - u^2 = 2 \times a \times x$. Rearrange the equation to make v the subject.

$v^2 - u^2 = 2 \times a \times x$

$v^2 = (2 \times a \times x) + u^2$

Add u^2 to both sides to get v^2 on its own.

$v = \sqrt{(2 \times a \times x) + u^2}$

Take the square root of both sides

Tip: There's an example of substituting into a rearranged form of this equation on the next page.

Substituting into equations

Once you've rearranged your equation, you'll probably need to substitute values into it to find your answer. Pretty easy stuff — make sure your values are in the right units — getting this wrong is a common mistake. Take a look at pages 18-19 for how to convert between different units.

Take a look at pages 18-19 for how to convert between different units.

Example

A train pulls out of a station and is initially travelling at 2.0 m/s. The train accelerates with a constant acceleration over a distance of 3.4 km. At this distance, the train reaches a final velocity of 150 km/h. Calculate the acceleration of the train.
Use the equation $v^2 - u^2 = 2 \times a \times x$. Give your answer in m/s².

Your answer needs to be in m/s², so you need to be using metres and seconds. Some of the given values are in different units, so you need to convert them.

$u = 2.0$ m/s

$x = 3.4$ km $= 3.4 \times 1 \times 10^3$ m $= 3400$ m

$v = 150$ km/h $= 150 \times 1 \times 10^3$ m/h $= 150\,000$ m/h
$\qquad\qquad\qquad\qquad = 150\,000 \div 3600$ m/s $= 41.66...$ m/s

Rearrange the equation $v^2 - u^2 = 2 \times a \times x$ to make a the subject:

$a = \dfrac{v^2 - u^2}{2 \times x} = \dfrac{41.66...^2 - 2.0^2}{2 \times 3400} = 0.254...$ m/s² $= 0.25$ m/s² (to 2 s.f.)

Tip: The values you put into an equation should be in the units given throughout the book, unless you're asked to give your answer in different units.

Tip: Converting all the values into the correct units <u>before</u> putting them into the equation stops you making silly mistakes.

Tip: Rounding to the correct number of significant figures is covered on page 15.

Formula triangles

If three terms are related by a formula that looks like $v = f \times \lambda$ or $f = \frac{v}{\lambda}$, then you can put them into a formula triangle like this:

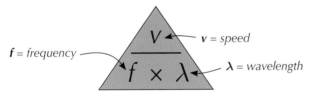

$f = frequency$ — $v = speed$ — $\lambda = wavelength$

Figure 2: *The formula triangle for $v = f \times \lambda$ — v on the top and $f \times \lambda$ on the bottom.*

- To use the triangle, put your thumb over the term you want to find and write down what's left showing. This gives you your formula (for example $f = \frac{v}{\lambda}$).

- Then put in the values for the other terms and work out the term you want.

Tip: For an equation with two terms multiplied together, these go on the bottom of the formula triangle (and so the other must go on the top). For an equation with one term divided by another, the one on top of the division goes on top in the formula triangle and the others go on the bottom (in any order).

Example

Give the equation for the time a device is on for (t), in terms of the energy transferred by the device (E) and its power (P), given the formula $P = \frac{E}{t}$

- As E is divided by t, E goes on top, leaving $P \times t$ on the bottom.

- Covering up t gives you $\frac{E}{P}$ so $t = \frac{E}{P}$.

Tip: Alternatively, you could work this out using the method for rearranging equations given on the previous page.

Tip: Alternatively, you could work this out using the method for rearranging equations given on the previous page.

---

3. Graphs

Results are often presented using graphs, as you've seen on pages 16-17.
They make it easier to work out relations between variables and can also
be used to calculate other quantities.

Linear graphs

Tip: The origin of a
graph is the point (0,0)
on the graph, i.e. it's the
point at which the x-axis
and y-axis meet.

You will most often come across linear graphs. A linear graph means that
the two variables plotted on the axes produce a straight line. If the line goes
through the origin (0,0), then the two variables are directly proportional.

Tip: A non-linear graph
is just any graph that's
curved.

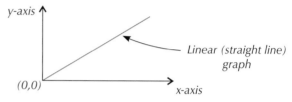

Figure 1: *A linear graph, which passes through the origin.*

Finding the gradient

The **gradient** (slope) of a graph tells you how quickly the variable on the y-axis
changes as the variable on the x-axis changes. It is calculated using:

Tip: On a distance-time
graph, the gradient
is the rate of change
of distance, which is
speed.

$$\text{gradient} = \frac{\text{change in } y}{\text{change in } x}$$

Example

Tip: There's more on
force-extension graphs
on page 324.

This linear graph shows the force acting on a spring against its extension.
The gradient of the line is equal to the spring constant of the spring.

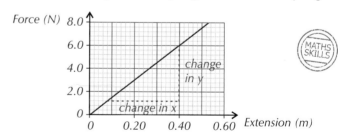

To calculate the gradient, pick two points on the line that are easy to read
and a good distance apart. Draw a line down from one of the points and
a line across from the other to make a triangle. The line drawn down the
side of the triangle is the change in y and the line across the bottom is the
change in x.

Change in y = 6.0 – 1.2 = 4.8 N   Change in x = 0.40 – 0.08 = 0.32 m

Spring constant = gradient = $\dfrac{\text{change in } y}{\text{change in } x} = \dfrac{4.8}{0.32} = 15$ N/m

---

y = mx + c

The equation of a straight line is given by:

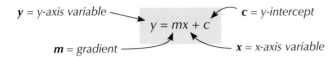

y = y-axis variable
c = y-intercept
$$y = mx + c$$
m = gradient
x = x-axis variable

The y-intercept is the point at which the line crosses the y-axis. If the straight line passes through the origin of the graph, then the y-intercept is just zero. You can use this equation to work out what the gradient and y-intercept values of a graph represent.

Example

A student is heating a block of aluminium with an electric heater in order to find its specific heat capacity. The expected shape of the graph from his experiment is shown. The change in temperature is the y-axis variable and the energy transferred to the aluminium is the x-axis variable.

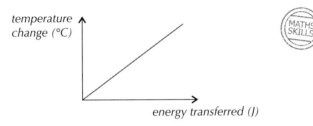

temperature change (°C)

energy transferred (J)

MATHS SKILLS

Tip: Take a look at pages 305-306 for more about this experiment.

The equation that relates temperature change and energy transferred is:

$$\Delta Q = m \times c \times \Delta\theta,$$

where ΔQ = energy transferred, m = mass of the aluminium, c = specific heat capacity of the aluminium and $\Delta\theta$ = temperature change.

This equation can't be compared to the equation of a straight line yet — the subject of the equation (see page 344) needs to be the y-axis variable, which in this case is $\Delta\theta$. So divide both sides of the equation by $m \times c$, to get:

$$\Delta\theta = \frac{1}{m \times c} \times \Delta Q$$

When you compare this to the equation of the straight line, you can see that the gradient is equal to $\frac{1}{m \times c}$:

Tip: You won't always need to rearrange an equation before you compare it to the equation of a straight line. For example, distance = speed × time or x = vt (+ 0), p.23. Comparing this to y = mx + c, it's easy to see that the gradient (m) of a distance-time graph is equal to speed (v).

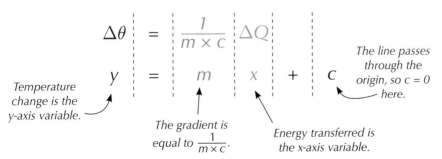

$$\Delta\theta \quad = \quad \frac{1}{m \times c} \quad \Delta Q$$
$$y \quad = \quad m \quad x \quad + \quad c$$

Temperature change is the y-axis variable.

The gradient is equal to $\frac{1}{m \times c}$.

Energy transferred is the x-axis variable.

The line passes through the origin, so c = 0 here.

Tip: You'll often find that the y-intercept is equal to zero, and that the graph passes through the origin. If c wasn't equal to zero, then the straight line would be shifted up or down, to pass through the y-axis at the value of c.

Once the student has plotted his data on a graph he can find the gradient, which can then be used to calculate the unknown value of c, as gradient = $\frac{1}{m \times c}$.

Curved graphs

For a curved graph, the gradient is always changing. So you can't use the same method as the one on page 346 to calculate the gradient — you would end up with an average gradient between the two points chosen.

To find the gradient of a curve at a point, you need to draw a tangent to the curve at that point. A tangent is a straight line that touches the curve at that point, but doesn't cross it. So to draw one, you position a ruler so that it just touches the curve at the point you're interested in, and draw a straight line. Then you just find the gradient of the tangent using the method for straight lines on page 346.

Figure 2: Make sure you use a really sharp pencil and a ruler whenever you're drawing graphs and tangents.

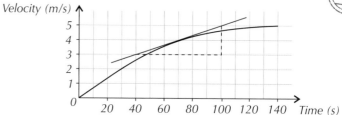

Figure 3: Drawing the tangent to a curve.

Tip: Another example of finding the gradient of a tangent is shown on page 28.

Example

The velocity-time graph of a cyclist is shown below. Find the acceleration of the cyclist at 70 s.

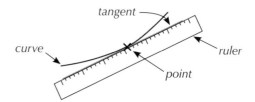

The rate of change of velocity is acceleration.
So the gradient of a velocity-time graph is acceleration.

A tangent to the curve at 70 s is drawn on the graph. Its gradient is:

$$\frac{\text{change in } y}{\text{change in } x} = \frac{5-3}{100-40} = \frac{2}{60} = 0.03333... = 0.03 \text{ (to 1 s.f.)}$$

So the acceleration at 70 s = 0.03 m/s² (to 1 s.f.)

Area under a graph

Sometimes the area between the curve or line and the horizontal axis of a graph represents a quantity. For example:

- The area under a velocity-time graph of an object is equal to the distance travelled by the object (page 31).

- The area under a linear force-extension graph for a stretched spring is equal to the energy transferred to the spring's elastic potential energy store.

You can find the area under a graph in two ways. The first is by breaking it up into triangles and rectangles, calculating the areas of these shapes and then adding together these areas. This is the best method for straight-line graphs. There's an example showing this on page 31.

Tip: The formulas for the area of a triangle and a rectangle are on the next page.

The second method is called the 'counting squares' method. Usually you'll use this method if you have a curved graph as the area under the curve won't split nicely into basic shapes. This method gives you an estimate of the area under the graph.

Tip: There's an example of using the 'counting squares' method on page 328.

These are the steps to work out an area by counting squares:

- First, calculate the value of one square. To do this, multiply the width of one square by the height of one square.

- Next count the number of small squares under the curve. If there are multiple squares that are partly under the graph, you can add them together to make whole squares (see the example below).

- Then multiply together the number of squares by the value of one square and ta-da, you have a good estimate of the area under the graph.

Tip: As you go through and count the squares, it helps to put a dot in the square once it's been counted. That way you don't lose track of what's been counted and what hasn't.

Example — **Higher**

The graph below is a velocity-time graph. You can estimate the distance travelled in the first 10 s by counting the number of squares under the graph (shown by the shaded area).

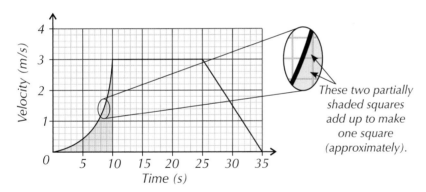

These two partially shaded squares add up to make one square (approximately).

Total number of shaded squares ≈ 32

Distance represented by one square = width of square × height of square
$$= 1 \text{ s} \times 0.2 \text{ m/s} = 0.2 \text{ m}$$

So total distance travelled in 10 s = 32 × 0.2 = 6.4 m

4. Geometry

You'll be expected to be comfortable with working out measurements of 2D and 3D shapes, such as areas, surface areas and volumes, in physics contexts.

Area

Make sure you remember how to calculate the areas of triangles and rectangles.

Tip: These come in handy when calculating the area under a graph.

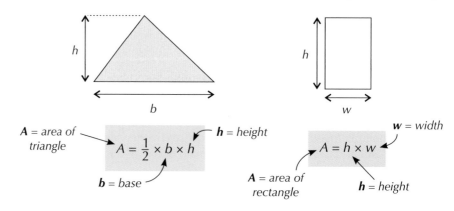

A = area of triangle
h = height
$A = \frac{1}{2} \times b \times h$
b = base
w = width
$A = h \times w$
A = area of rectangle
h = height

Surface area and volume

Tip: Make sure you don't forget any sides when finding the surface area. For a cube or cuboid, there are 6.

If you need to work out the surface area of a 3D shape, you just need to add up the areas of all the 2D faces of the shape. So, for example, if you need to work out the surface area of a cuboid, you just find the area of each rectangular face and then add them together.

Make sure you also remember how to calculate the volume of a cuboid:

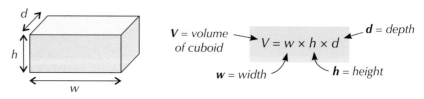

V = volume of cuboid
d = depth
$V = w \times h \times d$
w = width
h = height

Tip: You need to be able to calculate volumes to calculate densities (see page 297).

Example

A block of copper is shown. Calculate the volume and surface area of the copper.

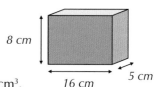

8 cm
16 cm
5 cm

Volume = $w \times h \times d$ = 16 × 8 × 5 = 640 cm³.

Surface area of front face = $h \times w$ = 8 × 16 = 128 cm².
Therefore the surface area of back face = 128 cm².

Surface area of right face = $h \times d$ = 8 × 5 = 40 cm².
Therefore the surface area of left face = 40 cm².

Surface area of top face = $d \times w$ = 5 × 16 = 80 cm².
Therefore the surface area of bottom face = 80 cm².

Total surface area = 128 + 128 + 40 + 40 + 80 + 80 = 496 cm².

Exam Help

1. The Exams

Unfortunately, to get your GCSE you'll need to sit some exams. And that's what this page is about — what to expect in your exams.

Assessment for GCSE Physics

To get your GCSE in physics you'll have to do some exams that test your knowledge of physics, your understanding of the Core Practicals and how comfortable you are with Working Scientifically. You'll also be tested on your maths skills in at least 30% of the marks.

All the content that you need to know is in this book. All the Core Practicals are also covered in detail and are clearly labelled, examples that use maths skills are marked up, and there are even sections dedicated to Working Scientifically, Maths Skills and Practical Skills.

Grading

When you sit your exams, you'll be given a grade between 1 and 9 based on your results. 9 is the highest grade, and 1 is the lowest. Which grades you can get will depend on which exams you sit — Foundation Tier, or Higher Tier.

If you take the Foundation Tier exams, you can get a grade between 1 and 5, with 5 being the maximum grade you can get. If you sit the Higher Tier exams, you can get a grade between 3 and 9.

The exams

You'll sit two separate exams at the end of Year 11. Remember that both will test your maths skills and you could be asked questions on Working Scientifically in either of them. You're allowed to use a calculator in both of your GCSE Physics exams, so make sure you've got one.

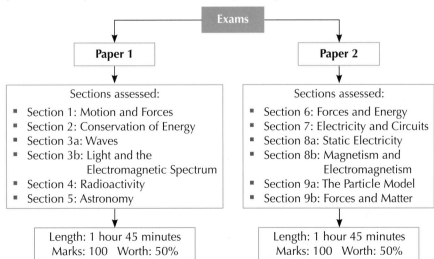

Exams

Paper 1

Sections assessed:
- Section 1: Motion and Forces
- Section 2: Conservation of Energy
- Section 3a: Waves
- Section 3b: Light and the Electromagnetic Spectrum
- Section 4: Radioactivity
- Section 5: Astronomy

Length: 1 hour 45 minutes
Marks: 100   Worth: 50%

Paper 2

Sections assessed:
- Section 6: Forces and Energy
- Section 7: Electricity and Circuits
- Section 8a: Static Electricity
- Section 8b: Magnetism and Electromagnetism
- Section 9a: The Particle Model
- Section 9b: Forces and Matter

Length: 1 hour 45 minutes
Marks: 100   Worth: 50%

> **Exam Tip**
> Make sure you have a good read through these pages. It might not seem all that important now but you don't want to get any surprises just before an exam.

> **Tip:** Working Scientifically is on pages 2-21, Maths Skills are on pages 340-350 and Practical Skills are on pages 333-339.

> **Exam Tip**
> The Higher tier papers target grades 4 to 9, however, if you just miss out on the marks needed for a grade 4, then you may be awarded a grade 3.

> **Exam Tip**
> As well as a calculator, you should make sure you've got a ruler for both exams. In Paper 1, where you might have to deal with ray diagrams, you'll need a protractor too. And don't forget the basics — a couple of black pens and sharp pencils.

> **Exam Tip**
> Use these section lists as a guide, but be aware that they may expect you to use basic physics knowledge from any part of the course in either exam.

2. Exam Technique

Knowing the science is vitally important when it comes to passing your exams. But having good exam technique will also help. So here are some handy hints on how to squeeze every mark you possibly can out of those examiners.

Time management

Good time management is one of the most important exam skills to have — you need to think about how much time to spend on each question. Check out the length of your exams (you'll find them on the previous page and on the front of your exam papers). These timings give you about 1 minute per mark, and 5 minutes spare to check your answers. Try to stick to this to give yourself the best chance to get as many marks as possible.

Don't spend ages struggling with a question if you're finding it hard to answer — move on. You can come back to it later when you've bagged loads of other marks elsewhere. Also, you might find that some questions need a lot of work for only a few marks, while others are much quicker — so if you're short of time, answer the quick and easy questions first.

Exam Tip
You shouldn't really be spending more time on a 1 mark question than on a 4 mark question. Use the marks available as a rough guide for how long each question should take to answer.

> **Example**
>
> The questions below are both worth the same number of marks but require different amounts of work.
>
> **1 (a)** Name **two** renewable energy sources.
>
> *(2 marks)*
>
> **2 (b)** Find the gradient of the graph when extension is 4 mm.
>
> *(2 marks)*
>
> Question 1 (a) only asks you to write down the names of two energy sources — if you can remember them this shouldn't take you too long.
>
> Question 2 (b) asks you to calculate a gradient — this may take you a bit longer than writing down a couple of names, and it might take a couple of attempts to get right.
>
> So if you're running out of time, it makes sense to do questions like 1 (a) first and come back to 2 (b) if you've got time at the end.

Exam Tip
Don't forget to go back and do any questions that you left the first time round — you don't want to miss out on marks because you forgot to do the question.

Reading the question

You've probably heard it a million times before, but make sure you always read the question carefully. It can be easy to look at a question and read what you're expecting to see rather than what it's actually asking you. Read it through before you start answering, and read it again when you've finished, to make sure your answer is sensible and matches up to what the question is asking.

Remember to pay attention to the marks available too. They can often give you a sense of how much work is needed to answer the question. If it's just a 1 mark question, it'll often only need a single word or phrase as an answer, or a very simple calculation. Questions with 4 or 6 marks are likely to require longer answers, which involve writing a clearly-structured paragraph or doing a more complicated calculation.

Exam Tip
The amount of space given for your answer should also give you an idea about how much you need to write.

Making educated guesses

Make sure you answer all the questions that you can — don't leave any blank if you can avoid it. If a question asks you to tick a box, circle a word or draw lines between boxes, you should never, ever leave it blank, even if you're short on time. It only takes a second or two to answer these questions, and even if you're not absolutely sure what the answer is you can have a good guess.

Example

Look at the question below.

5 (b)   A $^{18}_{5}B$ nucleus decays to $^{17}_{5}B$.
What type of radiation is emitted during the decay?

☐ **A** An alpha particle   ☐ **C** A beta-minus particle

☐ **B** A gamma ray   ☐ **D** A neutron

(1 mark)

Say you know that when an alpha or a beta particle is released, a new element is formed. As the element has not changed, you know the answer is not A or C.

That leaves you with a gamma ray or a neutron. If you're not absolutely sure what the answer is, just have a guess. You won't lose any marks if you get it wrong and there's a 50% chance that you'll get it right.

Calculations

Calculations can seem daunting if you're not so keen on maths, but they're often where a load of marks are hiding. And there are some dead easy ways to make sure you don't miss out on them.

Exam Tip
Take a look at p.404 to see which equations will be given on the Equation Sheet in the exam.

You'll be given an Equation Sheet in the exam that tells you some of the equations you might need. There are plenty of other equations you won't be given though — you'll be expected to remember them. Make sure you always write down any equation you use before you put any numbers into it.

Make sure you write down all your working. If the final answer is all you write down, and you get it wrong, that's all the marks gone. But if you write down all the steps that lead to the answer, and you've used the correct method, you'll be awarded marks for your working. Then you'll pick up most of the marks, regardless of whether your final answer's correct or not.

Exam Tip
You can do an estimate to check that an answer to a calculation is a sensible number. Check out page 343 for more on estimates.

3. Question Types

If all questions were the same, exams would be mightily boring. So really, it's handy that there are lots of different question types. Here's some information that'll help you work out exactly what type of answer a question requires...

Command words

Command words are just the bits of a question that tell you what to do. You'll find answering exam questions much easier if you understand exactly what they mean, so here's a brief summary of the most common ones:

Command word:	What to do:
Calculate	Use the numbers in the question to work out an answer.
Compare	Give the similarities or differences between two or more things.
Compare and contrast	Give at least one similarity and one difference between two or more things.
Complete	Fill in a gap in a table, or finish a diagram.
Describe	Write about what something's like, e.g. describe the trend in a set of results.
Determine	Use the data or information given to reach your answer.
Estimate	Calculate an approximate value, or find one from a graph or diagram.
Evaluate	Give the arguments both for and against an issue, or the advantages and disadvantages of something. You'll also need to give an overall judgement.
Explain	Make something clear, or give the reasons why something happens. The points in your answer need to be linked together, so you should include words like because, so, therefore, due to, etc.
Give / Name / State	Give a brief one or two word answer, or a short sentence.
Justify	Give a reason for your answer or for a given statement.
Predict	Say what you think will happen.
Show	Give clear evidence that supports a given statement.
Sketch	Draw without a lot of detail, e.g. for a graph you just need correctly-labelled axes, the general shape and the important features labelled.

Some questions will also ask you to answer using information from a particular figure (e.g. a graph, diagram or table) — if so, you must refer to the information you've been given or you won't get the marks.

Testing Practical Skills

The Core Practicals are eight specific experiments that you need to cover during your lessons. You'll be asked about them in the exams too. At least 15% of the total marks in your exams will test the practical skills that you will have learnt whilst doing Core Practicals. You may be tested on experiments you've done in class, or be asked to apply your knowledge of apparatus and techniques to new scenarios. There are a lot of different types of question you could be asked on these experiments. Here are some basic areas they might ask you about:

- Carrying out the experiment — e.g. planning or describing a method, describing how to take measurements or use apparatus.

- Risk assessment — e.g. identifying or explaining hazards associated with the experiment, or safety precautions which should be taken.

- Understanding variables — e.g. identifying control, dependent and independent variables.

- Analysing results — e.g. drawing conclusions based on sample results.

- Evaluating the experiment — e.g. making judgements on the quality of results, identifying where mistakes may have been made in the method, suggesting improvements to the experiment.

Core Practical questions won't be pointed out to you in the exam, so you'll need to make sure you know the practicals inside out, and can recognise them easily. For an example of a question testing your understanding of a practical, see page 241.

Exam Tip
The Core Practical questions are likely to have some overlap with Working Scientifically, so make sure you've brushed up on pages 2-21.

Levels of response questions

Some questions are designed to assess your ability to present and explain scientific ideas in a logical and coherent way, as well as your scientific knowledge. These questions often link together different topics, and are worth 6 marks. These questions will be marked with an asterisk (*).

This type of question is marked using a 'levels of response' mark scheme. Your answer is given a level depending on the number of marks available and its overall quality and scientific content. Here's an idea of how the levels may be described:

> **Example**
>
> **Level 0**
>
> A Level 0 answer has no relevant information, and makes no attempt to answer the question. It receives no marks.
>
> **Level 1**
>
> A Level 1 answer usually makes one or two correct statements, but does not fully answer the question. The points made are fairly basic and are not clearly linked together. These answers receive 1 or 2 marks.

Exam Tip
Make sure your writing is legible, and be careful with your spelling, punctuation and grammar — if an examiner can't read or understand what you've written, they can't give you the marks.

Level 2

A Level 2 answer usually makes a number of correct statements, with an explanation for most of them, but falls short of fully answering the question. It may miss a step, omit an important fact, or not be organised as logically as it should be. These answers receive 3 or 4 marks.

Level 3

A Level 3 answer will answer the question fully, in a logical fashion. It will make a number of points that are explained and related back to the question. Any conclusions it makes will be supported by evidence in the answer. These answers receive 5 or 6 marks.

Make sure you answer the question fully, and cover all points indicated in the question. You also need to organise your answer clearly — the points you make need to be in a logical order. Use specialist scientific vocabulary whenever you can. For example, if you're talking about the structure of the atom, you need to use scientific terms like 'the nuclear model'. Obviously you need to use these terms correctly — it's no good knowing the words if you don't know what they actually mean.

There are some exam-style questions that use this type of mark scheme in this book (marked with an asterisk). You can use them to practise writing logical and coherent answers. Use the worked answers given at the back of this book to mark what you've written. The answers will tell you the relevant points you could've included, but it'll be down to you to put everything together into a full, well-structured answer.

Section 1 — Motion and Forces

1. Distance, Displacement, Speed and Velocity

Page 24 — Fact Recall Questions

Q1 a) vector
 b) scalar
 c) vector
 d) scalar

Q2 If an object is travelling at a constant speed but is changing direction, then its velocity is changing.
Remember — speed only has a magnitude, but velocity has magnitude and direction.

Q3 a) 6 m/s
 b) 3 m/s
 c) 1.5 m/s

Q4 distance travelled (x) = speed (v) × time (t) where distance travelled is in m, speed is in m/s and time is in s.

Page 24 — Application Questions

Q1 a) Distance = 16 + 25 + 16 = **57 m**
 b) Displacement = **25 m south.**
 The eastern displacement of the car is cancelled out by the western displacement of the car, so the overall displacement of the car is directly to the south of its starting point. Remember to give both the magnitude and direction in your answer.

Q2 Typical walking speed = 1.5 m/s.
 $x = v \times t = 1.5 \times 18 = \textbf{27 m}$

Q3 a) Use the train's speed between stations A and B and the time taken to travel between them.
 $x = v \times t = 45 \times 120 = \textbf{5400 m}$
 b) Use the speed the train is moving at between stations B and C, and the distance between them. Change the distance into m:
 16.8 × 1000 = 16 800 m
 Then rearrange the distance equation:
 $x = v \times t$, so $t = x \div v = 16\,800 \div 60 = \textbf{280 s}$
 c) Total distance travelled = 5400 + 16 800
 = 22 200 m
 Total time taken to travel this distance = 120 + 280
 = 400 s
 $x = v \times t$, so $v = x \div t = 22\,200 \div 400$
 = 55.5 = **56 m/s (to 2 s.f.)**

2. Acceleration

Page 26 — Fact Recall Questions

Q1 $a = \dfrac{v - u}{t}$

Q2 m/s^2

Q3 10 m/s^2

Page 26 — Application Questions

Q1 $v - u = 10 - 25 = -15$ m/s
 $a = \dfrac{v - u}{t} = -15 \div 5 = \textbf{-3 m/s}^2$

Q2 Rearrange $a = \dfrac{v - u}{t}$ for v:
 $a \times t = v - u$
 $v = u + (a \times t)$
 $v = 0 + (4 \times 5) = \textbf{20 m/s}$

Q3 Rearrange $v^2 - u^2 = 2 \times a \times x$ for acceleration:
 $a = (v^2 - u^2) \div (2 \times x) = (7.1^2 - 5.6^2) \div (2 \times 38.1)$
 = **0.25 m/s^2**

Q4 Rearrange $v^2 - u^2 = 2 \times a \times x$ for distance (height):
 $x = (v^2 - u^2) \div (2 \times a) = (6.0^2 - 0^2) \div (2 \times 10)$
 = **1.8 m**
 $u = 0$ m/s because the apple is at rest just before it falls.

3. Distance/Time Graphs

Page 29 — Fact Recall Questions

Q1 The speed of the object.
Q2 It tells you that the object is stationary.
Q3 It represents acceleration (or deceleration).
Q4 Draw a tangent to the curve at the given time, and then calculate the gradient of the tangent.

Page 29 — Application Questions

Q1 *A* — It's increasing (the object is speeding up).
 B — It's not changing (the object is moving at a steady speed).
 C — It's decreasing (the object is slowing down).
 D — It's zero (the object is not moving).

Q2 For the first 10 seconds the graph will be curved with an increasing gradient. For the next 5 seconds it will be a sloped straight line.

Q3 a)

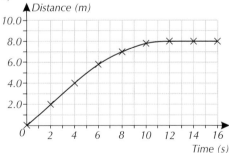

 b) $x = v \times t$, so
 $v = x \div t$
 = 4 ÷ 4 = **1 m/s**

c) Speed at 8 s is equal to the gradient of the tangent to the curve at that point.

E.g.

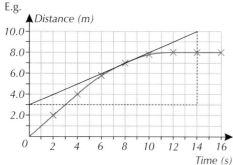

change in distance = 10 − 3 = 7
change in time = 14 − 0 = 14
gradient = 7 ÷ 14 = 0.5
So, speed at 8 s = **0.5 m/s**
(Accept 0.4-0.6 m/s)
Tangents are difficult to draw accurately, so often a range of answers are accepted.

4. Velocity/Time Graphs

Page 32 — Fact Recall Questions
Q1 The acceleration (of the object).
Q2 The distance travelled (by the object).

Page 32 — Application Questions
Q1 A — It's not changing (the object has a steady acceleration).
B — It's zero (the object is moving at a steady speed).
C — It's increasing (the object is speeding up, but not at a steady rate).
D — It's not changing (the object has a steady deceleration).
Q2 a) 4 m/s
b) Between 100 and 120 seconds.
It's the part where the graph has a negative gradient (sloping downwards).
c) The acceleration is equal to the gradient, so:
$$\text{gradient} = \frac{\text{change in the vertical}}{\text{change in the horizontal}} = \frac{8 - 4}{80 - 60}$$
$$= \mathbf{0.2 \ m/s^2}$$
d) Distance travelled between 0 and 20 s
= ½ × base × height = ½ × 20 × 4 = 40 m
Distance travelled between 20 and 60 s
= base × height = (60 − 20) × 4 = 160 m
So total distance travelled = 40 + 160 = **200 m**
Remember to break the area into separate shapes if you think it will make the calculation easier.
Q3

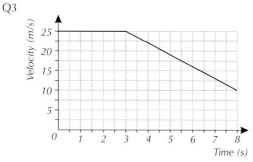

$$\text{Acceleration} = \text{gradient} = \frac{\text{change in the vertical}}{\text{change in the horizontal}}$$
$$= \frac{10 - 25}{8 - 3} = \mathbf{-3 \ m/s^2}$$
The acceleration is negative as the car is decelerating.

5. Newton's First Law

Page 34 — Fact Recall Question
Q1 a) Nothing will happen — it will remain stationary.
b) The object will accelerate (start moving) in the direction of the resultant force.
c) The object will keep moving at the same velocity.
d) The object will accelerate in the direction of its motion.
e) The object will decelerate.

Page 34 — Application Question
Q1 The resultant force is zero.

6. Newton's Second Law and Inertia

Page 36 — Fact Recall Questions
Q1 $F = m \times a$, where F = force in N, m = mass in kg and a = acceleration in m/s².
Q2 a) centripetal force
b) Towards the centre of the circle.
Q3 Inertial mass is the ratio of force over acceleration / a measure of how difficult it is to change the velocity of an object.

Page 36 — Application Questions
Q1 The car without the rock has a smaller mass, so it will win the race. Acceleration is inversely proportional to mass ($a = F ÷ m$), so a larger mass means a smaller acceleration for a given driving force.
Q2 $a = F ÷ m = 303 ÷ 1.5 = \mathbf{202 \ m/s^2}$

7. Weight, Mass and Gravity

Page 38 — Fact Recall Questions
Q1 Weight is the force acting on an object due to gravity.
Q2 Weight and gravitational field strength are directly proportional.
Q3 Weight = mass × gravitational field strength ($W = m \times g$).
Q4 A spring balance (or newton meter).

Page 38 — Application Question
Q1 a) $W = m \times g = 15 \times 10 = \mathbf{150 \ N}$
b) Its mass would stay the same.

8. Investigating Motion

Page 41 — Application Question
Q1 a) E.g. stand up during the experiment so that she can get out of the way of any falling weights.
b) To reduce the friction between the trolley and the track, so that any force applied will cause the trolley to move / so any applied force won't have to overcome friction before it moves the trolley.

c) $x = v \times t$ so $v = x \div t = 0.10 \div 0.2 = \textbf{0.5 m/s}$

d) $a = \dfrac{v - u}{t} = (2.0 - 0.5) \div 0.75 = \textbf{2 m/s}^2$

e) It should decrease.

The acceleration should decrease because $a = F \div m$. F is being kept constant, so as m increases a decreases.

9. Newton's Third Law

Page 43 — Fact Recall Question

Q1 When two objects interact, the forces they exert on each other are equal and opposite.

Page 43 — Application Question

Q1 No, as the two forces are not of the same type and they are both acting on the ball.

10. Momentum

Page 48 — Fact Recall Questions

Q1 The object's mass and velocity.

Q2 $p = m \times v$. p is momentum in kg m/s, m is mass in kg and v is velocity in m/s.

Page 48 — Application Questions

Q1 a) $p = m \times v = 0.1 \times 0.6 = \textbf{0.06 kg m/s north}$

Don't forget to give a direction.

b) $0.80 \div 1000 = 0.00080$ kg

$p = m \times v = 0.00080 \times 12 = \textbf{0.0096 kg m/s left}$

c) $p = m \times v = 5.2 \times 8.0 = \textbf{42 kg m/s down (2 s.f.)}$

Q2 The total momentum before and after the event is 0 kg m/s. Momentum depends on mass and velocity, so if the gas canister's velocity before the explosion is zero, the momentum is 0 kg m/s. Assuming it's a closed system, the total momentum after the explosion will be equal to the momentum before, so it must be 0 kg m/s as well.

Q3 $F = (mv - mu) \div t = 27 \div 3 = \textbf{9 N}$

Q4 a) Rearranging $p = m \times v$,

$v = p \div m = 3.04 \div 0.95 = \textbf{3.2 m/s south}$

b) Rearranging $p = m \times v$,

$v = p \div m = 45\,000 \div 2000$

$= 22.5 = \textbf{20 m/s east (to 1 s.f.)}$

Q5 a) Rearranging $p = m \times v$,

$m = p \div v = 31.5 \div 0.75 = \textbf{42 kg}$

b) Rearranging $p = m \times v$,

$m = p \div v = 210 \div 7.5 = \textbf{28 kg}$

Q6 $F = (mv - mu) \div t$

so, $t = (mv - mu) \div F = 32 \div 20 = \textbf{1.6 s}$

Q7 Say positive means in the direction the bullet travels.

Total momentum before = total momentum after.

Total momentum before = 0

Total momentum after = $(m_{gun} \times v_{gun}) + (m_{bullet} \times v_{bullet})$

So $0 = (1 \times -2) + (m \times 200)$

$m = 2 \div 200 = \textbf{0.01 kg}$

Q8 Say positive means to the right.

Total momentum after the collision = $m_{C+D}\, v_{C+D}$

$= (56.0 + 70.0) \times -1.50 = -189$ kg m/s

Total momentum before the collision

$= (m_C\, v_C) + (m_D\, v_D)$

$-189 = (56.0 \times 1.30) + (70.0 \times v_D)$, so:

$v_D = (-189 - 72.8) \div 70.0 = -3.74$ m/s

$= \textbf{3.74 m/s to the left}$

The minus sign means that the skier D moves to the left (because we said positive was to the right).

Q9 a) Take the direction of the paint ball to be positive.

$F = (mv - mu) \div t$

so $v - u = (F \times t) \div m$

$= (100 \times 0.05) \div 0.05 = 100$ m/s

u is 0 m/s so $v = \textbf{100 m/s}$

b) $F = (mv - mu) \div t$

so, $m = (F \times t) \div (v - u)$

$= (-100 \times 0.05) \div (-2.0 - 0)$

$= \textbf{2.5 kg}$

The force acting on the gun is equal in size to the force that acts on the paint ball due to Newton's Third Law. It acts to the opposite direction though, so it is negative.

11. Stopping Distances

Page 50 — Fact Recall Questions

Q1 The stopping distance is the distance covered by the vehicle in the time between the driver first spotting a hazard and the vehicle coming to a complete stop. It's the sum of the thinking distance and the braking distance.

The thinking distance is the distance the vehicle travels during the driver's reaction time.

The braking distance is the distance the vehicle travels after the brakes are applied until it comes to a complete stop.

Q2 Any three from: e.g. state of the car's brakes, the mass of the car, friction between the car and the road/state of the road (ice, water, oil, leaves etc. on the road)/state of the tyres.

Q3 a) Braking

b) Thinking

c) Thinking

d) Braking

Page 50 — Application Questions

Q1 Stopping distance = 15 + 38 = **53 m**

12. Stopping Safely

Page 53 — Application Questions

Q1 Force is the rate of change of momentum. This means to cause a large deceleration, a large force is needed. Large forces can cause injury to passengers. They can also cause the brakes to overheat and so not work as well. Large braking forces can also lead to the vehicle skidding.

Q2 a) 60 mph is double 30 mph.

Thinking distance is directly proportional to speed, so new thinking distance = $9.0 \times 2 = \textbf{18 m}$

b) Braking distance increases by the square of the scale factor of the speed increase, so new braking distance = 14.0×2^2 = **56 m**

Q3 $\frac{1}{2} \times m \times v^2 = F \times d$
$v^2 = (2 \times F \times d) \div m$
$v = \sqrt{(2 \times F \times d) \div m}$
$= \sqrt{(2 \times 10\,000 \times 15) \div 12\,000}$
$= $ **5 m/s**

Q4 $m \sim 1000$ kg, $t \sim 1$ s, $v = 12$ m/s, $u = 0$ m/s
$F = (mv - mu) \div t$
$= ((1000 \times 12) - (1000 \times 0)) \div 1 = 12\,000$
So force $\sim$ **10 000 N**

13. Reaction Times

Page 55 — Fact Recall Question

Q1 Sit with your arm resting on the edge of a table. Have someone hold a ruler end-down so that the 0 cm mark hangs between your thumb and forefinger. The ruler should be dropped without warning. Grab the ruler between your thumb and forefinger as quickly as possible. Measure the distance at which you have caught the ruler. Use $v^2 - u^2 = 2 \times a \times x$ and $a = (v - u) \div t$ with $a = g = 10$ m/s^2 to calculate the time taken for the ruler to fall that distance. This is your reaction time.

Page 55 — Application Question

Q1 a) Average distance = $(3.0 + 5.0 + 7.0) \div 3$
$= 15.0 \div 3$
$= $ **5.0 cm**
b) $v^2 - u^2 = 2 \times a \times x$
$x = 5.0$ cm $= 0.050$ m
so $v = \sqrt{(2 \times a \times x) + u^2} = \sqrt{(2 \times 10 \times 0.050) + 0^2}$
$= 1$ m/s
$a = (v - u) \div t$, so $t = (v - u) \div a = (1 - 0) \div 10$
$= $ **0.1 s**
Remember to convert the distance from cm to m.
c) E.g. They are tired from the school day, so their reaction time is longer.

Pages 59-60 — Motion and Forces
Exam-style Questions

1 a) Between 70 and 120 seconds *(1 mark)*
b) Acceleration = gradient
$= \dfrac{\text{change in the vertical}}{\text{change in the horizontal}} = \dfrac{10 - 6}{40 - 30}$
$= $ **0.4 m/s^2**
(3 marks for correct answer, otherwise 1 mark for correct method used for calculating the gradient and 1 mark for correct values read from graph)
c) $F = m \times a$
$= 980 \times 0.4$
$= $ **392 N**
(3 marks for correct answer, otherwise 1 mark for stating F = m × a and 1 mark for correct substitution into the equation)
It's fine if you write down equations in words instead of with symbols — you'll still get a mark for recalling the equation. It's best to use symbols when you can though, as they're quicker to write and clearer to rearrange.

d) The distance travelled between 30 and 40 s is equal to the area under the graph, which can be found by splitting the area up into a triangle and a rectangle:
Area = $(\frac{1}{2} \times b \times h) + (b \times h)$
$= (\frac{1}{2} \times 10 \times 4) + (10 \times 6)$
$= $ **80 m**
(3 marks for correct answer, otherwise 1 mark for statement of distance being equal to the area under the graph and 1 mark for correct method used for calculating the area)
You could also have read values from the graph and substituted them in to $v^2 - u^2 = 2 \times a \times x$.

2 a) i) $W = m \times g$ *(1 mark)*
ii) On Earth: $W = m \times g = 2300$
g on Earth is 10 N/kg, so
$m = W \div g = 2300 \div 10 = 230$ kg
On the Moon: $W = m \times g = 368$ N
$g = W \div m = 368 \div 230 = $ **1.6 N/kg**
(4 marks for correct answer, otherwise 1 mark for correct rearrangements of W = m × g, 1 mark for correct substitution into the rearranged equations and 1 mark for correct calculation of m)
b) $a = \dfrac{v - u}{t} = (0.42 - 0) \div 1.4 = $ **0.3 m/s^2**
(3 marks for correct answer, otherwise 1 mark for stating a = (v − u) ÷ t and 1 mark for correct substitution into the equation)
c) $F = m \times a = 230 \times 0.3 = $ **69 N**
(3 marks for correct answer, otherwise 1 mark for stating F = m × a or F = (mv − mu) ÷ t and 1 mark for correct substitution into the equation)

3 a) In a closed system/a situation where no external forces act, the total momentum before an event is the same as after the event *(1 mark)*.
b) i) $p = m \times v$ *(1 mark)*
ii) Say to the right is positive.
The blue ball is at rest, so it has zero momentum
Total momentum = momentum of white ball
$p = m \times v$, so total momentum = $(m_{white} \times v_{white})$
$p = 0.16 \times 0.5 = $ **0.08 kg m/s to the right**
(2 marks for correct answer, otherwise 1 mark for correct substitution into the equation)
iii) Total momentum before the collision = total momentum after the collision = 0.08 kg m/s
Total momentum after the collision
$= (m_{white} \times v_{white}) + (m_{blue} \times v_{blue}) = 0.08$
so $v_{blue} = [0.08 - (m_{white} \times v_{white})] \div m_{blue}$
$v_{blue} = [0.08 - (0.16 \times 0.1)] \div 0.16$
$= $ **0.4 m/s to the right**
(3 marks for correct answer, otherwise 1 mark for correct rearrangement and 1 mark for correct substitution into the rearranged equation)

4 a) $v^2 - u^2 = 2 \times a \times x$ so $a = (v^2 - u^2) \div (2 \times x)$
$a = (25^2 - 20^2) \div (2 \times 125) = $ **0.9 m/s^2**
(3 marks for correct answer, otherwise 1 mark for correct rearrangement and 1 mark for correct substitution into the rearranged equation)
b) i) (average) speed = distance ÷ time / $v = s \div t$
(1 mark)

ii) $t = s \div v = 450 \div 25 = \textbf{18 s}$
(3 marks for correct answer, otherwise 1 mark for correct rearrangement and 1 mark for correct substitution into the rearranged equation)

c) $\frac{1}{2} \times m \times v^2 = F \times d$ so $d = (m \times v^2) \div (2 \times F)$
$d = (25\,000 \times 30^2) \div (2 \times 125\,000) = \textbf{90 m}$
(4 marks for correct answer, otherwise 1 mark for correctly recalling and equating work done to energy in kinetic energy stores, 1 mark for correct rearrangement for distance and 1 mark for correct substitution into the rearranged equation)

d) $F = (mv - mu) \div t$
$= [(25\,000 \times 30) - (25\,000 \times 0)] \div 10$
$= \textbf{75\,000 N}$
(2 marks for correct answer, otherwise 1 mark 1 mark for correct substitution into the equation)

Section 2 — Conservation of Energy

1. Energy Stores and Transfers

Page 65 — Fact Recall Questions

Q1 Thermal energy store, kinetic energy store, gravitational potential energy store, elastic potential energy store, chemical energy store, magnetic energy store, electrostatic energy store and nuclear energy store.

Q2 For a closed system, the net change to the total energy in the system is zero.

Q3 Energy can be transferred usefully, stored or dissipated, but can never be created or destroyed.

Page 65 — Application Questions

Q1 a) Energy is transferred mechanically from the elastic potential energy store of the bow to the kinetic energy store of the arrow.

b) Energy is transferred by heating from the chemical energy store of the gas to the thermal energy stores of the soup (and the surroundings).

c) Energy is transferred electrically from the chemical energy store of the battery to the kinetic energy store of the motor / the blades of the fan.

Q2 10 J of the total energy input from the gravitational potential energy store has been dissipated or wasted, instead of being transferred usefully to the kinetic energy store. This is due to work done in overcoming friction and air resistance as the ball rolls down the hill, so energy will have been transferred to the thermal energy stores of the ball and surroundings.

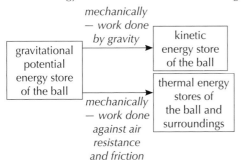

2. Kinetic and Potential Energy Stores

Page 68 — Fact Recall Questions

Q1 $KE = \frac{1}{2} \times m \times v^2$. KE is the kinetic energy in J, m is mass in kg and v is speed in m/s.

Q2 $\Delta GPE = m \times g \times \Delta h$. ΔGPE is change in gravitational potential energy in J, m is mass in kg, g is gravitational field strength in N/kg and Δh is change in vertical height in m.

Page 68 — Application Questions

Q1 $\Delta GPE = m \times g \times \Delta h = 25\,000 \times 10 \times 12\,000$
$= \textbf{3\,000\,000\,000 J}$

Q2 $m = 12.5 \text{ g} \div 1000 = 0.0125$ kg
Rearranging $KE = \frac{1}{2} \times m \times v^2$,
$v = \sqrt{\dfrac{2 \times KE}{m}} = \sqrt{\dfrac{2 \times 40}{0.0125}} = \textbf{80 m/s}$

Q3 Due to conservation of energy, the energy lost from the potato's GPE store is all transferred to its kinetic energy store, so $\Delta GPE = KE = 450$ J.
Rearranging $KE = \frac{1}{2} \times m \times v^2$,
$v = \sqrt{\dfrac{2 \times KE}{m}} = \sqrt{\dfrac{2 \times 450}{1}} = \textbf{30 m/s}$

If there had been air resistance, some energy would have been transferred to other stores, such as the thermal energy store of the air.

3. Reducing Unwanted Energy Transfers

Page 70 — Fact Recall Questions

Q1 Thick walls, made of a material with a low thermal conductivity, will transfer heat energy away from the building by conduction more slowly, meaning the building will cool more slowly.

Q2 a) Cavity walls are made up of an inner and an outer wall with an air gap in the middle. The air gap reduces the amount of energy transferred by conduction through the walls, because air is a thermal insulator.

b) Double-glazed windows have a double layer of glass separated by an air gap. Because air is an insulator it will reduce energy loss by conduction through the window.

c) Hot water tank jackets are made of insulating fibreglass wool, which traps insulating air. This reduces the energy transferred by conduction from the tank's thermal energy store.

Q3 E.g. a lubricant (oil or grease) can be used on the moving parts in a sewing machine to decrease the friction between them, and so decrease the unwanted energy transfers to thermal energy stores.

4. Efficiency

Page 73 — Fact Recall Questions

Q1 $\text{efficiency} = \dfrac{\text{useful energy transferred by the device}}{\text{total energy supplied to the device}}$

Q2 The amounts of energy transferred.

Page 73 — Application Questions

Q1 a) $\text{efficiency} = \dfrac{\text{useful energy transferred by the device}}{\text{total energy supplied to the device}}$

$= \dfrac{54}{90}$

$= \textbf{0.6}$

b) Useful energy transferred $= 800 - 280 = 520$ J

$\text{efficiency} = \dfrac{\text{useful energy transferred by the device}}{\text{total energy supplied to the device}}$

$= \dfrac{520}{800}$

$= \textbf{0.65}$

Q2 a) $\text{efficiency} = \dfrac{\text{useful energy transferred by the device}}{\text{total energy supplied to the device}}$

$= \dfrac{12.6}{36}$

$= 0.35$

percentage efficiency $= 0.35 \times 100 = \textbf{35\%}$

b) $\text{efficiency} = \dfrac{\text{useful energy transferred by the device}}{\text{total energy supplied to the device}}$

$= \dfrac{4.5}{7.5}$

$= 0.6$

percentage efficiency $= 0.6 \times 100 = \textbf{60\%}$

The energy transferred by heating to thermal energy stores and by sound isn't useful — only the energy transferred by light is.

Q3 a) Convert percentage efficiency into decimal efficiency:

efficiency $= 68\% \div 100 = 0.68$

Rearrange the equation:

$\text{efficiency} = \dfrac{\text{useful energy transferred by the device}}{\text{total energy supplied to the device}}$

total energy supplied to the device

$= \dfrac{\text{useful energy transferred by the device}}{\text{efficiency}}$

$= \dfrac{816}{0.68}$

$= \textbf{1200 J}$

b)

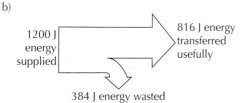

1200 J energy supplied

816 J energy transferred usefully

384 J energy wasted

The wasted energy is the difference between the supplied energy and the energy usefully transferred, i.e.
$1200 \text{ J} - 816 \text{ J} = 384 \text{ J}.$

Q4 E.g. lubricate the motor to reduce friction, and therefore reduce the energy transferred to thermal energy stores.

5. Energy Sources and Their Uses

Page 75 — Fact Recall Questions

Q1 Coal, oil and (natural) gas.

Q2 a) Any four from: wind, the Sun (solar), tides, hydro-electricity, bio-fuels.

b) E.g. they might produce less energy than non-renewable sources / a lot of them are less reliable because they depend on the weather.

Q3 E.g. renewable: bio-fuels
non-renewable: petrol/diesel/coal

Q4 Electromagnetic radiation from the Sun is used to heat water which is then pumped into radiators in the building.

6. Renewable Sources: Wind and Solar

Page 77 — Fact Recall Questions

Q1 The wind turns the blades of the turbine, which are connected to an electrical generator inside the turbine. This generates electricity as it turns.

Q2 E.g. wind turbines generate no electricity when there's no wind / they generate no electricity when the wind is too strong.

Q3 Supplying a device in a remote location with another source of energy could be very difficult and expensive.

Page 77 — Application Question

Q1 a) E.g. Solar cells, because the street light is remote, will get lots of sunshine during the day and requires a fairly small amount of electricity.

b) E.g. Wind power, because the sign will be exposed to wind and requires a fairly small amount of electricity.

7. Renewable Sources: Hydro-electricity, Tides and Bio-fuel

Page 80 — Fact Recall Questions

Q1 Hydro-electric dams and the dried up reservoirs can look unsightly, so they're often built in remote locations so they do not spoil the view of lots of people.

Q2 One advantage of using a tidal barrage to produce electricity is that e.g. it produces no pollution / tides are reliable / there are no fuel costs / running costs are minimal.
One disadvantage is that e.g. it prevents free access by boats / it spoils the view / it alters the habitat of the wildlife who live in the area / the height of the tide is variable, so lower tides provide less energy than the bigger tides / it doesn't work when the water level is the same either side of the barrage four times a day / initial costs are moderately high.

Q3 The use of bio-fuels is limited by the amount of available farmland that can be dedicated to producing them.

8. Non-renewable Sources

Page 82 — Fact Recall Questions

Q1 E.g. carbon dioxide and sulfur dioxide.

Q2 a) nuclear fuel

b) E.g. highly radioactive waste is produced, which is difficult to dispose of.
Possibility of nuclear disasters that can dramatically harm people/the environment.

9. Trends in Energy Resource Use

Page 84 — Fact Recall Questions

Q1 Appliances are being made more efficient, and people are more concerned about the amount of electricity they use.

Q2 Any two from: e.g. they're not as reliable as non-renewables / they can have large initial setup costs / a number of power stations that use renewable sources can only be built in certain locations / a lot of renewable sources cannot easily have their power output increased to meet demand.

Pages 86-87 — Conservation of Energy Exam-style Questions

1   a) $\Delta GPE = m \times g \times \Delta h$
        $= 5.0 \times 0.8 \times 10 = $ **40 J**
        (3 marks for correct answer, otherwise 1 mark for correct equation and 1 mark for correct substitution of values.)

    b) i)   **D** *(1 mark)*
       ii)
       $$v = \sqrt{\frac{2 \times KE}{m}} = \sqrt{\frac{2 \times 10}{5.0}} = \textbf{2 m/s}$$

       (3 marks for correct answer, otherwise 1 mark for correct rearrangement of equation and 1 mark for correct substitution of values.)

    c) How to grade your answer:

       Level 0:   There is no relevant information.
                  [0 marks]

       Level 1:   There is mention of either the energy stores or the transfer of energy mechanically, caused by work done by or against a force. The points are basic and not linked together. *[1 to 2 marks]*

       Level 2:   There is a description of the energy transfers that occur, including a description of how energy is transferred and between which stores. Some of the points made are linked together. *[3 to 4 marks]*

       Level 3:   There is a clear and detailed description of the way energy is transferred as the ball moves, including how energy is dissipated. The points made are well-linked and the answer has a clear and logical structure. *[5 to 6 marks]*

       Here are some points your answer may include:
       Energy is transferred from the gravitational potential energy store of the ball to the kinetic energy store of the ball as it rolls down the slope. This energy is transferred mechanically as gravity does work to move the ball.
       Some energy is transferred from the gravitational potential energy store of the ball to the ball's thermal energy store, as work is done against friction and air resistance.
       When the ball rolls along the flat surface, energy is transferred from the ball's kinetic energy store to its thermal energy store.

This is due to work being done against friction and air resistance.

2   a) Convert percentage efficiency into a decimal:
        efficiency = 62.5 % ÷ 100 = 0.625
        Rearrange the equation:

        $$\text{total energy supplied} = \frac{\text{useful energy transferred}}{\text{efficiency}}$$

        $$= \frac{93\,750}{0.625}$$

        $$= 150\,000 \text{ J}$$

        150 000 J ÷ 1000 = **150 kJ**
        (3 marks for correct answer, otherwise 1 mark for correct rearrangement of equation and 1 mark for correct conversion and substitution of values.)

    b) E.g. by insulating the kettle *(1 mark)*.

3   a) E.g. the thickness of the walls *(1 mark)*, and their thermal conductivity *(1 mark)*.

    b) Loft insulation reduces the amount of energy transferred by heating to the loft *(1 mark)*. Decreasing the amount of energy wasted in this way means that a higher proportion of the energy supplied by the heating system is transferred usefully to warm the main rooms of the house, so the efficiency of the house is increased *(1 mark)*.

4   a) i)   A non-renewable energy source is one that is not being replenished at the same rate as it is being used, so it will eventually run out *(1 mark)*.

       ii) Non-renewable energy sources:
            Coal (49.9%), Oil (2.4%), Gas (20.3%) and Nuclear (19.6%).
            Total percentage = 49.9 + 2.4 + 20.3 + 19.6
                             = **92.2%**
            (2 marks for correct answer, otherwise 1 mark for correctly identifying all of the non-renewable energy sources in the table)

    b) E.g. coal, oil and gas are the energy sources listed that emit the most harmful gases (e.g. CO_2, sulfur dioxide) when burned to generate electricity *(1 mark)*. A far greater percentage of Country 1's electricity comes from using these sources, so this country will produce more pollution *(1 mark)*.

    c) i)   Any one from: e.g. burning coal releases CO_2 into the atmosphere (which contributes to the greenhouse effect) / burning coal releases sulfur dioxide (which causes acid rain) / coal mining destroys the landscape *(1 mark)*.

       ii) E.g. coal is burnt in fireplaces to heat homes *(1 mark)*.

       iii) E.g. hydro-electricity / tides / bio-fuel *(1 mark)*

       iv) E.g. there might not be suitable places to build many damns / The country might not have enough suitable estuaries to build a lot of tidal barrages. / There might not be enough land available to grow bio-fuels as well as food crops *(1 mark)*.

Section 3a — Waves

1. Wave Basics

Page 89 — Fact Recall Questions

Q1   A

Q2 a) Transverse waves have oscillations that are perpendicular to the direction in which the wave travels. However, longitudinal waves have oscillations that are parallel to the direction in which the wave travels.

b) E.g. any electromagnetic wave, ripples on water, waves on a string, a spring wiggled up and down.

Q3 B and D

Q4 No. An object will bob up and down on the ripples rather than move across the water.

2. Features of Waves

Page 92 — Fact Recall Questions

Q1 a) The amplitude of a wave is the maximum displacement of a point on the wave from its undisturbed (or rest) position.

b) The wavelength is the distance between the same point on two adjacent waves.

c) The frequency is the number of waves passing a certain point per second.

d) The period is the time taken for one cycle of a wave to be completed.

Q2 Wavefronts are imaginary lines drawn through identical points on waves, e.g. through each crest. They're perpendicular (at right angles) to the direction in which the wave is moving.

Page 92 — Application Questions

Q1 The wavelength is the length of one full cycle. The distance shown on the diagram is only half a cycle, so the wavelength is twice the distance shown on the diagram, $2 \times 2.0 =$ **4.0 m**.

Q2 a) Amplitude = 1.0 cm, Period = 4.0 s

b) $f = 1 \div T = 1 \div 4.0 =$ **0.25 Hz**

3. Wave Speed

Page 94 — Fact Recall Questions

Q1 $v = \frac{x}{t}$, v = wave speed in m/s, x = distance in m, t = time in s

Q2 $v = f \times \lambda$, v = wave speed in m/s, f = frequency in Hz, λ = wavelength in m

Page 94 — Application Questions

Q1 $v = \frac{x}{t} = 100 \div 0.5 =$ **200 m/s**

Q2 $v = f \times \lambda = 15 \times 0.45 = 6.75 =$ **6.8 m/s (2 s.f.)**

Q3 $x = 90$ km $= 90\,000$ m
$v = \frac{x}{t}$, so $t = \frac{x}{v} = 90\,000 \div (3 \times 10^8) =$ **3×10^{-4} s**

Q4 $f = 3$ kHz $= 3000$ Hz
$v = f \times \lambda$, so $\lambda = v \div f = 1500 \div 3000 =$ **0.5 m**
Make sure the frequency is in Hz and the wavelength is in metres before you use the wave equation.

Q5 $v = f \times \lambda$, so $f = v \div \lambda = (3.0 \times 10^8) \div (7.5 \times 10^{-7})$
$=$ **4×10^{14} Hz**

Q6 $v = \frac{x}{t}$, so $x = v \times t = 340 \times 1.5 = 510$ m
Distance to mountain from boy
$= 510 \div 2 = 255 =$ **260 m (2 s.f.)**
The sound wave travels to the mountain and back, so you need to divide the distance by 2.

4. Measuring Waves

Page 97 — Fact Recall Questions

Q1 E.g. Use a signal generator connected to a speaker to make a sound of known frequency. Put two microphones next to the speaker. The microphones should be connected to an oscilloscope so that it displays a trace for each microscope. Slowly move one microphone away from the speaker. Its trace will shift sideways on the oscilloscope. Keep moving it until the two traces on the oscilloscope are aligned once more. At this point the microphones will be exactly one wavelength apart, so measure the distance between them. You can then use the formula $v = f \times \lambda$ to find the speed (v) of the sound wave passing through the air, using the wavelength you measured and the frequency of the signal generator.

Q2 E.g. Suspend a metal rod of known length using elastic bands. Tap the end of the rod with a hammer. Measure the frequency of the peak frequency wave of the rod by measuring the frequency of the loudest sound wave produced. To do this, use a microphone connected to a computer with the relevant software. Multiply the length of the rod by 2 to get the wavelength of the peak frequency wave. Finally, calculate the speed of the peak frequency wave in the rod using $v = f \times \lambda$. All the waves in the rod will travel at this speed.

Page 97 — Application Question

Q1 a) Wavelength on screen = $2.0 \div 4 = 0.5$ cm
The 1.0 cm line drawn on the bottom of the ripple tank has produced a 2.0 cm shadow, so shadow pattern of ripples is magnified.
Scale factor $= 2.0 \div 1.0 = 2.0$
So, actual wavelength $= 0.5 \div 2.0 = 0.25$ cm

b) $\lambda = 0.25$ cm, which is 0.0025 m
$v = f \times \lambda = 100 \times 0.0025 = 0.25$ m/s

5. Wave Behaviour at Boundaries

Page 98 — Fact Recall Questions

Q1 Absorption is when the wave's energy is transferred to the second material's energy stores.
Reflection is when the wave bounces back off the second material.
Transmission is when the wave carries on travelling through the second material.

Q2 Whether a material transmits, absorbs or reflects a wave depends on the wavelength of the wave.

6. Refraction

Page 102 — Fact Recall Questions

Q1 When a wave changes direction as it passes across the boundary between two materials. It happens when a wave crosses a boundary at an angle to the normal (Higher students could also add that a change in the wave's speed is needed for refraction to occur.)

Q2 E.g.

angle of incidence
angle of refraction

The exact angles aren't important, but it must bend towards the normal.

Q3 E.g. Place a rectangular glass block on a piece of paper and trace around it. Use a ray box or a laser to shine a ray of light at the middle of one side of the block at an angle to it. Trace the incident ray and mark where the light ray emerges on the other size of the block. Remove the block and, with a straight line, join up the incident ray and the emerging point to show the path of the refracted ray through the block. Draw the normal at the point where the light ray entered the block. Use a protractor to measure the angles of incidence and refraction.

Q4 It bends away from the normal.

Q5 Its wavelength increases. Its frequency doesn't change.

Page 102 — Application Questions
Q1

40°
60°

Q2 The angle of refraction is larger than the angle of incidence, so the ray has bent away from the normal. This shows that the light ray travels faster in the second material than in the first, so the light ray speeds up as it crosses the boundary between the materials.

7. Sound
Page 105 — Fact Recall Questions
Q1 The frequency stays the same and the wavelength increases.

Q2 E.g. the object's size / structure / shape.

Q3 The vibrating diaphragm in the speaker causes air particles to vibrate. These vibrations are passed through the air as a series of compressions and rare factions (a sound wave). When the sound wave reaches a person's ear, the air particles collide with the person's ear drum and cause the particles in it to vibrate. The vibrations are passed through the ear, then turned into electrical signal which are sent to the brain, resulting in the sound being heard.

Page 105 — Application Questions
Q1 Lead has a higher density than aluminium. So, when the sound wave moves from the lead to the aluminium, the speed of the wave will decrease. The frequency of the wave stays the same, so the wavelength must decrease.

Q2 Humans cannot hear such sounds because the human ear cannot convert waves of such a high frequency into vibrations of parts of the ear, due to the size, shape and structure of these parts.

8. Ultrasound
Page 108 — Fact Recall Questions
Q1 Ultrasound is sound waves with a frequency above 20 000 Hz (20 kHz).

Q2 Ultrasound waves can pass through the body, but whenever they reach a boundary between two different media (like fluid in the womb and the skin of the foetus) some of the waves are reflected back and detected. The exact timing and distribution of these echoes are processed by a computer to produce a video image of the foetus.

Q3 Ultrasound pulses can be sent from a submarine to the ocean floor. The ultrasound waves will reflect off the ocean floor, and can be detected when they reach the submarine again. Using the speed of ultrasound in water, and the time between sending the ultrasound and detecting the reflected waves, the distance to the ocean floor can be calculated.

Page 108 — Application Questions
Q1 Ultrasound waves can be directed at the tins. The ultrasound will partially reflect at each boundary between materials. In a tin without a plastic shard, the ultrasound should only reflect at the boundaries between the tin and the syrup (at the near side, and the far side). If a plastic shard is present, ultrasound will reflect off the plastic shard, and a reflected ultrasound pulse will be detected between the two expected reflected pulses from the sides of the tin.

Q2 $x = v \times t = 1720 \times (15.0 \times 10^{-6}) = 0.0258$ m
So the distance is $0.0258 \div 2 = 0.0129$ m = **12.9 mm**
Remember, the ultrasound pulse travels the distance between the transmitter and the boundary twice (there and back), so you need to divide the distance by two.

9. Infrasound
Page 111 — Fact Recall Questions
Q1 Infrasound is sound waves with a frequency below 20 Hz.

Q2 E.g. some seismic waves generated by earthquakes are infrasound waves. Looking at the places on the Earth's surface that these waves are detected, and the time taken for them to reach each point, gives scientists information about the Earth's core.

Q3 E.g. P-waves and S-waves.

Page 111 — Application Question
Q1 S-waves cannot travel through liquids, so if the seismometer was placed at the surface of the lake, S-waves could not reach it.

Pages 113-114 — Waves
Exam-style Questions

1 a) C *(1 mark)*
   b) B *(1 mark)*
   c) $T = 1 \div f = 1 \div 2$ *(1 mark)* = **0.5 s** *(1 mark)*
   d) wave speed = frequency × wavelength / $v = f \times \lambda$ *(1 mark)*
   e) $v = 2 \times 1.5$ *(1 mark)* = **3 m/s** *(1 mark)*
   f) E.g. they transfer energy or information / can be reflected / can be refracted *(1 mark)*.
   g)

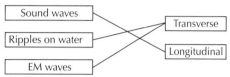

| List A | List B |

(2 marks for matching all three waves in List A correctly, otherwise 1 mark for matching two waves correctly.)

2 a) $80 \times 2 = 160$ mm *(1 mark)*
      160 mm = 160 ÷ 1000 = **0.16 m** *(1 mark)*
   b) Average frequency = $(1.3 + 1.8 + 2.0) \div 3$
         = 1.7 kHz *(1 mark)*
      $1.7 \times 1000 = 1700$ Hz
      $v = f \times \lambda = 1700 \times 0.16$ *(1 mark)*
         = 272 m/s *(1 mark)*
         = **270 m/s (2 s.f.)** *(1 mark)*

3 a) A *(1 mark)*
   b) The distance travelled by the pulse can be found by using $x = v \times t$.
      The speed, $v = 1500$ m/s, and the time between transmission and detection is
      $t = 20$ μs $= 0.000020$ s.
      So $x = v \times t = 1500 \times 0.000020$ *(1 mark)*
         $= 0.030$ m *(1 mark)*
      So distance is $0.030 \div 2 = $ **0.015 m** *(1 mark)*
      The distance travelled by the ultrasound pulse between transmission and detection is the total distance there and back. So you need to divide your calculated distance by two to find the answer you're looking for.

4 a) They are sound waves with frequencies below 20 Hz *(1 mark)*.
   b) There must be some liquid between points A and B *(1 mark)*. P-waves can pass through both solids and liquids *(1 mark)* but S-waves can only pass through solids *(1 mark)*.

5 For concrete:
   $v = f \times \lambda$, so $f = v \div \lambda$ *(1 mark)*
   $f = 3300 \div 3.3$ *(1 mark)* = 1000 Hz
   For the steel beam:
   $v = f \times \lambda$, so $\lambda = v \div f$ *(1 mark)*
   $\lambda = 6000 \div 1000 = $ **6.0 m** *(1 mark)*
   The frequency of the sound wave stays the same as it travels through the different materials.

Section 3b — Light and the Electromagnetic Spectrum

1. Reflection and TIR
Page 117 — Fact Recall Questions
Q1 E.g.

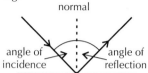

Q2 Specular reflection is when parallel waves are reflected in a single direction by a smooth surface. Diffuse reflection is when parallel waves are reflected by a rough surface (e.g. a piece of paper) and the reflected rays are scattered in lots of different directions.
Q3 Total internal reflection is where light is refracted so much that it is reflected back into a material instead of being transmitted into the new material.

Page 117 — Application Questions
Q1

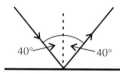

The angle of incidence is always equal to the angle of reflection.
Q2 Light rays reflected by the polystyrene will travel in random directions compared to each other (diffuse reflection), whereas rays reflected by the aluminium will all travel in the same direction (specular reflection).
Q3 a)

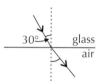

As you're only sketching, you don't need to work out the angle of refraction, it should just be larger than 30°.
   b)

As the angle of incidence is larger than the critical angle for glass, total internal reflection occurs and the two angles should be the same size.

2. Lenses and Images
Page 121 — Fact Recall Questions
Q1 The distance between the centre of the lens and the principal focus.
Q2 Diverging lens

Q3 E.g.

converging lens *diverging lens*

The converging lens should bulge outwards and the diverging lens should curve inwards.

Q4 The principal focus of a converging lens is the point where rays hitting the lens parallel to the axis all meet.
The principal focus of a diverging lens is the point where rays hitting the lens parallel to the axis appear to have come from.

Q5 Real and virtual images.

Q6 Its size compared to the object, which way up it is (upright or inverted) and whether it's real or virtual.

Q7 The more powerful a lens is, the shorter its focal length.

Q8 Make the lens more curved.

Page 121 — Application Question

Q1 a) A converging lens
b) The image is smaller than the object, inverted and real.

3. Ray Diagrams for Lenses

Page 126 — Fact Recall Questions

Q1

convex lens *concave lens*

Q2 a) Real, inverted, smaller than the object and between F and 2F on the far side of the lens.
b) Real, inverted and the same size as the object, positioned at 2F on the far side of the lens.
c) Real, inverted and bigger than the object, and beyond 2F on the far side of the lens.
d) Virtual, upright and bigger than the object and on the same side of the lens as the object.

Q3 Virtual, upright, smaller than the object and the same side of the lens as the object.
A diverging lens always produces a virtual image that's the right way up, smaller than the object and on the same side of the lens as the object, no matter where the object is placed.

Page 126 — Application Questions

Q1 a)

object
F *2F*
2F *F*
image

b) Real, inverted and bigger than the object.
c) A converging lens.

Q2 a)
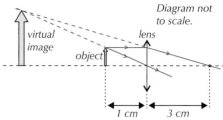

Diagram not to scale.

virtual image *lens*
object

|←1 cm→|← 3 cm →|

b) Converging lenses refract parallel rays of light so they meet at the principal focus of the lens. Diverging lenses refract parallel rays of light so they spread out and appear to come from a single point behind the lens (the principal focus).

c)

Diagram not to scale.

object *lens*
F
image

|←1 cm→|

d) Virtual, upright, smaller than the object and on the same side of the lens as the object.

4. The Electromagnetic Spectrum

Page 127 — Fact Recall Questions

Q1 Transverse

Q2 A continuous spectrum of all the possible wavelengths (or frequencies) of electromagnetic waves.

Q3 Gamma rays, X-rays, ultraviolet, visible light, infrared, microwaves, radio waves.

Q4 Gamma rays

5. Properties of EM Waves

Page 129 — Fact Recall Questions

Q1 Electrons falling to a lower energy level from a higher one and a nucleus releasing excess energy after a radioactive decay.

Q2 E.g. A hot object (the source) emits infrared radiation as it cools down. This radiation is absorbed by the air around it (the absorber) and transfers energy to the thermal energy stores of the air.

Q3 It can be absorbed, reflected or transmitted. No, the same thing won't always happen to any EM wave — different wavelengths may behave differently at the same boundary.

Q4 Refraction / dispersion

6. EM Radiation for Communication

Page 132 — Fact Recall Questions

Q1 Alternating current in a circuit is made up of oscillating electrons — these produce alternating electric and magnetic fields, or radio waves, of the same frequency as the current. These radio waves are emitted by a transmitter and absorbed by a receiver. The energy carried by the waves is transferred to the kinetic energy stores of electrons in the receiver. This causes the electrons to oscillate and, if the receiver is part of a complete circuit, generates an alternating current with the same frequency as the absorbed radio waves.

Q2 Radio waves and microwaves

Q4 Any two from: e.g. short range communications, TV remote controls, transferring information via optical fibres.

7. More Uses of EM Radiation

Page 135 — Fact Recall Questions

Q1 Microwaves and infrared radiation.

Q2 Infrared cameras detect the amount of infrared radiation emitted by an object. The hotter an object, the more infrared radiation it gives out in a given time. Infrared cameras turn the amount of radiation detected into an electrical signal, which can be displayed on screen as a picture.

Q3 Visible light

Q4 Ultraviolet

Q5 Any two from: e.g. medical X-rays, seeing inside of objects, airport security scanners.

Q6 E.g. sterilisation / detecting cancer / treating cancer

8. Dangers of EM Radiation

Page 136 — Fact Recall Questions

Q1 The higher the frequency of the radiation, the more potential danger it poses.

Q2 E.g. skin burns

Q3 Ultraviolet radiation

9. Visible Light and Colour

Page 139 — Fact Recall Questions

Q1 Its wavelength (or frequency).

Q2 Some (or all) wavelengths are absorbed and the rest (if any) are reflected.

Q3 a) none
b) all

Q4 A translucent material transmits and scatters light, whereas an opaque material doesn't transmit any.

Q5 It only transmits certain colours (wavelengths) and absorbs the others.

Page 139 — Application Questions

Q1 It most strongly reflects the wavelengths corresponding to the green part of the visible spectrum and absorbs the others.

Q2 The red light will appear red, but the green light will appear black.

Q3 The red bag only reflects red light which is absorbed by the blue filter, so the bag appears black. The blue buckle reflects blue light which is transmitted by the blue filter, so the buckle appears blue.

10. Radiation and Temperature

Page 144 — Fact Recall Questions

Q1 All objects.

Q2 The intensity of every wavelength increases and the peak wavelength decreases.

Q3 False. All objects are continually absorbing radiation. Objects that are warmer than their surroundings just emit a larger average power than they absorb, so they cool down even though they are absorbing radiation.

Q4 They are equal.

Q5 At night, that side of the Earth is facing away from the Sun, so less radiation is being absorbed than emitted.

Q6 E.g. two ball bearings are each stuck to one side of a metal plate with solid pieces of candle wax. The other sides of these plates are then faced towards a Bunsen burner. The sides of the plates that are facing towards the flame each have a different surface colour — one is matt black and the other is silver. The Bunsen burner is then turned on, and the plates are heated until one of the ball bearings falls.
The surface of the plate which a ball bearing falls from first is the better surface at absorbing radiation. In this example, the ball bearing would fall from the plate with the black surface first, because black surfaces are better absorbers of radiation than silver surfaces.

Page 144 — Application Questions

Q1 The Sun. Peak wavelength decreases as temperature increases, and the Sun has the lower peak wavelength of the two.

Q2 The ice cream is colder than the surroundings, so it absorbs a higher average power than it emits / it absorbs more radiation in a given time than it emits. This leads to a rise in its temperature. Eventually it will reach the same temperature as its surroundings (the room) and will be absorbing and emitting radiation at the same rate.

Pages 147-148 Light and the Electromagnetic Spectrum Exam-style Questions

1 a) Wavelength *(1 mark)*
   b) i) Ultraviolet *(1 mark)*
      ii) E.g. security pens / detecting forged bank notes / fluorescent lamps / disinfecting water *(1 mark)*
      iii) E.g. it can damage surface cells in skin, leading to skin cancer / it can damage surface cells in eyes leading to eye conditions or blindness *(1 mark)*.
   c) Radio waves *(1 mark)* and microwaves *(1 mark)*

2 a)

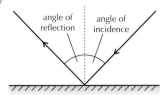

(1 mark for reflected ray drawn correctly, 1 mark for angles labelled correctly.)

Use a protractor to make sure the angle of incidence is equal to the angle of reflection.

b) The angles of reflection don't match the angles of incidence. / The normals aren't drawn perpendicular to points where the rays meet the rough surface. **(1 mark)**

c) Diffuse reflection **(1 mark)**

3 a) The whole surface of the can is the same temperature, as it is all heated by the same water, so the thermometer readings are equal **(1 mark)**. The amount of radiation emitted by an object depends on the properties of its surface — shiny silver is a worse emitter than matt black, so the sensor readings are different **(1 mark)**.

b) The thermometer readings would be lower than before, but they would still be equal to each other **(1 mark)**. The radiation readings would be lower than before, but the reading from the black surface would still be higher than from the silver surface **(1 mark)**. This is because at a lower temperature, the power radiated by the can would be less than before, but the black surface is still a better emitter than the silver surface **(1 mark)**.

4 How to grade your answer:

Level 0: There is no relevant information.
[0 marks]

Level 1: There is a brief description of how the ball will appear. The points made are basic and not linked together. **[1 to 2 marks]**

Level 2: There is an explanation of how the transmitted and reflected light relates to the appearance of the ball, but some details may be missing or incorrect. Some of the points made are linked together. **[3 to 4 marks]**

Level 3: There is a clear and detailed explanation of how the light transmitted and reflected relates to the appearance of the ball. The points made are well-linked and the answer has a clear and logical structure.
[5 to 6 marks]

Here are some points your answer may include:

Light with wavelengths corresponding to the red part of the visible light spectrum will be strongly reflected by the red part of the ball.

All wavelengths of visible light will be reflected equally by the white areas of the ball.

So, when viewed from point A, the ball will appear white with a red stripe, as normal.

Only red light will be transmitted by the red filter, so the whole ball will appear red when viewed from point B. The other colours reflected from the white part of the ball will be absorbed by the red filter.

When the red light transmitted by the red filter reaches the green filter, it will be absorbed. None of the light that has been reflected by the ball will be transmitted by the green filter, so the ball will appear black when viewed from point C.

5 a) The image is virtual **(1 mark)**, upright **(1 mark)** and smaller than the object **(1 mark)**.

b)

(5 marks available — 1 mark for correct symbol for diverging lens, 1 mark for object, lens, and principal focus in correct positions, 1 mark for correctly drawn rays parallel to the axis and through the centre, 1 mark for refracted ray traced back through principal focus, 1 mark for image drawn at intercept.)

c) 1.7 cm **(1 mark for any value between 1.6 cm and 1.8 cm)**

You need to measure the height of the image you've drawn, and then divide it by any scale factor you used to draw your diagram.

Section 4 — Radioactivity

1. Atomic Models

Page 151 — Fact Recall Questions

Q1 A positively-charged sphere with tiny negative electrons stuck in it (like fruit in a plum pudding).

Q2 In Rutherford's nuclear model there is a tiny, positively charged nucleus at the centre of the atom; most of the atom's mass is in the nucleus; the nucleus is surrounded by a 'cloud' of negative electrons; and most of the atom is empty space. The problem with having a cloud of electrons is that they would be attracted to the positive nucleus and the atom would collapse.

Q3 Bohr adapted the model to have the electrons orbiting the nucleus only at certain distances, called energy levels or shells.

Q4 a) Protons, neutrons and electrons.

b) Protons and neutrons are in the nucleus at the centre of the atom. Electrons orbit the nucleus at set distances from the nucleus.

Q5 About 1×10^{-10} m.

2. Subatomic Particles

Page 152 — Fact Recall Questions

Q1 neutron

Q2 –1

Q3 Positrons have a relative mass of $\frac{1}{2000}$ and a relative charge of +1.

Page 152 — Application Question
Q1 10

An atom is neutral, so it has an equal number of protons and electrons.

3. Electron Energy Levels
Page 154 — Fact Recall Questions
Q1 It absorbs electromagnetic radiation.
Q2 It leaves the atom (and becomes a free electron).

Page 154 — Application Question
Q1 Particle A has more protons than electrons, so it must be an ion. It has an overall charge of
(+17) + (–16) = +1.

Remember, electrons have a charge of –1 and protons have a charge of +1.

4. Isotopes and Radioactive Decay
Page 157 — Fact Recall Questions
Q1 Atomic number is the number of protons in the nucleus of an atom. Mass number is the number of protons and neutrons in the nucleus of an atom.
Q2 The charge is the same on each nucleus.

Isotopes of an element have the same number of protons.
Q3 a) Alpha, beta-minus, beta-plus, gamma rays and neutrons.
    b) alpha radiation
    c) alpha radiation

Page 157 — Application Questions
Q1 a) It has an atomic number of 53, and a mass number of 53 + 82 = 135, so it has the symbol $^{135}_{53}$I.
    b) $^{123}_{53}$I

This is the only option that shows an atom with 53 protons — which all isotopes of iodine must have. This isotope has 123 – 53 = 70 neutrons.
Q2 a) Radiation A, as it passes through the hand and radiation B doesn't.
    b) Radiation B, as it doesn't penetrate the hand.
    c) Gamma radiation, as it penetrates through all of the materials.

5. Nuclear Equations
Page 160 — Fact Recall Questions
Q1 Both total mass and total charge have to be the same on both sides of the equation.
Q2 The relative mass decreases by 1, and the charge stays the same.
Q3 a) A neutron becomes a proton plus an electron.
    b) A proton becomes a neutron plus a positron.

Page 160 — Application Questions
Q1 Alpha decay.
Q2 a) Beta-minus decay

b) $^{228}_{88}$Ra $\longrightarrow$ $^{228}_{89}$Ac + $^{0}_{-1}\beta$
Remember you need to balance the atomic and mass numbers on each side of the equation.
Q3 In beta-plus decay, the mass number doesn't change and the atomic number decreases by 1, so mass number of the new element is 11, and the atomic number is 5.

6. Activity and Half-life
Page 163 — Fact Recall Questions
Q1 Activity is measured in Becquerels (Bq). It always decreases over time.
Q2 Because the activity of a source never drops to zero — it will never have fully decayed.
Q3 Half-life is the time taken for half the undecayed nuclei to decay, or the time taken for the activity of a source to decay by half.

Page 163 — Application Questions
Q1 Initial activity = 32 Bq
After one half-life: 32 ÷ 2 = 16
After two half-lives: 16 ÷ 2 = 8
After three half-lives: 8 ÷ 2 = 4
Therefore, it will have dropped to 4 Bq after **3 half-lives**.
Q2 The initial activity is 120 Bq, so after one half-life it will have decreased to 60 Bq. Find 60 Bq on the activity axis and follow across to the curve and then down to the time axis.

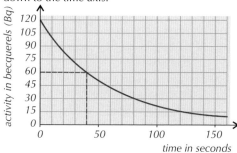

The half-life is **40 seconds**.

7. Background Radiation
Page 164 — Fact Recall Questions
Q1 Background radiation is low-level radiation that is around us at all times and in all places.
Q2 Naturally occurring unstable isotopes (e.g. in the air, food, building materials and rocks), radiation from space (cosmic rays), and radiation from man-made sources (e.g. nuclear weapons, waste and disasters).

8. Dangers of Ionising Radiation
Page 167 — Fact Recall Questions
Q1 E.g. cell/tissue damage / mutation of cells/cancer / cell death.
Q2 Irradiation is exposure to radiation from a radioactive source. Contamination is where unwanted atoms of a radioactive substance are present in or on another material.

Page 167 — Application Questions

Q1 Any two from e.g. wearing gloves whilst handling the source to prevent contamination / wearing shielding over his body whilst injecting the patient to prevent some of the radiation from the source irradiating his body / wearing a radiation badge to monitor his exposure to make sure it does not get too high.

Q2 Initially, there is no difference in the potential danger of (or risk from) the two sources as they both have the same activity. However, the activity of source A will fall to a safer level more quickly than source B as it has a shorter half-life. So source B, with the longer half-life, is potentially more dangerous, as it will have a higher activity than source A over time.

9. Uses of Ionising Radiation

Page 172 — Fact Recall Questions

Q1 Alpha radiation is used e.g. in fire (smoke) alarms. The radiation ionises air particles which then cause a current to flow. In the event of a fire, smoke blocks the flow of the ionised air particles, stopping the current and activating the alarm.
Beta radiation is used e.g. in paper thickness gauges. The radiation passes through the paper to a detector. If too much or too little radiation is detected, the rollers are adjusted to correct the thickness of the paper.
Gamma radiation is used e.g. in food sterilisation: to kill microbes at low temperatures without damaging the food.

Q2 a) A radioactive isotope is injected into or swallowed by a patient. The isotope gives out radiation which is detected using an external radiation detector and is used to track the progress of the isotope around the body. A computer can produce an image from the detected radiation showing where the radiation is most concentrated.

b) Gamma or beta emitters can be used as they can be detected outside the body.
The source should only have a half-life of a few hours, so that the radioactivity inside the patient disappears quickly after the test has been done.

Q3 The isotopes used in PET scanning have short half-lives. If they are transported to the hospital from elsewhere, they may not have a high enough activity to be useful by the time they reach the hospital.

Q4 a) External radiotherapy uses gamma sources, as the radiation needs to be able to penetrate the patient's body from the outside. Internal radiotherapy uses alpha or beta sources, which are more ionising than gamma so don't travel as far. This means they can do a lot of damage to the cells close to them without harming healthy cells far away from the tumour.

b) Sources for external radiotherapy don't enter the patient's body, so they can have long half-lives. This means that they don't have to be replaced frequently. Internal radiotherapy uses sources with short half-lives, to limit the time that radiation is emitted in the patient's body to reduce the harm to healthy cells.

Page 172 — Application Question

Q1 E.g. Carbon-11 could be used for PET scanning because it is a positron emitter. Its short half-life means that it won't stay radioactive inside the patient's body for too long after the scan.
E.g. Cobalt-60 could be used for equipment sterilisation / external radiotherapy. Both uses require a gamma emitter to kill microbes / cancer cells. Its long half-life means that it will last a long time in the machine without needing to be replaced.

10. Nuclear Fission and Fusion

Page 175 — Fact Recall Questions

Q1 A slow-moving neutron is absorbed by an unstable U-235 nucleus. The nucleus splits, forming two new 'daughter nuclei' (e.g. Kr-91 and B-143) and releasing energy. It also releases more neutrons.

Q2 Daughter nuclei.

Q3 Nuclear fusion is the creation of large, heavier nuclei from smaller, lighter nuclei joining together/ fusing, resulting in a loss of mass from smaller nuclei, accompanied by a release of energy. It's the opposite of fission, which is the splitting of large nuclei into smaller ones.

Q4 Nuclear fusion.

Q5 Fusion requires a lot of energy to overcome the electrostatic repulsion between two nuclei. This requires very high temperatures and pressures, which are difficult and expensive to create in a power station. Currently, fusion reactors take more energy to create and control fusion than the fusion reaction releases, meaning that it is not cost effective to use fusion to generate electricity.

Page 175 — Application Question

Q1 a) This is done using control rods made of, e.g. boron. They absorb excess neutrons produced during fission reactions, preventing them from being absorbed by and splitting other uranium nuclei. They are raised or lowered to create a steady rate of nuclear fission, where each fission creates one new fission.

b) This is done using a moderator made of, e.g. graphite. Only slow-moving neutrons are able to cause a fission reaction, so the moderator slows down fast-moving neutrons to make them move at the right speed to keep the chain reaction going.

10. Nuclear Power

Page 177 — Fact Recall Questions

Q1 Nuclear fission, nuclear fusion and radioactive decay.

Q2 The thermal energy released by the chain reaction is transferred to the thermal energy store of the moderator. This energy is then transferred to the thermal energy store of the coolant, and then to the thermal energy store of the cold water passing through the boiler. This causes the water to boil, which turns a turbine connected to a generator, causing electricity to be generated.

Q3 Unlike burning fossil fuels, nuclear fission does not release carbon dioxide, so it does not contribute to the greenhouse effect or global warming. Neither does it release sulfur dioxide that causes acid rain. However, the waste produced by nuclear fission is radioactive, and has a very long half-life, so will stay radioactive for a long time (possibly millions of years). This poses a risk to the environment if it leaks out from the power station or from where it's stored. There's also a risk of an explosion or other catastrophe. In terms of the fuel used, nuclear fission is cheaper than burning fossil fuels because there is much more energy released by the same amount of fuel. However, nuclear power plants are very expensive to build and dismantle, so start-up and decommissioning costs are high.

Pages 180-182 — Radioactivity
Exam-style Questions

1 a) The nucleus contains <u>protons</u> and <u>neutrons</u>.
OR
The nucleus contains <u>neutrons</u> and <u>protons</u>.
The numbers of protons and <u>electrons</u> in a neutral atom are equal.
(2 marks for all correct otherwise 1 mark for one correct answer.)

b) The nuclei of the two atoms will have the same positive charge but a different mass *(1 mark)*.

2 a)

Radiation type:	Made up of:	Stopped by:
Alpha particles	2 protons and 2 neutrons / He nucleus *(1 mark)*	Thin paper
Beta-minus particles *(1 mark)*	Electrons emitted from the nucleus	Thin aluminium
Gamma rays	Short-wavelength EM waves	Thick lead

b) Alpha radiation is the most ionising radiation and so if emitted inside the body it can badly damage cells in a localised area *(1 mark)*.

c) Its atomic number decreases by 2 *(1 mark)* and its mass number decreases by 4 *(1 mark)*.
It loses 2 protons and 2 neutrons.

d) A neutron changes into a proton plus an electron, which it emits *(1 mark)*.

3 a) The time it takes for half of the undecayed nuclei in a caesium-137 sample to decay is 30 years *(1 mark)*.
OR
The time it takes for the activity of a sample of caesium-137 to halve is 30 years *(1 mark)*.

b) 90 years = 3 half-lives
Activity after 1 half-life = 24 ÷ 2 = 12 Bq
Activity after 2 half-lives = 12 ÷ 2 = 6 Bq
Activity after 3 half-lives = 6 ÷ 2 = **3 Bq**
(3 marks for correct answer, otherwise 1 mark for the correct number of half-lives and 1 mark for halving the initial activity this number of times.)

c) Any two from: e.g. cosmic rays (accept radiation from space) / naturally occurring isotopes in food/ building materials/rocks/the air
(2 marks — 1 mark for each correct source.)

d) E.g. Radiation can be detected by a Geiger-Müller tube and counter, which records the count-rate — the number of radiation counts reaching it per second. / Radiation can be detected using photographic film — the more radiation the film's exposed to, the darker it becomes *(1 mark)*.

e) Beta-minus *(1 mark)*.

f) $^{137}_{55}\text{Cs} \rightarrow {}^{137}_{56}\text{Ba} + {}^{0}_{-1}\beta$ / $^{137}_{55}\text{Cs} \rightarrow {}^{137}_{56}\text{Ba} + {}^{0}_{-1}\text{e}$ *(1 mark)*

4 How to grade your answer:

Level 0: There is no relevant information. *[0 marks]*

Level 1: There is a brief explanation of how the method would detect cracks with no explanation of the type of radiation used. The points made are basic and not linked together. *[1 to 2 marks]*

Level 2: There is an explanation of how the method would detect cracks and some explanation of the type of radiation emitted or of an appropriate half-life of the radioactive isotope. Some of the points made are linked together. *[3-4 marks]*

Level 3: There is a clear and detailed explanation of how the method would detect cracks and the radiation type and half-life of the radioactive isotope are fully explained. The points made are well-linked and the answer has a clear and logical structure. *[5-6 marks]*

Here are some points your answer may include:
The radioactive isotope will give out radiation.
The detector will detect how much radiation is reaching it as it moves along above the pipe.
If there is a crack, the substance will leak out and collect outside the pipe.
This means there will be a higher concentration of the radioactive isotope around a crack.
Radiation will also not be absorbed by the pipe at this point — the radiation will pass through the hole.
This will be detected as a higher count rate by the detector.
So the engineer will know where the crack is located — it'll be directly below the detector when the reading increases.
The source used should be a gamma source.
Gamma radiation penetrates far into materials without being stopped and so will pass through the ground and reach the detector.
Alpha and beta radiation would be stopped by the ground, so they wouldn't reach the detector.
The source should have a short half-life.
This will ensure it does not continue emitting lots of radiation for a long time, which would possibly harm people/animals that come close to the pipes or the substance.

5 a) Ionising radiation enters living cells and collides with molecules. This can knock electrons off the atoms and molecules in the cell, damaging them *(1 mark)*. A high enough dose of radiation will cause the cell to be destroyed completely *(1 mark)*

b) i) The beta particles emitted by the source have a moderate penetration depth, and so can get through the plastic pellet casing to the cancer cells *(1 mark)*. Beta particles are also ionising, which means they can kill the patient's cancer cells when they are absorbed by them *(1 mark)*.

ii) The beta source must have a short half-life *(1 mark)*. If it had a long half life, the pellets couldn't be left in the patient as they would emit radiation that would damage healthy cells after the cancer cells had been killed *(1 mark)*.

c) The radiation will also kill healthy cells *(1 mark)*.

d) The source for external radiotherapy would need to emit gamma radiation rather than beta radiation *(1 mark)*, so that the radiation can penetrate through the body from the outside to reach the cancer cells *(1 mark)*. The source for external radiotherapy will need to have a long half-life rather than a short one *(1 mark)*, so it doesn't need to be replaced often / retains a useful activity level for a long time *(1 mark)*.

e) Keeping the machines in a shielded room reduces the risk of irradiation for nearby staff and patients *(1 mark)*.

6 a) i) a (slow-moving) neutron *(1 mark)*

ii) E.g.

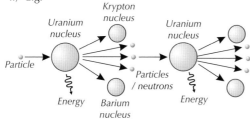

(1 mark for showing small particles/neutrons being produced when the uranium atom splits, 1 mark for showing these particles going on to cause at least one more fission.)

b) E.g. unlike burning fossil fuels, nuclear power does not produce carbon dioxide / sulfur dioxide, which is harmful to the environment because it causes global warming / acid rain *(1 mark)*. However, the products of nuclear fission are radioactive, so they can cause lots of harm to living things if the radiation reaches the nearby environment *(1 mark)*.

c) A moderator is used in a nuclear reactor to slow down the neutrons emitted when a uranium-235 nucleus splits *(1 mark)*. This allows the neutrons produced by the fission reaction to be absorbed by other uranium-235 nuclei and cause further fission *(1 mark)*. Control rods are placed into nuclear reactors to absorb some of the neutrons emitted when a uranium-235 nucleus splits *(1 mark)*. This ensures that the chain reaction is controlled and energy is released at a steady rate *(1 mark)*.

Section 5 — Astronomy

1. The Solar System and Orbits

Page 186 — Fact Recall Questions

Q1 The Earth is the centre of the Solar System and is orbited by the Sun and the other planets. The current model of the Solar System says that the Sun is the centre of the Solar System, and it is orbited by the planets, including Earth.

Q2 Mercury, Venus, Earth, Mars, Jupiter, Saturn, Uranus, Neptune.

Q3 A natural satellite is a naturally occurring (i.e. not man-made) object which orbits a more massive object. E.g. the Moon.

Q4 comet

Q5 gravity

Page 186 — Application Question

Q1 The speed of orbit would increase, as a greater force is acting, so a greater speed is needed to keep the Earth in a stable orbit.

2. The Life Cycle of Stars

Page 188 — Fact Recall Questions

Q1 Gravity causes clouds of dust and gas (a nebula) to be pulled together and form a protostar. Within the protostar, gravity increases the density and causes particles to collide more frequently, increasing the temperature. When the temperature is high enough nuclear fusion begins, causing the star to give out energy.

Q2 Main sequence stars are stable because the energy released by nuclear fusion provides an outward pressure (thermal expansion) which balances the force of gravity trying to pull everything inwards.

Q3 It will become a red giant. The red giant will eventually become unstable and eject its outer layer of dust and gas. This will leave behind a white dwarf.

Page 188 — Application Question

Q1 A black hole.

3. Observing the Universe

Page 190 — Fact Recall Questions

Q1 The larger the aperture, the higher the image quality.

Q2 Early telescopes were only able to detect visible light, but over time telescopes have been produced that can detect radiation across the whole range of the electromagnetic spectrum. Over time, technology improved so that larger telescopes could be created, which improved the quality of the measurements. Telescopes can now also be placed in space, which gets rid of issues caused by the Earth's atmosphere and pollution. Modern telescopes also work alongside computers, which allows huge amounts of data to be collected continuously and analysed quickly.

Q3 Being high up reduces the amount of the Earth's atmosphere that is above the telescope. This improves the image quality as there is less distortion of the light because of the atmosphere. Cities and towns produce light and air pollution. Light pollution makes it harder to see dim objects and air pollution can reflect or absorb incoming radiation.

4. Red-shift and CMB Radiation

Page 193 — Fact Recall Questions

Q1 a) The observed wavelength is greater than the wavelength of the light when it is emitted.
   b) Red-shift
   c) Generally, galaxies further away from the Earth have a greater red-shift than those closer to the Earth.

Q2 a) The Steady State theory says that Universe has no beginning and no end, whereas the Big Bang theory says that the Universe had a beginning and so has a finite age. The Steady State theory says that the Universe has always existed as it is now, and it always will do. As the Universe expands, new matter is constantly being created, so the density of the Universe is always roughly the same. The Big Bang theory says that initially, all matter in the universe occupied a very small space. This tiny space was very dense and so was very hot. This tiny space then exploded and space started to expand, causing the density of the Universe to decrease.
   b) Cosmic microwave background radiation provides evidence that the Universe had a beginning. Steady State theory states that the Universe has no beginning and no end, which means that CMB radiation can not be explained by Steady State theory.

Page 196 — Astronomy Exam-style Questions

1 a) The outwards pressure of the energy released by nuclear fusion/thermal expansion *(1 mark)* balances the inward force of gravity *(1 mark)*.
   b) The main sequence star begins to run out of hydrogen for fusion *(1 mark)* and expands to become a red supergiant *(1 mark)*. The red supergiant eventually becomes unstable as it runs out of fuel in its core, and explodes in a supernova *(1 mark)*, leaving behind a black hole *(1 mark)*.
   c) No, the Sun is not massive enough to become a (red supergiant and hence a) black hole *(1 mark)*.
   d) No, the less massive a star is, the longer it will spend on the main sequence *(1 mark)* because it uses fuel at a slower rate *(1 mark)*.

2 How to grade your answer:
   Level 0: There is no relevant information.
      [No marks]
   Level 1: There is a brief description of why the planet orbits and how the orbital speed is related to the orbital radius. The points made are basic and not linked together.
      [1 to 2 marks]
   Level 2: There is some explanation of why the planet

orbits and how the orbital speed is related to the orbital radius. Some of the points made are linked together. *[3 to 4 marks]*

Level 3: There is a clear and detailed explanation of why the planet orbits and how the orbital speed and orbital radius are related in a stable orbit. The points made are well-linked and the answer has a clear and logical structure. *[5 to 6 marks]*

Here are some points your answer may include:
There is a gravitational force of attraction between the planet and the star.
The gravitational force causes an acceleration of the planet towards the star.
The planet keeps accelerating towards the star, but the planet also has an instantaneous velocity (forward motion) that keeps it travelling in a circular path.
The closer the planet is to the star, the stronger the gravitational force between them.
A greater gravitational force requires a greater instantaneous velocity to keep the object in orbit.
So, to maintain a stable circular orbit, the closer the planet is to the star, the faster its orbital speed must be. The further away it is, the slower its orbit will be.

3 a) The wavelength of observed light from a source is longer than that of the light emitted by the source *(1 mark)* when the source is moving away from the observer *(1 mark)*.
   b) If light from most galaxies is red-shifted, then most galaxies are moving away from us *(1 mark)*. The larger the red-shift, the faster the galaxy is receding, so galaxies further away are moving away from us faster. This means that the Universe is expanding *(1 mark)*.
   c) Angular resolution = $\dfrac{\text{wavelength}}{\text{aperture}} = \dfrac{650 \times 10^{-9}}{10.0}$
      $= 6.5 \times 10^{-8}$ **radians**
      (2 marks for correct answer, otherwise 1 mark for correct substitution.)
   d) The Earth's atmosphere absorbs some frequencies of electromagnetic radiation, so by putting the telescope in space all frequencies of EM radiation can be detected *(1 mark)*. Air pollution can also absorb some radiation, as well as reflect it back into space. There is no air in space, so a space telescope is not affected by this *(1 mark)*. In space there is no light pollution, which on Earth makes it difficult to detect dim light sources in the sky *(1 mark)*.

Section 6 — Forces and Energy

1. Energy Transfers and Systems

Page 198 — Fact Recall Questions

Q1 A closed system is one in which the net change in total energy is zero.

Q2 By work done by forces, using electrical equipment and by heating.

Page 198 — Application Questions

Q1

electrically →	thermal energy store of the kettle's heating element	heating →	thermal energy store of the water
		→	thermal energy store of the kettle
		→	thermal energy store of the air

Q2 a) Energy is transferred mechanically from the gravitational potential energy store of the skier to the kinetic energy store of the skier. Some energy is dissipated out of the system.

b) Energy is transferred from the chemical energy store of the gas by heating to the thermal energy stores of the beaker and the water. Some energy is dissipated out of the system.

2. Work Done

Page 200 — Application Questions

Q1 $E = F \times d = 24 \times 14 = 336 \text{ J} = \textbf{340 J (to 2 s.f.)}$

Q2 a) $E = F \times d = 250 \times 20 = \textbf{5000 J}$

b) Rearrange equation:
$d = E \div F = 750 \div 250 = \textbf{3 m}$

c) $E = F \times d = 250 \times 2 = 500 \text{ J}$
If all of this is transferred to KE, then $KE = 500$ J.
Rearrange $KE = \frac{1}{2} \times m \times v^2$:
$$v = \sqrt{\frac{2 \times KE}{m}} = \sqrt{\frac{2 \times 500}{10}} = \textbf{10 m/s}$$

In real life, not all of the work done would be transferred to the kinetic energy store of the bike, so the speed would be lower.

Q3 $\Delta GPE = m \times g \times \Delta h = 0.1 \times 10 \times 0.3 = 0.3$ J
Work done by the force $= \Delta GPE = 0.3$ J
Rearrange equation:
$F = E \div d = 0.3 \div 0.5 = \textbf{0.6 N}$

3. Dissipation of Energy

Page 202 — Fact Recall Questions

Q1 During a mechanical process, some energy is dissipated to the thermal energy stores of the system and its surroundings when work is done to overcome friction or air resistance. This is wasteful, because the energy is not being transferred to useful energy stores.

Q2 $\text{efficiency} = \dfrac{\text{useful energy transferred by the device}}{\text{total energy supplied to the device}}$

Page 202 — Application Question

Q1 a) Find the energy usefully transferred to the lift's gravitational potential energy store:
$\Delta GPE = m \times g \times \Delta h = 2000 \times 10 \times 15 = 300\,000$ J
Energy supplied to lift = work done = 500 000 J
Then:
$\text{efficiency} = \dfrac{\text{useful energy transferred by the device}}{\text{total energy supplied to the device}}$
$= \dfrac{300\,000}{500\,000} = 0.6$

As a percentage, efficiency $= 0.6 \times 100 = \textbf{60\%}$

b) Lubricants would reduce the friction between the moving parts of the machinery, so that less energy is dissipated to the thermal energy stores of the parts and surroundings.

4. Power

Page 204 — Fact Recall Questions

Q1 Power is the rate at which energy is transferred.
You can also define power as the rate of doing work. Energy transferred and work done are the same thing.

Q2 $P = \frac{E}{t}$. P is power in watts, E is work done in joules and t is time taken in seconds.

Page 204 — Application Questions

Q1 a) $P = E \div t = 1500 \div 37.5 = \textbf{40 W}$

b) $7.98 \text{ kJ} \times 1000 = 7980$ J
$P = E \div t = 7980 \div 42 = \textbf{190 W}$

c) $6840 \text{ kJ} \times 1000 = 6\,840\,000$ J
9.5 minutes $\times 60 = 570$ s
$P = E \div t = 6\,840\,000 \div 570 = \textbf{12\,000 W}$

Q2 Lift B will lift the load in the least time. Since both lifts need to transfer the same amount of energy to perform the task, the lift with the larger power, B, will perform the task in less time, as it transfers more energy per second.

Q3 $P = E \div t$, so $t = E \div P$
$t = 1344 \div 525 = \textbf{2.56 s}$

Q4 $P = E \div t$, so $E = P \times t$
$E = 1240 \times 35 = \textbf{43\,400 J}$

5. Force Basics

Page 206 — Fact Recall Questions

Q1 A scalar quantity only has magnitude, but a vector quantity has magnitude and direction.

Q2 a) Vector
b) Vector
c) Scalar
d) Vector

Q3 E.g. friction between a car's tyres and the road / air resistance between the body of the car and the air / a normal contact force between a person sitting on a stool and the stool / tension in a dog's lead.

Q4 E.g. gravitational attraction between the Earth and the Moon / magnetic attraction between opposite poles of two bar magnets / electrostatic repulsion between hairs with a build up of static charge, making them stand on end.

Page 206 — Application Questions

Q1 The swimmer's feet exert a normal contact force on the wall, and the wall exerts an equal force on the feet in the opposite direction:

Wall

6. Finding the Resultant Force

Page 210 — Fact Recall Questions

Q1 A free body force diagram shows all the forces acting on an object, including the magnitude and direction of each force.

Q2 An object is in equilibrium if drawing all the forces tip-to-tail gives a complete loop.

Q3 Resolving a force means splitting the force into two component forces that are at right angles to each other. The combination of the two forces has the same effect as the original single force.

Page 210 — Application Questions

Q1 If the forward direction is the positive direction, then the resultant force = 87 − 24 = 63 N
So the resultant force is **63 N forwards**.

Q2 The boat is not in equilibrium as drawing all the forces to scale and tip-to-tail doesn't create a complete loop:

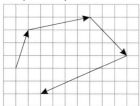

Q3 E.g.

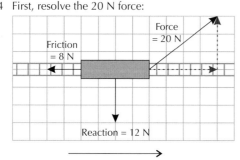

The weight and normal contact arrows should be vertical and pointing in opposite directions to each other. They should also be the same length. The force arrow should be horizontal. It could point in either direction and be any length, as you're not given its exact direction or magnitude.

Q4 First, resolve the 20 N force:

The frictional force that has a magnitude of 8 N is 2 squares long, so 1 square = 4 N.
The component of the pulling force in the direction of motion is 4 squares long, so has a magnitude of 4 × 4 = 16 N.
Resultant force in direction of motion = 16 − 8 = **8 N**.
You don't need to worry about the 12 N reaction force as it's at a right angle to the direction of the motion and doesn't contribute to the resultant force you're looking for.

7. Moments

Page 214 — Fact Recall Questions

Q1 The moment is the turning effect of the force.

Q2 moment of a force (Nm) = force (N) × distance normal to the direction of the force (m) (or $M = F \times d$)

Q3 The sum of all clockwise moments acting on the object must be equal to the sum of all anticlockwise moments acting on the object.

Q4 When a small force is applied at a large distance from the pivot, there will be an equal moment created on the other side of the pivot. Because moment = force × distance, if the distance is small it will mean a large force.

Q5 A gear is a circular disc with teeth. In machinery, it is interlocked with other gears in order to transmit the rotational effects of a force.

Page 214 — Application Questions

Q1 B, D and E.

Q2 $M = F \times d = 60.0 \times 2.70 = $ **162 Nm**

Q3 Calculate the total moments clockwise:
$M = F \times d = 420 \times 0.80 = 336$ Nm
Calculate the total moments anticlockwise:
$M = F \times d = 350 \times 1.40 = 490$ Nm
The total moment anticlockwise is larger than the total moment clockwise, and the difference is:
490 − 336 = 154 Nm
So you need an extra 154 Nm clockwise moment provided by the third child. Rearrange $M = F \times d$ for d, to find the distance from the pivot that the third child needs to sit:
$d = M \div F = 154 \div 308 = 0.5$ m
So the child should sit **0.5 m to the right of the pivot**.
Make sure you include which side of the pivot the child should sit in your answer. In this case, it's to the right of the pivot, because the moment needs to be clockwise for the seesaw to balance.

Q4 Any two from: the force could be moved further from the pivot / the force could be applied at a right angle to the lever / the pivot could be moved closer to the load.

Pages 217-218 — Forces and Energy Exam-style Questions

1 a) A closed system is one where there is no net change to the total energy of that system *(1 mark)*. The brother has a net gain in energy as a result of the push, so he is not a closed system *(1 mark)*.

   b) E.g. as the girl pushes her brother up the slide she will have to do work against friction *(1 mark)*. This transfers energy to the thermal energy stores of the brother, the slide and the surrounding air *(1 mark)*.

   c) i) To find the work done, add up all the energy transferred as a result of the work done:
      $E = 125 + 300 = $ **425 J** *(1 mark)*

      ii) $E = F \times d$, so rearranging:
      $F = E \div d = 425 \div 2.50 = $ **170 N**
      (4 marks for correct answer, otherwise 1 mark for correct equation, 1 mark for correct rearrangement, and 1 mark for correct substitution of values.)

2 a) A is more powerful than B, so it will transfer more energy in the same amount of time / transfer a given amount of energy in a shorter amount of time *(1 mark)*.

b) B is more efficient than A, so more of the energy it transfers will be transferred usefully / less of the energy it transfers will be wasted *(1 mark)*.

c) i) $t = 1$ minute $= 60$ s
$P = E \div t$, so rearranging:
$E = P \times t = 10 \times 60 = 600$ J
(4 marks for correct answer, otherwise 1 mark for correct equation, 1 mark for correct rearrangement, and 1 mark for correct substitution of values.)

ii) $9\% = 9 \div 100 = 0.09$
Rearranging the given equation:
Useful energy transferred by the device
= efficiency ×
total energy supplied to the device
$= 0.09 \times 600 = 54$ J
(3 marks for correct answer, otherwise 1 mark for correct rearrangement and 1 mark for correct substitution of values.)

3 a) i) $M = F \times d$ *(1 mark)*
ii) $M = F \times d = 32.0 \times 3.0 = 96$ Nm
(2 marks for correct answer, otherwise 1 mark for correct substitution of values.)

b) Calculate the moments of the other two forces:
$M = F \times d = 18.0 \times (3.5 + 1.5)$ *(1 mark)*
$= 90$ Nm *(1 mark)*
$M = F \times d = 4.0 \times 1.5$ *(1 mark)* $= 6$ Nm *(1 mark)*
So total moments anticlockwise $= 90 + 6 = 96$ Nm
The sum of clockwise moments (from a) = 96 Nm
This is equal to the sum of anticlockwise moments, so the plank of wood is balanced *(1 mark)*.
The plank's centre of mass is directly above the pivot, so the weight of the plank doesn't have any turning effect and you don't need to worry about it in your calculations.

c) The sum of clockwise moments would decrease if the force labelled X was applied at any other angle *(1 mark)*, so they would be less than the sum of the anticlockwise moments, and the plank would turn anticlockwise *(1 mark)*.

4 a) Contact force *(1 mark)*
b) Resolve the forces of both horses:

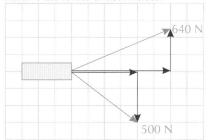

Find the scale of the diagram:
500 N = 2.5 cm, so 1 cm = 200 N
Measure the length of each component that is in the direction of the boat's motion (East):
Horse 1: East component = 3 cm
3×200 N = 600 N
Horse 2: East component = 2 cm
2×200 N = 400 N

So the total force provided by the horses in the direction of motion $= 600 + 400 = $ **1000 N**
(4 marks for correct answer, otherwise 1 mark for resolving the forces, 1 mark for working out the scale and 1 mark for finding the magnitude of the force provided by each horse in the direction of the boat's motion.)

c) Resistive force $= 1000 - 800 = 200$ N *(1 mark)*

Section 7 — Electricity and Circuits

1. Circuit Basics

Page 220 — Application Questions
Q1 E.g.

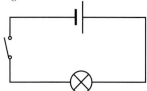

This is just one example of a correct circuit diagram — you could have the components in a different order in the circuit.

Q2 E.g.

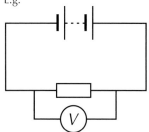

Remember that voltmeters are always connected across a component.

Q3 E.g.

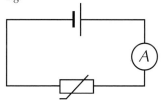

Remember that ammeters are always connected in series with a component.

Q4 Circuit B.
In the rest of the circuits, the lamp is in an incomplete part of the circuit. Don't worry about the extra bits coming off the circuit — as long as there's a complete cycle containing the lamp, current will flow through it and the lamp will light.

2. Current and Potential Difference

Page 222 — Fact Recall Questions
Q1 electrons
Q2 $Q = I \times t$, where Q = charge in coulombs (C), I = current in amperes (A) and t = time in seconds (s).
Q3 A source of potential difference.
Q4 Potential difference is the energy transferred per unit charge passed. It's measured in volts.

Q5 $E = Q \times V$, where E = energy transferred, Q = charge moved and V = potential difference.

Page 222 — Application Questions
Q1 $V = 12$ V, $E = 3600$ J
    $E = Q \times V$ so $Q = E \div V = 3600 \div 12 =$ **300 C**
Q2 $I = 0.20$ A, $Q = 50.0$ C
    $Q = I \times t$, so
    $t = Q \div I = 50.0 \div 0.20 =$ **250 s**

3. Resistance
Page 224 — Fact Recall Questions
Q1 Resistance is anything in a circuit that opposes the flow of current. It is measured in ohms, Ω.
Q2 A resistor heats up because the electrons that move through the resistor to cause a current collide with the lattice of ions that make up the metal. When an electron collides with an ion, it transfers energy to it, making the ion vibrate and the resistor heat up.

Page 224 — Application Question
Q1 $I = 0.015$ A, $R = 2.0$ Ω
    $V = I \times R = 0.015 \times 2.0 =$ **0.03 V**

4. LDRs and Thermistors
Page 226 — Fact Recall Questions
Q1 E.g.

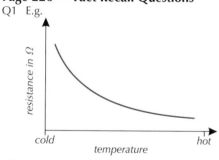

Q2 Increase the light intensity.
    An LDR is a light dependent resistor — its resistance decreases as the light hitting it gets brighter.
Q3 E.g. place the thermistor in a water bath and pour enough water into the bath to fully cover the thermistor. Turn on the water bath, so the water begins to heat up. Measure and record the temperature of the water using a digital thermometer, and measure the current through the circuit for every 5 °C increase in temperature. Use the p.d. of the power supply and the values of current you recorded to calculate the resistance of the thermistor at each temperature, using $R = V \div I$.

Page 226 — Application Question
Q1 E.g.

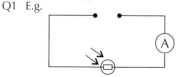

5. I-V Graphs
Page 230 — Fact Recall Questions
Q1 By reading off the value of current for the given p.d. from the I-V graph and substituting these values into $R = V \div I$.
Q2 E.g.

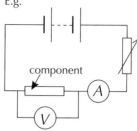

component

Q3 a) E.g.

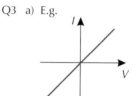

    b) E.g.

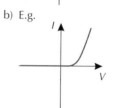

Q4 a) The resistance is initially high but drops as V increases, allowing current to flow.
    b) The resistance is very high, so current can't flow through a diode in this direction.

Page 230 — Application Questions
Q1 A diode.
Q2 $R = V \div I$. The graph is a straight line, so the resistance is constant, so just pick a point on the line and use the values of V and I to work out the resistance:
    E.g. $R = V \div I = 2 \div 0.25 =$ **8 Ω**

6. Series Circuits
Page 234 — Fact Recall Questions
Q1 Components are connected all in a line, end to end.
Q2 In series and in the same direction as each other (and any other cells in the circuit).
Q3 False, it is shared between all components.
Q4 It is always the same.
Q5 Ammeter
Q6 When a resistor is added in series, it has to take a share of the p.d.. This decreases the p.d. through each component, and hence decreases the current ($V = I \times R$). In a series circuit, the current is constant through each component, therefore the total current decreases, so the total resistance increases.

Page 234 — Application Question

Q1 a) 1.5 A

b) $V_1 = I \times R = 1.5 \times 7.0 = 10.5$ V = **11 V (to 2 s.f.)**

c) $V = V_1 + V_2$ so $V_2 = V - V_1 = 12 - 10.5 = $ **1.5 V**

d) $V = I \times R$ so $R = V \div I = 1.5 \div 1.5 = $ **1 Ω**

7. Parallel Circuits

Page 238 — Fact Recall Questions

Q1 Components are connected to the power supply separately to the other components (on their own branches).

Q2 It is the same across each component and across the power supply.

Q3 By adding up the current in every branch.

Q4 When two components are connected in series, the total resistance of the circuit increases compared to when they are connected in parallel.

Page 238 — Application Question

Q1 a) With the switch open, the circuit is just a simple series circuit with two resistors and an ammeter. The current in the circuit is 0.70 A and the total resistance is 12 + 8.0 = 20 Ω.
$V = I \times R = 0.70 \times 20 = $ **14 V**

b) i) The potential difference is the same on each branch of the parallel part of the circuit. So you can just find the voltage on the lower branch by using the resistance of, and current through resistor R_1.
$V = I \times R_1 = 0.50 \times 8.0 = $ **4.0 V**

ii) The total potential difference of the circuit is shared between resistor R_2 and the parallel loop with the other components on it. The potential difference across the parallel loop is 4.0 V and the total potential difference is 14 V, so the potential difference across resistor R_2 is 14 − 4.0 = **10 V**.

8. Investigating Circuits

Page 241 — Application Question

Q1 a) E.g.

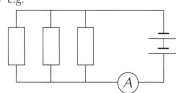

b)

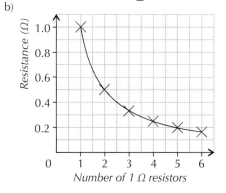

Number of 1 Ω resistors

c) The total resistance of the circuit decreases as the number of resistors connected in parallel increases. When a resistor is added in parallel, it has the same potential difference across it as the source. But by adding another branch, the current has more than one direction to go in. This increases the amount of current flowing. Using $V = I \times R$, an increase in current at a constant p.d. means a decrease in the total resistance.

9. Energy in Circuits

Page 243 — Fact Recall Questions

Q1 a) It is transferred to the thermal energy stores of the components and the surroundings.

b) E.g. use low resistance wires.

Q2 E.g. fuses / toasters / electrical heating.

Page 243 — Application Questions

Q1 E.g. energy is transferred electrically from the chemical energy store of the battery to the kinetic energy stores of the watch hands.

Q2 $V = 230$ V, $I = 3.0$ A, $t = 1$ hour
1 hour = $1 \times 60 \times 60 = 3600$ seconds
$E = I \times V \times t = 3.0 \times 230 \times 3600$
$= 2\,484\,000$ J = **2 500 000 J (to 2 s.f.)**

Q3 $E = 52\,800$ J, $V = 24$ V, $I = 8.0$ A
$E = I \times V \times t$ so $t = E \div (I \times V)$
$t = 52\,800 \div (8.0 \times 24) = 275$ s = **280 s (to 2 s.f.)**

10. Power of Electrical Appliances

Page 245 — Application Questions

Q1 Cooker B will transfer the most energy in 20 minutes because it has the highest power.

Q2 $P = I \times V = 3.0 \times 230 = $ **690 W**

Q3 $P = 2.0$ kW = 2000 W, $t = 30$ minutes = 1800 s
$P = E \div t$, so $E = P \times t = 2000 \times 1800 = $ **3 600 000 J**

Q4 $P = I^2 \times R$
$R = P \div I^2 = 40 \div (0.2)^2 = $ **1000 Ω**

Q5 Microwave A:
$P = E \div t$, so $E = P \times t = 900 \times (4 \times 60) = 216\,000$ J
Microwave B:
$E = P \times t = 650 \times (6 \times 60) = 234\,000$ J
So **microwave B** transfers the most energy.
Remember to convert the time into seconds before carrying out any calculations.

11. Electricity in the Home

Page 249 — Fact Recall Questions

Q1 Alternating current. The direction of charge in a.c. is constantly changing whereas in d.c. charges always move in one direction.

Q2 230 V, 50 Hz

Q3 The live wire carries current to a device.
The neutral wire carries current away from a device.
The earth wire is for safety, to protect against shocks and fires.

Q4 230 V

Q5 A connection between live and earth creates a large potential difference, which causes a large current to flow. This causes heating of wires, which could result in a fire. If a person provides the connection between live and earth, they will get an electric shock which could harm or even kill them.

Q6 Circuit breaker

Page 249 — Application Questions

Q1 Alternating current.

Q2 a) Fuses and switches should be connected to the live wire so that the supply of electricity can be stopped before it reaches a device. This prevents the device from becoming live/isolates the device.

   b) Fuses are used to isolate appliances, which stops a current being able to flow from the appliance to the earth. This means that there is no danger of getting an electric shock from the appliance / little danger of the appliance causing a fire.

Pages 252-253 — Electricity and Circuits Exam-style Questions

1 a) The resistance of the variable resistor can be increased or decreased, which will decrease or increase the current in the circuit *(1 mark)*.

   b) E.g. a fixed resistor / an LDR in constant light conditions *(1 mark)*.

   c) Choose a point on the graph and read off the values — e.g. I = 0.20 A when V = 1 V.
   $V = I \times R$
   So $R = V \div I = 1 \div 0.20 = $ **5 Ω**
   (3 marks for correct answer, otherwise 1 mark for correct method to calculate resistance, 1 mark for values read correctly from Figure 2)

   d) i) E.g.

   (1 mark)

   ii) When an electrical charge flows through a filament lamp, it transfers some energy to the thermal energy store of the filament *(1 mark)*, which is designed to heat up and glow. Resistance increases with temperature *(1 mark)*, so as more current flows through the lamp, the lamp heats up more and the resistance increases, so the I-V graph gets shallower *(1 mark)*.

2 a) The potential difference across the battery is the same as the potential difference across the motor V = 14 V *(1 mark)*.

   b) i) $Q = I \times t$ *(1 mark)*

   ii) The current passing through the motor is found by:
   $I_{motor} = Q \div t = 15 \div 30 = $ **0.5 A**
   (3 marks for correct answer, otherwise 1 mark for correct rearrangement and 1 mark for correct substitution)

   c) The components are in parallel, so the sum of their currents is equal to the total current:
   $I_{total} = I_{motor} + I_{lamp}$
   $1.2 = 0.5 + I_{lamp}$
   $I_{lamp} = 1.2 - 0.5 = 0.7$ A
   The p.d. is the same as the battery p.d. (14 V)
   $E = I \times V \times t$
   $= 0.7 \times 14 \times 240$
   $= 2352 = $ **2400 J (to 2 s.f.)**
   (4 marks for correct answer, otherwise 1 mark for correct calculation of current, 1 mark for correct substitution and 1 mark for correct unrounded result)

3 a) P.d. = 230 V *(1 mark)*,
   frequency = 50 Hz *(1 mark)*.

   b) i) $P = E \div t$ *(1 mark)*

   ii) Power = 2.55 kW = 2550 W
   $t = E \div P$
   $= 7\ 038\ 000 \div 2550$
   $= $ **2760 s**
   (3 marks for correct answer, otherwise 1 mark for correct rearrangement and 1 mark for correct substitution)

   c) $E = Q \times V$
   $Q = E \div V$
   $= 7\ 038\ 000 \div 230 = $ **30 600 C**
   (4 marks for correct answer, otherwise 1 mark for correct equation, 1 mark for correct rearrangement and 1 mark for correct substitution)

4 a) $P = I \times V$
   $I = P \div V$
   $= 575 \div 230 = 2.5$ A
   $P = I^2 \times R$
   $R = P \div I^2$
   $= 575 \div 2.5^2 = $ **92 Ω**
   (5 marks for correct answer, otherwise 1 mark for recalling $P = I \times V$, 1 mark for recalling $P = I^2 \times R$, 1 mark for correct rearrangement of equations and 1 mark for correct calculation of current)

   b) How to grade your answer:
   Level 0: There is no relevant information.
   [0 marks]

   Level 1: A description is given as to how the fault may cause a fire or how a fuse works in a circuit. The points made are basic and not linked together.
   [1 to 2 marks]

   Level 2: A description is given as to how the fault may cause a fire and how a fuse functions in a circuit. Some of the points made are linked together.
   [3 to 4 marks]

   Level 3: A full, clear explanation is given as to how the fault causes the wires to heat up, which could lead to a fire. A description is given as to how a fuse works and how this reduces the risk of a fire when a fault occurs. The points made are well-linked and the answer has a clear and logical structure.
   [5 to 6 marks]

Here are some points your answer may include:
The fault allows current to flow through the case of the kettle.
The earth wire is connected to the metal case, so a current flows through the earth wire.
This causes a large current to flow, because the resistance of the earth wire is low.
When a current flows through a wire, it causes the live wire to heat up as work is done against electrical resistance.
The larger the current, the more the live wire heats up.
This heating may lead to a fire if it is not stopped.
Fuses melt when the current through them exceeds their rating.
The larger current through the kettle would cause the fuse to melt.
This breaks the circuit and stops a current from reaching the kettle.
This stops the heating effect and prevents a fire from starting.

Section 8a — Static Electricity

1. Static Electricity

Page 257 — Fact Recall Questions
Q1 Negatively charged electrons may be rubbed off the first insulator and onto the other insulator (due to friction), leaving the first insulator with a positive charge.
Q2 a) repel
    b) attract

Page 257 — Application Questions
Q1 a) All her hairs have the same charge (the opposite charge to the hair brush), so they will all repel each other, causing them to stand on end.
    b) + 0.5 nC
Q2 When a static charge has built up on the TV screen, it attracts nearby dust particles in the air by induction. By reducing the static on the screen, less dust will be attracted to the screen over time.

2. Uses of Static Electricity

Page 259 — Application Question
Q1 The electrostatic spray gun is charged, so that the droplets it sprays all gain a static charge. As all of the droplets have the same charge, they repel each other, creating a fine, even spray.

3. Sparking and the Dangers of Static Electricity

Page 262 — Fact Recall Questions
Q1 A spark is when electrons jump between a charged and earthed object (because the p.d. between them is so large).

Q2 When raindrops and bits of ice bump together inside storm clouds, friction causes the top of the cloud to become positively charged and the bottom of the cloud to become negatively charged. This creates a huge potential difference between the cloud and the earth and a big spark (lightning).
Q3 E.g. it can cause a spark when refuelling vehicles, which could lead to a fire or an explosion if the spark ignites the fuel.
Q4 Where an object is connected to the ground by a conductor so a static charge cannot build up on it/ excess charge is removed from a statically charged object.

Page 262 — Application Questions
Q1 Electrons move from the ground, up the conductor and to the positively charged object.
Q2 As the student walks up the staircase, the friction between their feet and the carpet causes electrons to be rubbed off one and deposited on the other. This causes the student to become charged. There is then a large p.d. between the student and earth. The metal hand-rail is an earthed conductor, so a spark jumps between it and the student as the student goes to touch it. This causes the student to feel a shock.
Q3 When a large enough static charge has built up in a storm cloud, there is a large enough potential difference that electrons can travel between the ground and the cloud (lightning). The lightning rod is grounded and is made from a conductor, so it provides an easy path for the electrons to travel along. This means that lightning will strike the rod instead of the building, stopping e.g. fires being caused or other damage being done to the building.

4. Electric Fields

Page 265 — Fact Recall Questions
Q1 Away from positive charge and towards negative charge.
Q2

You should have at least three equally spaced straight lines between the two plates.
Q3 An object with a large static charge has a large potential difference between it and the earth. A large potential difference creates a strong electric field. The strong electric field interacts with the electric fields of electrons in the air particles, causing a strong force. The strong force removes electrons from the air particles (the air is ionised). This makes the air conductive, and allows charge to flow in the form of a spark.

Page 266 — Static Electricity
Exam-style Questions

1   a) The force felt between the positively charged paint droplets and the negatively charged car body is attractive, so the droplets are attracted to the car body *(1 mark)*. If the paint droplets and car body were uncharged, there would be no electrostatic force between the droplets and the car, so less paint would reach the car body resulting in more waste *(1 mark)*.

   b) The car has a large static charge and so there is a large potential difference between it and the earth *(1 mark)*. This causes a strong electric field *(1 mark)*. The electric field ionises air particles near the car, so that the air can conduct electricity *(1 mark)*. The engineer is an earthed conductor *(1 mark)*, so a spark jumps across the gap from the car to the engineer *(1 mark)*.

2   a) A large static charge causes a large potential difference, which can lead to a spark *(1 mark)*. Sparks can ignite the petrol, leading to a fire or an explosion *(1 mark)*.

   b) Metal is a conductor, so charges can flow easily through it *(1 mark)*. Connecting the tank to the metal bar means that the tank is earthed, so charges can flow between the ground and the tank *(1 mark)*. This prevents the build up of a static charge and so reduces the risk of sparks *(1 mark)*.

   c) When he touches the tank, electrons *(1 mark)* move from the ground, up the bar and through the tank to the man *(1 mark)*.

3   a) When the scarf and balloon are rubbed against each other, electrons are removed from the balloon and left on the scarf, giving the scarf a negative charge *(1 mark)*.

   b) The balloon would move away from the rod *(1 mark)* because the balloon and rod are both positively charged and repel each other *(1 mark)*.

   c) The electric field around the balloon interacts with the electric fields of the electrons in the wall *(1 mark)*. This causes an attractive force between the electrons and the balloon, so the electrons move slightly towards the surface of the wall *(1 mark)*. This creates a negative charge on the surface of the wall, which creates an electric field that interacts with the electric field around the balloon. This causes the balloon and the wall to be attracted to each other and stick together *(1 mark)*.

   d)

You should have a minimum of eight equally spaced lines.
(1 mark for equally spaced field lines pointing radially outwards from the sphere)

Section 8b — Magnetism and Electromagnetism

1. Magnets and Magnetic Fields
Page 269 — Fact Recall Questions
Q1 It's a region where magnets experience a non-contact force acting on them.
Q2 An induced magnet is a magnetic material which only becomes a magnet (with its own magnetic field) when it is placed inside another magnetic field.
Q3 Any three from: e.g. iron, steel, nickel, cobalt.
Q4

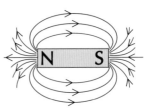

The field is strongest at the poles of the magnet.
Q5 a) Repel
   b) The magnetic fields of the two magnets interact with each other.
Q6 When not in the field of another magnet, the magnet in a compass points north. It is experiencing a magnetic force, so the Earth must have a magnetic field. For the Earth to have a magnetic field, its core must be magnetic.

2. Electromagnetism
Page 272 — Fact Recall Questions
Q1 The strength of the magnetic field increases.
Q2 The further away from a wire you get, the weaker the magnetic field is.
Q3 An electromagnet is a magnet whose magnetic field can be turned on and off with an electric current.
Q4 E.g. magnetic separators in recycling plants / to hold closed fridge doors / in cranes in scrapyards.

Page 272 — Application Questions
Q1 a) The current is flowing into the page.
   Curl the fingers of your right hand in the direction of the magnetic field (i.e. clockwise). Your thumb should point into the page.
   b) The magnetic field lines would also change direction — i.e. they'd point anti-clockwise.
Q2 a) When current flows in the circuit, the electromagnet has a magnetic field. The iron bolt is magnetised and attracted to the electromagnet so it moves towards it, bolting the door.
   b) When the circuit is opened, current stops flowing through the electromagnet. The electromagnet demagnetises and the iron bolt is no longer attracted to it. The spring pulls the iron bolt back across the doorway and the door can be opened.

3. The Motor Effect

Page 275 — Fact Recall Questions

Q1 Zero

The wire won't feel any force if it's parallel to the magnetic field — it'll experience the greatest force when it's at 90° to the magnetic field.

Q2 Any two from: by increasing the strength of the magnetic field / by increasing the current in the wire / by increasing the length of the wire inside the magnetic field.

Q3 The index finger is the field, the middle finger is the current and the thumb is the force (or motion).

Page 275 — Application Questions

Q1 a) Out of the page.
   b) Out of the page.
   c) Into the page.

Q2 Into the page.

Swapping both the current and the field will swap the direction of the force twice, with no overall effect.

Q3 $F = B \times I \times l$, so $l = F \div (B \times I)$
$l = 0.25 \div (0.20 \times 5.0) = 0.25$ m = **25 cm**

4. Using the Motor Effect

Page 279 — Fact Recall Questions

Q1 It reverses the direction of the current every half turn so that the force on each arm of the wire loop changes direction every half turn. This way the force is always acting in a direction that causes the coil to keep rotating.

Q2 By swapping the polarity of the d.c. supply or swapping the magnetic poles over.

It'll only be reversed if you swap one of these things. If you swap both it'll just carry on in the same direction. If you don't believe me, check it using Fleming's left-hand rule.

Q3 The paper cone of a loudspeaker is a attached to a coil of wire that sits around one pole of a permanent magnet, and is surrounded by the other pole. When a current flows through the coil, it experiences a force due to the motor effect. With an alternating current, the force changes direction every time the current does, moving the coil, and so the cone, backwards and forwards. This makes the air around the cone vibrate, creating variations in pressure (sound waves).

Page 279 — Application Question

Q1 a) anticlockwise
   b) It'll increase.
   c) The direction of rotation will be reversed.

5. Electromagnetic Induction

Page 284 — Fact Recall Questions

Q1 It's the creation of a potential difference across a conductor which is experiencing a change in an external magnetic field.

Q2 By causing a change in magnetic field by: moving a coil of wire into and out of a magnetic field / moving/changing an external magnetic field around a coil of wire.

Q3 E.g. by changing the direction of movement of the conductor/magnet / by reversing the polarity of the magnet.

Q4 Sound waves hit a flexible diaphragm that is attached to a coil of wire, wrapped around one pole of a cylindrical magnet, and entirely surrounded by the other pole. This causes the coil of wire to move back and forward in the magnetic field, which generates an alternating current. The generated current depends on the properties of the sound wave, so variations in sound are converted into variations in current.

Page 284 — Application Question

Q1 a) The windmill rotating will cause the axle, and therefore the coil of wire, to rotate. As the coil of wire turns inside the magnetic field, it cuts the field lines and a potential difference is induced across the ends of the coil of wire by the generator effect. The ends of the wire are connected to the bulb circuit by the slip rings, so a current will flow in the bulb circuit.
   b) Alternating current.

6. Transformers

Page 289 — Fact Recall Questions

Q1 An alternating potential difference/voltage.

Q2 When an alternating current flows through the primary coil it produces a magnetic field within the iron core. This field is constantly changing as the current changes direction, so it induces an alternating potential difference across the secondary coil by the generator effect. This p.d. will cause an alternating current to flow in the secondary coil if it is part of a complete circuit.

Q3 The electrical power input is equal to the electrical power output.

Page 289 — Application Questions

Q1 a) A step-up transformer — it has more turns on the secondary coil than on the primary coil.
   b) greater

Q2 The output power will be equal to the electrical power input, so $P = V_s \times I_s = 12 \times 10 =$ **120 W**.

Q3 $\dfrac{V_s}{V_p} = \dfrac{N_s}{N_p}$, so $V_s = \dfrac{N_s}{N_p} \times V_p = \dfrac{12}{8} \times 4 =$ **6 V**

Q4 $V_p \times I_p = V_s \times I_s$

So $I_p = \dfrac{V_s \times I_s}{V_p} = \dfrac{20 \times 100}{400} =$ **5 A**

7. The National Grid

Page 291 — Fact Recall Questions

Q1 A transformer changes the potential difference of an electrical supply. When electricity is transmitted, energy is lost through heating in the cables. This energy loss is greater for a higher current. Transmitting electricity at a high voltage reduces the current for the same amount of power, so transformers are used to increase the voltage, decrease the current and reduce the energy loss. Transformers are also used to decrease the voltage to safe levels again before the electricity reaches users.

Q2 A — power station
    B — step-up transformer
    C — pylons / electricity cables
    D — step-down transformer
    E — consumers

Page 291 — Application Question

Q1 a) 4.0 kA = 4.0 × 1000 = 4000 A
        $P = I^2 \times R = 4000 \times 3.0 =$ **48 000 000 W**
    b) Step-up transformers have more turns on their
        secondary coil than on their primary coil, so the
        p.d. across the secondary coil is larger than the
        p.d. across the primary coil, as $\frac{V_s}{V_p} = \frac{N_s}{N_p}$.

        Transformers are almost 100% efficient, so the
        input power is equal to the output power. This
        means that increasing the potential difference of
        the electricity decreases its current, as $P = I \times V$.
        This decreases the power lost due to the current
        heating the cable, as the power lost is proportional
        to the current squared ($P = I^2 \times R$). As power is the
        rate of energy transfer, this reduces the amount of
        energy wasted, which increases the efficiency of
        the national grid.

Pages 294-295 — Magnetism and Electromagnetism Exam-style Questions

1   a) A uniform magnetic field is one that has a constant
        strength everywhere (**1 mark**), so the magnetic
        field lines are evenly spaced, parallel, straight lines
        (**1 mark**).
    b) i)   Alternating current (**1 mark**)
        ii) Figure 1 (**1 mark**) shows an alternating
             potential difference, because the trace crosses
             the horizontal axis/the trace alternates between
             positive and negative (**1 mark**).
    c) E.g. increase the speed of the movement, so more
        field lines are being cut in a given time / increase
        the strength of the magnetic field, so there are
        more field lines to cut / add more coils of wire, so
        there are more wires to cut each field line.
        (**1 mark for correct method, 1 mark for a valid
        explanation of how this would increase the
        induced current**)

2   a) $V_p \times I_p = V_s \times I_s$ so $I_s = (V_p \times I_p) \div V_s$
        $I_s = (400 \times 50) \div 125 =$ **160 A**
        (**3 marks for correct answer, otherwise 1 mark
        for correct rearrangement and 1 mark for correct
        substitution.**)
    b) How to grade your answer:
        Level 0: There is no relevant information.
                  [0 marks]
        Level 1: There is a brief explanation of how
                  transformers are used in the national
                  grid. The points made are basic and
                  not linked together. **[1 to 2 marks]**
        Level 2: There is some explanation of both how
                  transformers are used in the national
                  grid and how energy lost to heating
                  relates to the current through a wire.
                  Some of the points made are linked
                  together. **[3 to 4 marks]**

Level 3: There is a clear and detailed
          explanation of how transformers
          are used to lower current before
          transmission and why this reduces the
          energy lost. The points made are well-
          linked and the answer has a clear and
          logical structure. **[5 to 6 marks]**

Here are some points your answer may include:
The national grid transfers lots of energy every
second, so it has a high power.
A high electrical power requires electricity to be at
a high potential difference or have a high current.
A high current causes wires to heat up, which
causes energy to be lost/dissipated to the
surroundings.
Transformers can increase the potential difference
of a supply.
Increasing the potential difference decreases the
current for a given power, and so decreases the
energy lost because of heating.
So using transformers makes the national grid
more efficient, as less energy is being wasted.
    c) E.g. If direct current is supplied, a magnetic
        field will be induced in the core but it won't be
        constantly changing (**1 mark**). If the magnetic field
        in the core isn't constantly changing, no potential
        difference will be induced in the secondary coil by
        the generator effect (**1 mark**).
    d) Rearranging $\frac{V_p}{V_s} = \frac{N_p}{N_s}$:
        $V_s = \frac{N_s}{N_p} \times V_p$
        $V_s = (30 \div 60) \times 100 =$ **50 V**
        (**3 marks for correct answer, otherwise 1 mark
        for correct rearrangement and 1 mark for correct
        substitution.**)

3   a) Reversing the direction of the magnetic field
        reverses the direction of the force caused by the
        motor effect (**1 mark**), so the motor turns in the
        opposite direction (anticlockwise) (**1 mark**).
    b) $F = B \times I \times l$
        $F = 0.20 \times 30 \times 0.0050$
        $F = 0.0030$ N
        There are four wires in total, and the above force
        on each wire, so the total force is
        $F = 0.0030 \times 4 =$ **0.012 N**
        (**2 marks for correct answer, otherwise 1 mark for
        correct calculation of the force for one wire.**)
    c) When the d.c. supply is turned on a current flows
        through the coil of wire (**1 mark**). When current
        flows through a wire, a magnetic field is produced
        around it, so the electromagnet becomes magnetic
        (**1 mark**).
    d) An alternating current supply would not be
        suitable because the direction of the current
        would be constantly changing (**1 mark**). This
        would cause the direction of the magnetic field to
        constantly change (**1 mark**), which would cause
        the direction of rotation of the coil (and hence
        the screwdriver) to constantly change, making it
        unable to function as intended (**1 mark**).

Section 9a — The Particle Model

1. Density

Page 298 — Fact Recall Questions
Q1 density = mass ÷ volume ($\rho = m \div v$)
Q2 Mass balance, eureka (or displacement) can and measuring cylinder.

Page 298 — Application Questions
Q1 The volume of the block is:
$0.030 \times 0.045 \times 0.060 = 0.000081$ m³
$\rho = m \div V = 0.324 \div 0.000081 =$ **4000 kg/m³**
Don't forget to convert the lengths into metres, or convert the mass to g if you want to find the answer in g/cm³.
Q2 From the diagram: $m = 10.8$ g, $V = 12$ ml $= 12$ cm³
$\rho = m \div V = 10.8 \div 12 =$ **0.9 g/cm³**

2. States of Matter

Page 300 — Fact Recall Questions
Q1 Solid, liquid, gas.
Q2 The particles in a solid are held close together by strong forces in a fixed, regular arrangement. The particles don't have much energy and so can't move around — they can only vibrate about fixed positions. In a liquid, the particles are still close to each other, but unlike in a solid, they're able to move past each other and form irregular arrangements as the forces of attraction between particles are weaker. The particles in a liquid also have more energy than in a solid — they can move in random directions at low speeds. There are almost no forces of attraction between particles in a gas so they can move far apart from each other. The particles have more energy than those in liquids and solids — they can move in random directions at high speeds.

Page 300 — Application Question
Q1 a) E.g. The balls represent the particles of a solid — they don't swap positions, they're close together and are arranged in a (fairly) regular pattern.
b) A gas.
c) The particles in a solid are packed closely together without much of a gap between them, like the balls in the box when the fan is switched off. So solids are generally quite dense (relative to the other states of matter) because they have lots of mass (particles) in a given volume. In a gas, the particles are spread much further apart, with large gaps between them, like the balls in the box when the fan is switched on. This means that gases are much less dense than solids, because there is less mass in a given volume.

3. Internal Energy and Changes of State

Page 303 — Fact Recall Questions
Q1 The internal energy of a system is the total energy that its particles have in their kinetic and potential energy stores.

Q2 The energy in the kinetic energy stores of the particles increases, which makes them move around faster.
Q3 The coldest temperature theoretically possible. At this temperature, particles have as little energy in their kinetic energy stores as it's possible to have.
Q4 Freezing, melting, boiling/evaporating, condensing and sublimating.
Q5 A physical change means that you don't end up with a new substance — it's the same substance as you started with, just in a different form.
Q6 Yes, a change of state does conserve mass. The number of particles in a substance doesn't change when the substance changes state. Only the arrangement and energy of the particles changes.

Page 303 — Application Questions
Q1 $89 - 273 =$ **–184 °C**
Q2 The system is changing state, e.g. freezing/condensing.

4. Specific Heat Capacity

Page 306 — Fact Recall Questions
Q1 The amount of energy needed to change the temperature of 1 kg of a substance by 1°C.
Q2 J/kg °C
Q3 Thermally insulated containers reduce unwanted energy transfers from the thermal energy store of the water to the surroundings. This will make the final result more accurate (as you assume in the experiment that all the energy transferred from the heater is transferred to the thermal energy store of the water).

Page 306 — Application Questions
Q1 $\Delta\theta = 100.0$ °C $- 20.0$ °C $= 80.0$ °C
$\Delta Q = m \times c \times \Delta\theta$
$= 0.200 \times 4200 \times 80.0 =$ **67 200 J**
Q2 $m = 400$ g $= 400 \div 1000 = 0.4$ kg
$\Delta\theta = 113$ °C $- 25$ °C $= 88$ °C
$\Delta Q = 70.4 \times 1000 = 70\ 400$ J
$\Delta Q = m \times c \times \Delta\theta$
$c = \Delta Q \div (m \times \Delta\theta) = 70\ 400 \div (0.4 \times 88)$
$=$ **2000 J/kg°C**

5. Specific Latent Heat

Page 309 — Fact Recall Questions
Q1 The amount of energy needed to change 1 kg of a substance from one state to another without changing its temperature.
Q2 J/kg
Q3 Specific heat capacity is related to a temperature rise of 1 °C, whereas specific latent heat is related to changes of state, where the temperature remains constant.

Q4 E.g. fill a beaker with crushed ice and place a thermometer into the beaker. Measure the initial temperature of the ice. Then, start a stop watch and turn on the Bunsen burner. Every twenty seconds, record the temperature and the current state of the ice. Continue this process until all of the ice has turned into water and the water then begins to boil. At this point, stop the stopwatch and turn off the Bunsen burner. Using your results, plot a graph of temperature against time for your experiment.

Q5

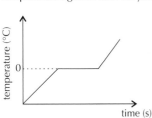

Page 309 — Application Questions

Q1 25.0 g $= 25.0 \div 1000 = 0.0250$ kg
$Q = m \times L = 0.0250 \times 334\,000 = 8350$ J

Q2 $Q = m \times L$ so $m = Q \div L = 4\,960\,000 \div 1\,550\,000$
$= \textbf{3.20 kg}$

6. Particle Motion in Gases

Page 312 — Fact Recall Questions

Q1 The particles move about at high speeds and collide with the walls of the container, exerting a force on them. Pressure is force per unit area, so the particles exert a pressure.

Q2 The higher the temperature of a gas, the higher the average energy in the kinetic stores of its particles (heating the gas will transfer energy into the kinetic stores of its particles). This means the particles will collide with the walls of a container more often and with greater speed, so they will exert a higher force. This means the pressure will be greater.

Q3 Inversely proportional

Q4 The pressure will decrease. This is because the particles will be more spread out, so there will be less frequent collisions with the walls of the container. This means the overall force exerted due to the collisions will decrease, and so will the pressure.

Q5 The temperature increases.

Page 312 — Application Questions

Q1 $P_1 \times V_1 = P_2 \times V_2$, so:
$P_1 = (P_2 \times V_2) \div V_1$
$P = (30 \times 110) \div 75 = \textbf{44 Pa}$

Q2 The volume of the balloon will decrease. When it is inside the refrigerator, the temperature of the helium inside the balloon will drop. Energy will be transferred away from the kinetic stores of the helium particles, and they will move more slowly. Less frequent collisions with the walls of the balloon means the gas pressure inside the balloon will decrease. When this pressure becomes less than the air pressure outside the balloon, the balloon will start to shrink until the pressures are balanced.

Pages 315-316 — The Particle Model
Exam-style Questions

1 a) **A** *(1 mark)*
   b) $V = m \div \rho = 450 \div 9 = \textbf{50 cm}^3$
      (3 marks for correct answer, otherwise 1 mark for correct rearrangement and 1 mark for correct substitution)
   c) **C** *(1 mark)*
   d) It is a liquid *(1 mark)*. It started off as a solid, but the flat spot on the graph shows the point at which it changes state and melts into a liquid *(1 mark)*.
      If there was a second flat spot on the graph, this would show another change of state, so the substance would've changed from liquid into gas.
   e) The mass is 450 g *(1 mark)*. This is because a change of state conserves mass (the number of particles doesn't change, they're just arranged differently) *(1 mark)*.

2 a) $P_1 \times V_1 = P_2 \times V_2$,
      so $V_1 = (P_2 \times V_2) \div P_1$
      $= (220 \times 30) \div 150 = \textbf{44 cm}^3$
      (3 marks for correct answer, otherwise 1 mark for correct rearrangement and 1 mark for correct substitution)
   b) When the volume decreases, the particles have less distance to travel between the walls, so they collide with the walls of the container more often *(1 mark)*. This means the total force exerted due to collisions increases, and so the pressure increases *(1 mark)*.
   c) Density before $= m \div V$
      $= 0.132 \div 44$
      $= 0.003$ g/cm^3
      You'll still get the marks for using an incorrect value of V from part a), as long as you do everything else right.
      Density after $= m \div V$
      $= 0.132 \div 30 = 0.0044$ g/cm^3
      So the difference in density
      $= 0.0044 - 0.003 = \textbf{0.0014 g/cm}^3$
      (4 marks for correct answer, otherwise 1 mark for correct rearrangement, 1 mark for correct calculation of density before and 1 mark for correct calculation of density after)
   d) $Q = m \times L$
      So $L = Q \div m$
      $= 5.0 \div (0.132 \times 10^{-3})$
      $= 37\,878.7...$ J/kg
      $37\,878.7... \div 1000 = 37.87... = \textbf{38 kJ/kg (to 2 s.f.)}$
      (4 marks for correct answer, otherwise 1 mark for correct rearrangement, 1 mark for correct substitution and 1 mark for correct numerical answer in J/kg)

3 a) E.g. care must be taken when handling the heating element and hot water to avoid being burnt *(1 mark)*.
   b) E.g. wrapping the beaker in a thermal insulator *(1 mark)*.

c) $\Delta Q = 189 \times 1000 = 189\,000$ J
$\Delta \theta = 100.0\,°C - 10.0\,°C = 90.0\,°C$
$\Delta Q = m \times c \times \Delta \theta$, so
$c = \Delta Q \div (m \times \Delta \theta)$
$= 189\,000 \div (0.50 \times 90.0)$
$= \mathbf{4200\ J/kg°C}$
(3 marks for correct answer, otherwise 1 mark for correct rearrangement and 1 mark for correct substitution)

4 a) Pumping air into the mattress means that the number of air particles inside the mattress will increase *(1 mark)*. This means there will be more frequent collisions between the air particles and the inside walls of the mattress — i.e. there will be an increase in gas pressure *(1 mark)*. As the gas pressure becomes greater than atmospheric pressure, the mattress/volume will expand, so that the pressure inside it remains at the same level as atmospheric pressure *(1 mark)*.

    b) Pressure is applied to the plunger of the foot pump by the gas inside the mattress, and so a force is exerted on it *(1 mark)*. Work is done against this force *(1 mark)*, which transfers energy to the kinetic energy stores of the air particles, increasing the temperature *(1 mark)*.

Section 9b — Forces and Matter

1. Fluid Pressure

Page 320 — Fact Recall Questions
Q1 Pressure is force per unit area.
Q2 pressure (Pa) = force normal to a surface (N)
           $\div$ area of that surface (m^2) ($P = F \div A$)
Q3 The force due to pressure acts normal (at 90°) to the surface of the fluid.
Q4 a) The pressure of a liquid increases with increasing depth.
    b) Pressure increases with depth because the weight of the liquid above adds to the pressure, and the greater the depth, the more liquid there is above.
Q5 Atmospheric pressure decreases with increasing altitude because as altitude increases the density of the surrounding air decreases and the amount of air above that point decreases. Both of these factors reduce the rate of collisions of air particles with a surface, and thus reduce the atmospheric pressure at that point.

Page 320 — Application Questions
Q1 Area needs to be converted from cm^2 to m^2:
    $320.0 \div 10\,000 = 0.03200$ m^2
    Rearrange $P = \dfrac{F}{A}$ for force:
    $F = P \times A = 101\,000 \times 0.03200 = \mathbf{3232\ N}$
Q2 $P = h \times \rho \times g = 5.0 \times 1030 \times 10$
    $= 51\,500 = \mathbf{52\,000\ Pa\ (to\ 2\ s.f.)}$

2. Upthrust

Page 322 — Fact Recall Questions
Q1 When the object is partially (or completely) submerged in the liquid, there will be forces acting on the object from all sides due to pressure in the liquid. The pressure from the liquid on the bottom of the object is greater than the pressure at the top of the object. Upthrust is the resultant upwards force from this.
Q2 Float.
Q3 Sink.
Q4 The object will never be able to displace an amount of water that is equal to its weight, so the object's weight will always be greater than the upthrust, and so it will sink.

Page 322 — Application Question
Q1 a) The density of the object is higher than that of the water, so the object will sink.
    b) The object has the same density as before, so will still sink.
    The object has a uniform density, so changing its volume won't affect the density. The volume of the object is not important, it's just the density that affects whether it will sink or float.

3. Forces and Elasticity

Page 326 — Fact Recall Questions
Q1 If only one force is applied to an object, then the object will just move in the direction of the force.
Q2 An elastic object can return to its original shape after all forces have been removed from it.
Q3 For an elastic distortion, once the distorting forces are removed, the object will return to its original shape. After an inelastic distortion, the object cannot return to its original shape once the forces are removed.
Q4 It means that force and extension are directly proportional to each other — if the force increased, the extension would increase by the same factor. The force-extension graph for a linear relationship is a straight line.
Q5 force exerted on a spring (N)
    = spring constant (N/m) × extension (m) ($F = k \times x$)
Q6 The limit of proportionality is the point beyond which the extension of an object will no longer be proportional to the force applied to the object.
Q7 All the energy is released, because all the energy transferred ends up in the spring's elastic potential energy store, and all of the energy is transferred out of that store when the spring is released.

Page 326 — Application Questions
Q1 Extension = 0.75 − 0.50 = 0.25 m
    $F = k \times x = 34 \times 0.25 = \mathbf{8.5\ N}$
Q2 Point B.
    The limit of proportionality is always the point at which a force-extension graph starts to curve.
Q3 a) Compression = 16 − 12 = 4 cm
       In metres, this is 4 ÷ 100 = 0.04 m
       Rearrange $F = k \times x$ for k:
       $k = F \div x = 0.80 \div 0.04 = \mathbf{20\ N/m}$

b) $E = \frac{1}{2} \times k \times x^2 = \frac{1}{2} \times 20 \times 0.04^2 = \textbf{0.016 J}$
c) Spring B's spring constant is higher than that of spring A.

You can work this out from $F = k \times x$. If x is smaller, then k must be larger to keep F the same.

4. Investigating Springs

Page 329 — Fact Recall Questions
Q1 A pilot experiment allows you to find the size of masses that should be used in order to record enough measurements to plot a straight line force-extension graph (the part of the graph up until the limit of proportionality is reached).
Q2 E.g. Safety goggles should be worn to protect the eyes if the spring snaps.
Q3 The work done is equal to the area under the force-extension graph.

Page 329 — Application Question
Q1 a)

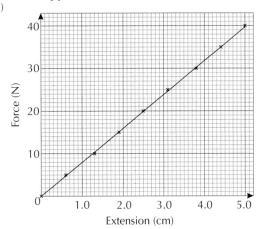

b) The area under the graph up to 2.5 cm extension is equal to the work done.
Area = area of triangle = $\frac{1}{2} \times$ base $\times$ height
Base = 2.5 cm = 2.5 ÷ 100 = 0.025 m
Height = 20 N
Area = $\frac{1}{2} \times 0.025 \times 20 = \textbf{0.25 J}$

Pages 331-332 — Forces and Matter Exam-style Questions

1 a) i) Force = spring constant × compression
or $F = k \times x$ **(1 mark)**
   ii) The weight of the mass is the force that is acting on the spring, so use the equation $F = k \times x$.
Calculate the compression first:
$x = 165 - 140$
$= 25$ mm
Convert the compression to m:
$25 ÷ 1000 = 0.025$ m
Then substitute the values into the equation for force:
$F = k \times x = 160 \times 0.025$
$= \textbf{4.0 N}$
(3 marks for correct answer, otherwise 1 mark for correct calculation of compression in m and 1 mark for correct substitution)
b) $E = \frac{1}{2} \times k \times x^2 = \frac{1}{2} \times 160 \times 0.025^2$
$= \textbf{0.05 J}$
(2 marks for correct answer, otherwise 1 mark for correct substitution)
c) i) Pressure = Force ÷ Area ($P = F ÷ A$) **(1 mark)**
   ii) F is the weight of the object = 4.0 N from part a)
$P = F ÷ A = 4.0 ÷ 0.025 = \textbf{160 Pa}$
(2 marks for correct answer, otherwise 1 mark for correct substitution)

If you get the wrong answer for part a), you won't lose marks for getting the wrong answer here, so long as you use the correct method.

2 a) When a force of 0.70 N was applied to the spring, the limit of proportionality of the spring may have been passed, and so the graph would have started to curve, and the data point would be in the right position **(1 mark)**. E.g. the student could increase the force acting on the spring to see whether the data points continue to follow the straight line of best fit, or whether the line of best fit should start to curve **(1 mark)**.
b) If the spring has been stretched too far, it will no longer distort elastically, and so it could not be used again for the same experiment **(1 mark)**.
c) Work done = area under the graph
Area = area of triangle
$= \frac{1}{2} \times$ base $\times$ height
Base = 15.0 ÷ 100 = 0.15 m
Height = 0.40 N
Area = $\frac{1}{2} \times 0.150 \times 0.40 = \textbf{0.03 J}$
(3 marks for correct answer, otherwise 1 mark for statement of work done = area under the graph and 1 mark for correct method to calculate the area)

3   a) $P = h \times \rho \times g$
       $= 0.700 \times 13\,500 \times 10.0 = $ **94 500 Pa**
       (2 marks for correct answer, otherwise 1 mark for correct substitution)

    b) How to grade your answer:
        Level 0:   There is no relevant information.
                   [0 marks]
        Level 1:   There is a brief explanation of either density or weight of air above a point contributing to atmospheric pressure. The points made are basic and not linked together. *[1-2 marks]*
        Level 2:   There is some explanation of both density and weight of air above a point contributing to atmospheric pressure. Some of the points made are linked together. *[3-4 marks]*
        Level 3:   There is a clear and detailed explanation of both density and weight of air above a point contributing to atmospheric pressure. The points made are well-linked and the answer has a clear and logical structure. *[5-6 marks]*

        Here are some points your answer may include:
        As altitude increases, the density of the air in the atmosphere decreases.
        This means that there are fewer air particles in a given space.
        So there are fewer collisions with a surface in a given time.
        This reduces the force, and thus pressure, on a surface.
        As altitude increases, there is also less atmosphere/air above the surface.
        So the weight of the air particles above the surface is less.
        This decreases the force on the surface, thus decreases the overall pressure on the surface.

4   a) i)   The liquid must be denser than the cube — objects float if their density is less than the density of liquid they are in *(1 mark)*.
        ii) When an object floats, its upthrust is equal to its weight *(1 mark)* so the upthrust acting on the block is 6.144 N *(1 mark)*.

    b) i) $P = F \div A$
             $P = 6.144 \div 0.0064 = $ **960 Pa**
             (3 marks for correct answer, otherwise 1 mark for correctly recalling P = F ÷ A and 1 mark for correct substitution)
        ii) $P = h \times \rho \times g$ so $\rho = P \div (h \times g)$
             $h = 5.00$ cm $= 0.0500$ m
             $\rho = 960 \div (0.0500 \times 10)$
             $= $ **1920 kg/m³**
        (3 marks for correct answer, otherwise 1 mark for correct rearrangement of P = h × ρ × g and 1 mark for correct substitution into the rearranged equation)

Glossary

A

Absolute zero
Theoretically the coldest temperature an object could reach. At absolute zero, particles have the minimum amount of energy in their kinetic energy stores. Absolute zero is at 0 K, or −273 °C.

Absorbed radiation dose
The amount of radiation (and so the amount of energy) absorbed by a person's body.

Absorption
When a wave transfers energy to the energy stores of a material.

Absorption spectrum
A spectrum showing visible light, with dark lines where certain frequencies have been absorbed.

Acceleration
A measure of how quickly velocity is changing.

Accurate result
A result that is very close to the true answer.

Activity (radioactivity)
The number of nuclei of a sample that decay per second, measured in Bq.

Alpha decay
A type of radioactive decay in which an alpha particle is given out from a decaying nucleus.

Alpha particle
A positively-charged particle made up of two protons and two neutrons (a helium nucleus).

Alternating current (a.c.)
A current where the charges are constantly changing direction.

Alternator
A device which generates an a.c. supply using electromagnetic induction.

Ammeter
A component used to measure the current through a component. It is always connected in series with the component.

Amplitude
The maximum displacement of a point on a wave from its rest position.

Angle of incidence
The angle the incident ray of a wave makes with the normal at a boundary.

Angle of reflection
The angle a reflected ray makes with the normal at a boundary.

Angle of refraction
The angle a refracted ray makes with the normal when a wave refracts at a boundary.

Anomalous result
A result that doesn't seem to fit with the rest of the data.

Aperture (of a telescope)
The diameter of the objective lens.

Artificial satellite
A man-made satellite normally orbiting the Earth in a fairly circular orbit.

Asteroid
A lump of rock and metals that orbits the Sun.

Atmospheric pressure
The pressure felt by any surface within the atmosphere, due to air molecules colliding with the surface.

Atom
A small particle that makes up matter. It is made up of a small, central, positively charged nucleus, consisting of protons and neutrons, surrounded by negatively charged electrons.

Atomic (proton) number
The number of protons in the nucleus of an atom.

Attraction by induction
See electrostatic induction.

Axis (of a lens)
A line passing through the middle of a lens, perpendicular to the lens.

B

Background radiation
The low-level radiation which surrounds us at all times, arising from both natural and man-made sources.

Beta decay
A type of radioactive decay in which a beta-minus or beta-particle is given out from a decaying nucleus.

Beta-minus particle
A high-speed electron emitted from the nucleus.

Beta-plus particle
A high-speed positron emitted from the nucleus.

Bias
Unfairness in the way data is presented, possibly because the presenter is trying to make a particular point (sometimes without knowing they're doing it).

Big Bang theory
The idea that the Universe began from a small, very hot and dense region of space, which exploded and has been expanding ever since.

Bio-fuel
A renewable energy resource made from plant products or animal dung.

Black hole
A super dense point in space that nothing can escape from.

Braking distance
The braking distance is the distance a vehicle travels after the brakes are applied until it comes to a complete stop, as a result of the braking force.

C

Calibrate
Measure something with a known quantity to see if the instrument being used to measure that quantity gives the correct value.

Carbon neutral fuel
A fuel is carbon neutral if it absorbs as much CO_2 from the atmosphere (when it's produced/grown) as it releases when it's burned.

Categoric data
Data that comes in distinct categories, e.g. type of energy source (coal, oil, wind).

Centripetal force
The resultant force that acts on any object moving in a circle. It acts towards the centre of the circle.

Chain reaction
A reaction which keeps going (without any outside input) because the products of the reaction cause further reactions (e.g. nuclear fission).

Circuit breaker
A circuit component that 'trips' and breaks the circuit when the current through it goes above a certain point. They are used to protect circuits and to prevent electrical fires and electric shocks.

Closed system
A system where the net energy transfer is zero.

Comet
A lump of ice and dust that orbits the Sun in a highly elliptical orbit.

Conduction
A method of energy transfer by heating where vibrating particles transfer energy through a material by colliding with neighbouring particles and transferring energy between their kinetic energy stores.

Conductor (electrical)
A material in which electrical charges can easily move.

Conservation of energy principle
Energy can be transferred usefully from one energy store to another, stored or dissipated — but it can never be created or destroyed.

Conservation of momentum
In a system where no external forces act (a closed system), the momentum before a collision is equal to the momentum after the collision.

Contact force
A force that only acts between touching objects.

Contamination
The presence of unwanted radioactive atoms on or inside an object.

Continuous data
Numerical data that can have any value within a range (e.g. length, volume or temperature).

Control experiment
An experiment that's kept under the same conditions as the rest of the investigation, but where the independent variable isn't altered.

Control group
A group that matches the one being studied, but where the independent variable isn't altered. The group is kept under the same conditions as the group in the experiment.

Control rod
A rod used to absorb excess neutrons to control the chain reaction in a nuclear reactor.

Control variable
A variable in an experiment that is kept the same.

Converging lens
A lens that bulges outwards and causes rays of light parallel to the axis to converge (come together) at the principal focus.

Conversion factor
A number which you must multiply or divide a unit by to convert it to a different unit.

Correlation
A relationship between two variables.

Cosmic microwave background (CMB) radiation
Radiation mainly in the microwave section of the electromagnetic spectrum that is present all over the Universe. It is thought to be leftover energy from the initial Big Bang explosion that has cooled over time.

Cosmic ray
Radiation from space.

Critical angle
The angle of incidence above which total internal reflection occurs.

Current
The flow of electric charge. The size of the current is the rate of flow of charge. It is measured in amperes (A).

D

Density
A substance's mass per unit volume.

Dependent variable
The variable in an experiment that is measured.

Diffuse reflection
When parallel waves are reflected by a rough surface (e.g. a piece of paper) and the reflected rays are scattered in lots of different directions.

Diode
A circuit component that only allows current to flow through it in one direction. It has a very high resistance in the other direction.

Direct current (d.c.)
A current where the charges only move in one direction.

Directly proportional
Two variables are directly proportional if an increase in one variable causes the second variable to increase by the same percentage.

Discrete data
Numerical data that can only take a certain value, with no in-between value (e.g. number of people).

Displacement
The straight-line distance and direction from a given position to an object's current position.

Distance/time graph
A graph showing how the distance travelled by an object changes over a period of time.

Dissipation
The transfer of energy to thermal stores of an object and its surroundings. Also called wasted energy.

Diverging lens
A lens that curves inwards and causes rays of light parallel to the axis to diverge (spread out) so they appear to have come from the principal focus.

Doppler effect
The observed change in wavelength and frequency of waves emitted by a source moving relative to the observer.

Dwarf planet
A planet-like object in space that orbits a star but which doesn't meet all of the rules for being a planet.

Dynamo
A device which generates a d.c. supply using electromagnetic induction.

Ear drum
The part of the ear which vibrates when sound waves enter the ear. It passes on these vibrations to other parts of the ear, which convert them to electrical signals that are sent to the brain.

Earth wire
The green and yellow wire in an electrical cable that only carries current when there's a fault. It stops exposed metal parts of an appliance from becoming live. It is at 0 V.

Earthing
Connecting a charged object to the ground using a conductor.

Efficiency
The proportion of energy supplied to a device which is usefully transferred.

Elastic distortion
An object undergoing elastic distortion will return to its original shape once any forces being applied to it are removed.

Elastic limit
The point beyond which objects are inelastically distorted.

Elastic object
An object which can be elastically distorted.

Electric field
The region around a charged object where, if a second charged object was placed inside it, a force would be exerted on both of the charges.

Electrostatic force
The non-contact force which acts to bring together opposite charges (attraction) / push apart like charges (repulsion).

Electromagnet
A magnet whose magnetic field can be turned on and off by an electric current.

Electromagnetic induction
The induction of a potential difference across a conductor which is experiencing a change in an external magnetic field. If the conductor is part of a complete circuit, this will cause a current to flow.

Electromagnetic (EM) spectrum
A continuous spectrum of all the possible wavelengths of electromagnetic waves.

Electron
A subatomic particle with a relative charge of −1 and a relative mass of 1/2000.

Electrostatic induction
Electrostatic attraction between a charged and an uncharged object. Caused by the induction of a small charge on the surface of the uncharged object.

Energy level
A fixed distance for the orbit of an electron around the nucleus of an atom, also called a shell.

Energy store
A means by which an object stores energy. Common energy stores are: thermal, kinetic, gravitational potential, elastic potential, chemical, magnetic, electrostatic and nuclear.

Equilibrium
A state in which all the forces acting on an object are balanced, so the resultant force is zero.

Eureka can
A beaker with a spout that is used to determine the volume of irregularly shaped objects. It is also known as a displacement can.

Fixed resistor
A resistor whose resistance doesn't vary with current.

Fleming's left-hand rule
The rule used to work out the direction of the force produced by the motor effect. Your first finger points in the direction of the magnetic field, your second finger points in the direction of the current and your thumb points in the direction of the force (or motion).

Fluid
A substance that can flow — either a liquid or a gas.

Focal length (of a lens)
The distance from the centre of a lens to its principal focus.

Force
A push or a pull on an object caused by it interacting with something.

Fossil fuel
The fossil fuels are coal, oil and natural gas. They're non-renewable energy resources that we burn to generate electricity.

Free body force diagram
A diagram that shows all the forces acting on an isolated object, the directions in which the forces are acting and their (relative) magnitudes.

Frequency
The number of complete waves passing a certain point per second, or the number of waves produced by a source per second. Measured in hertz, Hz.

Frequency density
The height of a bar on a histogram. It is found by the frequency divided by the class width.

Friction
A force that opposes an object's motion. It acts in the opposite direction to motion.

Fuse
A circuit component that contains a thin piece of wire which melts when the current through the fuse goes above a certain point. Fuses are used to protect circuits and to prevent electrical fires and electric shocks.

G

Gamma decay
A type of radioactive decay in which a gamma ray is given out from a decaying nucleus.

Gamma ray
A high-frequency, short-wavelength electromagnetic wave.

Gear
A circular disc with teeth round its edge. It can be used to transmit the rotational effect of a force.

Geiger-Müller tube
A particle detector that is used with a counter to measure count rate.

Geocentric model
A model of the Solar System, with the Earth at the centre being orbited by the Sun, Moon and the other planets.

Gravitational potential energy (GPE) store
Anything that has mass and is in a gravitational field has energy in its gravitational potential energy store.

Greenhouse effect
The process where greenhouse gases in the Earth's atmosphere block radiation from the Sun from leaving the atmosphere, causing global warming.

 H

Half-life
The time taken for half the undecayed nuclei in a sample of a radioactive isotope to decay.
OR
The time taken for the activity of a radioactive source to decay by half.

Hazard
Something that has the potential to cause harm (e.g. fire, electricity, etc.).

Heliocentric model
A model of the Solar System, with the Sun at the centre being orbited by the planets.

Hydroelectric power station
A power station in which a dam is built across a valley or river. This holds back water, forming a reservoir. Water is allowed to flow out of the reservoir through turbines at a controlled rate. This turns the turbines, which are attached to generators and can generate electricity.

Hypothesis
A possible explanation for a scientific observation.

 I

Independent variable
The variable in an experiment that is changed.

Induced (temporary) magnet
A magnetic material that only has its own magnetic field, and behaves as a magnet, while it is inside another magnetic field.

Inelastic distortion
An object undergoing inelastic distortion will not return to its original shape once the forces being applied to it are removed.

Inertia
The tendency of an object to remain stationary or continue travelling at a constant velocity.

Inertial mass
The ratio of the force on an object over its acceleration.

Infrasound
Sound with a frequency less than 20 Hz.

Instantaneous velocity
The velocity of an object at a particular moment in time.

Insulator (electrical)
A material in which electrical charges cannot easily move.

Internal energy
The total energy that a system's particles have in their kinetic and potential energy stores.

Intensity
The power per unit area, i.e. how much energy is transferred to a given area in a certain amount of time. Its units are W/m^2.

Ion
An atom in which the number of electrons is different to the number of protons, giving it an overall charge.

Ionising radiation
Radiation that has enough energy to knock electrons off atoms.

Irradiation
Exposure to radiation from an external source.

Isotopes
Atoms with the same nuclear charge but which can have different nuclear masses.

 K

Kinetic energy store
Anything that's moving has energy in its kinetic energy store.

Kinetic theory of matter
A theory explaining how particles in matter behave by modelling these particles as tiny balls.

 L

Law of reflection
That the angle of incidence always equals the angle of reflection.

Lever
A device that increases the distance between an applied force and a pivot. It transmits the rotational effect of a force.

Light-dependent resistor (LDR)
A resistor whose resistance is dependent on light intensity. The resistance decreases as light intensity increases.

Limit of proportionality
The point beyond which the force applied to an elastic object is no longer directly proportional to the extension of the object.

Live wire
The brown wire in an electrical cable that carries an alternating current from the mains. It is at 230 V.

Longitudinal wave
A wave in which the oscillations are parallel to the direction the wave travels.

Lubricant
A substance (usually a liquid) that can flow easily between two objects. Used to reduce friction between surfaces.

M

Magnetic field
A region where magnetic materials (like iron and steel) and current-carrying wires experience a force.

Magnetic flux density
The number of magnetic field lines per unit area. Its symbol is B and it is measured in tesla, T.

Magnetic material
A material (such as iron, steel, cobalt or nickel) which can become an induced magnet while it's inside another magnetic field.

Main sequence star
A star in the main sequence of its life, which is stable because the nuclear fusion in the star provides an outward pressure that balances the inward pull of gravity.

Mass (nucleon) number
The number of neutrons and protons in the nucleus of an atom.

Material interface
The boundary between two different materials.

Mean (average)
A measure of average found by adding up all the data and dividing by the number of values there are.

Median (average)
A measure of average found by selecting the middle value from a data set arranged in ascending order.

Mode (average)
A measure of average found by selecting the most frequent value from a data set.

Model
Used to describe or display how an object or system behaves in reality.

Moderator
A substance such as graphite that slows down fast-moving neutrons in a nuclear reactor.

Molecule
Two or more atoms joined together.

Moment
The turning effect of a force.

Momentum
A property of a moving object that is the product of its mass and velocity.

Motor effect
When interacting magnetic fields around two separate objects results in the movement of one of the objects.

N

National grid
The network of transformers and cables that distributes electrical power from power stations to consumers.

Natural satellite
A natural object which orbits a second, more massive object, e.g. a moon.

Nebula
A cloud of dust and gas in space.

Neutral wire
The blue wire in an electrical cable that completes the circuit and carries away current from the appliance. It is around 0 V.

Neutron
A subatomic particle with a relative charge of 0 and a relative mass of 1.

Neutron star
The very dense core of a star that is left behind when a red supergiant explodes in a supernova.

Newton's First Law
An object will remain at rest or continue travelling at a constant velocity unless it is acted on by a resultant force.

Newton's Second Law
The acceleration of an object is directly proportional to the resultant force acting on it, and inversely proportional to its mass. Often given as $F = m \times a$.

Newton's Third Law
When two objects interact, they exert equal and opposite forces on each other. These forces are the same type.

Non-contact force
A force that acts between objects without needing them to touch, usually as a result of interacting fields.

Non-renewable energy resource
An energy resource that is non-renewable cannot be made at the same rate as it's being used, so it will run out one day.

Normal (at a boundary)
A line that's perpendicular (at 90°) to a boundary at the point of incidence (where a wave hits the boundary).

Normal contact force
A force that acts between all touching objects, of equal size but opposite direction to the force exerted on one object by the other.

Nuclear equation
An equation showing the atoms before and after radioactive decay, and the radiation emitted, balanced in terms of mass and charge.

Nuclear fission
When an atomic nucleus splits up to form two smaller nuclei.

Nuclear fuel
Nuclear fuels (e.g. uranium and plutonium) release energy through nuclear fission reactions to heat water into steam, which drives turbines and generators to generate electricity.

Nuclear fusion
When two nuclei join to create a heavier nucleus.

Nuclear model
A model of the atom that says that the atom has a small, central positively-charged nucleus with negatively-charged electrons moving around the nucleus, and that most of the atom is empty space.

Nucleus
The centre of an atom, containing protons and neutrons.

 O

Opaque object
An object that doesn't transmit light.

Orbit
The path on which one object moves around another.

P

Parallel circuit
A circuit in which every component is connected separately to the positive and negative ends of the source p.d..

Peak wavelength
The wavelength of radiation emitted by an object that has the highest intensity.

Peer-review
The process in which other scientists check the results and explanations of an investigation before they are published.

Period (of a wave)
The time taken for one full cycle of a wave to be completed.

Permanent magnet
A magnetic material that always has its own magnetic field around it.

Permanent magnetic material
Magnetic materials that take a long time to lose their magnetism.

Physical change
A change where you don't end up with a new substance — it's the same substance as before, just in a different form. (A change of state is a physical change.)

Planet
A large object in space which orbits a star.

Positron
A subatomic particle with a relative charge of +1 and a relative mass of 1/2000. It is the antiparticle of an electron.

Positron emission tomography (PET scanning)
A medical imaging technique that detects the gamma rays produced during electron-positron annihilation.

Potential difference
The energy transferred per unit charge passed, measured in volts (V). Also known as p.d. or voltage.

Power
The rate of transferring energy (or doing work). Normally measured in watts (W).

Power rating
The maximum safe power an appliance can operate at.

Precise result
When all the data is close to the mean.

Prediction
A statement that can be tested and is based on a hypothesis.

Pressure
The force exerted normal (at right angles) to a surface per unit area of that surface.

Principal focus of a converging lens
The point where rays hitting the lens parallel to the axis all meet.

Principal focus of a diverging lens
The point where rays hitting the lens parallel to the axis appear to have come from.

Principle of moments
The statement that for a body in equilibrium, the total clockwise moments are equal to the total anticlockwise moments, and so the body will not turn.

Proton
A subatomic particle with a relative charge of +1 and a relative mass of 1.

Protostar
An early stage in the life cycle of a star. Protostars are formed when the force of gravity causes clouds of dust and gas to spiral together.

R

Radioactive decay
The random process of a radioactive substance giving out radiation from the nuclei of its atoms.

Radiotherapy
A treatment for cancer that uses ionising radiation to kill cancer cells.

Random error
A difference in the results of an experiment caused by unpredictable events, e.g. human error in measuring.

Range
The difference between the smallest and largest values in a set of data.

Ray
A straight line showing the direction of energy transfer of a wave, indicating the path along which the wave moves.

Ray diagram
A diagram that shows the path of a wave.

Reaction time
The time taken for a person to react after an event (e.g. seeing a hazard).

Real image
An image formed when light rays from a point on an object come together at another point — the light rays actually pass through that point.

Red giant
A type of star that is formed when a star around the same mass as the Sun expands as it starts to run out of hydrogen in its core.

Red supergiant
A type of star that is formed when a large star (with a mass much greater than the Sun) expands as it starts to run out of hydrogen in its core.

Red-shift
The shift in observed wavelength of light from a source moving away from a stationary observer. The wavelength is shifted towards the red end of the electromagnetic spectrum (the wavelengths get longer).

Reflection
When a wave bounces back as it meets a boundary between two materials.

Refraction
When a wave changes direction as it passes across the boundary between two materials at an angle to the normal.

Renewable energy resource
An energy resource that is renewable is one that is being, or can be, made at the same rate (or faster) than it's being used, and so will never run out.

Repeatable result
A result that will come out the same if the experiment is repeated by the same person using the same method and equipment.

Reproducible result
A result that will come out the same if someone different does the experiment, or a slightly different method or piece of equipment is used.

Resistance
Anything in a circuit that reduces the flow of current. Measured in ohms, Ω.

Resolution
The smallest change a measuring instrument can detect.

Resultant force
A single force that can replace all the forces acting on an object to give the same effect as the original forces acting altogether.

Right-hand thumb rule
The rule used to work out the direction of the magnetic field produced by a current. Your thumb on your right hand points in the direction of the current and the curled fingers of your right hand show the direction of the field.

Risk
The chance that a hazard will cause harm.

S

Satellite
An object which orbits a second more massive object.

Scalar
A quantity that has magnitude but no direction.

Scaling prefix
A word or symbol which goes before a unit to indicate a multiplying factor (e.g. 1 km = 1000 m).

Seismic wave
A wave which travels through (or over the surface of) the Earth when an earthquake occurs. Two important types are P-waves and S-waves.

Series circuit
A circuit in which every component is connected in a line, end to end.

S.I. unit
A unit recognised as standard by scientists all over the world.

Significant figure
The first significant figure of a number is the first non-zero digit. The second, third and fourth significant figures follow on immediately after it.

Solar cell
A device which generates electric currents directly from the Sun's radiation.

Solar System
The Sun and all of the objects that orbit it.

Solenoid
A coil of wire often used in the construction of electromagnets.

Sound wave
A longitudinal wave of vibrating particles caused by vibrating objects.

Spark
The passage of electrons across a (usually) small gap between a charged object and an earthed conductor (or the earth).

Specific heat capacity (SHC)
The amount of energy (in joules) needed to raise the temperature of 1 kg of a material by 1°C.

Specific latent heat (SLH)
The amount of energy (in joules) needed to change 1 kg of a substance from one state to another, without changing its temperature.

Specular reflection
When parallel waves are reflected in a single direction by a smooth surface.

Standard form
A number written in the form $A \times 10^n$, where A is a number between 1 and 10.

State of matter
The form which a substance can take — e.g. solid, liquid or gas.

Static charge
An electric charge that cannot move. It often forms on electrical insulators, where charge cannot flow freely.

Steady State theory
The idea that the Universe has no beginning or end. It has always looked as it does and always will do. As the Universe expands matter is created, so the density of the Universe remains constant.

Stopping distance
The distance covered by a vehicle in the time between the driver spotting a hazard and the vehicle coming to a complete stop. It's the sum of the thinking distance and the braking distance.

Supernova
The explosion of a red supergiant.

System
The object, or group of objects, that you're considering.

Systematic error
An error that is consistently made throughout an experiment.

T

Temporary magnetic material
Magnetic materials that lose their magnetism quickly.

Theory
A hypothesis which has been accepted by the scientific community because there is good evidence to back it up.

Thermal conductivity
A measure of how quickly an object transfers energy by heating through conduction.

Thermal insulator
A material with a low thermal conductivity.

Thermistor
A resistor whose resistance is dependent on the temperature. The resistance decreases as temperature increases.

Thinking distance
The distance a vehicle travels during the driver's reaction time (the time between seeing a hazard and applying the brakes).

Three-core cable
An electrical cable containing a live wire, a neutral wire and an earth wire.

Tidal barrage
A dam built across a river estuary, containing turbines connected to generators. When there's a difference in water height on either side, water flows through the dam, turning the turbines and generating electricity.

Total internal reflection (TIR)
When a ray is refracted so much at a boundary that it is reflected back into a material instead of being transmitted into the new material. Occurs when a wave travels into a less dense material at an angle of incidence larger than the critical angle of the material the wave is travelling through.

Tracer
A radioactive isotope whose path through a system can be followed. Medical tracers can be used to diagnose illness and medical conditions.

Transformer
A device which can change the size of an alternating voltage.

Transmission (of a wave)
When a wave passes across a boundary from one material into another and continues travelling.

Transverse wave
A wave in which the oscillations are perpendicular (at 90°) to the direction the wave travels.

Trial run
A quick version of an experiment that can be used to work out the range of variables and the interval between the variables that will be used in the proper experiment. Sometimes called a pilot experiment.

U

Ultrasound
Sound with a frequency greater than 20 000 Hz.

Uncertainty
The amount by which a given result may differ from the true value.

Uniform field
A field that has the same strength everywhere.

Upthrust
The resultant force acting upwards on an object immersed in a fluid, due to the pressure of the fluid being greater at the bottom of the object than at the top.

V

Valid result
A result that is repeatable, reproducible and answers the original question.

Vector
A quantity which has both magnitude (size) and a direction.

Velocity
The speed and direction of an object.

Velocity/time graph
A graph showing how the velocity of an object changes over a period of time.

Voltmeter
A component used to measure the potential difference across a component. It is always connected in parallel with the component.

Virtual image
An image that is formed when light rays appear to have come from one point, but have actually come from another — the light rays don't actually pass through that point.

W

Wave
An oscillation that transfers energy and information without transferring any matter.

Wave velocity
The speed and direction of a wave.

Wavefront diagram
A representation of a wave made up of a series of 'wavefronts'. These are lines drawn through identical points on a wave, e.g. through each crest, perpendicular to the wave's direction of travel.

Wavelength
The distance between the same point on two adjacent waves, e.g. from one crest to the next crest.

Weight
The force acting on an object due to gravity.

White dwarf
The hot, dense core left behind when a red giant becomes unstable and ejects its outer layer of dust and gas.

Work done
The energy transferred when a force moves an object through a distance, or by a moving charge.

Z

Zero error
A type of systematic error caused by using a piece of equipment that isn't zeroed properly.

Acknowledgements

Data acknowledgements

Edexcel specification reference points reproduced by permission of Edexcel and Pearson Education.

Data used to construct stopping distance diagram on page 52 from the Highway Code. Contains public sector information licensed under the Open Government Licence v3.0. http://www.nationalarchives.gov.uk/doc/open-government-licence/version/3/

Photograph acknowledgements

Cover photo © **valdezrl** - stock.adobe.com, p 5 **Alastair Philip Wiper**/Science Photo Library, p 7 **Belmonte**/Science Photo Library, p 8 **Trevor Clifford Photography**/Science Photo Library, p 9 **Philippe Plailly**/Science Photo Library, p 23 **Andy Williams**/Science Photo Library, p 25 **Alan and Sandy Carey**/Science Photo Library, p 34 **NASA/Joel Kowsky**/Science Photo Library, p 36 **Ashley Cooper**/Science Photo Library, p 38 **Martyn F. Chillmaid**/Science Photo Library, p 39 **Martyn F. Chillmaid**/Science Photo Library, p 41 **Martyn F. Chillmaid**/Science Photo Library, p 42 **Sheila Terry**/Science Photo Library, p 45 **Sputnik**/Science Photo Library, p 50 (top) **Ton Kinsbergen**/Science Photo Library, p 50 (bottom) **David Woodfall Images**/Science Photo Library, p 53 **CC Studio**/Science Photo Library, p 54 **Sputnik**/Science Photo Library, p 66 © iStock.com/**Tuayai**, p 73 **Sheila Terry**/Science Photo Library, p 74 **Ashley Cooper**/Science Photo Library, p 75 ©iStock.com/**RichardHayman13**, p 77 **Martin Bond**/Science Photo Library, p 79 (top) **Martin Bond**/Science Photo Library, p 81 **U.S. Coast Guard**/Science Photo Library, p 83 © iStock.com/**AMR_Photos**, p 89 **David Weintraub**/Science Photo Library, p 92 **Tek Image**/Science Photo Library, p 100 **Andrew Lambert Photography**/Science Photo Library, p 107 **Cavallini James/BSIP**/Science Photo Library, p 108 **NASA**/Science Photo Library, p 109 (bottom) **Zephyr**/Science Photo Library, p 115 **GIPhotostock**/Science Photo Library, p 116 (top) **GIPhotostock**/Science Photo Library, p 118 **David Parker**/Science Photo Library, p 119 **David Parker**/Science Photo Library, p 124 (top) **Lea Paterson**/Science Photo Library, p 129 **David Parker**/Science Photo Library, p 133 (right) **Mark Sykes**/Science Photo Library, p 134 Science Photo Library, p 143 **Cordelia Molloy**/Science Photo Library, p 149 **Emilio Segre Visual Archives/American Institute of Physics**/Science Photo Library, p 150 Science Photo Library, p 156 (top) **James King-Holmes**/Science Photo Library, p 160 Science Photo Library, p 163 **Trevor Clifford Photography**/Science Photo Library, p 164 **Lawrence Livermore Laboratory**/Science Photo Library, p 169 (bottom) **Oulette & Theroux, Publiphoto Diffusion**/Science Photo Library, p 170 (top) **Burger/Phanie**/Science Photo Library, p 171 **Dr P. Marazzi**/Science Photo Library, p 175 **EFDA-Jet**/Science Photo Library, p 176 **Energy**/Science Photo Library, p 177 © iStock.com/**TkKurikawa**, p 184 **Damian Peach**/Science Photo Library, p 187 (bottom) **National Optical Astronomy Observatories**/Science Photo Library, p 188 **European Southern Observatory**/Science Photo Library, p 190 **NASA**/Science Photo Library, p 192 **Emilio Segre Visual Archives/American Institute of Physics**/Science Photo Library, p 200 **Lee Powers**/Science Photo Library, p 203 © iStock.com/**DarthArt**, p 212 **Peter Menzel**/Science Photo Library, p 213 (top) **Trevor Clifford Photography**/Science Photo Library, p 213 (bottom) **Leonard Lessin, FBPA**/Science Photo Library, p 225 **Andrew Lambert Photography**/Science Photo Library, p 227 **Trevor Clifford Photography**/Science Photo Library, p 229 (bottom) **Martyn F. Chillmaid**/Science Photo Library, p 231 **GIPhotostock**/Science Photo Library, p 235 **GIPhotostock**/Science Photo Library, p 236 **Philippe Psaila**/Science Photo Library, p 244 **Martyn F. Chillmaid**/Science Photo Library, p 256 Science Photo Library, p 257 **Charles D. Winters**/Science Photo Library, p 269 **Dorling Kindersley/UIG**/Science Photo Library, p 271 **Andrew Lambert Photography**/Science Photo Library, p 273 **Trevor Clifford Photography**/Science Photo Library, p 277 **Martyn F. Chillmaid**/Science Photo Library, p 279 **Andrew Lambert Photography**/Science Photo Library, p 284 **Dorling Kindersley/UIG**/Science Photo Library, p 297 Science Photo Library, p 299 **Mehau Kulyk**/Science Photo Library, p 302 **GIPhotostock**/Science Photo Library, p 305 **Tony McConnell**/Science Photo Library, p 307 **Martyn F. Chillmaid**/Science Photo Library, p 308 **Adam Hart-Davis**/Science Photo Library, p 311 (left) **Ted Kinsman**/Science Photo Library, p 311 (right) **Ted Kinsman**/Science Photo Library, p 319 (top) **Geoff Tompkinson**/Science Photo Library, p 327 **GIPhotostock**/Science Photo Library, p 333 **GIPhotostock**/Science Photo Library, p 335 **GIPhotostock**/Science Photo Library, p 336 **Trevor Clifford Photography**/Science Photo Library, p 338 (top) Science Photo Library, p 339 Science Photo Library, p 341 © **David Maliphant**

Index

G

gamma decay 128, 157, 160
  nuclear equations 160
gamma rays 127, 128, 157, 160
  dangers 136, 165, 166
  uses 135, 169-171
gases 300
  doing work 312
  pressure 310-312, 319
gears 213
Geiger-Muller tubes 161
geocentric model 183
gradients 28, 346-348
  tangents 348
graphs 16, 17, 346-349
  areas under graphs 348, 349
  distance/time graphs 27, 28
  gradients 346-348
  velocity/time graphs 30, 31
gravitational potential energy (GPE)
    stores 61, 67, 200
gravity 37
  acceleration due to 26
  forces 37, 38, 184, 185
greenhouse effect 81

H

half-life 161-163
  effect on safety 167
hazards (in experiments) 7, 8, 336
hearing 104
heliocentric model 183
histograms 16
hydro-electric power stations 78
hypotheses 2, 3

I

images 120
  converging lenses 124
  diverging lenses 126
immersion heaters 337
independent variables 10
induced
  charge 256
  current 280-282
  magnets 267, 268
  potential difference 280-283
inelastic distortion 323, 324
inertia 36
infrared radiation 127
  dangers 136
  uses 132, 133
infrasound 109

insulation 69, 70
insulators (electrical) 254
intensity 140
intensity-wavelength distributions
    140, 141
interaction pairs 206
internal energy 301
ionising radiation 136, 156, 157
  dangers 136, 165
  uses 134, 135, 168-172
ions 154
irradiation 165, 166
isotopes 155
issues created by science 5
I-V graphs 227-229
  diodes 229
  filament lamps 228
  fixed resistors 228
  LDRs 229
  thermistors 229

K

kelvin scale 301, 302
kinetic energy stores 61, 66, 200
kinetic theory 299, 300
  changing state 302, 303
  gas pressure 310, 311
  internal energy 301
  temperature 301

L

law of reflection 115
LDRs 225, 226, 229
length (measuring) 333, 334
lenses 118, 119
  converging lenses 118, 122-124
  diverging lenses 119, 125, 126
  images 120
  power 121
  ray diagrams 122-125
levers 213
light gates 335
light pollution 190
lightning 260
limit of proportionality 324
limitations of science 6
linear electrical components 227
linear graphs 346, 347
lines of best fit 17
liquids 299, 300
  pressure 318, 319
  upthrust 321, 322
live wires 246-248
loft insulation 69

longitudinal waves 88, 89
loudspeakers 279
lubrication 70, 201

M

magnetic energy stores 61
magnetic fields 267
  forces 268, 269, 273-275
  flux density 274
  materials 267
  of bar magnets 268
  of current-carrying wires 270
  of solenoids 270, 271
  uniform fields 268
magnets 267
  electromagnets 270-272
  induced magnets 267, 268
  uses 271, 272
main sequence stars 187
mains supply 246
mass 37
  conservation in changes of state
    303
  inertial 36
  measuring 333
mass (nucleon) numbers 155
means (averages) 14
medians (averages) 14
medical imaging 135, 169, 170
microphones 284
microwaves 127
  dangers 136
  uses 131, 133
models 3, 4
moderators 174
modes (averages) 14
molecules (size of) 151
moments 211-213
momentum 44-47
motor effect 273-278
motors 276-278
multimeters 339

N

national grid 290, 291
natural satellites 184
nebulae 187
neutral wires 246
neutron decay 157, 160
neutron stars 188
neutrons 152, 155
  in fission reactions 173, 174
  nuclear decays 157
  nuclear equations 160

Equations Page

In each paper you have to sit for your Physics GCSE, you'll be given an equations sheet listing some of the equations you might need to use. That means you don't have to learn them (hurrah), but you still need to be able to pick out the correct equations to use and be really confident using them. The equations sheet won't give you any units for the equation quantities — so make sure you know them inside out.

The equations you'll be given in the exam are all on this page. You can use this page as a reference when you're doing the exam-style questions at the end of each section.

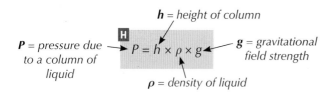

h = height of column

P = pressure due to a column of liquid

H $P = h \times \rho \times g$

g = gravitational field strength

ρ = density of liquid

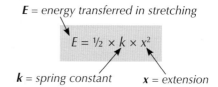

v = final velocity a = acceleration

$v^2 - u^2 = 2 \times a \times x$

u = initial velocity x = distance

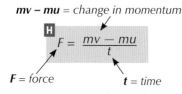

$mv - mu$ = change in momentum

H $F = \dfrac{mv - mu}{t}$

F = force t = time

E = energy transferred in stretching

$E = \frac{1}{2} \times k \times x^2$

k = spring constant x = extension

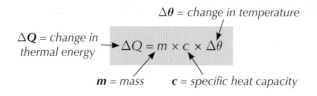

$\Delta\theta$ = change in temperature

ΔQ = change in thermal energy

$\Delta Q = m \times c \times \Delta\theta$

m = mass c = specific heat capacity

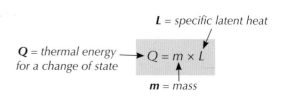

L = specific latent heat

Q = thermal energy for a change of state

$Q = m \times L$

m = mass

B = magnetic flux density l = length

H $F = B \times I \times l$

F = force on a conductor at right angles to a magnetic field carrying a current I = current

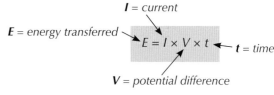

I = current

E = energy transferred

$E = I \times V \times t$ t = time

V = potential difference

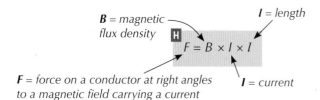

V_p = potential difference across primary coil

I_s = current in secondary coil

$V_P \times I_P = V_S \times I_S$

I_P = current in primary coil V_s = potential difference across secondary coil

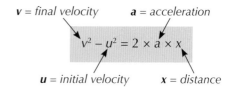

N_p = number of turns in primary coil

H $\dfrac{V_p}{V_s} = \dfrac{N_p}{N_s}$

N_s = number of turns in secondary coil

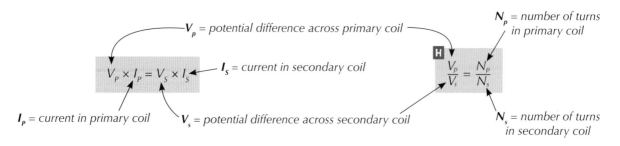

V_1 = volume 1 V_2 = volume 2

$P_1 \times V_1 = P_2 \times V_2$

P_1 = pressure at volume V_1 P_2 = pressure at volume V_2

PETB41